Practical Approach

by Charles Siegel

A Subsidiary of
Henry Holt and Co., Inc.

Copyright © 1994   MIS:Press
                    a subsidiary of Henry Holt and Company, Inc.
                    115 West 18 Street
                    New York, NY 10011

All rights reserved. Reproduction or use of editorial or pictorial content in any manner is prohibited without express written permission. No patent liability is assumed with respect to the use of the information contained herein. While every precaution has been taken in the preparation of this book, the publisher assumes no responsibility for errors or omissions. Neither is any liability assumed for damages resulting from the use of the information contained herein.

Throughout this book, trademarked names are used. Rather than put a trademark symbol after every occurrence of a trademarked name, we used the names in an editorial fashion only, and to the benefit of the trademark owner, with no intention of infringement of the trademark. Where such designations appear in this book, they have been printed with inital caps.

ISBN 1-55828-350-1

Printed in the United States of America.

10 9 8 7 6 5 4 3 2 1

Library of Congress Cataloging-in-Publication Data

Siegel, Charles
    Practical Approach : covers through version 3.0 / Charles Siegel.
      p. cm.
    Includes index.
    ISBN 1-55828-350-1
    1. Database management.   2. Lotus Approach for Windows.
    I. Title.
QA76.9.D3S56335 1994   94-26167
005.75'65--dc20   CIP

MIS:Press books are available at special discounts for bulk purchases for sales promotions, premiums, fund raising, or educational use. Special editions or book excerpts can also be created to specification.

For details contact: Special Sales Director
                       M&T Books
                       a subsidiary of Henry Holt and Company, Inc.
                       115 West 18 Street
                       New York, NY 10011

Contents

Introduction 1
    Is This Book for You? 1

Part I:
Up and Running 5

Chapter 1:
Approach: A Quick Tour 7
    What is a Database? 8
        Data Files and Approach Files 9
        Using Data Files 9
        Using Approach Files 10
    The Basics of the Approach Interface 11
    Creating Views 13

Practical Approach, 3.0

> Using The Assistants 13
> Forms 14
> Reports 15
> Mailing Labels 15
> Form Letters 16
> Worksheets 16
> Crosstabs 18
> Charts 18

Browse and Design Modes 19
> Working in Browse Mode 20
> Working in Design Mode 22
> Working in Preview Mode 26
> Working in Find Mode 27

A Glance at Approach's Menus 28
Creating a Working Directory 29

Chapter 2:
Creating a Database File 33

Creating a New File 34
> The Welcome Dialog Box 34
> The New Dialog Box 35
> The Field Definition Dialog Box 37

A Sample Database File 45
> What Fields Are Needed 46
> Creating a Sample File 49

Working with Existing Files 53
> Opening, Closing, and Saving a File 53
> Saving a File under a New Name 59
> Changing Field Definitions 61

Chapter 3:
Entering and Viewing Data 63

- How to Add Data 64
  - Adding New Records 65
  - Entering Data in Fields 66
  - Automatic Data Validation 69
- Viewing and Editing Records 70
  - Using the Status Bar to Move through the Records 71
  - Deleting Records 72
- Adding Sample Data 72
- Special Techniques 76
  - Other Features of the Browse Menu 76
  - PicturePlus Fields 79
- Automating and Validating Data Entry 88
  - Automatic Data Entry 89
  - Validating Entered Data 91
  - Other Features of Data Entry Options 94
  - Entry Options for your Sample Data 95

Chapter 4:
Changing the Design of a View 99

- An Overview of Design Mode 100
  - Using Design Mode 100
  - Objects 102
  - The Info Box 103
  - Other Features of Design View 104
  - Summary of the Overview 107
  - Saving Changes in Designs 108
  - Displaying Your Sample Form in Design Mode 108

Manipulating Objects 109
    Adding Objects 110
    Adding a Picture 111
    Selecting Objects 113
    Moving Objects 114
    Resizing Objects 115
    Deleting Objects 115
    Using the Edit Menu 115
    Changing Margins 116
Objects and Their Styles and Properties 117
    Graphic Objects 117
    Text 121
Working with Fields 126
    Adding a Field to a Design 126
    Field Styles and Properties 128
    Formatting Fields 133
    Creating Dialog Box Controls for Data Entry 139
    PicturePlus Fields and Their Properties 145
Formatting Shortcuts 147
    Fast Formatting 148
    Named Styles 149
Layout Tools 149
    Enlarging and Reducing the View 149
    Aligning Objects 150
    Grouping Objects 152
    Changing Stacking Order 153
    The Alignment Command 154
    Setting Tab Order 155

Chapter 5:
Creating Forms and Printed Output 157

Working with Several Designs 158
    Switching among Views 158
    Creating and Managing Views 159
Forms 160
    Creating a New Form 160
    Modifying Forms 164
    Designing a Sample Form 166
Reports 172
    Creating a Report 172
    Modifying Reports 177
    Designing a Sample Report 188
Mailing Labels 190
    Creating Mailing Labels 190
    Designing Sample Labels 196
Form Letters 198
    Creating Form Letters 198
    Modifying Form Letters 200
    Designing a Sample Form Letter 203
Printing Output 208
    The Print Dialog Box 209
    Print Setup Dialog Box 210

Chapter 6:
Using Sorts and Finds 213

Sorts: An Overview 214
    When to Sort on Multiple Fields 215
    Ascending and Descending Sorts 215

Sorting on a Summary Field 216
Sorting the Sample Records 217
Finds 219
Simple Finds 219
Finds Using Operators 226
Comparison Operators 226
Finds with Multiple Criteria 232
Special Features of Finds 238
The Find Icon Bar 246
Combining Sorts and Finds 247

Part II:
The Power User 251

Chapter 7:
Working with Relational Databases 253

Understanding Relational Databases 254
Data Normalization 256
The Key Field 263
Using Relational Databases in Approach 265
Joining Two Databases 266
Repeating Panels 270
A Sample Relational Database 276
Creating the Hours File 276
Working with a One-to-Many Relationship 277
Working with a Many-to-One Relationship 284
Views Based on a Many-to-One Relationship 285

Chapter 8:
Using Approach Formulas 291

What Is a Formula? 292

    Fields 293

    Operators 293

    Constants 298

    Functions 298

Using Calculated Fields 315

    Creating a Calculated Field 316

    Dependent Calculated Fields 318

    Changing a Formula in a Calculated Field 319

    Bad References 319

    A Sample Summary Report 319

Using Formulas in Finds 323

    Special Features of Formulas in Finds 323

    Finds Using Today( ) 323

    If Searches 324

Using Formulas to Automate and Validate Data Entry 324

    Using a Formula to Enter a Default Value 325

    A Validation Formula 325

Chapter 9:
Analyzing Your Data: Worksheets, Crosstabs, and Charts 329

Worksheets 330

    Creating a New Worksheet 331

    Changing the Design of a Worksheet 331

    Viewing and Working with Data in Worksheets 341

    The Worksheet Menu 343

A Sample Worksheet	344
Crosstabs	347
Creating a New Crosstab	348
Modifying a Crosstab	350
The Crosstab Menu	352
A Sample Crosstab	353
Charts	355
Creating a New Chart	355
Modifying a Chart	358
The Chart Menu	359
A Sample Chart	360

Chapter 10:
Speeding Up Your Work with Macros 363

Creating and Using Macros	364
Managing Macros	364
Defining a Macro	366
Actions that Macros Can Perform	367
Running a Macro	379
Sample Macros	381
Attaching Macros to Objects	386
Attaching Macros to Fields or Views	386
Creating a Macro Button	388
Using Formulas in Macros	391
Conditional Macros	392
Changing the Data in Records	394
Variables	396

Chapter 11:
Using Approach Utilities 399

The Spell Checker 400
    Spell Check in Browse Mode 400
    Spell Check in Design Mode 401
    Spell Check Options 401
    Correcting Errors 402

Named Styles 403
    Managing Named Styles 404
    Defining a Named Style 405

Customizing Approach 410
    Custom Menu Systems 411
    Custom Icon Bars 416
    Setting Preferences 418

Chapter 12:
Working with Other Database Applications 429

Files Types Used Directly by Approach 430
    Xbase Files 431
    Paradox Files 440
    Working with Other Lotus Applications 445
    Working with SQL 445
    Working with DB2-MDI 451
    Working with ODBC Sources 451

Importing and Exporting Data 452
    Importing Data 453
    Exporting Data 456
    The Field Mapping Dialog Box 458

Sharing Data on a Network 458
    Copying a Database to a Network 458
    Refreshing Your Data 460
    Record Locking 460
    Printing and Previewing Designs on a Network 462

Part III: Appendices 463

Appendix A: Installing Approach 465

System Requirements 466
Installing Approach 467

Appendix B: Reference Guide 469

Menu and Dialog Box Reference 469
    The File Menu 470
    The Edit Menu 494
    The View Menu 498
    The Create Menu 500
    The Browse Menu 524
    The Object Menu 529
    The Form Menu 531
    The Panel Menu for Forms 532
    The Report Menu 533
    The Panel Menu for Reports 535
    The Mailing Label Menu 535
    The Letter Menu 537
    The Worksheet Menu 537

Contents

The Crosstab Menu	541
The Chart Menu	543
The Tools Menu	545
The Window Menu	581
The Help Menu	581
The Formula Dialog Box	587
Operator, Constant, and Function Reference	588
Operators	588
Constants	590
Functions	590
Info Box Reference	604
Styles and Properties of Graphic Objects	605
Style and Properties of Text Objects	610
Styles and Properties of Fields	614
Styles and Properties of Views and their Components	638
Shortcut Keys	658
Shortcut Keys for Moving through the Database	660
Alternative Editor Shortcut Keys	660

Appendix C:
Windows Basics 663

Mouse Actions	664
Pop-Up Menus	664
Making Selections Using the Mouse	665
Making Selections Using the Keyboard	665
Shortcut Keys	666
Common Features of Windows Menus	666
Dialog Box Controls	667
Text Box	668

Lists	668
Drop-Down Lists	668
Checkboxes	669
Radio Buttons	669
Push Buttons	669
Working with Windows	670
Resizing and Moving Windows	671
Control Menus	671
The Scroll Bars	673
The Editor	674
Selecting Text	674
Cut and Paste	675
Undoing Errors	675
The Help System	676
Searching by Topic	676
Alphabetical Searches	678
The Help System Menus	679

Index 681

Introduction

Is This Book for You?

Approach is popular because it is both easy to use and a powerful, relational database management system.

Because of its ease of use, many small business owners use it to manage their own data. However, they find that, easy as Approach is to understand, the process of managing data is complex—they must understand a bit of relational database theory to know how to organize their data, and understand advanced features of Approach to use all of its power.

This book answers the questions that actual business users ask most frequently about Approach.

Part I is an introduction to the basics of Approach, which takes the form of a tutorial with exercises to give the reader experiences in features of the program that are essential to any application. It shows you how to:

- create a new database
- add and edit data
- create forms that speed data entry
- design reports, mailing labels, and form letters
- sort your data
- use finds to isolate data that meet certain criteria.

These chapters should be read as a tutorial, and they include exercises to give you hands-on experience with Approach.

Part II covers more advanced features of Approach, many of which people managing their own data must understand to use the program effectively.

It begins with an extensive discussion of relational databases, which does not concentrate on technical details of database theory but gives you the basic, common-sense theory that you need to manage the data used in most actual business applications.

Included are chapters on how to:

- create worksheets, crosstabs, and charts
- use Approach formulas
- save time by using macros
- use Approach's utilities
- work with other database applications
- use Approach on a network.

Many of these chapters can be used for reference and read as the need to use them arises.

In addition, the appendices include instructions on installing Approach, a tutorial on Windows basics for beginners, and a reference guide to Approach, which you can use to look up its features quickly while you are working with it.

This book is a complete guide to every feature of Approach, but it is organized in a way that is convenient for most readers. Part I covers the basics that you should know to work with even the simplest application, such as a mailing list. Part II begins with a chapter on relational databases, which you should understand to manage most business applications, and goes on to discuss power features of Approach, which you can learn as you need them.

This book is meant for people who use Approach practically, for people who want to put it to work for them as quickly and powerfully as possible.

Part I

Up and Running

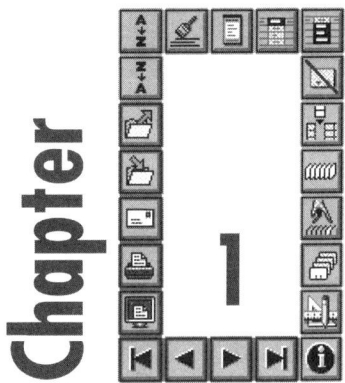

Approach: A Quick Tour

Before you look at Approach in detail, you should get a quick overview of how the program is organized. This chapter introduces all the basic features of Approach. It ends with an exercise that creates a subdirectory to hold the files you create to work with the sample data in this book. It assumes that you have used other Windows applications and that you know the most basic techniques for working with them, such as how to make selections from drop-down menus and how to use dialog boxes; if you do not know anything about Windows applications, you should see Appendix C for an introduction to them. This chapter covers:

- The basics of database terminology
- The difference between data files and Approach files
- The basic features of the Approach Interface
- The Views that Approach lets you work with: Forms, Reports, Mailing Labels, Form Letters, Worksheets, Crosstabs, and Charts
- Browse, Design, Preview and Find modes
- The Approach menu system
- Using the Windows File Manager to create a subdirectory

What is a Database?

A simple database is a collection of repetitive data, such as a list of names, addresses, and telephone numbers; a list of product names, prices, and descriptions; or any similar repetitive list. Before there were computers, this type of data used to be kept on sheets of paper, or on index cards, each printed with a form that has blank spaces to fill in each element of data. For example, a form might have a space for name, address, city/state/zip, and telephone number.

When you work with computerized databases, there are a couple of new terms that are used to refer to the same elements that were used on paper forms:

- *Field.* A field is one element of the data—what would have been filled into one blank space in a paper form. For example, a name or telephone number could be a single field. In general, for reasons you learn about in Chapter 2, when you are working on a computer, it is best to have separate fields for First Name and Last Name, and generally to break up the data into more fields than you would use on a paper form.

- *Record.* A record is all the data about one entity—for example, the name, address, and telephone number of one person. Everything that would have been recorded on a single index card or on a single form when you were working with paper files is one record of a computerized database.

It is often convenient to look at data as a table, rather than as a collection of separate forms. Approach automatically creates a standard Form and a standard Worksheet for all data files to display them in both these ways. When you look at data in tabular form, each row is a record—for example, one row holds the name and address of one person (see Figure 1.1). Each column is a field—for example, there is a column for First Name and a column for Address. The table as a whole is the file. In fact, a database file is often referred to as a table.

Chapter 1: Approach: A Quick Tour

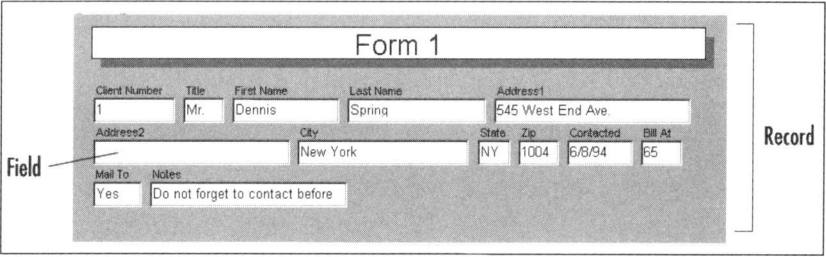

Figure 1.1 Data in a form and in a table.

Data Files and Approach Files

One key feature of Approach is the difference between Approach files and data files.

When you use Approach, you work directly with *Approach files*, which determine how you see the data it is displayed on the screen and printed in reports, mailing labels, and form letters. The files that actually hold your data are separate from the Approach files mentioned above, and are the same as data files used in other database management programs.

Using Data Files

Approach does not have its own data file format, which would only make it more difficult to exchange data among applications. Instead, it makes direct use of the most popular file formats. It uses *power key technology* to work seamlessly with data from dBASE IV, dBASE III +, Paradox, FoxPro, SQL Server, Oracle, and other popular formats.

With most database programs, you must import data in other formats, converting it to the program's format before you can use it. By contrast, Approach uses these formats directly. It can even join different types of data files to create a relational database.

Because it uses data from other programs with no conversion, Approach can be used as a front end to applications in a network environment, on a stand-alone computer. It makes it easy to use data files created in applications that are difficult to work with. Because you do not change the original format of the data, other people on the network can continue to use data files with the programs where they were created.

Approach is also the easiest Windows application to use if you are creating a database from scratch. You can create dBASE, Paradox, and FoxPro files from within Approach.

If you are working on a network and have the necessary software, you can create several additional types of files, such as SQL Server files.

Using Approach Files

Approach creates its own Approach Files, which have an APR extension, while using data file formats from other programs.

Earlier versions of Approach used Approach files that have the extension VEW (because they consist of views.) Approach 3.0 can automatically convert these to APR files.

You work with these Approach files to change the way the data is displayed or used. The Approach file, which includes data entry forms, reports, mailing labels, and form letters, are accessible only from within Approach. It is easy to create new designs and to use the data in any of these ways within Approach.

Data that you add or edit is saved in the original file format—dBASE, Paradox or whatever—and can be accessed by any program using that format.

Chapter 1: Approach: A Quick Tour

The front end of data entry forms, reports, mailing labels, and form letters is used only in Approach.

Most of this book focuses on Approach files, as it assumes you are doing most of your work using Approach. It mentions only a few features of the underlying data files, the features that you need to know when you are working in Approach. Chapter 12 discusses the distinctive features of all the different types of data files that you can use under the Approach View file. If you are working on your data using some other application as well as Approach, you should read the parts of Chapter 12 that cover its features.

The Basics of the Approach Interface

The Approach interface is very easy to use.

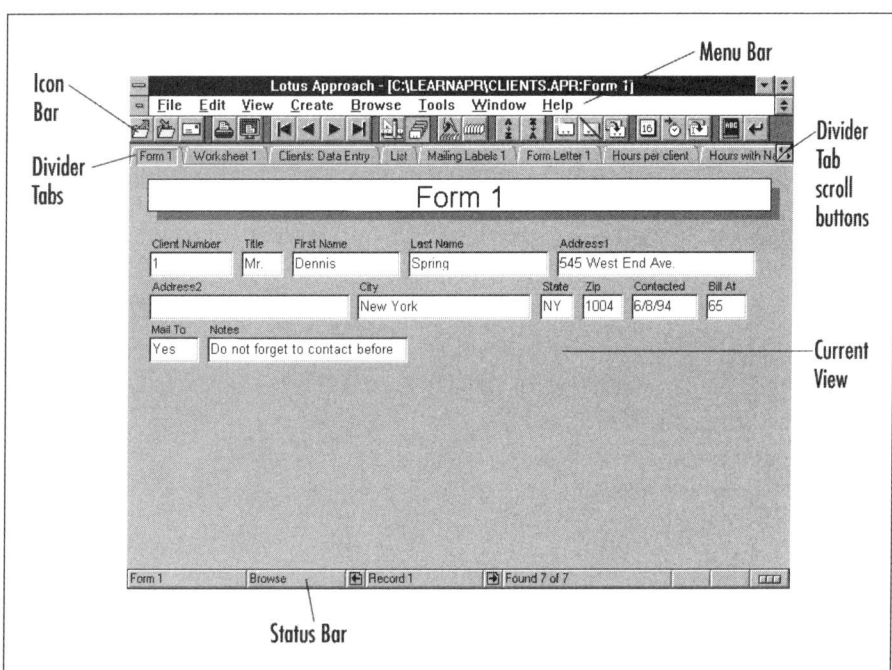

Figure 1.2 Important features of the interface.

Practical Approach, 3.0

Figure 1.2 shows some important features of the Approach interface:

- *The Current View.* One View of the data is displayed when you open the file.
- *Divider tabs.* Above the current View, divider tabs are displayed with the name of all the Views in the Approach file. These tabs look like the tabs that are used to divide sections of a notebook. You can switch to a different view of the data simply by clicking its tab.
- *Divider tab scroll buttons.* If there are too many divider tabs to fit on the screen, scroll buttons are displayed to their right, which you can click on to scroll the tabs left or right to view hidden tabs.
- *The Menu Bar.* Approach has drop-down menus like other Windows applications. Click one of the options on the menu bar, such as **File** or **Edit**, to display all the options on that menu.
- *The Icon Bar.* There is also an Icon Bar, like other Windows applications. Clicking an icon is a quicker way of choosing the most important menu options.
- *The Status Bar.* Like other Lotus Applications, Approach has an active Status Bar. Its features not only indicates the current status of the application, but can also be used like menu options or icons. For example, you can click the **View indicator** of the Status Bar to display a pop-up menu (see Figure 1.3) and select a View from this pop-up menu to switch to that view.

Figure 1.3 Using the Active Status Bar.

One other feature of the Approach interface you may not be familiar with is the Help button (in the upper right corner of its dialog boxes). This button has a question mark on it, and you can click it to get help on the dialog box. Apart from this feature, Approach's dialog boxes work like those of other Windows applications: if you are not familiar with the controls used in Windows dialog boxes, see Appendix C for more details.

Creating Views

When you first create a data file in Approach or open a data file that was created in another application, it automatically creates two views of the file:

1. The standard Form lets you view one record on the screen.
2. The standard Worksheet lets you view the records in tabular form.

You can create additional views of the data by choosing: **Form**, **Report**, **Mailing Label**, **Form Letter**, **Worksheet**, **Crosstab**, or **Chart**. from the Create menu.

Using The Assistants

When you choose one of these menu options, Approach displays an Assistant that helps you create the view. Assistants differ, depending on what type of view you are creating, but the Form Assistant illustrates a few features of all of them (see Figure 1.4).

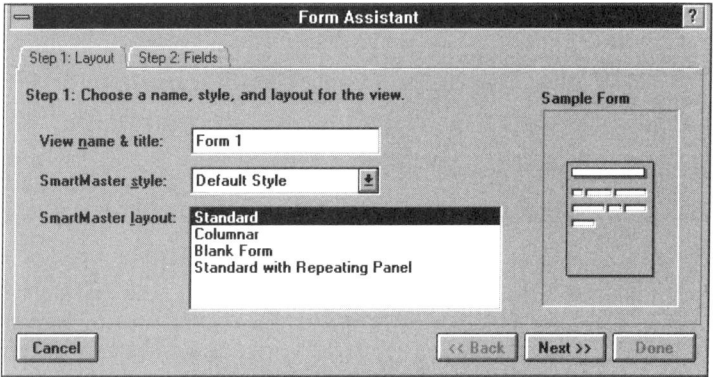

Figure 1.4   The Form Assistant.

As you can see, the Assistant breaks up the work of defining the view into a few steps, and it has the familiar divider tab interface, which lets you display each step simply by clicking the tab. As an alternative to using the tabs, you can use the <<Back or Next>> button to go through the steps in sequence: click **<<Back** to go to previous step or **Next>>** to go to the following step. Each step has controls, such as text boxes, drop-downs menus, and lists, which you can use to define features of the View you are creating. When you have finished defining the View, click **Done**, and Approach creates and displays it. You can also click **Cancel** at any time to close the Assistant without saving your work.

In later chapters of this book, you look in detail at how to create each of the types of View. At this point, you should glance at each to get a general idea of what Approach can do.

Forms

Forms are used primarily to display and edit data on the screen one record at a time. Although you can edit data in the Worksheet view, a single record may sometimes span many screens horizontally because of a large number of fields or large field size. This can be cumbersome to work with. The Form view lets you see as much of the record as possible. Form design is covered in Chapters 4 and 5.

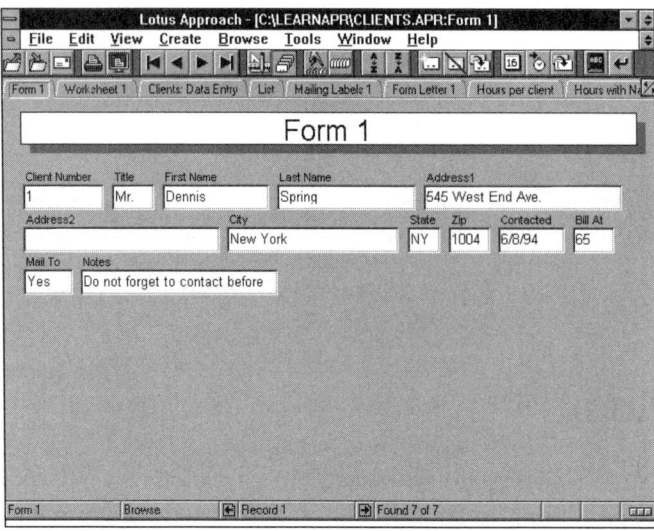

Figure 1.5   The standard form.

Approach automatically creates the standard form for a database (see Figure 1.5). Notice that the fields are arranged as close together as possible, so the screen can display all of the fields in one record, or as many of its fields as possible.

Reports

Reports are used primarily to print data, though you can also use them to display and edit data on the screen. You can create reports that have the fields arranged in a number of different ways, and reports that group data and include totals for groups or for the entire database (see Figure 1.6). Report design is covered in Chapter 5.

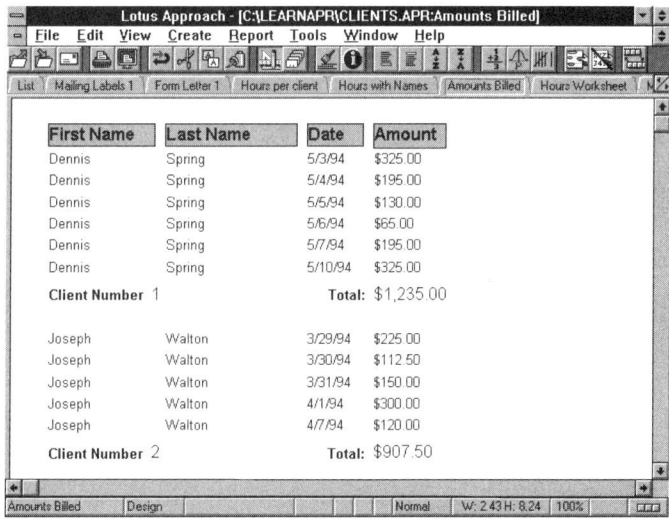

Figure 1.6 A grouped report with totals.

Mailing Labels

Approach automatically lays out mailing labels in many standard formats, and lets you create custom mailing labels. In addition to printing labels, you can display them on the screen and edit the data in them (see Figure 1.7). Mailing Label design is covered in Chapter 5.

Practical Approach, 3.0

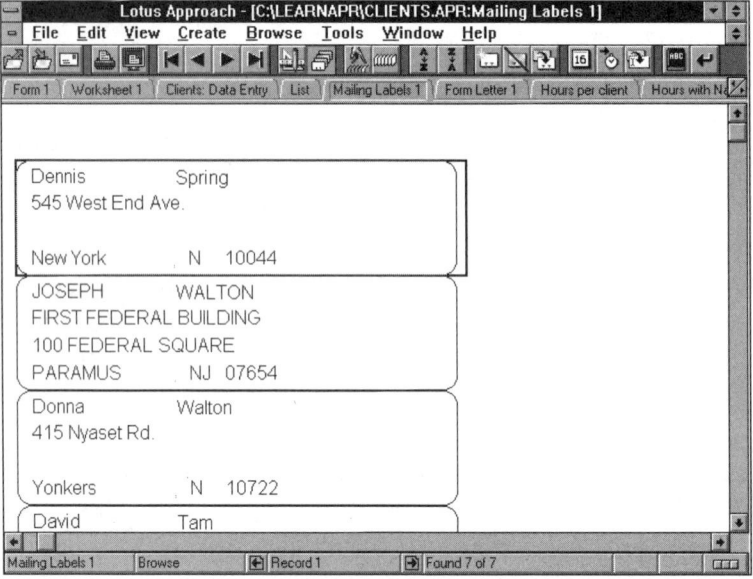

Figure 1.7 Mailing Labels displayed on the screen.

Form Letters

You can create form letters within Approach itself, without using a separate word processing application. It is easy to include fields in your database as part of the text. A form letter can be printed or displayed on the screen (see Figure 1.8). Form Letter design is covered in Chapter 5.

Worksheets

An Approach worksheet displays the data in tabular form, with a row for each record and a column for each field. You can use Approach worksheets to add, edit, or view data, but they also have some features of spreadsheets and are useful for analyzing data (see Figure 1.9). Worksheets are covered in Chapter 9.

Chapter 1: Approach: A Quick Tour

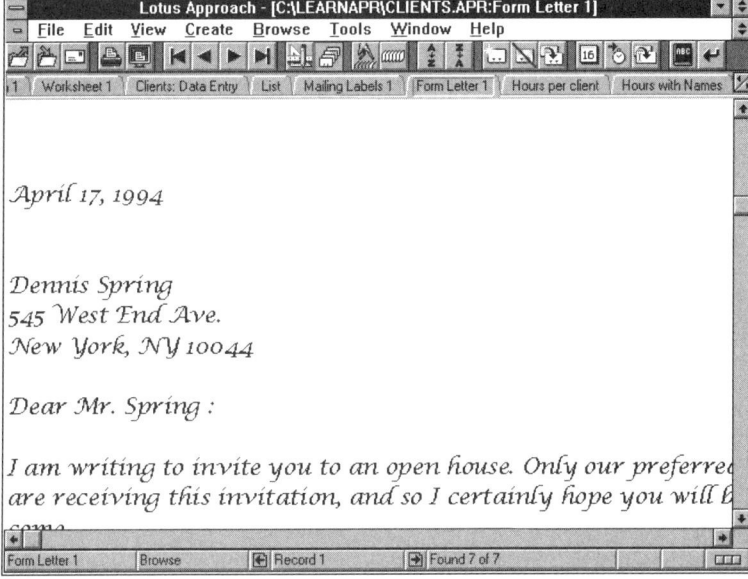

Figure 1.8 A Form Letter displayed on the screen.

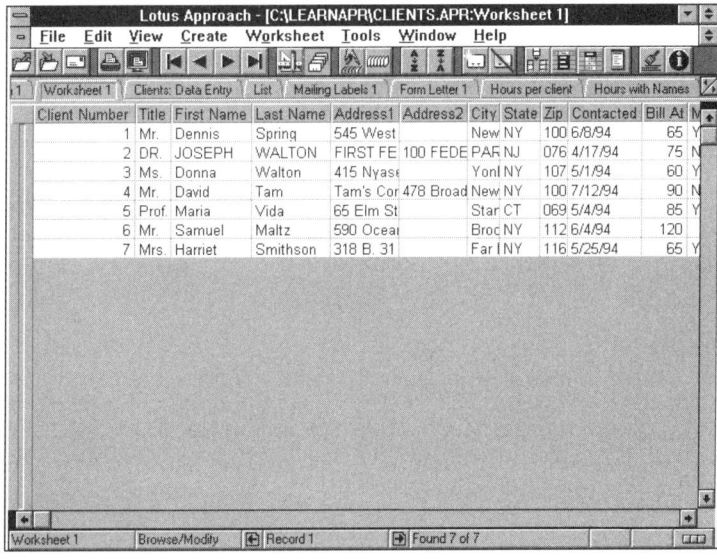

Figure 1.9 A Worksheet.

Crosstabs

A crosstab displays data in cross tabulated form, depending on the data in two fields (see Figure 1.10). The content of one field is listed at the top of each column, the content of another is listed at the left of each row, and the cells contain summary data based on their columns and rows.

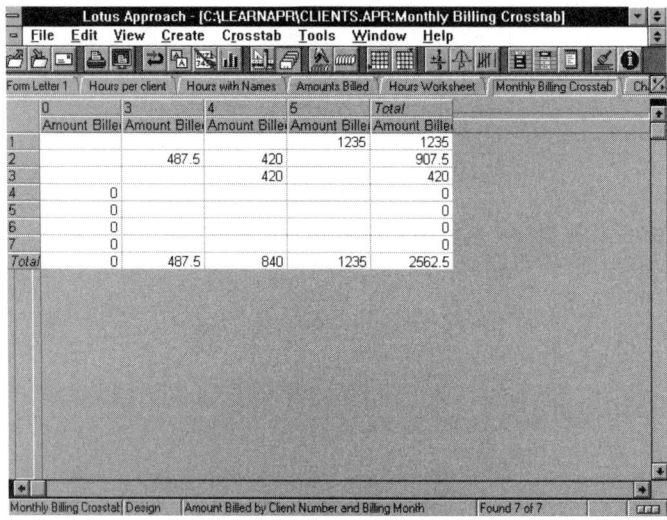

Figure 1.10 A crosstab.

For example, if you sell a number of products in different countries, and you have a database that records sales, with one field in each record for the product and another field in each record for the country where it is sold, you can create a crosstab with the names of the countries at the top of the columns, the name of the products at the left of the rows, and the number of products sold in each country tabulated in the cells.

Because their cells contain summary data, crosstabs cannot be edited. Crosstabs are covered in Chapter 9.

Charts

Approach can create charts based on databases or crosstabs, including bar graphs, line graphs, area graphs, and pie graphs (see Figure 1.11). These charts make the meaning of data clearer by presenting it in visual form.

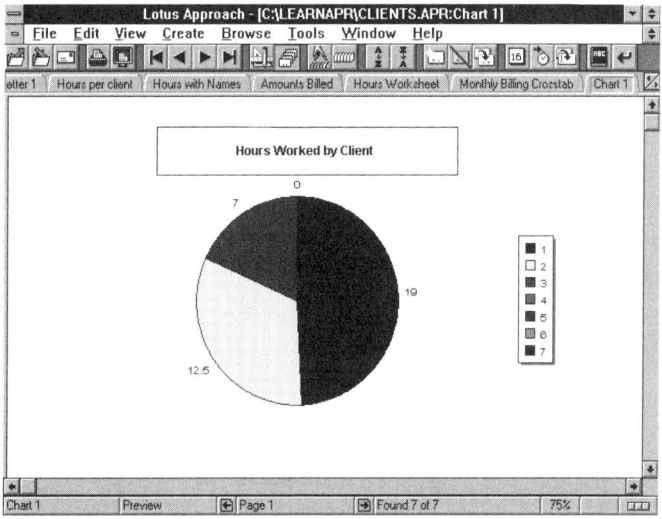

Figure 1.11 A chart.

Browse and Design Modes

Once you have created Views, you work with them in Browse mode and Design mode:

- *Browse mode*. Lets you view and edit data, move through the file, sort the file in any order you specify, find specific records or groups of records, and produce printed output.
- *Design mode*. Lets you rearrange the design of the current view. When you are working with most types of View, you can move the fields of the database easily by using the mouse, and you can add text and other objects, such as lines, rectangles, check boxes, and push buttons. You can also resize all these objects, change their colors, and manipulate them in other ways.

You can switch to Design or Browse mode by choosing **Design** or **Browse** from the View menu, by clicking the Icons, or by clicking the **Mode indicator** of the Status bar to display a pop-up menu that includes all the modes (see Figure 1.12).

Practical Approach, 3.0

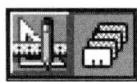

Figure 1.12 The Design and Browse icons.

In addition to these two modes, there is a *Preview* mode that you can use to display a View as it will look when it is printed. There is also a *Find* mode, which you can use to search for data, but these are not as fundamental to using Approach as Design and Browse.

All of these modes are discussed in detail in later chapters, but you should take a quick look at them now.

Working in Browse Mode

A typical Approach view displayed in Browse mode displays the data in the database (see Figure 1.13). You can get a general idea of how to use Browse simply by looking at its icon bar.

The most important Browse mode icons are:

 Open File. Is used to open a file.

 Save Approach File. Can be used to save the design of an Approach File.

 Send Mail. Can be used to send mail, if you have a mail application installed.

 Print. Is used to print the view.

 Preview. Is used to switch to Preview mode.

 Start Arrow. Moves the focus to the first record of the file.

Chapter 1: Approach: A Quick Tour

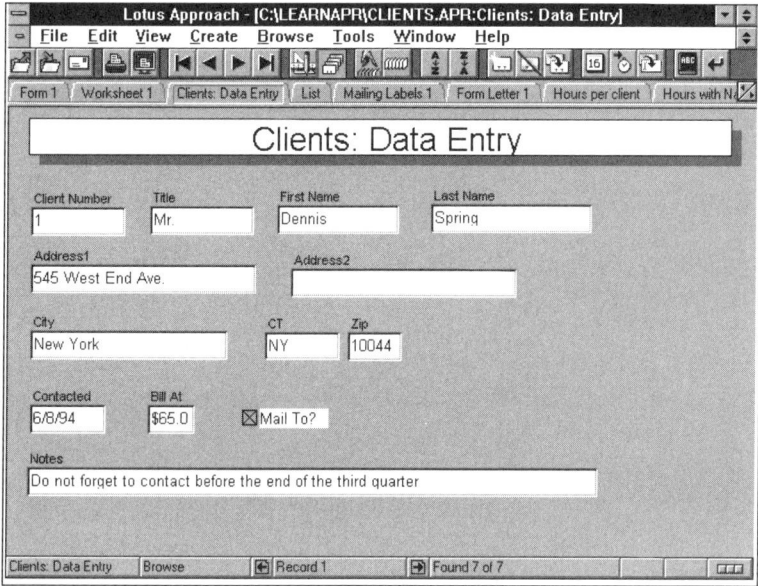

Figure 1.13 A View in Browse mode.

- *Back Arrow.* Moves the focus to the record before the current record.

- *Forward Arrow.* Moves the focus to the record after the current record.

- *End Arrow.* Moves the focus to the last record of the file.

- *Design.* Is used to enter Design mode.

- *Browse.* Is used to enter Browse mode.

- *Find.* Is used to enter Find mode, so you can you enter criteria to specify which records are displayed.

Show All. Displays all the records once again.

 Sort Ascending and Sort Descending. Lets you sort the records instantly, so the records are arranged with the values in the current field in ascending or descending order.

 New Record. Adds a blank record to the file, so you can add new data to it.

 Delete Record. Deletes the current record, removing it permanently from the file.

You can begin to appreciate Approach's ease of use simply by looking at these icons. They let you do almost everything that you need to do to work with data simply by pointing and clicking.

Working in Design Mode

You can display a field in Design mode in two different ways. Figure 1.14 shows the same view that was illustrated above displayed in Design mode with data showing, and Figure 1.15 shows it without data showing. With data showing, design mode looks like Browse mode. Without data showing, the fields are replaced by objects that include the name of the field surrounded by a dotted line. You can change a View in Design mode with or without data showing, depending on which is easier for what you are currently doing. To switch between the two, choose **Show Data** from the View menu.

Whether or not data is showing, you can manipulate objects easily by using the mouse. You can simply click and drag an object to resize it or to move it somewhere else in the design, as you do with objects in many Windows applications.

The icon bars in Design mode differ a bit, depending on what type of design you are working on. There are a few features of design mode that are even more important than the icon bar and that are common to most designs.

Chapter 1: Approach: A Quick Tour

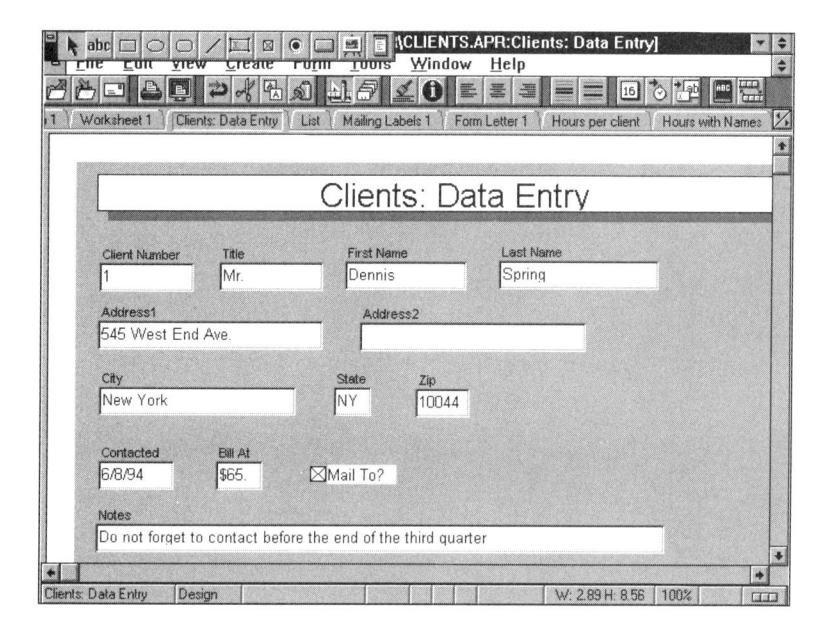

Figure 1.14 Design mode with data showing.

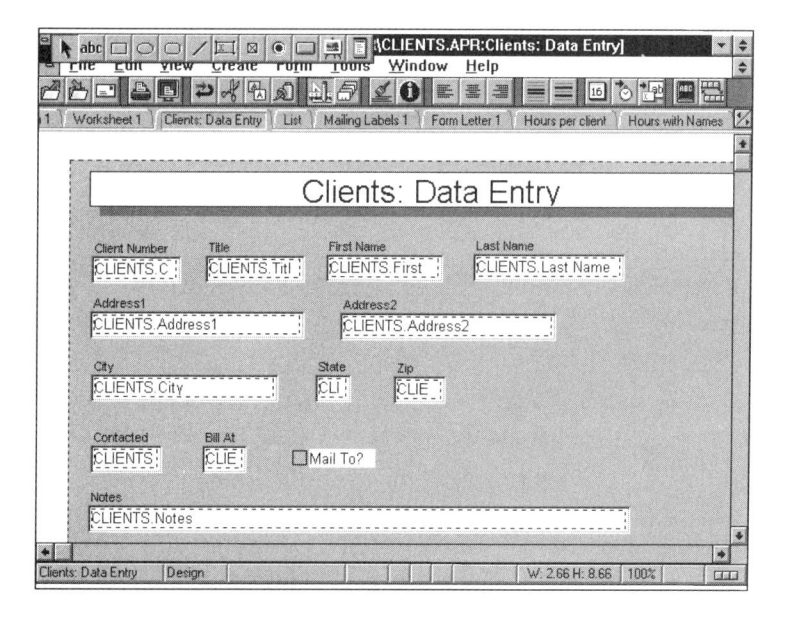

Figure 1.15 Design mode without data showing.

The Drawing Tools

You can add new objects to a view by working in Design mode using the drawing tools and the Add Field box (see Figure 1.16).

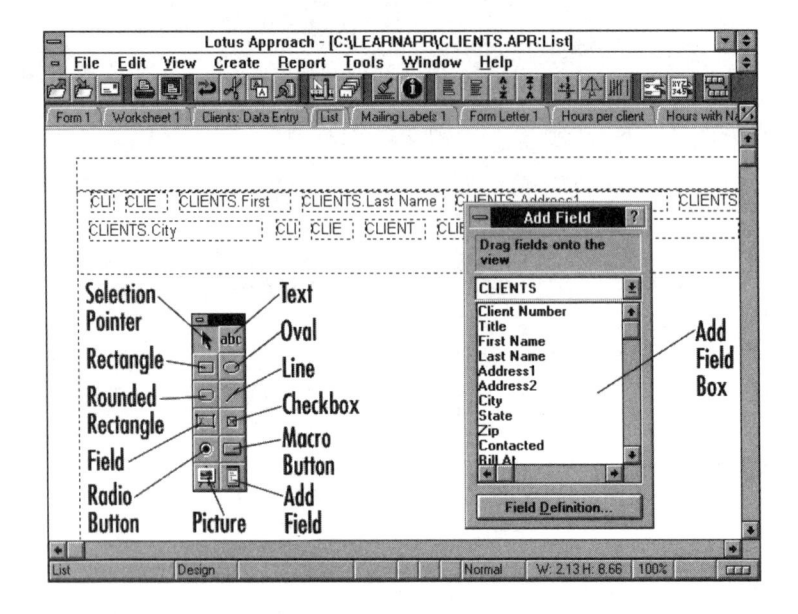

Figure 1.16 The Drawing Tools and Add Field Box.

Approach provides the following drawing tools:

- *Selection Pointer.* When you select the other tools to add new objects to a design, your mouse pointer changes from a pointer to some other form. You can click **Selection Pointer** at any time to make it a pointer again and to stop adding the object.
- *Text.* Used to add text to a design. Select it, then click and drag anywhere on the design to create a text box. Type the text into this box.
- *Graphics.* Includes the Rectangle, Oval, Rounded Rectangle, or Line tools, let you add simple graphic objects. Select one of these tools, and then simply click and drag to place one of these graphic objects anywhere on the design.
- *Field.* Lets you place a field in the design. If necessary, the same field can be placed in the design several times.

- *Checkbox.* Lets you place a check box in the design, to make it easy for the user to enter data in a field that holds the values true or false.
- *Radio button.* Lets you place a group of radio buttons in the design, to make it easier for the user to choose among multiple values for a field.
- *Macro Button.* Lets you place a push button in the design. You can attach a macro to the push buttons, so you can execute a series of commands simply by clicking the button.
- *Picture.* Lets you add a PicturePlus field to your design. Version 1 of Approach included a Picture field which held graphic images. Now you can also add sound, video, and other advanced effects in these fields, if you have other Windows applications to create them, and so they are called PicturePlus fields.
- *Add field.* Displays the Add Field Box, so you can use it to add a field to the design. The Add field box gives you an easy way of adding fields to a design: simply click and drag a field from this box to place it in the design.

The Info Box

You can change certain styles and properties of the objects in a View or of the View as a whole by working in Design view with its Info Box. An Info Box has the same sort of divider tab interface as other features of Approach (see Figure 1.17). You can display panels with specifications for different features of the object by clicking the appropriate tab.

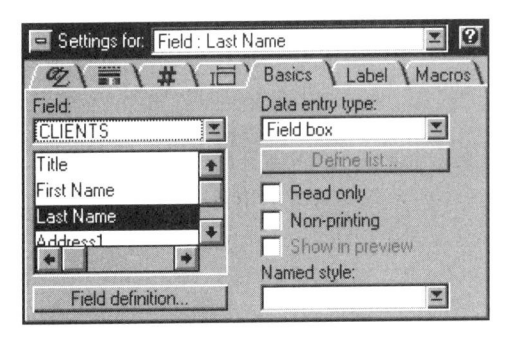

Figure 1.17 An Info Box.

There is one panel of the Info Box for a Field. You can use it to select the field's colors and a number of features of its borders. A similar panel is included in the Info Box for many types of objects.

The styles and properties included in an Info Box depend on the type of object and type of view it is used for. Info Boxes are discussed in detail in Chapters 3, 4, and 9, where you learn to design different types of views.

Working in Preview Mode

Preview mode displays the view as it looks when it is printed (see Figure 1.18).

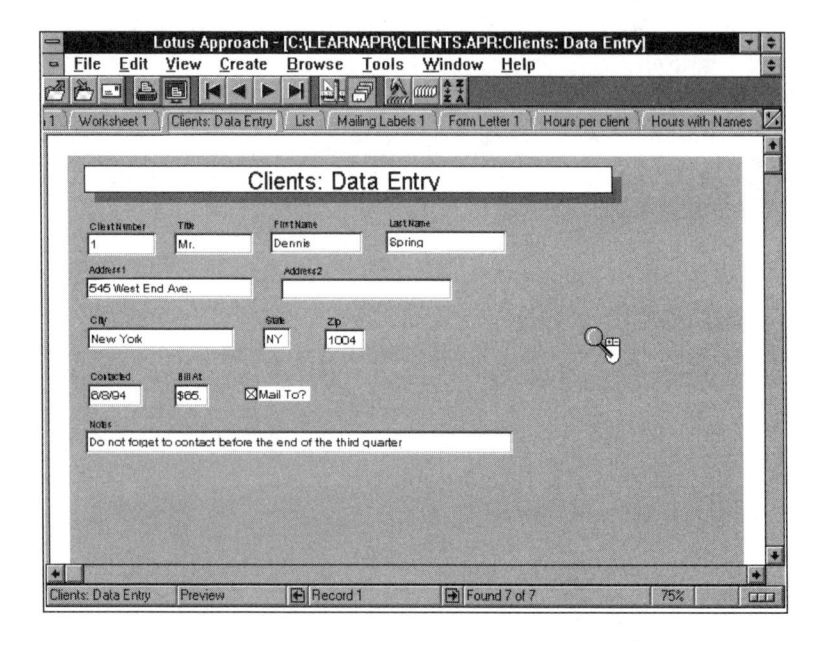

Figure 1.18 Preview Mode.

Initially, the view is displayed at 75 percent of its actual size. It is easy to change its size:

- The pointer changes to the form shown in the illustration to show that you can simply click the design to make it larger or right-click it to make it smaller.
- The percent of actual size is shown on the status bar, and you can click it to display a pop-up that lets you choose among available zoom sizes, from 25% to 200%.

Working in Find Mode

When you are in Browse mode, you can choose **Find** from the Browse menu to display a Find Request (see Figure 1.19).

In Find mode, Approach displays one record from the current view, with all of its fields blank, so you can enter criteria in the fields to determine which records to find.

For example, you can enter **CA** in the State field to find the records of people from California, or you can enter **John** in the First Name field and **Smith** in the Last Name field to find the record for John Smith. After you have finished the find, only the records that match the criterion are displayed; the others are temporarily hidden.

You can choose **Show All** from the Browse menu or click the **Find All** icon to display all the records again.

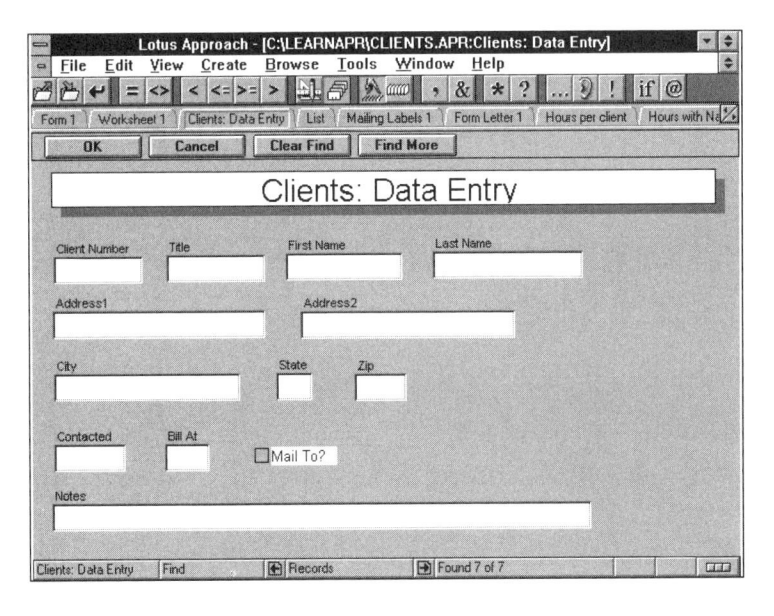

Figure 1.19 A Find Request.

The icon bar in Browse mode makes it easier to enter formulas needed for more sophisticated finds. Finds are covered in detail in Chapter 6 of this book.

A Glance at Approach's Menus

Approach has pop-up menus like other Windows applications. All of the options of the menu system are described in Appendix B. But for now glance at the main features of Approach's menu, to see how it is organized:

- *File.* Used for the same file operations that it commonly performs in Windows applications, such as creating, opening, and closing files, and printing.
- *Edit.* Used for the editor operations, such as **Cut** and **Paste**, that are common to Windows applications. It is also used to duplicate or delete a form or other view.
- *View.* Changes the display in ways that may be convenient when you are creating a design. For example, you can use the View menu to display the Info Box and the Drawing tools when you are in design view.
- *Create.* Displays the Assistant in order to create a new Form, Report, Mailing Label, Form Letter, Worksheet, Crosstab, or Chart. It is also used to join the files of a relational database and to change the definition of the fields of a database.
- *Browse.* This menu is displayed only when you are in Browse mode, is used to add or delete records, and to perform finds to isolate sets of records, to sort records, and to perform a few other tasks that are useful when you are viewing data.
- *Object.* A menu for the specific type of view you are working on (such as the Form Menu or the Report Menu) is displayed instead of the Browse menu when you are in Design view. These menus help you change the design of specific objects or of the view as a whole.
- *Tool.* Works with Approach utilities, for example, to check spelling or to create and run Macros.
- *Window.* Arranges windows and moves from one window to another. Like other Windows applications, Approach can open multiple databases at the same time, each in a different Window, and the Window menu lets you work with them all.
- *Help.* Lets you use the Approach Help System, which is like the help systems of other Windows applications.

All menu options require that you first select one of the options listed above to pop-up a submenu, and then select an option from the submenu. To describe this sort of selection, this book says (for example), "choose **Copy** from the Edit menu" to mean that you first choose **Edit** from the Main menu, and then choose **Copy** from the Edit submenu.

Creating a Working Directory

This chapter has given you an overview of Approach. In the rest of this book, you look at its features in detail and work with sample data. Before you go on, you should create a directory to hold the files that you will create as you use this book.

Directories are a convenience for organizing your files. You can think of the directory system as an inverted tree. At the top is the root directory, represented by the character \. You can create other directories under the root directory, or under any other directory.

When a directory system is displayed by the Windows File Manager, notice that all of the directories under the root directory are listed alphabetically. In addition, the Approach directory has two subdirectories under it, Icons and Samples (see Figure 1.20).

You can think of directories as folders. Notice that, in the illustration, the Approach folder is open (and the folder and directory name are highlighted) to indicate that the files displayed in the right panel are in this folder. In addition, the Icons and Samples folders are shown in the right panel; these folders are in the Approach folder.

It is easy to create a new directory by using the File menu of the Windows File Manager. By default, the new directory is a subdirectory of the directory that is selected when you create it, so you must be sure the root directory is selected.

In this exercise, the directory is created on disk drive C, the hard disk of most systems. If your hard disk is partitioned, or you have multiple hard disks, you may want to use some other disk for your sample data instead of C.

Practical Approach, 3.0

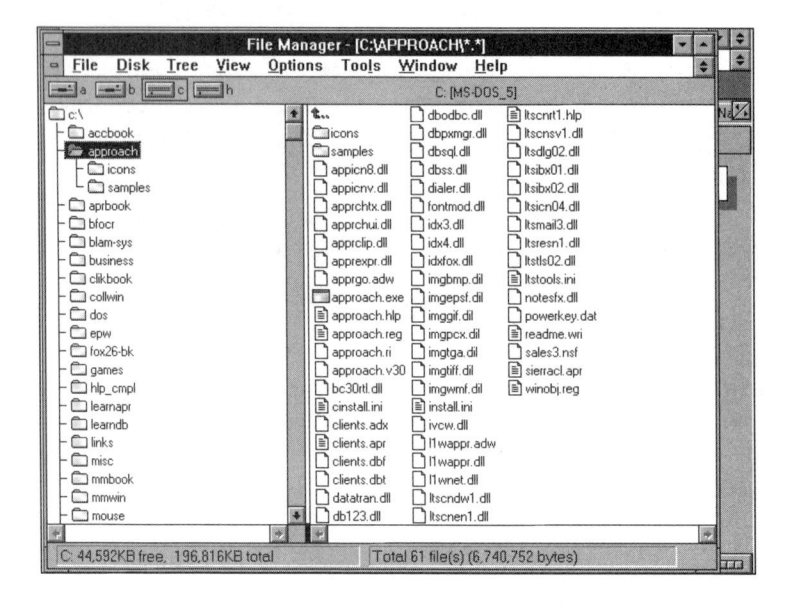

Figure 1.20 A directory system.

1. If necessary, start your computer and start Windows. Bring the Main window of the Windows Program Manager to the front or open it if necessary (you can do this by choosing **Main** from the Window menu of the Program Manager's menu system). Double-click the **File Manager** icon (or highlight this icon and press **Enter**) to use the File Manager.

2. Make sure that C is the current drive. If it is not, click on the **C drive** icon near the upper-right corner of the File Manager icon. (Or, if you want to use some other drive, make it the current drive.)

3. Click the root directory, **C:**, at the top of the left panel of the File Manager to make it the current directory. It should be highlighted and its folder open.

4. Choose **Create Directory** from the File menu to display the Create Directory dialog box. The cursor should be in the name text box. Type: **learnapr** (see Figure 1.21). Then press **Enter** (or select the **OK** push button).

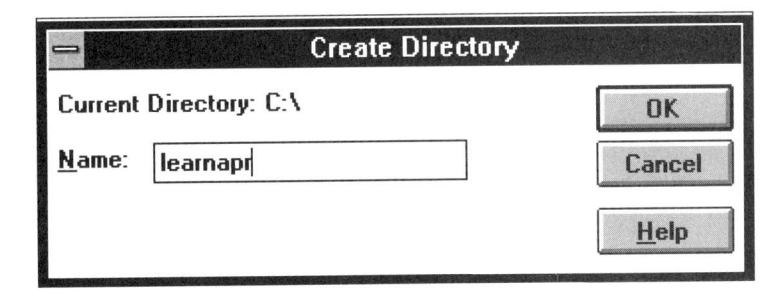

Figure 1.21 Creating a new directory.

5. The new directory should be added to the directory tree of the File Manager in alphabetical order. Choose **Exit** from the File menu to close the File Manager.

All the exercises in this book use this directory. When you are done with this book, you can use the File Manager to get rid of all sample data you add in the exercises. Simply highlight learnapr in the directory panel and press **Del**. Windows asks for confirmation before deleting all the files and removing the directory.

Chapter 2

Creating a Database File

In the last chapter, you learned that a database is like a folder of paper forms that are printed to show you where to fill in the data. Before you can work with sample data, you must define the fields of the database, which is like deciding what data you should leave spaces for on the paper forms. In this chapter, you learn to define the fields of a sample database. In later chapters, you enter sample data in this file and create custom data entry forms, reports, and other designs that use this sample database.

To create a sample database file in this chapter, you learn:
- How to use the New dialog box to name the file
- How to use the Field Definition dialog box to specify the fields in the file
- The data files that can underlie an Approach File
- The data types available in Approach
- How to decide what fields you should use to hold your data
- How to open and close an Approach file
- How to change the definition of fields in a file you have already created

Creating a New File

To create a new file, you can begin by using either the Welcome dialog box or the New dialog box. Then you must use the Field Definition dialog box to specify the names and types of its fields.

The Welcome Dialog Box

When you start Approach, by default, it displays the Welcome dialog box that lets you open an existing file or create a new one (see Figure 2.1).

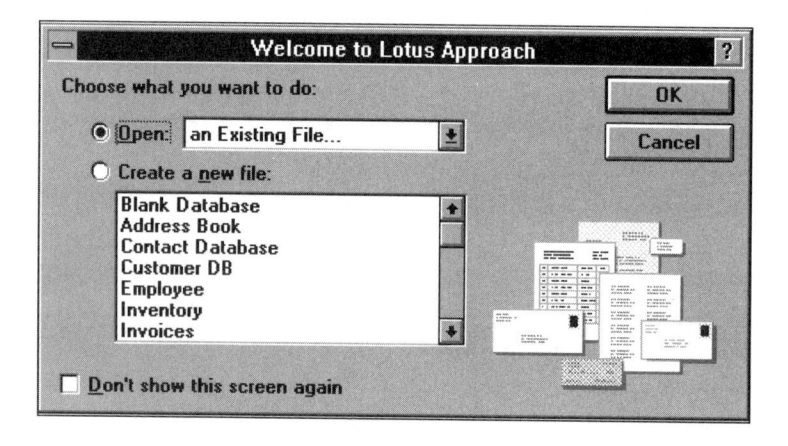

Figure 2.1 The Welcome dialog box.

SHORTCUT — You can select the checkbox at the bottom of this dialog box if you do not want Approach to display it again. Many people find it more convenient to bypass this dialog box and go directly to the menu system when you start Approach. If the dialog box is not displayed in your version of Approach, it simply means an earlier user selected this checkbox.

To create a new database, select either **Blank Database** or one of the templates in the list in the bottom half of this dialog box: the templates are discussed below in the section on the New dialog box.

Chapter 2: Creating a Database File

SHORTCUT — You do not need to click the **Create a new file** radio button. When you make a selection from this list, Approach automatically selects it for you.

Select **OK**, and Approach displays the **New** dialog box, which is covered next, so you can name the File.

The New Dialog Box

You can also create a database file in Approach by choosing New from the File Menu to display the New dialog box (see Figure 2.2).

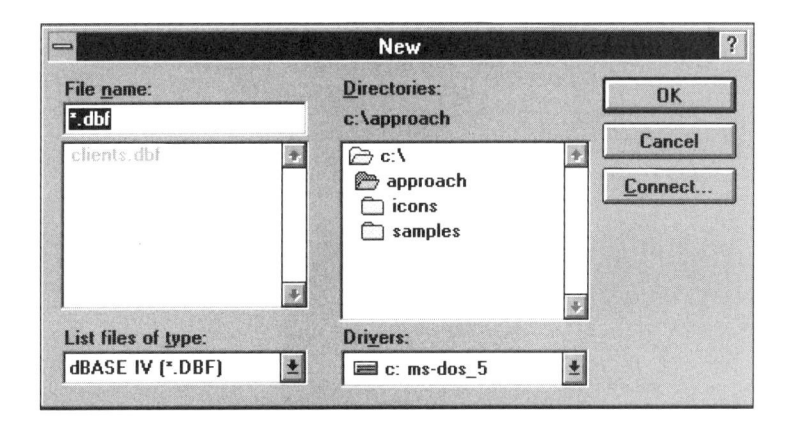

Figure 2.2 The New dialog box.

As you can see in the illustration, you use this dialog box to specify the file's name and the disk drive and directory that it is kept in. If you have seen similar dialog boxes in other Windows applications, you should just glance at the description in this section and then go on to the next section.

Selecting a Drive and Directory

You use the Drives drop-down menu of this dialog box to select the disk drive that you want the file to be kept on.

The directories of the selected drive are displayed in the Directories list. You can make a directory the *current directory* by double-clicking it in this list. This is sometimes called *opening a directory*.

For example, you can double-click the root directory to display all the directories under it. Use the scroll bar to scroll through this list of directories and double-click on the one you want to use as the current directory and display the directory under it.

In Figure 2.2, for example, Approach is the current directory, and only the two subdirectories under it are displayed. The rest of the directories under the root directory are not.

Selecting File Type

You must select the type of the file you want to create from the List files of type drop-down. The file types available are dBASE III +, dBASE IV, FoxPro, and Paradox. If you are working on a network and have the appropriate software, you can use other file types that are added to this drop-down menu and can be selected like any other file type.

The features of all these different types of files are discussed at length in Chapter 12 of this book; you need to know most of them only if you are working with your data using some other database program as well as Approach. The features you generally need to know to create and use files within Approach are covered in this chapter. The default file type is dBASE IV. It is the most commonly used in Approach applications and so it is used in the exercises in this book.

This drop-down list includes the files extensions after the name of the file type. FoxPro, dBASE IV, and dBASE III + all have the extension DBF, though there are some minor differences between them. Paradox files have the extension DB.

Naming the File

When you select a file type, all files with that extension are displayed in the File Name list.

An asterisk followed by that extension is displayed in the File Name text box. For example, ***.db** is displayed if you select **Paradox**. The asterisk is the wildcard character that stands for any series of characters.

WARNING: You can select one of the existing files from this list, and its name is displayed in this text box. However, if you create a new file with the same name as an existing file, Approach either destroys that file and all the data it contains or refuses to create the file—depending on the file type.

This list is added primarily for compatibility with other dialog boxes that are similar to this one. On occasion, you might want to select a file name from this list and then edit it in the text box so it is no longer the name of an existing file.

Normally, however, you simply type the name of a new file in the File Name text box. File names can be no more than eight characters and cannot contain blank spaces. The name must also have the same extension as the type selected in the List files of type drop-down menu, or Approach does not let you create it.

SHORTCUT: If the name has no extension, the appropriate extension is added to it. The easiest way to create a file is to type a name and omit the extension.

Other Features of the New Dialog Box

The New dialog box has one other control, the Connect button, which displays dialog boxes that let you define network connections for the various file types. These dialog boxes are covered in Chapter 12.

This button does not apply to you if you are working on a stand-alone computer, and even if you are working on a network, you generally can ignore this push button and use the default network connection.

Once you have selected the drive, directory and file type of the new file and entered its name, select **OK** (or press **Enter**) to define the fields of the new file.

The Field Definition Dialog Box

When you select **OK** from the New dialog box, the Field Definition dialog box is displayed, which lets you define the fields on the new database (see Figure 2.3). As you can see, this dialog box has the title Creating New Database followed by the database name.

Practical Approach, 3.0

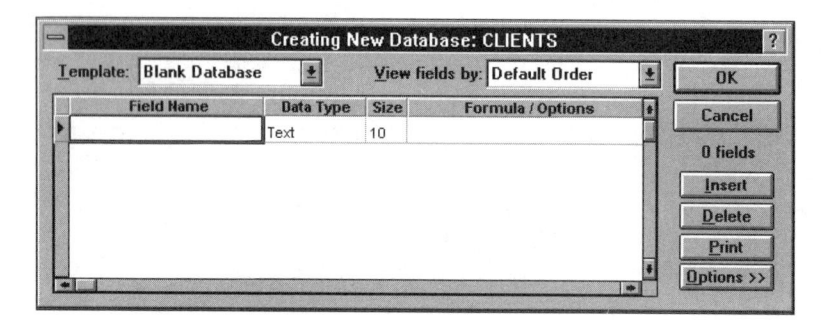

Figure 2.3 The Field Definition Dialog Box.

To define a field, you enter its Name, select its **Data Type**, and enter its Size in the appropriate columns.

If you select the **Options** button, you can use an expanded form of the dialog box to enter options for each field. The options you select are automatically displayed in the Formula/Options column, to the right of the field. These options are used to validate data and automate data entry, rather than to define the fields themselves, and they are covered in Chapter 3.

To define the database, you simply use this dialog box to list a Field Name and Data Type for all the fields in the database, and a Size for fields that require one.

Press **Tab** to move the focus to the next column, or simply click to move to it. If the focus is in the Size column, pressing **Tab** again adds a new row and moves the focus to its field name column, making it easy to enter definitions for all the fields.

As a beginner, you will type in the name and use the Data Type drop down to select a Data Type. If that Data Type does not require a Size, Approach enters **Fixed** in the Size column. If it does require one, Approach enters a default Size, which you can edit.

> **SHORTCUT** Rather than using the drop-down menu to select a Data Type, you can simply Tab to that column and press the first letter of the data type you need, after you are accustomed to the available data types. Tabbing among columns and typing specifications is the fastest way to define a database.

If you enter an invalid specification for a field, Approach displays a warning (see Figure 2.4). It does not let you move the focus out of that row until you correct the error.

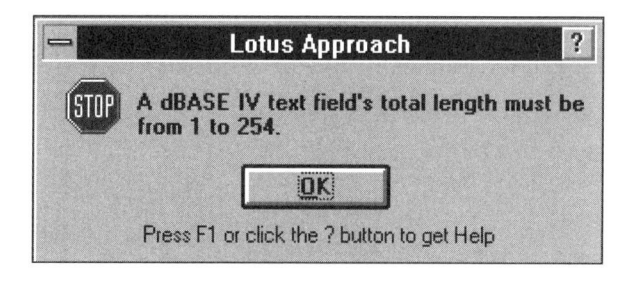

Figure 2.4 Approach does not let you enter invalid specifications.

Defining Fields

Now you have an overview of this dialog box, and you can look in more detail at how to specify fields.

Field Names

The field names that are valid depend on the type of file that you are creating. FoxPro, dBASE III+, and dBASE IV all use the same type of file (with the extension DBF) and all have the same limitations on field names. Paradox uses a different type of file (with the extension DB) and has different rules for naming fields:

- *dBASE and FoxPro.* Field names can be up to 32 characters long and can use any characters, including blank spaces and special characters such as commas and periods.
- *Paradox.* Most field names can be up to 25 characters long; the names of Time, Memo, Boolean, and PicturePlus fields can be up to 18 characters. Field names can contain letters, numbers, blank spaces, commas, periods, and arithmetic signs. There are some special characters they cannot contain.

WARNING: The rules for dBASE and FoxPro databases only apply in Approach. FoxPro and dBASE themselves allow field names of up to 10 characters long, which can include letters, numbers, or the underscore character, but cannot include other special characters or blank spaces. If you create a dBASE field name in Approach that does not obey these rules, the field name will be different if you use that file in another dBASE compatible application.

The requirements for field names for various file types are covered in more detail in Chapter 12, but you should have no trouble naming fields if you remember the requirements listed above.

There is no need to spend time memorizing these requirements. As you have seen, if a field name is not valid, Approach displays an error message when you try to move the focus to another row.

Data Types

Approach files let you use a wide variety of field types, which you select from the Data Type drop-down menu. However, not all of these can translate into fields in the underlying file, so data entered in some field types may not be accessible if you use files from Approach in dBASE, FoxPro, or Paradox. This is an issue that you do not need to worry about if you are only using Approach to work with your data.

Approach's Data Types are:

- *Boolean.* Holds only two values, logical true and logical false, generally displayed as **Yes** and **No**.
- *Calculated.* Holds the result of a calculation. Calculations can be performed on numeric or other types of fields. Before you use this field type, you must know about advanced features of Approach, such as Operators and Functions, and so it is covered in Chapter 8. Calculated fields exist only in the Approach File, not in the underlying database file.
- *Date.* Holds a date. Only valid dates can be entered.
- *Memo.* Holds any amount of text, unlike Text fields, whose length must be specified. Memo fields can be used to hold large amounts of text, as Text fields have limitations on their size, or they can be used when the amount of text stored in the field varies greatly from record to record—for example, in a field used to hold notes on each record.

- *Numeric.* Holds numbers that you may want to perform calculations on. For data such as zip codes, which are made up of numbers but which you never want to perform calculations on, it is best to use Text fields. The Size of a numeric field (including the number of decimal places it has) must be specified when you define the field. Only valid numbers can be entered.
- *PicturePlus.* Holds pictures or sound, animation, and other types of data. It is described in more detail in Chapter 3, which discusses how to add data to a PicturePlus field.
- *Text.* Holds any characters, including letters, numbers, and special characters. The Size of a Text field must be specified when you define the field. The field does not hold more than the number of characters you specify, and it includes that many characters even if the data you enter is shorter than the length you specify, adding extra blank space characters to fill the length.
- *Time.* Holds a time, precise to a hundredth of a second. Only valid times can be entered.
- *Variable.* Holds temporary data used in a calculation. This advanced field type is covered in Chapter 10. Variable fields exist only in the Approach File, not in the underlying database file.

As you can see, the field types you use most often are Text, Numeric, and Date fields. Boolean, and Memo fields are often useful for special purposes. The data in any of these field types can be used in dBASE, FoxPro or Paradox 4.0, but memo fields cannot be used by earlier versions of Paradox.

Approach PicturePlus, Calculated, and Variable fields cannot be accessed by any of the other programs.

For more details on compatibility of Approach field types with other programs, see Chapter 12.

Field Size

Most fields are a constant size (such as Boolean or Date fields), or have no specific size (such as PicturePlus or Memo fields). When you select one of these as the Data Type, Approach displays **Fixed** in that field's Size column.

You must always specify the size of text fields, and you must specify the size of number fields for dBase files, but not for Paradox or SQL files.

The sizes that are allowed are discussed below, but there is no need to memorize these size requirements. Just remember that a size is required if the word **Fixed** not displayed in the Size column. If you enter an invalid size, Approach displays an error message explaining the size requirement, so you should just glance at the size limits listed below to get a general idea of what they are.

dBASE and FoxPro

When you are defining a dBASE or FoxPro database, you must specify a size for both Text and Numeric fields:

- *Text Fields.* In dBASE and FoxPro files, a text field can be any length from 1 to 254 characters.
- *Numeric.* When you define a Number field for dBASE or FoxPro files, you must use the size column to indicate both the number of integer digits and the number of decimal places that the field holds. A Number field can have up to 19 digits and up to 15 decimal places.

Enter the number of digits, followed by a decimal point, followed by the number of decimal places. For example, to hold dollar amounts up to hundreds of dollars, enter the Size **3.2** to allow three places left of the decimal point and two places right of the decimal point.

> **NOTE** If you leave out the decimal point and second number, Approach assumes that no decimal places are allowed.

Later, when you are doing data entry, Approach uses the size you defined as follows:

- It does not let you enter a number larger than the number of integers you specify. The number of integers you enter here determines the maximum magnitude of the number you can enter.
- If you enter more decimal places than the definition allows, Approach rounds or truncates the number to fit the specification. The number of decimal places you enter here determines the maximum precision of the number you can enter.

NOTE: If you are familiar with dBASE or FoxPro, you should remember that number fields for these file types are defined differently in Approach than in these programs. In dBASE or FoxPro, the length of the field represents its total length, including both the number of integers and the number of decimal places, and the decimal point. In Approach, the length represents only the number of integers, the number of decimal places is specified separately, and the decimal point is not counted in the length.

Paradox

For Paradox files, a *text field* can be any length from 1 to 255 characters. You do not specify the length of a number field.

If you create or use a Paradox file in Approach, it must have a Key field. A *Key field* is a unique identifier field, such as an employee number. Key fields in Paradox can be made of a single or multiple fields and must not hold duplicate values. Key fields are useful in relational databases, and they are described fully in Chapter 7.

When you are finished defining the fields of a Paradox file and select **OK**, Approach displays the Choose Key Field dialog box. You must select one or more of the fields from the list and select the **Add Key Field** button to designate it as a Key field.

If you select the **Cancel** button from this dialog box, Approach returns you to the Field Definition dialog box. If necessary, you can add a new field there to be used as the Key field. Approach does not create the file without a Key field.

NOTE: If you use an existing Paradox file that does not already have a Key field, Approach also displays the Choose Key Field dialog box and requires you to select a Key field.

Editing Specifications of Field Definitions

When you are defining a database, it is easy to edit the specifications that you have already entered.

Move the focus to the cell you want to change by pressing **Tab** and **Shift+Tab** to move to the next and previous column, or simply by clicking the cell with the mouse. Edit it or type over it using the usual Windows editing methods.

Practical Approach, 3.0

Inserting a New Field

To insert a new field in the structure of the database, click the **Insert** button to add a new, blank row above the row where the focus currently is, and enter the specifications for the field in that row.

Deleting a Field

To delete a field, first select its row by clicking the selection box to its left and the row is highlighted (see Figure 2.5). Then click the **Delete** button to delete it.

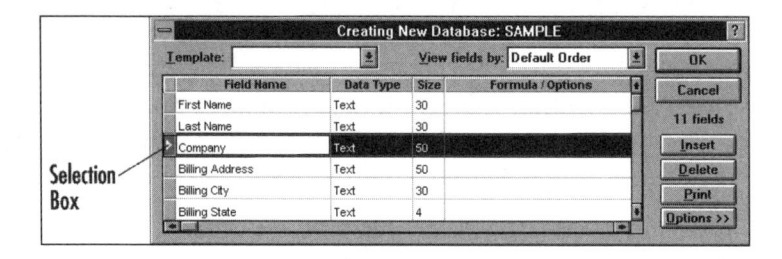

Figure 2.5 Selecting a row.

Changing Field Order

To change the order of fields that you have already defined, first select the row of a field that you want to move by clicking the selection box to its left. When the row is highlighted, you can click and drag the selection box up or down to move the row to a different location in the field list. The pointer is displayed as a hand when it is in the location where it can be used to move the row.

Using Templates

Approach comes with a collection of templates that you can use as the basis of new databases that you are defining. A template is simply a typical definition of a commonly used database file: for example, there are templates set up to keep track of Addresses, Contacts, Customers, Employees, Inventory, and the like.

Use the Template drop-down menu to select one of these templates. The entire definition is entered in the dialog box, for example, the field definitions for the Address Book template (see Figure 2.6).

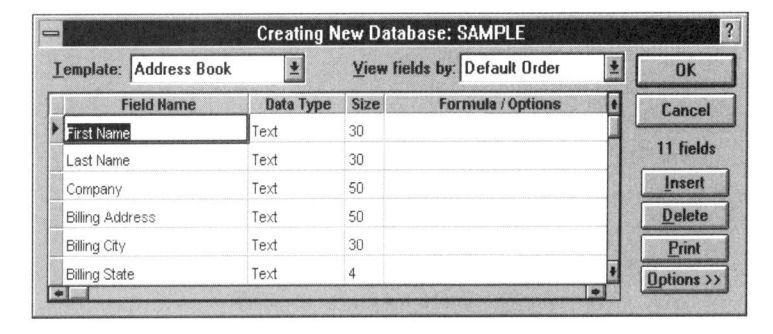

Figure 2.6 The Address Book template.

After selecting a template, you can modify it using the methods described above, so it fits your specifications exactly.

Field Order

If you are modifying a database that has a large number of fields, it is sometimes hard to find the field that you want to change. You can use the View fields drop-down menu to change the order in which fields are displayed. It has the following options:

- *Default Order.* Lists the fields as you entered them in their actual order in the database.
- *Field Name.* Lists the fields alphabetically by field name.
- *Data Type.* Lists the fields alphabetically by data type.
- *Custom Order.* When this is selected, you can drag the fields up and down in the list to rearrange them.

Any of these options only changes the order in which fields are displayed in this dialog box—not their actual order in the database. Though it can be very useful on occasion, this feature is not needed when you are defining most databases.

A Sample Database File

Creating a database file using Approach is fairly simple, and you now have more than enough background to create a sample file.

The sample application that you work with in this book is a list of clients used by a professional who bills by the hour. It must hold the clients' names, addresses, the date of the last contact, the rate at which the client is billed, a field indicating whether the client is on a special mailing list, and a field to hold notes. It must also keep track of the dates on which you worked for each client, and the number of hours worked on each date.

Before you begin creating this application on the computer, though, you should analyze its requirements in more detail. A short time spent analyzing before you begin work can save you many hours spent changing the application once you are using it.

What Fields Are Needed

First, think carefully about what data you need and about how to break down your data into separate fields.

Necessary Data

The data that is needed in this application was outlined above, but in a real application, you would spend some time developing a list of the data that you need for the application, before you begin to create the database file. Even with the data outlined for you, as it is here, there are still some questions to decide upon.

For example, do you need to keep a record of a title, such as Mr., Ms., or Dr. for each client? For many applications, this is not necessary, but if you write form letters and want to begin them with a salutation such as Dear Mr. so-and-so, then you need a field to hold the title. Let's assume that we do want to write this sort of form letter and that we need to include a Title field in the database.

You should try to anticipate the ways in which the data is to be used so that you can decide in advance what data you need. It takes more time to go through the database after you have done the initial data entry and add a title for each client, than it does to enter the titles from the start.

Breaking Down the Data into Fields

You must also anticipate how you will use your data in order to decide how to break it down into fields.

Any data that you want to use as the basis of a sort, for example, should be in a field by itself. People computerizing their own businesses actually have made the error of creating a single field for Name, entering all of their data, and then realizing that they could not list the names alphabetically without having the last name in a separate field. People have been forced to re-enter hundreds or even thousands of names because of this error.

> **NOTE** As a general rule, it is best to break up the data into more fields rather than fewer, to give yourself the ability to manipulate the data in more ways. In addition to separate fields for First Name and Last Name, you should always have separate fields for City, State, and Zip code, rather than a single CSZ field, so you can search for records by state and sort by zip code if necessary.

Having additional fields does slow down data entry a bit, however, and many people find it a nuisance to press **Tab** to move to the new field, so you should not add extra fields unnecessarily.

It is common to have a single field for both First Name and Middle Initial, for example. If you are writing form letters where you address people by first name, you must put the first name and middle initial in separate fields so your letters begin *Dear John* instead of *Dear John Q*. In the sample application, however, you are using a title and last name in the form letters, and we will assume that you do not need to use the first or middle name alone elsewhere, so that you do not need separate fields for first name and middle initial.

One-to-One Relationships

Finally, there is one very important feature of database design that people who are not computer professionals often overlook; there must be a one-to-one relationship among the fields of a database file.

In the sample application every client has one title, one first name, one last name, one last-contact date, and so on. There is a one-to-one relationship among all these data elements.

On the other hand, you can contract to do many jobs for each client, so you may have many different sets of work days and work hours for each. Work days and work hours are in a many-to-one relationship with the other data on clients.

How should you record the data on work days and hours? You obviously do not want to have one field for work day and hours in each record, so that you would have to create a new record for a client each day that you work for that client. Doing this would involve tremendous duplication of data. You would have to re-enter the client's name, address and the like for every day.

You might be tempted to create a record for each client with space for a large number of days and hours. It could have fields for the client's name and address, and fields for the date of day one, the hours of day one, the date of day two, the hours of day two, and so on through day fifty or one hundred. If you did this, however, you would waste disk space on blank fields if you had a client that you did only one or two days of work for. Even more important, it would be difficult to create reports summarizing the total number of hours that you worked for each client, because each day's hours would be recorded in fields with a different name.

Database theory has shown that the best way to handle this sort of many-to-one relationship is by keeping the data in two files, which are related by using some common *Key field*, such as a Client Number.

In the sample database, one file would hold the Client Number and all the basic data on the client, such as name, address, and last contact date. The second would hold the client number and the data on the dates worked for the client and the number of hours worked on each date—the data that is in a many-to-one relation with the data in the first file. Then, you could use the Client Number to relate the two in order to produce data entry forms or reports that include the name and other basic data for a client, plus a list of the dates worked and hours worked for that client.

This is called a *relational database* because it involves relating multiple files. Relational databases are needed for most practical business applications, for anything more complex than a simple mailing list. They are covered in Chapter 7.

For now, you simply create a single-file database without the days and hours worked for each client. Once you have learned how to use Approach to work with this single-file database, it will be easy for you to create the second file and to learn to work with a relational database.

You include a Client Number field in the file you create in this chapter, to make it easier to use it in a relational database later.

Chapter 2: Creating a Database File

WARNING — Until you have learned about relational databases, you should remember to look for one-to-one relationships among all data elements when you are designing a database. If the fields are not in a one-to-one relationship, you should not try to manage the data using a single-file database.

Creating a Sample File

The analysis has gone far enough that you should be able to identify the fields of the sample file and the data type of each.

Table 2.1 Fields and data type.

Fields	Data type	Fields	Data type
Client Number	Number	State	Text
Title	Text	Zip	Text
First Name	Text	Last Contact	Date
Last Name	Text	Billing rate	Number
Address1	Text	Mailings	Boolean
Address2	Text	Notes	Memo
City	Text		

In general, it is best to leave two lines for an address, so that you can record addresses that have a company name as their first line. The reasons for including all the other fields listed here (and for leaving out fields to hold the dates and hours worked on each job) were described above in the section on analysis.

We use a dBASE IV file to hold the sample data, since this is the default and the most common file type. You might try working with other file types on your own.

You can use another file type for the sample file in the exercises in this book if you have a special reason to use it in your work. You may find there are only minor variations from the instructions on creating and using a dBASE file, that are listed in the exercises in this book.

NOTE: Before you do this exercise, you must create a directory named **\LEARNAPR** to hold the database file. If you have not already done so, go back to the last section of Chapter 1, which tells you how to create this directory (or create it on your own, if you are familiar with DOS or with the Windows File Manager). If you have not yet installed Approach, see Appendix A.

Create the new database file as follows:

1. If necessary, start Approach by double-clicking on the icon in the Windows file manager. You can use the Welcome dialog box to create the new file by selecting **Blank Database** from its list and then selecting **OK**. Alternatively, if Approach is running, choose **New** from the File menu. In either case, the New dialog box is displayed, which lets you name the file.

2. Select the **\learnapr** directory from the Directories list. If necessary, use the Drives drop-down menu to select the drive where you created this directory. Double-click the **C:** directory (or Root directory of another disk) at the top of the directory tree to display all the directories under it. If necessary click the **Scroll Bar** until you can see the learnapr directory. Double-click **\learnapr** so it is displayed as the only directory under **C:**, with its folder open.

3. At the File Name, enter **clients.** Since you are creating a dBASE file, Approach automatically adds the extension DBF (see Figure 2.7). Select **OK** to display the Field Definition dialog box.

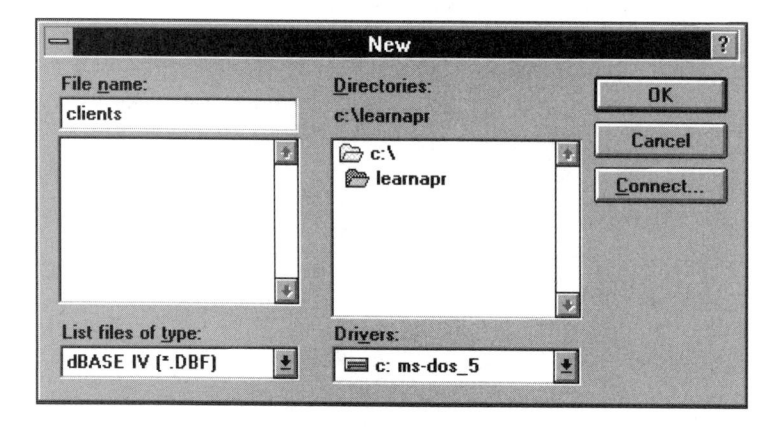

Figure 2.7 Naming the new file.

Chapter 2: Creating a Database File

4. You might want to try looking at some of the templates that are provided. Select **Address Book** from the Template drop-down menu and scroll through the fields. Select other templates if you want. When you are done, choose **Blank Database** (the first option on this list). After you have created a database from scratch, it is easy to modify templates.

5. The cursor should already be in the Field Name text box. Type **Client Number**. Select **Numeric** from the Data Type drop-down list. As the Size, enter **3**.

6. Now, enter the definition of the Title field. Press **Tab** to move to the next row. Type **Title.** Leave Text as the Data Type. As the Size, enter **5**. Press **Tab** to move to the next row.

7. To define the first name field, type **First Name** in the Field Name column leave Text as the Data Type, press **Tab** twice, and enter **15** as the Size. Next, define the first name field. Press **Tab** to move to the next row, and type **Last Name** as the Field name. Press **Tab** twice to move to the Size text box and type **20**. Press **Tab** to move to the next row.

8. To add the two address fields, type **Address1** as the name, press **Tab** twice, type **30** in the Size text box, type **Address2** as the name, press **Tab** twice, type **30**, and press **Tab** again to move to the next row.

9. Add the City, State, and Zip fields in the same way. Type **City** as the Name and **25** as the Size. Type **State** as the name and **2** as the size. Type **Zip** as the Name and **5** as the Size.

10. The next field holds the date of the last contact. In the Name text box, type **Contacted,** and select **Date** from the Data Type drop-down list. **Fixed** is automatically entered in the Size column.

11. The next field holds the rate at which you bill this client. In the Name text box, type **Bill At**. Select **Numeric** from the Data Type drop-down list (or **Tab** to the Data Type column and press **N**). Assuming that your rate can be over one hundred dollars, enter **3.2** as the Size.

12. The next field specifies whether the client is included in your regular mailings. Enter **Mail To** as the name, and select **Boolean** as the type. The Size is Fixed.

13. Finally, add a field to hold general notes. **Tab** to the next row, at the field name, type **Notes**, and as the Data Type, select **Memo**.

14. That is all of the fields in the sample database Field Definition dialog box (see Figure 2.8). Not all the fields you defined are visible in the list in the dialog box. Select **OK** to create the new file.

Practical Approach, 3.0

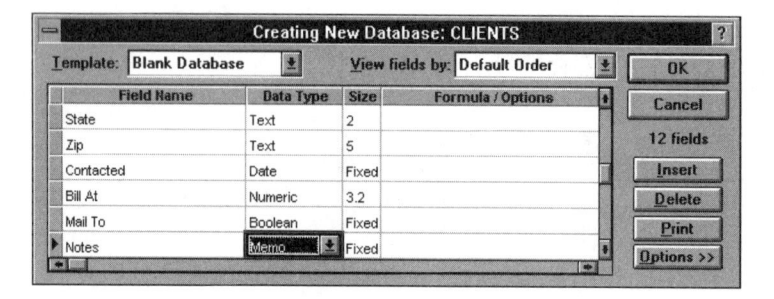

Figure 2.8 Defining the fields for the clients database.

15. Approach displays the standard data entry form (Form 1) that it creates for the new database (see Figure 2.9).

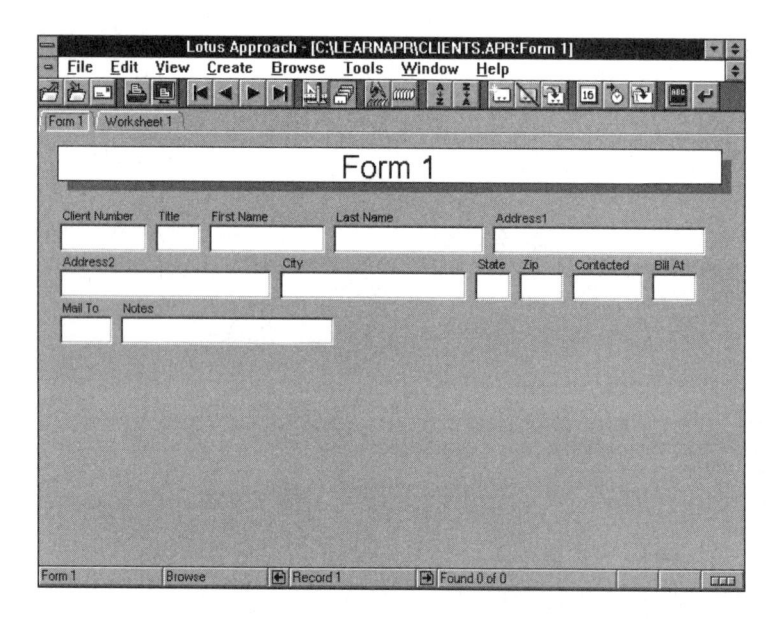

Figure 2.9 The default form for the clients database.

Notice that Approach creates two views of the database automatically, which you can use by clicking their divider tabs, **Form 1** and **Worksheet 1**. Look at both of these and now you will learn to use the Form in Chapter 3, though the Worksheet has advanced features that are covered in Chapter 9.

Working with Existing Files

Now that you have created a sample file, you should look at the basic ways of manipulating a file: opening, closing, saving and deleting it. You do all of these things by using the File menu, and they all use very similar dialog boxes.

Opening, Closing, and Saving a File

You open and close files in Approach much as you do in other Windows applications. However, there is an additional complication when you save a file, which occurs because of the difference between the underlying database file and the Approach file. You have just created a dBASE IV file, with a DBF extension. Approach automatically creates an Approach file with an APR extension to hold forms and other designs you create.

When you finished the last exercise, Approach automatically created an Approach File named CLIENTS.APR. You can see its name, followed by Form 1, the name of the current view, in the Approach title bar.

The file CLIENTS.DBF was saved when you created it. Data is also saved automatically when you enter it. But the Approach file, which holds any forms or other designs that you create, must be saved explicitly before it is closed, or changes that you have made in it since it was last saved are lost.

> **WARNING**
> If you are used to other database programs which require you to save changes that you made in your data, you may lose data until you get used to the fact that Approach saves data automatically as you do data entry. If you are looking through a file and accidentally change the data in a field of one record, for example, you should choose **Undo** from the Edit menu or press **Esc** immediately to correct the accidental change.

Saving an Approach File

You can save a Approach file at any time by choosing **Save Approach File** from the File menu. In addition, Approach asks you if you want to save the Approach file when you close it, and you can save it simply by selecting the **Yes** button.

The first time you save a newly created Approach file, Approach displays the Save Approach File dialog box (see Figure 2.10). This dialog box is very similar to the New dialog box you learned about earlier in this chapter. By default, it saves the Approach file in the same drive and directory as the original file, and it gives it the same name as the original file, but with an APR extension.

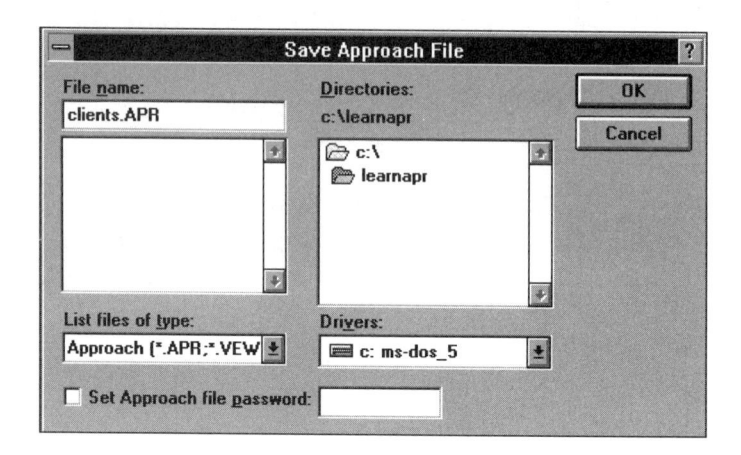

Figure 2.10 The Save Approach File dialog box.

In this dialog box, the List Files of Type drop-down menu only includes Approach files. The Set Approach File Password check box is used primarily on networks, and so it is covered in Chapter 12.

In general, it is best to use the default settings of this dialog box. Use this dialog box to change the name, drive and directory only if you have a special reason to.

Opening a File

You can open a file by choosing **Open** from the File menu to display the Open dialog box (see Figure 2.11). You can also choose **An Existing File** from the Open drop-down menu of the Welcome dialog box to display the Open dialog box.

This dialog box is also very similar to the New dialog box you learned about earlier in this chapter. Use the Drives drop-down menu and the Directories list in the same way to select the drive and directory of the file you want to open, and the List files of type drop-down menu to select the file type. Descriptive information about the deselected file is displayed in the File information box.

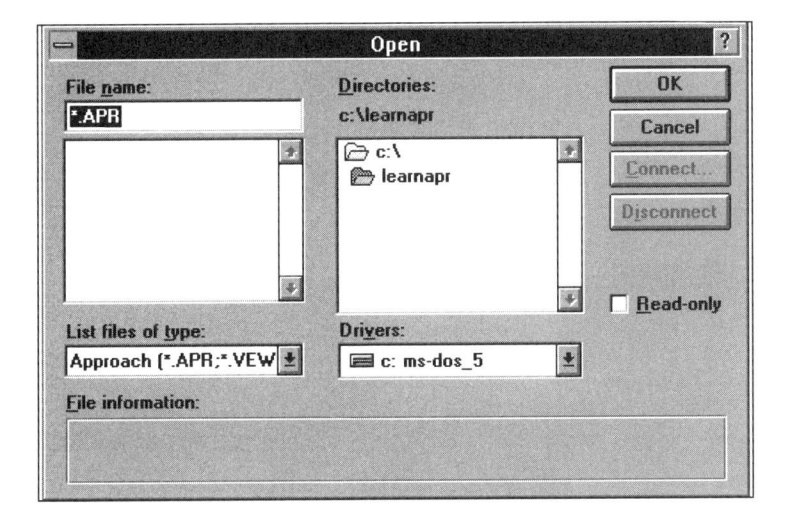

Figure 2.11 The Open dialog box.

All files of the type selected are displayed in the File Name list. When you select a file in this list, its name is displayed in the File Name text box, and you can select **OK** to open it. You can also open a file simply by double-clicking its name in the list.

The default file type is Approach files, which displays the files you have already worked with in Approach, but you can also use the List files of type drop-down menu to open files from other programs.

> **NOTE** An Approach file is automatically created for any database file you open if it does not already have one—for example, if you are opening a file that was created in dBASE and not used before in Approach. You should open that Approach file rather than the original database file when you use it again, so that you can use any forms or reports you created for it.

Opening Commonly Used Approach Files

Approach lists the names of the five most recently used Approach files at the end of the File menu. You can open any of them simply by selecting one. When one of these file names is highlighted, its full path name is displayed in the status bar.

The names are numbered, and the numbers are underlined to indicate that you can use them as shortcut keys. If, like most people, you have one file that you always use, you can open it by pressing **Alt+F** to display the File menu and then pressing **1** to open the last file you used.

Only Approach files are added to the File menu. Selecting one of them is the easiest way to open commonly used files.

The Welcome dialog box also includes the names of the five most recent files on its Open drop-down menu. To open one, select it from this drop-down menu and select **OK**.

Opening Multiple Files

You can open multiple Approach files at the same time. Approach opens each in its own window. The file's name and the name of the form being used are displayed in the window's title bar.

You can work with these windows in all the ways that you work with the Document windows of any Windows application. For example, you can Resize, Move, Maximize or Minimize them. If you are not familiar with how to work with document Windows, see Appendix C.

When you open a file, its name is added to the Window menu. Select the file name from the Window menu to bring its window to the top. You can also choose **Arrange Windows** from the Window menu to stack the windows so you can see all of their title bars, then it is easy to click the one you want to bring to the top.

Closing a File

You can close the file in the current window at any time by choosing **Close** from the File menu. If you made changes in it, you are asked if you want to save the Approach file. You must select **Yes** to save changes in forms and other designs since it was last saved.

You can also close a file by choosing **Close** from the Control menu of the window it is displayed in.

Deleting a File

To delete a file, choose **Delete** from the File menu to display the Delete File dialog box (see Figure 2.12). Use the controls to select a file, just as you do in the New, Open and Save View dialog boxes. After you select **OK,** Approach displays a warning that asks you for confirmation before deleting the file.

Chapter 2: Creating a Database File 57

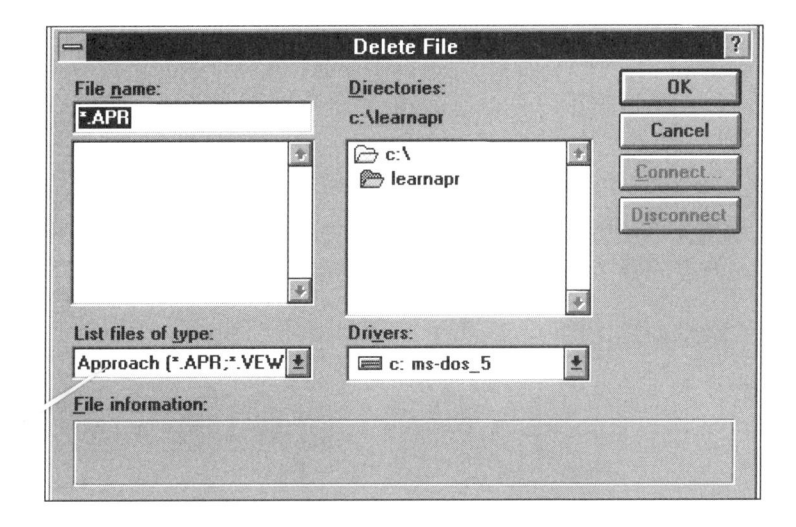

Figure 2.12 The Delete File dialog box.

Approach does not let you delete a file that is currently open. If you select it, a warning is displayed telling you to close the file before deleting it.

If you are deleting an Approach file, first it asks whether you want to delete the Approach file and then asks if you want to delete the database file that it is based on. You can delete the Approach file but save the database file.

An Exercise

If you are not familiar with other Windows applications, you should try closing and opening the file you just created. In the exercise, you do not save the Approach file, so you can see clearly the difference between the Approach file and the underlying database file that you created.

1. Choose **Close** from the File menu. Approach displays a dialog box asking if you want to save the Approach file. Select **No**. If Approach displays the Welcome dialog box, click **Cancel**.

2. Choose **Open** from the File menu to display the Open dialog box. Learnapr should be the current directory: if it is not, then select it from the Directories list. Notice that the Approach files are the file types displayed, and that none are displayed in the file list, because you did not save the Approach file when you closed it.

3. From the List Files of Type drop-down menu, select **dBASE IV (*.DBF)**. Now, the file clients.dbf is displayed in the File Name list (see Figure 2.13). Double-click it. Approach opens the DBF file and automatically creates the clients.APR file with Form 1 and Worksheet 1 again.

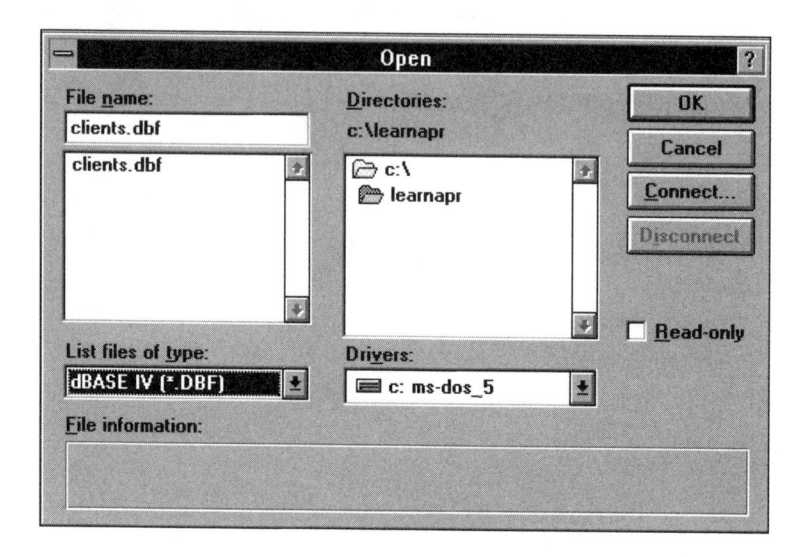

Figure 2.13 Opening a data file.

4. Choose **Close** from the File menu. When asked if you want to save the APR file, select **Yes**.

5. The Save View dialog box is displayed: select **OK** to use the same name (with the extension APR), directory, and drive as the DBF file.

6. Open the Approach file. Either use the Open drop-down menu of the Welcome dialog box or the File menu. The option 1 **CLIENTS.APR** has been added to both.

7. Now, try selecting this Approach file. First choose **Close** from the File menu to close it; Approach does not delete it if it is open. If necessary, choose **Cancel** to eliminate the Welcome dialog box. Then choose **Delete File** from the File menu. Select **clients.apr** from the File Name list and select **OK**. When asked if you really want to delete clients.APR, select **Yes**. Then, when it asks if you really want to delete the database CLIENTS, select **No**.

8. Choose **Open** from the File menu. No Approach files are displayed in the Open dialog box. From the List files of type drop-down menu, select **dBASE IV (.DBF)**. Select the File Name **clients.dbf** and select **OK**.

9. Approach opens the database file and creates a new Approach file for it. Choose **Save Approach File** from the File menu (or click the **Save Approach File** icon). Because this is a new Approach file, the Save View dialog box is displayed. Select **OK** to save the file as clients.apr or choose the **Save Approach File** button from the toolbar menu.

These exercises give you a very clear grasp of the difference between an Approach file and the Data file underlying it.

You did not lose anything by deleting the Approach file, because Approach created the default designs of Form 1 and Worksheet 1 for you each time you opened the data file and created a new Approach file.

WARNING If you had created any Views of your own, however, they would have been lost when the Approach file was deleted, as would any Calculated or Variable fields or macros.

Saving a File under a New Name

As in other Windows applications, you can save an Approach file under a different name by choosing **Save As** from the File menu to display the Save Approach File As dialog box (see Figure 2.14). The Approach file is also retained with its original name, so that this option gives you two copies of the file.

NOTE If you choose this option when you are using a relational database, Approach displays the Save As dialog box repeatedly to let you rename each joined file.

Most of the features of this dialog box are the same as those of the Save View dialog box, described above. Enter the name of the new file in the File Name text box. Use the Directories list and the Drives pop-up menu to select the directory and drive where it is to be saved. The List files of type drop-down menu includes only one option: Approach files. The Set View Password check box lets you enter a password in the text box to its right to prevent unauthorized users from opening the Approach file with a new name.

Practical Approach, 3.0

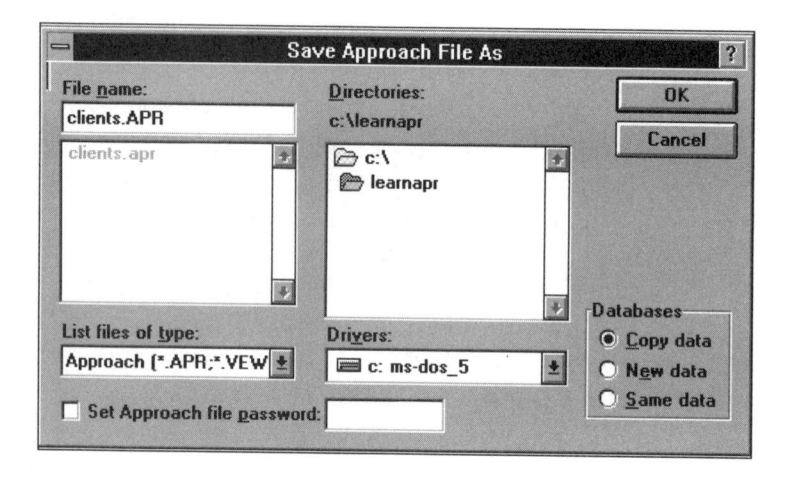

Figure 2.14 The Save Approach File As dialog box.

The Approach File As dialog box has one additional feature that the Save View dialog box does not have. The Databases radio buttons give you three options for saving your data files.

- *Copy Data.* Creates a duplicate of both the Approach file and the database file, including all of the data it is holding.
- *New Data.* Creates a copy of the Approach file and Database file, but without any data.
- *Same Data.* Creates a copy of the Approach file but not of the Database file. The new Approach file still uses the old Database file.

Whichever of these you select, you can use the Save View As dialog box to specify the location of the new Approach file.

If you choose **Copy Data** or **New Data**, (the two options that also create a new database file), then you must also specify where to save the new Database file. When you select **OK**, the Save Database As dialog box is displayed (see Figure 2.15).

Use this dialog box in the familiar way. Enter the name of the new file in the File Name text box. Use the Directories list and the Drives pop-up menu to select the directory and drive where it is to be saved. Use the List files of type drop-down menu to select the type of file that you are creating. If you select **Cancel** rather than saving the database file, then Approach does not create the new Approach file.

Chapter 2: Creating a Database File

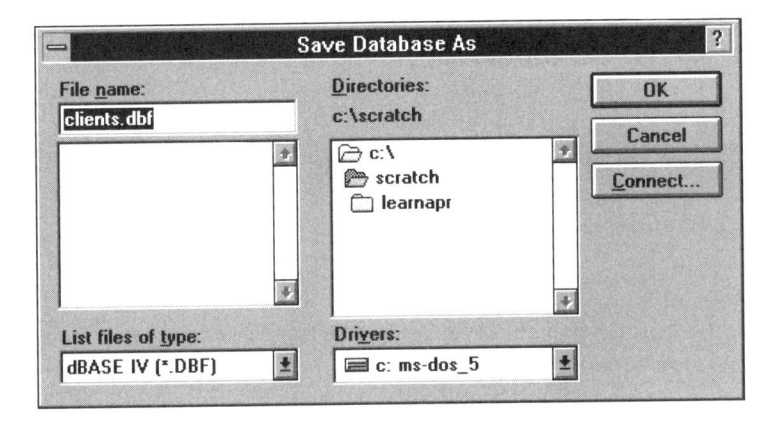

Figure 2.15 The Save Database As dialog box.

Changing Field Definitions

If you need to change the field definitions you created initially, you can modify a file at any time, by choosing **Field Definition** from the Create menu to display the Field Definition dialog box (see Figure 2.16). As you can see, this is the same dialog box you used to create the file, with all the specifications of the current database listed in it. You can add, delete, or change fields just as you did when you were first creating a file.

Figure 2.16 The Field Definition Dialog Box.

If you are working with a relational database, you can use the Database drop-down menu to choose another data file. Approach displays the specifications for its fields.

There is one very important difference between creating and modifying field definitions. If you modify field definitions after you have added records, there is a danger of losing data, if you change the field length or field type.

Changing Field Length

You can obviously lose data by decreasing the length of a text or numeric field so that it is too short to hold some data you have entered. Any data that does not fit in the new length is *truncated*; letters or digits that do not fit are discarded, and the rest are retained.

WARNING Changing the length of a field is particularly dangerous if you reduce the number of integers in a numeric field. The new data differs from the old by one or more orders of magnitude, but when you look through the data, there is no way of knowing that it has changed.

There can be minor loss of data if you truncate a text field, and there is only a loss of precision if you reduce the number of decimal places in a numeric field.

Changing Field Type

If you change the field type, Approach substitutes blank values for any values that it cannot convert to the new field type. Only two types of conversion are possible without data loss:

- Numeric fields can be changed to Text fields without losing data.
- Text fields can be changed to Numeric fields without losing data if all the characters are numbers.

In any other case, data is lost.

Adding New Fields

If you add a new field to the database, it is not added to the standard form or worksheet or to any other views that have already been created. However, Approach automatically displays the Add Field box to make it easy for you to add the field to the current view. The Add Field box is covered in Chapter 4.

Chapter 3

Entering and Viewing Data

Now that you have created a sample database file, you will try entering data into it. Often, you can speed data entry by creating custom data entry forms, a feature of Approach that is covered in Chapter 4. This chapter covers the basics of entering and viewing data in Approach. It also discusses a few special techniques used to speed data entry and to enter PicturePlus fields. This chapter discusses:

- Adding records to your database
- Entering and editing data in different types of fields
- Moving through your database to view records you have entered
- Deleting records from your database
- Using special features of the Browse menu to speed data entry
- Entering data in PicturePlus fields, including linked and embedded objects (OLE)
- Automating data entry by defining Default Values for fields
- Validating the data that is entered

How to Add Data

When you finish defining the fields of a database, Approach automatically creates a standard form named Form 1 and a standard Worksheet named Worksheet 1. Both of these include all the fields of the database. It displays the standard form, which you can use in Browse mode to add data, and the Form 1 and Worksheet 1 Divider tab, which you can click to display either of these views (see Figure 3.1).

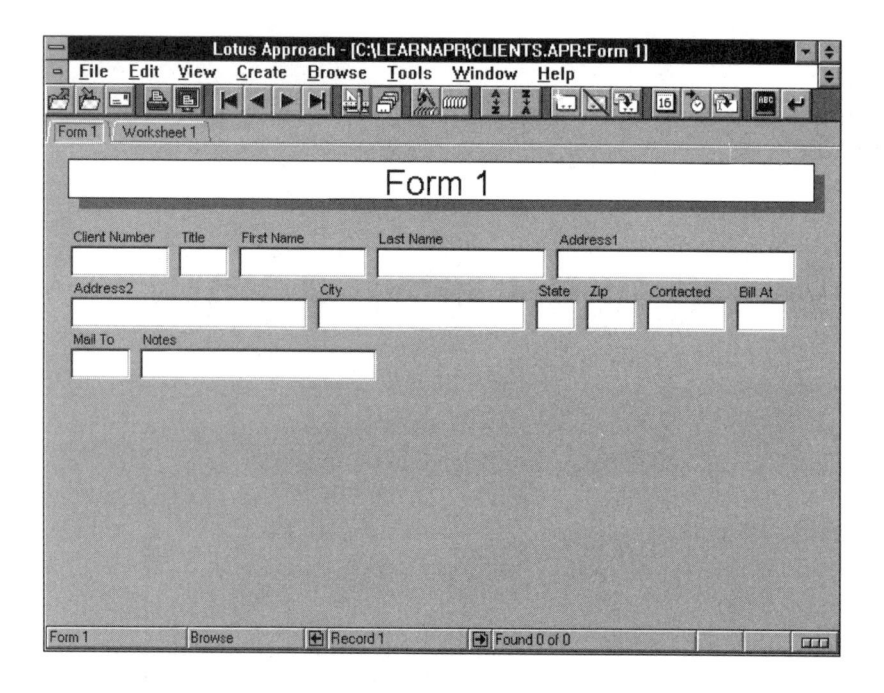

Figure 3.1 The Standard Form.

You can shift to Design mode and customize this form, as you will learn to do in Chapter 4, but first you should get some experience adding and viewing data using the standard form. You will look briefly at the standard worksheet: because data is entered differently in Worksheets than in other views, they are covered in detail in Chapter 9.

Chapter 3: Entering and Viewing Data 65

Adding New Records

Once your database is opened and displayed in Browse mode, you can add records in three different ways:

1. Click **New Record** on the icon bar.
2. Choose **New** from the Browse menu.
3. Press **Ctrl+N** (the shortcut key for the New command of the Browse menu).

SHORTCUT
If you are entering a series of records, after beginning in one of the listed above you can simply continue to press **Tab** after entering data in the last field of a record, and Approach automatically adds an additional record.

Approach does not let you add a new record or move to another field if you have entered invalid data in the current field—for example, if you enter all letters in a number field. Instead, it displays a message describing your error (see Figure 3.2).

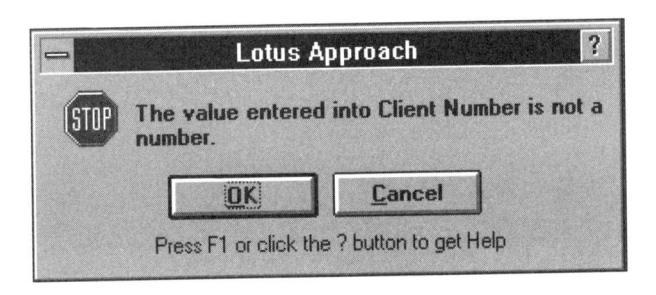

Figure 3.2 The message if you try to enter invalid data.

Approach automatically saves the data you have entered in a record when you:

- Add a new record.
- Move the focus to a different record.
- Press **Enter** or click the **Enter icon** of the icon bar.

In general, you do not have to think about saving the file to avoid data loss. You can press **Enter** if you want to save changes while you are in the midst of working on one record, but there is rarely a need to do this.

> **WARNING** Because Approach saves changes automatically, you must correct any errors before leaving the record, to avoid saving mistakes. You can cancel changes you made in the current record by pressing **Esc**.

Entering Data in Fields

The field that you can edit or add data to has a cursor (or insertion point) in it, and is called the *current field*. Use the usual Windows Editor keys to add data to the fields of your database. For example, use the **Left Arrow** and **Right Arrow** keys to move the cursor within a field, or click any location in the field with the mouse to move the cursor there. New data that you type is inserted at the location of the cursor, and any existing data is pushed to the right to make room for it.

Press **Del** to delete the character to the right of the insertion point, or **Backspace** to delete all the character to the left of the insertion point. In either case, any existing characters to the right of the cursor are pulled leftwards to fill the gap.

If data is selected (highlighted), pressing **Del** or **Backspace** deletes it all, any character you type replaces it, and using a cursor movement key deselects it.

Press **Tab** to move to the next field and **Shift+Tab** to move to the previous field. When you first tab to a field that has data in it, all the data in the field is selected (highlighted) and anything you type replaces it. Press a cursor movement key to deselect data already in the field, if you do not want it replaced by anything new that you type.

You can also move among fields by clicking them with the mouse; the insertion point is placed where you click, so you can edit the field. If you double-click a field, its entire contents are selected, so anything you type replaces it.

> **SHORTCUT** The mouse is often useful for editing data, but when you are entering new records, it is generally easiest to use the **Tab** key, so you can move from field to field without interrupting your typing.

There are special considerations that you must bear in mind when you enter data in certain types of fields. PicturePlus fields are the most complex, and have their own menu instead of the Browse menu, and so are covered in a separate section later in this chapter. Others are covered here.

If you are not familiar with the basic editing techniques that have already been discussed, which are used in virtually all Windows applications, you should read the section on *The Editor* in Appendix C before going on.

Boolean Fields

Boolean fields can only accept the values true and false (or Yes and No). You may enter:

- **N**, **n**, **No**, **no**, or **0** to represent false.
- Any other characters to represent true.

When you leave the field, Approach displays the data as **Yes** or **No**.

Date Fields

Enter Date fields as numbers separated by some non-numeric character in the order month/day/year. This order depends on the window's International setting, and you can change the default by changing this setting in Windows. You can enter up to ten characters in the field to specify the date completely; two for the month, two for the date, and four for the year, in addition to the two separators.

You can omit some of these characters to save typing:

- Type one or two numbers for the year, and Approach assumes you mean that year of the twentieth century.
- Leave out the year and Approach assumes you mean the current year.
- Leave out the year and month, and Approach assumes you mean the current year and month. That is, you can type just one number to enter a date of the current month.
- Press the **Spacebar** to enter the current month, day, or year. Which one is entered depends on where the cursor is.

You do not have to include leading zeroes in the month, date, or year.

When you move the cursor out of the field, the date is displayed in the format specified using the field's Info Box, which is covered in Chapter 4.

Memo Fields

You can type as much text as you want into a Memo field, but Approach only displays the text that fits into the field boundaries.

To enter a long body of text in a Memo field, simply continue typing. The field scrolls automatically to accommodate your entire entry.

To view the text in a Memo field, make it the current field and use the Arrow keys to scroll through it. You can also resize the Memo field to make it easier to view its data, as you learn to do in Chapter 4.

Numeric Fields

If you type only text in a Numeric field, it displays a warning that your entry is not a number, when you try to leave the record. It refuses to move to another field as long as the data in the field in invalid.

If you enter numbers and characters in a Number field, Approach uses the first complete number in your entry as the value of the field, and discards the text and any later numbers you entered. For example, if you enter **xx99yy88**, it makes 99 the value of your field.

WARNING You lose data if you enter Social Security numbers or telephone numbers in a Numeric field in their usual format. If you enter Social Security numbers in the format **999-99-9999**, Approach only saves the first three numbers. They are interpreted as the first complete number before the first hyphen, which is the first non-numeric character. Likewise, if you enter **(212)284-1059** as a telephone number, it saves only 212 and discards the rest. As you see in Chapter 4, the Info Box for number fields lets you display numbers in this format, but they must be entered without the hyphen.

Because of the difficulty of entering and editing telephone numbers and Social Security numbers without including these formatting characters, it is generally best to store them in text fields.

NOTE: As a general rule, it is best to use numeric fields only for numbers that are used in calculations or sorted numerically, and these do not require any special characters.

When you move the cursor out of the field, Approach displays the number in the format specified using the field's Info Box. You can also use the Info Box to change the field's input format.

Text Fields

You can type any characters in a Text field. The only limitation is the length of the field.

Time Fields

A Time field can hold up to 12 characters, representing hours, minutes, seconds, and hundredths of a second, in the format HH:MM:SS.00. Notice that colons must be used to separate all of the elements of a Time field, except hundredths of a second, which must be preceded by a decimal point. You can enter just hours and minutes, just hours, minutes and seconds, or the full time including hundredths of a second.

NOTE: You can enter time in 12 hour format by including AM or PM at the end or in 24 hour format with or without AM and PM included.

When you leave the field it is displayed using the format specified in the field's Info Box.

Automatic Data Validation

Approach validates the data you enter in any of these field types. An error message is displayed when you try to move the focus out of the field if :

- You have entered text that is too long to fit into a Text field.
- A date is entered (such as **2/30/94**) that does not exist in a Date field.
- If only non-numeric characters in a Numeric field are entered.

- If there is any other invalid entry.

NOTE: Approach does not let you leave the field until the data is valid. However, you can press **Esc** to cancel the entry rather than correcting the data.

Numeric fields are a partial exception. As you learned above, they accept any entry that includes a number, even if it also includes non-numeric characters, but they save only the first complete number in the entry and discard the rest. You can also define special validation rules for fields, which are covered at the end of this chapter.

Viewing and Editing Records

The simplest way to view and edit records is by using the SmartIcons, on the Approach icon bar (see Figure 3.3). These icons are available only in the Browse mode.

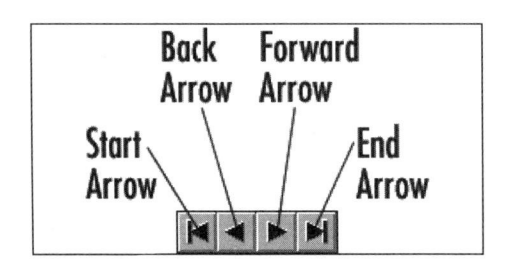

Figure 3.3 Icons for viewing and editing records.

As you learned earlier, you can move among the records and view them, by clicking the arrow icons:

Start Arrow. Select **Start** (a left-pointing arrow with a vertical line to its left) to move immediately to the first record of the file.

Back Arrow. Select **Back** (a left-pointing arrow) to display the record before the record currently displayed.

Chapter 3: Entering and Viewing Data

Forward Arrow. Select **Forward** (a right-pointing arrow) to display the record after the record currently displayed.

End Arrow. Select **End** (a right-pointing arrow with a vertical line to its right) to move immediately to the last record of the file.

SHORTCUT

To move through a series of records quickly, you can click **Back Arrow** or **Forward Arrow** and hold down the mouse button.

There are also keyboard equivalents for all of these buttons:

- Press **Ctrl+Home** or **Ctrl+End** to go to the first or last record.
- Press **PgUp** or **PgDn** to go to the previous or next record.

Once you have moved to the record you want to view, you can make any field the *current field* by clicking it or tabbing to it, and then you can edit it in the usual ways.

NOTE

If you are viewing the records in Print Preview mode, the **Back Arrow** and **Forward Arrow** move you to the previous or next screen rather than the previous or next record. The difference from Browse mode is significant only if your records are large enough to take up more than one screen.

Using the Status Bar to Move through the Records

You can also use the arrows on the status bar to move to the next record or the previous record (see Figure 3.4).

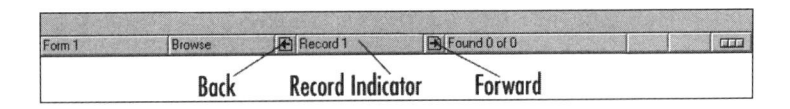

Figure 3.4 The status bar in Browse Mode.

The status bar also contains the record indicator that displays the number of the current record. Click it to display the Go to Record dialog box (see Figure 3.5). Simply enter a number in this dialog box and click **OK** to go immediately to the record with that number.

Figure 3.5 The Go to Record dialog box.

Deleting Records

You can also use either the icon bar or the Browse menu to delete selected records. Select the **Delete Record** icon or choose **Delete Record** from the Browse menu to delete the selected record, removing it from the file.

Ordinarily, doing either of these deletes just the current record, but you can also select multiple records in reports by holding down **Shift** or **Ctrl** when you click them. Then use either one of these options to delete all selected records.

Adding Sample Data

You have learned the basic techniques needed to enter, edit and view most data. Later in this chapter, you learn some special techniques for entering and viewing data, including the complex methods used to enter PicturePlus fields.

First, however, you should enter a few records in the sample database that you created in Chapter 2. This gives you a bit of practice with the basics of data entry before going on to more advanced techniques, and you have some sample data to work with in later exercises.

Enter a few records, as follows:

Chapter 3: Entering and Viewing Data

1. If necessary, start Approach, and use the Welcome to Lotus Approach or the File menu to open the CLIENTS.APR database you created in Chapter 2. The standard form (Form 1) should be displayed in Browse mode, with a blank record for you to enter data in.

2. Press **Tab** to make Client Number the current field; type **1**. Press **Tab** again to make Title the current field; type **Mr**. To make First Name the current field press **Tab**, and type **Dennis**. Press **Tab** to move to the Last Name field, and type **Spring**. To move to Address1 press **Tab** again, and type **545 West End Ave**. Press **Tab** twice to move beyond Address2 to the City field, and type **New York**. Press **Tab** to move to the State field, and type **NY**. Press **Tab** to move to the Zip field, and type **10044**.

3. The next few fields are different data types, and you should try entering them in a way that illustrates their default display: you learn how to specify the format in which they are displayed later in this chapter. Press **Tab** to move to the Contacted field, which is the date of last contact, and type **06/08/94**. Press **Tab** again to move to the next field, and notice that the date changes to 6/8/94, without the leading zeroes. The Bill At field represents your billing rate, a dollar amount, so try entering it as **$65.00**. When you press **Tab,** the amount changes to **65**. In the Boolean Mail To field type **y**. When you press **Tab**, it changes to **Yes**.

4. In the Notes field, type **Do not forget to contact before the end of the third quarter.** Notice that when you reach the edge of the field boundary, the text scrolls left so you can continue typing. This is a Memo field, which can hold an indefinite amount of text. The data for this record has all been entered (see Figure 3.6).

5. Use the same method to enter the three records listed below. Begin by pressing **Ctrl+N** to add a new record. Remember, after you have begun adding records, the fastest way to add more is by continuing to press **Tab** when you are done with one record in order to add another. Note that the first record should be entered in all capital letters; assume that you want the data entered with only the first letter of each word capitalized, but that someone makes this common error when they enter this record.

Practical Approach, 3.0

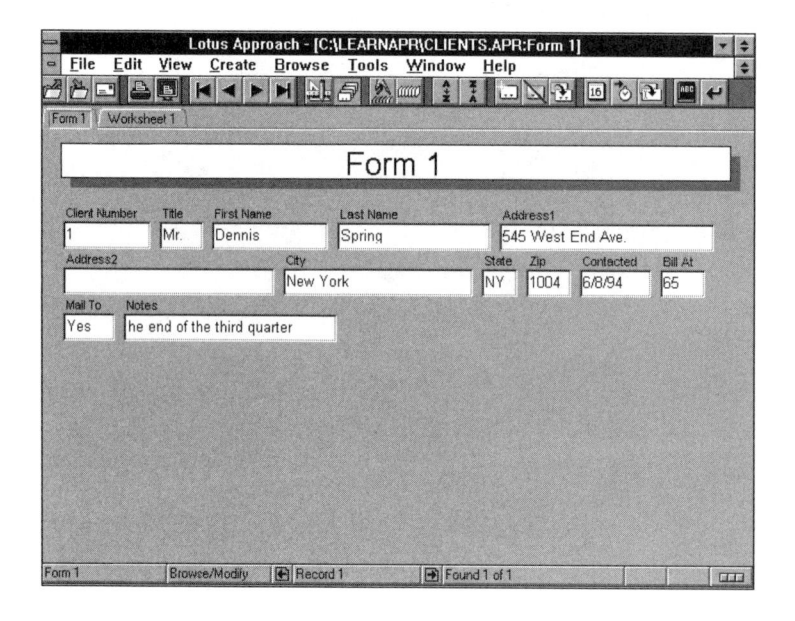

Figure 3.6 The first record.

The first record:

```
Client Number: 2
Title: DR.
First Name: JOSEPH
Last Name: WALTON
Address1: FIRST FEDERAL BUILDING
Address2: 100 FEDERAL SQUARE
City: PARAMUS
State: NJ
Zip: 07654
Contacted: 4/17/94
Bill At: 75
Mail To: No
Notes: (none)
```

The second record:

```
Client Number: 3
Title: Ms.
First Name: Donna
Last Name: Walton
```

```
Address1: 415 Nyaset Rd.
Address2: (none)
City: Yonkers
State: NY
Zip: 10722
Contacted: 5/1/94
Bill At: 60
Mail To: Yes
Notes: Call frequently. Prospecting necessary.
```

The third record:

```
Client Number: 4
Title: Mr.
First Name: David
Last Name: Tam
Address1: Tam's Computer Shack
Address2: 478 Broadway
City: New York
State: NY
Zip: 10010
Contacted: 7/12/94
Bill At: 90
Mail To: No
Notes: Sometimes slow in paying bills.
```

The first two of these records have the same last name, because it is almost inevitable that you will have a last name repeated in a sizable database; though you are working with only a few sample records, they should represent this reality.

6. Try moving through the records, by clicking the **Arrow** buttons and making the menu selections. Move through the records until you are comfortable using the controls.

7. Try looking at the data as it is displayed in Worksheet 1. Click the **Worksheet 1** Divider tab to display that View (see Figure 3.7). When you are done looking at this view, click the **Form 1 Divider** tab to return to the default form.

You can see that the standard worksheet, Worksheet 1, gives you a convenient way of looking at your data in tabular form. You learn to work with data in Worksheets in Chapter 9.

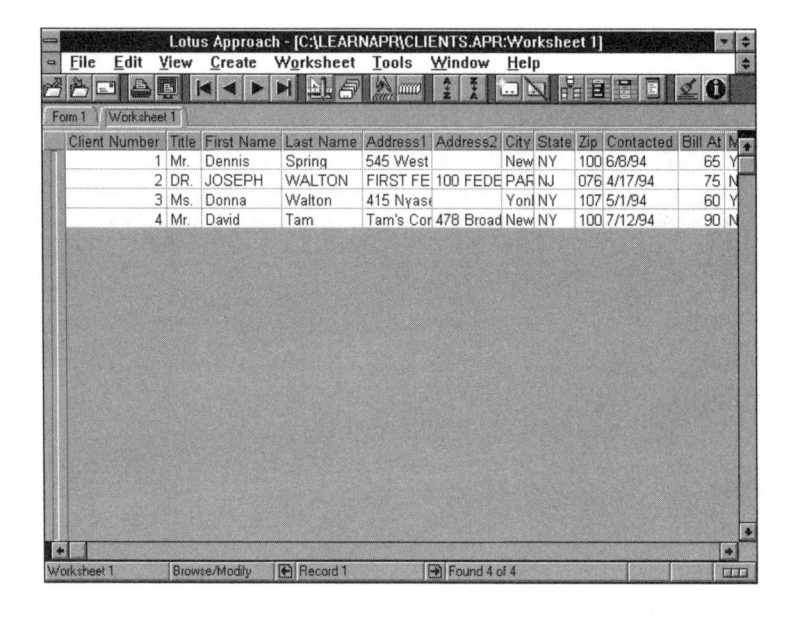

Figure 3.7 Displaying the Data in Worksheet 1.

Special Techniques

You have learned all the basics of how to add and view data in a file. This section covers some special techniques used to alter the way that data is displayed, to speed data entry, and to work with PicturePlus fields.

Other Features of the Browse Menu

The Browse menu also has a number of special features that can be used to speed data entry (see Figure 3.8). Though some of them are most useful in combination with techniques that you learn in later chapters, you should look at them now.

Finds and Sorts

The first five options on the Browse menu are used for Finds and Sorts.

When you perform a Find, Approach displays only records that match some criterion you specify—for example, you can display only your clients

Chapter 3: Entering and Viewing Data

who live in New York State. When you choose **Show All** from the Browse menu, all the records are displayed again.

When you perform a Sort, Approach displays the records in the order you specify. Finds and Sorts are covered in detail in Chapter 6.

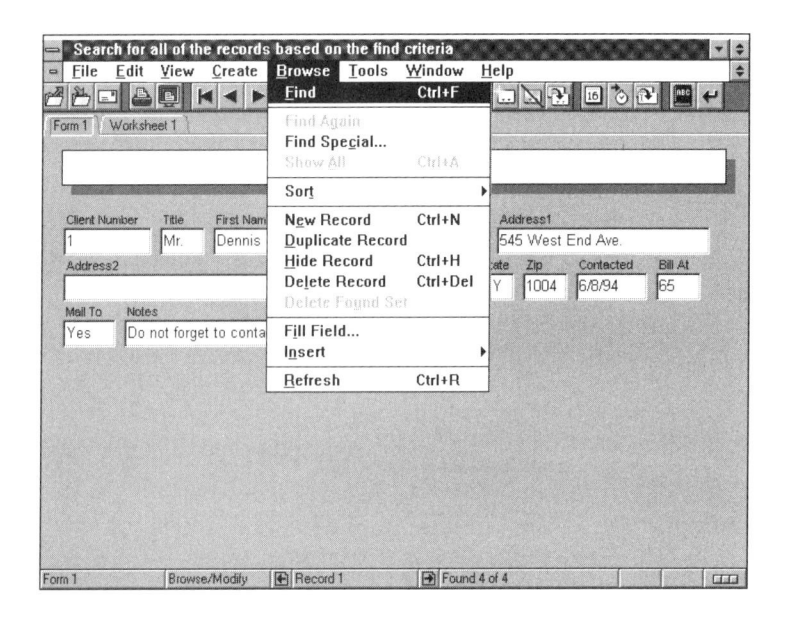

Figure 3.8 The Browse menu.

Refreshing the Screen

Choose **Refresh** from the Browse menu to display the data with all changes included. This is useful if you are sharing data on a network and other users have made changes. Chapter 12 includes a detailed discussion of using Approach on networks.

Duplicating a Record

If new records are similar to existing ones, it is often easier to duplicate the existing records and then edit them.

You can choose Duplicate Record from the Browse menu or click the Duplicate Record icon to add a new record that is a duplicate of the current record. This technique works regardless of which record is the current record. Thus, it is more powerful than the equivalent feature in many database applications, which only lets you duplicate the last record added.

Deleting the Found Set

Choose **Delete Found Set** from the Browse menu to delete all the records that are displayed after doing a find. Needless to say, this is often the fastest way of deleting a number records that can all be displayed as the result of a Find.

Hiding a Record

Choose **Hide Record** from the Browse menu to hide the selected record, so it is not displayed and is not accessible in Reports, Finds, or Sorts. Ordinarily this hides just the current record, but you can also select multiple records in reports by holding down **Shift** or **Ctrl** when you click them.

Filling a Field

Choose **Fill Field** from the Browse menu to change the value of the selected field of all the records in the found set to the value you enter (see Figure 3.9). Any data located in these fields previously, is lost. This option is most useful in combination with a Find, though it can be used to change the value of a field in all the records of the database.

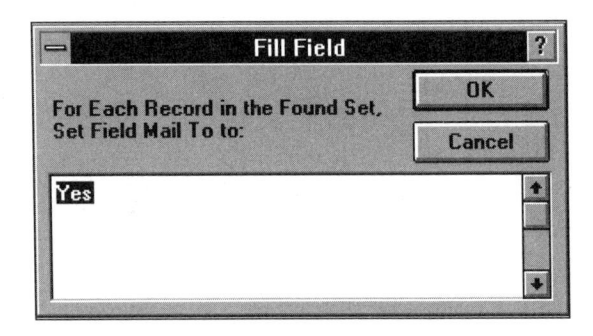

Figure 3.9 The Fill Field dialog box.

This option is accessible only when you are in browse mode with a field selected as the Current field.

Inserting Commonly Used Values

The Insert command makes it easy for you to enter a few values that are commonly needed in data entry. Choose **Insert** from the Browse menu to display a submenu with the following options:

Today's *Date*. Enters the date in the current field.

Current Time. Enters the time in the current field.

Previous Value. Enters the same value in the current field that it has in the previous record.

There is also an icon on the icon bar that is equivalent to each of these selections, which is shown to the right of each.

PicturePlus Fields

PicturePlus fields are entered differently from other fields because they hold pictures, sound, and other kinds of data that you cannot simply type into the field.

In general, you create the PicturePlus field in some other Windows application that lets you work with drawings, sound or video. You can then enter data in the PicturePlus field in several ways.

You can also define a PicturePlus field so you can use the mouse to draw in it while you are working in Approach, but you cannot make sophisticated drawings this way. Because they are generally created in other applications, you will not add a PicturePlus field to your sample database. In an actual application, you might find PicturePlus fields very convenient to hold scanned photographs or charts and other graphics.

This chapter covers all the methods of adding PicturePlus fields, so you can use them in your own applications. Skim through all these methods for now. Then, if you do use a PicturePlus field in an actual application, come back to this section and choose the easiest method of adding it.

Pasting from a File

One way to enter data into a PicturePlus field is by pasting it from a file.

When you are entering or editing data in Browse mode and the PicturePlus field is the current field, choose **Paste from File** from the Edit menu to display the dialog box (see Figure 3.10). Use this dialog box to select the file that holds the application. Use the Directories list and the Drives pop-up list to select the directory and drive where that file has been saved.

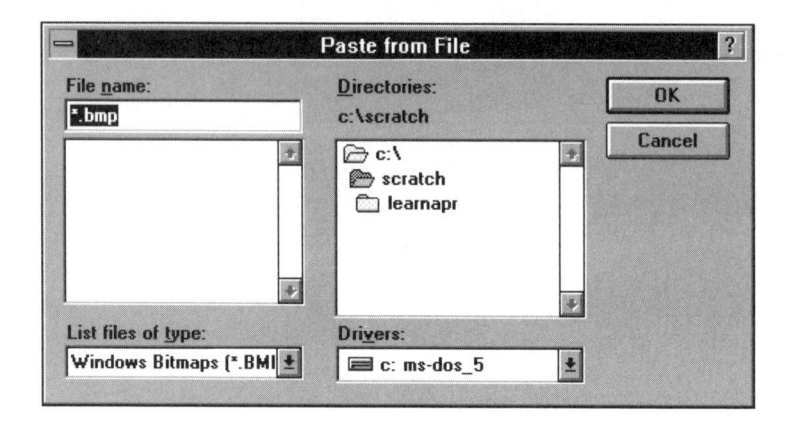

Figure 3.10 The Paste from File dialog box.

Use the List Files of Type drop-down menu to select the type of file that you are opening. The options and their extensions are:

- Windows Bitmaps (BMP)
- Windows Metafiles (WMF)
- TIFF Files (TIF)
- Paintbrush Files (PCX)
- Encapsulated PostScript Files (EPS)

When you select a file type, a field skeleton including its extension is displayed in the File Name text box. All files in the current directory with that extension are listed below. Select the file that you want to open from this list, or just enter its name in the File Name text box, and select **OK** to enter it in the PicturePlus file. Of course, before you enter a PicturePlus field in this way, it must have been created and saved in a file using some other application. For example, you can create Bitmap (BMP) files or PCX files by using Windows Paintbrush, an accessory which comes with Windows, or by using many other paint applications.

NOTE: This method of entering data in PicturePlus fields is most useful if you have already created a series of pictures using some other application. For example, you might use it if you have scanned photographs of all the people in your database, using a program that stores them on one of the file types listed previously.

Copy and Paste

You can also copy and paste PicturePlus fields from some other application.

Open the other application, select the picture or other object that you want in your PicturePlus field, and choose **Copy** from the Edit menu (or **Cut** from the Edit menu, if you want to remove the original) from its menu system. By doing this, you place the picture in the Windows clipboard.

Return to Approach, either by closing the other application or by choosing **Switch** from the Control menu and using the Task List to switch to Approach (or by holding down **Alt** and pressing **Tab** until Widows gives the option of switching to Approach). If you close the other application, it may display a dialog box asking if you want to save the clipboard; select **Yes**. Within Approach, make the PicturePlus field where you want to store this picture the current field. Choose **Paste** from the Edit menu to place the picture in that field. After you paste it into the field, a copy of it remains in the clipboard, so you can also paste it into other PicturePlus fields. Or, you can copy a different picture into the clipboard.

NOTE: This method is useful if you are creating or modifying each picture in some other application as you are adding them to Approach records, and if you do not want to change the pictures again after storing them in Approach.

OLE Objects

If you are creating pictures in other applications and you want to modify them again after storing them, you should use OLE objects. That retains a connection between the original object and the copy that you placed in Approach.

OLE stands for *Object Linking and Embedding*. As the name indicates, there can be two different connections between the original object and the copy you place in Approach.

- *Linking.* If an object is linked, then any changes you make to it in the original application are reflected in the copy. For example, if you have a PicturePlus field that contains graphs of data from an Excel spreadsheet as linked OLE objects, then whenever there are changes in the original spreadsheets that change these graphs, the graphs also change automatically in Approach. Likewise, changes made in Approach change the original.
- *Embedding.* If an object is embedded, then you must double-click it in Approach to launch the original application and make changes in the object. For example, if you have a PicturePlus field that contains graphs of data from an Excel spreadsheet as embedded OLE objects, then you can simply double-click one of these graphs in Approach to use Excel with this graph open, so you can modify it. On the other hand, if there are changes in the original spreadsheets made solely through Excel that change these graphs, they are not reflected in Approach. Only changes made using the embedded object are reflected in that object.

PicturePlus Options

If a PicturePlus is the current field in the field list of the Field Definition dialog box, you can click the **Options** button to display the PicturePlus options panel (see Figure 3.11).

Allowing OLE Objects

Use the Allow OLE objects checkbox to specify whether OLE objects can be added to this PicturePlus field. By default, this checkbox is selected and OLE objects can be added.

The Default Object Type

If OLE objects are allowed, you can also select a default object type from the list in this dialog box. If there is a default object type, double-clicking a blank PicturePlus field automatically launches the application that lets you create the default object.

The types of objects available in this list depend on the other Windows applications that you have installed.

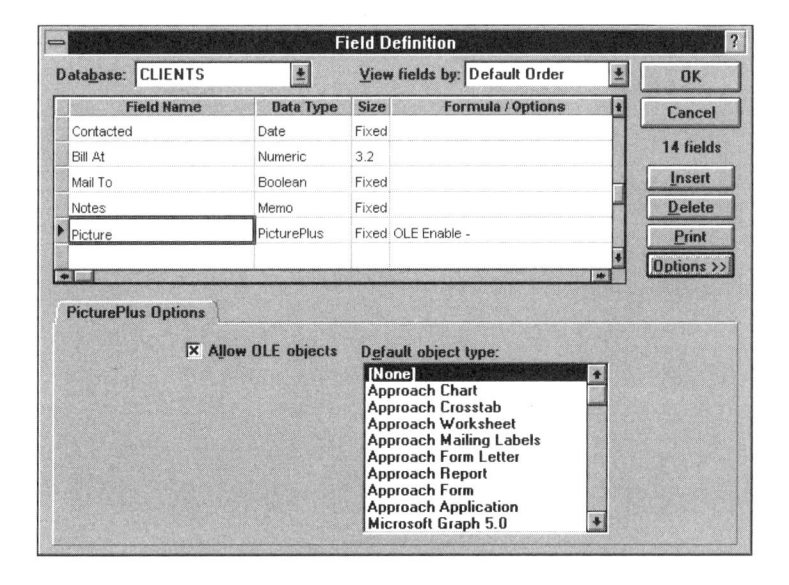

Figure 3.11 The PicturePlus Options panel.

Paste Special

There are many ways of adding embedded OLE objects, but only one way of adding Linked OLE objects. Choosing **Paste Special** from the Edit menu gives you the option of linking or embedding.

Use Paste Special in much the same way you use ordinary Copy and Paste:

1. Open the other application, select the picture or other object you want in your PicturePlus field, and choose **Copy** from the Edit menu (or **Cut** from the Edit menu) of its menu system to place the picture in the Windows clipboard.

2. Return to Approach without closing the other application. Make the PicturePlus field (where you want this picture stored) the current field. Then choose **Paste Special** from the Edit menu to display the Paste Special dialog box (see Figure 3.12).

If necessary, use the As list to select the format in which you want the object to be pasted. The **Paste Special** command of the Edit menu is accessible only when the object in the clipboard can be pasted in more than one format. It should be active for all linkable objects.

Practical Approach, 3.0

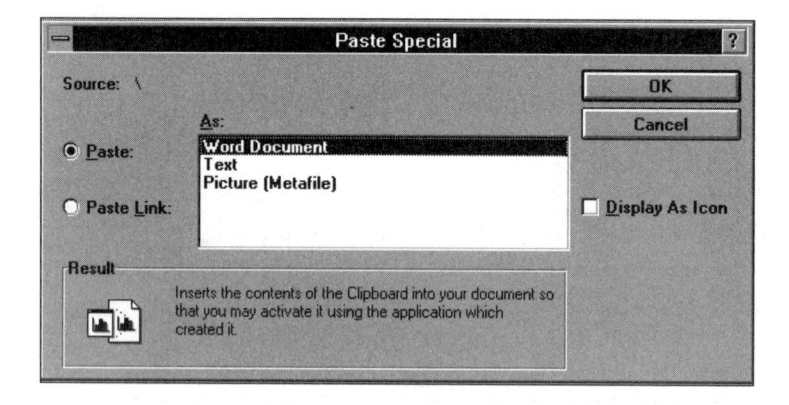

Figure 3.12 The Paste Special dialog box.

> **NOTE** Select the **Paste** radio button to add the object to the field as an embedded object, or select the **Paste Link** button to add it to the field as a linked object.

Paste and Paste from File

If OLE objects are allowed, then when you Paste an object from a file or Copy and Paste an object, it is added as an embedded OLE object.

Drag and Drop

In some cases, it is extremely convenient to use drag and drop to place embedded OLE objects in the PicturePlus fields.

Open the Windows File Manager by double-clicking its icon in the Main window of the Windows Program Manager. Select the directory that holds the file you want to place in the PicturePlus field. Then resize the File Manager's window and the Approach Application window so you can see them both. Then, simply click the name of the file you want in the File Manager, hold down the mouse button, drag the file's name to the Approach PicturePlus file where you want to place it, and release the mouse button to place the picture in the field as an embedded OLE object.

Chapter 3: Entering and Viewing Data 85

> **NOTE** If you have a large number of files in the same directory that you want to store in PicturePlus fields as embedded OLE objects, this is the quickest way to store all of them.

Insert Object

You can also add an embedded object to a PicturePlus field by selecting the field and then choosing **Object** from the Create menu to display the Insert Object dialog box. If you select the **Create New** button, Approach displays the Insert Object dialog box as shown in Figure 3.13.

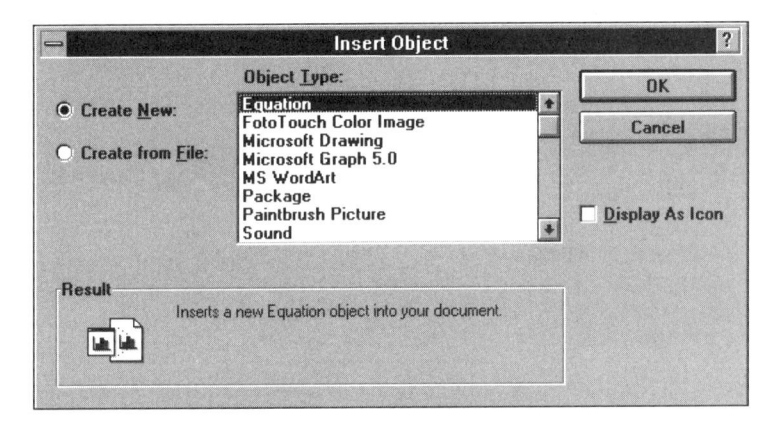

Figure 3.13 The Insert Object dialog box.

Select the type you want from the Object Type list (or simply double-click the object type in the list) to launch the application used to create that object. The Object Types that are available depend on what other Windows applications you have installed.

If you want the object to be displayed as an icon, the user must double-click to display the actual picture or other data in the field. Select the **Display as Icon** checkbox.

After you have finished using the other application to create and save the object, exit from that application. Most applications display a dialog box asking whether you want to update the object. Select **Yes** to embed the object in Approach in its current form.

If you select the **Create from File** button, the Insert Object dialog box is displayed as shown in Figure 3.14. Simply enter the name of the file that holds the object in the File text box, or click **Browse** to display the Browse dialog box, which you can use just like the Open dialog box to select a file.

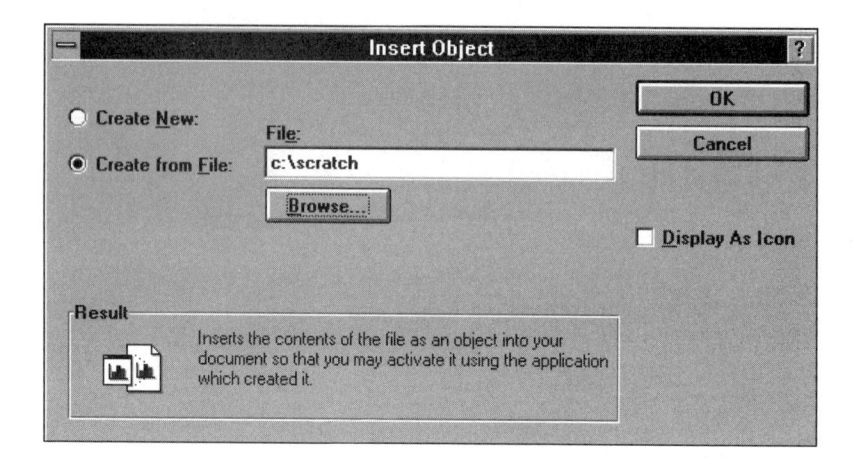

Figure 3.14 The Insert Object dialog box.

Drawing in a PicturePlus Field

You can draw directly in a PicturePlus field if you select the **Allow Drawing** checkbox in the Basics panel of the PicturePlus fields Info Box (see Figure 3.15).

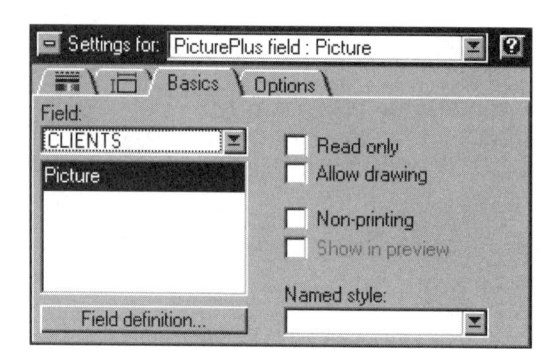

Figure 3.15 A PicturePlus field's Info Box.

To display this Info box:

- In Browse mode, select the PicturePlus field and choose **Style & Properties** from the PicturePlus menu.

- In Design mode, select the PicturePlus field and choose **Style & Propertie**s from the Object menu or simply double-click the **PicturePlus field.**

If this option is turned on, you can simply move the pointer to the PicturePlus field when you are entering data, hold down the mouse button, and move the pointer to draw a line. This option obviously can only be used to enter crude drawings, and is useful only on occasion.

Deleting an Object from a PicturePlus Field

To delete an object from a PicturePlus field, select the field in Browse mode and choose **Clear** from the Edit menu to delete it.

WARNING: When you clear an object from a PicturePlus field in this way, you cannot restore it by choosing **Undo** from the Edit menu, as you can when you delete text from other types of fields.

The PicturePlus Menu

When the current field in Browse mode is a PicturePlus field, the Browse menu is replaced by the PicturePlus menu (see Figure 3.16). As you can see, this menu has the same options as the Browse menu, plus two extra commands:

- *Style & Properties*. Displays the Info Box for the PicturePlus field, which was described briefly in the section on *Drawing in a PicturePlus Field*.

- *Edit OLE object*. If the PicturePlus field contains an OLE object, this command launches the application in which it was created so you can edit it.

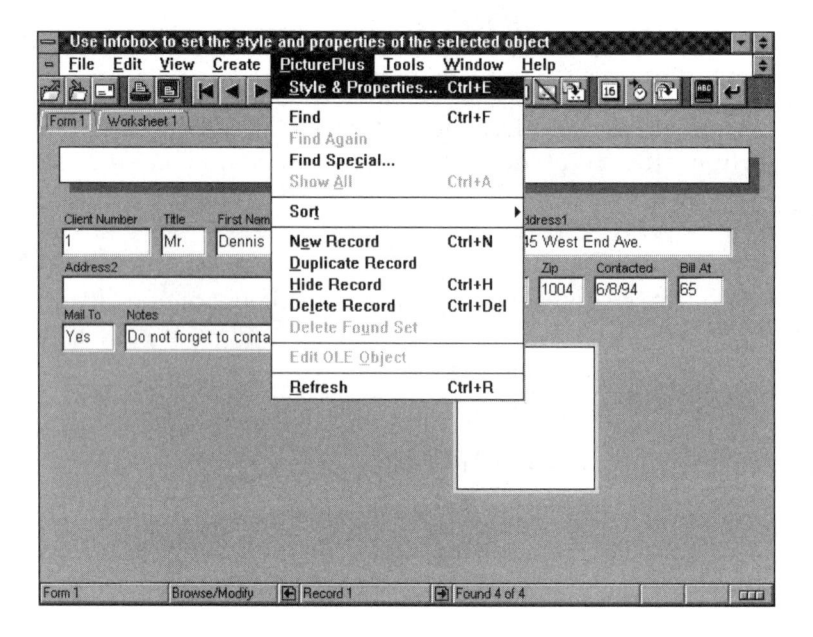

Figure 3.16 The PicturePlus menu.

Automating and Validating Data Entry

You have already looked at options for PicturePlus fields. For other data types, you can click **Options** in the Field definition dialog box to display this dialog box in an expanded form. This includes panels that give you two ways to improve data entry:

1. You can automate the entry of data in a field that has only one possible value, such as the current date, or in a field that often has the same value.

2. You can validate the entry of data that has a range of values, such as a number that has a maximum and minimum acceptable value.

You can use these panels when you are first creating a database. It is very common to overlook them until you are designing forms and thinking about ways to speed data entry. They can be used at any time by choosing **Field Definition** from the Create menu.

After displaying the Field Definition dialog box, simply click **Options,** place the cursor in any field in the list, and use the panels below to automate or validate data entry in that field.

Automatic Data Entry

Use the Default Value panel of this dialog box to enter data in the field automatically when you add new records (see Figure 3.17).

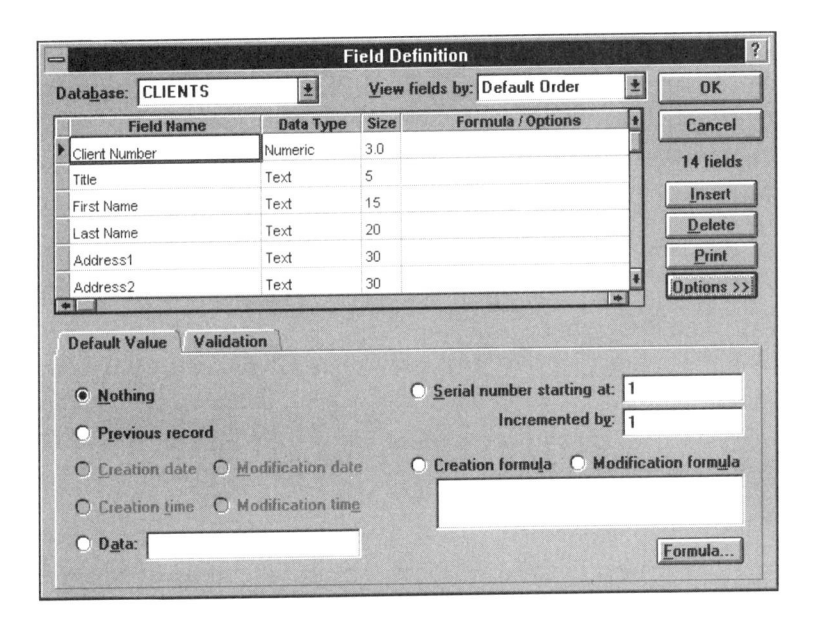

Figure 3.17 The Field Definition dialog box.

This is useful if that field always has the same data. The default value can also be edited before the record is saved, so it can be used for fields with data that is usually the same. For example, if most of your clients are from the same state, but some clients are from other states, it is easiest to have Approach enter the state name automatically. You can just skip that field when you enter most records, and you can replace it in the records where it is different.

Remember, when you tab to a field, data already in the field is selected (highlighted), so anything you type replaces it with no extra effort.

Nothing

The **Nothing** radio button is selected by default; nothing is added automatically. You can also select this button to eliminate automatic data entry that you set up earlier.

Previous Record

Select **Previous Record** to automatically enter the data in the same field of the previous record. This option could be useful if you enter lists of data that have the same value in some field—for example, if you are managing a membership organization and you get lists of new members from each state to enter. You just have to enter the name of each state once, when you began working on that state's list.

Dates and Times

The four radio buttons that follow let you automatically enter the date the record was created, the time it was created, the date it was modified last, and the time it was modified last.

The Modification Date, for example, might be useful to record your last contact with a client, assuming that you usually modify clients' records when you call them. The Creation Date might be useful to record the date that an employee was hired, assuming that you usually create records for employees on the same day that you hire them.

Data

Select **Data** to enter some specific data in the field by default. Type the data in the text box to its right.

This option is useful in any field that usually has the same data, such as the city and state that clients live in.

Serial Numbers

The Serial Number radio button can only be used for number fields and automatically enters a number larger than the number in the previous field.

By default, the series of numbers that is entered automatically starts at one and is increased by one in each record, but you can use the text boxes to the right of this radio button to specify a different starting number and a different amount that it is increased by. This option could be useful for entering client numbers or the numbers in any key field.

Formula

Use the **Creation Formula** or **Modification Formula** buttons to enter a value that is based on an Approach Formula, either when the record is first created or whenever it is modified. You must enter the formula in the text box below the radio buttons or click **Formula** to display the Formula dialog box, which you can use to generate it.

Formulas are an advanced feature of Approach, which are discussed in Chapter 8.

Validating Entered Data

Click the **Validation** Divider tab to display the panel used to validate the data that is entered in the field (see Figure 3.18).

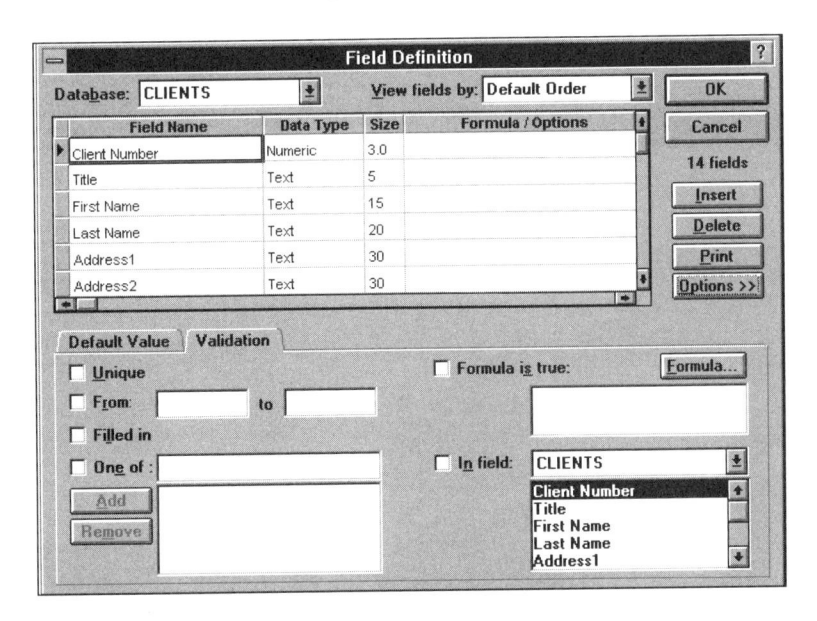

Figure 3.18 Creating validation rules.

Before using any of these options, remember that Approach automatically validates data entry based on data type. You cannot enter an invalid date in a Date field. The first step to ensuring that valid data is entered is to use the proper field type. The Validation panel lets you add additional validation rules.

Unique Values

Select **Unique** to require a value in the field that is different from the value in that field in any other record of the database.

This option is essential for the key fields of certain files in relational databases.

Specifying a Range of Entries

To specify a range of values that may be entered in the field, select **From... to**. Enter the lowest acceptable value in the text box to its immediate right, and the highest acceptable value in the text box further to the right.

This option could be useful in the Bill At field of your Clients file, assuming that you have some minimum and maximum rate that you charge.

Requiring an Entry

Select the **Filled in** checkbox to require that some value be entered in the field, and that the field may not be left blank. This option also is essential for the Key fields of certain files in relational databases.

Listing Valid Values

Select **One of** to specify a list of valid values for the field. Type each valid value in the text box to the right of this checkbox, and select **Add** to add it to the drop-down menu of all valid values. To remove a value from this list, select it and select **Remove**.

This option is useful if there are a limited number of values that can be entered in a field, but more than you could select using a drop-down menu. For example, it is quicker to type a state's name than to select it from a drop-down menu. You could use this option if you wanted to type state names but, for some reason, had to be absolutely sure all the state names you entered were valid.

Using a Formula

Select **Formula is true** to require that the value satisfy a formula. You can enter this formula in the text box to its right or select the **Formula** push button to generate it using the Formula dialog box.

Formulas are an advanced feature of Approach, which are discussed in Chapter 8.

Requiring Values in a Field of Another File

Use **In field** to require that the data entered in this field must already be in some field of another database file. Select the name of the other file from the drop-down menu to the right of this checkbox, and the name of the field that the value must be in from the list below it. This option is also essential for the Key fields of certain files in relational databases.

Error Messages

After you validate data in any of these ways, Approach does not let you move the cursor out of the field as long as it has invalid data in it.

When you press **Tab** or click another field a dialog box is displayed (see Figure 3.19). This dialog box tells you what type of data you must enter in the field. Select **OK** to return to the form with the cursor still in the field. Select **Cancel** to stop entering data.

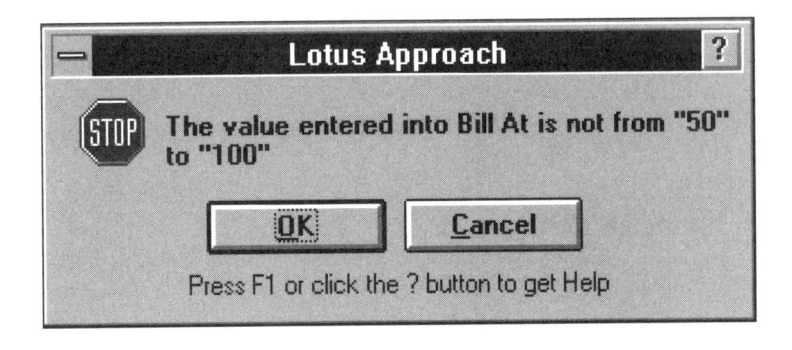

Figure 3.19 An error message requiring valid data.

NOTE: If you try to enter data in a field several times and keep getting error messages, select **Cancel** to cancel all changes to the record, and then try adding the new record (or editing the old one) again. If you still cannot enter a valid value, select **Cancel** and look at the Data Entry Options dialog box to see what is wrong with the validity check you entered.

Other Features of Data Entry Options

There are a couple of other features that are common to both automation and validation of data entry.

Changing Data Entry Options

You can change the options for automating and validating data entry at any time, in the same way that you created them. Just use the Data Entry Options dialog box to specify a new option for the field. Changing Data Entry Options does not effect data already in a field, until you try to edit it. It applies to newly entered data.

WARNING: Validation rules also prevent you from tabbing through a field of an existing record if that record has invalid data in it. Approach does not let you leave the field until the data is valid. After changing a validation rule or creating a new one, you will not have any problem scrolling through the records of your database, but you should not tab through individual fields of older records if the rule was not meant to apply to earlier data.

Combining Automation and Validation

Since data that is entered automatically can be edited by the user, it sometimes makes sense to use both panels of this dialog box for the same field. For example, you could use the default value panel to enter a client number automatically and use the validation panel to make sure it is both filled in and unique, so you do not mistakenly delete a client number or edit it.

Entry Options for your Sample Data

You can automate and validate data entry for your sample data in the following ways:

The Client Number key field can be entered automatically as a serial number. As you see in Chapter 7, the Key field of this database must be unique, and some value must be entered in it. Entering its value as a serial number automatically enters unique values, but these might be edited or deleted inadvertently, so it is a good idea to include validation for it also.

Let's assume that most of your clients are from New York state. You can enter this value automatically, and then you can edit it if necessary. You always bill at rates between $60.00 and $120.00. You can validate data to make sure it is in this range, in order to reduce the chance of error.

1. Choose **Field Definition** from the Create menu to display the Field Definition dialog box, and click **Options** to display it in expanded form. Client number should already be selected in the Field list. Select **Serial Number**, and since you have already entered four records, enter **5** in the Starting At text box to its right. Then click the **Validation** divider tab and select the **Unique** and **Filled In** checkboxes (see Figure 3.20).

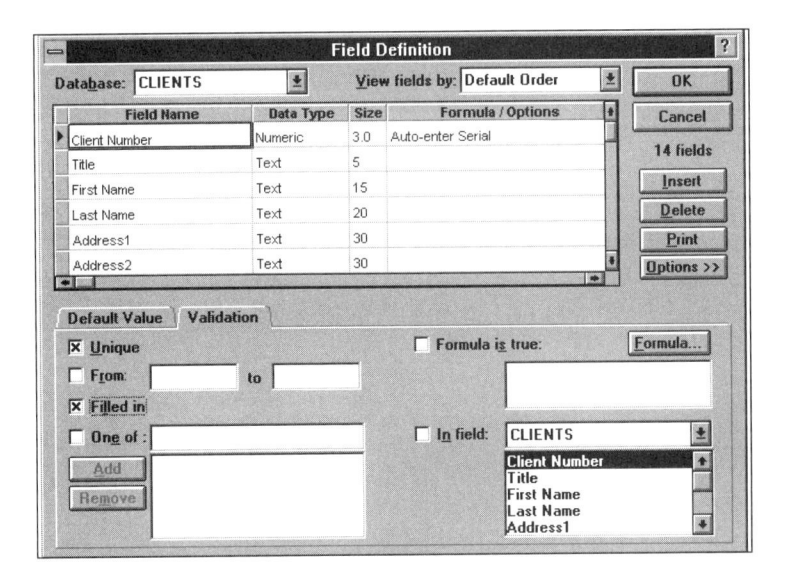

Figure 3.20 Validating entries in the Client Number field.

2. Select the State field in the Field Definition dialog box. If necessary, click the **Default Value** tab. Select **Data,** and enter **NY** in the text box to its right (see Figure 3.21).

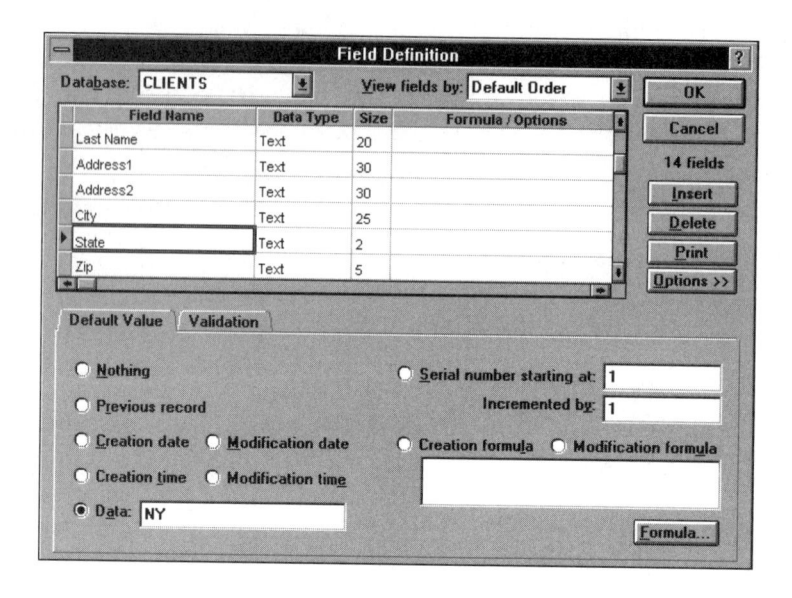

Figure 3.21 Specifying data to be entered automatically.

3. Select the Bill At field in the list in the Field Definition dialog box. Click the Validation tab. In the Validation panel, select the **From** checkbox, enter **60** in the checkbox immediately to its right, and enter **120** in the checkbox to the far right (see Figure 3.22). Then select **OK** to return to the design.
4. Notice, when you select another field, the options that you entered for the current field are entered in its Formula/Options column. Click **OK** to close the Field Definition dialog box.

If you would like, you can switch to Browse mode, if necessary, and click **New Record** to test these features with a new record. When you are done, press **Esc** to eliminate the new record.

The changes that you made in the Field Definition dialog box apply when you use any view to make changes to the data. In Chapter 4, you see that you

Chapter 3: Entering and Viewing Data

can also make data entry faster and more accurate by creating forms that include drop-down menus, checkboxes, and radio buttons. These can be used to enter data when there are a limited number of possible entries in a field.

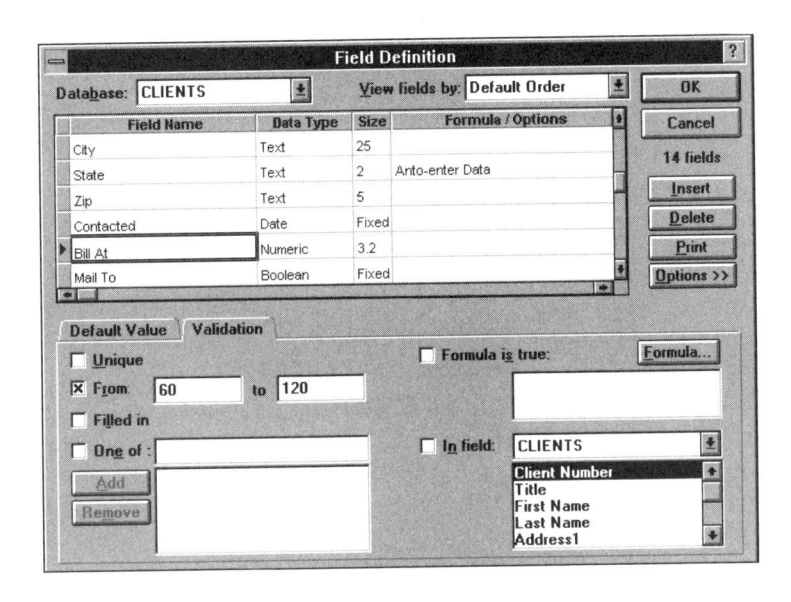

Figure 3.22 Specifying a range of valid entries.

They also combine automation and validation, automating data entry by letting the user click the control to select a value, and validating data by only giving the user valid values to choose among.

In general, if you want to improve data entry in a field, it is best to use the Default Value panel of the Field definition dialog box to enter a value in it automatically. If this is not possible, the second best option is to create a data entry form with a drop-down list, radio buttons, or checkbox, to speed data entry and control the values entered very precisely. Finally, the third best option is to use the Validation Rules panel of the Field Definition dialog box, which gives you looser control over the values entered.

Chapter 4

Changing the Design of a View

Now that you have entered and viewed data using the standard form that Approach creates when you define a database, you can appreciate the extra power that you gain by designing custom forms. In this chapter, you learn how to change the design of Forms and other views.

As you read this chapter, you should display Form 1 (the standard form that you created in the last chapter) in Design mode, so you can use it to test the techniques you are reading about. After learning these techniques in this chapter, you apply them when you learn to create new Forms, Reports, Labels, and Form letters in Chapter 5.

In this chapter, you learn to:

- Add objects such as text, graphic objects, pictures, and fields to the design of a view
- Move, resize, and delete objects

- Add check boxes, radio buttons, and drop-down lists to replace fields, in order to save time in data entry
- Make layout work easier by using the grid, rulers, and other special design tools
- Use the Info Box of objects and of the form as a whole to change colors, typefaces, and other styles and properties.
- Use the Info Box of fields to control the format in which data is displayed
- Change the order in which the cursor moves from field to field when you press the **Tab** key

An Overview of Design Mode

Design mode is so rich and has so many features, that you should begin by looking generally the ways in which you can use it to modify the design of Forms, Reports, Mailing Labels, and Form Letters.

This chapter begins with an overview of design mode, which helps you see clearly how each of its features is used when you look at them in detail later in the chapter.

Using Design Mode

As you know, you can toggle from Browse mode to Design mode by clicking the **Design** button of the icon bar or by choosing **Design** from the View menu.

Once you are in Design mode, you can view the layout in two different ways:

- When you view it Showing Data, the view is displayed with the data included as it is in Browse mode (see Figure 4.1).
- When you view Without Data, the contents of each field is represented by a dotted line with the field name in it and other features of the design are shown as in Browse mode (see Figure 4.2).

Chapter 4: Changing the Design of a View

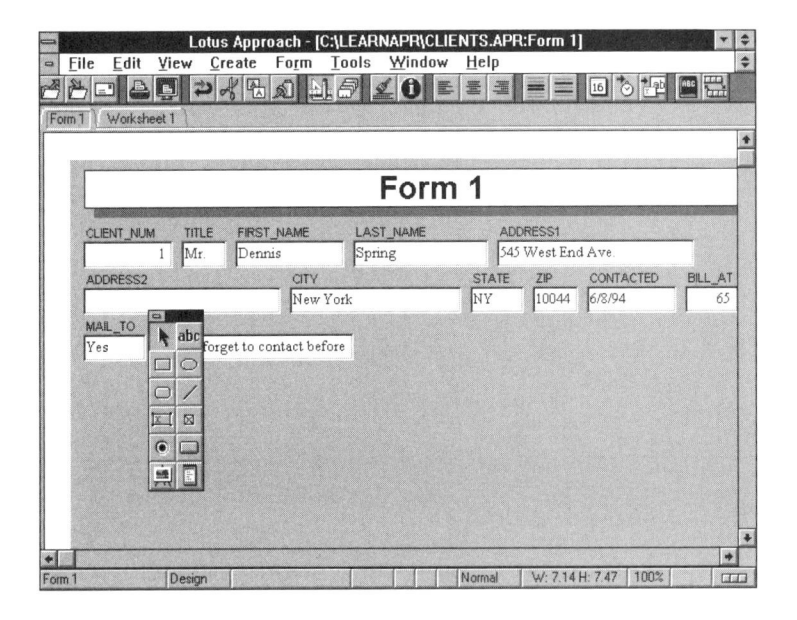

Figure 4.1 Design mode showing data.

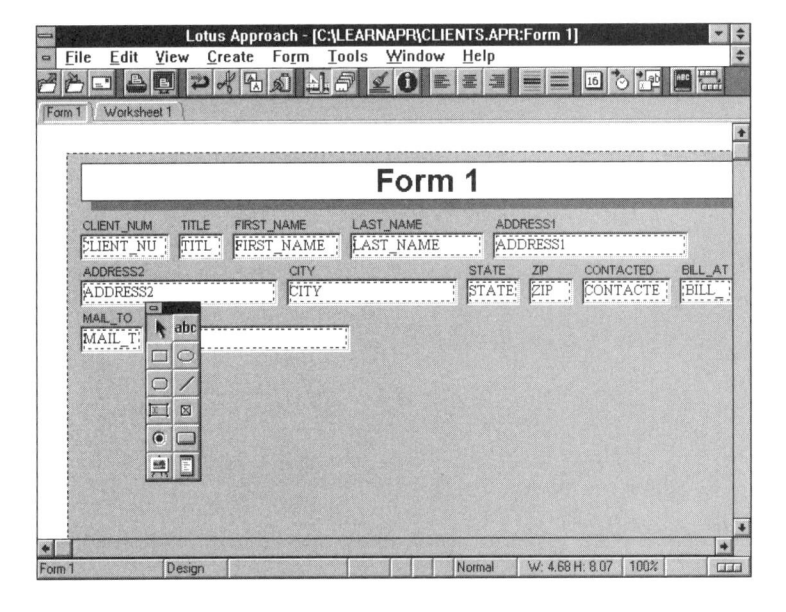

Figure 4.2 Design mode without data.

You can toggle between these two displays by choosing **Show Data** from the View menu. In either case, you can add new objects or modify existing ones in similar ways, and you can choose whichever you feel most comfortable with.

> **NOTE** Beginners often find it easiest to work without showing data, so they do not confuse Design and Browse mode. After you are accustomed to working in Design mode, you will probably prefer working with the data showing, so you can see exactly how the view looks in Browse mode.

Objects

The design of a view is made up of objects. For example, the name of each field is displayed above the field as a label in Design mode—just as it was displayed in Browse mode. Each field and its label are a single object.

Likewise, the box at the top of the standard form, with the title Form 1 in it and shadow behind it, is a single object.

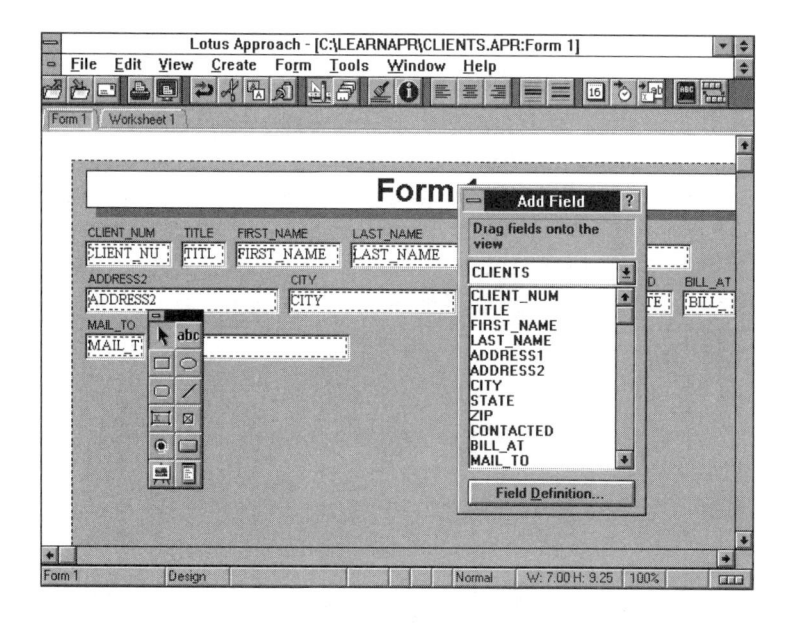

Figure 4.3 The drawing tools and Add Field box.

You can use the drawing tools to add other objects. When you switch to Design mode, this extra toolbox of drawing tools is displayed (see Figure 4.3). Use these tools to add additional text objects, graphic objects such as rectangles and lines, fields, checkboxes, radio buttons, and push buttons to designs.

You can also select the final drawing tool to display the Add Field Box (see Figure 4.3). Then you can add new fields to the design simply by clicking and dragging them from this box to the location where you want them in the design.

All of these objects can be manipulated in similar ways. For example, they can all be selected, resized, or moved very easily using the mouse.

SHORTCUT You can also Cut or Copy and Paste selected objects in the usual way, by using the Edit menu or the icon bar. The Undo command of the Edit menu (or the equivalent icon) is also extremely useful to undo the last change you made. For example, choose **Undo** to return an object you just moved to its original location, to restore an object you just resized to its original size, or to eliminate an object you just placed. (The object must still be selected for Undo to work.)

The Info Box

You can display an Info Box with specifications for all the Style and Properties box of an object or of the entire form is several ways:

- Double-clicking the object or a part of the form that does not have any objects.
- Click the object or a part of the form that does not have any objects to select it, and then choose **Style and Properties** from the Object menu.
- Select the object or form then click the Info Box icon.

Once the Info Box is displayed, it remains open until you select **Close** from its Control menu. As you select different objects, the Info Box changes and contains information on the style and properties of the object that is selected.

Info Boxes have a Divider tab interface which lets you view and modify many different features of the object (see Figure 4.4). The Info Box for a field lets you control the fonts using the panel shown in the figure, and also has panels that let you control its borders, its format, its size, and other properties.

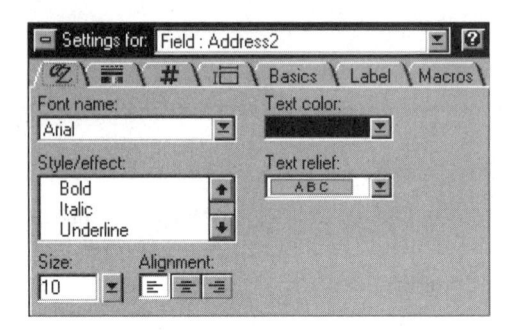

Figure 4.4 The Info Box for a Field.

Its drop-down list lets you display the settings for the entire form (or other design) or for a section of the design that the object is in (if the design has multiple panels), as well as for the selected object itself.

If a Divider tab of an Info Box is already selected, you can click it again to shrink the Info Box (see Figure 4.5). This makes it easier to get it out of the way while you are working on the design. Click any of the Divider tabs again to restore the Info Box to full size with the panel for that Divider tab displayed.

Figure 4.5 Shrinking the Info Box.

Other Features of Design View

To get an overview of Design mode, glance at a few more features to be covered in more detail later in this chapter.

The Object and Form Menu

When you enter Design mode for a form, the Browse menu is replaced by a Form menu if the entire Form is selected, or by an Object menu if an object is selected (see Figure 4.6). If you are working with other types of views, a Report, Mailing Label, or Form Letter menu is displayed rather than a Form menu, if the entire View is selected. These menus let you display an Info Box, help you manipulate objects, and have other features.

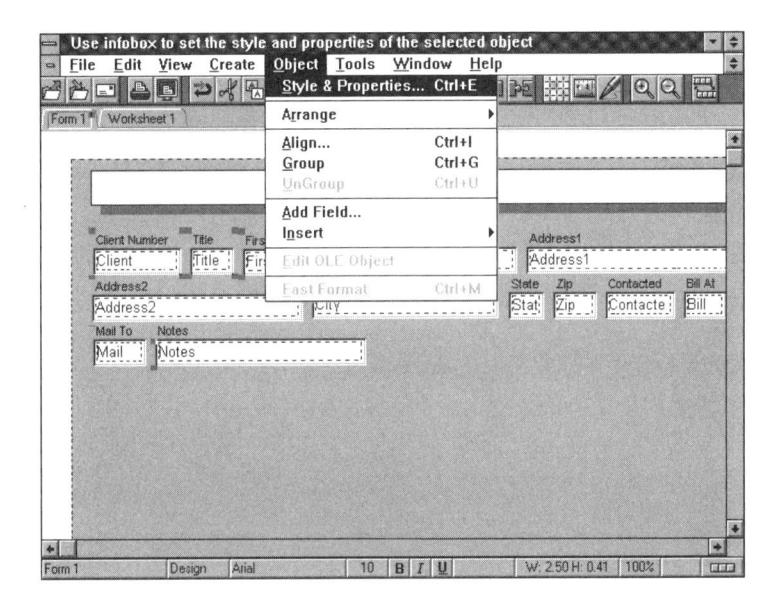

Figure 4.6 An Object menu.

The Shortcut Menu of Objects

You can also select an object and display the menu for it in a single step by right-clicking it (see Figure 4.7). As you can see, the Shortcut menu has the same commands as the Object menu. It also has the Cut, Copy, and Paste commands from the Edit menu. You can use this shortcut menu to select and Cut or Copy an object with a single movement.

Practical Approach, 3.0

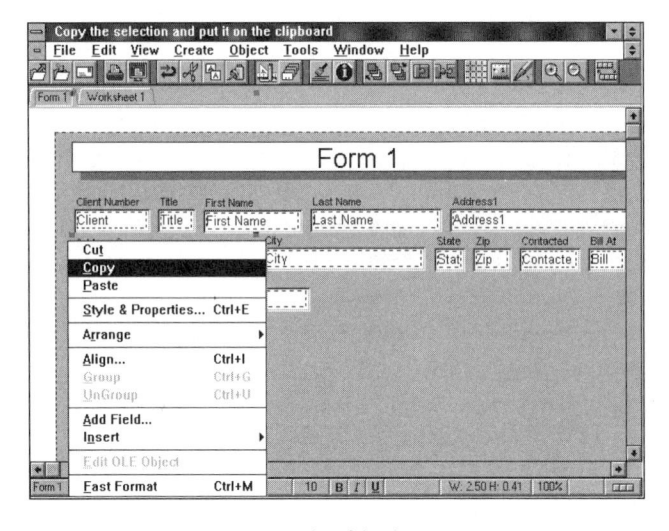

Figure 4.7 Display of the Shortcut menu.

The View Menu

To help you to place object up in exactly the locations you want, you can use the View menu to display gridlines and rulers (see Figure 4.8). The View menu also lets you display or hide other features of Design mode and basic features of the Approach interface, such as the SmartIcons, Status Bar, and View Tabs.

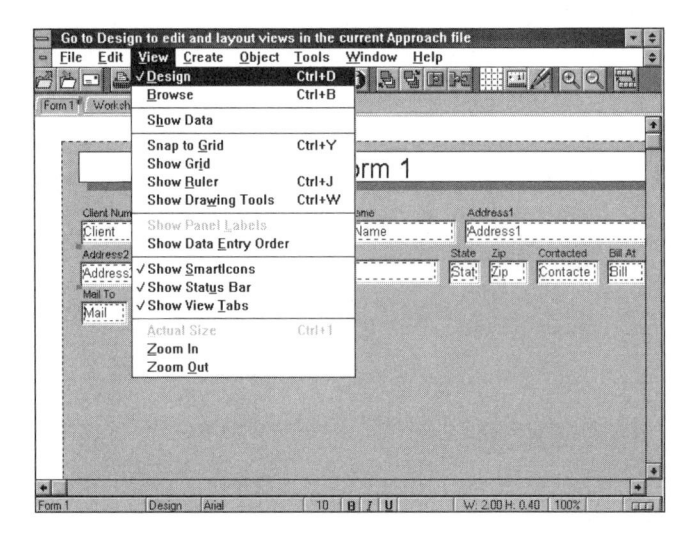

Figure 4.8 The View menu.

Chapter 4: Changing the Design of a View

In addition, you can also use the View menu or the icon bar to enlarge or reduce the size of the design, to make it easier to work on.

Icon Bars

Because it has so many features, Design View has two icon bars (see Figure 4.9). You can switch between the two by clicking the icon at the far right, the **Next SmartIcon** icon.

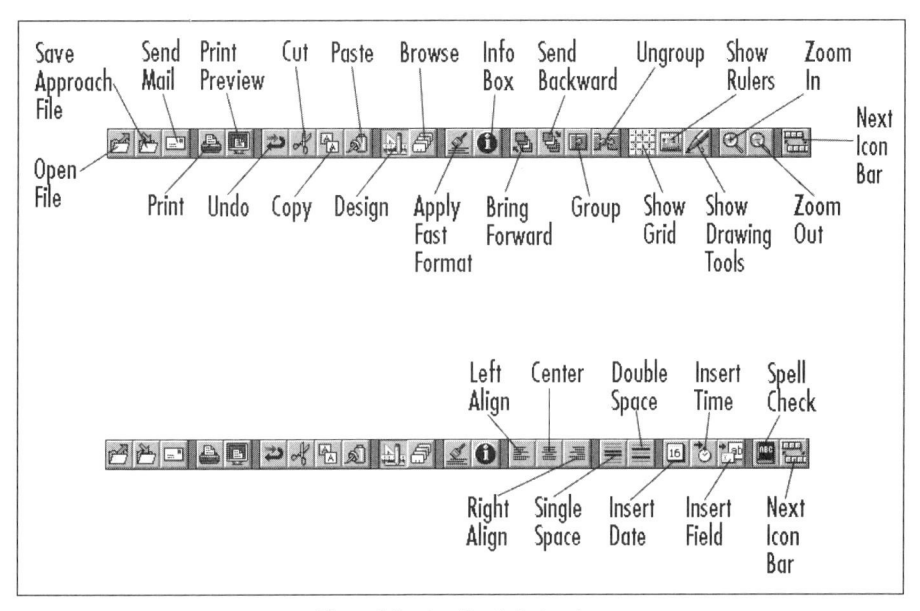

Figure 4.9 Icon Bars in Design view.

If you cannot find one of the icons described in this chapter on the Icon bar, click this icon to display the alternative icon bar.

Approach displays slightly different icon bars when you use different types of views in Design mode. This chapter covers icons that are important for a number of views. Chapter 5 covers icons used for specific types of views.

Summary of the Overview

Those are the basic features of Design mode. You should remember that you can do the following:

- Add objects using the drawing tools or the Add Field Box.
- Control the style and other properties of objects by using the Info Box.
- Manipulate objects using the mouse or the **Cut**, **Copy**, **Paste**, and **Undo** commands of the Edit menu.
- Use special layout tools accessible through the View menu.

This general outline makes it much easier for you to see the importance of each of the features of design mode, as they are discussed in more detail below.

Saving Changes in Designs

Remember you must save an Approach file to keep the changes you made in its designs. You can do this by choosing **Save Approach File** from the File menu.

If you have not saved changes to a view, Approach displays a dialog box asking if you want to save the Approach File when you close it or exit from Approach. You simply select **Yes** to save the View.

WARNING: If you are working on a complex design, however, you should save the Approach File periodically, by choosing **Save Approach File** from the File menu, so that you do not lose your work if your computer is turned off accidentally—for example, because of a power failure.

Saving the Approach File frequently also lets you go back to an earlier stage of the design if you make changes in it that were mistaken. Close the Approach File without saving it to discard the changes since you saved it last.

Displaying Your Sample Form in Design Mode

Look at Form 1 in Design mode, while you are reading the detailed descriptions of how to change designs so that you can experiment with the features that you are reading about. While you are learning, you will probably prefer to use design mode without data showing, and you should begin by displaying the design in this way.

Chapter 4: Changing the Design of a View

1. If you have not done so already, start Approach, and open CLIENTS.APR to view Form 1. Initially the Form is displayed in Browse mode. Click the **Design** icon or choose **Design** from the View menu to display it in Design mode.
2. To display the design without the data, choose **Show Data** from the View menu (see Figure 4.10).

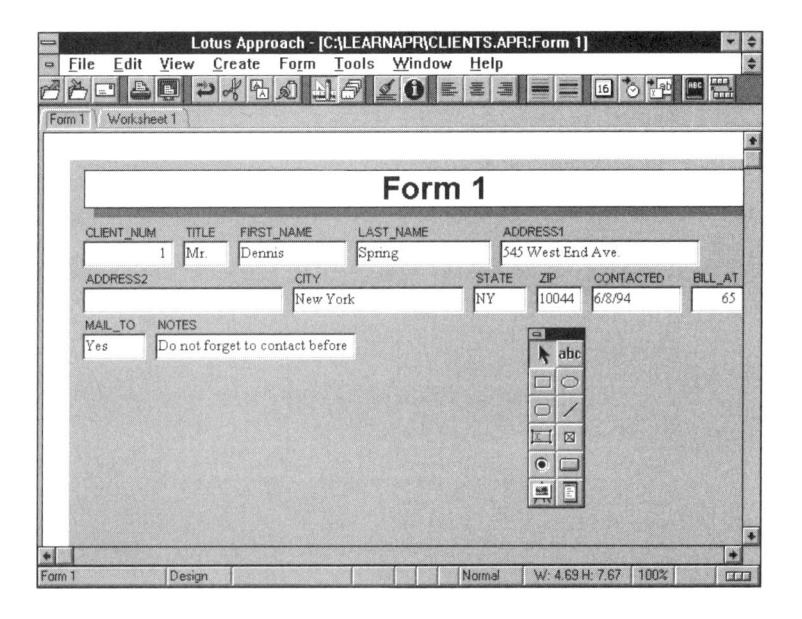

Figure 4.10 Displaying the form in design mode.

> **NOTE** You may want to look at the form both with and without the data as you read, to see which you prefer. The Show Data command of the View menu is a toggle: you can also choose it again to display the data.

Manipulating Objects

Now that you are done with the overview of design mode, begin by looking in detail at the simplest and most basic ways of manipulating objects, the things that you will do constantly as you change the designs of views.

Try doing these things as you read the descriptions that follow. Remember that you can undo the last change you made by choosing **Undo** from the Edit menu or clicking the **Undo** icon while the object remains selected.

You can also make a number of changes in the design as you read this chapter, and then close the file without saving changes in order to preserve the original design of the view.

Adding Objects

As you know, the drawing tools let you add text, graphic objects, fields, check boxes, push buttons, or PicturePlus fields (or other OLE objects). You can also create any of these by choosing **Drawing** from the Create menu and then choosing the name of the appropriate object from the submenu.

In general, after using the tool or menu, you click and drag to place the objects. Because each object is added a bit differently, each is covered in more detail below.

You can double-click a tool to add multiple cases of the same type of object. After you click and drag to add the object once, the button remains down, and the mouse pointer remains in the form that you use to add that object. You can click and drag again to create another object of the same type. You can keep adding the same type object repeatedly until you click the **Selection Pointer** tool to return the pointer to its default form.

The Add Field Box

As an alternative to using the drawing tools, you can add fields to a design by clicking the **Add Field Box** tool or choosing **Add Field** from the Form menu to display the Add Field Box (see Figure 4.11). The Add Field box is displayed and can be used as a substitute for either the Field or the PicturePlus drawing tool.

To add fields to the design, you can simply click and drag them from this box to the location where you want them. This box remains open until you choose **Close** or choose **Add Field** from the Form menu again, and you can continue to work on other parts of the design while it is displayed.

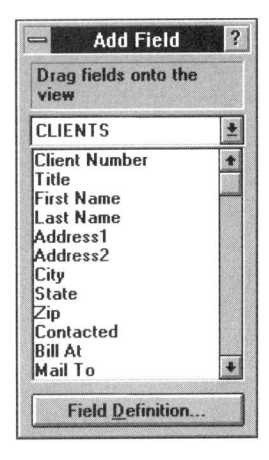

Figure 4.11 The Add Field Box.

Notice that the Add Field Box also includes a Field Definition button, which you can click to display the Field Definition dialog box. You can use this dialog box to modify the structure of the database, using the methods described in the section on *Changing Field Definitions* in Chapter 2.

WARNING: Remember, you can lose data if you change the definitions of fields in an existing database.

Adding a Picture

In addition to including a PicturePlus field from the database, you can add a picture to the design. A PicturePlus field and a Picture are used for different purposes:

- A PicturePlus field holds a picture or other object that is different for each record. For example, you might want to add a PicturePlus field to your Client database to hold a scanned photograph of each client.
- A picture added to the design remains the same, regardless of which record is displayed. For example, you might want your company logo displayed at the top of a data entry form.

You can add a picture to a view by pasting it from a file or from the clipboard

Pasting a Picture from a File

To paste a picture from a file:

- First click the location in the design where you want its upper left corner to be. If you do not click a location before pasting it, it is placed in the upper left corner of the design, and you can click and drag it to move it.
- Then choose **Paste from File** from the Edit menu to display the dialog box, and use it to select the file that contains the picture.

Pasting a Picture from the Clipboard

To paste a picture from the clipboard:

- First open the source application, select the picture there, and then choose **Copy** (or **Cut**) from the source application's Edit menu.
- Then return to Approach and click the location in the design where you want the picture's upper left corner to be located.
- Choose **Paste** from the Edit menu or click the **Paste** icon to add the picture there.

A Picture in a Design versus Picture in a Field

These are two methods of pasting a picture in a design can also be used to add pictures to a PicturePlus field.

The major difference is that you add pictures to a PicturePlus field in Browse mode—adding the pictures to this field is part of the job of adding data to the database. On the other hand, you add pictures to a view in Design mode—adding pictures is part of the job of creating the design.

Thus, the PicturePlus drawing tool simply adds a frame to the design that is used to display data from the PicturePlus field of each record. By contrast, a picture that is part of the design is added to it directly.

Selecting Objects

You can select an object simply by clicking it. Handles appear at its corners to indicate that it is selected (see Figure 4.12).

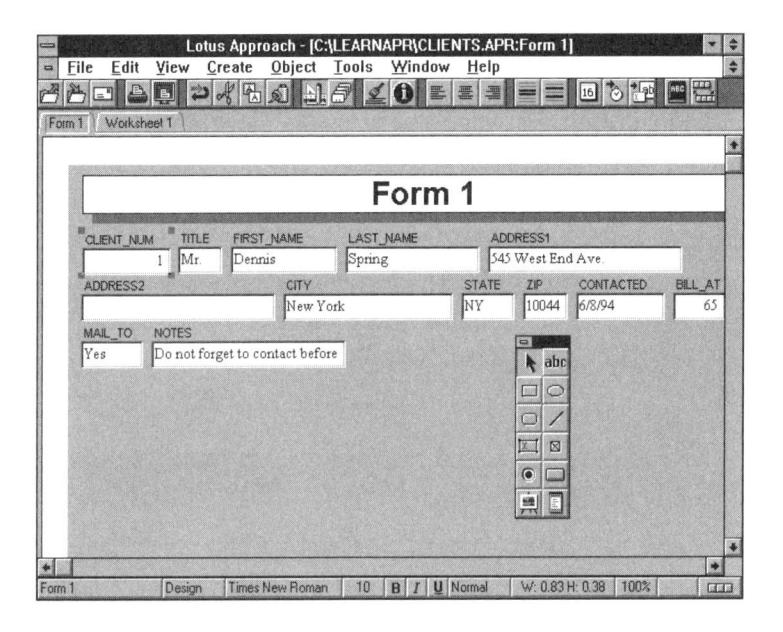

Figure 4.12   Handles indicate that the Client Number field is selected.

You can deselect an object by clicking anywhere in the window outside of the object. The handles around it disappear. You automatically deselect an object when you select another object.

Multi-Selecting Objects

You can also select multiple objects by holding down the **Shift** key as you click objects. Previously selected objects are not deselected. Handles are added to all selected objects.

When you click without holding down **Shift** anywhere in the window outside of one of the selected objects, all of the selected objects are deselected.

Selecting a Group of Objects

You can also select a group of objects that are next to each other simply by clicking and dragging around the group. Move the pointer to a location beyond one corner of the group, and hold down the mouse button as you drag to a location beyond the opposite corner of the group. A dotted line is temporarily displayed as a rectangle around the area while you drag it (see Figure 4.13). When you release the mouse button, the rectangle disappears, all of the objects that were totally surrounded by it are selected and have handles added.

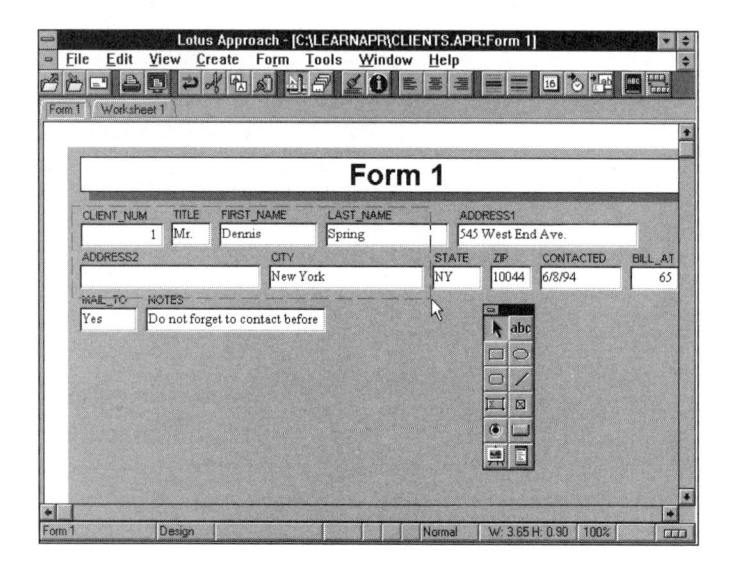

Figure 4.13 Selecting multiple objects.

If an object was only partially surrounded by the rectangle, it is not selected.

You can deselect all of these objects by clicking anywhere in the window that is not within a selected object. You can also select additional objects without deselecting them by holding down the **Shift** key as you click them.

Moving Objects

You can move an object simply by clicking and dragging it. When you click it, handles appear to indicate that it is selected. Hold down the mouse button and drag the mouse to move it.

You can also *nudge* selected objects—move them a small distance—by using the arrow keys. This is often the easiest way to align objects.

If you have already multi-selected objects, you can move them all by clicking and dragging any one of them or by using the arrow keys. They all move the same distance in the same direction. If any other objects that are not selected happen to be surrounded by the selected objects, they are not moved.

Resizing Objects

You can resize a selected object very easily by clicking and dragging its handles. Drag one of the lower handles downward or one of the upper handles upward to make it taller, or drag one of the handles left or right to make it wider. Drag a handle outward diagonally from the corner to make it both taller and wider.

Just move the mouse pointer to a handle, click it, and hold the mouse button down while you drag.

If multiple objects are selected, you can resize any one of them by clicking and dragging its handles. You can only resize one object at a time.

Deleting Objects

You can delete a selected object in any one of three ways:

- Press **Del**.
- Press **Backspace**.
- Choose **Clear** from the Edit menu.

If multiple objects are selected, all are deleted.

Using the Edit Menu

You can choose **Cut** from the Edit menu or click the **Cut** icon to delete selected objects and place a copy of them in the clipboard. You can choose **Copy** from the Edit menu or click the **Copy** icon to leave the selected objects in the design and place a copy of them in the clipboard.

Once an object is in the clipboard, you can place it in any location in a design simply by clicking that location and then choosing **Paste** from the Edit menu or clicking the **Paste** icon.

Finally, it is worth re-emphasizing that you can undo the operations described in this section (and most other design operations) by choosing **Undo** from the Edit menu, or clicking the **Undo** icon.

Changing Margins

The entire surface of a design is also treated like an object in some ways.

You can click the margin of the design, and solid double lines are displayed to indicate that the margin is selected (see Figure 4.14). You can also click the margin if you are showing data, even though it is not displayed as a dotted line, to select it and display it as double lines. Then click and drag these lines to change the margin settings. Simply drag them up, down, left or right to make the margins wider or narrower. The text and other objects in the design move to reflect the changed margin. For example, if you make the upper margin wider, they all move downward. You cannot drag the corners to change two margins at once; you can change only one margin setting at a time.

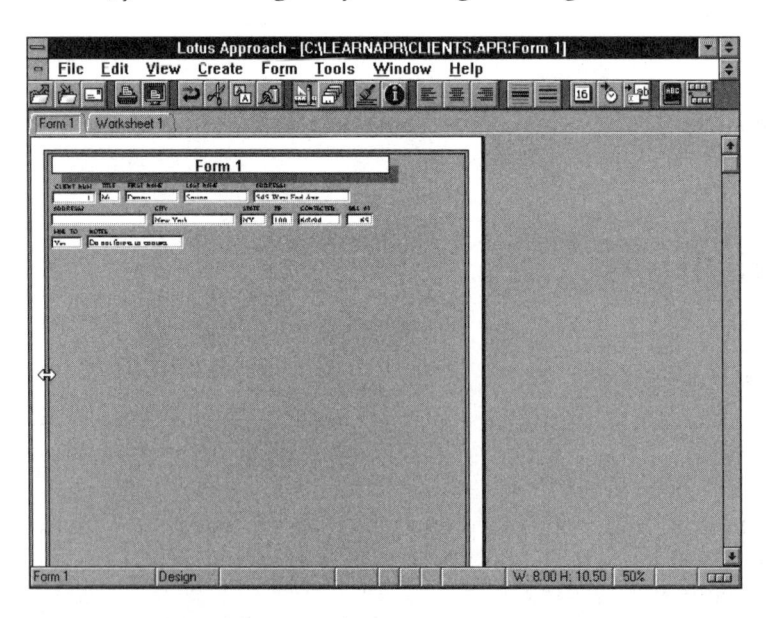

Figure 4.14 A design with its margin selected (zoomed out).

In fact, when you click and drag margins, you resize the entire printable area of the form, and you can do the same with other designs, such as reports and mailing labels. Thus, you resize the entire area of a design in just the same way that you resize other objects.

> **NOTE** The margin remains selected when you zoom out to see more of the page, or it can be selected after you have zoomed out (see Figure 4.14). In most cases, if there are many objects already in the design, it is best to view the design at 25% or 50% of its actual size when you change margins.

Objects and Their Styles and Properties

Now that you have looked at the general methods of manipulating objects, you can begin to look at how to work with specific types of objects—both how to add them to a design and how to use the Info Box to control their styles and properties.

In this section, you look at the simpler examples—graphic objects, text objects, and picture objects—and at the features that are used to specify the style of many different types of objects. Because field objects are more complex, they are discussed in a section of their own.

Graphic Objects

Rectangles, ovals, rounded rectangles, and lines are the simplest objects that you add to designs.

To add one of these, simply click the appropriate drawing tool (see Figure 4.15). Then, when you move the pointer to the Design window, it becomes a cross hair. Click at one corner of the object, hold down the mouse button, and drag the pointer to the opposite corner. The object is displayed and its size varies as you drag. When you release the mouse button, the pointer is restored to its usual form, and the object you just created is selected.

Practical Approach, 3.0

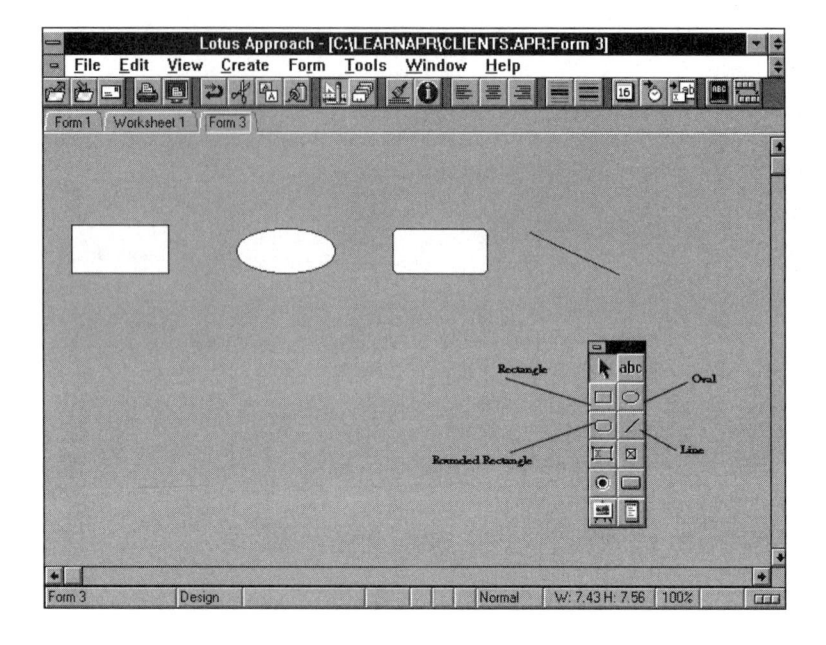

Figure 4.15 The tools for adding graphic objects and the objects.

When you add a rectangle, oval, or rounded rectangle, you must drag from one corner to the opposite corner of the object.

When you add a line, you drag from one end to the opposite end of the line. Lines can be horizontal, vertical or diagonal, and you can change their slope as well as their size by clicking and dragging one of the handles.

> **NOTE** If you hold down the **Shift** key while you create a rectangle or rounded rectangle, Approach draws a precise square or rounded square. Likewise, if you hold down **Shift** when you draw an oval, Approach draws a circle. If you hold down **Shift** when you draw a line, it makes the line precisely horizontal, vertical or diagonal at a 45 degree angle.

Styles and Properties of Graphic Objects

The styles and properties for graphic objects are also among the simplest for any objects. All have similar Info Boxes, except lines, which are even simpler than the others because they do not have a fill color. The Figures 4.16 and

4.17, which show the styles and properties for a rectangle, also apply to other graphic objects, though some settings are missing for lines.

Borders and Colors

The first panel of the Info Box lets you specify settings for borders and colors (see Figure 4.16). Use the drop-down menus to select a border width between hairline and 12 points, a border color, a fill color, and a shadow color. The frame drop-down lists display graphics that let you use a solid line, double line, several types of dotted lines for frames, or shading that gives the frame a raised or lowered appearance.

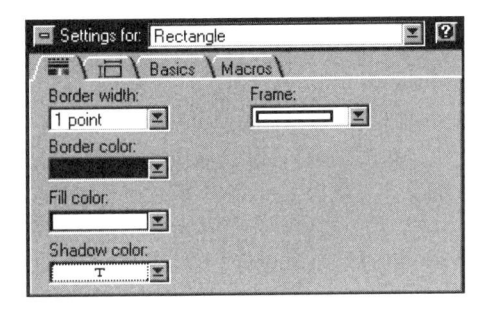

Figure 4.16 The first panel of the rectangle Info Box with a color palette displayed.

All of the palettes used to select colors simply display a variety of colors, and you can click one to select it. The sample color on their upper left appears white but has the letter T in it to indicate that it is transparent. Choosing this color lets you see whatever is behind the object. When you place a graphic object, by default, its shadow is this color, so it is not visible; if you want the object to have a shadow, select any other shadow color.

Size, Location, and Slide Options

The second panel of this Info Box displays the size, location, and printing slide options of the object (see Figure 4.17).

You can edit the numbers in the Width and Height text boxes to change the size of the object, or edit the numbers in the Top and Left text boxes to change its location. Generally, however, it is easier to change size and location by clicking and dragging: these numbers change accordingly.

Practical Approach, 3.0

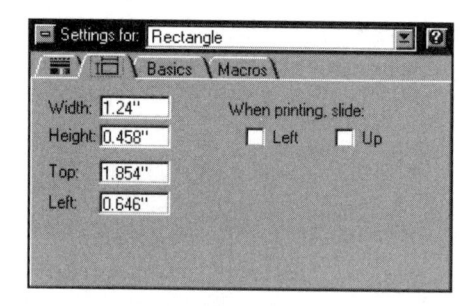

Figure 4.17 The second panel of the rectangle Info Box.

The Left and Up boxes in this panel can be used to close up spaces between objects when you print. This is used most commonly with field objects. A couple of typical uses are:

- If the Last Name field is placed to the right of the First Name field, there ordinarily are extra spaces between the two, because the First Name in most records does not fill the entire width of its field. Select **When printing, slide: Left** to eliminate extra spaces between it and the First Name.
- If fields are placed below a field that does not always contain data, such as the Address2 field in your sample database, you can select **When printing slide: Up** to close up the blank line that would be left by an empty Address2 field.
- You could also use these check boxes in the same way if you place graphic objects to the right or below a field.

Because these options are almost always needed for Mailing Labels, they both are automatically turned on for the fields in label designs.

Basic Features

The Basics panel lets you specify that an object should not be printed (see Figure 4.18). If you select the **Non-printing** checkbox, **Show in preview** is enabled, and you can select it if you want to display the object in print preview mode, even though it in not printed. This panel also includes a drop-down menu that lets you apply a named style to the object. Named styles are covered in Chapter 11.

Chapter 4: Changing the Design of a View

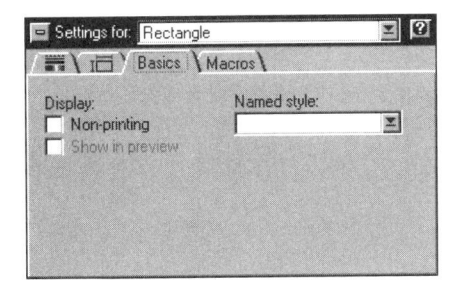

Figure 4.18 The Basics panel for the rectangle Info Box.

Macros

The Macros panel lets you attach a macro to the object, so the macro is performed whenever the used clicks this object (see Figure 4.19). Macros are covered in Chapter 10.

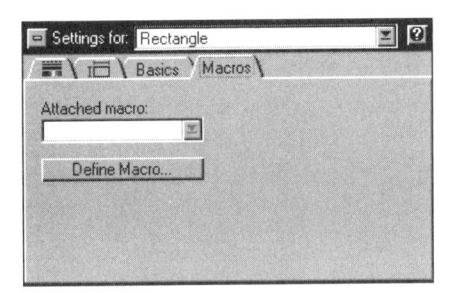

Figure 4.19 The Macros panel for the rectangle Info Box.

Text

You can add text to a design in a two-step process:

1. First, create a *text frame*. To do this, click the **Text** tool. Click and drag in the design window just as you would do to create a rectangle. The pointer becomes an insertion bar, like that used when you edit text. When you release the mouse button, the text frame is displayed as a rectangle with a cursor in it.

2. Enter text in the text frame. You can simply type in the text, or you can paste text in the text frame that you cut or copied from some other location. Use the usual methods of editing to modify the text. When you are done, click anywhere outside of the text frame to remove the insertion point and return the pointer to its usual form.

> As a quicker way of adding text, simply click the **Text** tool, click anywhere on the design, and type the text. The text box expands to accommodate the text you are entering. When you are done, click anywhere outside the text object.

You can select a text object at any time and move it or use the handles to resize it as you would any other object. When you manipulate it in this way, the text frame is affected. If you resize the text that you entered in it is word-wrapped to fit into the new size of the text frame.

How to Edit Text

To edit the text in a text object that you added earlier, click the **Text** tool. The pointer changes to an insertion bar, as always. Then you can click an existing text object to display it with its text frame around it and an insertion point in it, as it was displayed when you first added it.

> After clicking a text object to select it, you can simply click it again to place an insertion point in it and edit it.

When the text object is displayed in this way, you can change the text in the same way that you did when you first added it. Use the usual editing methods to change the text. When you are done, click anywhere outside the text object to return the pointer to its usual form.

Style and Properties of Text Objects

Approach lets you control styles and properties of the text itself when you are editing a text object, and styles and properties of the object as a whole when it is selected but does not have an insertion point in it.

The Text Editing Info Box

When you are first entering a text object or editing text in a text object, A Text menu is displayed instead of the Object menu, and lets you use the Text Editing Info Box, (see Figure 4.20). You can display this Info Box in the usual way, by clicking the **Info Box** tool or choosing **Style & Properties** from the text menu at any time while you are editing text.

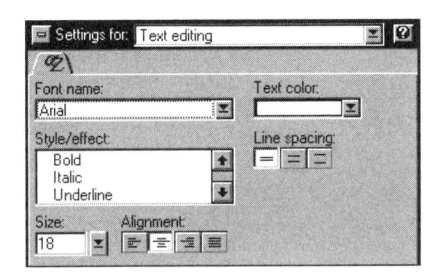

Figure 4.20 The Text Editing Info Box.

Select a font, such as **Arial** or **Roman**, from the Font name list. Select styles such as **Bold** or **Italic** or effects such as **Underline** or **Strikethrough** from the Style/effect list. You can select multiple styles and effects: when you select one, it is checked, and you can select it again to remove the effect. Select a size expressed in points, from the Size list. The options available in these lists depend on which fonts you have installed under Windows, and they may differ from the illustration.

Use the **Alignment** buttons in the Alignment area to specify if the text should be centered within its text frame, or aligned to the left or right edge of the text frame. The Line spacing buttons let you select single space, one-and-a-half space, or double space. The Text color drop-down list displays a color palette, like the one you looked at above in the section on graphic objects, that lets you select the color of the letters.

NOTE: You can also use this Info box to change the typeface of part of the text within a text object. First select (highlight) the text you want changed. Then choose **Text Style** from the Style menu to display the dialog box. (In this case, you cannot use the dialog box by double-clicking the object, as the pointer is an insertion bar.) Changes you make in **Font**, **Font Style**, **Size**, and **Effects** apply only to the selected text, though changes in Alignment still apply to all the text in the object.

When you are editing text, the Text Menu gives you an alternative way of choosing styles, such as Bold or Underline, as does the Icon bar.

The Text Object Info Box

When you have selected a Text Object but are not editing the text, Approach displays the Text object Info Box (see Figure 4.21). As you can see, the first panel of this Info Box is the same as the Text editing Info Box that you just looked at, which lets you control the font and other features of the text.

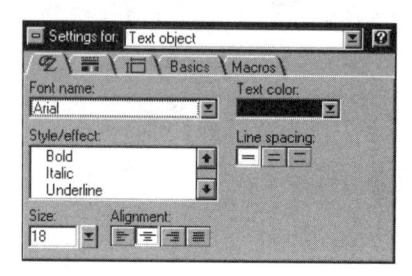

Figure 4.21 The Text object Info Box.

The four panels of this Info Box are similar to the ones used for a Rectangle. They let you control border, fill color, shadow color and frame, control size, location, and slide properties. It lets you control basics such as whether the object is non-printing and whether it has a named style, and the last one lets you attach a macro. For more details on all of these, see the section on *Styles and Properties for Graphic Objects,* above.

Using The Status Bar and Icon Bar to Work with Text

If you are editing text or have selected an object that includes text, you can also use the features from the Status Bar to change its typeface, size, and turn on or off boldface, italics, and underlining (see Figure 4.22).

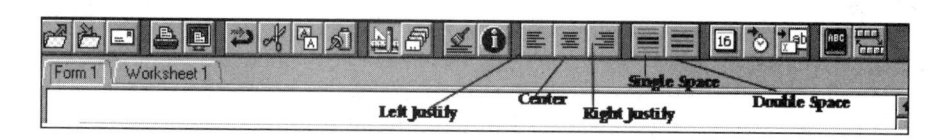

Figure 4.22 The Status Bar for working with text.

The following icons are also useful shortcuts for working with text (see Figure 4.23). You may have to click the **Next Smarticon** icon to display these icons.

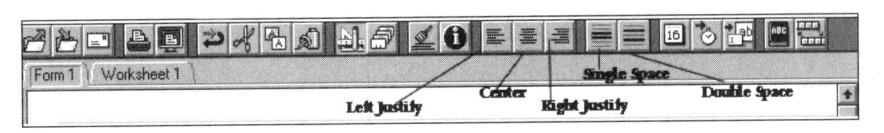

Figure 4.23 SmartIcons for working with text.

Adding a Date, Time, Page Number, or Field to a Text Object

Approach also lets you add the date, time, page number or the contents of a field to a text object.

To add one of these, first select a text object or place the insertion point in a text object that you are editing.

Choose **Insert** from the Text or Object menu and select either **Date**, **Time**, **Page#**, or **Field** from the submenu, or click the equivalent icon of the Icon bar, to place one of these in the text object. (You may have to select the **Show Next SmartIcon** icon to display these icons.) If you choose **Field**, the Add Field Box is displayed, and you can click and drag the field you want into the Text Object.

Approach places the symbol <<DATE>>, <TIME>>, <<#>> or the name of the field surrounded by double angle brackets into the text object, when it is displayed in Design mode with Show Data off.

It displays the actual date, time, page number or contents of a field in Browse mode or in Design mode with Show Data on.

The first three of these are particularly useful in printed reports, which have multiple pages and which you may print several times while you are designing them. It is useful to know the date and time that each was printed. You may want to use one or more of them by themselves in text objects.

> **NOTE** If you put any of these in text objects along with other text, it moves and is word-wrapped as you edit the rest of the text. This is the primary advantage of inserting a field in a text object, rather than adding the field itself as an independent object. When you to create form letters, all the fields you add are inserted as text objects, to make it easy for you to reformat and edit the form letter.

You can edit or change the Type Style of the page number, time, date, or field just as you do with any text object. Select it and make changes in it, just as if it were a part of the ordinary text.

Finally, even though they are text objects, you can format the page number, date, or field as you do number, date, and text fields. Select it and then use the methods of formatting described later in this chapter in the section on *Working With Fields*.

Working with Fields

In many ways, fields are similar to the other objects you have looked at: they are added in a similar way and they have many of the same styles and properties as graphic and text objects. They are more complex than the objects that you have looked at before:

- They let you format the data displayed in the field, for example, to display text in all capital letters or display numbers as currency.
- They let you create controls like those used in dialog boxes, such as drop-down lists and radio buttons, to make data entry easier.

In addition to the basics, these more advanced features of fields are covered in this section. PicturePlus fields, which work differently from other fields, are covered at the end of the section.

Adding a Field to a Design

In most cases, you can add all the fields you need to a design when you first create it. All the fields of the database are automatically included in the default form. There are cases, however, when you must add a field to a design—for example, if you change the field definition of the database by adding fields to it, and you must add the new fields to existing forms.

Using the Add Field Box

SHORTCUT

The simplest way to add a field is to use the Add Field Box (see Figure 4.24). Display this box by clicking the **Add Field Dialog** tool of the Drawing tools or by choosing **Add Field** from the Form or Object menu. You can simply click and drag a field from this box to a location in the design in order to place the field there.

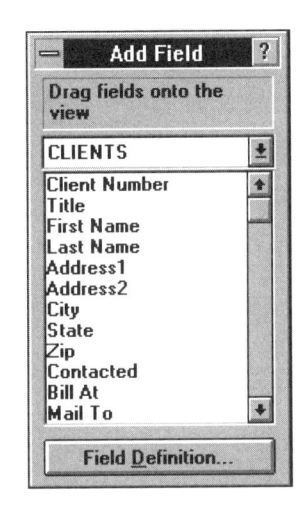

Figure 4.24 The Add field box.

Use the database drop-down list to select another file or a relational database and display its fields in the list. You can also click the Field definition button to display the Field definition dialog box, discussed in Chapter 2, and use it to add a new field or change the definition of existing fields in the database.

Using the Fields Tool

You can use the Fields of the Drawing Tools to add a field to a view. This method is rather like adding a text object or a picture:

- Create a Field frame in the usual way. Select the **Field** tool. The pointer becomes a cross hair. Click and drag to place the frame.

- Use the Info Box to specify which field the frame holds, as well as to set its style and properties, if you want to. By default, Approach places the first field in the database in the frame, but you can use the Field list in the Basics panel of its Info Box to select any field to be displayed in the frame (see Figure 4.25). Here too, you can use the database drop-down list display fields from another file or click the **Field definition** button to display the Field definition dialog box.

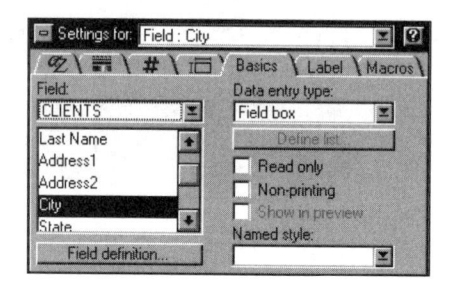

Figure 4.25 The Basics panel of the Fields Info Box.

Field Styles and Properties

The Info Box for fields is more complex than for other objects and has seven panels, some of which are the same as the panels for other types of objects that you have already learned about.

Basic Properties

You can use the controls in the Basic panel of the Info Box to change the contents of any field in the design—even to change the fields placed in the design when it created the default form. You can think of the field that is displayed in it as one property of the field frame, which you can change as you do any other property. As you can see in Figure 4.25, the Basics panel also includes the following features:

- A checkbox to make the Field read-only, which you can select to prevent users from editing the field. This is particularly useful if you create a field that has data entered in it automatically that you do not want to be changed by mistake, such as key fields in relational databases.

- Checkboxes to make a field non-printing and to display a non-printing field in preview mode, and the drop-down menu that lets you apply a Named style, which you have seen in the Basics panel of other types of objects.
- A Data entry type drop-down list, which lets you create drop-down lists, checkboxes, and other special controls to make it easier to enter data in the field. You can also create these controls using the Drawing Tools, and they will be covered later in this chapter.
- The Named style drop-down list gives you a quicker way of applying a style to a field, and it is discussed briefly later in this chapter and in more detail in Chapter 11.

Fonts

The first panel of the Field Info Box is used to specify font and other typographical effects and is similar to the equivalent panel used for Text Objects, which you looked at previously (see Figure 4.26).

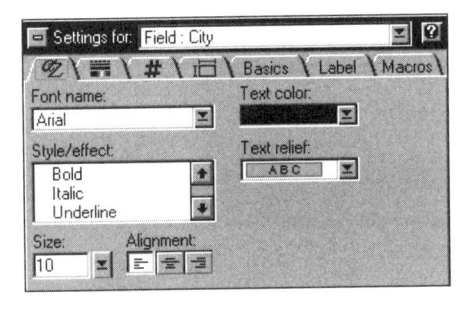

Figure 4.26 Specifying the Fonts of a Field.

Borders

The second panel is used for specifying the borders of the field, and it has the same features that you looked at earlier in the section on Text Boxes, plus a couple of additional features.

You can add border lines on any or all of the field's four edges (see Figure 4.27). Use the check boxes in the Borders area to specify if a line should be displayed at the top, bottom, left, or right edge of the Field frame or as a baseline under the text itself. There is also a checkbox that you can select to specify that the border should enclose the field's label.

Practical Approach, 3.0

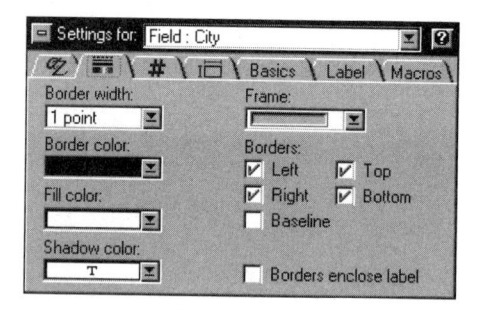

Figure 4.27 Specifying the Borders of a Field.

Format

The third panel lets you specify the format of the field, and it differs for different data types. Formats for all data types are discussed below, in the section on Formatting Fields.

Size and Location

The next panel specifies the size and location of the field and the slide options, like the equivalent panel for graphic objects and text objects (see Figure 4.28).

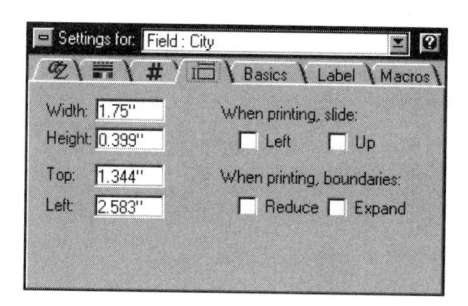

Figure 4.28 Specifying the Size and Location of a Field.

There are checkboxes to control the boundaries of the object when it is printed:

- Select **Reduce** if you want the text frame to shrink when the data in the field is not large enough to fill the frame.

- Select **Expand** if you want the text frame to expand when it is not large enough to hold the data in the field. This can be used if you make a frame too small to hold the data in all the fields, and it is particularly useful for text fields.

WARNING: If you use the Reduce or Expand checkbox, you must adjust the slide properties of other objects in the View accordingly, or it will not print as you expected.

In mailing labels the reduce property is needed so that there is not a gap between the First Name and Last Name if the first name is not long enough to fill the entire field, or a similar gap between the City field and the State and Zip fields. But the slide Left property must also be turned on, otherwise the Last Name and State and Zip fields would not slide over to fill the gap. These properties are turned on automatically for all fields when you create mailing labels.

For other types of view, you must think carefully about how Reducing or Expanding the size of a field affects other objects in the design.

Label

The Label panel, shown Figure 4.29 lets you specify how the field's label is displayed:

- You can control the font, color, and other typographical effects of the label, as you do with any text.
- You can change the label that is displayed by editing in the Label text box. By default, the field's name is used as the label and displayed in this box.
- You can also use the Label position drop-down menu to locate the label above, below, left, or right of the field; or choose **No label** from this drop-down list to eliminate the label.

Practical Approach, 3.0

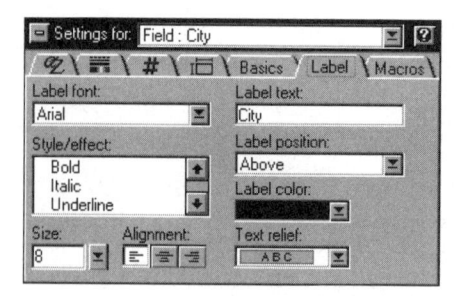

Figure 4.29 The Label Panel.

Macros

The Macros panel of the Field Info Box works a bit differently from the Macros panel of some other objects (see Figure 4.30). You can attach macros to other objects so they are executed when the object is clicked. You have more precise control with Fields. You can attach a macro so it runs:

- When the focus enters the field (before the user edits its value).
- When the focus leaves the field (after the user has had the chance to edit its value).
- When data changes.

This makes it possible to control the data entered in a field very closely and to display a prompt before the user enters data. Macros are covered in Chapter 10.

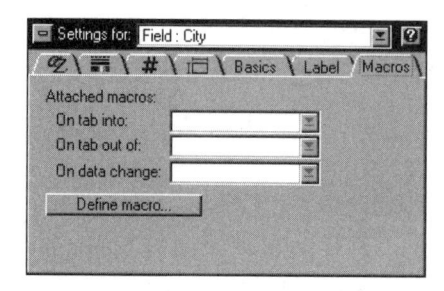

Figure 4.30 The macros panel of the Field Info Box.

Formatting Fields

You have seen that the Info Box for Fields includes a panel to control the field's format.

You will find this panel useful to change Approach's default display of fields. For example, when you added data to the Bill At field in the last chapter, you wanted it displayed with a leading dollar sign and two decimal places because it represented an amount of money. Even when you entered it that way, Approach used the standard numeric format, which displays only significant decimal places.

You can use a field's Info Box to change its format so its data is displayed in the way you want. You can also choose whether or not the field should be displayed in this format when you enter data in it.

Format Types

The options that you have for formatting a field depend on its Data Type, and on the Format type you choose for it. You must use the Format type drop-down menu to choose among the Format types that are available for each Data Type.

Fields that are the Text data type can use any Format, since a Text field can hold any characters. Most other Data Types only give you the option of one format type besides the default format. Memo fields cannot be formatted.

After you choose a Format type from this drop-down list, controls are displayed in the panel that lets you specify all the options for formatting that type of data.

NOTE
When you do any formatting, the Info Box displays a sample of the format you are creating, in its lower left corner. In addition, it has a Show data entry format checkbox, which you can select to display the format in the field itself as you change it in the Info Box. This checkbox is enabled only when the **Show Data** option of the View menu is on.

Removing Formatting

Fields of every data type have a Display as entered option on this drop-down list, which you can choose to display data without formatting. You can use this option to remove formatting that you specified previously.

Despite its name, this option actually displays data in the default formats that you learned about in Chapter 3. For example, it displays **Yes** or **No** in Boolean fields, and it displays numeric data with only significant decimals, regardless of how the data was entered.

The panel has no other controls when this option is selected from the drop-down menu (see Figure 4.31).

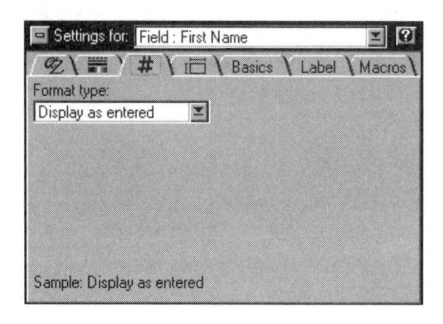

Figure 4.31   Using the Format type drop-down to remove formatting.

Date Formats

If you are formatting a field that is the Date or Text Data Type, you can select the **Date Format** from the Format type drop-down list to display the following options (see Figure 4.32).

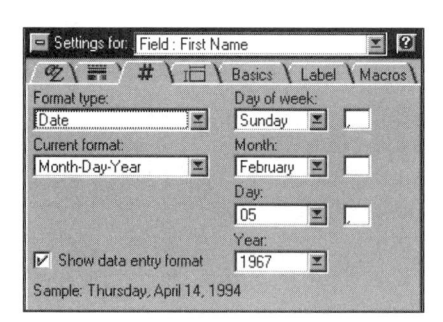

Figure 4.32   Formatting dates.

The Current Format drop-down menu controls what is displayed in the rest the Info Box. Its first three options, **Day-Month-Year**, **Month-Day-Year**, and **Year-Month-Day**, control the order of the drop-down list in the right half of the Info

Box. The **Day-Month-Year** is selected by default, and the list to the right, under the Day of week, are in this order, as is the sample date at the bottom of the panel. In America, it is more common to begin a date with the month: if you select **Month-Day-Year**, the drop-downs under Day of the week and the sample date changes to this order. Likewise, if you choose **Year-Month-Day**, which some computer applications use for sorting chronologically, the order of the drop-downs and the sample date changes accordingly.

The fourth option on the Current format drop-down list, Other, gives you a different set of controls to create different types of date format. For example, you can display the quarter of the year a date is in.

Day, Month, and Year Formatting

In most cases, you may want to display the month, day and year of a date. Use the Current format drop-down list to select **Day-Month-Year**, **Month-Day-Year**, or **Year-Month-Day**, to control the order of the date elements. Then choose the formats for each element from the list to its right, and enter the separators you want to use between date elements in the text boxes next to them. You have the following options:

- *Day of the week*. Select a three-letter abbreviation of the day (such as **Sun**), the full name of the day (such as **Sunday**) or select the blank option if you do not want to display the day.
- *Date*. Select a display with or without leading zeros or no display.
- *Month*. Select a three-letter abbreviation (such as **Feb**), the full name of the month (such as **February**) the number of the month with leading zeroes (such as **02**), the number of the month without leading zeroes (such as **2**) or no display of the month.
- *Year*. Select the full year including the century, the last two numbers of the year without the century, or no display of the year.

Enter any (or no) characters in the text boxes between these data elements to be used as separators.

Other Date Formatting

If you select **Other** in the Current format drop-down list, different controls are displayed (see Figure 4.33). You use them to specify a format that represents different periods of the year: quarters, trimesters, halves of the year, or periods. For example, you can format a date so Approach displays it as Third Quarter 1993 or as 2nd Trimester 1993.

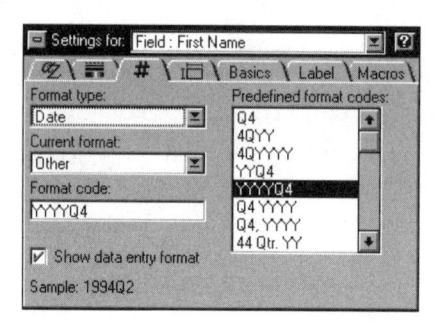

Figure 4.33 Specifying other date formats.

The Format code text box contains a code that specifies how a date is formatted, which consists of three parts: a number, text, and a year format.

The number specifies how many periods the year is broken up into, and how the number of the period is displayed:

- Which number is used determines how many periods there are: use the number 4 to display quarters, 3 to display trimesters, 2 to display halves, or 1 to display the year.
- How many numbers are used determines how the number of the period is displayed. Use one number to display it as a number such as 1, two numbers to display it as an ordinal number such as 1st, and three numbers to display it in a written out form, such as first.

The second part of the code is text, and it is used literally in the display—for example, you could use the Quarter or Trimester display that is part of the result.

The third part of the code is a year format, either YY to display the last two digits, or YYYY to display all four digits of the year.

Thus, the code 4 Qtr YY would display a result such as **1 Qtr 93** or **3 Qtr 92**, and the code 333 Trimester YYYY would display a result such as **First Trimester 1993** or **Second Trimester 1992**.

You can either select the format you want from the list of Predefined format codes a drop-down list or type a custom format in the Format Code text box.

Time Formats

If you are using the Info Box for a Time or a Text field, you can choose **Time** as the Format type to display the following controls (see Figure 4.34).

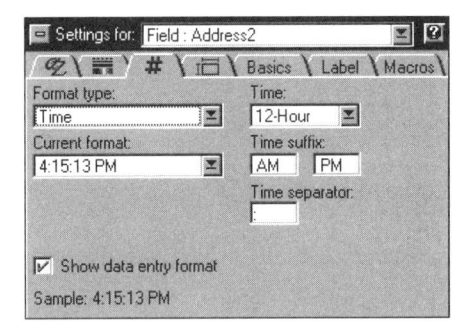

Figure 4.34 Formatting times.

Use the Current format drop-down list to select the elements of the time that are displayed. You can display time accurate to the hundredth second, to the second, to the minute, or just display the hour.

Use the Time menu to specify whether to use 12 hour or 24 hour time.

If 12 hour time is used, you can edit Time suffix to change the usual AM and PM that is displayed by default following times in the morning and afternoon. Enter up to three letters to be used, instead of each. If 24 hour time is used, only one Time suffix text box is displayed. You can enter a suffix in the box that is displayed following all times. You can leave these boxes blank if you do not want any suffix displayed, and this is the default for the 24 hour clock.

The Time separator text box is issued for separators between these elements. By default, a colon is used, but you can enter any character or series of characters to be used as a separator. The separator is only used between hours, minutes, and seconds; hundredths of a second are preceded by a decimal point if they are included.

Numeric Formats

If you are using the Info Box for a Numeric or a Text field, you can choose Numeric as the Format type to display the following controls (see Figure 4.35).

Practical Approach, 3.0

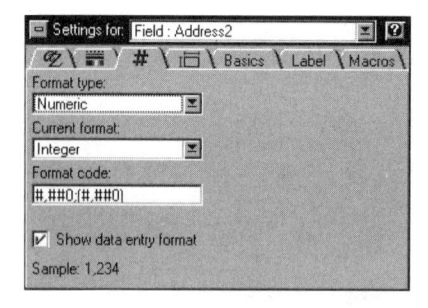

Figure 4.35 Formatting numbers.

Use the Current format drop-down menu to select one of Approach's built-in formats. The options include:

- *Integer.* Uses a comma separator and does not display decimal places.
- *General.* Uses a comma separator and displays two decimal places.
- *Currency.* Is like Integer but with a leading dollar sign.
- *Currency with decimals.* Is like General but with a leading dollar sign.
- *Percent with decimals.* Displays the number as a percentage with decimals.

NOTE

The Current format drop-down menu also includes formats for Telephone numbers, Social Security numbers, and extended Zip codes. To use these, however, the data must have been entered only as numbers, and the hyphens or parentheses must be added by the formatting.

When you select any of these Format types, a code for it is displayed in the Format code text box. In these codes, 0 (zero) specifies a digit that is always displayed. It is displayed as a zero if there is no number in that location. On the other hand, # (the number sign) specifies an optional digit that is displayed only if there is a number in that location. You can edit these codes to fine tune the format types that Approach provides—for example, to display more or fewer digits, to change the separator, and the like.

Text Formats

If you are using the Info Box for a Text field, in addition to all the other Format types, you can choose **Text** as the Format type to display the following controls (see Figure 4.36).

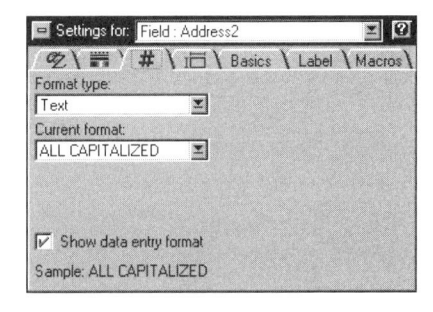

Figure 4.36   Formatting text.

The Current format drop-down menu is simply used to specify whether text is displayed in all capital letters, all lowercase letters, or lowercase letters with a capital letter at the beginning of each word. Its options are self-explanatory: ALL CAPITAL LETTERS, all lower-case letters, and First Letters Capitalized.

Creating Dialog Box Controls for Data Entry

The Basics panel of a Field's Info Box includes a Data entry type drop-down menu, which lets you create drop-down lists, Field boxes with lists, checkboxes, and radio buttons that can be used to enter data in the field (see Figure 4.37).

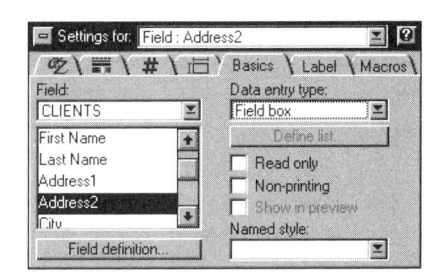

Figure 4.37   The Data entry type drop-down list.

There are also drawing tools that let you add check boxes, radio buttons, and push buttons to designs. Push buttons are attached to macros and used to take actions, and so they are covered in Chapter 10 of this book, which discusses macros. All the other types of dialog box controls can be used to increase the speed and accuracy of data entry, and so they are covered here.

The ease with which you can add these controls to designs is one of the most powerful features of Approach.

Drop-Down Lists

You must use the Data entry type drop-down list of a field's Info Box to create a drop-down list that lets the user select the values to add to the field. There are two types of drop-down lists available:

- Select **Drop-down list** if you want to restrict the user to only the values that can be selected from the drop-down list.
- Select **Field box & list** if you want the user to have the option of either typing in the text, or selecting one of the options of a drop-down list.

Either of these can speed data entry. The first gives you complete control over the values that the user can enter, ensuring that valid data is entered.

When you select one of these options, Approach displays the Drop-Down List dialog box or the Field Box and List dialog box, which is identical to it (see Figure 4.38). Either of these lets you specify the values in the drop-down list: the only difference is whether the final control also includes a Field Box.

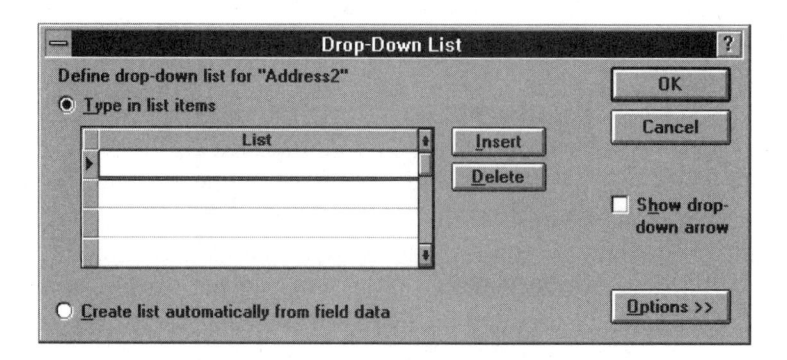

Figure 4.38 The Drop-down List dialog box.

You can specify the values that can be chosen from the drop-down list by creating custom values or by using values that are in a database field. Creating custom values is a very simple process. Using database field values sometimes can be more complex but often can speed your work. Look at how to add values in these two different ways. Once they are added, the values in the list can be manipulated in a similar way.

Custom Values

To create custom values, simply enter them in the list. You can modify this list in the same way that you do a field definition list. Click **Insert** to its right to insert a new, blank row above the current one. Use the field selection box at the left of each row to select (highlight) a row. Once a row is selected, click **Delete** to remove it, or click and drag its selection box to change field order. Apart from that, use the usual Windows editing keys to enter or change data.

When you are done, select **OK** to create a drop-down list that lets the user select from the values that you typed. That is all that you need to do to create most drop-down lists.

Database Field Values

If you have a longer list of values, you can often save time by selecting the **Create list automatically from field data** radio button. Approach automatically adds all of the values currently in this field to the List. Then you can edit the list in the usual ways, to add more values or remove existing ones.

In most cases, this is all you need to do to create a value list instantly. There are a few cases, however, where you must use the expanded form of the dialog box (see Figure 4.39).

If there are no values in the field, Approach automatically displays the expanded form of this dialog box when you select **Create list automatically from field data**. You can also display the dialog box in this form by selecting **Options**. This enlarged form of the dialog box lets you add values from fields other than the current one to the value list simply by selecting that field in the Field list. The values in the field you select replace any values already in the value list. If you are working with a relational database, you can use the database drop-down list to include values from a field in another database that is joined to the current one. Relational databases are covered in Chapter 7.

Practical Approach, 3.0

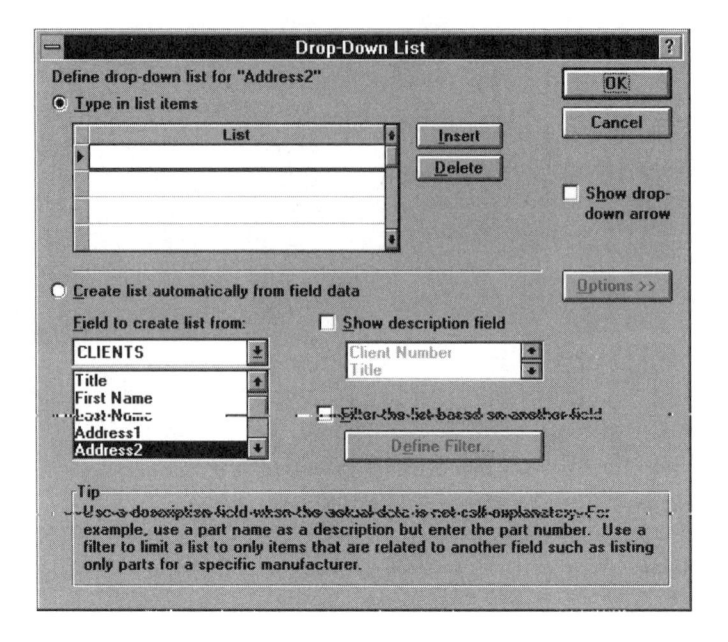

Figure 4.39 The Expanded Value List dialog box.

If you select **Show description field** the Field list under it is activated and can be used to add descriptions from a field to the List list, which are used to represent the actual values stored in this field. For example, you can select the **Client Number** field from the list on the left (as the actual value to be entered), and select the **Last Name** field from the list on the right (as the value to be used as a description). Then the List displays the last names of clients, but when you select one, the client number is entered in the field.

WARNING Descriptions from fields obviously cannot be used to enter new data. It is meant to be used when the data is already in another database file. Note that to use it, you must be sure that there is a unique value in each description field. You could not actually use it to enter Client numbers as described in the example above, because some Clients have the same last names. You could use it to enter display a Part Description field and enter values in a Part Number field, as the tip in the dialog box says, only if each part has a unique description.

You can use the Define Filter button to limit the list. When selected the Define Filter dialog box is displayed, which simply lets you choose a field to filter by. This feature is useful only in relational databases. For example, if you have one database that lists teachers and the courses they teach, you can use a filter to create a drop-down list with only the courses taught by one teacher.

Modifying a Drop-Down List

After you have finished defining a drop-down list, you can no longer display its dialog box by using the Data entry type drop-down list. If you want to modify its definition, select the **Define list** button under this drop-down to display its dialog box, and change it using the methods described above.

Check Boxes

You can create a checkbox in two ways.

Choose the **Checkbox** drawing tool and click and drag to define the location and size of the checkbox and display the define checkbox dialog box (see Figure 4.40). Or choose **Checkboxes from field Data** entry type drop-down list to display the Define Checkbox dialog box (see Figure 4.41).

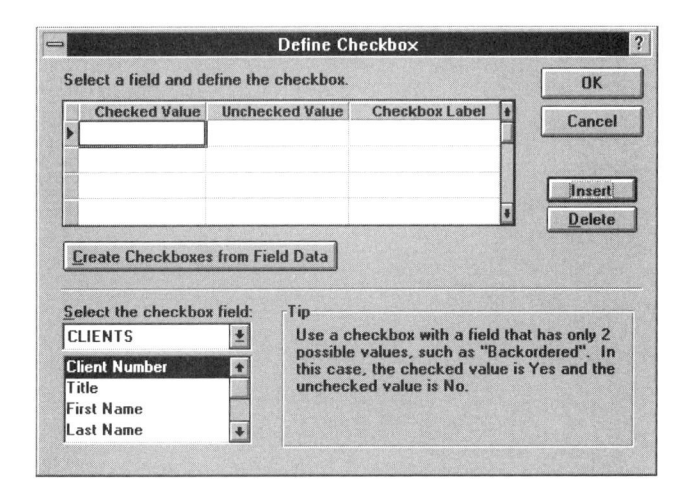

Figure 4.40 The define checkbox dialog box using the drawing tool.

Practical Approach, 3.0

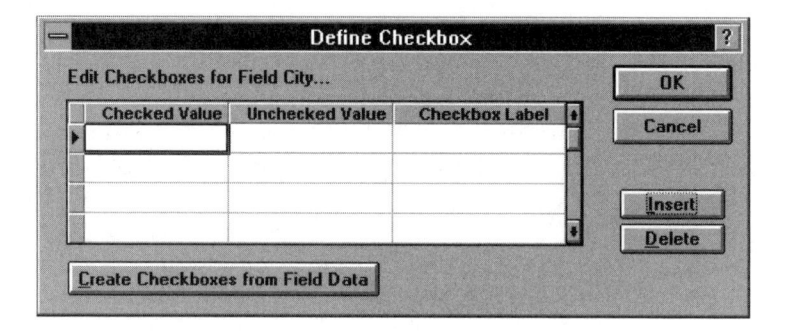

Figure 4.41 The define checkbox dialog box using the Info Box.

As you can see, the only difference between these two is when you use the drawing tool, the dialog box includes a list that lets you select a field that the checkbox uses to enter data in. When you use the Info Box, this list is not included, because the checkbox enters data in the field whose Info Box is displayed.

To define a checkbox, you generally should just enter a Checked Value, Unchecked Value, and Checkbox label in one row of the list in this dialog box. Checkboxes are generally used to enter values in Boolean field—enter **Yes** as the Checked Value, **No** as the Unchecked Value, and some Label that explains to the user what the checkbox does.

It is also possible to create a group of checkboxes associated with a single field by entering multiple rows in this list. You can edit the values in the list as you do in the Drop-down list dialog box. You can automatically fill the list with all the values already in some field by clicking the button. If you do this, you should give each row of the list a Checked Value, no Unchecked Value, and a Label that indicates what the checked value is, so that users can select one of the checkboxes in the group to enter its value in the field.

WARNING Users are not accustomed to using checkboxes in this way. To let the user choose among multiple values in this way, it is best to create a group of radio buttons to avoid confusion.

Radio Buttons

Like checkboxes, radio buttons can be created in two ways:

1. Choose the **Radio Button** drawing tool and click and drag to place the radio buttons and display the Define Radio Buttons dialog box.
2. Choose **Radio buttons** from the Data entry type drop-down list to display the Define Radio Buttons dialog box (see Figure 4.42).

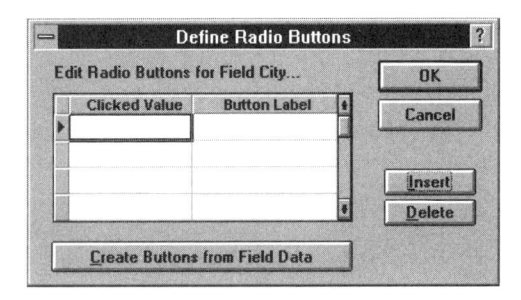

Figure 4.42   The define Radio Buttons dialog box using the Info Box.

The only difference between the two is that, when you use the drawing tool the dialog box includes a list that lets you select a field that the checkbox is used to enter data in. When you use an existing field's Info Box, this list is not needed.

To define a group of Radio Buttons, you should simply enter a list of Clicked Values and a Label associated with each. You can edit the values in the list as you do in the Drop-down dialog box. It is sometimes useful to fill the list with all the values already in some field by clicking the **Create Buttons from Field Data** button.

Approach creates a group of radio buttons, and the user can select one to enter its value in the field. As with all radio buttons, one and only one must be selected. Selecting one automatically deselects others.

NOTE
It is generally useful to use the Label panel of the Info Box to give a label to the entire radio button group, in addition to the labels for individual buttons.

PicturePlus Fields and Their Properties

You can place a PicturePlus field in a design using a two step process, as you do ordinary fields.

1. Create the frame as you do other objects.
2. Select the **PicturePlus** tool. The pointer becomes a cross hair and you can click and drag to place the picture frame. Release the mouse button and the Info Box is displayed for the Picture Plus object with Basics panel showing (see Figure 4.43).

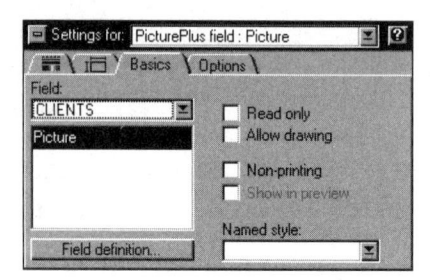

Figure 4.43 The Info Box for Picture Plus field.

Select the PicturePlus field that holds the picture or other object from the list of fields in this panel. If necessary, use the drop-down list to select a different database file.

If there is not already a PicturePlus field in the database, you can use the **Field Definition** push button to display the Field Definition dialog box. You can use this to change the definition of the fields in the database, if you need to add a new PicturePlus field to the database. This is the same dialog box that you use to create a new database or to modify an existing database.

SHORTCUT: As with other fields, you can also add a PicturePlus field to a design in a single step by displaying the Add Field box and clicking and dragging the field from it to the design.

The Basics Panel

In addition to specifying which field it holds, the Basics panel of the Info Box for a PicturePlus field controls the following styles and properties:

- Select the **Read Only** check box to prevent the user from launching the applications that the OLE object was created in and editing it.

- The **Allow Drawing** check box can be selected or deselected to control whether the user can draw a picture in the field with the mouse.
- The **Non-printing** and **Show in preview** checkboxes and the Named style drop-down list work as they do for other types of objects.

The Options Panel

Use the Options panel of this Info Box to specify how Approach handles pictures that do not fit in the frame you created for them (see Figure 4.44). You can specify what is done both for pictures that are too large and for those that are too small.

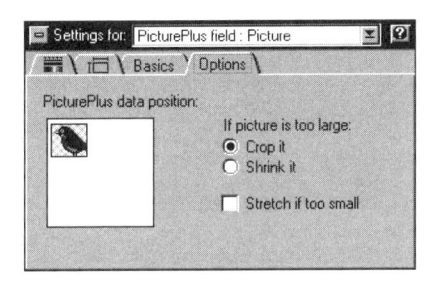

Figure 4.44 The Options Panel.

- *Too Large*. The radio buttons give you two options for handling pictures that are too large to fit in their frame. You can select **Crop it**, so that it remains its original size but not all of it is displayed, or select **Shrink it**, so all of it is displayed but in reduced size.
- *Too Small*. This checkbox gives you options for handling pictures that are too small. Select **Stretch if too small** to proportionally fill the entire frame, or leave it unselected to leave the picture its original size.

Formatting Shortcuts

Now that you have looked at all the styles and properties that you can set for a field, you can see that it could involve a tremendous amount of work to change a large number of properties in all the fields in a design.

There are two faster methods of formatting that you can use to apply all the necessary properties to a field at once.

Practical Approach, 3.0

Fast Formatting

You can use the Fast Format command to copy all the styles and properties of one object and apply them to another object.

Select the object whose styles and properties you want to copy, and then choose **Fast Format** from the Object menu or click the **Apply Format** icon. The pointer is displayed as a paintbrush (see Figure 4.45). You can simply click other objects to apply the same style and properties to them.

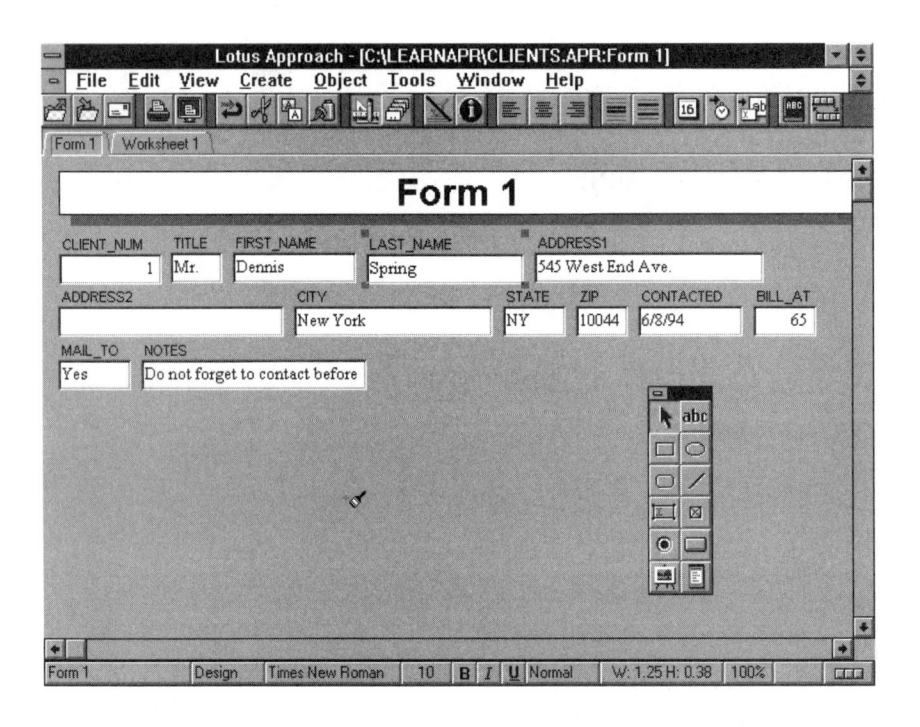

Figure 4.45 The Pointer is displayed as a brush when you apply a Fast Format.

You can continue to use as many objects and fast format as you want to. When you are done, choose **Fast Format** from the Object menu, again, to turn off the Fast Format feature.

Named Styles

You have already seen that the Basic panel of Info Boxes has a Named style drop-down list. Approach includes a utility that lets you specify a group of styles and properties and give them a name. Then, you can apply all of these styles and properties to an object simply by selecting that named style from this drop-down list.

The Named Styles utility is discussed at length in Chapter 11, which covers Approach utilities.

Layout Tools

You have learned all you need to know about designing objects themselves. There are also a number of tools on the View and Object menu which are useful in controlling the layout of designs. They let you place objects more precisely, group them, control their stacking order, and tab order.

Enlarging and Reducing the View

It is often useful to enlarge the design so that you can work on details more precisely, or to reduce the design so that you can see the entire layout. As you know, you can do this by using the two magnifying glass icons on the icon bar of the Design window. There are also menu options that do the same thing:

- Choose **Zoom In** from the View menu to display the design in a larger size. This option is equivalent to selecting the **Zoom In** icon on the icon bar.
- Choose **Zoom Out** from the View menu to display the design in a smaller size. This option is equivalent to selecting the **Zoom Out** icon of the icon bar.
- Choose **Actual Size** from the View menu to display the design in its actual size. This option is only accessible if you previously enlarged or reduced the size of the design.

150 *Practical* Approach, 3.0

NOTE You may have to select the **Show Next SmartIcon** icon to display these icons.

The Status bar indicates whether or not the view has been zoomed. For example, it says 75% after you have zoomed out once, to reduce the view to three-quarters of its actual size. You can click **Status Bar** to display the pop-up menu which lets you choose among the available sizes of the View (see Figure 4.46).

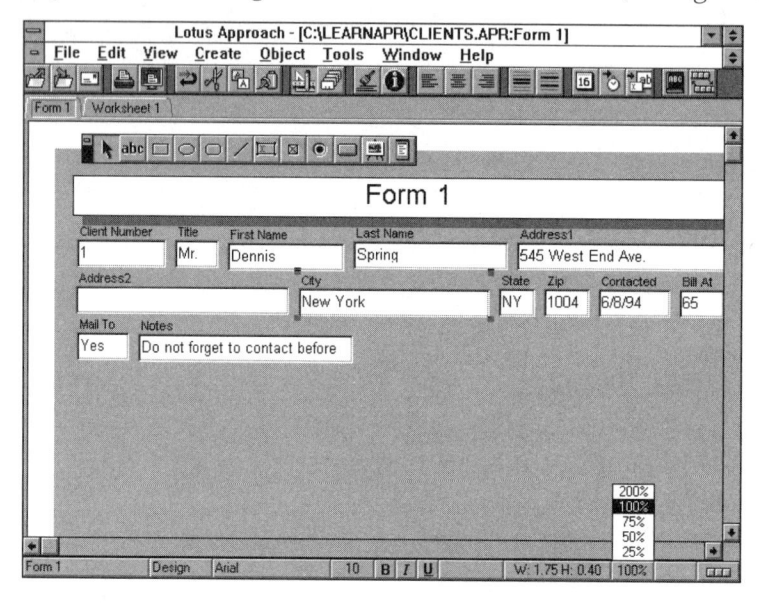

Figure 4.46 Using the Status Bar to zoom in or out.

NOTE You can manipulate the objects of designs in all the usual ways whatever the size of the display. Zooming is meant solely to make it easier for you to Design a view and does not affect the way the view is printed or displayed in Browse mode.

Aligning Objects

Several features of the View menu change the Design window in ways that make it easier to align objects. There is also an option on the Object menu that directly controls the alignment of objects.

The Grid

By default, when you are working on a design, objects are automatically aligned with a grid of horizontal and vertical lines. If you place an object so that its edge is not on one of these lines, it moves so that it is aligned with the nearest grid lines.

Displaying the Grid

You can display this grid (or hide it if it is already displayed) by choosing **Show Grid** from the View menu. Like other options on the View menu, the Show Grid command has a checkmark next to it when it is on.

You can also display or hide the grid by clicking the **Show/Hide Grid lines** icon. If the lines are showing, this icon is displayed with a line across it to show that it now can be used to hide gridlines. You may have to select the **Show Next SmartIcon** icon to display this icon.

Enabling the Grid

You can enable or disable the grid by choosing **Snap to Grid** from the View menu. Like other options on the View menu, the Snap to Grid command has a checkmark next to it when it is on.

If the Snap to Grid option is off, objects can be placed anywhere. They do not move to the nearest grid lines when you place them.

It is easier to create neat designs if the **Grid** option is on. There are often occasions when you want to turn it off to place one or two objects, and to turn it on when you place the rest.

The Ruler

You might find it easier to lay out objects precisely if you choose **Show Ruler** from the View menu to display rulers at the upper and left edges of edge of the Design window. Hairlines on both rulers indicate the current location of the pointer.

This option is also a toggle, and can be selected again to eliminate the rulers.

You can also display or hide the rulers by clicking the **Show/Hide Grid** ruler tool. If the ruler is showing, this tool is displayed with a line across it, to show that it now can be used to hide the rulers. You may have to select the **Show Next SmartIcon** icon to display this icon.

Other Features of the View Menu

The View menu has Show Drawing Tools, Show SmartIcons, Show Status Bar, and Show View Tabs options. They are toggles that you can select to hide or display the toolbox of drawing tools, the icon bar, the Status bar, and the Divider tabs you use to switch among views. Though it is occasionally useful to remove these features temporarily to give you more room to work, they are all vital to creating designs.

If you suddenly find that one of them is missing, it just means that you have chosen the command that controls it by mistake. Simply choose the command again to display the feature.

Grouping Objects

It is often useful to group objects, so that they all are manipulated together.

You learned earlier that you can multi-select objects and move them together. If you expect to work on several objects together, design the form with them grouped more permanently in order to avoid the work of reselecting them and eliminate the chance of error.

> **NOTE** Even if you have something as simple as a report title with a line under it, it is a good idea to group the two objects to avoid future errors, if you are going to be doing much work on the design.

To group objects:

1. Select all the objects you want grouped.
2. Choose **Group** from the Object menu to combine all of the selected objects into a group, which must be selected, moved and manipulated as a single object.

Select the group and choose **Ungroup** from the Object menu to separate objects that you have grouped previously, so each can be selected and manipulated individually.

Instead of choosing these menu options, you can click the **Group** and **Ungroup** icons. You may have to select the **Show Next SmartIcon** icon to display these icons.

Changing Stacking Order

When you place objects in a design, the ones that you placed more recently seem to be in front of the ones that you placed earlier. If you move two objects to the same location, the one that you placed more recently hides the one that you placed earlier anywhere that they overlap. This is called the *stacking order* of objects.

There are times when you want to change stacking order. For example, imagine that you placed text in a design and then decide that you want to have an oval filled with color behind that text to emphasize it. When you place the oval in the same location as the text, you will not be able to see the text at all. You have to change the stacking order so the text appears to be in front of the oval.

If you choose **Arrange** from the Object menu, it displays a submenu with four options that let you change stacking order. You must select the object whose stacking order you want to change. Then choose **Arrange** from the Object menu and one of the following submenu options (or use the icon shortcuts):

- Choose **Bring to Front** to make the selected object appear to be in front of all other objects.
- Select **Send to Back** to make the selected object appear to be behind all other objects.
- Choose **Bring Forward** or click the **Bring Forward** icon to make the selected object appear one layer further forward compared with other objects.
- Select **Send Backward** or click the **Send Backward** icon to make the selected object appear to be one layer further backward compared with other objects.

You may have to select the **Show Next SmartIcon** icon to display these icons.

You can change stacking order by right-clicking an object to select it and display its shortcut menu, which has an Arrange command that has the same submenu options.

In some cases, you may have to move an object that is hiding the object whose order you want to change to select it, and then move it back after you have changed the stacking order. There is usually a way around this, though. For the example mentioned above, where the text is entirely hidden, you could select the oval and send it to the back.

The Alignment Command

There are cases when you can let Approach align objects for you, rather than moving them by hand to lay them out.

Select the objects that you want to be aligned. Choose **Align** from the Object menu to display the Align dialog box that you use to specify the alignment of the objects (see Figure 4.47).

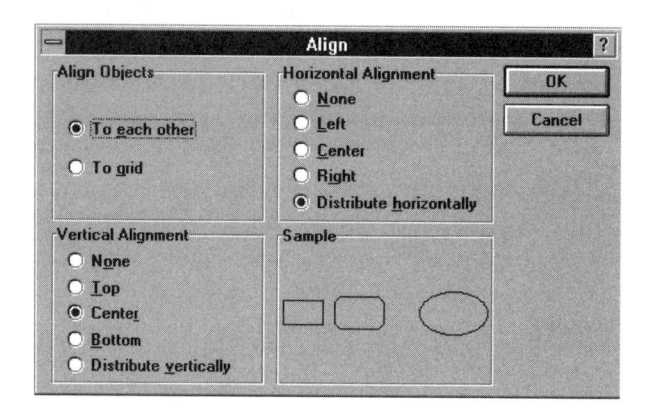

Figure 4.47 The Align dialog box.

Use the radio buttons in the Align Objects area to determine if the objects are aligned with each other or aligned with the lines of the grid. Use the radio buttons in the other areas to determine the vertical and horizontal alignment of the object with the grid, or with each other.

For example, if you select **To each other** in the Align Objects area, and you select **Top** in the Vertical Alignment area, the top edges of the objects are lined up with each other. Likewise, if you select **Left** in the Horizontal Alignment area, the left edges of all the objects are lined up with each other.

On the other hand, if you select **To Grid** along with these other radio buttons, these edges of the objects are lined up with the grid lines.

The Distribute Horizontally and Distribute Vertically radio buttons arrange the objects with equal space between them.

The objects in the Sample area are arranged to illustrate the alignment chosen.

Setting Tab Order

As you have seen, the default data entry form lists the fields from top to bottom in the same order that you specified when you defined the database file. When you press **Tab**, the cursor moves from the top to the bottom of the form.

As you design a form, however, you may move fields around and add new fields. By the time you are done, you might find that the cursor jumps back and forth across the screen when you press **Tab** to do data entry.

You can choose **Show Data Entry Order** from the View menu to specify the order in which you move among fields when you press the Tab key. If you choose this option, a box with a number is displayed on top of each field to show the order in which it is accessed (see Figure 4.48).

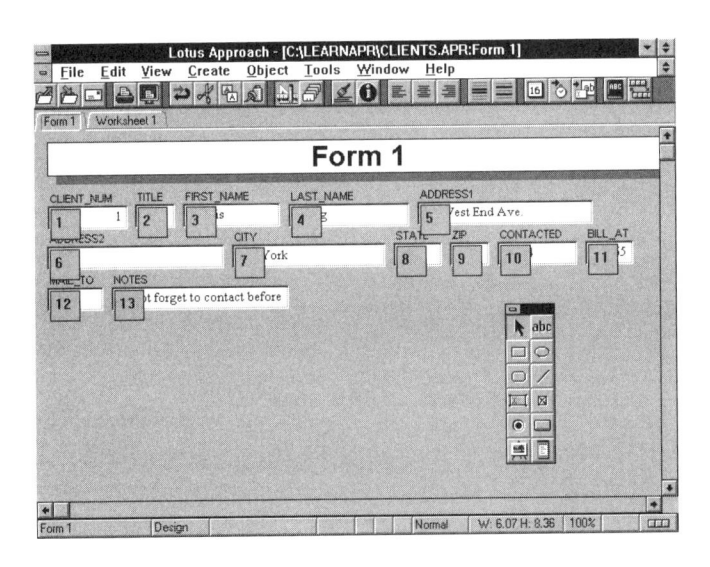

Figure 4.48 Specifying tab order.

You can simply edit the numbers to change the order.

SHORTCUT: As a quicker way of changing the tab order of a large number of fields, you can double-click the border of a square to remove the numbers from all the squares. Then simply click the squares in the order that you want, and they are numbered in that order.

Choose **Show Data Entry Order** from the View menu again to remove the display of tab order numbers.

Chapter 5

Creating Forms and Printed Output

In this chapter you learn about creating new forms, reports, mailing labels and form letters. You begin by using one of the Approach Assistants to place fields on the new design and define some of its other basic features. Then you work with the new objects in the ways you learned about in the last chapter—though each type of view has a few features that are specific to it. You already know how to place, move and resize objects, how to specify the styles and properties of objects, how to work with text, and how to work with field objects in the four major types of views, forms, reports, mailing labels, and form letters.

In this chapter you learn to create these four types of views, and you learn about features specific to each one of them. You also learn to print views. (The three other types of views, Worksheets, Crosstabs, and Charts, are designed and used differently, and so they are covered in Chapter 9.) This chapter discusses:

- How to duplicate, rename, and delete a view
- How to create new forms
- How to create standard and columnar reports
- How to create summary reports
- How to create mailing labels with standard and custom layouts

- How to create form letters
- How to set up the printer and to print output

Working with Several Designs

Up to this point, you have worked primarily with Form 1. In this chapter, you create new reports, labels, and form letters, and work with multiple views.

NOTE One important point to keep in mind is that you can edit the data in any of the views you create in this chapter (except in form letters, where you cannot edit fields because they are added to the view as text objects). If you are displaying your mailing labels and see that a name is spelled wrong, you can correct the spelling right on the label design. You do not have to return to the data entry form, as you do in most database products. This is one very convenient feature of Approach that is missing from most database management systems.

Though the title of this chapter refers to *forms and printed output*, you can actually use all the designs discussed here except form letters for data entry as well as printing them. In fact, later in this chapter, you create a report design that is meant to be used primarily for viewing and entering data.

Switching among Views

When you create new views, a new divider tab is displayed for each. As you know, you can simply click a **Tab** to switch to that view.

When you switch among views, the cursor remains on the same record (as long as you stay in Browse mode and the views are based on the same database file). Sometimes, it is easiest to edit data by using one design to scroll through the database and find the record you want, and then switch to another design to edit that record.

WARNING Remember that choosing **Show View Tabs** from the View menu removes the Divider tabs that you use to switch among views. If you do this by mistake, you can simply choose **Show View Tabs** again to display the Divider tabs.

Creating and Managing Views

In general, you create the views discussed in this chapter by choosing one of the first four options on the Create menu:

1. Form
2. Report
3. Form Letter
4. Mailing Labels

Approach displays an Assistant to help you. The Assistants used for different types of views will be discussed in detail in later sections of this chapter.

Duplicating a Design

If a new design is similar to an existing one, it is often easiest to begin creating it by duplicating the existing design and then making the modifications you want.

When you are in Design mode, you can choose **Duplicate Form** from the Edit menu to create an exact duplicate of the current design. This option is displayed as **Duplicate Form**, **Duplicate Report**, or **Duplicate Labels** depending on the type of design that is currently being displayed, and you can use it to create a duplicate of any design.

This design is automatically given a default name, such as Form 2, or Report 2.

Renaming a Design

You might want to change this default name or the name you gave to a design.

You can do this by displaying the Basics panel of the Info Box for the Form or other design and editing the view name. The Info Box for each type of view is covered in detail later in this chapter.

Deleting a Design

When you are in Design mode, choose **Delete Form** from the Edit menu to delete the view that is currently being displayed. This option is displayed as **Delete Form**, **Delete Report**, or **Delete Labels** depending on the type of view that is currently being used.

> **NOTE** Most users find it difficult to remember that this option is on the Edit menu. Since it is sometimes needed, you should note its location in the menu system.

Forms

You have already worked with Form 1, the standard form that Approach creates automatically. Now you should look at how to create a new form from scratch and get experience with the techniques of changing the design of a view that you looked at in Chapter 4 by creating a custom data entry form.

> **NOTE** The key feature of a form is that it displays one record on the screen at a time or, prints one record on a page. This distinguishes forms from reports, which display or print multiple records. If you remember this defining feature of forms, it is easier for you to understand the types of form that Approach lets you create.

Creating a New Form

To create a new form, choose **Form** from the Create menu to display the Form Assistant (see Figure 5.1). This Assistant contains basic elements that are shared by the Assistants you use to create other types of design.

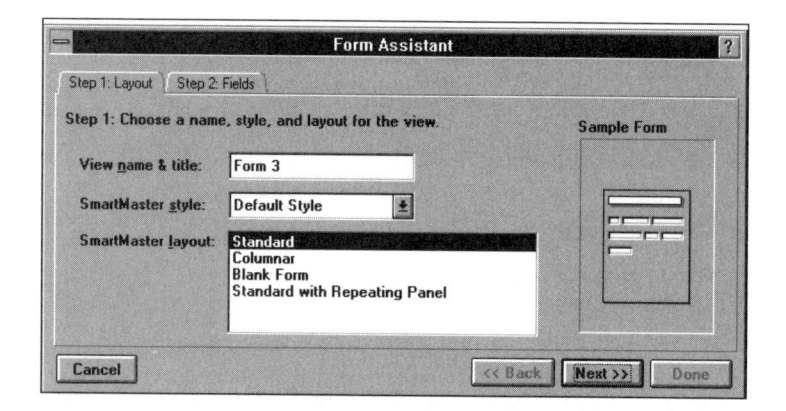

Figure 5.1 The Form Assistant.

Chapter 5: Creating Forms and Printed Output

Notice it has the a *divider tab interface* that you use to display each step in designing the Form. Every Assistant has a similar interface, which breaks up the design problem into a few simple steps. You can display any step by clicking its tab, or you can click the **<<Back** or the **Next>>** button to display the previous or next step. When you have made selections for every step, click the **Done** button to generate the form.

To create a form enter the name of the new form in the Name text box, or use the default name, such as Form 2, that Approach suggests; this name is used as the form's title. The style you choose is shown in the sample box on the right. Use the Smart Master style drop-down to choose a style for the appearance of the report.

Types of Form

Use the SmartMaster layout list to select the type of form you want to create. The Assistant lets you create the following types of forms.

Standard

A *standard form* has the fields laid out next to each other, on several lines if necessary, with the name above each, so they take up as little room as possible (see Figure 5.2). This is the same layout as the standard form that is generated automatically.

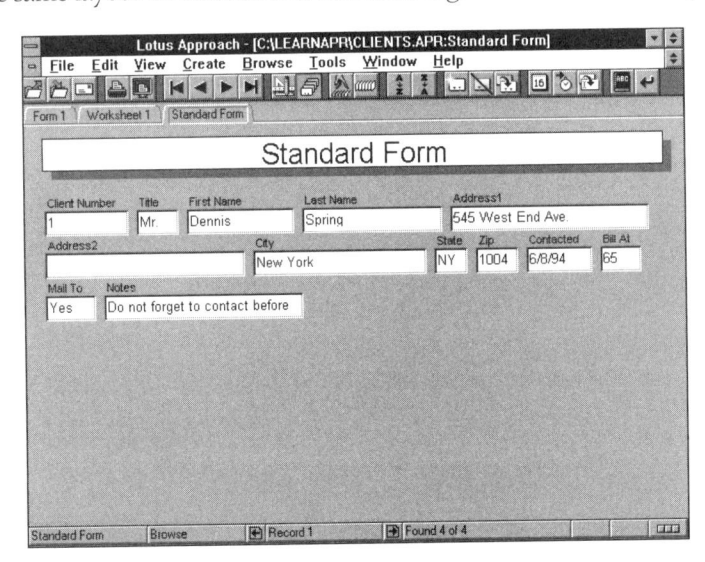

Figure 5.2 A Standard Form.

Columnar

A *columnar form* has the fields laid out one above the other, with the name above each (see Figure 5.3). All the fields and their names are laid out in one or more columns.

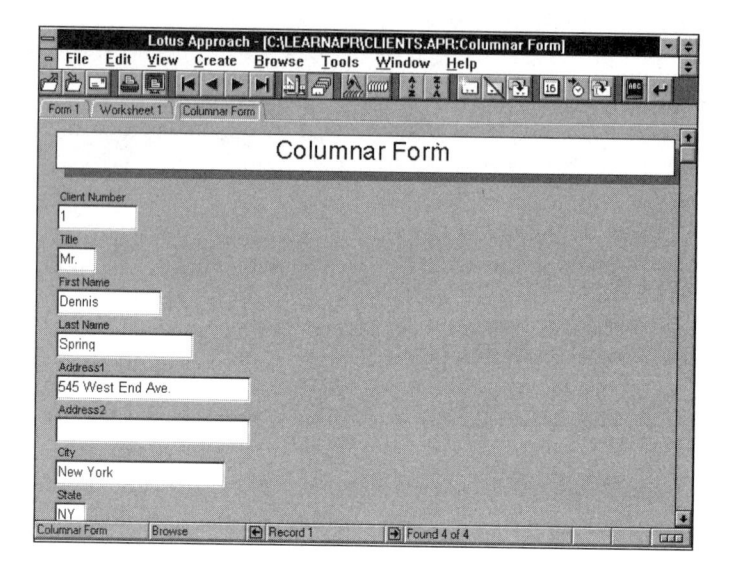

Figure 5.3 A columnar form.

> **NOTE** Remember, a form always displays only one record on the screen. As you see later in this chapter, if you want data as a list with a number of records displayed on the screen, you can use a report. A form cannot display multiple records on a screen in this way.

Other Types of Form

The Assistant also lets you create the following types of forms:

- *Blank Form.* Begins with no fields or title in the form. Add objects to the form using the methods described in Chapter 4.
- *Standard with Repeating Panel.* Includes the fields from the current database at the top of the panel and the fields from a second, related database below it. This option is used for relational databases.

Chapter 5: Creating Forms and Printed Output

Though you may want to begin with a blank form in special cases, it is usually easiest to let the assistant add the fields you want to the form, rather than adding each manually.

Including Fields in Forms

The second step of the Form Assistant lets you choose which fields to include in the form (see Figure 5.4). Select each field to be included in the form from the Database Fields list and select **Add** to add it to the Form Fields list—or simply double-click a field in the Database Fields list to add it to the Form Fields list. Select a field in the Form Fields list and select **Remove** to remove it from the list.

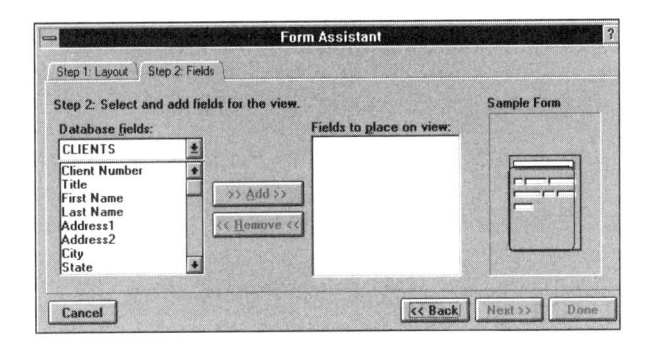

Figure 5.4 Adding fields to the form in the For Assistant.

If you are working with a relational database, use the Database drop-down list to display fields from other database files in the Database Fields list.

Selecting Multiple Fields

You can select multiple fields in either of these lists in several ways:

- Hold down the **Ctrl** key while you click fields to multi-select fields in either of these lists; new fields are selected without the others being deselected.

- Select one field and then hold down the **Shift** key while you click another field, in order to select all the fields in the list from the first to the second.

- Click and drag through the field list. For example, you can select all of the fields by clicking the first, holding down the mouse button, and dragging through the entire list.

In any case, you can select **Add** or **Remove** to add or remove all the selected fields.

Creating the Form

When you select **Done,** Approach displays a form with the name and fields that you specified.

NOTE Fields are included in the form in the same order that you added them to the list in Step 2 of the Assistant.

Modifying Forms

After creating the Form with the Assistant, you can work in Design mode to make further changes in it, using the techniques discussed in Chapter 4. There are a few special features of Forms in Design View, which are covered here.

The Info Box for Forms

If you have displayed the Info Box by choosing **Styles & Properties** from the Form menu or by clicking the **Info Box** icon, and if an entire form (rather than an individual object) is selected, the Form Info Box is displayed (see Figure 5.5).

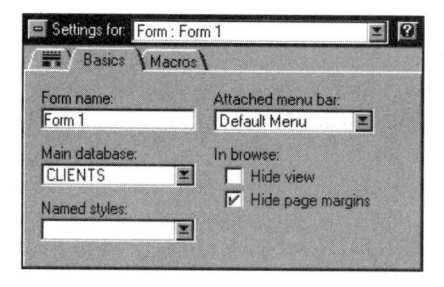

Figure 5.5   The Form Info Box.

The Basics panel of this Info Box lets you control the following features of the form:

Chapter 5: Creating Forms and Printed Output

- *Form name:* Use the Form name text box to change the name of the form. Simply edit the existing name, or replace it with a new name.
- *Main database:* The Main database drop-down lets you specify the main database of a form. This is used only if you are working with a relational database.
- *Named styles:* The Named styles drop-down lets you apply a named style to the form, like the equivalent drop-down for individual objects.
- *Attached menu bar:* Use the Attached menu bar drop-down to display the short menus or a custom menu rather than the default menu whenever the user switches to this view. This feature is useful only if you are setting up an application for a novice, and it is covered in Chapter 11.
- *Hide view:* Select the **Hide view** checkbox if you do not want this view to be displayed in Browse mode. This feature is useful only if you are setting up an application for a novice and you password protect the Approach file so some users cannot switch to design mode. Chapter 11 covers setting up applications with password protection.
- *Hide page margins:* The **Hide page margins** checkbox is selected by default. If you deselect it, the margins are displayed in Browse mode—the fields on the form are shifted right, for example, because the left margin is included in the screen.

The Info box also has a panel that lets you control borders and colors, which works like the equivalent panel of fields (see Figure 5.6). Notice that, like fields, Forms have check boxes that let you display their left, right, top, or bottom border.

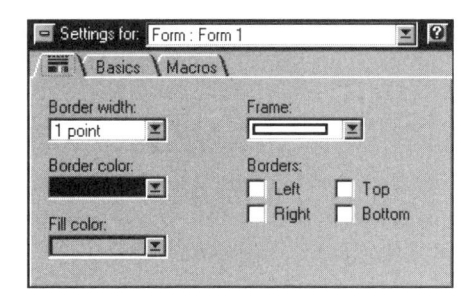

Figure 5.6 The borders and colors panel.

Finally, the Info box has a Macros panel that lets you run a macro automatically when you switch into or out of this view. Macros are covered in Chapter 10.

The Form Menu

When you display a form in design view and the entire form (rather than an individual object) is selected the Form menu is added to the Menu bar where the Browse menu usually is (see Figure 5.7).

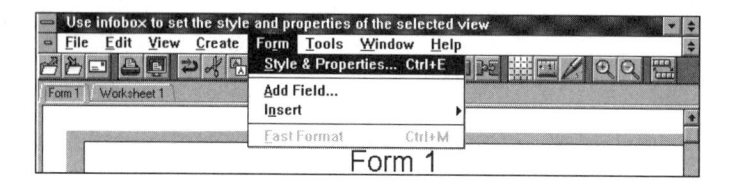

Figure 5.7 The Form Menu.

The Form menu has the following options:

- *Style & Properties.* Displays the Info Box.
- *Add Field.* Displays the Add Field Box.
- *Insert.* Lets you insert the Date, Time, Page Number, or value of a field in a text object.
- *Fast Format.* Lets you apply a Fast Format to an object.

The Form icon bar has features that can be used for other types of view.

Designing a Sample Form

That is all you need to know to create a new form. After using the Assistant to create it, you can use techniques you learned in Chapter 4 to redesign it and make it easier to use.

In this exercise, you create a form to use for data entry. You begin by creating a columnar form and then rearrange the fields so that they are all visible on the screen at the same time but are not as cluttered as they are in the standard form. You also should format the currency field, so it is displayed with a dollar sign and two decimal places.

Chapter 5: Creating Forms and Printed Output

In addition, you can create controls to speed data entry in two fields:

- Since Mail To is a Boolean field, you can use a check box to make it easier to enter data in it.
- You can create a drop-down list to choose values for the Title field, since it has only a limited range of values.

Remember, you already added features to automate and validate data entry in the Clients database. This form makes data entry even easier and more accurate.

1. Choose **Form** from the Create menu to display the Form Assistant. As the View name and title, enter **Clients: Data Entry**, and as the SmartMaster layout, select **Columnar** (see Figure.5.8).

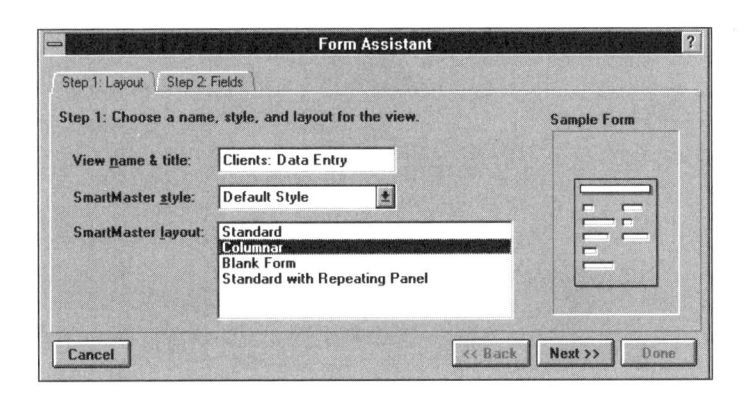

Figure 5.8 The Form Assistant dialog box for a new form.

2. Click the tab for **Step 2: Fields**. Click and drag through the Database fields list to select all the fields, and click **Add** to add them all to the Fields to place on view list. Click **Done** to generate the new Form. When Approach is finished creating the form, click the **Design** icon to switch to Design mode, if necessary, and choose **Show Data** from the View menu to display it without data.
3. The illustration shows the initial layout of the fields (see Figure 5.9). Click and drag the fields to rearrange them (see Figure 5.10).

Practical Approach, 3.0

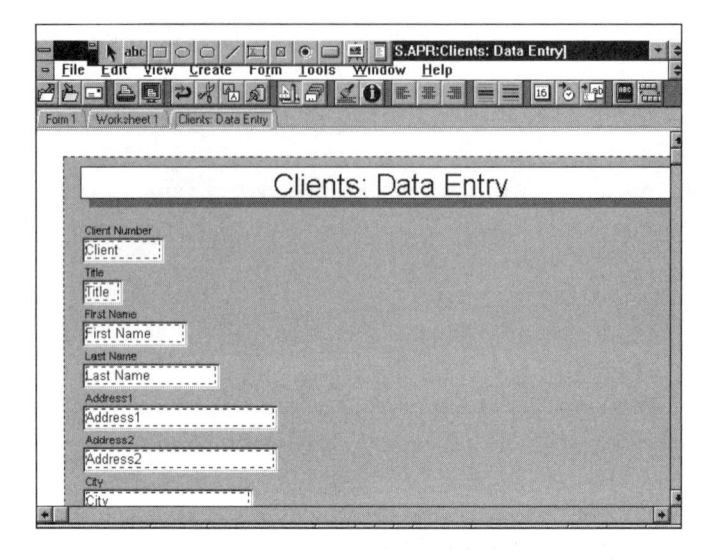

Figure 5.9 The initial layout of the form.

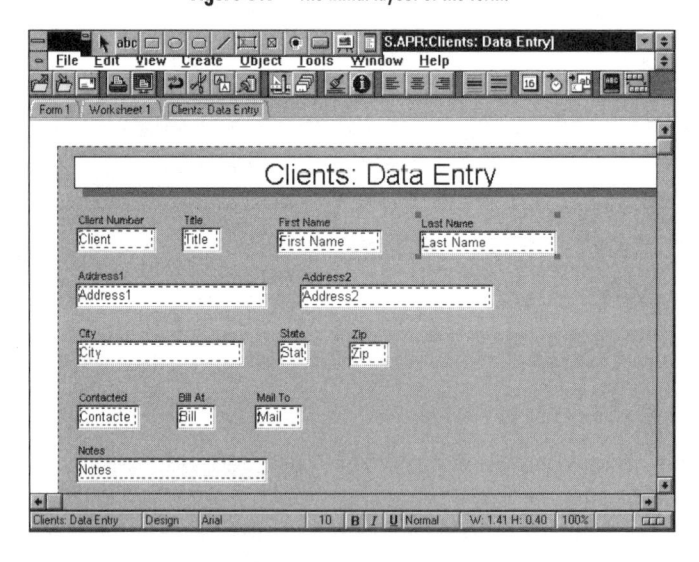

Figure 5.10 The rearranged fields.

4. Now, format the Bill At field as currency. Double-click to display its Info Box. Click the third Tab in the Info Box, which has the symbol # on it, to display the format panel, and select **Numeric** from the Format type drop-down. Then select **Currency decimal** from the Current format

Chapter 5: Creating Forms and Printed Output 169

drop-down. Notice that the Format code is $#,##0.00;($#,##0.00), indicating that two decimal places and at least one integer digit are displayed, and that negative numbers are in parentheses.

5. You can create a drop-down list to make entries in the **Title** field. Click that field to display its Info Box, and click **Basics**. Select **Field box and list** from the Data entry drop-down, so you can type in the title rather than selecting it from a drop-down in case you have some client (for example, a foreigner) with a title that you did not anticipate. The Field Box and List dialog box are displayed. In the List, type **Mr.**, **Ms.**, **Mrs.**, **Miss**, **Dr.**, and **Prof.** (see Figure 5.11). (All of the options in the list are not shown.) Then select **OK** to return to the design. Click and drag one of the handles of the Title field to make it wider—it should extend almost to the First Name field to make the drop-down look best.

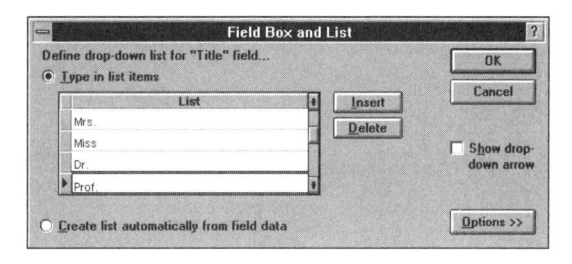

Figure 5.11 Creating a drop-down list in the List and Field Box and dialog box.

6. You can create a check box to enter data in the Mail To field. Click it to display its Info Box. Select **Checkboxes** from the Data entry type drop-down to display the Define Checkbox dialog box. In the Checked Value column, enter **Yes**, in the Unchecked Value column, enter **No**, and in the Checkbox label, enter **Mail To?** (see Figure 5.12). Then select **OK**.

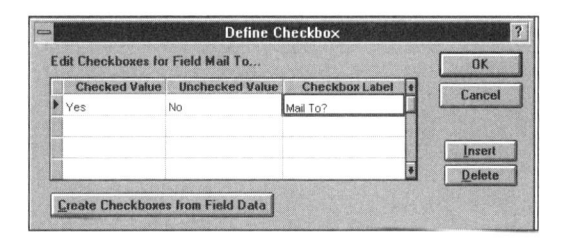

Figure 5.12 The Define Checkbox dialog box.

7. Select the **Notes** field and click and drag one it its handles to make it wider. You have completed the design of the form (see Figure 5.13).

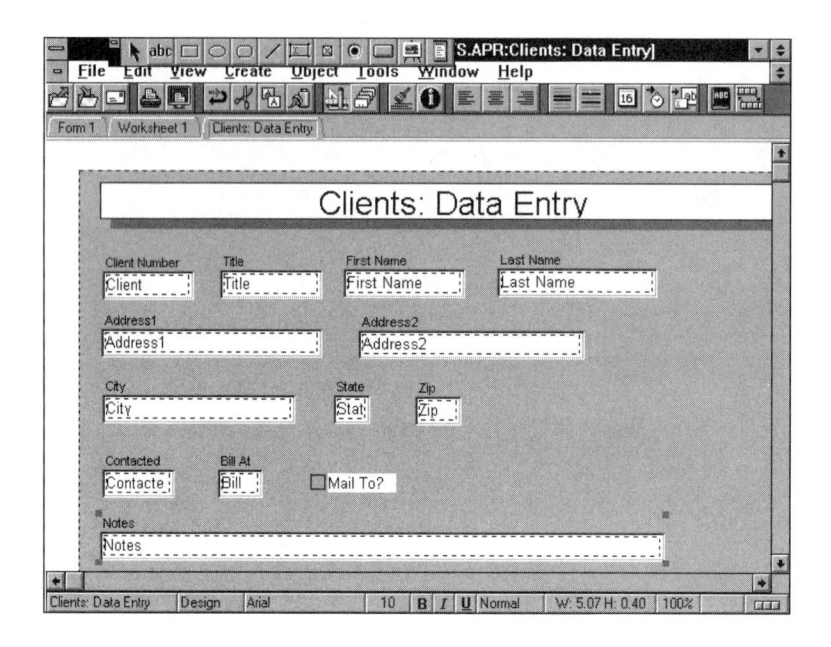

Figure 5.13 The Clients:Date Entry form completed.

8. Now, try entering sample data. Click the **Browse** icon to return to Browse mode. Notice that the check box has an X in it to indicate that you entered **Yes** as its value in this field. Select the **New Record** icon to add a record to the database. Notice that the Client Number and the State are already entered.

9. Press **Tab** and the cursor moves to the Title field and displays its drop-down list. Press **Down Arrow** to select **Prof.** (or use the mouse to drop down the list and select **Prof.**), and then press **Tab** to move to the next field. As the first name, type **Maria** and press **Tab**. As the last name, type **Vida** and press **Tab**. As Address1, type **65 Elm St.**, and press **Tab** twice to skip Address2 and go to the City field. Type **Stamford**, and press **Tab**. The default value in the State field is selected; type **CT** to replace it, and press **Tab**. As the Zip, type **06905**, and press **Tab**. In the Contacted field, type **5/4/94** and press **Tab**. In the Bill At field, type **85** and press **Tab** twice to skip the Notes field and go to the Mail To field. Press the **Spacebar** to place a check in the field.

10. In order to get accustomed to the form you created and have data to use in future exercises, enter a couple of additional records. The instructions have you enter the last record without using the mouse. Try pressing **Ctrl+N** to add new records and using the same method of data entry when you enter the following records, to see if you find it easier to work only with the keyboard:

The first record:

```
CLIENT NUMBER: 6
TITLE: Mr.
FIRST NAME: Samuel
LAST NAME: Maltz
ADDRESS1: 590 Ocean Ave - Apt. 5H
ADDRESS2: (none)
CITY: Brooklyn
STATE: NY
ZIP: 11226
CONTACTED: 6/4/94
BILL AT: 120
NOTES: (none)
MAIL TO: No
```

The second record:

```
CLIENT NUMBER: 7
TITLE: Mrs.
FIRST NAME: Harriet
LAST NAME: Smithson
ADDRESS1: 318 B. 31 St.
ADDRESS2: (none)
CITY: Far Rockaway
STATE: NY
ZIP: 11601
CONTACTED: 5/25/94
BILL AT: 65
NOTES: (none)
MAIL TO: Yes
```

Be sure to save the changes in the Approach file either by choosing **Save Approach File** from the File menu or by selecting **Yes** from the dialog box that is displayed when you close the View or Exit, asking if you want to save the Approach file.

Reports

A Report is a view that displays multiple records on the screen or prints multiple records on the same page, unlike a form, which displays only one record at a time. This is a useful way to print data, but it can also be a useful way to display data.

> **NOTE** Despite the name, you should not think of reports as views that are intended solely to be printed. In fact, later in this section, you create a report meant to be used to edit and display data on screen.

Reports can be complex, because when you are viewing multiple records at the same time, it is often useful to group them and to add summary data on each group, or to add summary data to all the records.

Creating a Report

Choose **Report** from the Create menu to display the Report Assistant (see Figure 5.14), which is used to create a new report. This Assistant works very much like the Form Assistant.

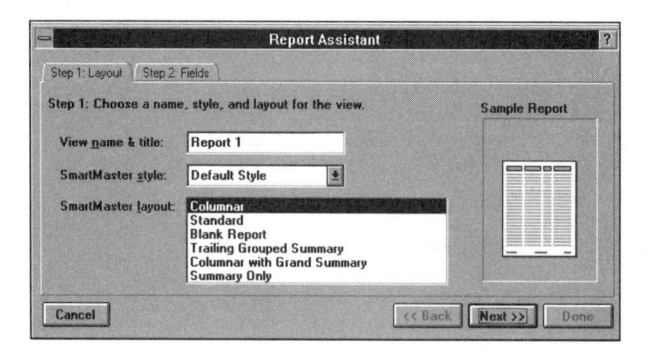

Figure 5.14 The Create Report Assistant dialog box.

Enter the name of the new report in the View name and title text box. You can use the default name, such as Report 2, that Approach suggests, but it is generally better to give reports descriptive names, to make it easier for you to select them when you are switching among views. The name is also used as the default title of the report that Approach generates, but this text object can be edited.

Choose a style from the SmartMaster style drop-down, as you do when you are creating a form.

Types of Reports

Use the SmartMaster layout list to choose what type of report you want to create. Approach lets you create Columnar, Standard, and several types of summary reports.

Columnar Reports

A columnar report displays each field in a column, so all the fields of a record are next to each other. The name of each field is displayed as a header at the top of each column, with all the records below it, and the date and time is displayed as a footer at the bottom of the screen (see Figure 5.15). If you print the report, the header and footer are printed at the top and bottom of every page, and when you view the report on the screen, they are displayed in the same location as you scroll through the records.

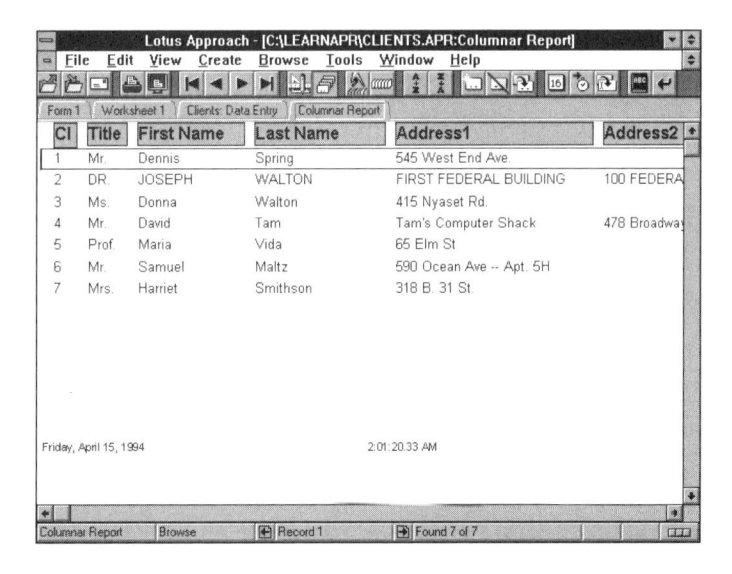

Figure 5.15 The columnar report layout.

Standard Reports

Like the standard form, a standard report displays fields next to each other, running onto additional lines if necessary (see Figure 5.16). There is one major difference between a standard report and a standard form. Forms have one record per page, and reports do not. Unlike the standard form, the standard report displays multiple records on the screen and prints multiple records on a page.

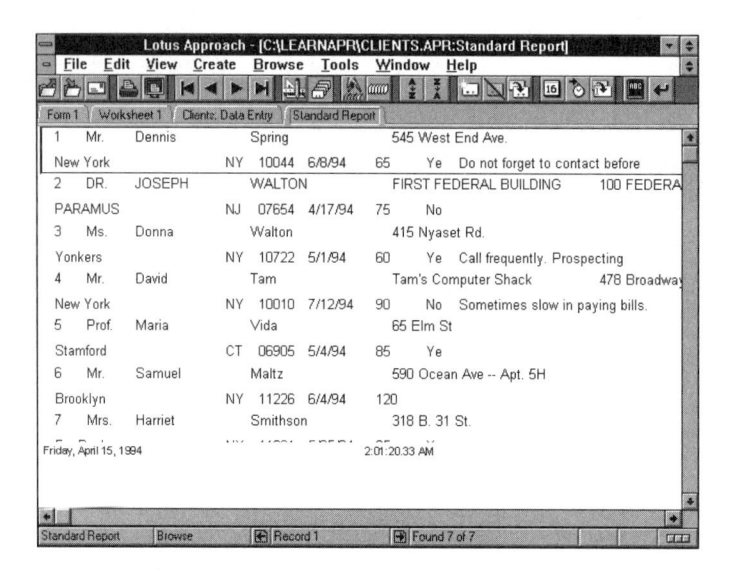

Figure 5.16 Standard report layout.

As you can see in the Figure 5.16, this makes the standard report seem cluttered, but you learn to remedy this problem below in the section on *Panels of a Report*.

Summary Reports

The assistant lets you create several types of summary report: Trailing Grouped, Columnar with Grand Summary, Summary only, and Summary.

The Assistant lets you create the most commonly used types of summary report, but you can also add summary panels to existing reports and create different types of summaries. You can create leading summaries that are displayed at the beginning of each group, as well as trailing summaries displayed at the end of the group. These are covered in detail later in this chapter, in the section on *Adding Summaries to Reports*.

The three types of summary reports that the Assistant creates all are defined in similar ways.

Trailing Grouped Summary

This is a *columnar report* that groups the records on the basis of the value of some field and includes a summary at the end of each group. For example, you might want to group the records by state and include a summary with the number of clients in each state.

If you choose **Trailing Grouped Summary** as the layout, Approach adds two extra panels to the Report Assistant, in addition to the panels you use to define the layout and to select fields that are included in the report. The new panels let you define the summary that follows each group and the grand summary at the end of the report.

Step 3:Trailing Summary lets you define the trailing summary that follows each group (see Figure 5.17).

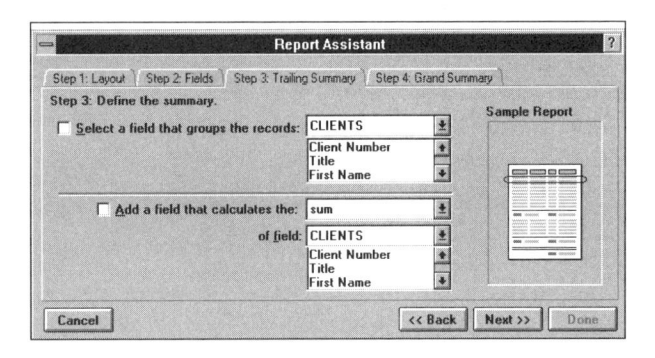

Figure 5.17 Defining the Trailing Summary.

- Use **Select a field that groups the record:** to select a field that the group is based on.
- Use the **Add a field that calculates the:** to select the type of summary you want. The options include value, average, number of items, sum, smallest item, largest item, standard deviation, variance, and net present value.

You must select these checkboxes to include them. For example, if you want to group the report but not to include a summary field, you can choose **Select a**

field that groups the records: but not select the other checkbox in the dialog box.

To calculate the average rate you charge clients from each state, for example, select the **State** field as the field to group on, select **Average** from the drop-down, and select **Bill At** in the lower field list.

Step 4:Grand Summary lets you add a grand summary that appears at the end of the report (see Figure 5.18). It is similar to the bottom half of **Step 3:Trailing Summary** (see Figure 5.17). You simply select the type of calculation to be performed and the field it is to be performed on.

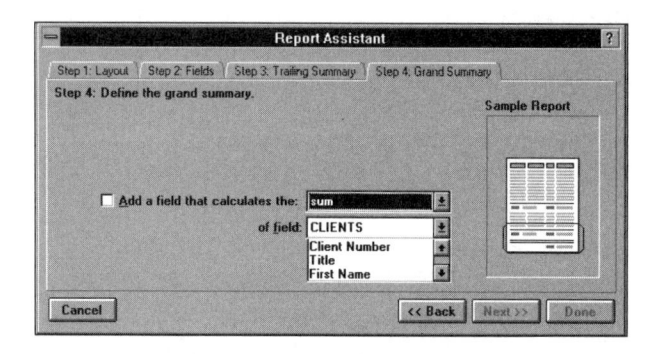

Figure 5.18 Defining the grand summary.

Columnar with Grand Summary

This is a *columnar report* with just one summary, at the end of the report, summarizing the values in all the records.

If you use the first panel of the Report Assistant to choose **Columnar with Grand** Summary as the SmartMaster layout, Approach adds one extra panel to the Assistant the Grand Summary panel. This panel is identical to the one shown in Figure 5.18 above and is used in the same way to define the final summary.

Summary Only

This is a report that only includes summaries, not data on individual records. For example, you might want a report on the number of clients from each state, without data on individual clients. If you use the first panel of the Report Assistant to choose **Summary Only** as the SmartMaster layout, Approach adds one extra panel to the Assistant. This panel is identical to the one shown in Figure 5.18 and is used in the same way to define the field that the report is grouped on and the type of summary included for each group. The report that is generated includes only the group summaries, not individual records from that group.

Blank Report

The *Report Assistant*, like the Form Assistant, gives you the option of creating a blank report and adding all fields and other objects manually. It is usually easier to use the Assistant to create the basic design of the report before modifying it.

Including Fields In Reports

Use **Step 2:Fields** of the Report Assistant to specify which fields should be included in the report, just as you do with Forms. For more information, see the section on *Including Fields in Forms*.

Modifying Reports

You can modify reports in the same ways that you do forms, as covered in Chapter 4. However, they do have a few added features.

Panels of a Report

Because they are made up of multiple records, reports are divided into multiple Panels. You can choose **Show Panel Labels** from the View menu or click the **Show Panel Labels** icon the to display a label for each panel in the report. Choose **Show Panel Labels** or click the icon again to hide the labels. (When the labels are displayed, the icon has a line across it, to show that it now is used to hide the labels.)

You can select these panels and resize them or change their styles and properties, as you do other objects. The Info box for a panel lets you control its colors and borders or to apply a named style to it, like the Info Boxes of many other objects.

> Because panels have other objects in them, it is sometimes hard to select the panel rather than an object inside of it. If you display the panel labels, you can click its label to select the panel.

The Body Panel of a Standard Report

You learned earlier that there is one difference between a standard form and standard report: the standard report displays multiple records on the screen and prints multiple records on a page. For this reason, the report seems cluttered unless you leave space between records.

The fields of a standard report are in a panel named *Body* (see Figure 5.19). By default, there is no space under the fields in this panel, and the report seems cramped when you display its data, as you saw earlier in Figure 5.16.

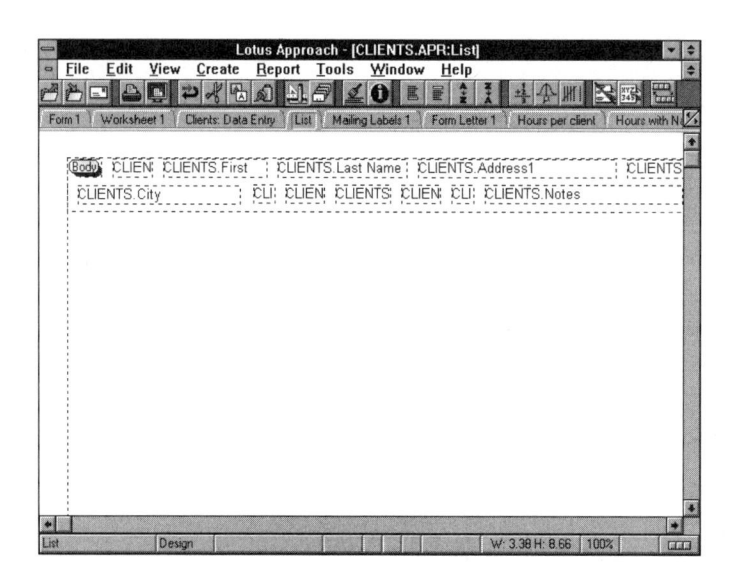

Figure 5.19 The Body Panel of a standard report created by an Assistant.

To leave space between records, select the body panel and click and drag its lower edge downward to make it larger (see Figure 5.20). This leaves extra space under the records, so the report no longer seems cramped (see Figure 5.21).

You can also work with the footer panel, which holds the date and time, if you scroll downward in Design View.

Panels of a Columnar Report

You learned earlier that a columnar report has titles at the top of the page and the field's contents listed below them. The titles are printed at the top of each

Chapter 5: Creating Forms and Printed Output

page when you print the report, and remain in place at the top of the screen when you scroll through records.

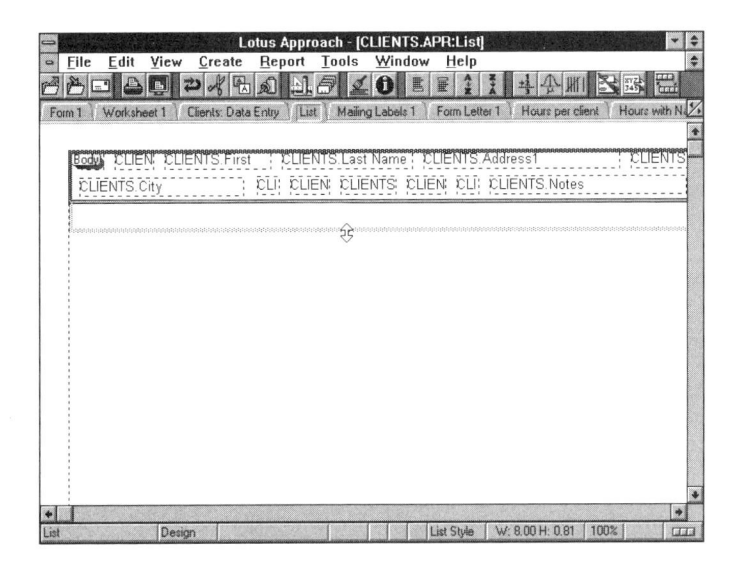

Figure 5.20 Resizing the Body Panel.

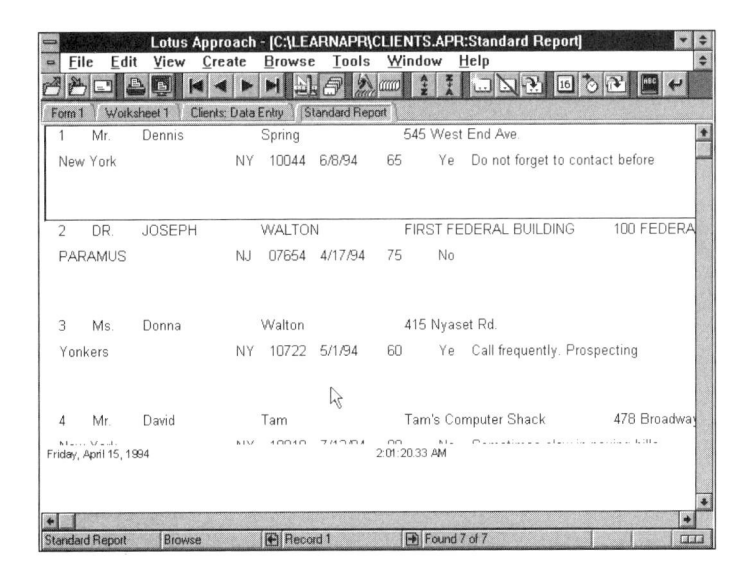

Figure 5.21 The records are no longer cramped.

As illustrated, the titles are in a header panel, and the fields are in a Body panel (see Figure 5.22). You can apply this sort of header to any report. You can resize or change the style and properties of the Header panel of a columnar report as you do any panel.

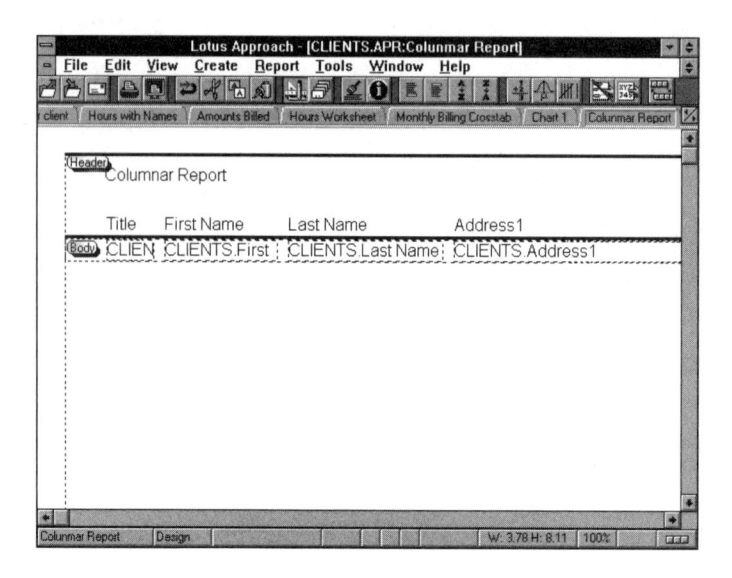

Figure 5.22 Panel labels of a columnar report.

In addition, the columnar report (like the standard report) has a footer panel at the bottom of the page with the date and time, which you can work with if you scroll down to the bottom of the report in Design View.

Adding Summaries to Reports

If you create a summary reports using the Report Assistant, Approach adds the appropriate panels to the report.

You can add summary panels to a report You can add the types of panels that the Assistant automatically adds. But you can also add additional types of panels that let you produce summaries that are more powerful and varied than those the Assistant creates automatically.

Chapter 5: Creating Forms and Printed Output

As you will see in the section on *Info Boxes for Summary Panels*, you can use an **Info Box** to give any existing panel these same varied properties.

You may add the summary in two steps:

1. Add a summary panel to the report.
2. Define the calculation included in it.

Creating a Summary Panel

To add a summary panel to a report, display the report in Design mode. Then choose **Summary** from the Create menu to display the Summary dialog box (see Figure 5.23).

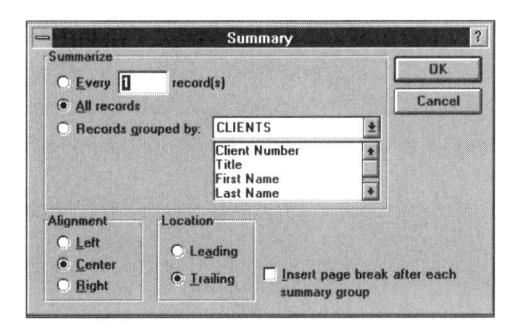

Figure 5.23 The Summary dialog box.

The radio buttons in the Summarize area of this dialog box let you select what groups of records the summaries are based on:

- *Every __ record(s):* Gives a summary for groups based on a number that you enter in the text box. For example, if you enter **10** in the text box, the report includes summary information on every ten records in the database.
- *All records:* Gives summary information on all the records in the database. This is equivalent to a Grand Summary created by the Report Assistant.

- *Records grouped by:* Summary information based on any field you specify. Select the field in the list of fields and, if necessary, the database from the drop-down list. The records are sorted on this field, and summary information is given for every value in the field. This is equivalent to a Group Summary created by the Report Assistant.

The two sets of radio buttons in this dialog box give you more control over how the summary information is displayed.

The *Alignment* radio button can be used to Left align, center, or right align the summary. The Location radio button lets you choose:

- *Leading.* Displays the summary before each group of records
- *Trailing.* Displays the summary after each group of records.

NOTE Trailing summaries are generally used when the summary panel includes some sort of calculation, such as the sum or average of some value in the group. Leading summaries are generally used to include the value in some field as part of the heading for the group. For example, if you group records by state, you can include a leading summary panel that says something like "Clients from NY."

You can select **Insert page break after each Summary Group** if you want each group to begin on a new page, a feature that can be useful for long reports.

Select **OK** to place a repeating panel in the report.

SHORTCUT You can also add a summary panel by clicking the **Leading** or **Trailing Summary Panel** icon (see Figure 5.24). Then you can use its Info Box to specify the same properties that are specified in the Summary dialog box, such as whether it totals all records or records grouped on a field.

Adding a Summary Calculation

In addition to creating the panel, you must add a summary calculation to it.

In Chapter 8, you learn to use an Approach Formula to create a calculated field based on a summary function, which lets you create very powerful summary calculations. After using the Field Definition dialog box to create the field, place it in the panel in the same way that you place any field on a report.

Chapter 5: Creating Forms and Printed Output

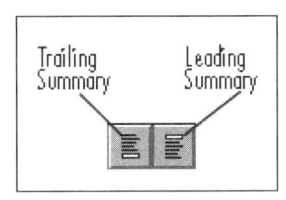

Figure 5.24 Icons for adding a summary calculation.

> **NOTE** There are two icon bars for reports in Design mode, as there are for forms in Design mode. You may have to click the **Next SmartIcon Bar** tool to display these icons.

Changing a Summary Panel

When a report includes a summary panel, either one created by the Assistant or one you added yourself, you can select it, resize it, move it, or delete just as you do other types of panels in reports.

You can also change the style and properties of a Summary panel by using its Info Box. The first panel lets you specify the style of its borders and fill color, like the equivalent panels in many Info Boxes. The Basics and Display panels control the same properties as the Summary dialog box (see Figure 5.25 and Figure 5.26). They are displayed when you add a summary panel by choosing **Summary** from the Create menu.

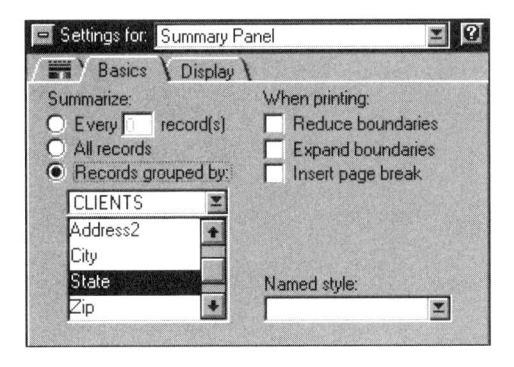

Figure 5.25 The Basics panel.

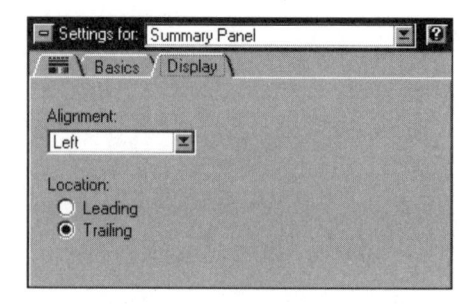

Figure 5.26 The Display Panel.

The Basics panel includes checkboxes that let you Reduce Boundaries and Expand Boundaries when printing and to apply named styles; these properties also apply to fields and were discussed in Chapter 4.

When a **Panel** is selected the Browse menu is replaced with a Panel menu, which has similar options to the Report menu.

Working with Columns of a Report

When you create a columnar report, columns are initially placed in the report in the order that you added the fields in the Assistant.

> **NOTE** To change the size or order of the columns, you must work with the data showing, rather than the field names. Then, choose **Turn On Columns** from the Report menu.

Once you have turned columns on, you can select, resize, and move columns just as you do other objects:

- Click the column to select it. It is highlighted to show that it is selected.
- Click and drag the right edge of a selected column to make it narrower or wider.
- Click and drag a selected column to move it.

When you resize or move a column, its header is also resized or moved.

The Info Box for Reports

When you display Styles and Properties and the entire report (rather than an individual object) is selected, Approach displays the Report Info Box (see Figure 5.27).

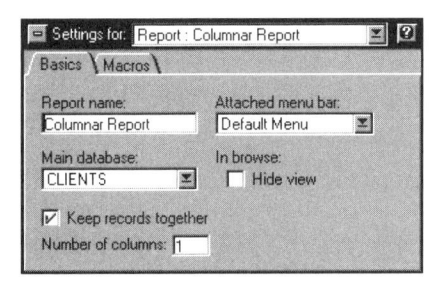

Figure 5.27 The Report Info Box.

The Report Info box has the following options in the Basics panel:

- *Report name:* Use the Report name text box to modify the name of the report. Simply edit the existing name, or replace it with a new name.
- *Main database:* This drop-down lets you specify the main database of a report. It is used only if you are working with a relational database, and is covered in Chapter 7.
- *Attached menu bar:* Use the Attached menu bar drop-down to display the short or custom menu rather than the default menu whenever the user switches to this view. This feature is useful only if you are setting up an application for a novice, and it is covered in Chapter 11.
- *Hide view:* Select **Hide view** if you do not want this view to be displayed in Browse mode. This feature is useful only if you are setting up an application for a novice and you password protect the Approach file so some users cannot switch to design mode. Chapter 11 covers setting up applications with password protection.
- *Keep records together:* If the **Keep records** together checkbox is selected (as it is by default) records are not separated by page breaks. A record that cannot fit in the current page begins on a new page.
- *Number of columns:* The Number of columns text box lets you specify the number of columns in the report. Rather than creating a columnar report

with a separate column for each field, for example, you can create a report with the data in just a few columns. Specify the number of columns you want to use, begin with the standard report layout, and then move some fields to the other columns, or copy the data to repeat it across the page.

The Report Menu

When you are working with a report in design mode, the Browse menu is replaced by a report menu (see Figure 5.28). Many of its options are also on the object menu when you select an Object in a report, in addition to the commands included on the Object menu of objects in a form.

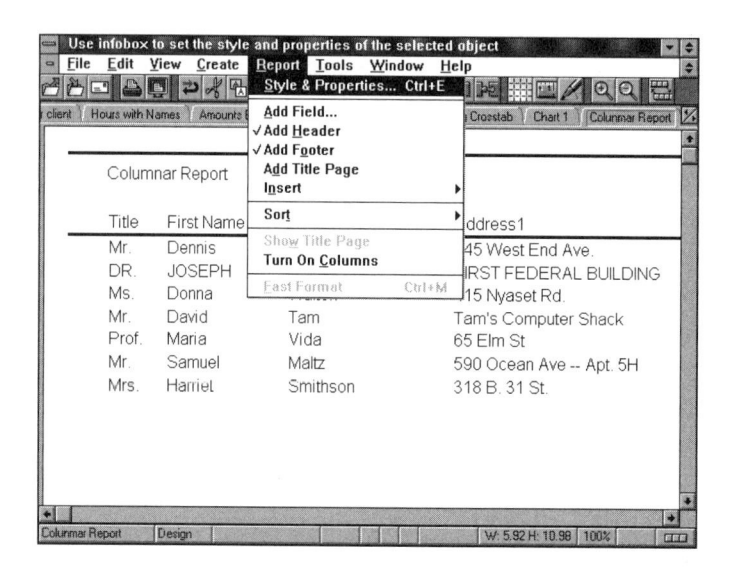

Figure 5.28 The Report menu.

As you can see, the Report menu has some options that are the same as the Form menu:

- *Style & Properties.* Displays the Info Box.
- *Add Field.* Displays the Field Box.
- *Insert.* Lets you add the Date, Time, Page number, or value of a field to a text object.
- *Fast Format.* Lets you apply a fast format to an object.

The report menu also has some unique features, which you have not looked at yet.

Headers, Footers and Title Pages

Because reports are meant to be printed, it is often useful for them to have a separate title page, a header, or footer on each page. You can add or remove these by using the Report Menu.

As you have seen, the Assistant generates reports with a footer panel, and it also includes a header panel in a columnar report.

You can add or remove the header, footer, or a separate title page by choosing **Add Header**, **Add Footer**, or **Add Title Page** from the Report menu. All these options are toggles, so you can select them again to remove them.

To display the title page after adding it, choose **Show Title Page** from the Report menu.

> **WARNING**
> If you remove a header, footer, or title page, any objects that were already added to it are removed and cannot be restored by selecting the menu option again. For example, if you generate a columnar report and remove the header, you lose the names of the fields at the top of the columns. If you choose **Add Header** from the Report menu to restore the header, Approach adds a blank header, without the field names in it.

Sort

Because a report displays multiple records, you sometimes want to control the order in which they are displayed.

Use the **Sort** option on the Report menu like the Sort option on the Browse menu. Choose **Sort** from the Report menu and:

- Choose **Ascending** from the submenu to sort in Ascending order on the current field.
- Select **Descending** from the submenu to sort in Descending order on the current field.
- Choose **Define** from the submenu to display the Sort dialog box and use it to define the sort. The Sort dialog box is covered in Chapter 6.

SHORTCUT — You can also Sort in Ascending or Descending order simply by selecting the field that you want the sort to be based on and then clicking the **Sort Ascending** or **Sort Descending** icon.

Turn On Columns

You can choose **Turn On Columns** from the Report menu to select, move, and resize columns of a report. The **Show Data** option must be on for you to work with columns.

Designing a Sample Report

Since you add and manipulate objects in a report just as you do in a form, that is all you need to know to design reports that do not include summaries.

You should bear in mind that some features of form design that you learned about in Chapter 4—particularly the ability to add a page number and the current date—are most useful in printed reports.

In this section, you create a sample report that is used to browse and edit data rather than being printed out. As an exercise, create a standard report, so you can use it to view multiple records and edit them just as you do a form.

1. Open **Clients.Apr**, if it is not already open. Choose **Report** from the Create menu to display the Report Assistant. Enter **List** in the View name and title text box. Keep the default style. As the layout, select **Standard**.

2. Click the **Step 2: Fields** divider tab. Click and drag to select all the fields in the Database Fields list. Select **Add** to add them all to the Fields to place on view list. Choose **Done** to create this new report.

3. If necessary, click the **Design** Icon and choose **Show Data** from the View menu to display the design without data. This report is almost in the form that you need. Just enlarge the panel a bit, so the records do not seem cramped, and to remove the date and time, which is automatically added in the footer of the report, since you are using this report for on-screen data entry rather than printing it. Select the panel and then click and drag its lower border downward (see Figure 5.29). Then choose **Add** Footer from the Report menu to turn off this option and remove the footer.

Chapter 5: Creating Forms and Printed Output

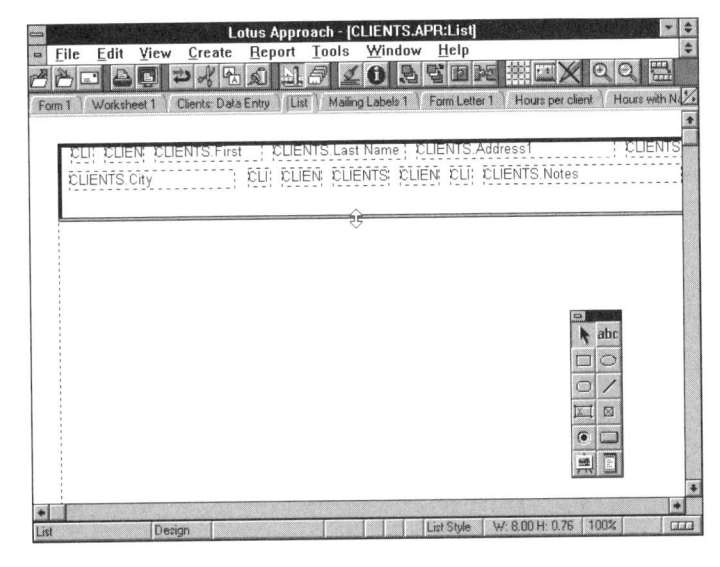

Figure 5.29 Enlarging the Panel of the Report.

4. Now, click the **Browse** icon to see the report in Browse mode (see Figure 5.30). Try clicking a name to place an insertion point in it and tabbing among fields. You can see how easy it is to scroll through and edit the database in this view.

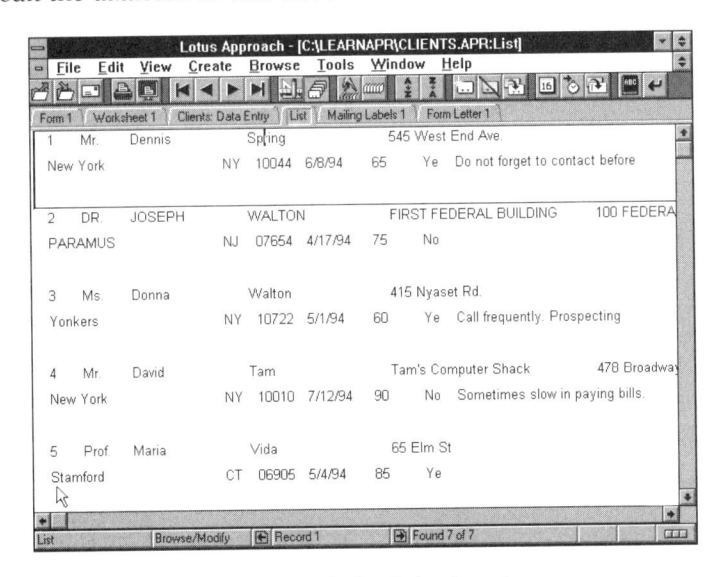

Figure 5.30 The data displayed using List.

Mailing Labels

Mailing labels are created like other designs, except that you must specify the type of label form that you are using and place the fields in precise locations in the form that Approach creates.

It is very easy to format labels automatically for most standard label forms. You simply choose the Avery number of the label you want and the number of lines in the label.

One convenience in labels is that fields automatically slide left and up to close up empty spaces between them. Remember you can select fields in a design and then choose **Slide Left** from the Style menu if you do not want extra spaces between fields; likewise, you can choose **Slide Up** from the Style menu if you do not want a blank line when there is no data in a field.

Mailing labels automatically have these two settings turned on, because you almost always want them in labels. If you select a field and look at the Style menu, you see a check next to these options to indicate that they are toggled on. You can toggle them off by selecting them, but you must do so for each field individually.

Creating Mailing Labels

To create mailing labels choose **Mailing Label** from the Create menu to display the Mailing Label Assistant.

Standard Label Layouts

The Basics panel of the Assistant is displayed, which is used for creating standard label layouts (see Figure 5.31). If you are using Avery forms or compatible label forms by other manufacturers, this panel is all you need to create most labels.

The feature that makes it so easy to create labels with Approach is the Label type drop-down at the bottom of this panel. You can use this to select any standard Avery label form and automatically lay out your labels to fit on that form. This list includes Avery labels for diskettes, audio tapes, video tapes, shipping labels, several types of name tags, and several kinds of index cards as well as mailing labels.

Chapter 5: Creating Forms and Printed Output

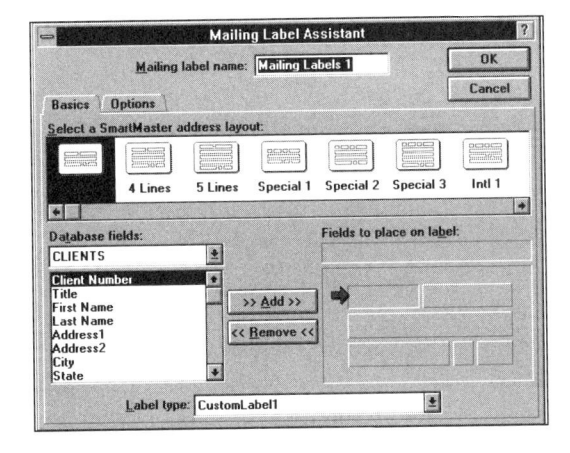

Figure 5.31 The Basics Panel of the Mailing Label Assistant.

All of these are listed by Avery number. If you use Avery labels, the most popular type of mailing label, you should simply look at the number on the package your labels come in, and select the same number from this drop-down list.

The size of each type of mailing label is listed to the right of the Avery number. If you use some other brand of mailing label, find the one that is the same size as your labels, and the layout is probably the same. You can select the **Options** button to view all the features of this Avery layout and compare them with your label.

In addition, enter the name of the new mailing labels in the Mailing label name text box (or use the default name, such as Mailing Labels 2, that Approach suggests). Unlike Forms and Reports, Mailing labels do not have titles, but it is still useful to enter a descriptive name here, to make the View's divider tab easier to recognize.

Select a SmartMaster layout, and that layout is displayed in the Fields to place on label box, at the lower right. These SmartMaster layouts indicate the basic layout of the label. For example, the first is a typical three line label, with spaces for first and last name on the first line, the address on the second line, and spaces for city, state, and zip on the third line. The second is a similar four-line label, with two lines for address, and the third is a similar five-line label. The others are special-purpose labels.

As you can see, there is a Database fields list and an Add button to the left of the Fields to place on label box, which you use to place fields in each of the spaces in it. You can click one of these spaces to display an arrow to its left, select a field to be included in the labels from the Database Fields list, and select **Add** to add it where the arrow points. (Alternatively, simply double-click a field in the Database Fields list to add it.)

SHORTCUT When you add a field to the label, the arrow moves to the next space, so you can add another field. The fastest way of adding fields to the label is simply to double-click them one after another, to add the ones you need.

To remove a name that has already been added, select it and select **Remove,** or simply double-click it. If you are working with a relational database, use the Database drop-down list to display fields from other database files in the Database Fields list. You can add fields from all joined database files to the mailing labels.

Use the Label type drop-down list to select any standard Avery label layout, and your labels are automatically sized to fit on that form.

Label Options

If your labels are not a standard layout, you can create custom labels by using the panel of the Mailing Label Assistant that is displayed after you select the **Options** divider tab (see Figure 5.32). This part of the dialog box also lets you control the arrangement of the labels.

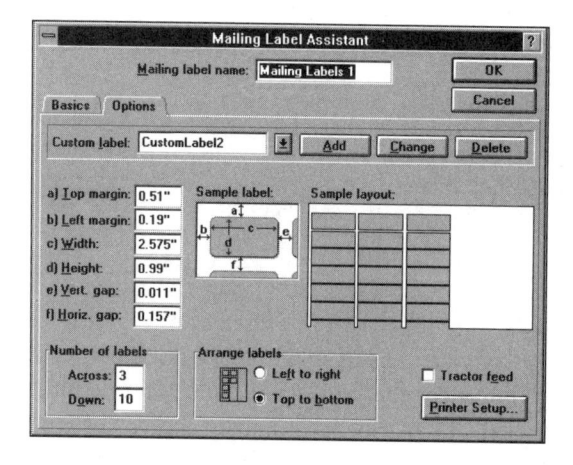

Figure 5.32 Creating a custom label layout in the Mailing Label Assistant.

Custom Label Layouts

The text boxes with the letters from a to f are automatically filled out with the specifications of the Avery label selected in the Label Code drop-down.

> **NOTE** If you are creating custom labels, you should begin by selecting the Avery labels that are the closest to what you need. Then use these text boxes to indicate the page margins, the width and height of each label, the size of the gaps between labels, and the number of labels across and down.

Notice that the Sample label box shows what each of these settings refers to. The Sample layout area to the right displays an example of the options you specify.

If you are creating custom labels, you may also have to use the Number of Labels text boxes to change the number of labels across and down. In addition, you should select the **Tractor feed** checkbox if you are working continuous form labels, rather than labels on separate, single-page forms.

Other Label Options

You can also use the **Options** panel to set other options, either for standard Avery labels or for custom labels.

Use the radio buttons in the Arrange Labels area to specify the order in which records are printed out on the labels (or displayed in the label forms on the screen). Select **Left to Right** to have them printed across each row, beginning with the top row of each page. **Top to bottom**, selected by default, prints them down each column, beginning with the left column of each page.

Select **Printer Setup** to use the Print Setup dialog box, described at the end of this chapter in the section *Printing Output*.

Modifying Mailing Labels

When you select **OK** from the Create Mailing Labels dialog box, a label is displayed with the layout and fields that you specified. You can work on the mailing labels in Design Mode in the same ways that you use with other Views. For example, you can add rectangles, text, or even pictures to the mailing label design. You can move, resize and change the style and properties of fields, display the rulers or other design tools, and so on.

WARNING: You can also click the margin of the label in Design mode to select it, as you do with other panels in designs. It is displayed as a double line, which you can click and drag to resize the label. But it is very difficult to make labels that are the proper size in this way, and you should avoid using this feature.

The Mailing Label Info Box

If you display the Info Box and select **mailing label**, rather than one of the objects in it, Approach displays the Mailing labels Info Box (see Figure 5.33).

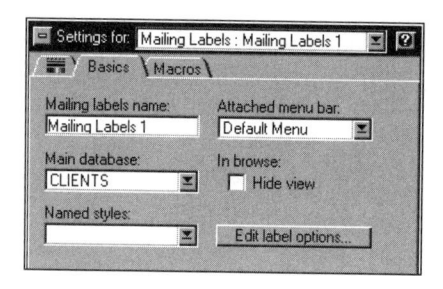

Figure 5.33 The Basics Panel of the Mailing Labels Info Box.

The Basics panel Mailing Label drop-down features are:

- *Mailing Label name.* Changes the name of the View.
- *Main.* Selects its main database. This only applies if you are working with relational databases.
- *Named styles.* Applies a named style to the labels.
- *Attached menu bar.* Displays either the Default menu, the Short menus, or a custom menu when this view is displayed. The Short menu or a custom menu is useful if you are setting up an application for a beginner, and do not want them to be able to use all of Approach's features. They are discussed in Chapter 11.
- *Hide view.* Use this checkbox if you do not want this view to be displayed in Browse mode. This option is only useful if you are setting up an application for novices.
- *Edit label.* Displays the Mailing Label Options dialog box (see Figure 5.34). This dialog box is identical to the Options panel of the Assistant.

Chapter 5: Creating Forms and Printed Output

It can be used to change options of existing labels, just as the Assistant is used to create options for new labels.

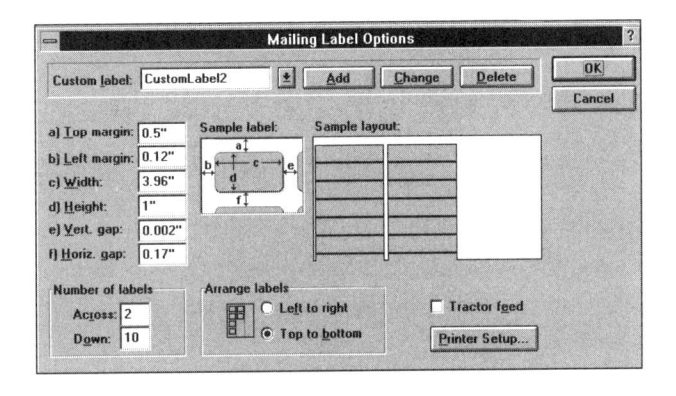

Figure 5.34 The Mailing Label Options dialog box.

> **NOTE** This dialog box is useful if you have laid out mailing labels, printed a test copy of them, and found that there are minor differences from your mailing labels. You can change the layout without starting again from scratch.

The Mailing Labels dialog box has a panel that lets you control the labels borders, which works like the equivalent panel in other Info Boxes. It has a panel that lets you attach macros to the view, that are executed when you switch into or out of it. Macros are discussed in Chapter 10.

The Mailing Label Menu

When you are working on Mailing Labels in Design View the Browse menu is replaced with the Mailing Label menu (see Figure 5.35), which includes the following options:

- *Style & Properties.* Displays the Info Box.
- *Add Field.* Displays the Add Field Box.
- *Insert.* Inserts the Date, Time, Page Number, or value of a field in a text object.

Practical Approach, 3.0

- *Sort.* Applies a quick sort or custom sort to the records in the view.
- *Fast* Format. Applies a Fast Format to an object.

You are already familiar with these options from the Form or Report menu.

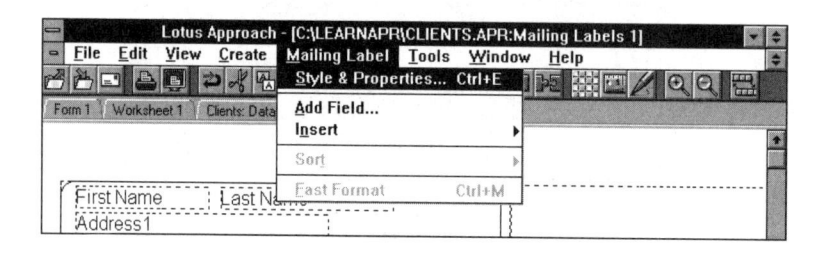

Figure 5.35 The Mailing Label menu.

Designing Sample Labels

Now, it should be easy for you to create labels for your sample database:

1. Choose **Mailing Label** from the Create menu to display the Mailing Label Assistant. Since you have two address lines, you need a four-line label. Click the **4 Lines** SmartMaster Address Layout.

2. A four-line form is displayed for you to add fields to, and the arrow is pointing at the space where the first name should be. Double-click the **First Name** field in the Database fields list to add it to the label and move the arrow to the next space. Likewise, double-click the Last **Name**, **Address1**, **Address2**, **City**, **State**, and **Zip** fields in sequence to add them all to the label.

3. Leave the default name, Mailing Labels 1. Select **Avery 5161, 1" X 4"** from the Label type drop-down list. If you have another type of Avery label and want to try printing these sample labels, select the number on your package. The final design is shown in Figure 5.36. Select **OK** to display the in label form and, if necessary, click the **Browse** icon to view them in Browse mode, as shown in Figure 5.37.

4. Click a field, and you see that you can edit it, just as you do a form; you can add data to a blank Address2 field.

Chapter 5: Creating Forms and Printed Output

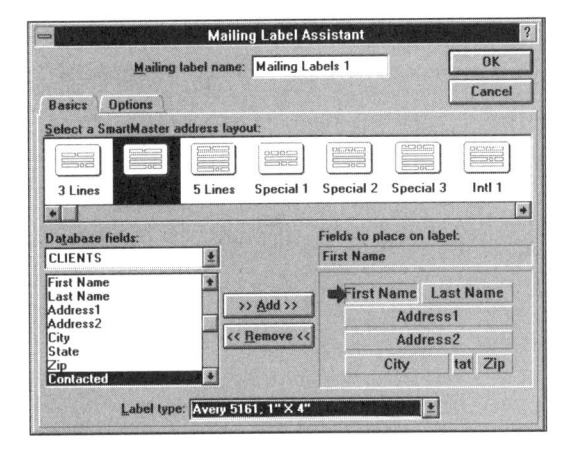

Figure 5.36 Creating new mailing labels.

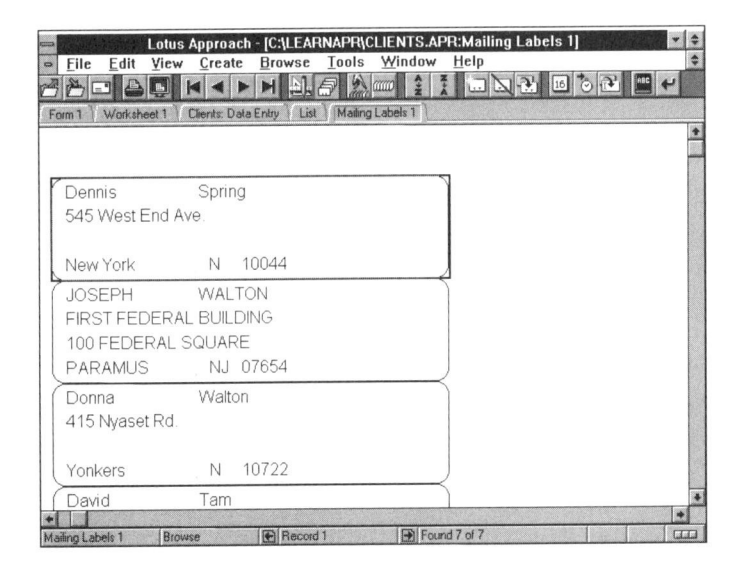

Figure 5.37 The labels in Browse mode.

5. Click **Print Preview** to view the labels in Print Preview mode (see Figure 5.38). Notice that, because the Slide Left and Slide Up features are automatically turned on when you create mailing labels, the extra spaces and blank lines are eliminated when you print the labels.

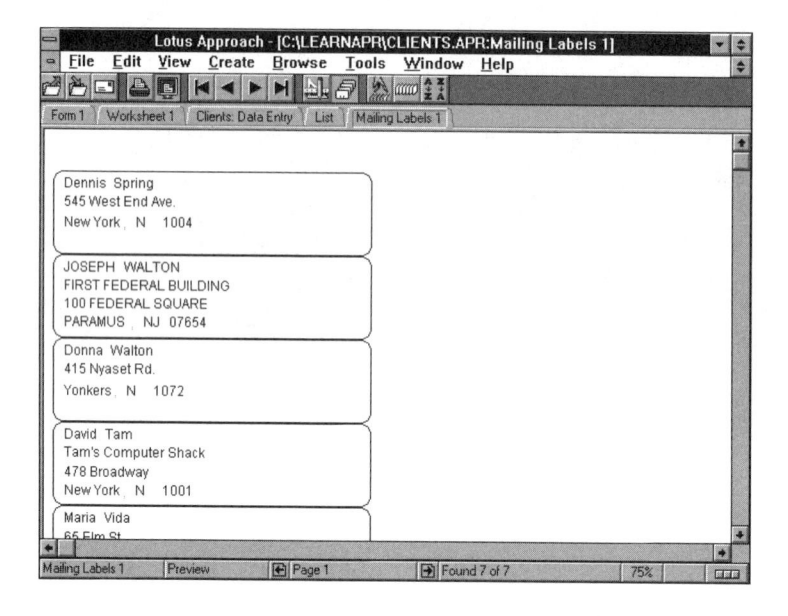

Figure 5.3 The labels in Print Preview mode.

Form Letters

Form letters are like other Views except that the fields you select in the Assistant when you first create them are added to the design as text rather than as separate objects. If you view it in design mode with Show Data off, they are surrounded with double brackets, like the page number and date that you insert in a text box, rather than as separate objects. The body of the Form letter is a single text object, with these fields included in it.

In fact, a form letter is simply a large text object, like the text objects you can add to a Form, which takes up a full page. You can work with it as you do with any text object, to create the continuous of a letter up to one page long.

Creating Form Letters

To create a new Form Letter, choose **Form Letters** from the Create menu to display the Form Letter Assistant (see Figure 5.39).

Chapter 5: Creating Forms and Printed Output

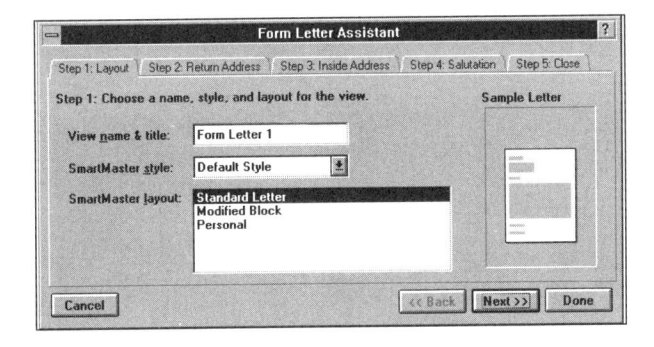

Figure 5.39 The Form Letter Assistant.

Though it has more steps than the other Assistants you have looked at, it is very easy to use.

- **Step 1:Layout the View name & title** lets you enters the name of the new form letter (or use the default name, such as Form Letter 2) and select a SmartMaster style and SmartMaster layout, as you do with other Assistants. You can see the style and layout you choose in the Sample Letter box to the right.
- **Step 2:Return Address** includes a text box where you can fill in a return address. Or select **None** to omit the return address.
- **Step 3:Inside Address** lets you add the name and address of the person you are writing to (see Figure 5.40). As you can see, this works like the Mailing Label Assistant, except that you select the Address layout from a drop-down list.

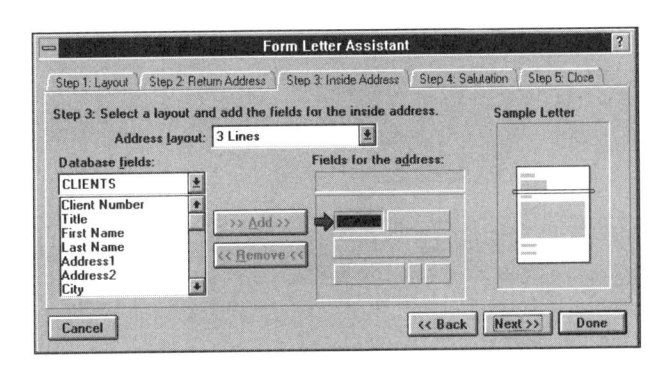

Figure 5.40 Adding Inside Address to a form letter.

- **Step 4:Salutation** lets you add a Salutation (see Figure 5.41). Edit the text box if you want to use a different salutation than Dear or a different punctuation other than a colon, and select up to two fields from the field lists to include as part of the salutation.
- **Step 5:Close** includes a text box where you can add a closing.

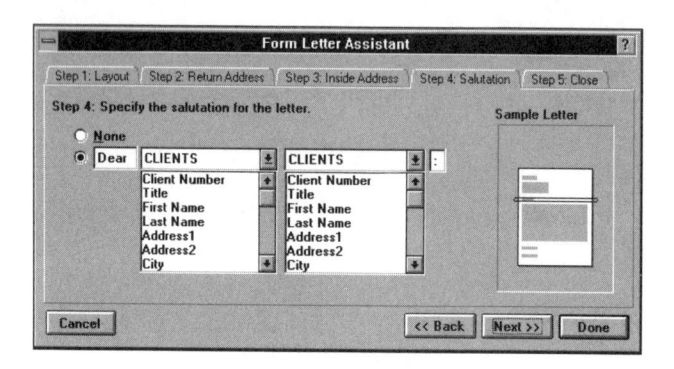

Figure 5.41 Adding a Salutation.

Since the closing and return address are simply text, you might find it easier to type them into the form letter after creating it than to enter them in the Assistant.

Modifying Form Letters

Because the body of the Form letter is a single text object, with the fields and other text that you added included in it, you do not modify it as you do other designs.

You do not move fields by clicking and dragging them with the pointer, for example, as you do objects in other designs. Instead, you move them as you would any text. For example:

- Place the cursor to their left and type new text to push them right, or delete text to their left to pull them left.
- Press **Enter** to move them to the next line as you would move any text in a document that you are editing.
- Use **Cut** and **Paste** to change their order.

You can treat the fields as if they were text and you can also type any other text within the body of the document.

Adding Fields

If you do not add enough copies of a field when you create the form letter, you can use **Copy** and **Paste** to add more, or you can choose **Insert** from the Letter menu and **Field** from the submenu to add the field as a text object.

> **WARNING** You can also choose **Add Field** from the Letter menu to display the Add Field box, and then click and drag a field from it to the form letter, as you do when you create other types of views. However, it is added as a separate field object, not as part of the text of the letter, and so it is hard to work with.

Formatting Fields

Even though fields in Form Letters are text, you can format them as you do fields.

Select (highlight) the field or fields that you want to format, and, if necessary, choose **Style & Properties** from the Text menu or click the **Info Box** icon to display the Info Box.

The Text editing info box is displayed, but it also has a formatting panel (see Figure 5.42).

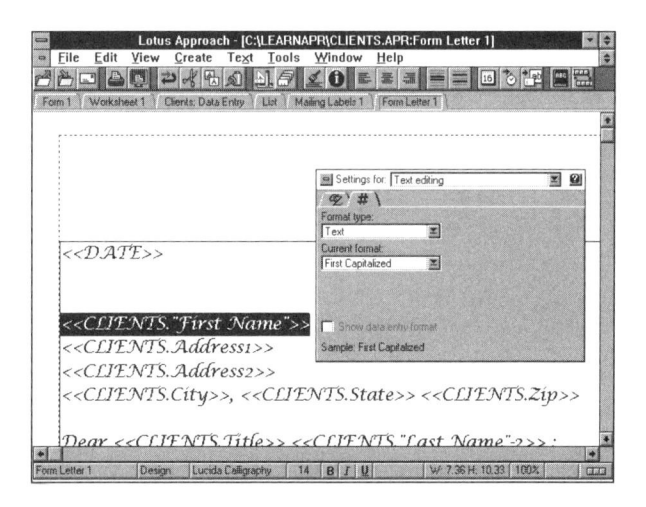

Figure 5.42 Formatting a field that is a text object.

This panel is the same as the one included on the Info Box for Field objects, discussed in the section on *Formatting Fields* in Chapter 4.

Editing Form Letters

Edit a form letter like any other text object, using the methods described in the section on *Text* in Chapter 4.

Because fields are added as text rather than as field objects, you cannot edit them in Browse mode. This is the reason that you cannot use form letters to edit your data.

The Form Letter Info Box

Select the Form letter as a whole and, if necessary, choose **Style & Properties** from the Text menu or click the **Info Box** tool to display the Form Letter's Info Box (see Figure 5.43).

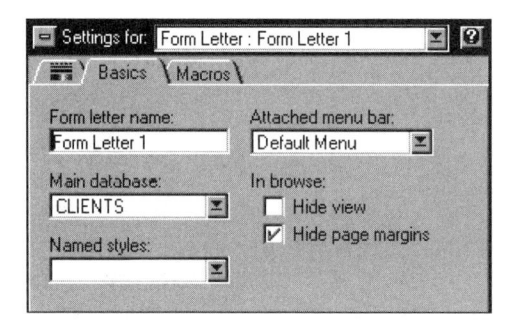

Figure 5.43 The Form Letter Info Box.

As you can see, the Basics panel, like the Basics panel of many other Views, lets you rename the form letter, select its main database, apply a named style to it, select the menu bar used with it, and hide view or margins in Browse. Unlike other objects, the margins are not hidden in Browse by default, because you generally want to know how a form letter will look when it is actually printed.

The Info Box also has a panel to control borders and colors, and a panel to control macros, which work like the equivalent panels on the Info Boxes of other Views.

Chapter 5: Creating Forms and Printed Output **203**

The Letter Menu

When you are working on a Form Letter in Design View, Approach replaces the Browse menu with the Letter menu (see Figure 5.44). The Letter menu includes the following options:

- *Style & Properties.* Displays the Info Box.
- *Add Field.* Displays the Add Field Box.
- *Insert.* Inserts the Date, Time, Page Number, or value of a field in a text object.
- *Fast Format.* Applies a Fast Format to an object.

You are already familiar with these options from the menu's of other types of views.

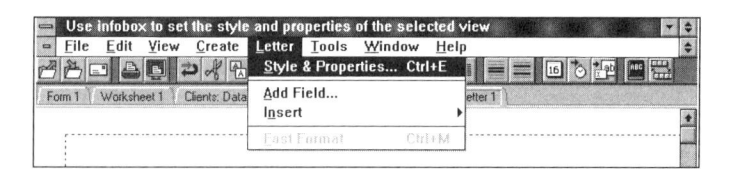

Figure 5.44 The Letter menu.

Designing a Sample Form Letter

Now, try creating the rudiments of a sample form letter. Since fields in form letters are placed as text rather than as fields, you should get used to the ways you place and manipulate them. You enter a bit of text at the beginning to give you a feel for how to enter form letters in Approach.

1. Choose **Form Letter** from the Create menu to display the Form Letter Assistant. Leave the defaults in **Step 1:Layout** and **skip Step 2: Return Address**.
2. Click **Step 3: Inside Address** to add the name and address of the addressee. Select **4 Lines** from the Address layout drop-down. Then double-click all the fields from **First Name** to **ZIP** in the Database Fields list in turn to add to them to the address, as you did when you were creating mailing labels.

3. Click **Step 4: Salutation.** Leave Dear in the text box, and select **Title** in the first Database Fields list and **Last Name** in the second field (see Figure 5.45).

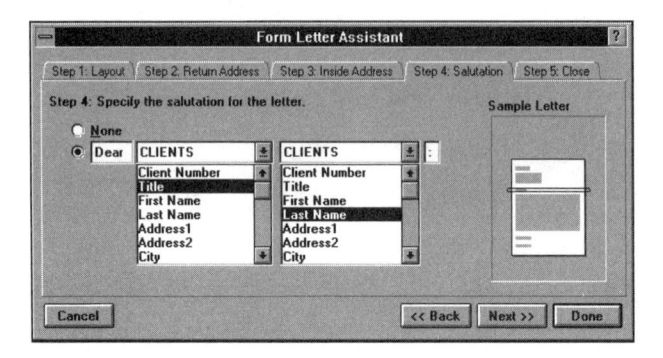

Figure 5.45 Creating the Salutation.

4. Select **Done** to create the form letter. If necessary, select the **Design** icon to display it in Design mode. Choose **Show Fields** from the View menu to view the symbols for the objects instead of the content of the Fields off (see Figure 5.46).

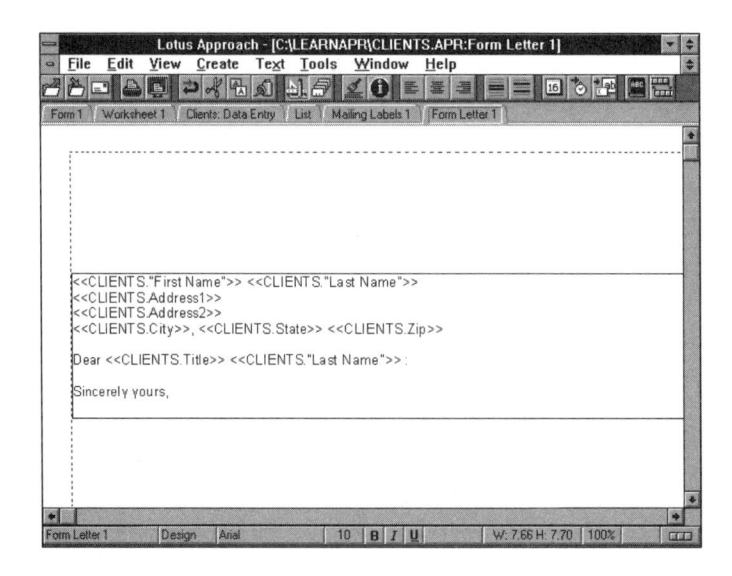

Figure 5.46 The initial form letter design.

Chapter 5: Creating Forms and Printed Output **205**

5. Now, you need to make the panel that holds the text larger, so it will hold the entire letter. Click the text object that holds the text to select it. Then click and drag one of its handles downward to make it larger, until you reach the bottom of the page. Make sure the left and right edges of the text object remain lined up with the left and right margins of the page.

6. You might want to add the date at the beginning of the letter. Scroll upward. Click the left edge of the first line, left of the First Name field to place the insertion point there. Choose **Insert** from the Text menu and Date from the submenu (or click the **Insert Date** icon) to add the date there, and press **Enter** three times to skip two lines after the date.

7. Since you do not want the date to be displayed as mm/dd/yy at the beginning of a letter, you should format it. Select (highlight) the Date field by clicking and dragging over it. Then, if necessary, click the **Info Box** icon to display the Info Box and click the field format type. From the Format type, select **Date**. The default date format is what you need, except that you do not want the day of the week displayed and do not want leading zeroes in the date. Select the day of the week drop-down (which has Sunday displayed on it), and select the **Blank Option** from the drop-down list. Then edit the text box to its right, to delete the comma that is currently in it. Finally, from the Day drop down, select the option that has the number without a zero before it (see Figure 5.47).

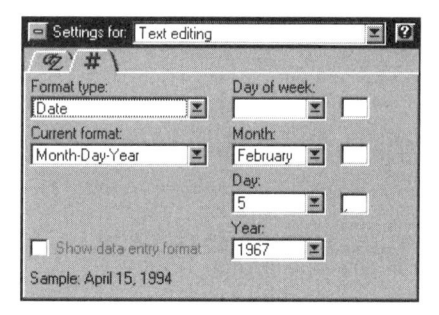

Figure 5.47 Formatting the date in text editing.

8. Formatting the name and address is also important, because a form letter is one case where you do not want to have incorrect capitalization. It would look a bit strange for a letter to begin "Dear DR. WALTON." To avoid this problem, you should format all the fields except the State

field so the first letter of each word is capitalized. Click and drag to select the fields from First Name to City (but not STATE). From the Format type drop-down of the Info Box, select **Text**, and as the Current format, select **First Capitalized** (see Figure 5.48). Likewise, click and drag to select the entire salutation line, and format it with First Capitalized also.

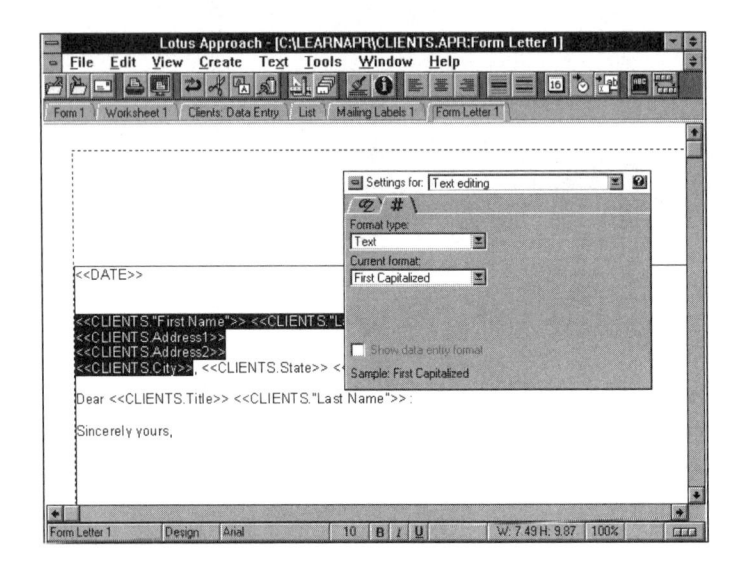

Figure 5.48 Formatting text in the form letter.

9. Now, try typing the beginning of a letter. Move the cursor to the line following the salutation, and press **Enter** to skip a line. Then press **Tab** to indent and type:

   I am writing to invite you to an open house. Only our preferred clients are receiving this invitation, and so I certainly hope you will be able to come.

   Notice that the text automatically wraps to the next line when it reaches the right margin, as it does with any word processor.

10. Choose the typeface for the text. Select all of the text and fields in the form letter by clicking and dragging over them—beginning with the date at the top and continuing to the end. Click the tab that displays the Fonts panel of the Info Box. If you have it, you can try selecting

Chapter 5: Creating Forms and Printed Output

Lucinda Calligraphy from the Font list and **14** point from the Size list; otherwise, select some other font (see Figure 5.49). Of course, you would include more text in an actual form letter.

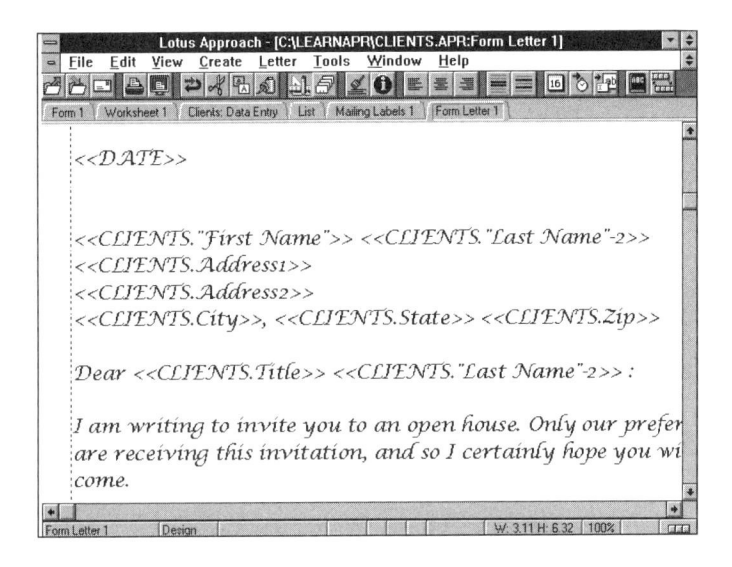

Figure 5.49   The final design of the form letter.

11. Select the **Browse** icon to see what an actual letter looks (see Figure 5.50). Press **PgDn** to view the letter for all the records, so you can see that all the names are capitalized correctly, including the one that was entered in all capitals. Click one of the fields to see that you cannot edit it, as you can edit the fields in other designs. You might also want to select **Print Preview** to view the design as an entire page.

You can see that you type a form letter just as you type any letter using a word processor. It has features, such as field formatting, that are not available when you do mail merge using a word processor and that are extremely useful when you are creating form letters.

If you want to test other features of form letters, you can try adding another type of object to the design. For example, to underline the letter's date, you could simply go back to Design mode, click the **Line** icon, and click and drag to place the line under the date. If necessary, you could move or resize the line, as you would any object in an Approach design.

Practical Approach, 3.0

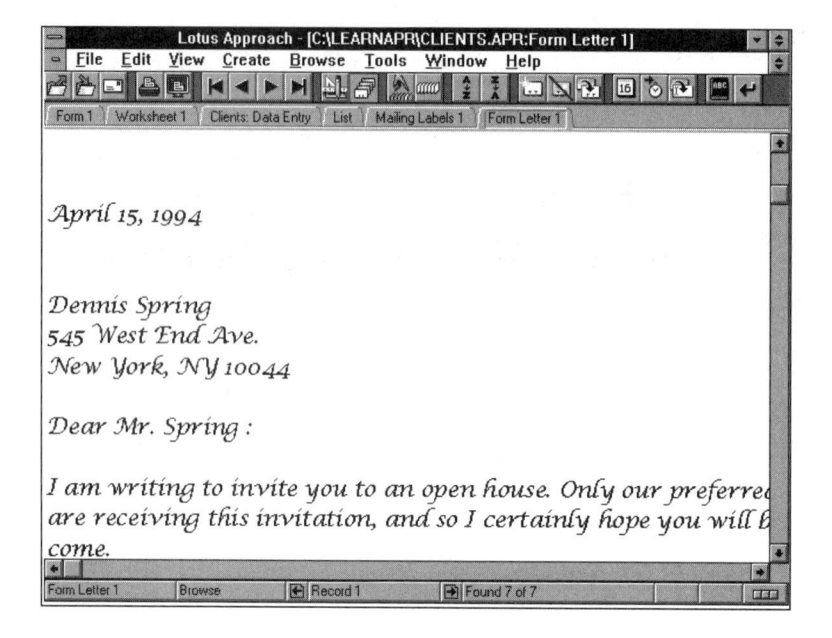

Figure 5.50 The letter in final form.

WARNING

Remember, graphic objects like this do not move when you add new text or reformat the text. If the text changes, you may also have to move graphic objects so they are still in the right location. It is best not to add them until the end, when you are sure that the text is correct.

Printing Output

As you know, all the designs covered in this chapter except for form letters can be browsed and edited on the screen as well as printed. You even created a Report, named List, which you intend to use to edit data on screen and not to print.

Yet, you will want to print the mailing labels, form letters, and most of the reports you create. There are two dialog boxes used to print Approach designs, Print and Print Setup, which are similar to the equivalent dialog boxes in other Windows applications.

The Print Dialog Box

Choose **Print** from the File menu to display the Print dialog box in order to print the current document. You can also display the Print dialog box simply by selecting the **Printer** icon of the icon bar.

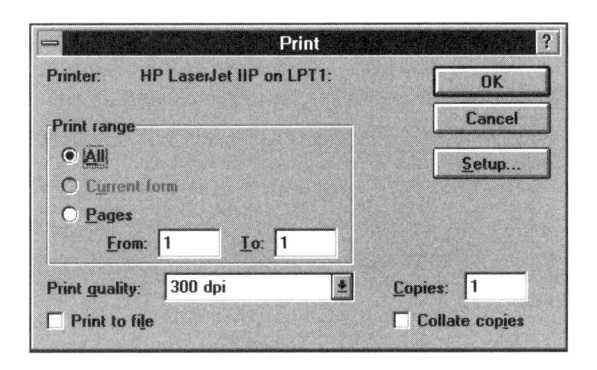

Figure 5.51 The Print dialog box.

To avoid wasting time and paper, it is always good to select Print Preview before printing, so you can see if there are any errors in the design. As you know, you can do this by clicking the **Preview** icon or choosing **Preview** from the file menu.

The printer that the report is sent to is described at the top of the Print dialog box.

Use the radio buttons in the Print Range area to select how much of the current database is printed:

- Select the **All** radio button to print all of the records in the found set (or the entire database if you have not done a Find) as they are displayed in the current view.
- Select the **Current Form** radio button to print the record currently being displayed.
- Choose the **Pages** radio button and enter numbers in the From and To text boxes to specify which pages should be printed. Use the **Print Quality** drop-down list to specify the resolution of the printout. On

some printers, you can use lower resolution to print a rough draft more quickly.

Use the **Copies** text box to specify how many copies are printed. If you are printing multiple copies, you can select the **Collate Copies** checkbox to have them collated.

Select the **Print** checkbox **to File** to save the formatted version of the document to a file rather than sending it to the printer. If you select this checkbox, then when you select **OK** to print the database, Approach displays the Print to File dialog box (see Figure 5.52). Use this dialog box in the familiar way to specify the file where the document should be saved.

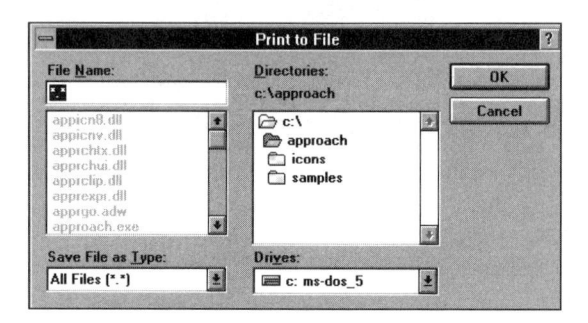

Figure 5.52 The Print to File dialog box.

Once you have printed a view to a file, anyone can print it, even if they do not have Approach, by sending the file to the printer. You can print it from the DOS prompt, for example, by entering the command **COPY FILENAME PRN**; of course, you must use the actual name of the file rather than the word FILENAME.

Print Setup Dialog Box

You can also choose **Print Setup** from the File menu to use the Print Setup dialog box (see Figure 5.53).

Use the radio buttons and drop-down list in the Printer area to select a printer, if you have more than one. Notice that the default printer is described under the first radio button. If you select **Specific Printer**, you can use the drop-down list under it to select any printer that is available to your system.

Chapter 5: Creating Forms and Printed Output

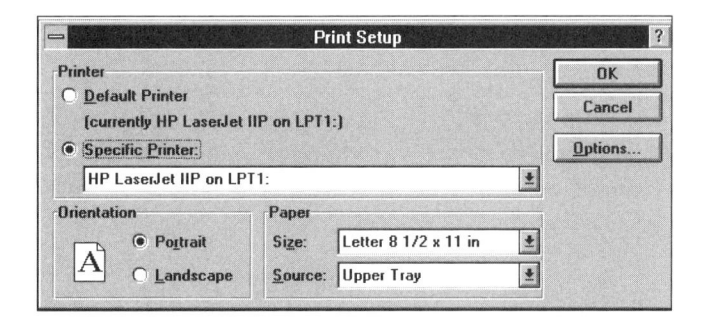

Figure 5.53 The Print Setup dialog box.

Use the radio buttons in the Orientation area to select **Portrait** (upright) or **Landscape** (left-to-right) orientation.

> **NOTE** Landscape orientation is often useful for printing columnar reports, to fit all the fields across one page. The pop-ups in the Paper area let you specify the size of paper that is being used and the source of the paper (the upper or lower tray of the printer or manual feed).

The **Options** push button displays an Options dialog box, which depends on your printer. No matter what type of printer you have, the Options dialog box includes a Help button, which you can click on for information on how to use it.

Using Sorts and Finds

In the last chapter, you learned to create designs, to determine which fields are displayed and how they are arranged on the screen. In this chapter, you learn about sorts and finds, which determine which records are displayed, and the order in which they are arranged.

Sorts and Finds are particularly useful in combination with printed output. For example, before you produce mailing labels, you might want to do a Sort, so they are in zip code order, or you might want to do a Find, to do a mailing to only some of the people in your database. Sorts are very easy to understand. Basic Finds are also easy to understand, but Approach also lets you use more complex and more powerful Finds. This chapter covers:

- Sorting records on a single field in ascending and descending order
- Using the Sort dialog box to define a sort
- Finding records that match a single criterion
- Finding records with a range of values
- Finding records that match multiple criteria, using a logical AND
- Finding records that match any one of several criteria, using a logical OR
- Using Sounds Like Finds and Wildcard Finds
- Using special finds to isolate records with unique or duplicate values
- Combining Sorts and Finds

Sorts: An Overview

Sorts, which determine the order in which the records are displayed, are extremely easy to use. Choose **Sort** from the Browse menu, and then from the submenu choose:

- **Ascending** to instantly sort on the current field in ascending order.
- **Descending** to instantly sort on the current field in descending order.
- **Define** to use the Sort dialog box to define a custom sort order.

You can also click **Sort Ascending** or **Sort Descending** icons to instantly sort on the current field in ascending order.

To create a custom sort order, use the Sort dialog box (see Figure 6.1). Simply select each field that the Sort is based on from the Database fields list, and select **Add** to add the field to the Fields to sort on. If you are working with a relational database, it may be necessary to use the drop-down list above it to select the database the fields are in, in order to base a sort on fields from multiple files. To remove a field from the Fields to sort on list, select it, and select **Remove.**

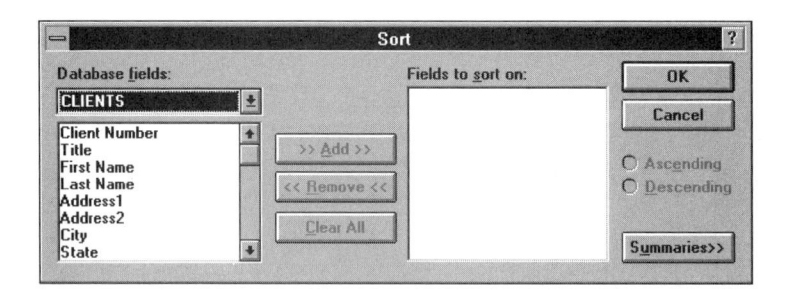

Figure 6.1 The Sort dialog box.

SHORTCUT You can also add a field to the Sort list simply by double-clicking it in the Fields list, or remove it by double-clicking it in the Sort list.

When to Sort on Multiple Fields

Many Sorts need to be based on only one field. To produce mailing labels in Zip Code order, you just need to sort on the **Zip** field. You do not need to use the Sort dialog box to define this sort.

NOTE Some sorts, however, must be based on several fields. To Sort names in alphabetical order, you must base the Sort on the Last Name field, but you must also use the First Name field as a tie-breaker in case two people have the same last name.

In your sample database you want Donna Walton to come before Joseph Walton. To do this, you must add **Last Name** as the first field in the Sort list and **First Name** as the second field. The second field in the Sort list is used as a tie-breaker, and it is only taken into account if two records have the same value in the first field.

You might want to use more complex Sorts. If you want to list your clients by state, and you want the clients within each state to be listed alphabetically, then you would have to add **State**, **Last Name** and **First Name** to the Sort list.

Ascending and Descending Sorts

Choose the **Ascending** or **Descending** radio buttons of the Sort dialog box for each of its fields to determine if that field is to be sorted from smallest to greatest, or from greatest to smallest value.

If you are using the Sort dialog box and select **Descending** for one field, and then highlight a second field, the Ascending radio button is selected again to indicate that the second field is still sorted in ascending order. These radio buttons work independently for each of the fields in the Sort list.

Ascending sorts arrange records from the smallest value in the field to the largest—from the earliest date to the latest date or from the smallest number to the largest number.

Descending sorts arrange fields from the largest to the smallest order. They are often useful for dates, to put the most recent dates at the top of the list.

If you do an ascending sort on a Boolean field, all records with **No** in the field are placed before all records with **Yes** in the field.

Text fields are sorted in alphabetical order. Approach does not give you the problems you have with some database management programs, which use ASCII order. They consider all uppercase characters to come before all lowercase characters. Approach sorts in proper alphabetical order even if fields are capitalized differently.

> **NOTE** Sorts are case sensitive. for SQL data and for Paradox data, if an index file exists.

You cannot sort on a Memo field.

Sorting on a Summary Field

If you have created summary fields and want to sort on them, click **Summaries** in the Sort dialog box to display it in the extended form (see Figure 6.2).

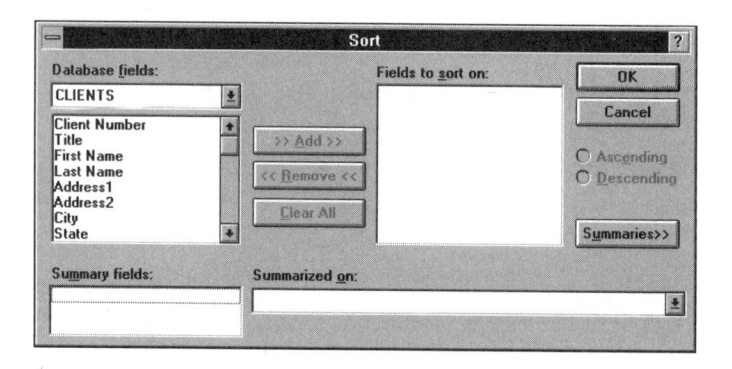

Figure 6.2 Creating sorts with summaries.

The Summary fields list includes all summary fields you have created for your database. If you have created a summary field that is used in more than one panel, you can use the Summarized on drop-down to select which one the sort is based on.

Summary fields are covered in Chapter 8.

Sorting the Sample Records

Try sorting your sample database in a few commonly used orders. You can sort your records in zip code order, to use in a mailing. Then sort in alphabetical order by name, to make it easier to look up clients.

1. Begin by viewing the Clients database in Browse mode. Click the **List** divider tab to view multiple records.
2. Place the cursor in the Zip field and choose **Sort** from the Browse menu and **Ascending** from the submenu (or click the **Sort Ascending** icon) to sort the records. Zip codes are arranged from smallest to largest (see Figure 6.3).

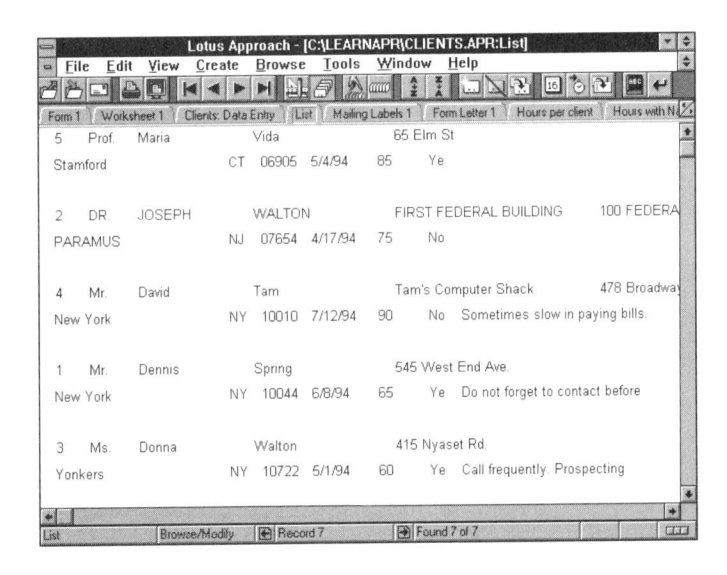

Figure 6.3   The records sorted in zip code order.

3. Now, sort in alphabetical order by name, choose **Sort** from the Browse menu and **Define** from the submenu to display the Sort dialog box. If necessary, double-click fields already in the **Fields to sort on** list to remove them. Then double-click the **Last Name** field to add it to this list, and the **First Name** to add it too (see Figure 6.4). Select **OK** to sort the records, and notice that they are arranged alphabetically by name (see Figure 6.5).

Practical Approach, 3.0

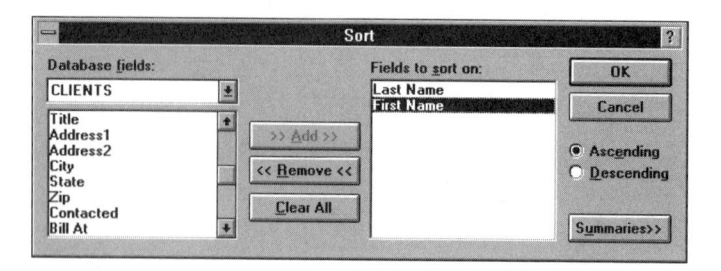

Figure 6.4 Sorting alphabetically by name.

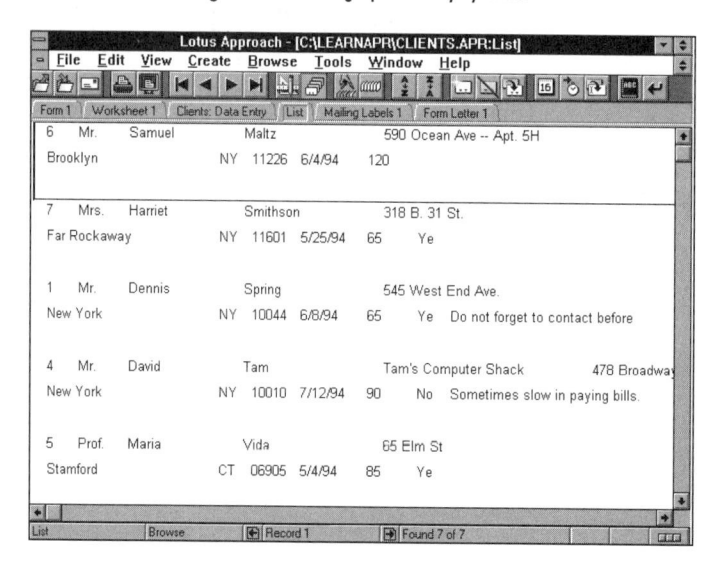

Figure 6.5 The records sorted in this order.

Scroll down to see that Joseph Walton comes after Donna Walton, as it should in alphabetical order, despite its incorrect capitalization. In database programs that sort in ASCII order, it would come first, because the capital A that is its second letter comes before the small a that is the second letter of Donna Walton in ASCII order.

There is no need for an exercise for descending sort, or for sorts that combine ascending and descending order, because they are so easy to do. Simply select a field in the Sort list, and select the **Descending** radio button to sort on that field in descending order. When you select each field, the **Ascending** or **Descending** radio button is selected, depending on the sort order of that field. Thus, you can change the sort order of each field independently.

Finds

The basics of the Find operation are very simple. It is as easy to do most Finds as it is to do a sort. Approach also lets you use many advanced features to do more sophisticated finds.

Simple Finds

To do a Find, you must be viewing a database in Browse mode. Select the **Find** icon on the icon bar or choose **Find** from the Browse menu to display a Find Request Form and use Find mode.

The Find mode has its own icon bar and four special buttons at the top of the view, below the divider tabs (see Figure 6.6). The most important feature of Find mode is the Find request form.

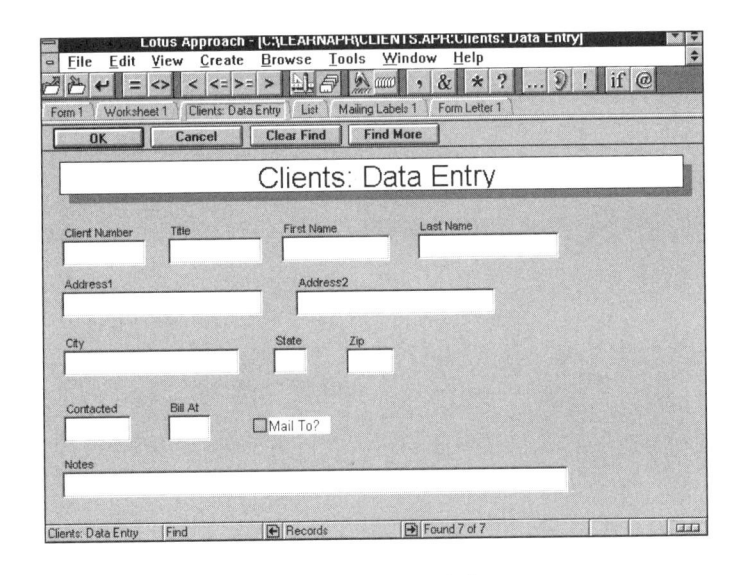

Figure 6.6 Doing a find.

The Find Request Form

The Find Request Form is laid out just like a single record of the current view. To do a simple Find, just fill in the value that you want to find in the appropriate field of the find request. Then press **Enter**, click **OK**, or select the **Enter** icon on the icon bar. Approach returns to Browse mode, but only the records that have the value you entered in that field are accessible.

The Found Set

The status bar always has a *Found message* near its right edge. Before you do a Find, the message says something like **Found 86 of 86**, meaning that you have a total of 86 records in the database, and that all of them are accessible. After you do a Find, this message says something like **Found 10 of 86**, meaning that you have a total of 86 records in the database and 10 of them are accessible.

> **NOTE** After you begin using Finds, you should get in the habit of looking at the Found message on the status bar whenever you perform some major operation, such as printing mailing labels or a report, to make sure that you have not inadvertently excluded some records.

The accessible records are called the *found set*. The found set might include either one or many records, depending on why you are doing the Find. For example:

- If you are looking up a client by name, you would fill in the last name in the **Last Name** field of the Find Request, and (assuming you have only one client with that name), Approach displays only one record after you press **Enter**.
- If you want to do a mailing to all your clients who live in a certain state, you would fill in the name of the state in the **State** field of the Find Request, and Approach would display all the records from that state.

The found set does not change when you switch between views, even if the view you switch to does not include the field that the Find was based on.

When you are done using this limited number of records in the found set, use the **Find All** icon on the icon bar (to the right of the Find icon) or choose **Show All** from the Browse menu to display all the records again. The message on the status bar indicates that all of the records are accessible again.

> **NOTE** No matter which records are in the found set when you begin, new Finds apply to all the records in the database, not just to the records in the current found set. You do not have to select the **Find All** icon before filling out a new Find Request (or editing the last one), even if you want to find records not in the current found set.

Finds for Different Field Types

If you are searching for text, there is a match as long as the text in the database begins with the same letters as the value you enter in the Find Request.

In addition, there generally is a match even if capitalization is different.

Later you see that you can search for exact matches, but it is usually easiest to use this default method. If you are searching for someone by name, you can enter just the first few letters of the name, without capitalizing the first letter.

For other types of fields, enter the value in the Find Request just as you would during data entry. To find a value in a date field for example, enter a date in the form mm/dd/yy, as you would during data entry. You cannot query PicturePlus fields.

Other Essential Features of Finds

Later in this chapter, you look at more advanced features of Finds, but there are a few other features that are essential even for simple Finds, which you should look at now:

- *Canceling a Find Request*. You can cancel a Find Request by pressing **Esc** or clicking the **Cancel** button. Approach displays the Browse screen once again, rather than the Find Request Form.
- *Clearing a Find Request*. If you have begun filling out a find request and you want to start over, you can click **Clear Find** to remove all criteria that you have entered.
- *Finding Again*. Choose **Find Again** from the Browse menu to display the Find Request Form with all the values that were entered for the last Find. You may want to do this if you did not enter the right criterion for the last Find so you can edit the criterion. In addition, if you added or deleted records since the last Find, the found set would be different after doing a Find with the same criterion.
- *Finds using Controls*. If you have created a view that uses a control, such as a checkbox or radio buttons, for data entry, you can use the control in a Find. If you have created a checkbox to enter data in a Boolean field, you can select it in the find request to find all the records that have **Yes** entered in that field.

- *Hiding Records.* In addition to doing a Find Request, you can hide individual records by selecting one or more records and then selecting **Hide** from the Browse menu. This is often useful for fine tuning a Find. Before doing a mailing to all the clients who live in a certain state, you might want to look through the records one by one and see if there are any individual clients whom you would want to exclude from the mailing by hiding their records.

Basic Finds Using Your Sample Data

Before going on to more advanced Finds, you should be sure you understand the basics by trying a few sample Finds.

1. Try looking up a client by name. If necessary, click the **view divider tab** to display the Clients: Data Entry form. Click the **Find** icon to display a Find Request. Click the **Last Name** field to add a cursor there, and enter VIDA (see Figure 6.7). Then press **Enter** (or select the **Enter** icon) to view that client's record (see Figure 6.8). Note that the status bar says Found 1 of 7 as you have only one client with that name, and that a match was found even though you did not capitalize the name as it is in the record.

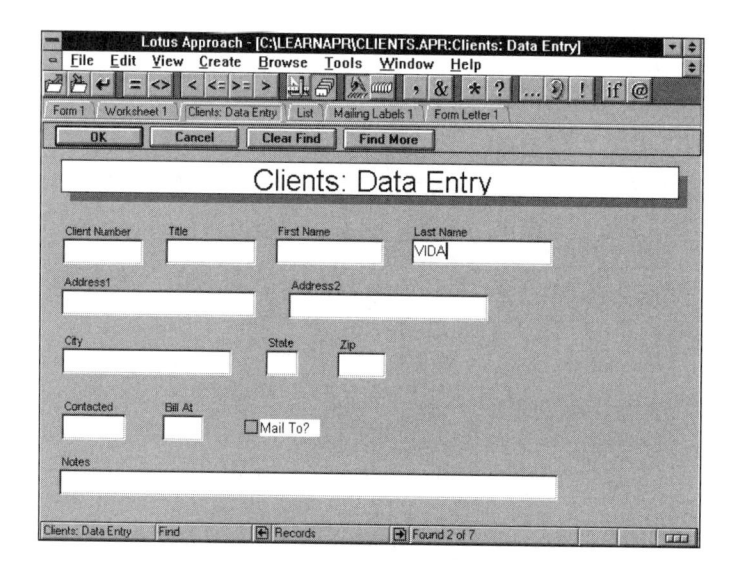

Figure 6.7 Looking up a client by name.

Chapter 6: Using Sorts and Finds

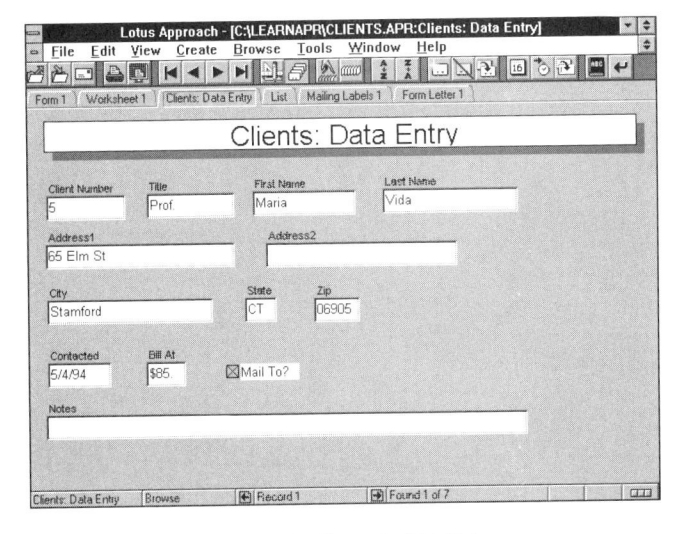

Figure 6.8 The result of this Find.

2. Try looking up all the clients in one state. Click the **State** field to add a cursor there, and type **NY** (see Figure 6.9). Then press **Enter**. Click the **List** divider tab, so you can see that only the records from New York state are in the Found set (see Figure 6.10). Note that none of these records was part of the found set before you did this Find.

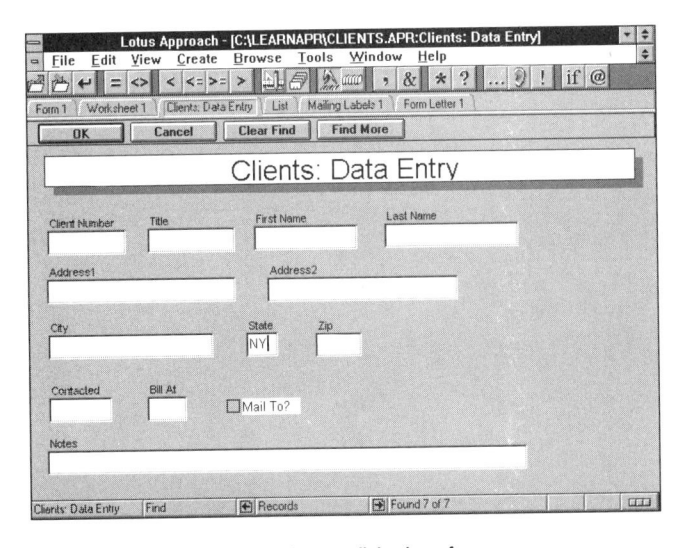

Figure 6.9 Looking up all the clients from a state.

Practical Approach, 3.0

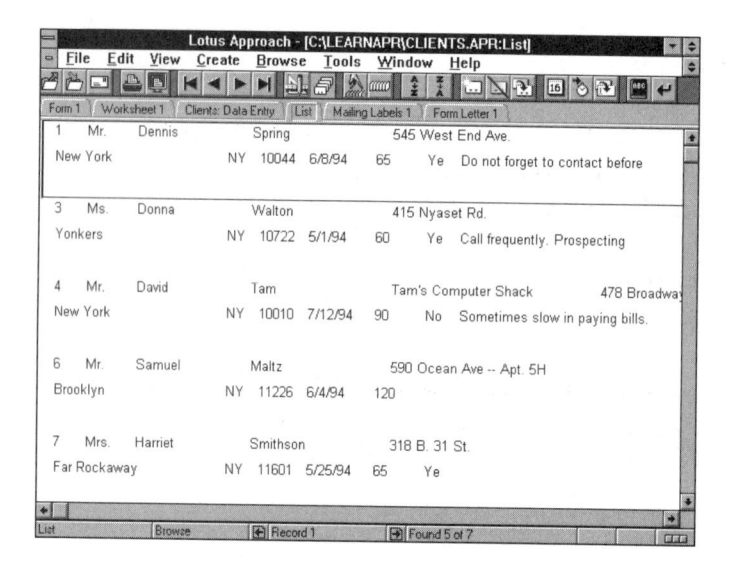

Figure 6.10 The result of this Find.

3. Do a find to get ready for a mailing. Click the **Clients: Data Entry** divider tab. Select the **Find** icon to display a Find Request. Click the checkbox in the **Mail To** field to select it (see Figure 6.11). Then press **Enter**.

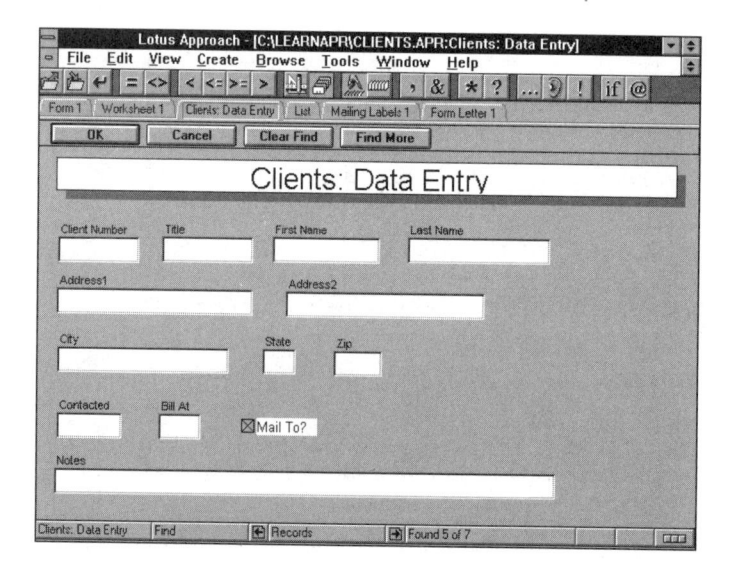

Figure 6.11 Looking up all the clients on your mailing list.

4. Click the **List** divider tab to confirm that only records that have **Yes** in this field are included in the found set (see Figure 6.12). Now, assume you decide to mail to all these clients except Donna Walton. Click any field in the record for Donna Walton, and choose **Hide Record** from the Browse menu. The status bar now reads Found 3 of 7, and this record has been removed from the found set. In an actual application, you would now click the **Mailing Labels** 1 divider tab, and choose **Print** from the File menu to print the labels.

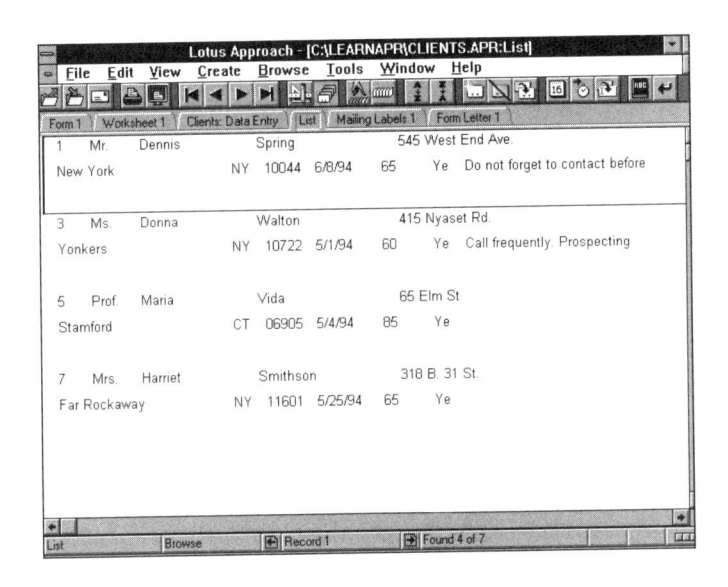

Figure 6.12 The results of this Find.

5. Click the **Find All** icon to view all the records again.

Now that you have learned the basics of using Finds, you can go on to learn advanced features of Finds in the next few sections. These involve adding more complex criteria in the Find Request. Since they are all entered using the same techniques you have just practiced, the following sections simply have illustrations of sample Find Requests and their results, rather than step-by-step exercises. You should enter some of the examples as you read, to reinforce your learning.

Finds Using Operators

Approach *operators* and *functions* are both used in *formulas*, an advanced feature of Approach which is covered in detail in Chapter 8. Operators can be entered in Finds by typing them or selecting them from the icon bar.

A few operators are essential in Finds to search for a range of values or for an exact match in a text field, and they are simple enough to introduce here.

SHORTCUT All of these operators are available on the icon bar of the find environment, and you can enter them at the location of the insertion bar simply by clicking the appropriate icons.

Comparison Operators

Several types of Finds use what are called *comparison operators* or *relational operators*, which are listed in Table 6.1. Most of them may look familiar to you, since they are also used in mathematics. The only unusual operator in this table is the ... (within a range) operator, which requires two values, a minimum before it and a maximum after it. The other operators take only one value that is placed after them.

Table 6.1 Comparison (or Relational) Operators Used in Finds.

Operator	Meaning
=	is exactly equal to
<>	is not equal to
<	is less than
<=	is less than or equal to
>=	is greater than or equal to
>	is greater than
...	is within a range

Chapter 6: Using Sorts and Finds

After looking at the Finds that use these relational operators, you look at a couple of operators sometimes used in Finds with multiple criteria, and at a couple of special operators used in Finds.

Finding a Range of Values

Often, you want to search for a range of values rather than for a single value. You might want to find all the clients that you have not contacted since a certain data, or all clients that you bill between $60 and $80 per hour.

The operators <, >, <=, and >= are used in the obvious way to find a range of values. To find dates before or after June 1, 1994, use the formula **< 6/1/94** or **> 6/1/94** (see Figure 6.13 and Figure 6.14).

NOTE In all of these examples, the Find Request is shown in the Data Entry view, so you can see which fields the operators are in, and the result is shown in the List view, so you can see all of the records in the Found set.

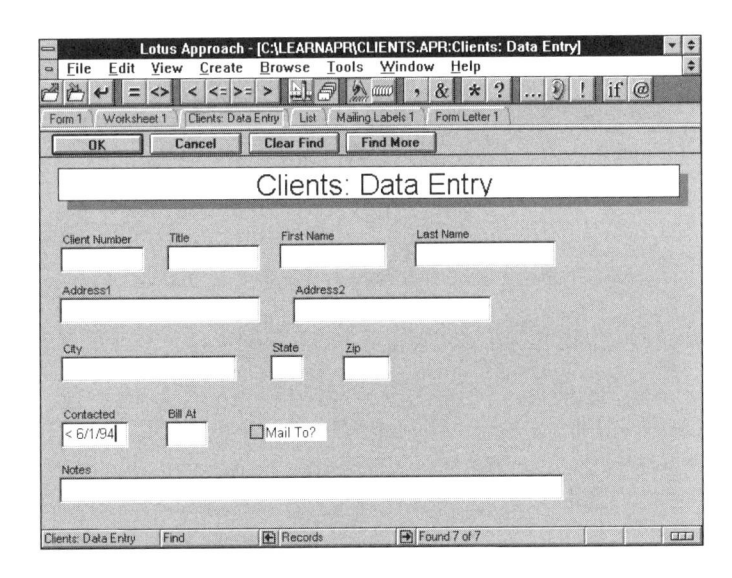

Figure 6.13 A Find using the < operator.

Practical Approach, 3.0

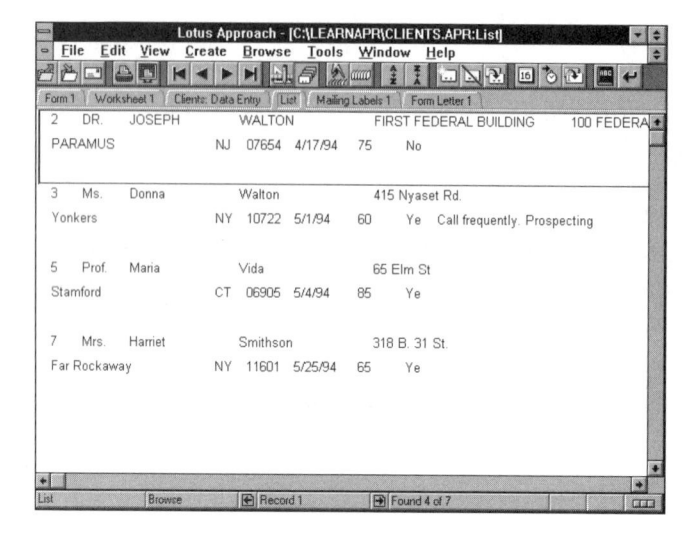

Figure 6.14 The result of this Find.

Remember, when you are using these formulas in finds, you must think a bit more precisely than you do when you use their meanings in regular speech. Ordinarily, if you say that you want all amounts greater than $50, you want to include amounts that are exactly $50. You cannot do this by using the formula > 50. You must use the more precise >= 50.

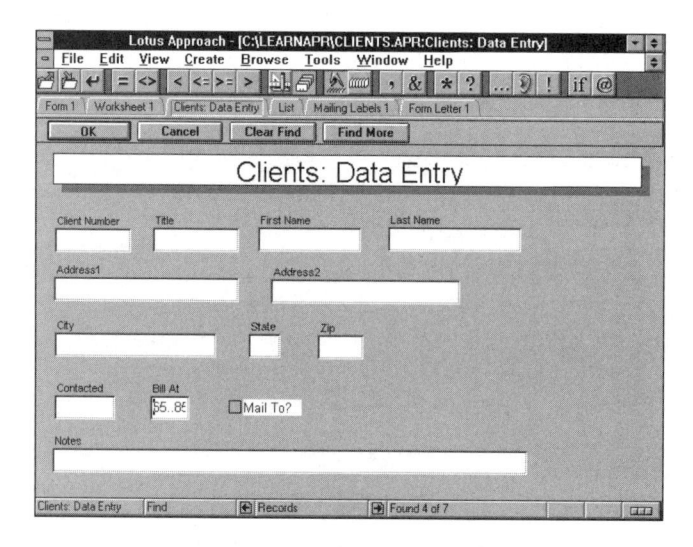

Figure 6.15. A Find using the ... operator.

The ... operator is used to find values that fall in a range between two values, which are listed before and after it. To get some date in the year 1994, you could use the formula 1/1/94 ... 12/31/94. Notice that the clients whom you bill exactly $65 or exactly $85 per hour are included in the found set (see Figure 6.15 and Figure 6.16).

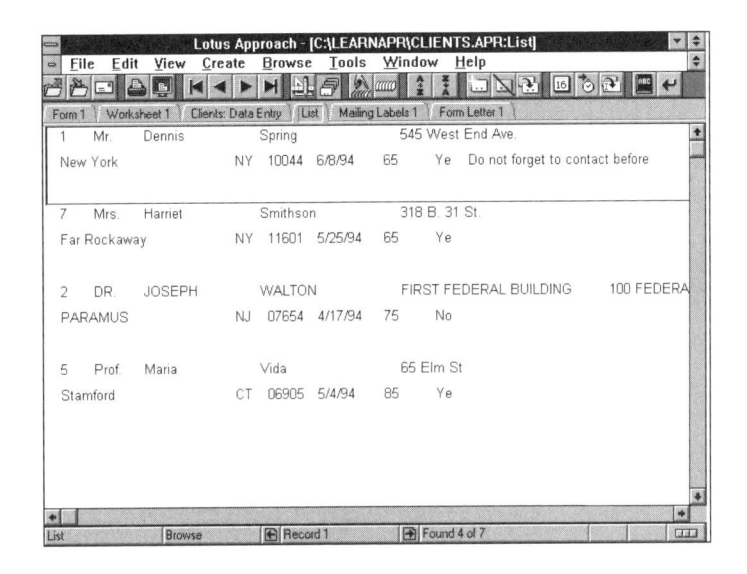

Figure 6.16 The result of this Find.

Finding an Exact Match

The = (*is exactly equal to*) operator can usually be left out. As you know, you can simply type a value in one of the fields of a Find Request to find all the records with the same value in that field.

This operator is useful in finding an exact match in a text field. Remember that, by default, text fields are included in the found set if they begin with the same letters as the criterion in the Find Request. This can save you typing, but sometimes it gives you records you do not want.

If you want the records for people named Smith, and you enter this name in the Last Name field of the Find Request, Approach includes people named Smithfield, Smithson, Smithe, and any similar name in the found set.

To find only the records that match exactly, use the = operator. Enter **=Smith** as the criterion.

Finding Records That Do Not Match

The <> (*is not equal to*) operator lets you find records that do not match a value. Thus, you can enter **<> NY** in the STATE field to find the records of all your clients who are not from New York (see Figure 6.17 and Figure 6.18).

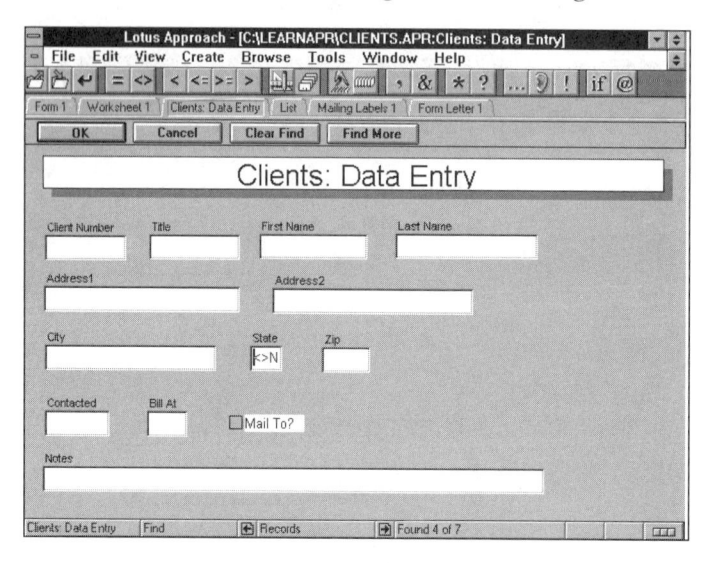

Figure 6.17   A Find using the <> operator.

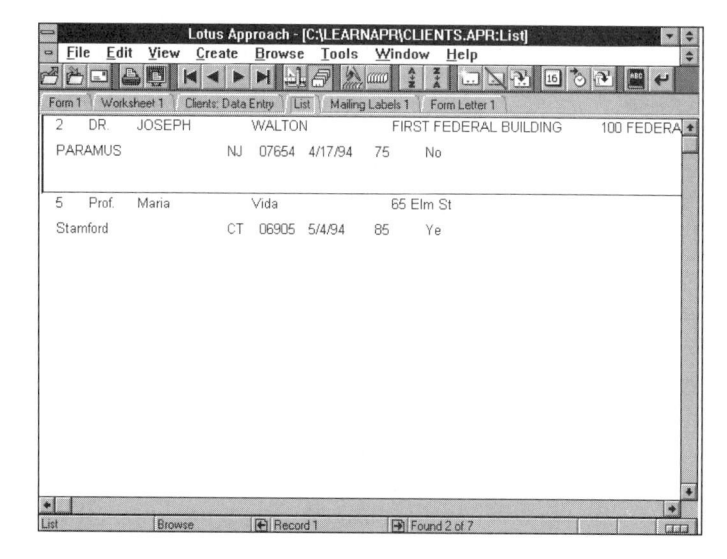

Figure 6.18   The result of this Find.

Chapter 6: Using Sorts and Finds

This operator is often useful as a complement to another search. If you are doing a mailing to all of your clients, but you have slightly different brochures for those who live in New York and those who do not, you can do finds to produce two sets of mailing labels. One set with the criterion NY, and the other with the criterion <>NY in the State field.

Blank Fields and Non-Blank Fields

You can find all the records that have one field blank by including just the = operator in that field of the Find Request. You can read this as "is equal to nothing." A query to find the records with no data in the Address2 field (see Figure 6.19 and Figure 6.20).

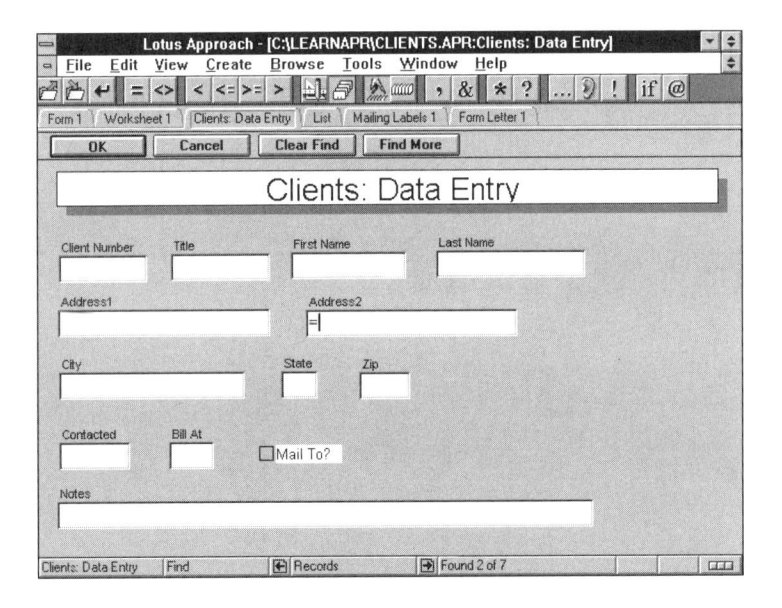

Figure 6.19 A Find using the = operator to search for blank fields.

Practical Approach, 3.0

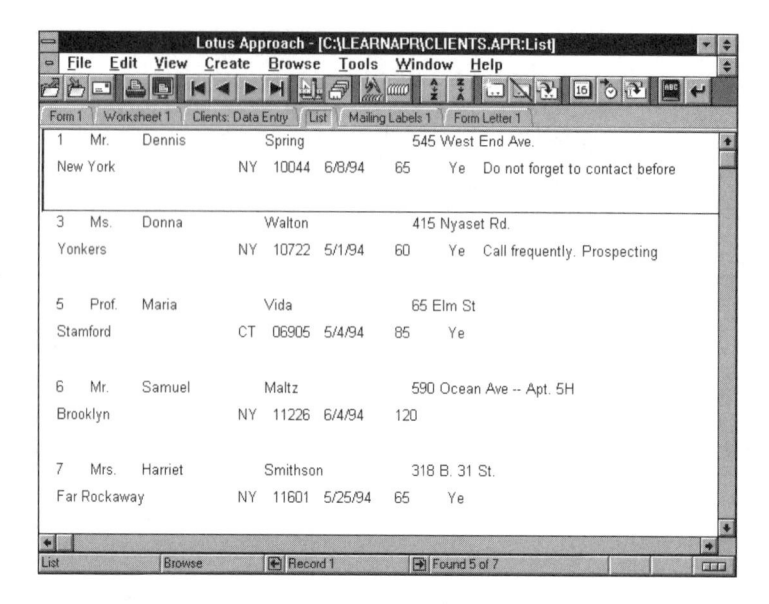

Figure 6.20 The result of this Find.

Likewise, you can find all the records that have an entry in some field by including just the <> operator in that field of the Find Request. Read this as "is not equal to nothing."

Finds with Multiple Criteria

So far, you have only looked at Finds that involve a single criterion, but there are also cases where you want to find records that match several criteria. These Finds fall into two categories:

1. *Logical AND.* Used to find the records that match all of the criteria. For example, you might want to find clients who live in New York state and have not been contacted recently.
2. *Logical OR.* Used to find the records that match any one of the criteria. For example, you might want to find clients who live in New York or in New Jersey.

The logical AND is exclusive; the more criteria you add, the fewer records you find that match. The logical OR is inclusive; the more criteria you add, the more records you with find that match.

NOTE: Whether a find uses a logical AND or a logical OR does not necessarily depend on whether you use the word "and" or "or" when you describe it in ordinary speech. If you were speaking colloquially, you might say that you want to find the records from New York or New Jersey, but you might just as well say that you want to find the records from New York and New Jersey. However you describe it colloquially, this find involves a logical OR, because there will be a match if either of the criteria is satisfied.

Logical AND

Most finds that involve a logical AND have the criteria in different fields, and so Approach makes these very easy to do.

With Criteria in Different Fields

To do a Find that uses a logical AND with criteria in different fields, simply type the criteria into the appropriate fields of the Find Request. Records will be found only if all of the criteria are matched.

To do a mailing to all your clients who live in New York state and whom you have not contacted since June 1994, enter **NY** in the State field and **< 6/1/94** in the Contacted field of the Find Request (see Figure 6.21 and Figure 6.22).

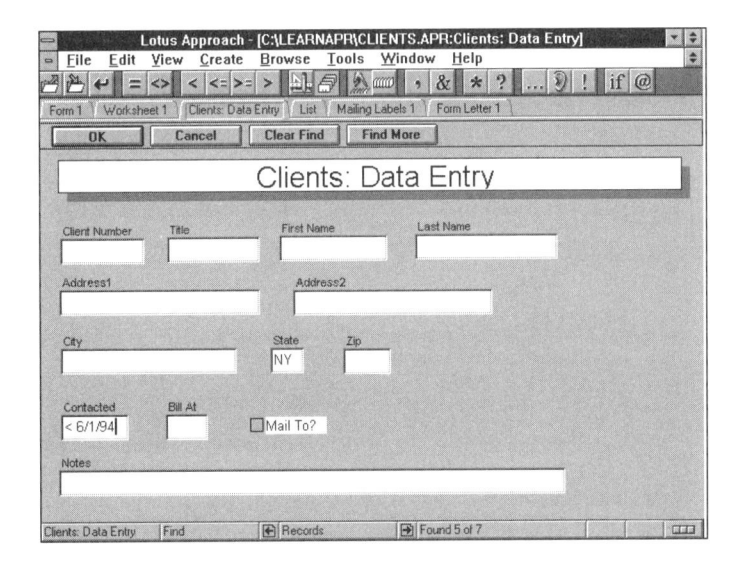

Figure 6.21 An ordinary Find with a logical AND.

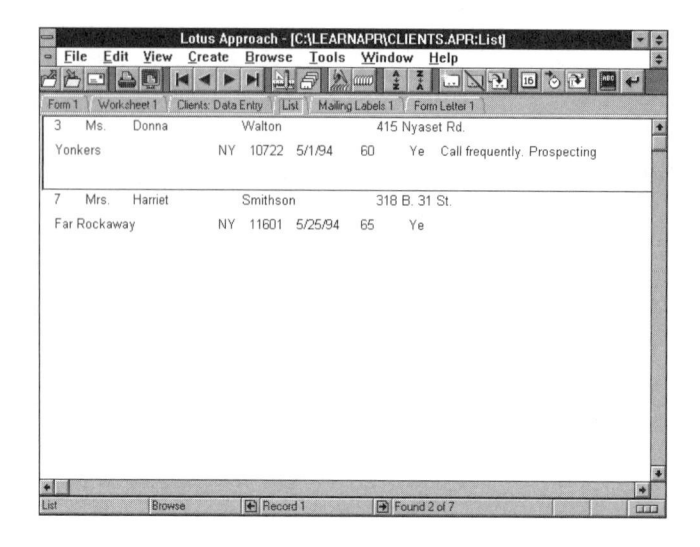

Figure 6.22 The result of this Find.

With Criteria in the Same Field

If the criteria are in the same field, you must use an & (logical AND) operator between them, so Approach knows they are two separate criteria. Do a Find to display the records of clients who are billed at more than $65 and less than $85 per hour (see Figure 6.23 and Figure 6.24).

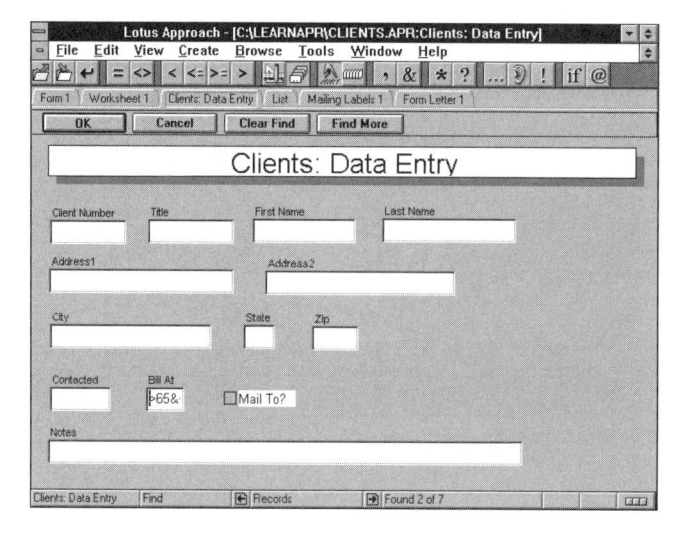

Figure 6.23 A Find with a logical AND and criteria in the same field.

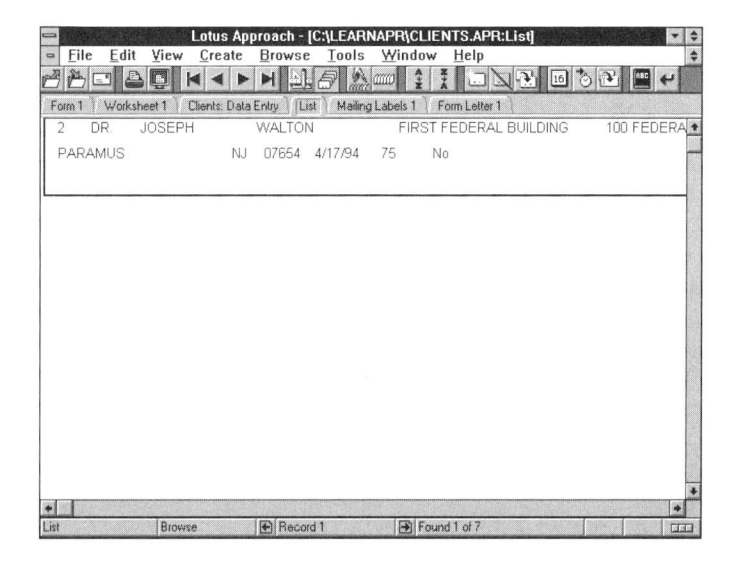

Figure 6.24 The result of this Find.

> **NOTE** Notice that, unlike the similar Find that you did using the ... (*within a range*) operator, this Find does not include the records that are billed at exactly $65 or exactly $85. You could have gotten the same result as the earlier range query by using the criterion >= 65 & <= 85 instead of > 65 & < 85.

Logical OR

Most finds that involve a logical OR have the criteria in the same field, and so Approach makes these very easy to do.

With Criteria in the Same Field

To do a find using a logical OR with criteria in the same field, type the criteria in the field separated by commas. Records are found if any of the criteria is matched.

To do a mailing to your clients who live in New York or in New Jersey, enter **NY, NJ** in the State field of the Find Request (see Figure 6.25 and Figure 6.26).

Practical Approach, 3.0

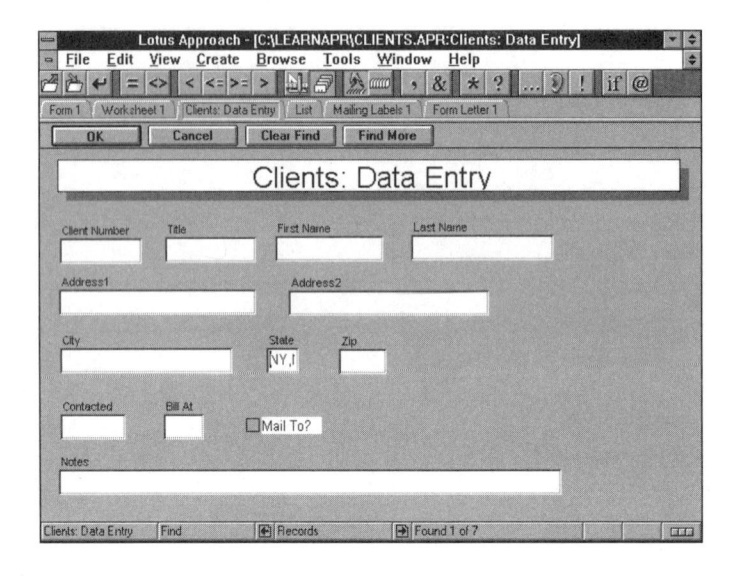

Figure 6.25 An ordinary Find with a logical OR.

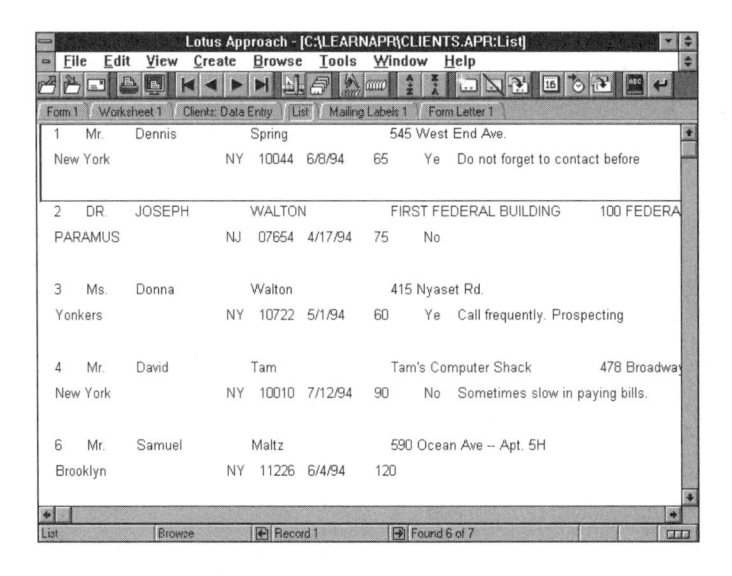

Figure 6.26 The result of this Find.

With Criteria in Different Fields

On occasion, you might want to do a find that involves a logical OR that has the criteria in different fields. To do this sort of Find, you must use the **Find More** option of the Browse menu.

When you are doing a find and the Find Request is displayed, the first option of the Browse menu becomes Find More instead of Find, and you can use it to call up new Find Requests.

> **SHORTCUT**
> You also can display new Find Requests by clicking the **Find More** button or clicking the **Find** icon while doing a Find.

All the records that match the criteria on any Find Request are included in the found set.

Imagine you want to do a mailing to the clients who are usually on your mailing list and also to all the clients who live in New Jersey. Call up a **Find Request** as usual and enter **Yes** in the Mail To field to include the clients on your usual mailing list. Then choose **Find More** from the Browse menu to call up another **Find Request**, and enter **NJ** in the State field (see Figure 6.27). When you press **Enter** to execute the Find, the found set includes all the records that match either criterion (see Figure 6.28).

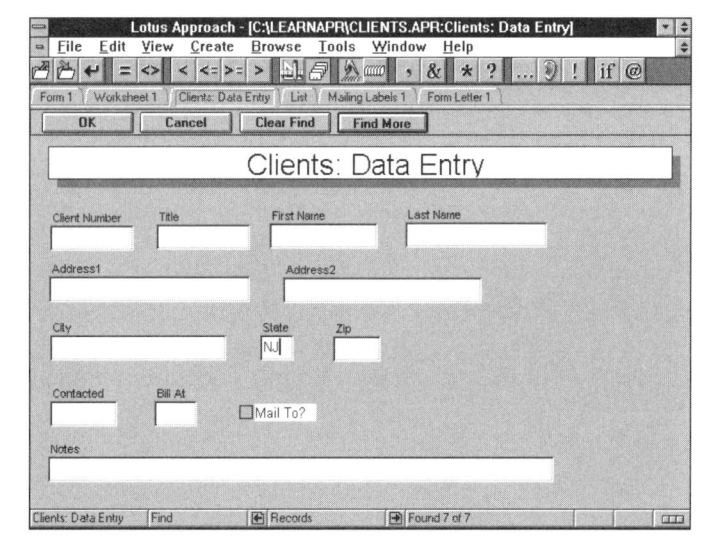

Figure 6.27 A Find with a logical OR and criteria in different fields.

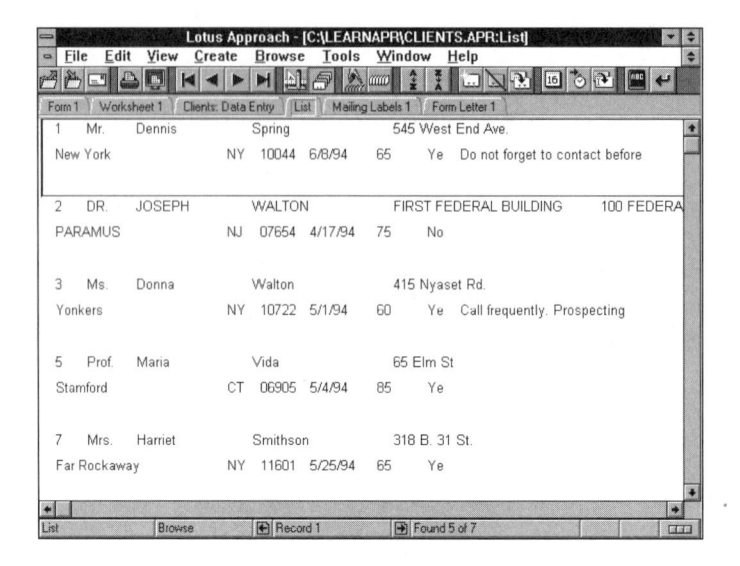

Figure 6.28 The result of this Find.

Special Features of Finds

You have looked at all the major features of Finds, but Approach also has a few special features that give Finds more power. To use these features, you must include other operators or special characters in the criterion of the find.

Case-Sensitive Matches

By default, as you have seen, Approach ignores the difference between capital and lowercase letters when you are doing a Find. This is true even when you use the = (*is exactly equal to*) operator.

If you want the find to take capitalization into account, include the ! operator before the criterion that you enter in the Find Request (see Figure 6.29 and Figure 6.30).

Chapter 6: Using Sorts and Finds

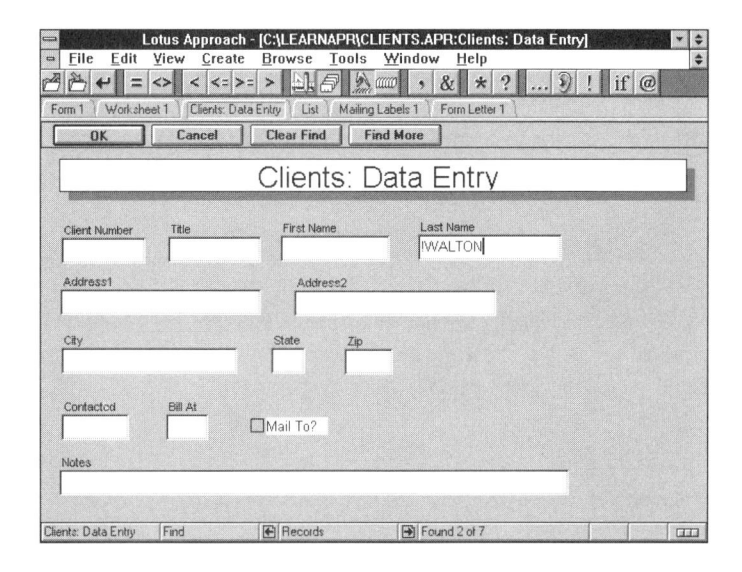

Figure 6.29 Exact matches ignore capitalization.

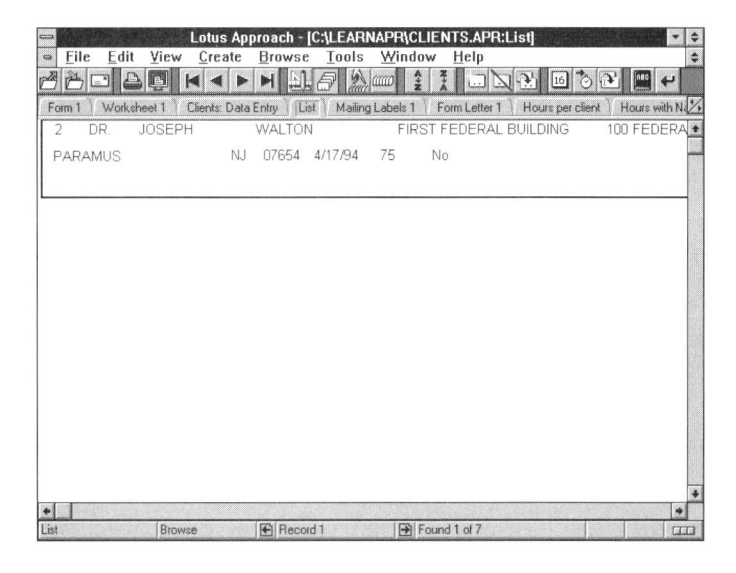

Figure 6.30 The result of this Find.

Wildcard Searches

There may be times when you want to do inexact searches—searches for fields that have only some of the same characters as the criterion you enter in the Find request. To do this, you can use these two *wildcard* characters:

- ? matches any single character.
- * matches any string of characters, from zero to an indefinite number.

You may be familiar with these wildcards, as they are also used in DOS and Windows.

For example, the criterion SM?TH matches SMYTH as well as SMITH. The criterion SM*TH also matches SMOOTH.

NOTE Remember that you do not generally need to use wildcards at the end of a word, because by default, a text field matches the criterion if its initial characters match. For example, you do not need to use SMITH* to match SMITHSON as well as SMITH; it matches even without the *, as long as you do not use the = operator.

You might want to use * at the beginning of a word. For example, you could use *SON to match SMITHSON, PEARSON, and the like. And you might want to use the ? at the end of a word to specify that it must have a certain number of characters added to match. For example, SMITH??? matches SMITHSON and SMITHERS, but it does not match SMITHSONIAN or SMITH.

NOTE The * wildcard is very useful for finding a word in a longer string. To find all the clients who live on Elm St., you can enter ***Elm*** as the criterion in the Address 1 field. This is invaluable in longer text fields.

Sounds Like Finds

Another form of inexact match that is often useful is the Sounds Like Find.

Enter the operator ~ before the criterion in the Find Request, and there is a match in every record whose entry in that field sounds like the criterion. For example, if you enter the criterion **~WILTAN** or **~WALDON** in the Last Name field, Approach finds the records for Walton (see Figure 6.31 and Figure 6.32).

Chapter 6: Using Sorts and Finds

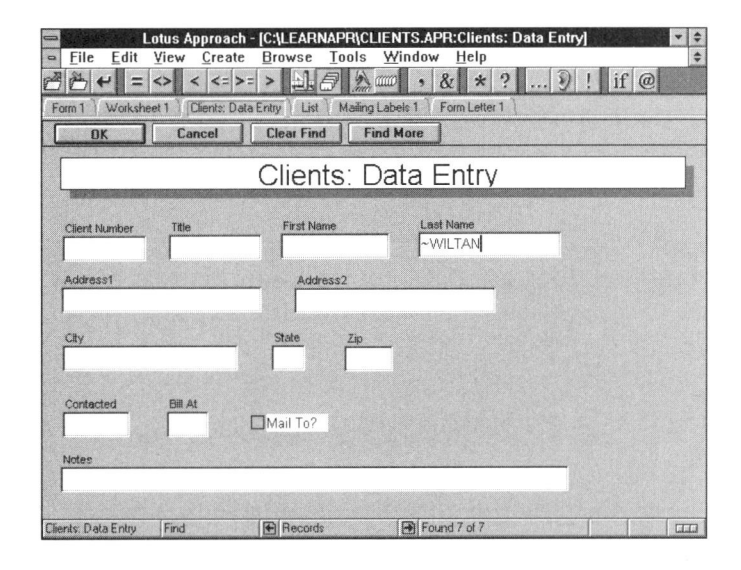

Figure 6.31 A Find using the ~ (sounds like) operator.

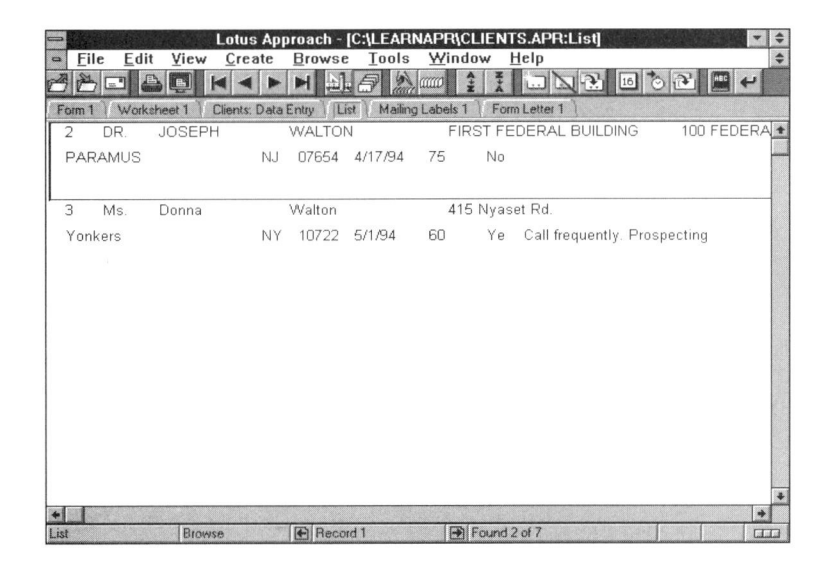

Figure 6.32 The result of this Find.

This feature is particularly useful if you know the pronunciation but not the spelling of a name you want to look up.

If Searches

If Searches let you enter a complex formula as the criterion in the Find Request, and so they are covered in Chapter 8.

You can also use Approach functions in Finds if you precede them with the character @. *Functions* are one element of formulas and are also covered in Chapter 8.

Finding Duplicate or Unique Values

In addition to the usual Finds that use the Find Request form, Approach provides a dialog box that lets you do special purpose finds. Choose **Find Special** from the Browse menu to display the Find Special dialog box, which lets you find records that have duplicate or unique values in one or more fields (see Figure 6.33).

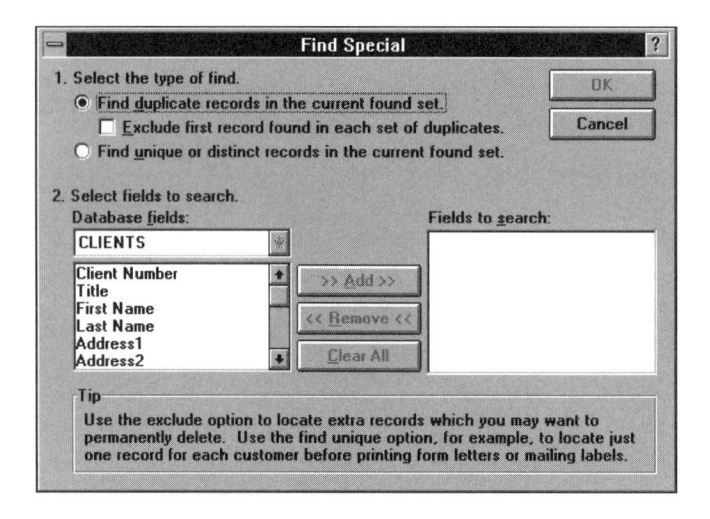

Figure 6.33 The Find Special dialog box.

You must add the fields that you want checked for duplicates or unique values to the Fields to Search list. Do this in the usual way. Select a field in the Fields list and select the **Add** button or simply double-click it in the Fields list to add it to the Fields to Check list. If you are working with a relational database, you can add fields from related databases by using a database drop-down list above the Fields list. To remove a field from the Fields to Check list, select it and select the **Remove** button.

> **NOTE** The Find isolates records that have unique or duplicate values in all the fields you add to the list. Thus, if you want to find unique or repetitive records, you should add all the fields to the list.

Finding Unique Values

Select **Find unique or distinct records in the current found set** to find records with unique values in these fields—values in the fields that are not duplicated in any other records in the current found set.

A search for unique values in the State field with the result of this Find are shown in Figure 6.34 and Figure 6.35). You can see how useful this would be if you have a large database and simply want a list of all the states that your clients live in.

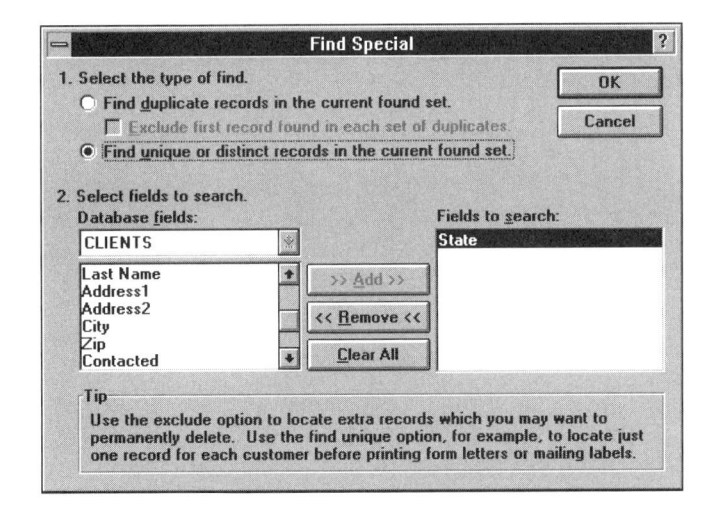

Figure 6.34 Searching for Unique Values.

Practical Approach, 3.0

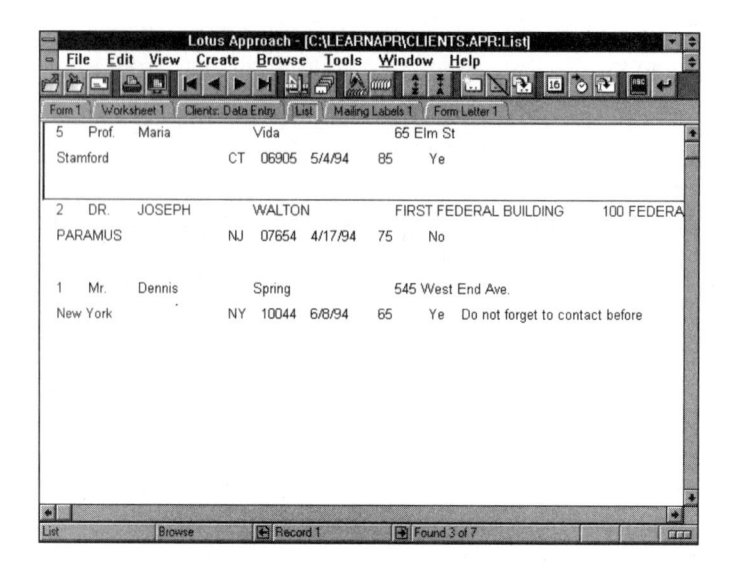

Figure 6.35 The result of this Find.

Finding Duplicate Values

Select **Find duplicate records in the current found set** to find records with duplicate values in these fields—the same values in these fields in multiple records in the current found set.

If you select the **Find duplicate** radio button, you can also select the **Exclude first record** checkbox, and one record with duplicate data is not included in the found set.

This checkbox makes it easy for you to delete duplicate records. Find records with the same data in all their fields, and select this checkbox so one record in each set of duplicates is not included in the found set. Then choose **Delete Found Set** from the Browse menu to delete the duplicates and keep one record on each person or other entity.

If you perform a find for records of people with the same last name, without selecting the **Exclude first record** checkbox, (see Figure 6.34 and Figure 6.36). As you can see, the Find Duplicates dialog box ignores capitalization, just as ordinary finds do (see Figure 6.36 and Figure 6.37).

Chapter 6: Using Sorts and Finds

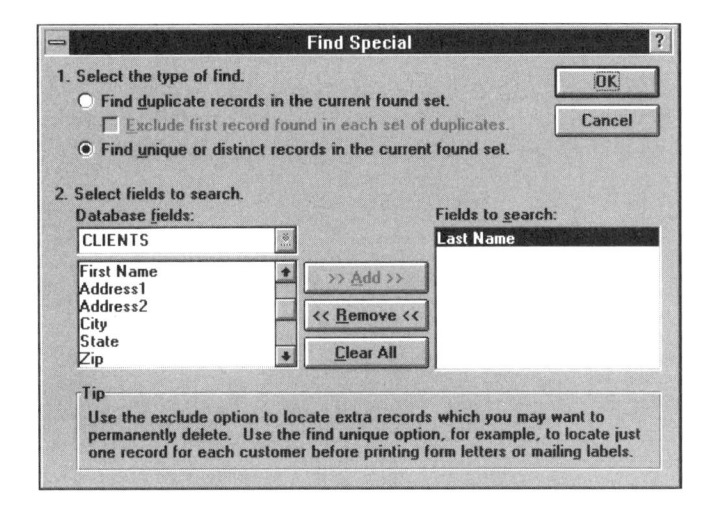

Figure 6.36 Searching for duplicate last names.

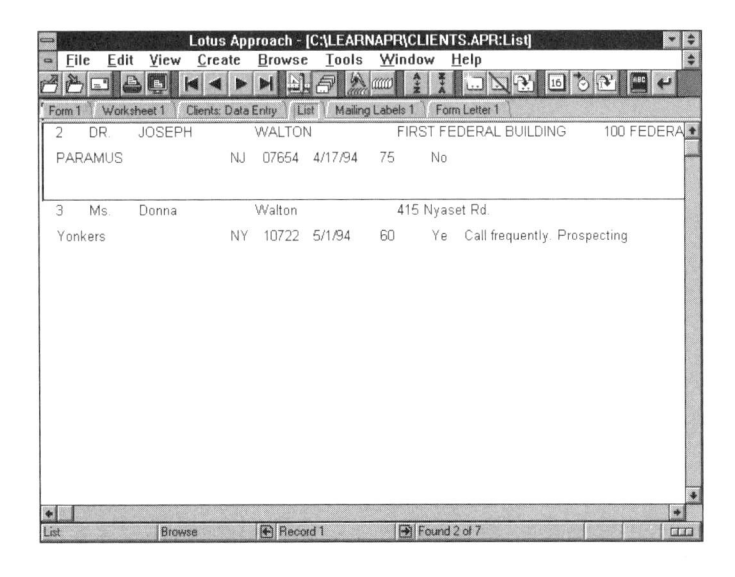

Figure 6.37 The result of this Find.

The Find Icon Bar

As you have seen, when you are in Find mode a special Icon bar is displayed, which is useful for adding operators and other special characters to the Find (see Figure 6.38).

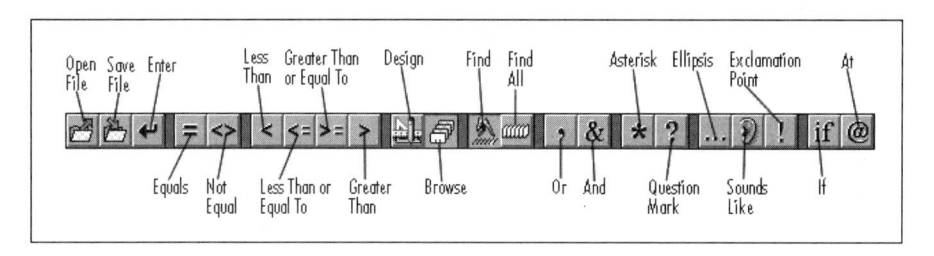

Figure 6.38 The Icon bar in Find mode.

You have gone over all these operators and special characters in the course of this chapter, and you can look at this icon bar as a review:

- *Open File icon.* Used to display the Open dialog box to open a file. It is equivalent to choosing **Open** from the File menu.
- *Save File icon.* Used to close the current Approach file. It is equivalent to choosing **Save Approach File** from the File menu.
- *Enter icon.* An alternative to pressing the **Enter** key, which you must do to perform the find.
- *Equals icon.* Used to enter the = operator in the Find request, to find records that identically match the criterion.
- *Not Equal icon.* Used to enter the <> operator in the Find request, to find records that do not match the criterion.
- *Less Than icon.* Use this to enter the < operator in the Find request, to find records that are less than the criterion.
- *Less Than Or Equal To icon.* Use this to enter the <= operator in the Find request, to find records that are less than or equal to the criterion.
- *Greater Than icon.* Used to enter the > operator in the Find request, to find records that are greater than the criterion.
- *Greater Than Or Equal To icon.* Use this to enter the >= operator in the Find request, to find records that are greater than or equal to the criterion.

- *Design icon.* Used to enter Design mode and cancels the Find. It is equivalent to choosing **Design** from the View menu.
- *Browse icon.* Use this to enter Browse mode and cancel the Find. It is equivalent to choosing **Browse** from the View menu.
- *Find icon.* Used to display a Find Request, which you can use to do a find. It is equivalent to choosing **Find** from the Browse menu. It always appears to be depressed on the icon bar for Browse mode.
- *Find All icon.* Use this to display all the records once again and cancel the Find.
- *Or icon.* Used to enter the operator , (comma), which lets you find records that match any one of multiple criteria.
- *And icon.* Is used to enter the operator & which lets which let you find records that match more than one criterion.
- *Asterisk icon.* Use this to enter the wildcard character *, which is used to match any string.
- *Question Mark icon.* Used to enter the wildcard character ?, which is used to match any single character.
- *Ellipsis icon.* Used to enter the ... operator, which is used to match a range of values.
- *Sounds Like icon.* Is used to enter the Sounds Like operator, which is used to find values that sound like the criterion.
- *Exclamation Point icon.* Use this to enter the ! operator, to do case-sensitive finds for character data.
- *If icon.* Is used to enter the If operator, which lets you enter a logical expression as a criterion.
- *At icon.* Used to enter the character @, which is needed before expressions in Finds.

Combining Sorts and Finds

There are often occasions when you want to combine a Find and a Sort—if you want to do a mailing to all of your clients in one state and want the mailing labels in zip code order. To do this, you must do the Find first and then the Sort, because doing a find (or selecting **Find All**) changes the order of the records.

New users often are confused by this point, so you should try it to get a feel for it:

1. If necessary, select **Find All** and click the **List** divider tab to view all the records in list form. Click the **Last Name** field of one of the records and click the **Sort Ascending** icon to sort the records alphabetically by last name.

2. Now, select the **Find** tool. Enter **>= a** in the Last Name field of the Find Request, so that all the records are included. Press **Enter** to do the Find, and note that the fields are no longer sorted.

3. To illustrate the right way to combine a Find with a Sort, try producing mailing labels. Select **Find** in the Mail To field of the Find Request. Enter **Y**, and press **Enter** to find only the records on the mailing list. Then click the **Zip** field to place the cursor in it, and click the **Sort Ascending** icon. Finally, click the **Mailing Labels 1** divider tab and click the **Preview** icon to display the records in the form of mailing labels sorted in Zip order and ready to print (see Figure 6.39).

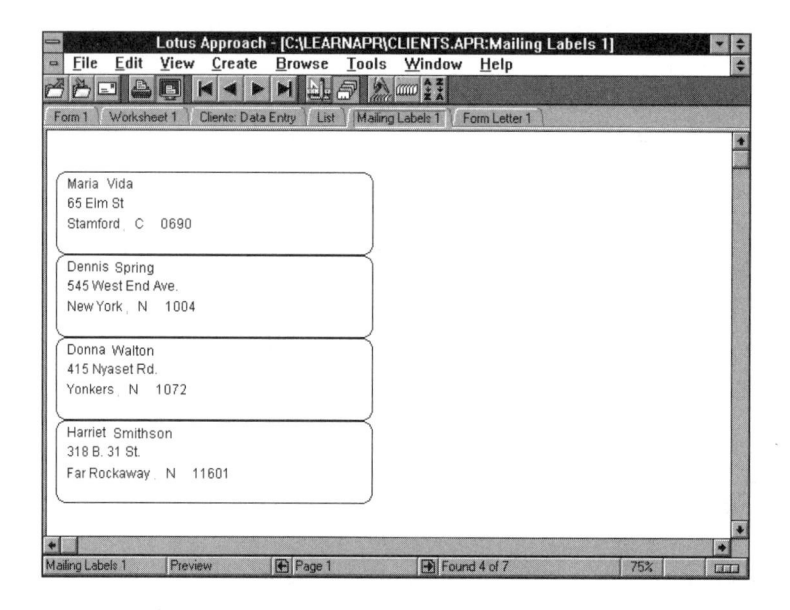

Figure 6.39 First Find and then Sort to keep the records in proper order.

WARNING: New users often fall into the trap of sorting first and then doing a find, and sometimes they do not realize that the records are in the wrong order until after they have printed out many pages of data.

After doing this exercise, you should be able to avoid this sort of problem in your work.

Part II

The Power User

Chapter 7

Working with Relational Databases

When you were first creating a sample database file, you learned you should be sure each field of a file has a one-to-one relationship with all of the others. If there is not a one-to-one relationship, you should break up the data into a number of database files, and relate these files to each other using a common key field, such as a client number. Because it involves relating files, this sort of database is called a *relational database*.

Now that you have learned all the basic operations you need to work with a single database file in Approach, it should be easy for you to perform the same operations on a relational database. After you have learned to join files into a relational database, you work with them in many of the same ways as you do with any database. In this chapter, you learn:

- The basics of relational database theory
- The difference between one-to-one, one-to-many, and many-to-many relationships

- How to break down a many-to-many relationship into two many-to-one relationships
- How the same data can be used in either a one-to-many or a many-to-one relationship
- How to join database files in Approach to create a relational database
- How to work with a one-to-many relationship by creating a form with a repeating panel
- How to work with a many-to-one relationship by adding fields from a related file to a form or other view
- How to add and edit the data in a relational database, to sort a relational database, and to work with it in other ways

Understanding Relational Databases

Computer scientists discovered an unexpected benefit of computerization when corporations began using computers to keep their records in the 1950s and 1960s. People had always expected that computerization would make it easier to find records, sort records, and use records in different forms, for example, as reports and as mailing labels. When record keeping began to be computerized, computer scientists discovered that it also was possible to avoid keeping all of the repetitive data that businesses had kept when they had used paper files.

When records are kept on paper, a large corporation might have a dozen different forms, used by a dozen different departments, each of which had the same basic data. The department in charge of payroll might have a file with each employee's name, address, social security number, wages and hours worked. The department in charge of benefits might have a file with each employee's name, address, social security number, and the benefits for which each was qualified. The department in charge of training might have a file with each employee's name, address, social security number, skills, and training courses taken.

It is not hard to imagine that a large business might have ten or more forms, each used by a different department, and each with the same basic data for each employee.

This repetition requires extra work in adding and maintaining records. When new employees are hired, all the data on them has to be entered ten times on ten different forms. And when employees move, their addresses have to be changed ten times.

The repetition also creates anomalies. It was found that there are often inconsistencies in the names and addresses on different forms. One might include a middle name and another might not. One address out of ten might be changed incorrectly when an employee moved.

Computer scientists devised several methods for eliminating this repetition. The early ones were complex and could only be used by advanced computer programmers. By the 1970s, however, relational databases emerged as the simplest and most powerful method of avoiding repetition.

> **NOTE** Relational databases involve breaking down data so it is stored in several different database files; this is called data normalization. Then the data in the different files is related by using a common key field, such as an employee number or a client number, in all of the files.

In the example we just looked at, there could be one file with the employee number and all the basic data on the employee, such as name, address, social security number, and telephone number. There could be a second file with the employee number, the wages and the hours worked each week for that employee, assuming that you record the wages for each week. There could be a third file with just the employee number and the benefits to which that employee was entitled.

Then, to produce a report on wages, you relate the file that holds wages and hours worked, to the file that holds basic data on employees. You join the two files based on the common key field. Each record holding wages and hours is connected, for the purposes of this report, with the record that has the same employee number in the file that holds basic data, so you can see the name, address, and social security number of the employee for each wage record.

Likewise, to view the benefits for which the employees are qualified, you use the employee number to join the file that holds data on benefits with the file that holds basic data. You can see the name and address of each employee along with the benefits to which that employee is qualified.

There is a tremendous savings in the amount of time needed for data entry. When you hire a new employee, you need to enter the basic data only once; rather than entering all the basic data ten times in ten files, you need only to enter the employee number in these ten files. When an employee moves, you only have to change the address once; the employee number never changes.

Data Normalization

Before you can work with a relational database, you must know exactly how to break down the data. Computer scientists have invented rules of database normalization, but it is possible to normalize most data using common sense. You can do this by looking carefully for one-to-one relationships and for the other two possible types of relation among data that require you to break down the file into several files: the one-to-many relationship and the many-to-many relationship.

One-To-Many Relationships

One-to-many relationships are very common in ordinary business applications.

This is the sort of relationship that you have in an example of wage records you just looked at. Every employee earns many weeks of wages. The name, address, and other basic data on each employee are in a one-to-one relation with each other, but weekly wage records are in a many-to-one relation with this basic data.

Though you might not recognize it at first, the wage rate may also be in a many-to-one relation with the other data, because the wages of employees can change over time. Whether the wages should be kept in the same file with the hours worked, or in the file with basic data on employees depends on the individual case.

If you change different employees' wages at different times, you must keep the hourly wage for each week in the same file as the hours worked that week. If you keep the current wage in the file with the basic information on employees, you could not use this figure to calculate the total wages that the employee earned during some period in the past, since the wage might have changed since then. You must copy it into the file with each week's hours worked in order to have a record of past wages.

If you change wages only once a year, however, you might want to have a separate file with the wages for each employee for each year. This file could have only the employee number, the year, and the employee's wages for that year. The file with hours worked each week could have only the employee number, the date the week ends, and the number of hours worked that week. Both of these files are in a one-to-many relation with the basic data on employees, but it is a different one-to-many relation; one changes each week, and the other changes only once a year.

Theory and Common Sense

Even if wages did change once a year, keeping each year's wages in a separate file rather than in the same file as weekly hours worked would eliminate repetitive data entry, but it would make it more complicated to join files to produce reports.

> **NOTE** According to the theory of database normalization, it is best to keep it in a separate file, to avoid repetition. Whether you actually want to keep it in a separate file depends on how you feel about the trade-off between repetition and complexity. Many people might be willing to store some repetitive data in order to simplify the process of joining files. Common sense should take priority over database theory.

One example of the need for common sense is the question of city, state, and zip code. Because city and state depend on zip code, database theory says that you should enter only the zip code in your database, and join it with a database that holds the city and state of each zip code, so that you do not have to enter the same city and state name twice if you have two addresses in the same zip code.

Notice that there is a one-to-many relationship here, and so you can save on data entry in theory by breaking the data into two files. In reality, though, for the average user, maintaining this separate file would add so much extra complexity and do so little to eliminate repetition that it is virtually never done.

A Sample One-to-Many Relationship

As you probably have already realized, the client database that you have used as an example through this book also involves a one-to-many relationship. You do many days of work for each client.

You have already created a Clients database file to hold the basic information on clients, such as name and address. Later in this chapter, you create a second file named Hours to hold the dates that you worked for each client, and the number of hours you worked on each date.

The basic information included in the Bill At field includes the hourly rate you charge each client. This rate may change over time, and so it should also be entered for each day's work (as the wage in the last example should be entered for each week's work).

You should look at the relation between the data in the two files now, to help you understand how a one-to-many relationship works. A few records from the Client file and the corresponding records from the Hours file are illustrated; most fields of the Clients file are omitted, and only the client number and name are shown (see Figure 7.1). When Approach works with this data, it must find all the records in the Hours file with the same key field (Client Number) as each record in the Client file. In the illustration, the lines indicate which records in the two files are associated.

Clients File			Hours File			
Clienno	Fname	Lname	Clientno	Date	Hours	Rate
1	Dennis	Spring	1	5/04/94	3	65
			1	5/05/94	2	65
			1	5/06/94	1	65
			1	5/07/94	3	65
			1	5/09/94	5	65
2	Joseph	Walton	2	3/30/94	1.5	75
			2	3/31/94	2	75
			2	4/01/94	4	75
3	Donna	Walton	3	4/08/94	1	60
			3	4/09/94	4	60

Figure 7.1 A one-to-many relationship.

NOTE The Hours file may have anywhere from zero to an indefinite number of records for any record in the Clients file. You may work any number of days for a given client, or you may have entered a new client for whom you have not yet done any work. On the other hand, there must be a record in the Clients file for each record in the Hours file. You cannot record the number of hours you worked for a client unless you have a clients name and an address to which you can send a bill.

Many-to-Many Relationships

Many-to-many relations are also fairly common in business applications.

Imagine that you do not deal with your clients yourself but have employees deal with them. If each client was assigned permanently to one employee, then you would still have a one-to-many relationship. Each client works with one employee, and each employee works with many clients.

On the other hand, if any employee were able to deal with any client, then you would have a many-to-many relationship. Each client may deal with many employees, and each employee may deal with many clients.

The way to work with a many-to-many relationship of this sort is to break it up into two one-to-many relationships. You do this by creating an additional file that links the two files involved.

In the example, you would have an Employee file, which includes the employee number and the basic data (such as name and address) for the employee, and you also have a Client file, which includes the client number and the basic data (such as name and address) for each client. You would also create a Jobs file that link these two. The Jobs file could contain the client number, the date the work was done, the number of hours worked, the bill rate for that job, the rate the employee was paid for that job, and the employee number of the person who did that job. This assumes that employees are paid by the hour and that their wage can change, so that it must be recorded for each job, like the client's billing rate.

Notice that the many-to-many relationship between employees and clients has been broken up into two one-to-many relationships, because the Jobs file is in a one-to-many relation to each of the two other files (see Figure 7.2).

- One employee may do many jobs, and each job is done by only one employee.
- One client may have many jobs done, and each job is done for only one client.

You can use key fields to join the files and produce reports just as you do when you are working with one-to-many relationships.

For example, for the purpose of billing clients, you use the client number in the Client file and the client number in the Jobs file to join the two files. Then you can produce a report with each client's name and address, and the dates, hours, and billing rates for that client. This is exactly the same as the one-to-many relationship between the Clients and Hours file that you looked at previously.

Clients File			Hours File							
Clienno	Fname	Lname	Clientno	Date	Hours	Rate	Empno	Empno	Fname	Lname
1	Dennis	Spring	1	5/04/94	3	65	1	1	John	Doe
			1	5/05/94	2	65	1			
			1	5/06/94	1	65	2	2	Jane	Smith
			1	5/07/94	3	65	2			
			1	5/09/94	5	65	2			
2	Joseph	Walton	2	3/30/94	1.5	75	2			
			2	3/31/94	2	75	2			
			2	4/01/94	4	75	3	3	Chris	Jones
3	Donna	Walton	3	4/08/94	1	60	3			
			3	4/09/94	4	60	3			

Figure 7.2 Breaking up a many-to-many relationship into two one-to-many relationships.

For the purpose of paying employees, you use the employee numbers in the Employee file and the Jobs file to join the two files, so you can produce a report with each employee's name and address, and the date, hours, and wage rate for that job. This is a one-to-many relationship, just like the one you use to bill the client.

Other Types of Relationships

There are also more complex cases, with multiple one-to-many and many-to-many relationships. Imagine that, rather than providing a service to clients, your employees sold products to regular customers. Then, you would not only need an Employee file and a Customer file, like the ones described above; you would also need a Products file, with the product number, description, and price of each of your products.

To work with even the most complex cases, you must look for the many-to-many relationships among files and break each down into two one-to-many relations. Ultimately, even the most complex cases can be broken down into a large number of one-to-many relationships.

Later in this chapter, you do exercises that show you the different ways you can work with the one-to-many relationship between the Clients and Hours file. Because any data can be broken down in this sort of relationship, these exercises teach you the techniques you need to know to work with more complex cases.

Before going on to learn the techniques that you use to work with relational databases there are a few more basic points about relationships among files that you should understand.

Many-to-One Relationships

Often, it is also useful to organize data in many-to-one rather than in one-to-many relationships. This does not involve a difference in the way that the data is normalized or in the data itself–just in the way that you use the data to create a form or report.

When you create a one-to-many relationship, as you have seen, you use the one file first, and then join the many file to it. This relationship means that there are many records of the second file that must be displayed in combination with each record of the first. For example, you would display many records of the days and hours you worked for each client on the same form as each client's name and address. This is done by using the Clients file as the *main file* of a form and adding a *repeating panel* to the form to hold multiple records from the Hours file.

When you create a many-to-one relationship, on the other hand, you use the many file as the *main file,* and join the *one file* to it. In a many-to-one relationship there is one record in the Clients file for each Record in the Hours file—one client whom you worked for during those hours (see Figure 7.3).

You do not need a repeating panel to create a report or other design based on a many-to-one relationship. For example, you can create a form using the Hours file, which shows the day and hours worked for each job, as the main file, and add fields with the name of the client you did that job for to each record in the Hours file.

> **NOTE**
> With a one-to-many relationship, you must use a repeating panel, with all the jobs for a client on a single form. With a many-to-one relationship, you can display each job on a separate form, with the client's name and address. There is no difference in the data, just in the way that you want to use it.

Hours File				Clients File		
Clientno	Date	Hours	Rate	Clienno	Fname	Lname
1	5/04/94	3	65	1	Dennis	Spring
1	5/05/94	2	65			
1	5/06/94	1	65			
1	5/07/94	3	65			
1	5/09/94	5	65			
2	3/30/94	1.5	75	2	Joseph	Walton
2	3/31/94	2	75			
2	4/01/94	4	75			
3	4/08/94	1	60	3	Donna	Walton
3	4/09/94	4	60			

Figure 7.3 A many-to-one relationship.

Because there is one client for each record in the Hours file, you can add fields from the Clients file to forms based on the Hours file, use them to sort the records from the Hours file, and so on.

Obviously, though, you should not simply add fields from the Hours file to forms based on the Clients file, because there is not a unique value in the Hours file for each record in the Clients file.

One-to-One Relationships

Finally, you should know that you can also join files in a one-to-one relationship.

As you know, it is generally best to keep all the fields that are in a one-to-one relation with each other in a single file, rather than breaking them up in this way and then relating them.

> **NOTE** There might be rare cases where you have some reason to break up data into files that are in a one-to-one relation to each other. Generally it is better to keep all the data in one file and to exclude fields that you do not need from the forms and reports you use to work on the file. Excluding the fields from the file itself just creates unnecessary complexity.

You may find it useful to join files that have a one-to-one relation if you have data in a file that was gathered independently, which happens to have some fields (such as social security number) that can be used as a key field.

The Key Field

Before you go on to look at how to work with relational databases, you should take a moment to look at the sort of data that should be used as a key field.

WARNING In general, it is best to use some arbitrary value, such as an employee number as a key field. Novices are sometimes tempted to use a meaningful field, such as the last name, as the key field, but this is never a good idea. It creates problems if a second person must be added who has the same last name as someone already in the database. Also, it creates problems if someone changes his or her name; you have to re-enter the data in every file in the relational database. This is just the sort of repetitive data entry that relational databases are meant to avoid.

The only possible exception is social security number or some other number (such as a business taxpayer identification number) that is sure to be unique and unchanging, because it is actually used as the key field in some other database. Even this can create problems if you have a client who is not from this country and does not have a social security number. It also creates extra data entry, since you do not need as long a number as a unique identifier for all your employees or clients, as the federal government needs to keep track of everyone in the country.

Since you always break a relational database down into files that have a one-to-many relationship, you must be aware of the constraints on the key field in both of the files in this sort of relationship. These constraints are obvious when you consider the way that this sort of relationship works, thinking about the examples that you looked at above.

Note that the key field must have data entered in it in every record of both the one and the many file; otherwise that record cannot be related to records in the other file. Every client must have a client number, or you have no way of keeping track of the jobs you do for that client. Every job must have a client number, or you have no way of knowing which client you did the job for.

Though both require an entry, there are different constraints on the data that may be entered in the one and the many file.

Key Fields in the One File

The key field in the one file must be unique for each record. There must be only one record in this file for each record in the many file.

In the sample database, the Client file must have only one record with each client number; that is, every client must have a different client number. If you have an entry in the Hours file, Approach must find only one client to bill for those hours. If there were two records in the Client file with the same client number, there would be no way to know which one a record in the Hours file should be joined with. You would not know which of the two clients to bill for those hours of work.

WARNING

In addition, the value in key fields in this file must never be changed, or there will be massive loss of data. Imagine that you have one hundred records in the Hours file with Client Number 1, and you change the client number of Client Number 1 in the Client file. You suddenly would not know whom to bill for any of the hundred jobs done for Client Number 1. The jobs are still listed in the Hours file, but they are orphans without an equivalent record in the Clients file.

Key Fields in the Many File

The key field in the many file must have a value that is in some field in the one file. There must be data in the one file to relate to each record in the many file.

In the sample database, you should not enter a job in the Hours file with a client number unless there is a client with that client number. You must have a record in the Client file, so there is someone to bill for the job.

Notice that, unlike records in the one file, records in the many file can have their client number changed without massive data loss. If you discover that you entered hours for Client Number 1 when you actually did the work for Client Number 2, you can simply change the Client Number in the record in the Hours file to 2, so it is joined with the appropriate record in the Clients file.

Using Relational Databases in Approach

When you work with a relational database in Approach, first you must create its database files, as you create any database file. Then you use the Join dialog box to join the files.

When you create a form, report, or other design for this database, you must decide which to use as the *main database* file and which to use as the *detail database* file. When you finish using the Assistant to create the view, Approach displays a dialog box that lets you select the main database file for that design. You can also select the **Main database** drop-down on the Basics panel of the View's Info Box to change the main database (see Figure 7.4).

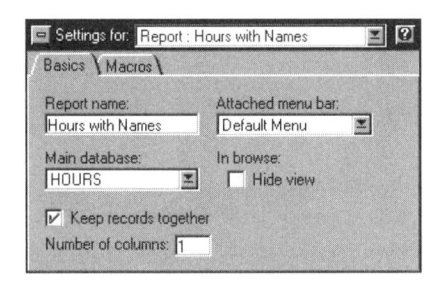

Figure 7.4 Selecting the main database.

You can use the same join and create designs based on either a one-to-many or a many-to-one relation as follows:

- To create a one-to-many relationship, select the one file as the main database and the many file as the detail database. Use a form with a repeating panel, as explained above, in order to display the many records of detail database file along with each record of the main database file. For example, make the Client database the main database, and use the repeating panel to display all the jobs you have worked for each client under that client's name and address.
- To create a many-to-one relationship, select the many file as the main database and the one file as the detail database. Add fields from the detail file to forms or other designs in the usual way. As you have learned, many dialog boxes have a drop-down list above the fields list

that lets you select a different database file to use fields from it. For the reasons discussed above, you can use this drop-down list to add a field to the design when you are working with a many-to-one relationship, but not when you are working with a one-to-many relationship.

In this section, you learn how to join two databases and how to create a design with a repeating panel. Use of the drop-down list to select files from another file is so similar to what you have learned earlier that it does not need special treatment. It is illustrated in the next section, which includes exercises where you work with both a one-to-many and a many-to-one relationship.

Joining Two Databases

To join two database files, choose Join from the Create menu to display the Join dialog box. A field list for the database you are currently using is included in the dialog box (see Figure 7.5).

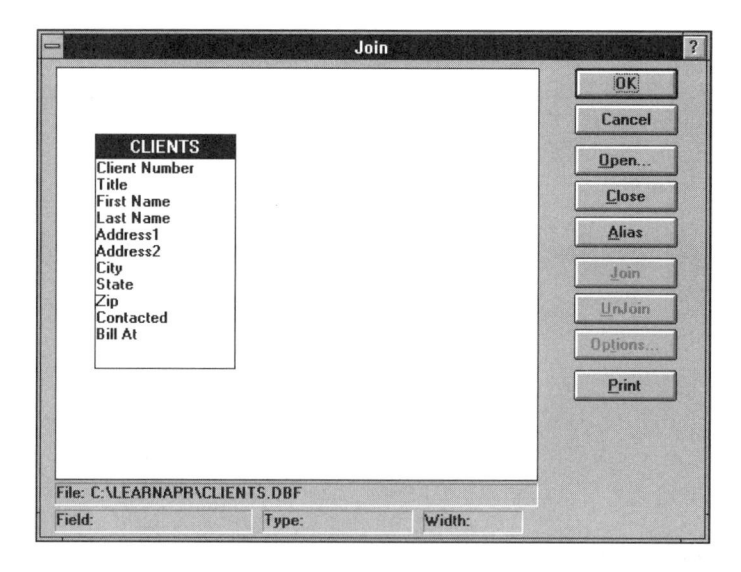

Figure 7.5 The Join dialog box.

Select **Open** to display the Open dialog box. Select the other file in the usual way (see Figure 7.6).

Chapter 7: Working with Relational Databases

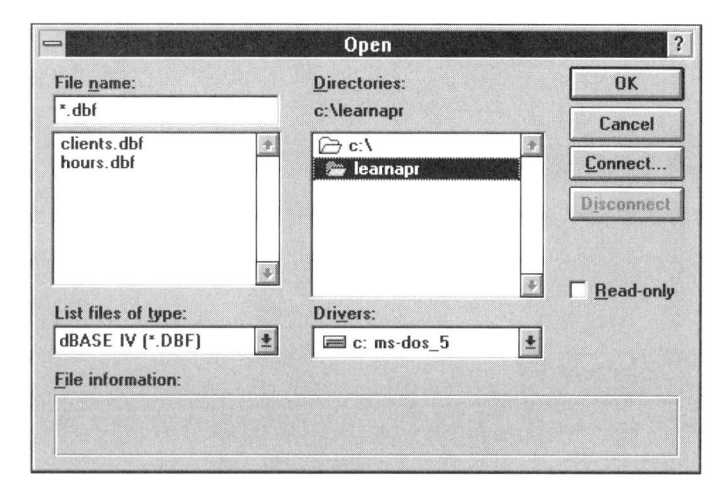

Figure 7.6 Selecting the detail file.

When you select **OK**, the second file is added to the Join dialog box. Both files are displayed as lists of fields with the file name in their title bars. Simply select the key fields that you want to use to join the files, and select the **Join** button. A line joins the two fields where the Clients database files are joined using the Client Number field as key field (see Figure 7.7).

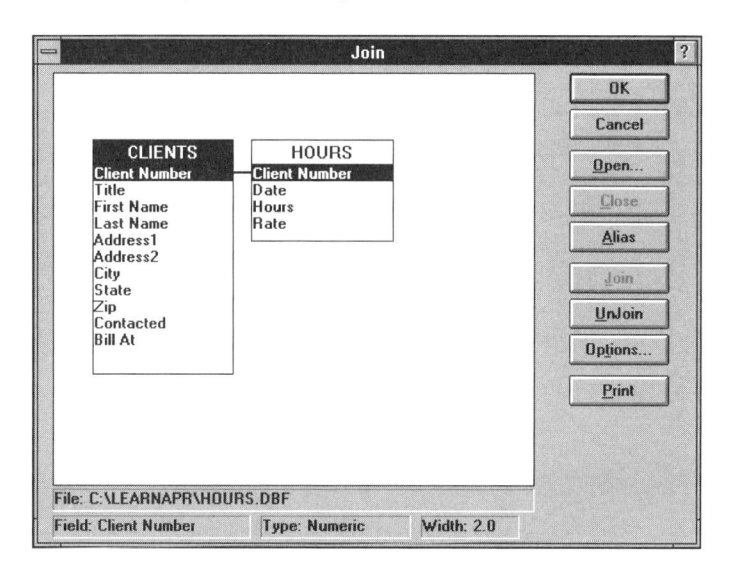

Figure 7.7 Joining two files.

Though the key fields are not required to have the same name or type, the join is less likely to have problems if you make them the same data type and length. Most users also find it easiest to give them the same name.

If it makes it easier for you to work with the files, you can move these field lists simply by clicking and dragging their title bars. You can also select a field list by clicking its title bar, and then selecting the **Close** push button to remove it from the dialog box. This option is accessible if the selected file is not joined to another file.

Unjoining Databases

To eliminate a join that you have created, first select it in the Join dialog box. A join is automatically selected in this way when you first create it, and you can select it at any time by clicking the line that represents the join. This line is thicker when the join is selected.

When a join is selected, the **UnJoin** button is enabled, and you can click it to eliminate the join.

If you have created forms or repeating panels based on the join, they are removed when you eliminate this join. Approach displays a dialog box warning you that this will happen and asks for confirmation before it eliminates the join.

The Relational Options Dialog Box

You can specify data entry options for a join by double-clicking it or by selecting it and then selecting **Options** to display the Relational Options dialog box (see Figure 7.8).

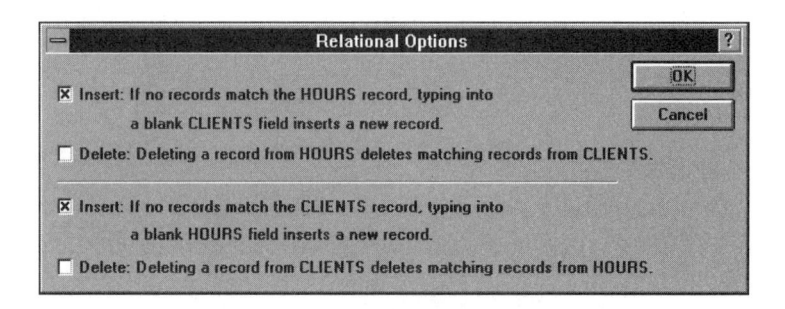

Figure 7.8 The Relational Options dialog box.

As you can see from the illustration, Approach lets you automatically insert or delete records in both the detail and main file when records are inserted or deleted in the other file.

It makes sense to select all of these check boxes if the two files have a one-to-one relation. Then whenever a new record is inserted in or deleted from either file, a corresponding record is added to or deleted from the other file. The two files work just like a single file, where you must add or delete all the fields of a record at once.

> **WARNING** If you are using a many-to-one or a one-to-many relationship, it is dangerous to select either of the **Delete** check boxes—and particularly dangerous to select the check box that deletes the records of the one file whenever the corresponding record is deleted in the many file. Imagine deleting one record of the hours that you worked for a client (perhaps because you entered it by mistake) and having the client record deleted automatically; you could no longer find the person to bill for any job that you have ever done for that client in the past.

Both **Insert** check boxes are selected by default. You will see that it is useful to have records added to the many file automatically when you are using a form with a repeating panel. There are cases where you would want to add a new record to the one file whenever you add one to the "many file," so you can enter data in both at the same time. Usually, however, it is best to set up a database so you cannot enter any record in the "many file" unless there is already a corresponding record in the "one file": even if you validate data in this way, there is no harm to having the **Insert** checkbox selected.

Using an Alias Join

The Alias button is an advanced feature of the Join dialog box, which lets you join a database to itself.

If you click **Alias**, it adds a second copy of the database to this dialog box. The numbers 1 and 2 are added to the name of the database in the title bar of the two lists in the Join dialog box, but the name of the database does not change anywhere else.

You can join these two copies of the same database just as you join any two databases.

This is useful only in special cases. For example, if some of your employees manage others, you could have an Employee Number and a Manager Number field in the database. In the Manager Number field, you could enter the employee number of the person who manages that employee. Then you could join the database to itself, by joining the Manager Number field to the Employee Number field, and create a form which displays the name of each manager and a repeating panel under it that lists all the employees he or she manages.

Most users do not need this advanced feature of joins.

Printing the Join

You can select the **Print** button to display the Print dialog box and print the contents of the Join dialog box. The Print dialog box was covered in Chapter 5.

Repeating Panels

After you have done a join to create a one-to-many relationship, you may create a form for the one file that includes a repeating panel in it to hold the corresponding records for the many file.

> **NOTE** When you create forms for relational databases, the file names are included before the field names in Design mode, separated from them with a period, so you know which file each field in the form is from. For example, the First Name field of the Clients file is displayed as Clients.First Name.

Using the Form Assistant

The easiest way to create a form with a repeating panel is by using the Form Assistant. Select **Form** from the Create menu to display the Assistant, and select **Standard with Repeating Panel** as the SmartMaster layout. Approach adds an extra step to the Assistant: Step 3: Panel.

Use steps 1 and 2 in the usual way to specify the layout of the form and its Fields. Bear in mind, though, that the Fields panel should only be used to select the fields from the one file that you want to include in the form.

Then choose **Step 3: Panel** to select and add the fields that are included in the repeating panel (see Figure 7.9). You can see that this panel works just like Step 2, but you should use it only to select fields from the many file.

Chapter 7: Working with Relational Databases

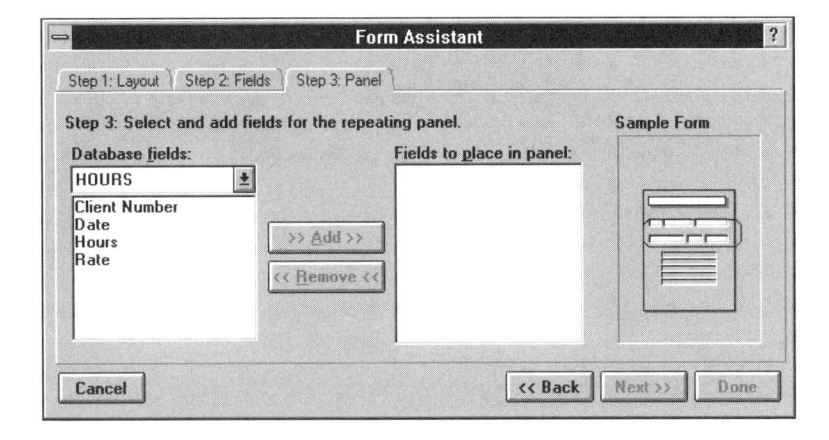

Figure 7.9 Specifying fields for the repeating panel.

When you select **Done**, Approach generates a form with a repeating panel.

Adding a Repeating Panel to a Form

You can also add a repeating panel to an existing form. Display a form that is based on the one file in Design view. Then choose **Repeating Panel** from the Create menu to display the Add Repeating Panel Dialog box (see Figure 7.10).

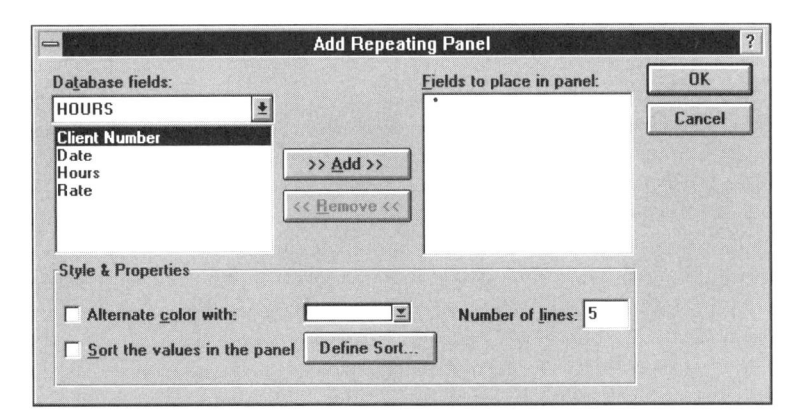

Figure 7.10 The Add Repeating Panel to Form dialog box.

Use this dialog box in the usual way to select the fields to include in the repeating panel.

The Style & Properties panel of this dialog box let you select properties of the repeating panel that you can also control using its Info Box. They are covered below in the section on *The Info Box for a Repeating Panel*.

Choose **OK** to add the panel to the Form.

Working with a Repeating Panel

In either case, a repeating panel is added to the form (see Figure 7.11).

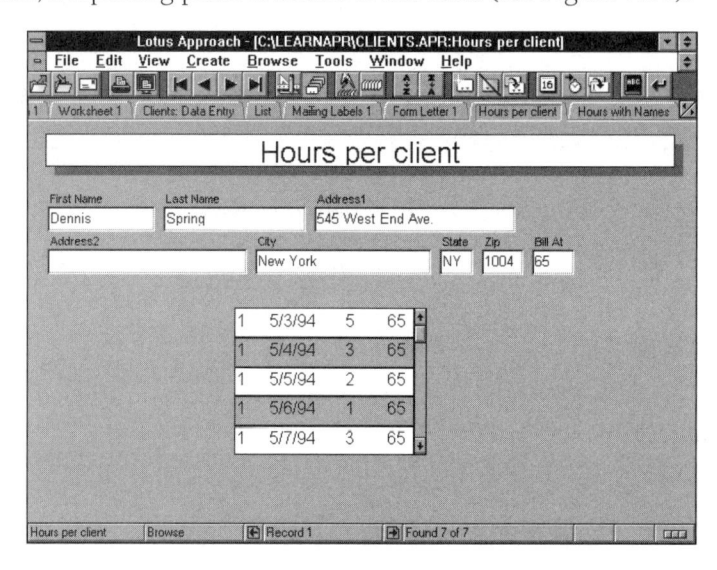

Figure 7.11 A repeating panel.

You can manipulate the panel as you do other objects in a Form. You can also manipulate the individual field objects in it.

Selecting a Repeating Panel

Select the panel by clicking its border. It is given a dark border to indicate that it is selected (see Figure 7.12). Notice the border of the entire panel is darkened, and there is also a highlighted border around the first line of the panel. The border around the first line is used to resize the panel.

> **SHORTCUT** If the Show Data option is turned off, you can click anywhere on the repeating panel to select it. In general, it is easier to work with repeating panels if Show Data is off.

Chapter 7: Working with Relational Databases

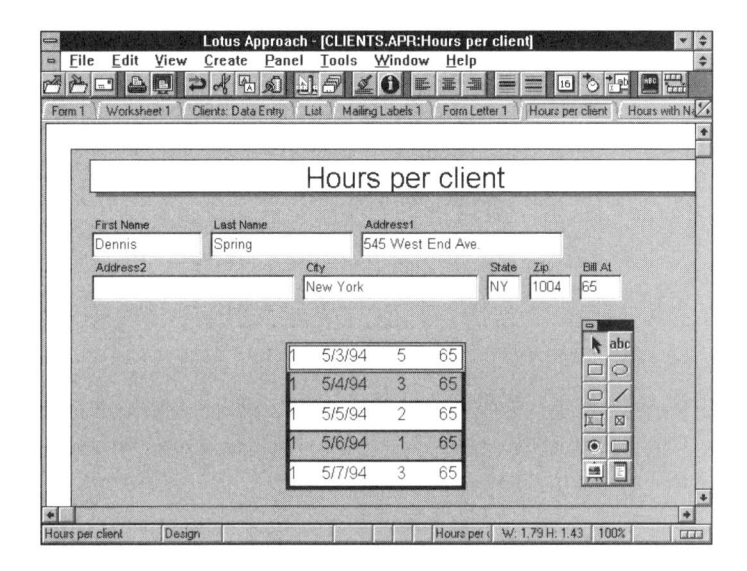

Figure 7.12 Selecting a Repeating Panel.

Moving a Repeating Panel

Once it is selected, you can simply click and drag the panel to move it. When you move the pointer to the selected panel, it is displayed as a hand, to indicate that it is in a location where it can be used to move an object.

Resizing a Repeating Panel

To resize a repeating panel, you must click and drag the border of its top line–not the border of the panel as a whole. The pointer is displayed as a two headed arrow when it is on the border of the top line, to show that you can resize the panel.

Resize the panel as you do other objects:

- Click and drag the sides of this border left or right to make it narrower or wider.
- Click and drag the top or bottom of this border up or down to make it taller or shorter. When you do this, you resize the single line whose border you are dragging, and all the other lines of the panel automatically become the same size.

- Click or drag the corners of this border to resize both height and width simultaneously.

Whichever edge you drag, the upper-left corner of the panel remains in the same place. If you drag the left border rightward, for example, when you are done, the panel is narrowed by the amount you have dragged it, but the left edge remains in the same place—as if you had dragged the right edge to narrow it.

To keep the panel properly centered, you can move it after resizing it.

The Info Box for a Repeating Panel

Display a Repeating Panel's Info Box as you do the Info Box for any object. Select the panel and, if necessary, choose **Style & Properties** from the Panel menu, or click the **Info Box** icon.

Use the Basics panel of the Info Box to specify the following properties (see Figure 7.13):

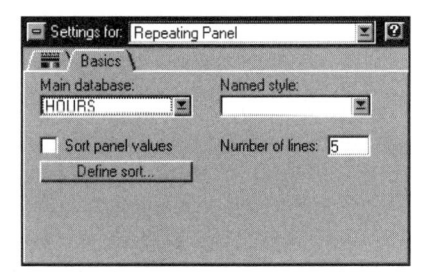

Figure 7.13 The Basic properties of a Repeating Panel.

- Use the **Main database** drop-down to select the main database of the panel. *Do not* confuse this with the main database of the entire form, which is the one database of the "one"-to-many relationship. The main database of the panel is the "many" database of the one-to-"many" relationship that the form is based on. You might want to change the main database of the panel if you are using a more complex relationship, that has other databases joined to the fields displayed in the panel, such as the many-to-many relationship described above.

- Use the **Number of Lines** text box to specify how many lines should be included in the repeating panel. If there is more data than can be displayed in this number of lines, a scroll bar is added to the repeating panel, so you can scroll through all the data.

- Use the **Named style** drop-down to apply a named style to the panel.
- Use the **Sort** panel values checkbox if you want to control the order of the records in the panel. Click the **Define sort** button to display the Sort dialog box, and use it to define the sort order.

The borders and colors panel of the Info Box has features similar to those used by other types of object (see Figure 7.14).

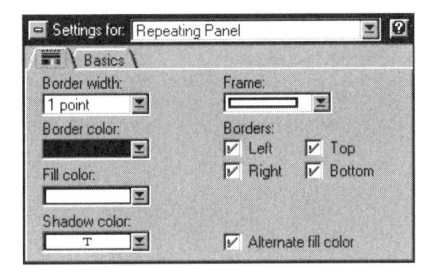

Figure 7.14   The colors and borders properties of a repeating panel.

In addition you can select the **Alternate Panel Background With** checkbox to display alternating lines in the repeating panel with different background colors, if this makes it easier to view. Use the **Fill color** drop-down to select a color or pattern to be used for every second line in the repeating panel. It alternates with white lines.

> **NOTE** If you are using the menu to add a repeating panel to an existing form, many of these properties can also be set in the Add Repeating Panel to Form dialog box, covered previously. If you use the Assistant to create the panel, you must set these properties using the Info Box.

Working with the Field Objects in a Repeating Panel

All the fields that you selected in the dialog box are included in the repeating panel as individual field objects. As in columnar reports, the field objects are displayed only once if you turn Show Data off, but the data is repeated for every record in the file. If there are more records than fit in the repeating panel, a scroll bar is added to its right, which you can use to view them all.

You can work with these field objects as you do with the fields in any design:

- Click a field object to select it.
- Click and drag a handle of a selected field object to resize it.
- Click and drag a field object to move it.
- Double-click a field object or select a field object and choose **Field style** to use the Field Style dialog box to specify the style of the field.
- Select a field object to use its Info Box to format the data displayed in the field, specify the fill color, line style, and other properties and styles of the field.

NOTE: You must resize a repeating panel and its fields in tandem. For example, if you make the panel wider and higher, you should also resize the fields so they fit in it properly.

A Sample Relational Database

Now, you understand enough about relational database theory and about the techniques that Approach uses to handle relational databases. You can begin doing hands-on work with sample data. In the rest of this chapter, you will:

1. Define the fields of an Hours database file, to record the number of hours that you have worked for each client.
2. Use the Clients database and join the Hours database to it.
3. Create a data-entry form for it based on a one-to-many relationship that includes a repeating panel.
4. Create a design for it based on a many-to-one relationship.

Creating the Hours File

As you know, the Hours database file should contain fields for the date worked for a client, the number of hours worked, the client number of the client, and the rate you billed at. Create the file as follows:

Chapter 7: Working with Relational Databases

1. Choose **New** from the File menu to display the New dialog box. Enter **hours.dbf** in the File Name text box. If necessary, select **learnapr** as the directory.
2. Approach displays the Field Definition dialog box. Enter **Client Number** in the Name column. Select **Numeric** as the type. Enter **2** as the length, and **0** as the number of decimal places. Select the **Add** push button to add it to the fields list.
3. For the second field, enter **Date** as the field name, select **Date** as the type, select **Add** to add this field to the list. Next, enter **Hours** as the field name, select **Numeric** as the type, enter **1** as the length, and **2** as the number of decimal places. Finally, for the third field enter **Rate** as the name, select **Numeric** as the type, enter **3** as the length, and **0** as the number of decimal places (see Figure 7.15). Select **OK** to create the file.

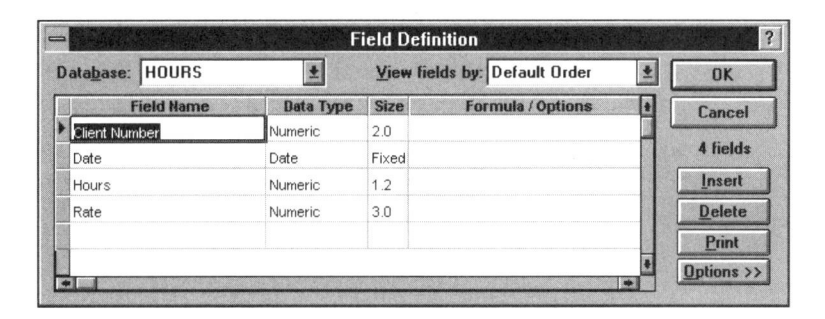

Figure 7.15 Defining the fields of the Hours database.

Working with a One-to-Many Relationship

Before designing views, you must relate the new Hours file to the Clients file.

1. Choose **Join** from the Create menu to display the Join dialog box. The Clients file is displayed.
2. Add the Hours file to the Join dialog box. Select **Open** to display the Open dialog box. Select the **hours.dbf** file from the File Name list. Select **OK** to return to the Join dialog box. The Hours file is added.
3. Join the two files. Click the **Client Number** field of the Clients file. Click the **Client Number** field of the Hours file. Both fields are high-

lighted to show they are selected. Click the **Join** button, and Approach adds a line between the two fields to show they are joined (see Figure 7.16). Select **OK**.

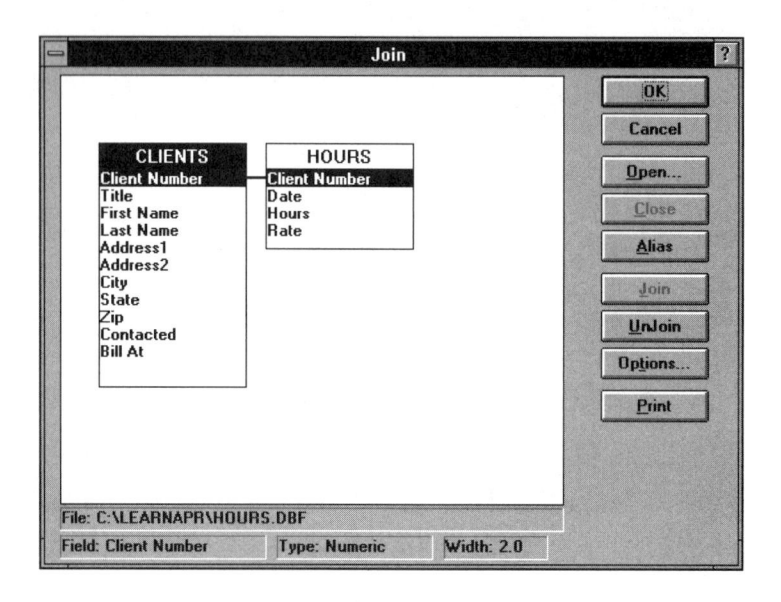

Figure 7.16 The two files are joined.

Creating a Form with a Repeating Panel

Now that you have joined the two files, you can create a data entry form with a repeating panel, based on a one-to-many relationship.

1. Choose **Form** from the Create menu to display the Form Assistant. In Step1:Layout, enter the name **Hours per client** in the view name & title text box. Leave Default Style as the SmartMaster style, and select **Standard with Repeating Panel** as the SmartMaster layout.

2. Click the **Step 2: Fields** divider tab. As the Fields for the view, select **First Name**, **Last Name**, **Address1**, **Address2**, **City**, **State**, **Zip** and **Bill At** fields in the Database fields list, and select **Add** to add them to the Fields to place on view list.

3. Click the **Step 3: Panel** divider tab. Select all the fields from the Hours table in the Database fields list, and click **Add** to add them all to the

Chapter 7: Working with Relational Databases

Panel Fields list (see Figure 7.17). Click the **Done** button to create the new Form (see Figure 7.18).

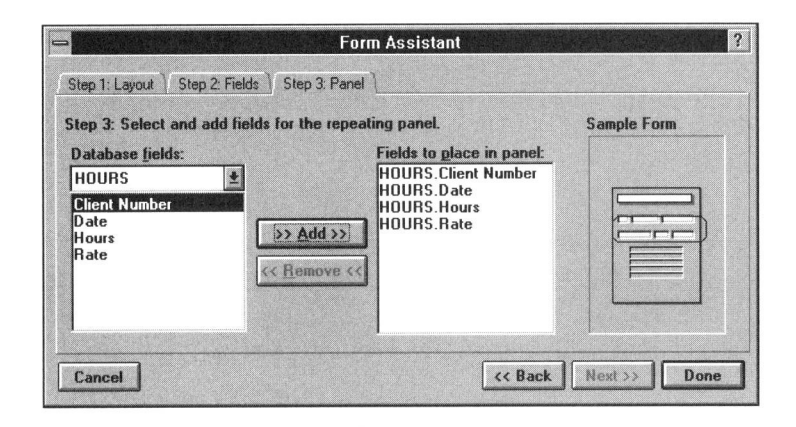

Figure 7.17 Creating the new form.

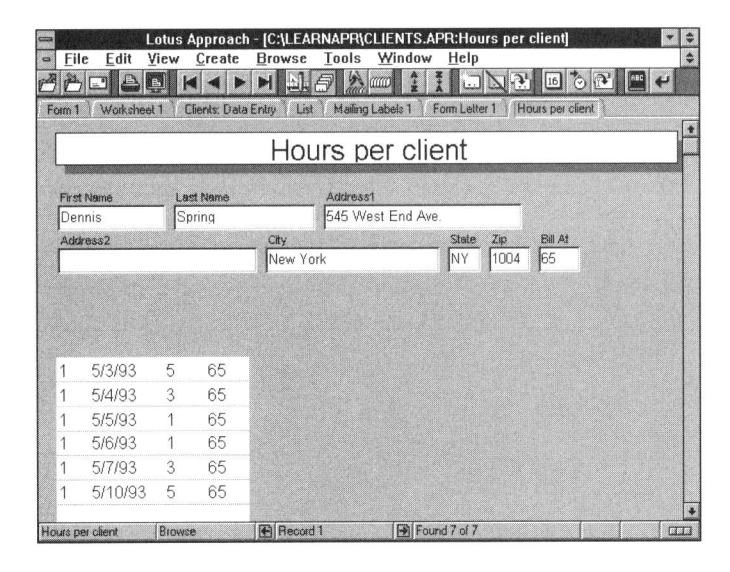

Figure 7.18 The Hours per Client form.

4. If necessary, click the **Design** icon to switch to design mode, and click the **Info Box** icon to display the Info Box. Select the repeating panel. In the Basics Panel of the Info Box, enter **5** in the Number of Lines text

box. In the other panel, select **Alternate fill color**, and **Select All of the Borders** checkboxes.

5. Click and drag the border of the repeating panel to resize it. Remember you must click its upper line, which is highlighted with a lighter color than the rest of the panel. Resize and move the panel, so that the repeating panel is centered below the fields already on the form, with a bit of space above it for column headings (see Figure 7.19).

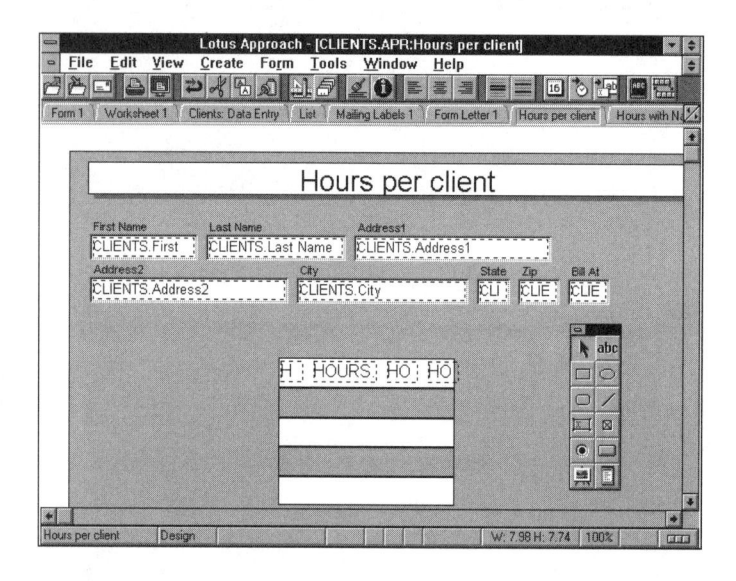

Figure 7.19 Locating the repeating panel.

6. Now, click the **Text** drawing tool. Click and drag to a place a text object above the repeating panel that is a bit wider than the repeating panel. Use the Info Box to select **8 points** as the font size. Type **Client No.** at the left of the text object, press the **Spacebar** to move the cursor until it is over the Hours.Date field, and type **Date**. Press the **Spacebar** to move the cursor until it is over the Hours.Hours field, and type **Hours**. Press the **Spacebar** to move the cursor until it is over the Hours.Rate field, and type **Rate** (see Figure 7.20).

Chapter 7: Working with Relational Databases

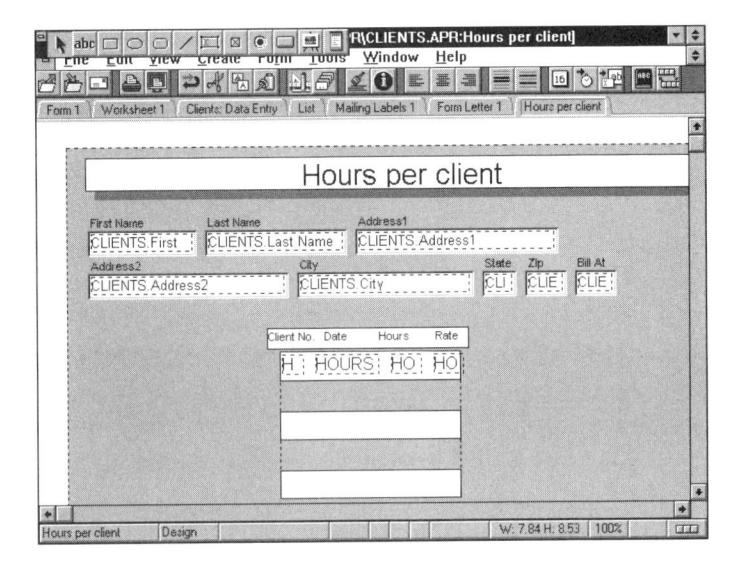

Figure 7.20 The final design of the form.

Working with Data

Now that you have created a data entry form, you can add some sample data to the Hours file.

1. Click the **Browse** icon to view the new form in Browse mode. Try clicking the **Arrow** icons to view a few records. Notice that if you display any record in the main database and click the Client Number field of the repeating panel, the client number is added to it automatically (see Figure 7.21). If you do this, press **Esc** to cancel data entry, so you do not add a record to the Hours file with just the client number in it.

2. Click the **Start Arrow** to view Dennis Spring's record, and add some sample data to the Hours file. Since the Client Number is entered automatically, click the **Date** field in the first line of the repeating panel. Type **5/3/94**. Press **Tab** to move to the Hours field, and type **5**. Press **Tab** to move to the Rate field and type **65**, the rate in the Bill At field.

3. Now that you have entered one record in the Hours file, click the **New Record** icon or choose **New Record** from the Browse menu. Approach adds a second record to the repeating panel, also with a Client Number of 1. In this record, enter **5/4/94** as the Date, **3** as the number of Hours, and **65** as the Rate.

Practical Approach, 3.0

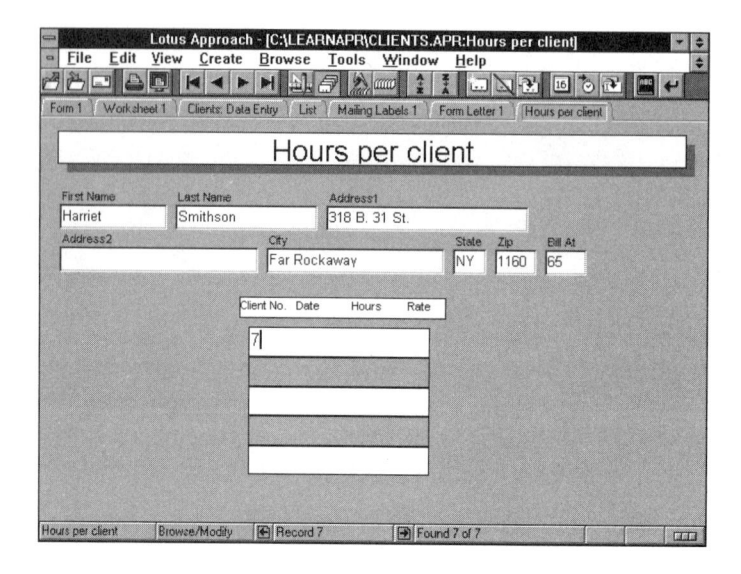

Figure 7.21 The Hours per Client form in Browse mode.

4. Keep adding new records to the repeating panel in the same way, and make the following entries:

   ```
   DATE         HOURS     RATE
   5/05/94      2         65
   5/06/94      1         65
   5/07/94      3         65
   5/10/94      5         65
   ```

   Of course, all have the client number of **1** added automatically. You have added enough records for this client to see the Scroll Bar that is added to the repeating panel when it has more than the five records you specified it should display (see Figure 7.22).

5. Click the **Next Arrow** to move to the next record, for Joseph Walton. The Client Number of **2** automatically is entered in the Client Number field of the repeating panel as you enter the following records:

   ```
   DATE         HOURS     RATE
   3/29/94      3         75
   3/30/94      1.5       75
   3/31/94      2         75
   4/01/94      4         75
   ```

Chapter 7: Working with Relational Databases

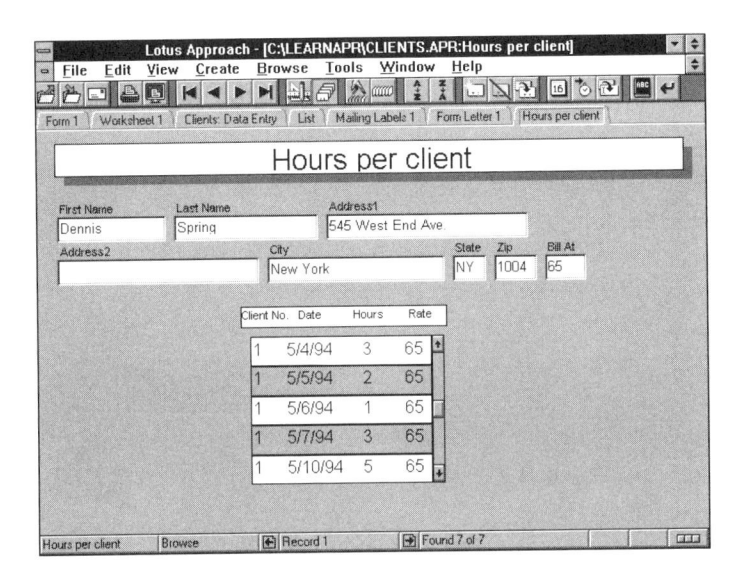

Figure 7.22 A scroll bar is added to the repeating panel.

6. Click the **Next Arrow** again and add data for just one more client: Donna Walton. Enter the following records in the repeating panel:

DATE	HOURS	RATE
4/7/94	2	60
4/8/94	1	60
4/9/94	4	60

   Of course, you must leave the Client Number as **3** in all the records.

7. That is enough records for purposes of illustration, though you can also add hours for other clients if you would like. You should try clicking the arrows in the icon bar and pressing **Tab** and **Shift+Tab**, trying out other features of the form, so you can see how it works. Try adding a new record when the cursor is in one of the fields of the Clients file. You see that Approach adds a new record for that file—not to the repeating panel, as it did when you were entering data with the cursor in the repeating panel.

8. Try changing a Client Number in the repeating panel. Approach displays a warning dialog box stating the field is used in a join (see Figure 7.23).

NOTE: In serious applications, it is best to make the Client Number field, or a similar key field in a repeating panel, into a Read Only field, so it can not be changed by mistake. As you know, you can do this by selecting Read Only in the Basics panel of its Info Box. Then the value that is entered automatically can never be changed. In fact, in this application, you do not even need to include the Client Number in the repeating panel, though it was included in the exercise so you can see how it works.

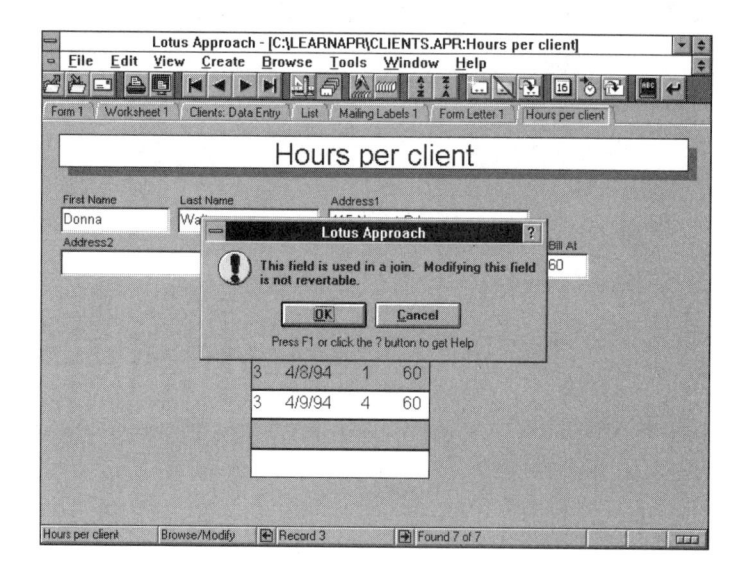

Figure 7.23 Approach warns you not to change data in the key field.

Working with a Many-to-One Relationship

Now you should try creating a many-to-one relationship by creating a report that uses the Hours file as the main file and the Clients file as the detail file. You get a clearer idea of the difference between a many-to-one and a one-to-many relationship when you see that you can look at the same data in both ways.

Remember, when you are working with a many-to-one relationship, you can add fields from the detail file to a design simply by using the drop-down list to select the file's name. Those fields are displayed for each record in the many file.

WARNING: As you learned earlier, there can be massive loss of data if you change the key field in a record of the one file of a relational database. For this reason, it is dangerous to add the key field from the one file to a design based on a many-to-one relationship. Displaying multiple copies of this key field, one for each record in the many file, makes it more likely to be edited by mistake.

Views Based on a Many-to-One Relationship

In the following exercise you create a columnar report based on a many-to-one relationship, so it is easy to see all the records at once. The same method can be used to add fields from the detail file of a many-to-one database to any design.

1. Choose **Report** from the Create menu to display the Report Assistant. As the View name and title, enter **Hours with Names**. Leave the Default Style. As the SmartMaster layout, leave **Columnar** selected.

2. Click the **Step 2: Fields** divider tab. Clients should already be selected in the Database drop-down. Double-click **Last Name** and **First Name** in the Database Fields list to add them to the Fields to place on view. Select **Hours** from the Database drop-down, select **Date**, **Hours** and **Rate** in the Database Fields list, and click **Add** to add them to the Fields to place on view list (see Figure 7.24). Select **Done** to generate the report.

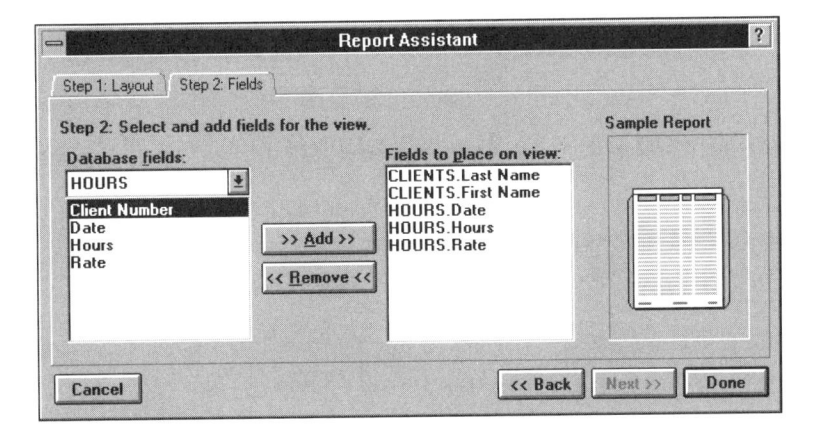

Figure 7.24 Adding fields from both files to a report.

3. When Approach displays a dialog box to let you select the main database, select **Hours.** The report is shown in Figure 7.25.

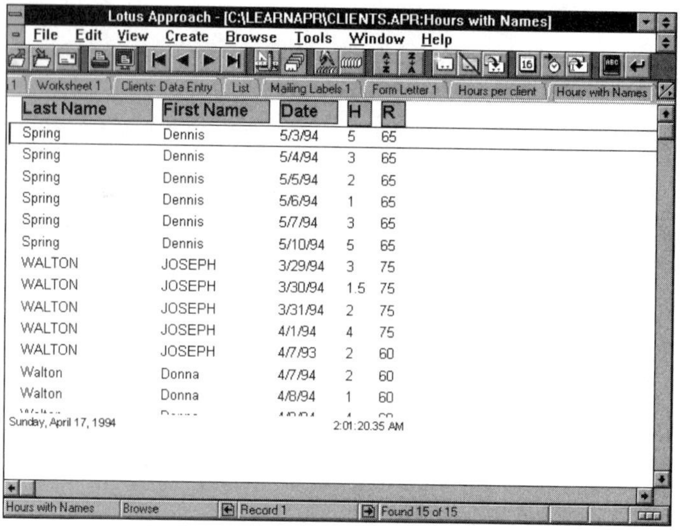

Figure 7.25 A columnar report with Hours as the main database.

Now you can see why you have to use the many database as the main database in this sort of report on a many-to-one relationship. It is of no use displaying one record for each record in the Clients table and only one matching record in the Hours table displayed to its right, while the other records from the Hours table are hidden. The purpose of this sort of report is to display the records from the Hours table with a bit of extra data from the Clients table (such as the name) added to each one.

Other Uses of Fields from the Detail File of a Many-to-One Relationship

You have seen, when you are working with a many-to-one relationship, you can add fields from the detail file to a report or other view, just as you add fields from the main file. Likewise, when you are using any dialog box that has a file drop-down list, you can use fields from the detail file just as you do fields from the main file if you are working with a design based on a many-to-one relationship.

As an example, try sorting the records in the report you just created, first using a field from the main file and then fields from the detail file as the basis of the sort.

1. Sort the data by date, so the work you did earliest is displayed first. Place the cursor in the Date field, and click the **Sort Ascending** icon. The report is sorted by date, from earliest to latest (see Figure 7.26).

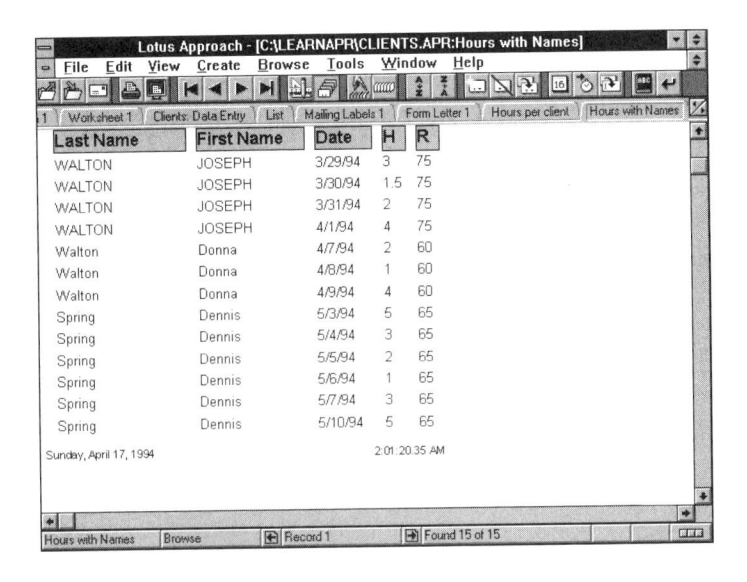

Figure 7.26 A sort based on a field in the main file.

2. Sort the report alphabetically by name. Choose **Sort** from the Browse menu, and **Define** from the submenu. If necessary, remove the Date field form the Sort list and select **Clients** from the Fields drop-down list. Double-click the **Last Name** and **First Name** fields to add them to the Sort list. Select **OK**. The report is sorted by name.

You can also use records from both files as the basis of a single sort. Just select one file from the drop-down list and add fields from it to the Sort list, then select the other file from the drop-down list and add fields from it to the Sort list. When all of the fields are added, select **OK**.

Adding a Validity Check

You should also validate the data entered in the Hours file. Now that you are using this sample data, you see how obvious it is that the key field in the many *file should* be checked against the key field in the one file. You cannot work for a client unless there is a client with that number.

1. Choose **Field Definition** from the Create menu to display the Field Definition dialog box. Select **Hours** from the Database drop-down to display its field definitions. Click **Options** to display the dialog box its enlarged form.
2. Click the **Validation** divider tab of this dialog box. In the Validation panel, click the **In field** check box. The drop-down list should already display the Clients file, and the **Client Number** field should be selected in the Field list below it, if not, select it (see Figure 7.27). Select **OK** to return to the Field Definition dialog box, select **OK** again to return to the Field Style dialog box, and select **OK** again to return to the design.

Now, a user will not be able to enter invalid data in this field. You should generally include a similar validity check for the key field on the many file in a one-to-many relationship.

You can also use records from both files as the basis of a single sort. Just select one file from the drop-down list and add fields from it to the Sort list, then select the other file from the drop-down list and add fields from it to the Sort list. When all of the fields are added, select **OK**.

Adding a Validity Check

You should also validate the data entered in the Hours file. Now that you are using this sample data, you see how obvious it is that the key fields in the many file should be checked against the key field in the one file. You cannot work for a client unless there is a client with that number.

1. Choose **Field Definition** from the Create menu to display the Field Definition dialog box. Select **Hours** from the Database drop-down to display its field definitions. Click **Options** to display the dialog box in its enlarged form.
2. Click the **Validation** divider tab of this dialog box. In the Validation panel, click the **In Field** check box. The drop-down list should already display the Clients file, and the **Client Number** field should be selected in the Field list below it, if not, select it (see Figure 7.27). Select **OK** to return to the Field Definition dialog box, select **OK** again to return to the design.

Chapter 7: Working with Relational Databases

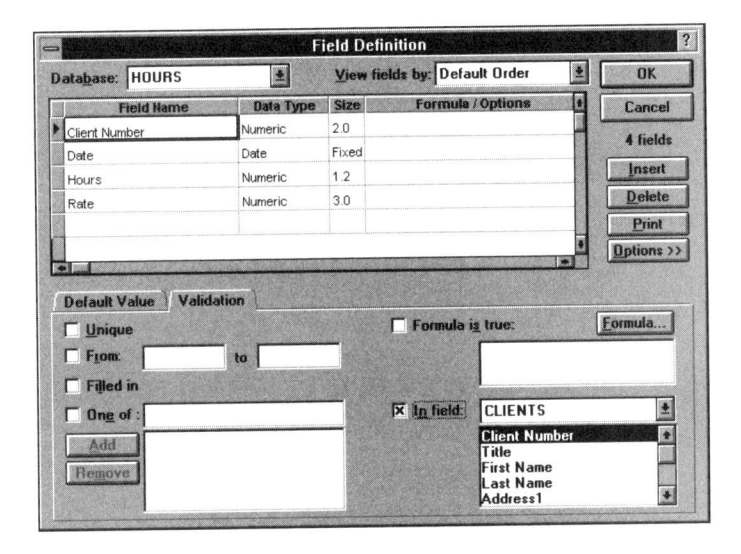

Figure 7.27 Setting up the validity check.

Now, a user will not be able to enter invalid data in this field. You should generally include a similar validity check for the key field on the many file in a one-to-many relationship.

Chapter 8

Using Approach Formulas

In the first part of this book, you glanced at several features of Approach that require the use of formulas. It is best to learn the basics of using the program before you go on to this more advanced topic. Now that you have learned how to use Approach, you can learn how formulas can be used to add more power to features of the program that were covered earlier. This chapter describes how to create and apply formulas. It covers:

- Understanding the elements that make up a formula
- Using the Formula dialog box to generate formulas
- Using operators in formulas
- Using functions in formulas
- Creating calculated fields
- Using formulas in Finds
- Using formulas to validate data entry
- Using formulas in designs and summary reports

What Is a Formula?

A *formula* is a type of calculation used by Approach. In general, you can either type a formula into a text box or generate it using the Formula dialog box (see Figure 8.1).

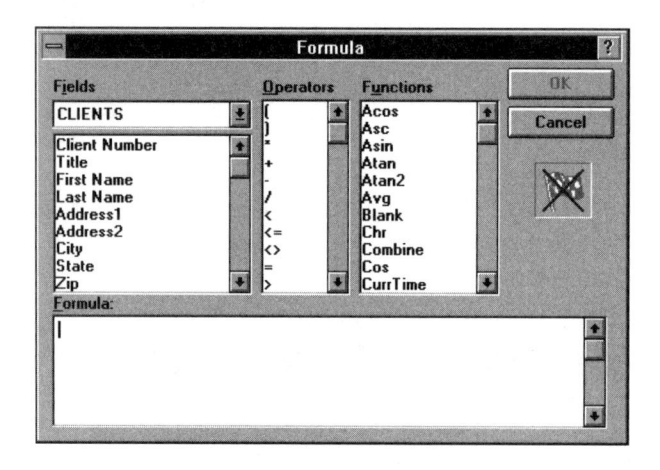

Figure 8.1 The Formula dialog box.

Formulas consist of three elements that you can see in the lists of the Formula text box in the illustration.

- *Fields.* Fields of a database, such as Last Name or Bill At.
- *Operators.* Symbols such as + (plus) or <> (not equal to).
- *Functions.* Special calculations, such as Abs (the absolute value of) or Avg (the average of).

There are also two other elements you can add to formulas:

- *Constants.* Always have the same value, including numbers (such as 2) and words. These are not selected from lists but simply typed into the Formula text box.
- *Variables.* Can be added to formulas by including a variable field in your database.

Variables are useful in macros, and are covered later in Chapter 10. In this section, you look at each of the other elements of formulas individually. After you understand formulas, you will look at the different ways they are used in the rest of this chapter.

One handy feature of this dialog box is that the **OK** button is activated only if the formula displayed is valid. In addition, a finish flag is displayed but is crossed out as long as the formula is invalid. When you have a valid formula, **Enter** is enabled and the flag is displayed without the X over it.

Fields

You already know what fields are, and you need to learn only one new point before using them in formulas.

> **NOTE** You must enclose the name of a field in double-quotation marks if it includes a space or any of the following special characters: ?, #, +, -, <, >, (,), period, or comma, or if it begins with a number. For example, you must refer to the Last Name field as "**Last name**" in formulas, so Approach knows that both words comprise a single field name.

When you add this type of field from the fields list in the Formula dialog box, Approach automatically adds the quotation marks.

Operators

Operators are used to perform simple calculations, like those done in arithmetic or elementary logic. There are three basic types of operators:

1. *Arithmetic operators* are used to do addition, subtraction, and the like.
2. *Comparison operators* are used to check whether a value is equal, smaller, or greater than another.
3. *Logical operators* are used to combine Boolean values (yes or no).

Formulas are also classified as arithmetic, comparison, or logical, depending on what operator they use.

Arithmetic Operators

The arithmetic operators probably look familiar to you from mathematics or from other computer programs (see Table 9.1). They are the same as the operators used in elementary arithmetic or in algebra, except that the asterisk is used for multiplication.

Table 9.1 The Arithmetic Operators.

Operator	Meaning
+	addition
-	subtraction
*	multiplication
/	division
( )	precedence

Arithmetic Formulas

The arithmetic operators are all used in the familiar way. For example, Bill At + 10 would give a result ten greater than the amount in the Bill At field, and 500 * 10 would give the result 5000.

Both of these examples are simple *arithmetic formulas*. Their result is numeric, but you can also use arithmetic formulas that perform addition and subtraction on dates and on times as follows:

- *Dates.* The number added to or subtracted from a date represents a number of days. For example, Contacted + 30 gives a result thirty days later than the date in the Contacted field.
- *Times.* The number added to or subtracted from a time represents hundredths of a second. However, calculations on times are based on a 24-hour clock. You can only add times up to midnight and cannot accumulate a total of more than 24 hours, without beginning again with zero.

Order of Precedence

The order in which operations are performed affects the result. For example, 2 * 10 + 5 could give two different results, depending on whether you multiply or add first:

- You could multiply 2 * 10 to total 20, and then add 5, for a total of 25.
- You could add 10 + 5 to total 15, and then multiply by 2 for a total of 30.

By default, multiplication and division are performed before addition and subtraction, so the formula 2 * 10 + 5 actually gives the result 25.

You can change the default by using parentheses. Operations in parentheses are performed first. For example, 2 * (10 + 5) gives the result 30.

It is easy to remember this order of precedence if you remember that it is the same in algebra. Though you may never have thought about it, you automatically multiply before adding or subtracting in algebra; for example, if x equals 10, then 2x + 5 equals 25. Likewise, you use parentheses to change order of precedence in algebra just as you do in Approach. For example, if x equals 10, then 2 (x + 5) equals 30.

Comparison Operators

You learned about the *comparison operators* earlier, because they are used in Finds (see Table 9.2).

Table 9.2 The Comparison Operators

Operator	Meaning
=	equal to
< >	not equal to
<	less than
>	greater than
< =	less than or equal to
> =	greater than or equal to

Comparison formulas always give a Boolean result: Yes or No. For example, the formula Bill At = 65 gives the result Yes if the amount in the Bill At field is 65 or the result No if the amount in the Bill At field is anything else. The formula 10 = 20 always gives the result No, and the formula 10 < 20 always gives the result Yes.

Logical Operators

The *logical operators* are used to combine or manipulate Boolean values and give the results Yes or No (see Table 9.3).

Table 9.3 The Logical Operators.

Operator	Meaning
AND	Yes if both values are Yes
OR	Yes if either value is Yes
NOT	Yes if the value is No; No if the value is Yes

AND and **OR** are both used to combine two Boolean values: **AND** gives the result Yes only if both are Yes, and **OR** gives the result Yes if either is Yes. For example:

- ("Bill At" > 80) AND (State = 'NY') gives the result Yes only if a client in your sample database is billed at a rate of greater than $80 and is from New York. The AND formula is true only if both conditions are true.
- ("Bill At" > 80) OR (State = 'NY') gives the result Yes if a client in your sample database is billed at a rate of greater than $80 or is from New York. The **OR** formula is true if either condition is true.

NOTE AND excludes records. There are fewer people who are billed at more than $80 AND are from New York than there are people who are billed at more than $80. On the other hand, OR includes more records; there are more people who are either billed at more than $80 OR are from New York than there are people who are billed at more than $80.

In the examples above, **AND** and **OR** were used to combine formulas based on comparison operators, which give the result Yes or No. They can also be used with Boolean fields, which contain the value Yes or No. For example ("**Bill AT**" > 80) OR "**Mail To** " would be true for every client who is either billed at more than $80 or who is on your mailing list. With a Boolean field, you do not need to use a comparison operator in a formula such as "**Mail To**" = 'Yes' to return the value of Yes or No, because Mail To already has the value Yes or No.

In addition, since a logical formula itself returns Yes or No, you can use it within a larger, more complex logical formula. For example, the formula ((**"Bill To"** > 80) OR (State = 'NY')) AND "**Mail To**" is true for any client who is billed at more than $80 **OR** is from New York **AND** who is also on your mailing list.

Notice the nested parentheses here. Parentheses indicate order of precedence in logical formulas, as they do in arithmetic formulas, and precedence can make a difference here too. The example would not be true for any client who is not on the mailing list. On the other hand, the formula (**"Bill At"** > 80) OR ((State = 'NY') AND "**Mail To**")) even though it only changes the location of the parentheses, would be true for any client who is billed at more than $80, regardless of whether they are on the mailing list.

WARNING

It is generally best to use parentheses in logical formulas rather than relying on default order of precedence, because the parentheses make the formulas easier for you to read even if they are not needed to change the value. Logical formulas are complex enough that you are likely to make errors if you rely on default order of precedence.

Finally, the **NOT** operator reverses any Boolean value: it makes Yes into No and makes No into Yes, however simple or complex the expression that gives the Yes or No result. Since "Mail To" is true for anyone who is on the mailing list, **NOT** "**Mail To**" is true for any client who is not on the mailing list. Likewise, NOT(("**Bill To**" > 80) OR ((State = 'NY') AND "**Mail To**")) results in Yes for all the clients for whom ("**Bill At**" > 80) OR ((State = 'NY') AND "**Mail To**") results in No.

Constants

You have already looked at some constants in the examples above, probably without noticing it. In the formula **"Bill At" > 80**, for example, 80 is a constant. Unlike a value in a field, which is different for different records, the value of a constant always remains the same. It is simply typed into the formula.

Like fields, constants can be of a different type and are entered as follows:

- *Text constants.* Must be enclosed in single quotation marks, for example, 'Smith'. Text constants are also called *strings*.
- *Date constants.* Must be enclosed in single quotation marks and entered as numbers separated by hyphens in the order month-day-year, for example, '2-14-93', assuming you are using the American date setting in Windows.
- *Time constants.* Must be enclosed in single quotation marks with hours, minutes, and seconds separated by colons, and hundredths of a second separated by a decimal point, for example, '12:00:00.00'.
- *Boolean constants.* Must be enclosed in single quotation marks and entered as either **'Yes'** or **'No'**.
- *Numeric constants.* Are simply entered as numbers, without commas or other separators. Scientific notation may not be used.

Numeric constants were used in examples above, because they are the simplest and do not require any explanation. Other constants may be used in the same way. Comparison formulas using date and text constants, such as **Contacted < '1-1-93' and State <> 'NY'**, are formed just like the comparison formulas using number constants you looked at earlier.

Functions

Functions can add a tremendous amount of power to formulas. Many functions perform mathematical calculations more complex than those you can do using the arithmetic operators, such as summarizing or averaging a field in all the records of a database, using logarithms, or finding statistical variance. Others let you work with text; for example they let you pull certain letters out of a text string. Others convert data from one type to another (for example, text to date) or specify the current date or the current time.

As you see when you look at the lists of functions, most functions work on some value that you specify, which is called a *parameter* (or sometimes an *argument*) and placed in parentheses following the function.

NOTE People often say that a function converts the value in a parameter to some other value, but it is important to note that there is no permanent change to the original value. If you use a field as the parameter of a function, the original value remains in that field in the database; the value is changed only within the formula itself, not in the original.

For this reason, though both are correct, it is more precise to say that a function *returns* a value, rather than that it converts a value.

The Parameters of Functions

The *Upper function* converts text to uppercase, and it must be followed by a single parameter that is text. Thus, **Upper("First Name")** returns the contents of the First Name field in all uppercase letters, and **Upper('sam smith')** returns **SAM SMITH**. Both of these have text as a parameter; "First Name" is a text field (enclosed in double quotation marks, because it has a space in its name), and 'sam smith' is a text constant (enclosed in single quotation marks, as text constants always are).

Different functions require parameters of different data types, and it is common to include the type of the parameter in parentheses after the function. For example, the **Upper** function is often written as **Upper(text)** to show that it requires text as a parameter.

Some functions have several parameters, which must be separated by commas. For example, **Left(text, number)** returns a number of letters from the beginning of the text that is specified by the number. **Left('sam smith',3)** returns the first three letters of the text: **sam**.

Some functions do not take parameters. **Today( )** returns the current date (as indicated by the computer's system clock). As you can see, these functions are still followed by parentheses, even though they are empty, so Approach knows that they are functions.

You can also use formulas as the parameters of functions, if they return the correct data type. Since **Left('sam smith',3)** returns **sam**, **Upper(Left('sam smith',3))** returns **SAM**.

Nested Functions

When one function is used as the parameter of another function in this way, they are called *nested functions*.

These are sometimes confusing, but you can decipher them if you remember to evaluate them from the inside out. In the example you just looked at, you must begin by figuring out what value **Left('sam smith',3)** returns. Once you realize that this returns **sam**, it is obvious the **Upper( )** of it is **SAM**.

> **NOTE** Notice that there must always be an equal number of left and right parentheses in nested functions, since each individual function has one left and one right parenthesis. Often this requires two or more closed parentheses at the end, as in the example. The most common error in entering complex functions of this sort is leaving out parentheses, and if you have problems getting one right, you should try counting the left and right parentheses.

The Listing of Functions

Approach has a very rich set of functions. They are all described in the following subsections, which list them by their use, but you should not try to learn them all. Just glance through the rest of this section to get a general idea of what you can do using Approach functions, and come back to it later when you need it.

This listing begins with the types of functions you use most commonly, such as summary functions, and ends with the functions that typical business users need least frequently, such as trigonometric functions.

> **NOTE** The listing for each function begins with the function and the type of data it uses as parameters. The **Fill( )** function requires two parameters, the first text and the second a number, and so it is listed as **Fill(text, number)**. Note that this refers to the type of data needed, not the field type. If a function requires a number as its parameter, you can use a text field as long as that field holds numbers as its data.

In a few cases, there are parameters that are optional, and they are placed in square brackets. There are also functions with an indefinite number of parameters, and this is indicated by listing two parameters of that type followed by an *ellipsis (...)* to show that the list may continue indefinitely.

NOTE: In the listings and examples, parameters are delimited by commas. Actually, Approach uses the delimiter specified in the List Separator setting in the International dialog box of the Windows' Control Panel. *Comma* is the standard delimiter in the United States, but many countries use a semicolon (;) instead. You must use the delimiter specified in the International dialog box to separate parameters.

Summary Functions

Summary functions are invaluable for adding summaries to reports, and their use is described later in this chapter. In addition to the commonly used summary functions listed in this section, Approach also includes a few financial and statistical summary functions. They are included in separate sections because they are not often needed in business applications.

When you use summary functions, you use the Summarize On drop-down list of the Formula dialog box to define which records they apply to; this is called the *range of the summary*.

SAverage(Number Field)

The *Summary Average* function returns the average values of the specified field in all the records in the range of the summary. The parameter must be a number field. **SAverage("Bill At")** returns the average rate at which you bill clients.

SCount(Field Name)

The *Summary Count* function returns the number of records that have a value in the specified field in the range of the summary. The parameter must be a field name. **SCount("Client Number")** returns the total number of records in the range of the summary, as every record must have a client number.

SMax(Number Field)

The *Summary Maximum* function returns the maximum value of the specified field in the records in the range of the summary. The parameter must be a number field. **SMax("Bill At")** returns the highest rate at which you bill any client.

SMin(Number Field)

The *Summary Minimum* function returns the minimum value of the specified field in the records in the range of the summary. The parameter must be a number field. **SMin("Bill At")** returns the lowest rate at which you bill any client.

SSum(Number Field)

The *Summary Sum* function returns the sum of the values of the specified field in all the records in the range of the summary. The parameter must be a number field. **SSum(Hours)** returns the total number of hours you worked.

Conversion Functions

Conversion functions return data of one field type as another field type. Many functions can work only on a specific type of data. However, you can use them on data of a different type if you use one of the conversion functions to return it as the type needed.

Date(Number1, Number2, Number3)

The *Date* function converts data from numeric to date. The three parameters represent month, day, and year, and they must be a valid date. **Date(12, 15, 1993)** returns **12-15-93**.

DateToText(Date, Format)

DateToText returns a date in text form. The format of the date is specified by a string, with repeated *Ms* representing the month, repeated *Ds* representing the day, repeated *Ys* representing the year, and spaces and commas or other delimiters included. **DateToText(Contacted,'MMM. DD, YY)** would return Feb. 12, 94, if **2/12/94** is in the Contacted field.

NumToText(Number, Format)

The *NumToText* function returns a number in text form. The format of the text is determined by the Format parameter, which is made up of zeros specifying required digits and number signs representing optional digits. **NumToText(2,#00.00)** returns the text string **02.00**, and **NumToText(2,##0.00)** returns the text string **2.00**.

TextToBool(Text)

The *TextToBool* function returns text as a Boolean value. It returns No if the first character in a string is F,f,N,n,0. Otherwise it returns Yes.

TextToDate(Text)

The *TextToDate* function returns text as a date value. The parameter must be a valid date in the format MM/DD/YY.

TextToTime(Text)

The *TextToTime* function returns text as a time value. The parameter must be a valid time in the format HH:MM:SS.00.

Time(Hours, Minutes, Seconds, Hundredths)

The *Time* function converts numeric to date data. The four parameters represent hour, minute, second, and hundredths of a second, and they must be a valid time.

Text Functions

The *Text* functions are useful for manipulating text; for example, for capitalizing it in the way you want, or for using only part of a text string.

Asc(Text)

The *ASCII* function returns the ASCII number of the first character of the text used as its parameter. Generally, a single character is used as the parameter. **Asc('A')** returns **65** and **Asc('Albert')** returns **65**.

Chr(Number)

The *Character* function returns the ASCII character for a number. **Chr(65)** returns **A**.

Combine(text, text ...)

The *Combine* function concatenates all the text strings used as parameters into a single text string. **Combine('Hello', ' world')** returns **Hello world**.

Fill(Text, Number)

The *Fill* function returns a text string containing the text that is repeated as many times as the number specifies. **Fill('x', 10)** returns **xxxxxxxxxx**, and **Fill('Hello ', 2)** returns **Hello Hello**.

Left(Text, Number)

The *Left* function returns a number of characters from the beginning of the specified text that is equal to the specified number. **Left('Hello world', 5)** returns **Hello**.

Length(Text)

The *Length* function returns the number of characters in the specified text, including spaces, numbers, and special characters, as well as letters. **Length('John Smith')** returns **10**.

Like(Text, Text)

The *Like* function compares the two text values and returns Yes if they are the same or No if they are different. The comparison is case insensitive. The second parameter can include the *wildcard* characters; a question mark (?) to represent any character, and an asterisk (*) to represent any number of characters (including zero characters). For example:

- **Like ("Last Name", 'SMITH')** returns Yes if the name in the Last Name field is Smith.
- **Like ("Last Name", 'SMITH*')** returns Yes if the name in the Last Name field is Smith, Smithson, Smithers, or anything else beginning with Smith.
- **Like("Last Name", 'SM?TH')** returns Yes if the name in the Last Name field is Smith, Smyth, and so on.

All of these match regardless of capitalization of the name in the field.

Lower(Text)

The *Lower* function converts all letters in text to lowercase but does not affect other characters. **Lower('Smith')** returns **smith**.

Middle(Text, Number, Number)

The *Middle* function returns a string of characters taken from the specified text, beginning at the position specified by the first number, and containing the number of characters specified by the second number. **Middle('Smith',2,3)** returns **mit**.

Text Functions

Text functions are used for manipulating or comparing text strings.

Position(Text, Text, Number)

The *Position* function searches the first text specified for the first occurrence of the second text specified beginning at the location specified by the number. It returns a number indicating its position. **Position('Smithson', 's', 2)** returns **6**.

Prefix(Text, Text)

The *Prefix* function returns Yes if the characters at the beginning of the second text string match the first text string. **Prefix('Sm', 'Smith')** returns **Yes**.

Proper(Text)

The *Proper* function converts the first letter of each word in text to upper case and all other letters to lower case. **Proper('JOHN Q. SMITH')** returns **John Q. Smith**.

Replace(Text, Number, Number, Replacement Text)

The *Replace* function replaces characters in the text with different characters. The first number specifies the starting position of the text that is being replaced, and the second number specifies the number of characters. The replacement text can be a different size than the number of characters it replaces. For **Replace('of their party', 10, 4, 'countr')** returns **of their country**, because it replaces part, four characters beginning with the tenth character of the string, with **countr**.

Right(Text, Number)

The *Right* function returns a number of characters from the end of the specified text that is equal to the specified number. **Right('Hello world', 5)** returns **world**.

Span(Text, Text)

The *Span* function returns the number of characters in the first text string before the first character that is not contained in the second text string. For example,

- Span('John Smith', 'Johnson') returns **4**.
- Span('54623456', '456') returns **3**.

Notice that the function ignores the order of the characters.

Soundslike (Text, Text)

The *Soundslike* function returns Yes if the first text string sounds like the second text string. **Soundslike ('Walton', 'Waldon') returns Yes**.

SpanUntil(Text, Text)

The *SpanUntil* function returns the number of characters in the first text string before the first character that is also in the second text string. For example

- SpanUntil('John Smith', 'Johnson') returns **0**.
- SpanUntil('54623456', '123') returns **3**.

Notice the function ignores the order of the characters.

Translate(Text, Character, Character)

The *Translate* function in the specified text string, replaces all occurrences of the first character with the second character. **Translate('6/23/93', '/', '-') returns 6-23-93**.

Trim(Text)

The *Trim* function returns the text without any leading or trailing blanks. **Trim(' John Smith') returns John Smith**.

Upper(Text)

The *Upper* function converts all letters in the text to lower case but does not affect other characters. **Upper('Smith') returns SMITH**.

Logical Functions

The first two *logical functions* listed here are extremely useful for letting you place either of two values in a design, depending on whether some condition is met. For example you could use the **If( )** function to add an extra message at the bottom of the mailing labels of your higher paying clients, and a different message in the same place for the rest of your clients.

Blank(FieldName, Value)

The *Blank* function returns the second value if the field is blank. Otherwise returns the field's value. **Blank(ADDRESS2, 'xxx')** returns **xxx** if the Address2 field is blank, or returns the content of the Address2 field if it is not blank.

If(Boolean Condition, Value1, Value2)

The *If* function. If the Boolean condition is Yes, it returns the first value. If it is No, it returns the second value. The condition must be a Boolean value; the other two parameters can be any value. **If (Bill At > 90, 'Hello', 'Goodbye')** returns **Hello** if the Bill At field contains an amount greater than 90 or returns Goodbye **if it does not.**

IsBlank(Fieldname)

The *IsBlank* function returns **Yes** if the field is blank and No if there is data in it. **IsBlank(Address2)** returns **Yes** if there is not a second address line in the record.

IsLastRecord( )

The *IsLastRecord( )* function returns **Yes** if the record is the last record in the found set in the current sort order and returns **No** if it is not.

Date Functions

Date functions are useful for working with date values. Many are indispensable if you need to pull just the day, month, or year out of a date value.

Day(Date)

The **Day** function returns the day of the month from a date. **Day('12-15-93')** returns **15**.

DayName(Number or Date)

The *DayName* function returns the name of the day of the week in text form. The parameter may be either a date or a number from 1 to 7, with 1 returned as **Sunday** and so on. **DayName('12-15-93')** returns **Wednesday**, and **DayName(2)** returns **Monday**.

DayOfWeek(Date)

The *DayOFWeek* function returns the day of the week in number form, with 1 returned as **Sunday** and so on. **DayOfWeek('12-1 5-93')** returns **4**.

DayOfYear(Date)

The *DayOfYear* function returns the number of days from the beginning of the year to the specified date, with January 1 returned as **1** and so on. **DayOfYear('2-1-94')** returns **32**.

Month(Date)

The *Month* Function returns the month of the specified date in number form, with January returned as **1** and so on. **Month('12-15-93')** returns **12**.

MonthName(Date or Number)

The *MonthName* returns the month in text form. The parameter can be either a date or a number from 1 to 12, with 1 returned as **January** and so on. **MonthName('12-15-93')** returns **December**, and **MonthName(2)** returns **February**.

Today( )

The *Today* function returns the current system date.

WeekOfYear(Date)

The *WeekOfYear* function returns the number of the week of the specified date, with January 1 being in Week 1 and so on. **WeekOfYear('1-8-94')** returns **2**.

Year(Date)

The *Year* function returns the year of the date in number form. **Year('12-15-93')** returns **1993**.

Time Functions

The *Time* functions are useful for working with time values. Like the Date functions, many of the time functions are indispensable if you need to pull just the hour, minute, or second out of a time value.

CurrTime( )

The *Current Time* function returns the time on the system clock.

Hour(Time)

The *Hour* function returns a number representing the hour of a time value. **Hour('12:03:25.32')** returns **12**.

Hundreth(Time)

The *Hundreth* function returns a number representing the hundredths of a second of a time value. **Hundreth('12:03:25.32')** returns **32**.

Minute(Time)

The *Minute* function returns a number representing the minutes of a time value. **Minute('12:03:25.32')** returns **3**.

Second(Time)

The *Second* function returns a number representing the seconds of a time value. **Second('12:03:25.32')** returns **25**.

Financial Functions

Financial functions instantly calculate present value, future value, and do other financial calculations. These often require an interest rate, and for the sake of simplicity, the examples use interest rates of 12% a year, so it is easy to see that the periodic interest rate is .01 (1%) per month.

> **NOTE** Remember, though, any numeric formula can be used as the parameter of a function, so that you do not have to calculate the monthly interest rate. You can simply leave them in fractional form. For example, if the interest rate is 9.5% a year, the monthly interest rate is .095/12, and you can simply include this fraction in the function as the parameter representing the periodic interest rate.

FV(Number1, Number2, Number3)

The *Future Value* function returns the future value of a series of periodic payments at a constant interest rate after the number of periods you specify. The first parameter is the periodic payment, the second parameter is the interest rate during each period, and the third parameter is the total number of periods. If you invest $100 per month for a year at an annual interest rate of 12%, the periodic payment is 100, the interest rate per period is .01 (1% is 12% a year, divided by 12 months per year), and the total number of periods is 12. Thus, the value of the investment at the end of the year is **FV(100, .01, 12)**.

NPeriods(Number1, Number2, Number3)

The *Number Of Periods* function returns the number of periods needed to pay a principal with a constant periodic payment at a constant interest rate. The first parameter is the interest rate, the second number is the principle that must be paid, the third number is the periodic payment. If you are paying a debt of $120,000 at 12% interest with a payment of $1000 per month, the monthly interest rate is .01 (1% is 12% divided by 12 months per year), the principal is $120,000, and the periodic payment is $1000. The number of months you need to pay it is **NPeriods(.01, 120000, 1000)**.

PMT(Number1, Number2, Number3)

The *Payment* function returns the amount of the periodic payment needed to pay off a specified principal at a constant periodic interest rate, with a specified number of periodic payments. The first parameter is the principal, the second parameter is the periodic interest rate, and the third parameter is the number of periods in which the principal must be paid. If you are paying a debt of $120,000 at 12% interest by making monthly payments for 15 years, then the principal is $120,000, the monthly interest rate is .01 (1% is 12% divided by 12 months per year), and the number of periods is 180 (15 years times 12 months per year). The monthly payment is **PMT(120,000, .01, 180)**.

PV(Number1, Number2, Number3)

The *Present Value* function returns the present value of a series of periodic payments with a constant interest rate over a specified number of periods. The first number represents the periodic payment, the second number represents the periodic interest rate, and the third represents the number of periods. If an annuity pays $1000 per year for 10 years, and the discount rate is 10% per year, then the periodic payment is $1000, the periodic interest rate is .1 (10%), and the number of periods is 10. The present value of the annuity is **PV(1000, .1, 10)**.

SLN(Number1, Number2, Number3)

The *Straight Line Depreciation* function calculates the straight line depreciation of an asset. The first number is the asset's cost, the second is its salvage value, and the third is its life. Straight line depreciation is calculated as (cost - salvage) / life. If you buy an asset for $1000 and scrap it after 3 years of use for a salvage value of $100, its yearly straight-line depreciation is **SLN(1000, 100, 3)**.

SNPV(Number field, Number)

The *Summary Net Present Value* function returns the net present value of a series of periodic future payments as a given discount rate; future payments can be either negative (indicating money you must pay) or positive (indicating money paid to you) or both. The first parameter is the name of the field that holds the future payments. The second parameter is the discount rate. For example, if a field named Payments had one record for each year's projected net gain or loss on an investment in future years, and if the discount rate were 10% (.1), then you could calculate the present value of the investment as **SNPV(Payments, .1)**.

Statistical Functions

A few *statistical* functions, such as Avg( ), are useful for the typical business user. Most are used primarily in scientific applications.

Avg(Number, Number, ...)

The *Average* function returns the average of all the parameters. There can be any number of parameters, all of which must be number values. **Avg(10,20,30)** returns **20**.

STD(number, number, ...)

The *Standard Deviation* function returns the standard deviation of all the parameters, a measure of how widely the values are dispersed from the average value. There may be any number of parameters, all of which must be number values.

SSTD(Number Field)

The *Summary Standard Deviation* function returns the standard deviation of the values in the field used as the parameter in all the records in the range of the summary. The parameter must be a number field. Standard Deviation is a measure of how widely the values are dispersed from the average value.

SVAR(Number Field)

The *Summary Variance* function returns the variance of the values in the field used as the parameter in all the records in the range of the summary. The parameter must be a number field.

Var(Number, Number, ...)

The *Variance* function returns the variance of all the parameters. There can be any number of parameters, all of which must be number values.

Mathematical Functions

Mathematical functions are not frequently needed in business applications.

Abs(Number)

The *Absolute Value* function returns the absolute value of a number, the positive equivalent of the number. **Abs(5)** returns **5** and **Abs(-5)** returns **5**.

Exp(Number)

The *Exponentiation* function calculates **e** to the power of the number value.

Factorial(Number)

The *Factorial* function returns the factorial of an integer, that integer multiplied by each smaller positive integer. **Factorial(3)** returns **6**, because 3 * 2 * 1 equals 6.

Mod(Number, Number)

The *Modulus (Remainder)* function returns the remainder (modulus) left when the first number is divided by the second to give an integer result. **Mod(14,4)** returns **2**, because 14 / 4 equals 3 with a remainder of 2.

Ln(Number)

The *Natural Logarithm* function returns the natural logarithm of a positive number–the logarithm to the base **e**. The value returned is the power to which e must be raised to produce the number.

Log(Number)

The *Logarithm* function calculates the common or decimal logarithm of a number–the logarithm to the base 10. The value returned is the power to which 10 must be raised to produce the number.

Pi( )

The **Pi** function returns **3.14159…**, the ratio of the circumference to the diameter of a circle.

Pow(Number, Number)

The *Power* function returns the value of the first number raised to the power of the second number. **Pow(3, 2)** returns **9**.

Random( )

The *Random* function returns a random number between 0 and 1. Often you multiply this by some power of ten, and round the result to get the random integer you really want to use.

Round(Number, [Number])

The *Round* function returns the value of the first number rounded to the number of decimal places specified in the second number. If the second number is omitted (or if it is zero), Approach rounds the number to the nearest integer. For example:

- **Round(2.643)** returns **3**.
- **Round(2.643,1)** returns **2.6**.
- **Round(2.643,2)** returns **2.64**.

Sign(Number)

The *Sign* function returns **-1** if the number specified is negative, **1** if the number specified is positive, and **0** if the number specified is zero. **Sign(15)** returns 1 and **Sign(-100)** returns **-1**.

Sqrt(Number)

The *Square Root* function calculates the square root of a number. **Sqrt(9)** returns **3**.

Trunc(Number, [Number])

The *Truncate* function returns the first number truncated to the number of decimal places specified by the second number. If the second number is omitted (or if it is zero), Approach truncates the number to an integer. For example:

- **Trunc(9.97463,1)** returns **9.9**.
- **Trunc(9.97463)** returns **9**.

Trigonometric Functions

Like other mathematical functions, *trigonometric* functions are not generally needed in business applications. Note that these functions generally measure angles in radians, and so they are often used in combination with the Pi( ) function, listed under Mathematical functions above. You can use the Degree( ) and Radian( ) functions to do the conversions needed to work with angles in degrees, rather than radians.

Acos (Number)

The *Arccosine* function returns the trigonometric arccosine of an angle expressed in radians.

Asin(Number)

The *Arcsine* function returns the trigonometric arcsine of an angle expressed in radians.

Atan(Number)

The *Arctangent* function returns the trigonometric arctangent of an angle expressed in radians.

Atan2(Number1, Number2)

The *Arctangent2* function returns the arctangent of an angle whose sized expressed in radians is number1 / number2 in radians.

Cos(Number)

The *Cosine* function returns the cosine of an angle expressed in radians.

Degree(Number)

The *Degree* function converts angles measured in radians to degrees. The parameter represents the number of radians. As the **Acos( )**, **Asin( )**, and **Atan( )** functions all return angles measured in radians, they can be nested within the **Degree( )** function to return the result in degrees.

Radian(Number)

The *Radian* function converts angles measured in degrees to radians. The parameter represents the number of degrees. As the **Cos( )**, **Sin( )**, and **Tan( )** functions all require parameters measured in radians, the **Radian( )** function can be nested within them to use them on angles measured in degrees.

Sin(Number)

The *Sine* function returns the sine of an angle expressed in radians.

Tan(Number)

The *Tangent* function returns the tangent of an angle expressed in radians.

Using Calculated Fields

One common use of formulas is in calculated fields. After you have created a calculated field, you can add it to a view like any other field, in order to display some calculated value in a form or report. If you know in advance what calculated fields you will need, you can create them when you are first defining the fields of a database.

It is common to discover that you need calculated fields when you are creating reports or other designs, however. You can create them by choosing **Field Definition** from the Create menu, and later use the **Field** drawing tool or **Add Field** to place them in the design.

> **NOTE** Calculated fields are listed in Italic type in the Add Field box. Calculated fields in views cannot be edited, though: to change their value, you must change the value of a field they are based on.

Creating a Calculated Field

Create a calculated field just as you create any other field, by using the Field Definition dialog box. Enter the name of the Calculated field in the **Field Name** column and select **Calculated** from the Data Type drop-down list. Approach automatically displays the Field definition dialog box in the expanded form to let you specify the calculation the field is based on (see Figure 8.2). When you are done defining the field, the formula that you generate is automatically entered in the Formula/Options column for the field.

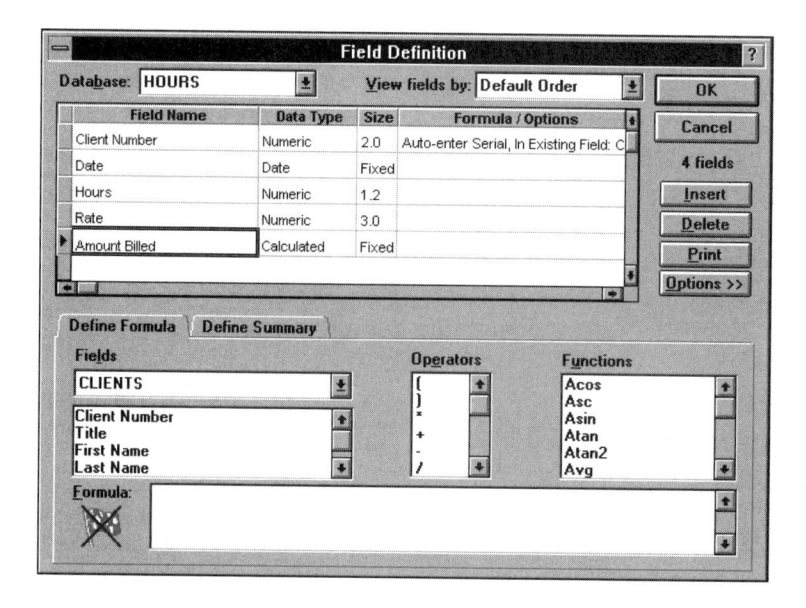

Figure 8.2 The Field Definition dialog box for a Calculated field.

The Define Formula Panel

The Define Formula panel works just like the Formula dialog box. Select **Fields**, **Operators**, and **Functions** from the lists to place them in the Formula text box or just type them a formula in the formula text box. Constants must be typed in.

> **NOTE** You use just this panel if you are creating a calculated field to display some value for each record of the database.

Let's say you want a form that displays the total cost of each days work you recorded in your Hours database. Though the database just has fields to hold the number of hours worked and the rate at which you billed for each day's work. You just need to create a calculated field, which you might call Amount Billed and to give it the value **Hours.Hours * Hours.Rate**, so that it contains the total billed for the day; that is the number of hours worked multiplied by the hourly billing rate. Then you can add this field to designs, just as you add any other field. You can create a form or report that displays the Amount Billed calculated field for each day just as easily as you create one to display the Hours or Rate field.

Since this type of calculated field displays a value for each record, it cannot be used in the summary panel of a report, and it cannot include one of the summary functions.

The Define Summary Panel

You must use a calculated fields with a summary function to calculate a value that summarizes the values in an entire range of records.

Let us say you want to determine the total number of hours you worked for the year. You would use the Summary Sum function, the **Ssum( )** function covered earlier in this chapter to create a calculated field with the formula **Ssum(Hours.Hours)** to summarize the value in the Hours field in all the records in the hours database.

When you create a calculated field with a summary function, you must also use the **Define Summary** panel of the Field definition dialog box to select the range of fields the summary is based on (see Figure 8.3). The Summarize on drop-down in this panel is accessible only if the field's Formula, as defined in the Define Formula panel, is based on a summary function.

Practical Approach, 3.0

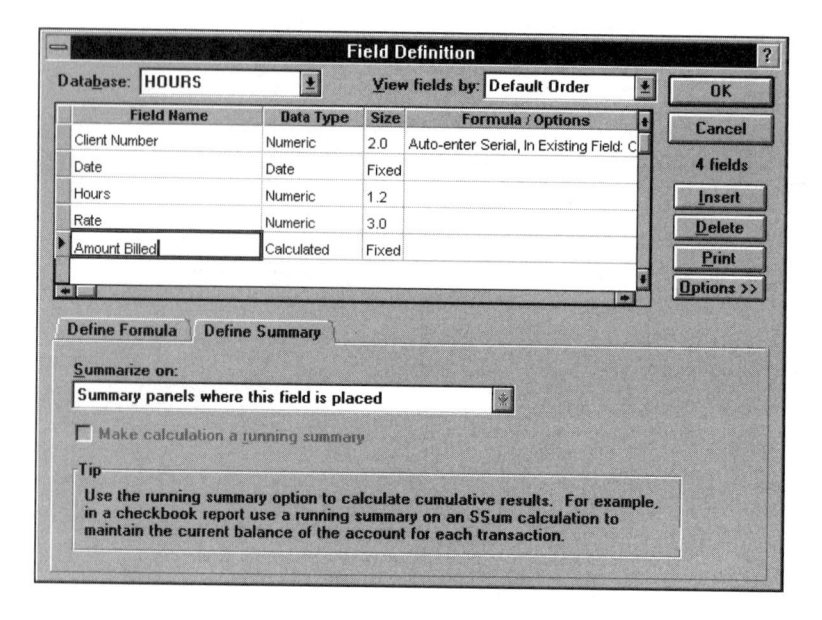

Figure 8.3 The Field definition dialog box.

By default, the range of fields depends on the panel where the field is placed–for example, if you place it in a group summary panel in a grouped report, it summarizes values for each group. You can also use the Summarize on drop-down to create a summary for all records in a database file or in all database files included in a relational database.

Select the **Make calculation a running summary** checkbox to create a cumulative summary. If you are summarizing by group, the calculated field would ordinarily just summarize the values in the group that it follows. If you select this checkbox, the summary at the end of each group includes all the records up to that point, both those in the group and those in preceding groups.

Dependent Calculated Fields

You can also use a calculated field within a calculated field. If you created a calculated field named Amount Billed to display the amount billed in each record of the Hours file, as described above, then you could create a calculated field with the formula **Ssum("Amount Billed")** to calculate the total that you billed all clients. You would create this field in just the same way that you create a field to summarize all the hours you worked. Any calculated field that depends on another calculated field in this way is called a *dependent calculated field*.

Changing a Formula in a Calculated Field

To change the formula in a calculated field, display the Field Definition dialog box, select the field, and click **Options**. The Formula dialog box is displayed, which you can use in the usual way to specify a new formula for the field.

When you change the formula in this way, Approach recalculates all data in this calculated field and in any dependent calculated fields that are based on it.

> **NOTE** You cannot change the formula in a calculated field that is used in a join. If you try, Approach displays a dialog box saying it cannot be changed.

Bad References

If you delete a field used in a formula, the formula becomes meaningless. For example, if you deleted the Hours.Hours field, there would no longer be any way to calculate the Amount Billed field described above. In this case **Bad Field Reference** is displayed in the calculated field instead of displaying a value.

A Sample Summary Report

You can get a clear idea of how summary reports are organized if you create one using the Assistant and then look at the calculated fields that are generated to display the summaries.

Lets say that you wanted a summary report to specify the total that you billed each client in your sample database, plus the grand total by billed all your clients. You have fields for Hour and Rate in each record of the Hours database. To calculate the dollar amount billed for each record, and you must create a calculated field called Amount Billed using the formula **Hours * Rate**, as described earlier in this chapter.

To calculate the total billed each client, you can create a summary report that groups all of these records by Client Number, with a summary for each client as well as a grand total of the entire amount you billed. You must group by client number rather than by name, because more than one client may have the same name.

To create this report by using the Assistant to generate a Trailing Grouped Summary report:

1. Create the Amount Billed field. Choose **Field Definition** from the Create menu to display the dialog box, and, if necessary, select **Hours** from the Fields drop-down. Then scroll down to the end of the Field list to add a new field to the Hours database. As the Field Name, type **Amount Billed**. As the Data Type, select **Calculated**. The dialog box is displayed in expanded form, to let you specify the formula. Select **Hours** from the Fields drop-down. Click the **Hours** field to add it to the formula, click the * operator to add it to the formula, and click the **Rate** field to add it to the formula (see Figure 8.4). Then select **OK**.

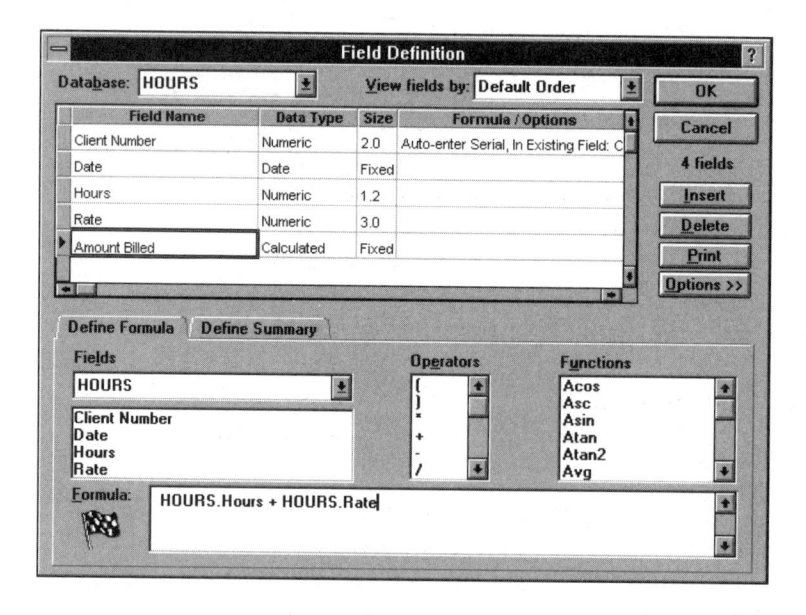

Figure 8.4   The formula for the Amount Billed field.

Chapter 8: Using Approach Formulas **321**

2. Choose **Report** from the Create menu to display the Report Assistant. For the View Name and Title, enter **Amounts Billed**. For the SmartMaster layout, select **Trailing Grouped Summary**.

3. Click the **Step 2: Fields** divider tab. Add the **First Name** and **Last Name** fields to the Fields to place on View list. Then use the drop-down to select the **Hours table**, and add the **Date** and **Amount** billed fields to the Fields to place on View.

4. Click the **Step 3: Trailing Summary** divider tab. Select **Client Number** as the field for the grouping to be based on. Leave sum in the drop-down as the calculation, and select the **Hours** database and the **Amount Billed** field in the list below (see Figure 8.5).

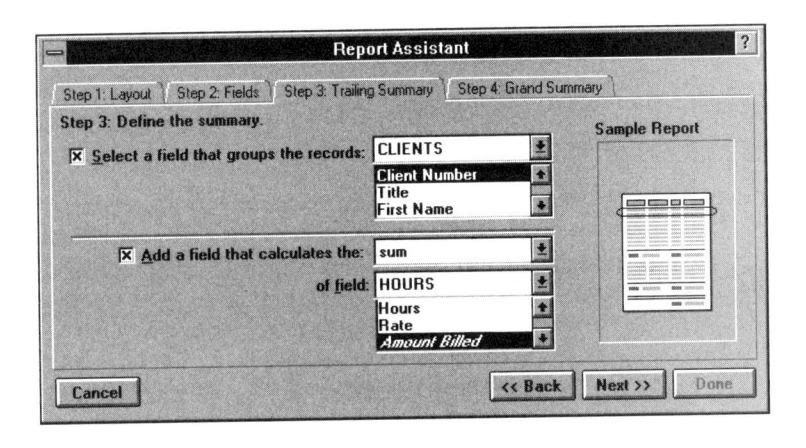

Figure 8.5 Specifying the Trailing Summary.

5. Next, click **Step 4: Grand Summary** divider tab. Leave sum in the drop-down as the calculation, and select the **Hours** database and the **Amount Billed** field in the list below, as you did in the previous panel. Select **Done** to generate the report. Select **Hours** as the main Database (see Figure 8.6).

6. To see how Approach creates these totals, choose **Field Definition** from the create menu to display the Field Definition dialog box, and click its options button to display it in expanded form. Select **Hours** from the Database drop-down, and scroll down through the fields, so you can see that Approach created two summary fields named Auto_Sum_of_Amount_Billed. Both of these use the summary formula

SSum("Amount Billed") (see Figure 8.7). The only difference is that one is in a panel where it calculates a total for the group, and the other is in a panel where it calculates a total for all the records.

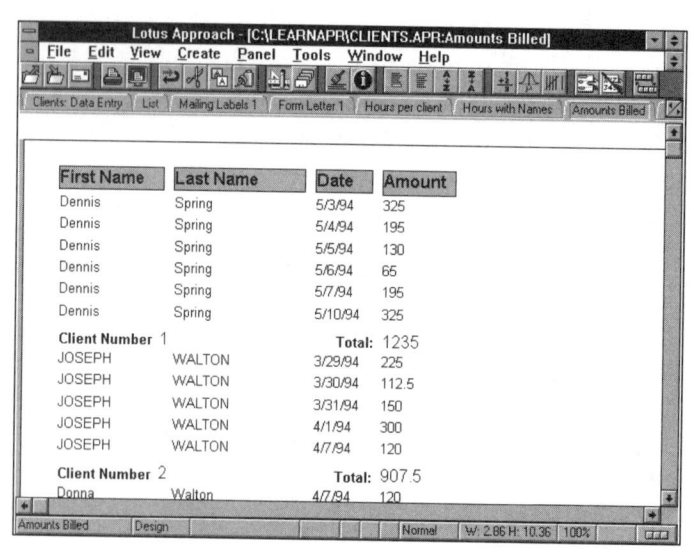

Figure 8.6 The design created by the Assistant.

7. Select **Cancel** to close the Field definition dialog box.

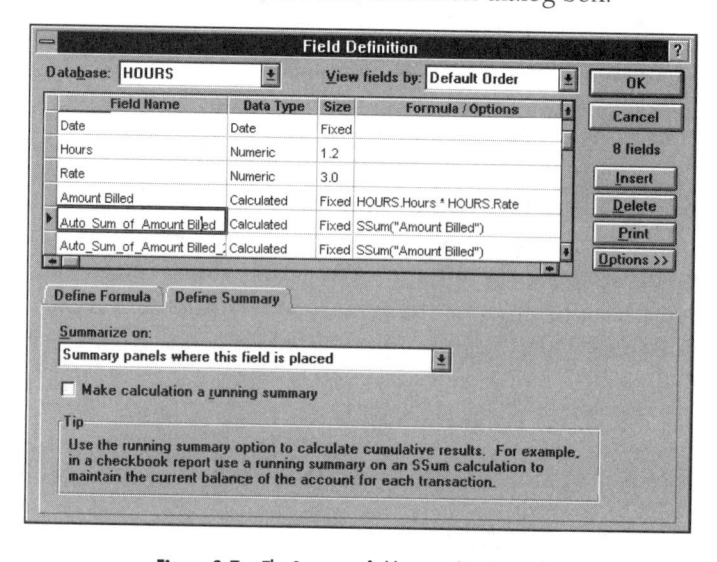

Figure 8.7 The Summary fields created in Approach.

Using Formulas in Finds

As you saw when you first learned about Finds, they often include simple formulas using the comparison operators. To find clients whom you bill at $90 per hour or more, you enter the criterion **>= 90** in the **Bill At** field of the Find Request.

You can also use more complex formulas in Finds, with any of the features described in this chapter. Here, we look at two uses of formulas in Finds that many people find useful. As you read them, you should also think about whether there are any functions and operators that might be useful in the Finds you need to do.

Special Features of Formulas in Finds

There are two differences between formulas in Finds and other formulas in Approach.

You do not have to include delimiters when you enter constants in a Find. You can simply type a name in the text field or the word Yes in a Boolean field to find all the records with that value. You do not have to enclose the value in single quotation marks, as you do when you use constants in formulas.

Because text constants are not enclosed in quotation marks, functions in finds must be preceded with the symbol @, so Approach knows that they are functions and not text. You will see an example of this in a moment.

Finds Using Today( )

The *Today( )* function returns the current system date; this function is often useful in Finds. If you want to do a mailing to clients whom you have not contacted for the last 90 days, you can use the criterion **< @Today( ) - 90** in the Find Request (see Figure 8.8). Note that the function must be preceded by the symbol @ in a Find. This function is particularly useful when you use the Find in a macro, because you can run the macro repeatedly without changing the date.

Practical Approach, 3.0

Figure 8.8 A Find using the Today( ) function.

If Searches

If Searches let you enter a complex formula using the if operator in a Search Request. The **if** operator can be followed by any formula that returns a Boolean value. The formula is simply placed in parentheses following 'if.' This operator is particularly useful for comparing values that are in different fields. To find jobs that were billed at a lower rate than the client's current billing rate, you could use the criterion **if(Hours.Rate <> Clients.Bill At)**. This criterion could be entered in any field of the find request.

> **NOTE** Though it is followed by parentheses, the **if** operator should not be confused with the **If( )** function, which takes the form **If(Boolean condition, value1, value2)** and returns **value1** if the condition is true, or **value2** if the condition is false.

Using Formulas to Automate and Validate Data Entry

In Chapter 3, you learned to automate and validate data entry in simple ways. You can use formulas to automate and validate data entry in more advanced ways.

Using a Formula to Enter a Default Value

You can use a Formula to enter a default value in a text, numeric, date, time, or Boolean field. Begin by displaying the Default Value panel of the Field Definition dialog box. (Choose **Field Definition** from the Create menu, to display this dialog box, and select **Options**). In the Default Value panel, select:

- The **Creation Formula** radio button to enter the result of a formula in this field whenever you add a new record to the database.
- The **Modification Formula** radio button to enter a value in this field whenever you edit the record.

In either case, enter the Formula in the text box, or click **Formula** to display the Formula text box and use it to generate the formula.

Using a formula to create a default value is similar to using a calculated field, except that the result of the calculation (like any other default value) can be edited. In most cases, it is best to use a calculated field. If you are calculating the amount billed to each client, you do not want a user to be able to edit the result, so that it is not actually equal to Hours * Rate. There may be occasional special cases, however, where you want the added flexibility of being able to edit the result of the calculation.

A Validation Formula

To use a formula to validate the date entered in a field, begin as always by using the **Validation Panel** of the Field Definition dialog box. Choose **Field Definition** from the Create menu, to display this dialog box, select **Options**, and click the **Validation** divider tab.

Select **Formula is True** and either enter a formula in the text box to its right or click **Formula** and use the Formula dialog box to generate the formula that is displayed in this text box. The formula must result in a Boolean value, and data entry is allowed only if its result is Yes.

Imagine that you have many different billing rates for your clients, but all are multiples of 5, such as $65, $70, $75, and so on. You could validate the data entry by using the **Modulus (or Remainder)** function, which takes the form **Mod(number,number)** and returns the remainder left when the first number is divided by the second. Create this validation formula as follows:

1. Choose **Field Definition** from the Create menu. Click **Options** to display the Field Definition dialog box in expanded form. If necessary, select **Clients** from the Database drop-down. Click the **Bill At** field to place the focus in it.

2. Click the **Validation** divider tab. Then select **Formula is true**. Click **Formula** to display the Formula dialog box. Click **Mod()** in the function list, and click the **Bill At** field. Then type the number **5** after the comma in the function's parentheses. Press **End**, click the = and type **0** to enter the formula **Mod(Clients."Bill At", 5) = 0** (see Figure 8.9). Select **OK** to return to the Field Definition dialog box, and **OK** to save the change in the Field Definition.

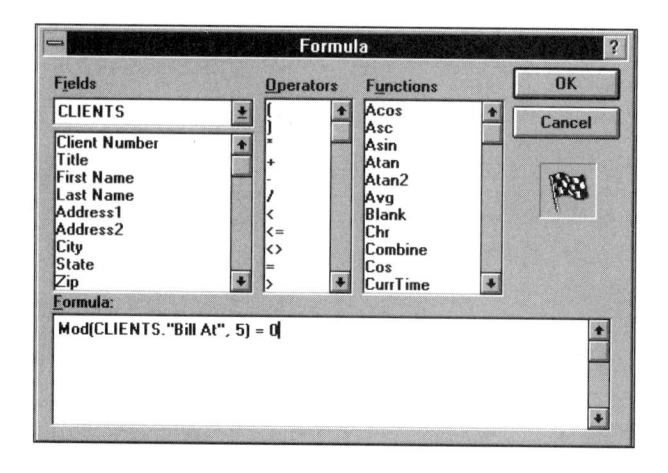

Figure 8.9 Using a formula to validate data entry.

3. To test the validation rule, display the **Clients:Data Entry** form in Browse mode and press **Ctrl-N** to add a new record. Try entering a value the cannot be divided by 5 in the Bill At field. When you try to move the cursor out of the field, Approach displays an error message (see Figure 8.10). Select **Cancel** to remove the new record.

You usually do not need this sophisticated a form of data validation, but Approach formulas provide it when it is needed.

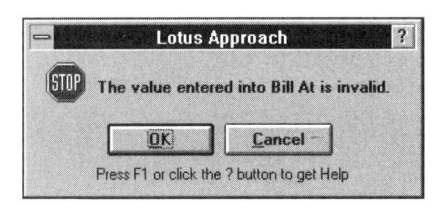

Figure 8.10 Approach displays an error message if you enter invalid data

Analyzing Your Data: Worksheets, Crosstabs, and Charts

The types of views that you have worked with in earlier chapters, Forms, Reports, Mailing Labels and Form Letters, are made of the same objects, so you can change their designs and edit their data in similar ways. In this chapter, you look at three other types of view that are used differently—Worksheets, Crosstabs, and Charts. These three views are useful for analyzing data and are related to each other. You can create a crosstab from a worksheet and a chart from a crosstab. This chapter covers:

- Creating a Worksheet using the Assistant
- Changing the design of a Worksheet
- Changing the Style and Properties of a Worksheet
- Adding and editing data in a Worksheet

- Creating a Crosstab using the Assistant
- Creating a Worksheet from a Crosstab
- Changing the Style and Properties of a Crosstab
- Creating a Chart using the Assistant
- Creating a Chart from a Crosstab

Worksheets

A worksheet arranges your data in the form of a table, which is used like a spreadsheet in some ways (see Figure 9.1). If you are familiar with spreadsheet applications such as Lotus 1-2-3, you will recognize the methods that are used to select a range of cells in an Approach worksheet and divide it into two panels that can be scrolled separately. Worksheets also make it easy to add columns that contain formulas with calculations based on data in other columns, without creating new calculated fields, which makes them particularly useful for analyzing data.

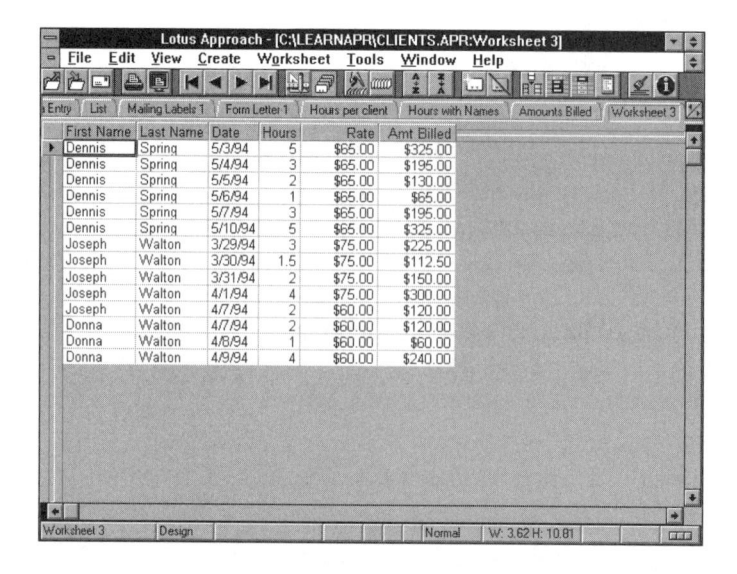

Figure 9.1 A Worksheet.

Creating a New Worksheet

Create a new worksheet as you do other designs, by choosing **Worksheet** from the Create menu to display the Worksheet Assistant (see Figure 9.2).

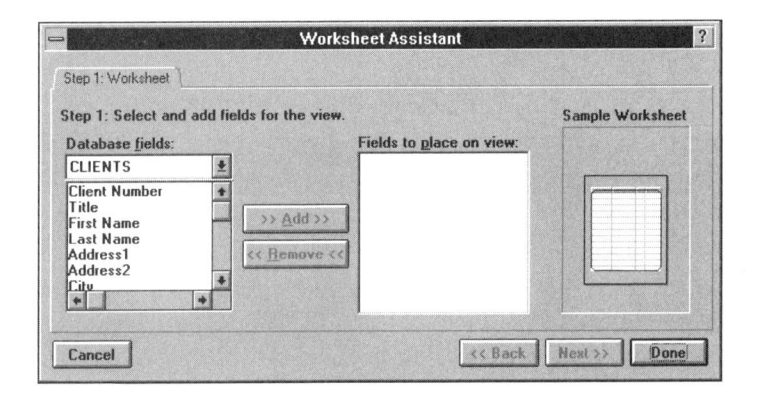

Figure 9.2 The Worksheet Assistant.

As you can see, the Worksheet Assistant has only one panel, similar to ones you use to select fields in other Assistants. The Assistant creates a column with the data from each field that you select and use the fields' names as the titles at the head of each column.

If you use fields from more that one database, Approach displays the Define Main Database dialog box when you are done, and you can use its drop-down to select the main database.

Changing the Design of a Worksheet

It is easy to change the design of a Worksheet—for example, to edit column titles or change the size or order of columns. Unlike the other views that you have already learned about, Worksheets can be redesigned in either Browse or Design mode.

If a file is password protected, however, the designs of its worksheets can be changed only in Design mode. Password protection (covered in Chapter 11), can be used to let some users edit data without being able to redesign views. You can require users to enter a password to switch to Design mode. It would defeat the purpose of password protection to allow users to change the design of a worksheet in Browse mode, and so the design features discussed below are disabled in Browse mode if password protection is added to the file.

Unless there is password protection, you can change a worksheet in the ways described below in either Design or Browse mode. This makes the Worksheet behave more like a spreadsheet.

Selecting Parts of a Worksheet

It is useful to select columns of a worksheet to work with them in the ways described below, and to select individual cells and ranges of cells in a worksheet to work with data.

Select parts of a Worksheet in the following ways:

- To select a *single cell,* click on it. A box is displayed around it to show it is selected.
- To select a *range of cells,* click and drag over them. They are displayed in black (except for the current cell, which has a dark border around it) to show they are selected.
- To select a *column,* click its header. It is displayed in black (except for the current cell, which has a dark border around it) to show it is selected.
- To select *multiple columns,* click and drag over their headers. They are displayed in black (except for the current cell, which has a dark border around it) to show they are selected.
- To select a *row,* click to the left of the row. It is displayed in black (except for the current cell, which has a dark border around it) to show it is selected.
- To select the *entire Worksheet,* click the box in its upper left corner.

In addition, if a row or cell is selected, an arrowhead is displayed to the left of that row: this is called the *row marker.*

There are occasions, sometimes, when you want to select just a column header or just column cells, rather than selecting the entire column. Do this in the following ways:

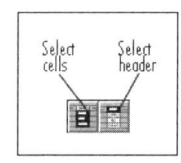

Figure 9.3 The icons for selecting column cells or headers.

- To select just a column header, first click the **Header** to select the entire column. Then click the **Select Header** icon (see Figure 9.3) or choose **Select** from the Worksheet menu and **Header Only** from the submenu. Alternatively, you can select just the column header by double-clicking it or by holding down **Ctrl** while you click it.
- To select just the column cells, first click **Header** to select the entire column. Then click the **Select Cells** icon (see Figure 9.3) or choose **Select** from the Worksheet menu and **Cells Only** from the submenu.

Working with Columns and Rows

When you first create a Worksheet, each column contains the data from one field. You can also add columns with additional fields or columns to hold calculations. Working with columns is central to changing the way that data is displayed in the Worksheet.

In addition, you may want to resize both columns and rows, if you want to use a larger typeface.

Adding a Field to a Worksheet

To add a field to a Worksheet, click the **Add Field** icon of the icon bar or choose **Add Field** from the Worksheet menu to display the Add Field Box (see Figure 9.4).

You can use the **Add Field Box** with worksheets just as you learned to do with other types of designs: simply click and drag a field from this box to the worksheet to add it to the worksheet. Approach adds a new column to the worksheet to hold the new field.

Inserting a Formula Column

You can also add a blank column to a Worksheet, which you can use to hold a calculation.

Practical Approach, 3.0

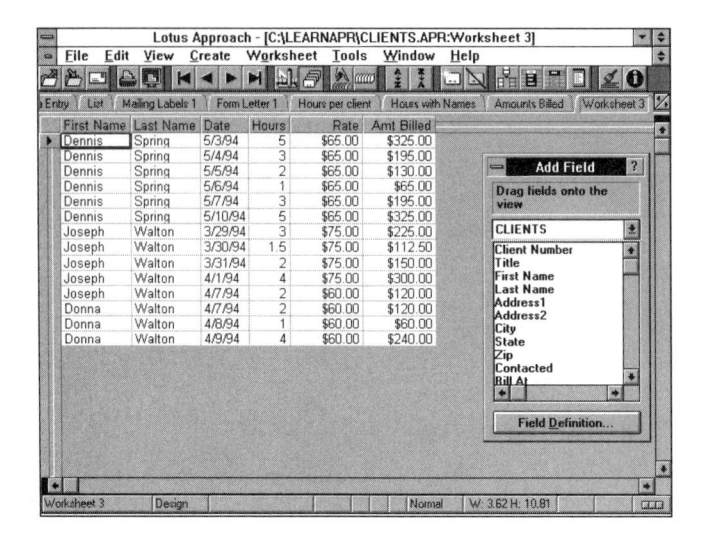

Figure 9.4 Using the Add Field Box with a Worksheet.

Adding a Blank Column

To add a column, simply place the pointer at the edge of an existing column and the very top of the column header, so it is displayed as a wedge (see Figure 9.5). You can simply click to add a new, blank column to the Worksheet (see Figure 9.6).

Figure 9.5 The pointer is displayed as a wedge where you can add a new column.

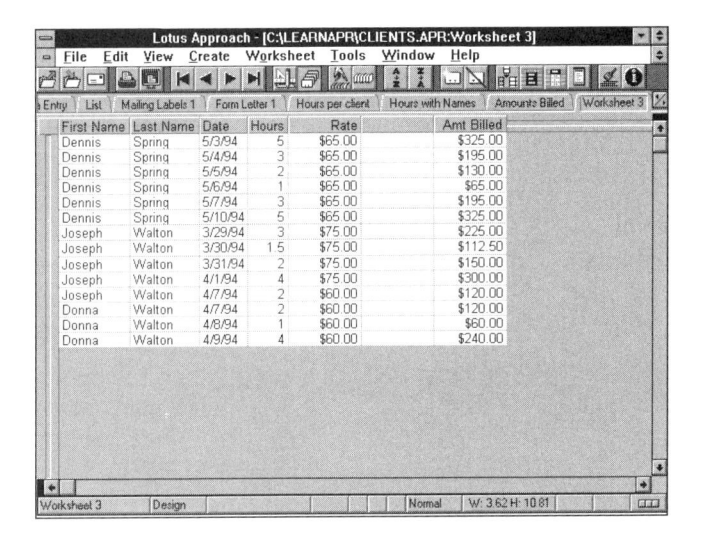

Chapter 9: Analyzing Your Data: Worksheets, Crosstabs, and Charts 335

Figure 9.6 Adding a blank column.

You can also add a blank column to the right of the current column by clicking the **Insert Column** icon or by choosing **Add Column** from the Worksheet menu.

Adding a Calculation

Once you have added a blank column, simply type a formula in any of its cells. Press **Enter** and a value based on that formula is entered in all of the cells of the column. Formulas were covered in Chapter 8.

In the illustration, the formula **Hours * Rate** was entered in one of the cells of a blank column added to the right of the other columns, and this column was given the heading Amt Billed (see Figure 9.7). As you can see, each cell in the column displays a value that is equal to the amount in the row's Hours field times the amount in the row's Rate field.

Removing a Column from a Worksheet

To remove a column from the Worksheet, click its header to select the column. After the column is selected, move the pointer to its header again—the pointer is displayed as a hand to show that it can be used to move the column. Click and drag the header upward, outside of the Worksheet and release the mouse button to remove that column from the worksheet (see Figure 9.8).

Practical Approach, 3.0

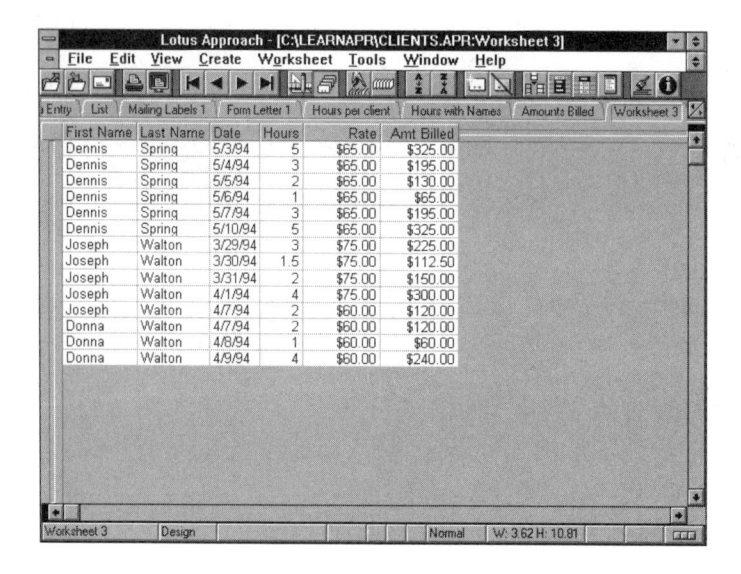

Figure 9.7 The Amount Billed field with a Formula.

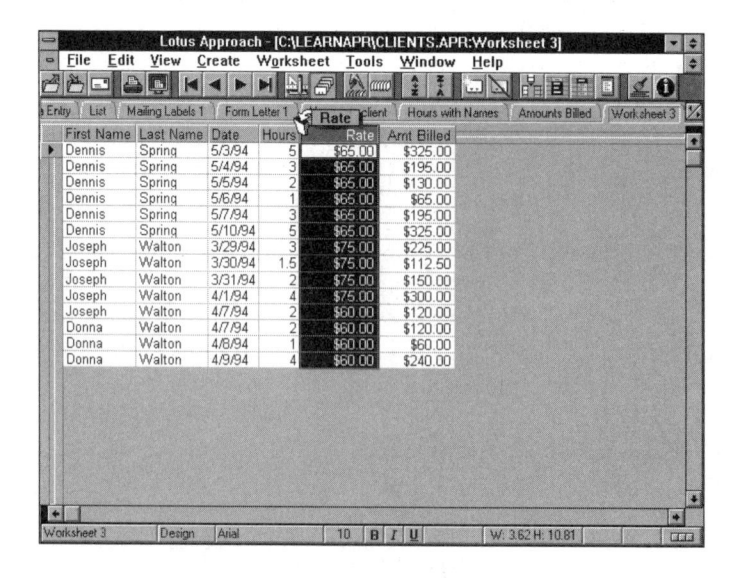

Figure 9.8 Removing a Column from a Worksheet.

Chapter 9: Analyzing Your Data: Worksheets, Crosstabs, and Charts

Use this method to remove either a field or a formula column from the Worksheet.

> **NOTE:** You can restore the column to the Worksheet by choosing **Undo** from the Edit menu.

You can also remove a column by selecting it and pressing **Del**. Again, you can undo the change by choosing **Undo** from the Edit menu.

Moving Columns

To move a column, click its header to select the column. Then move the pointer to its header again—the pointer is displayed as a hand to show that you can move the column. Click and drag the header left or right to move the column, changing the order of columns in the worksheet. The column's title is displayed and a vertical line to indicate its current location as you drag it (see Figure 9.9).

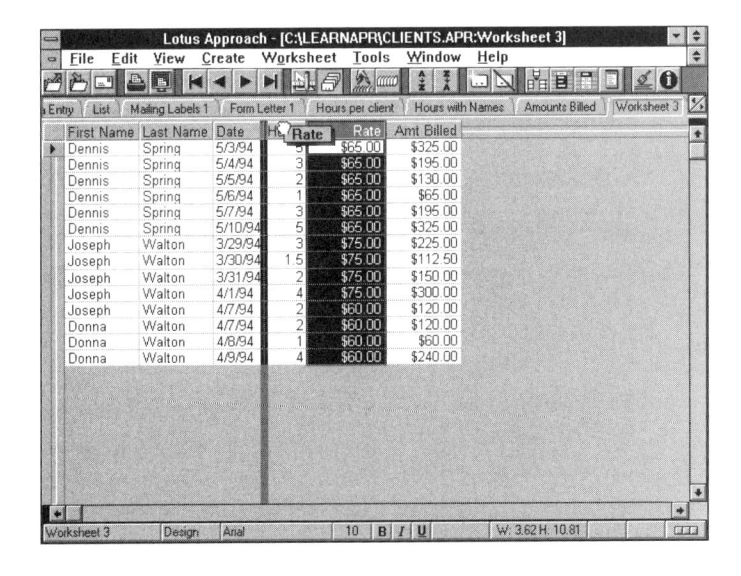

Figure 9.9 Moving a Column.

Choose **Undo** from the Edit menu to return the column to its previous location.

Editing a Column Header

By default, a column that contains field data has the field's name in its header, and a formula column has nothing in its header.

You can edit the text in the header in the following ways:

- Select only the header, not the entire column: you can do this either by clicking the header twice or by selecting the column and clicking the **Select Header** icon. Then click the header again to place an insertion bar in it.
- Select the column, and then choose **Edit Column Label** from the Worksheet menu to place an insertion bar in the header.

Once it has an insertion bar in it, you can use the usual windows editing methods to edit it.

Resizing Columns and Rows

Columns and rows are resized using similar methods. The major difference is that columns may be resized individually, while all rows must be the same size. You can choose **Undo** from the Edit menu to undo either change.

Resizing a Column

To resize a column, simply move the pointer to the right edge of its header. The pointer is displayed as a vertical line with arrows pointing left and right. Then you can drag rightward to make the column larger or leftward to make it smaller.

Resizing a Row

To resize all rows in the worksheet, move the pointer to the lower edge of any row. The pointer is displayed as a horizontal line with arrows pointing up and down. Then you can drag downward to make the row larger or upward to make it smaller.

NOTE: When you release the mouse button, all of the rows are displayed in the new size.

Styles and Properties of Worksheets

As with other types of View, you can choose **Style & Properties** from the Worksheet menu or click the **Info Box** icon to display the Info Box for a Worksheet or for individual columns. In general, these are both similar to other Info Boxes.

The Info Box for the Worksheet

Usually, unless one or more columns are selected, Approach displays the Info Box for the Worksheet. The Basics panel of this Info Box lets you rename the view, select its Main database and menu bar, and Hide it in browse (see Figure 9.10).

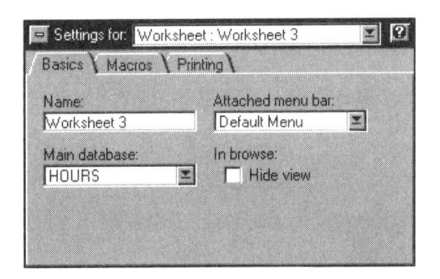

Figure 9.10 The Basics Panel of the Info Box for the Worksheet.

The Macros panel lets you specify Macros that run when you switch into or out of the view. Macros are covered in Chapter 10.

The Printing panel lets you set specifications that are useful when you print the Worksheet (see Figure 9.11).

The options for the Printing panel are as follows:

- *Print title:* Select the **Print title** checkbox and enter a title in the text box to its right if you want a title above the printout of the worksheet.
- *Print grid:* Select the **Print grid** check box if you want the print out to include the grid of lines between the cells of the Worksheet.
- *Print date and Print Page number:* Select these checkboxes if you want the printout to include the current date and page numbers.

Practical Approach, 3.0

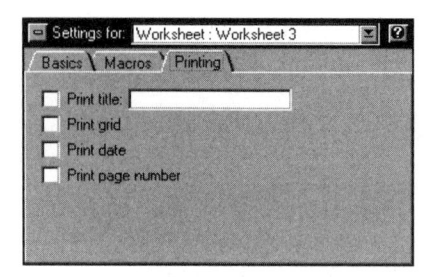

Figure 9.11 The Printing Panel for the Worksheet.

The Info Box for Columns

If columns are selected, Approach displays the Info Box shown Figure 9.12.

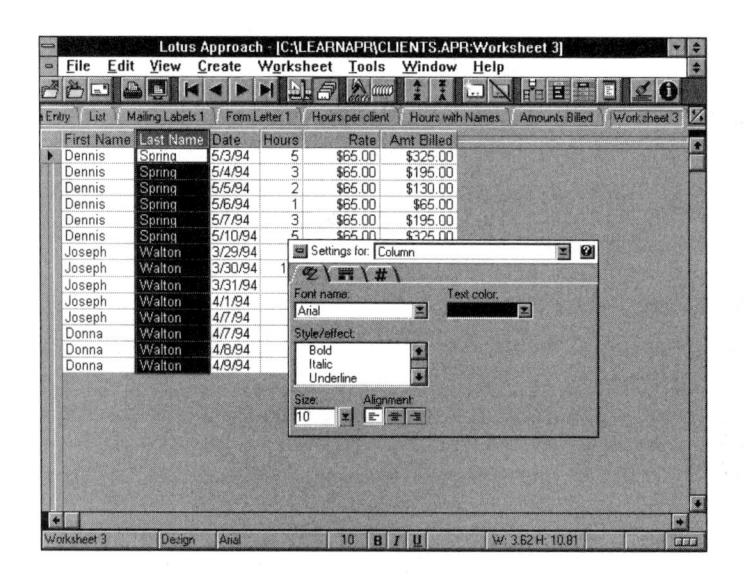

Figure 9.12 The Worksheet Info Box for Columns.

The Panels for this Info Box have the following features:

- The first panel lets you select the typeface, size, style, alignment and other effects of its font.

- The second panel lets you select the fill color and border color of the column—this border color applies to the entire column, not to individual cells.
- The third panel lets you format data, and its options depend on the data type.

> **SHORTCUT** These styles and properties apply to columns, but you can apply them to the entire Worksheet by clicking and dragging across the column headings to select all the columns of the Worksheet and then using the Info Box.

The Info Box for Headers

If you are editing the text in the header of columns, an Info Box is displayed with Fonts, Lines and a Colors panel, which you can use to specify properties for the header.

Viewing and Working with Data in Worksheets

Though you move among cells a bit differently in Worksheets than in other Approach views, you edit data in much the same way.

Editing Data

To replace the contents of any cell, simply select the cell and type over its contents.

> **WARNING** By default, there is no insertion bar in the selected cell of a Worksheet and its contents is not highlighted. Yet, if you type anything, it immediately replaces the contents of the cell. To cancel this change, you can simply press **Esc**.

To edit the data in the cell of a **Worksheet**, double-click it to place an insertion bar in it. The data in the cell is selected, so anything you enter replaces it. However, as with other Window editors, you can use any of the cursor movement keys to deselect the data, so that what you type is inserted.

Moving among Cells

If a cell is selected but does not have an insertion point in it, you can use the arrow keys to move right, left, up or down, to the next cell. You may also press

Tab or Shift+Tab to move right or left one cell and PgUp and PgDn to move up or down.

If a cell has an insertion point in it, the **Arrow** keys move the insertion point within the cell. You must press **Tab** or **Shift+Tab** to move right or left and **PgUp** and **PgDn** to move up or down.

If a range of cells is selected, you may also press **Enter** to move down a cell and to continue to the next column when you reach the end of a column. You may move the focus through all the cells of a selected range column by column by pressing **Enter** repeatedly. You may move the focus through all the cells of a selected range row by row by pressing **Tab** repeatedly.

Using the Pane Divider

SHORTCUT

If a database has a large number of records, you may want to divide the Worksheet in two separate panes, so you can see records from both parts at the same time.

To do this, you simply have to click and drag the pane divider (see Figure 9.13). The pointer is displayed as a two-header arrow, pointing up and down, when you can click and drag the pane divider.

Figure 9.13 A Worksheet divided into two panes.

Chapter 9: Analyzing Your Data: Worksheets, Crosstabs, and Charts

When you first open a Worksheet, the pane divider is at the very top of the right scroll bar, so there is only one pane. You can:

- Click and drag it down to open a second pane.
- Click and drag it at any time after a second pane is open to resize the panes.
- Click and drag it back to its original position to close the top pane and leave only one pane visible again.

The two panes have separate scroll bars, so you can choose which records you want to see in each independently.

The Worksheet Menu

When you are using a worksheet, either in Browse or in Design mode, the Browse menu is replaced by the Worksheet menu (see Figure 9.14).

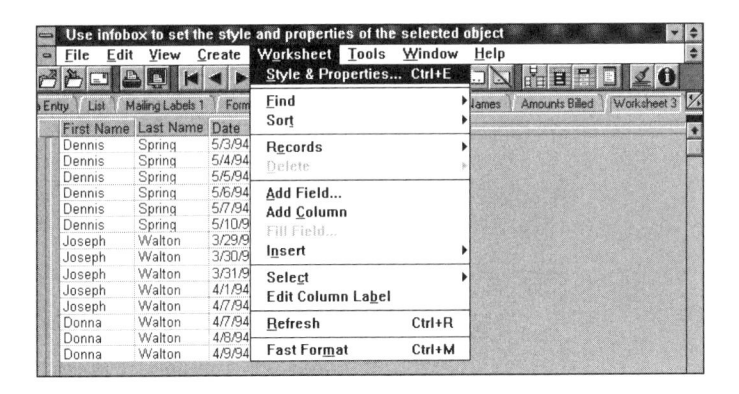

Figure 9.14 The Worksheet menu.

Because you can design a worksheet in either Browse or Design mode, this menu includes some Commands that you are familiar with from the Browse menu, as well as special Worksheet commands. It includes the following commands:

- *Style & Properties:* Displays the Info Box.

- *Find:* Displays a submenu with the options **Find**, **Find Again**, **Find Special**, and **Show All**, which work like the same options of the Browse menu.
- *Sort:* Displays a submenu that lets you sort the records in Ascending or Descending order based on a single field or fill out the Sort dialog box to create a custom sort order.
- *Records:* Displays a submenu with the options **New**, **Duplicate**, or **Hide**, which work like the equivalent options on the Browse menu.
- *Delete:* Displays a submenu with options that let you delete **Selected Records** or the entire **Found Set**. You must select (highlight) a row to delete it.
- *Add Field:* Displays (or hides) the Add Field box. You can click and drag fields from this box to the Worksheet to add new columns with the data from those fields.
- *Add Column:* Adds a blank column to the right of the currently column.
- *Fill Field:* Fills all the values in a field with a value, like the **Fill Field** command of the Browse menu.
- *Insert:* Displays a submenu that lets you insert the date, time or previous value in a field, like the Insert command of the Browse menu.
- *Select:* Displays a submenu with the options **Header Only** and **Cells Only**, used to select just the header or just the cells of the currently selected column.
- *Edit Column Label:* Places an insertion point in the header of the currently selected column, so you can edit its label.
- *Refresh:* Displays current data, including any changes that have been made by other people on a network, like the **Refresh** command of the Browse menu.
- *Fast Format:* Lets you apply a fast format, you can do when you are designing other views.

A Sample Worksheet

Now, try creating a sample worksheet to display the hours worked and billing rates on each of your jobs and add a formula column that calculates the amount billed. You can use the Assistant to place the columns as you want

Chapter 9: Analyzing Your Data: Worksheets, Crosstabs, and Charts

them, with the name at the left of each row. Make the Hours database the main database, so a record is displayed in the worksheet for each record in it.

1. Choose **Worksheet** from the Create menu to display the Worksheet Assistant. The fields from the Clients database should be displayed in the Database fields list: double-click the **First Name** and **Last Name** fields to add them both to the Fields to place on view list. Then select **Hours** from the Database fields drop-down, and double-click the **Date**, **Hours**, and **Rate** fields to add them to the Fields to place on view list (see Figure 9.15). Select **Done**.

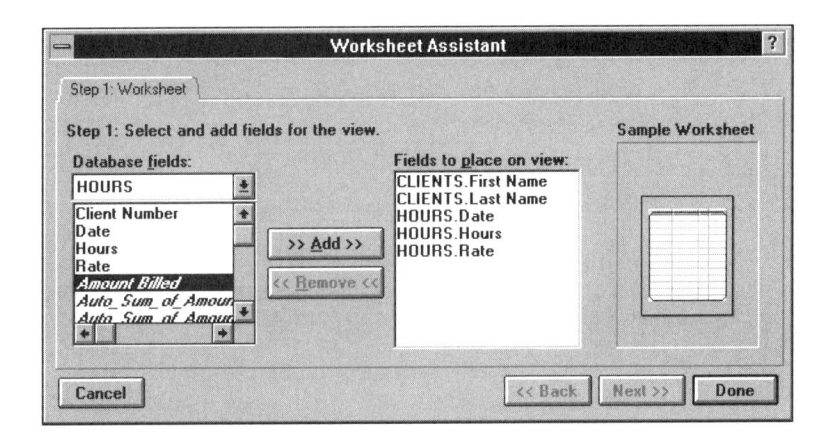

Figure 9.15 Using the Worksheet Assistant

2. Approach displays the Define Main Database dialog box. Select **Hours** from the Main Database drop-down and select **OK**. Approach creates the Worksheet (see Figure 9.16).

3. Now, name the Worksheet. If necessary, click the **Info Box** icon to display the Info Box for the entire Worksheet. Enter **Hours Worksheet** in the Name text box of the Basics panel. You may also want to click and drag to narrow the columns a bit.

4. Insert a blank row to hold a formula. Move the pointer to the upper right edge of the Rate column header, so it is displayed as a wedge, and click to add a blank column. Click any cell in the new column to select it, type **Hours * Rate** in it, and press **Enter**. The result of this calculation is displayed in every cell of the column (see Figure 9.17).

Practical Approach, 3.0

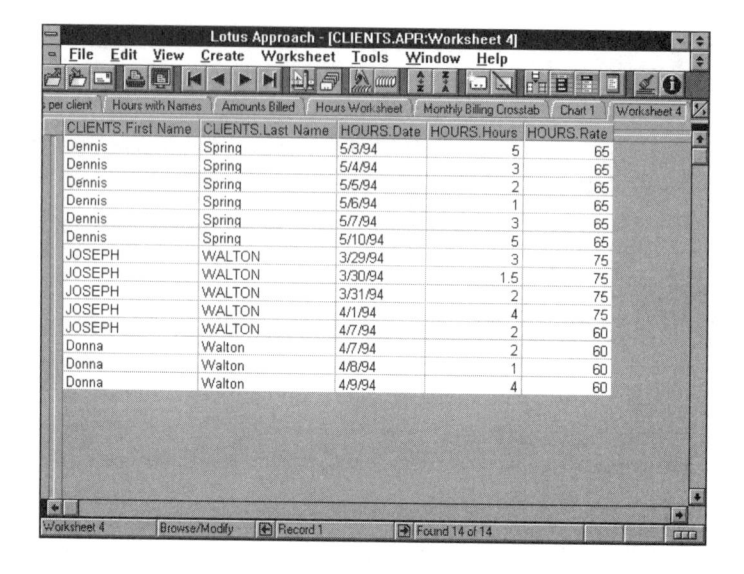

Figure 9.16 The Worksheet generated by the Assistant.

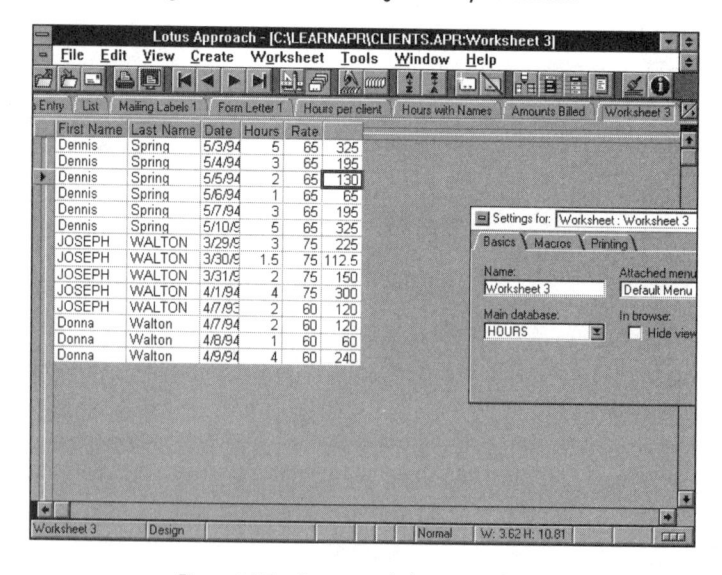

Figure 9.17 Entering a calculation in a column.

5. Click the new column's header to select the column, click **Select Label** to select only the column's header, and then click the header again to place an insertion point in it. Type **Amt Billed** as the column's header.

6. Format the text properly. Click and drag across the headers of the **First Name** and **Last Name** columns to select them both. The Info Box should already be displayed. Click its format panel and select **Text** from the Format type drop-down. Then select **First Capitalized** from the Current format drop-down. The Names should all be capitalized correctly.

7. Now, click and drag across the headers to select the Rate and Amt Billed columns. Select **Numeric** from the Format type drop-down, and select **Currency** with decimals from the Current Format drop-down. In addition, display the **Fonts** panel of the Info Box and select **Right Alignment** for both.

8. To add a final touch to the formatting, click and drag the right edges of the headers of any columns that need to be resized, and close the Info Box (see Figure 9.18).

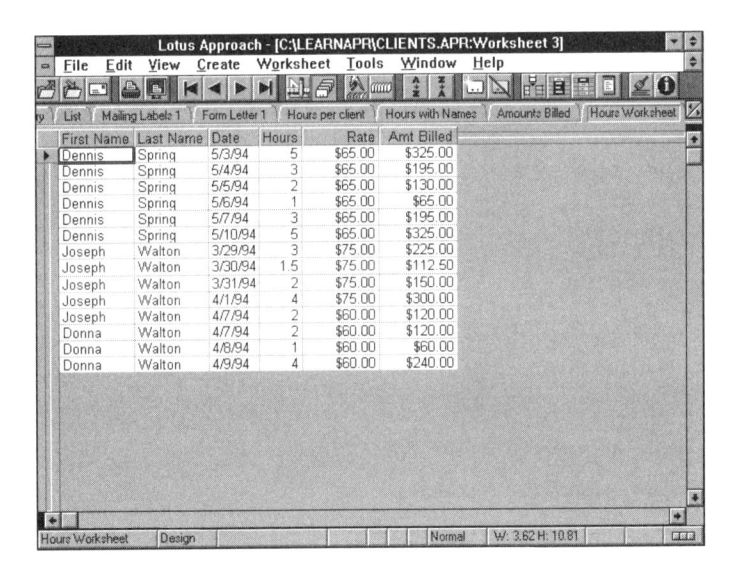

Figure 9.18 The final design of the Worksheet.

Crosstabs

A crosstab is a table that summarizes the data in database by cross-tabulating it. It uses the values from one field as the labels of the table's columns, and the values of another field as the labels of the table's rows. Each cell of the table holds a summary of all the records that have the row and column title in those fields.

For example, a crosstab that summarizes the amount billed to clients by month uses the month as column titles and the Client numbers as row titles. Each cell has the total amount billed to that client in that month, with the first column for the clients who have no billing month.

You can see that Approach also adds a total column and row. The column at the right summarizes the total billed to each client. The bottom row summarizes the total billed each month.

There are many types of data that crosstabs can display very effectively. If you sell a number of different products world-wide, for example, a crosstab is the most effective way of showing your total sales for each product in each country.

Creating a New Crosstab

You can create a crosstab by using the Assistant or by converting a Worksheet into a crosstab.

The Crosstab Assistant

Choose **Crosstab** from the Create menu to display the Crosstab Assistant (see Figure 9.19).

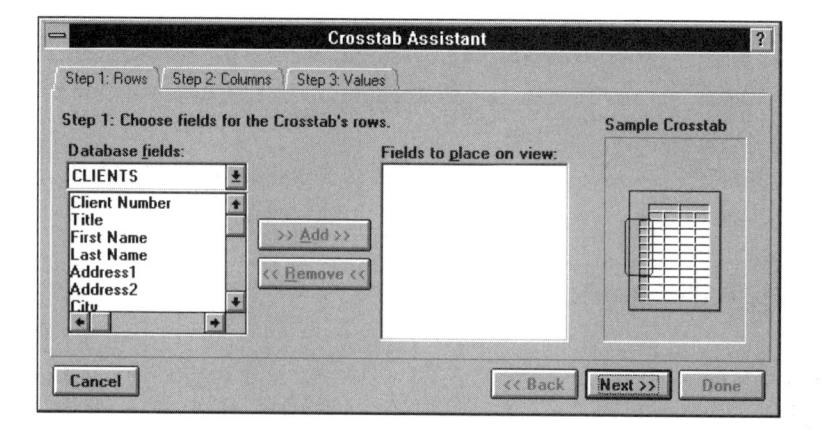

Figure 9.19 The Crosstab Assistant, Step 1: Rows.

As you can see in Figure 9.19, Step 1: Rows lets you choose one or more fields whose values are used as labels for the rows of the crosstab. Ordinarily, you would choose one field—for example, the **Client Number** if you want each cell to display information on each client.

> **NOTE** If you choose more than one field, Approach nests them. For example, if you choose **State** as the first field and **City** as the second, Approach creates a row for each city but groups the cities by state.

The Crosstab Assistant, Step 2: Columns, is identical to Step 1: Rows and is used to choose one or more fields whose values are used as labels of the crosstab's columns.

Step 3: Values, lets you define the values that are displayed in the cells of the crosstab. You use the drop-down to choose a Summary function, such as **average**, **number of items**, or **sum**, and you use the field list to choose a field (see Figure 9.20).

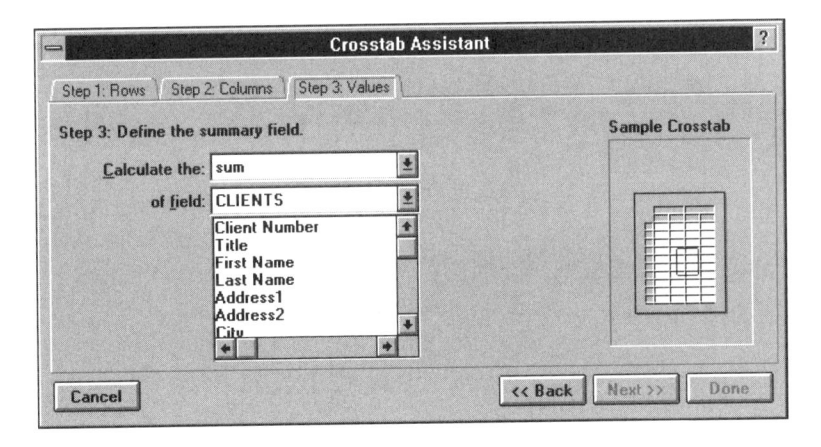

Figure 9.20 The Crosstab Assistant Step 3: Values.

Converting a Worksheet to a Crosstab

> **SHORTCUT** It is very easy to convert a worksheet into a crosstab. Simply drag the heading of one of the worksheet's columns to its left edge, where the contents of its fields are used as the basis of the crosstab's rows.

If you have a Worksheet that lists the amount of hours worked for each client and it includes a column with the state each client lives in, for example, you can convert it into a crosstab that shows the number of hours worked for clients in each state simply by dragging the header of the state column to the left edge of the worksheet.

When you create a crosstab in this way, Approach automatically displays the sum of the values.

Modifying a Crosstab

After you have created a crosstab, you can work with it in many of the same ways you do with worksheets, though there are some differences. The major difference is that you cannot edit the values in cells of a crosstab, because they are all based on calculations.

Like a Worksheet, a Crosstab can generally be modified in either Browse or Design mode. If the Approach File is password protected, though, you must use the password to switch to Design mode in order to modify the Crosstab.

Styles and Properties of Worksheets

As with other types of View, you can choose **Style & Properties** from the Crosstab menu or click the **Info Box** icon to display the Info Box for a Crosstab or for individual columns or rows. These are similar to the Info Box for Worksheets.

The Info Box for the Crosstab

Unless columns or rows are selected the Info Box displays the Crosstab Info box (see Figure 9.21).

This Info Box is the same as the Worksheet Info Box:

- *Basics panel*. Lets you rename the view, select its **Main database**, select its menu bar, and **Hide** it in browse.
- *Macros panel*. Specifies Macros that run when you switch into or out of the view.
- *Printing panel*. Lets you add a title, date and page number to the printout and include the grid of lines between the cells of the Crosstab.

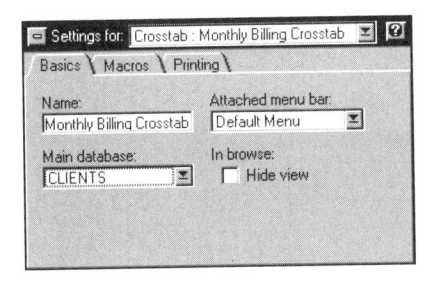

Chapter 9: Analyzing Your Data: Worksheets, Crosstabs, and Charts

Figure 9.21 The Info Box for the Crosstab.

The Info Box for Columns and Rows

If columns or rows are selected, an Info Box is displayed that is similar to the Info Box for columns of Worksheets (see Figure 9.22).

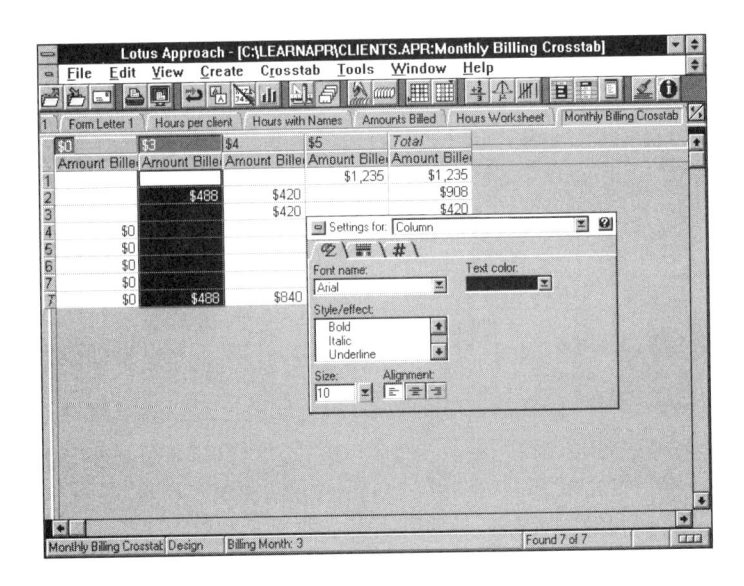

Figure 9.22 The Info Box for Columns or Rows of a Crosstab.

Its panels are similar to ones you have used in many other dialog boxes. They let you specify fonts, borders and colors, and field formatting.

> **NOTE:** Whether you apply these to columns or to rows depends on which summary you want to emphasize.

The Info Box for Headers

You can select the header of a column or row in a crosstab the same way you select the header of a column in a worksheet.

If just the Header of a columns or row is selected, the Info Box for Headers is displayed, which is similar to the Info Box for columns or rows. Use it to specify the font, color and border, and formatting of the header.

The Crosstab Menu

When you are using a Crosstab in either Browse or Design mode, the Browse menu is replaced by the Crosstab menu (see Figure 9.23).

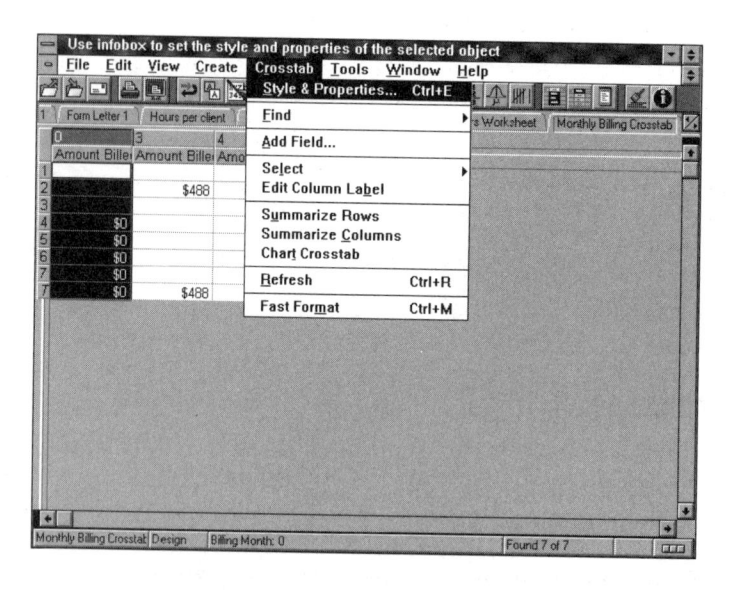

Figure 9.23 The Crosstab menu.

This menu includes the following commands:

- *Style & Properties:* Displays the Info Box.
- *Find:* Displays a submenu with the options **Find, Find Again, Find Special**, and **Show All**, which work like those options of the Browse menu.
- *Add Field:* Displays the **Add Field** box. You can click and drag fields from this box to the Worksheet to add new columns with the data from those fields.
- *Select:* Displays a submenu with the options **Header Only** and **Cells Only**, used to select just the header or just the cells of the currently selected column or row.
- *Edit Column Label:* Places an insertion point in the header of the currently selected column, so you can edit its label.
- *Summarize Rows:* Adds a Total column to the right of the other columns, which contains totals of the amounts in each row. Crosstabs created by the Assistant already have a Total column.
- *Summarize Columns:* Adds a Total row below the other rows, which contains totals of the amounts in each column. Crosstabs created by the Assistant already have a Total row.
- *Chart Crosstab:* Generates a chart based on the crosstab. Charts are covered in the final section of this chapter.
- *Refresh:* Displays current data, including any changes that have been made by other people on a network, like the Refresh command of the Browse menu.
- *Fast Format:* Lets you apply a fast format, as you can do when you are designing other views.

A Sample Crosstab

Now, try creating a simple crosstab that plots the amount billed to each client each month. Before you can use the Crosstab Assistant, you must create a calculated field whose value contains just the month from the Date field from the Hours database, so you can use it as the head of the Crosstab columns.

1. Choose **Field Definition** from the Create menu. In the Field Definition dialog box, select **Hours** from the Database drop-down. To add a new

field to the database, scroll down if necessary, click the blank cell at the bottom of the Field Name column and type the name **Billing Month**. As the Data Type, select **Calculated**. Approach displays the Define Formula panel. First, select **Month** from the function list. Then use the Fields drop-down of this panel to select the **Hours** database, and click the **Date** field in the Fields list under it. Approach generates the Formula (see Figure 9.24). Select **OK**.

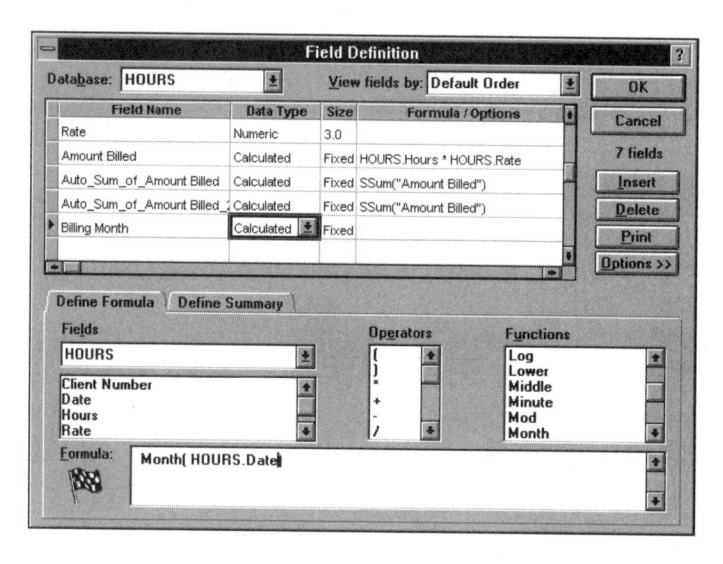

Figure 9.24 Creating a calculated field.

2. Next, choose **Crosstab** from the Create menu to display the Crosstab Assistant. In Step 1: Rows, double-click **Client number** to select it as the field used as the basis of the Crosstab's rows. Click the **Step 2: Columns** divider tab, and then select **Hours** from the Database fields drop-down, and double-click **Billing Month** in the fields list, to choose it as the basis of the Crosstab's columns.

3. Click **Step 3: Values**. Leave **Sum** in the Calculate drop-down. Select **Hours** from the Fields drop-down and **Amount Billed** from the fields list under it (see Figure 9.25). Then select **Done** to generate the Crosstab (see Figure 9.26).

4. If necessary, click the **Info Box** icon to display the Info Box for the entire crosstab. As the Name, enter **Monthly Billing Crosstab**. Then select all the columns, display the Format panel of the Info Box, select

Numeric as the Format type, and select **Currency** as the Current Format. Now, so that Headers are not formatted as currency, choose **Select** from the Crosstab menu and **Header Only** from the submenu to select only column headers; in the Format panel of the Info Box, select **Display as Entered** as the Current Format, so that headers are displayed without formatting. If you would like, you could also edit the headers so they display the names of the months instead of their numbers.

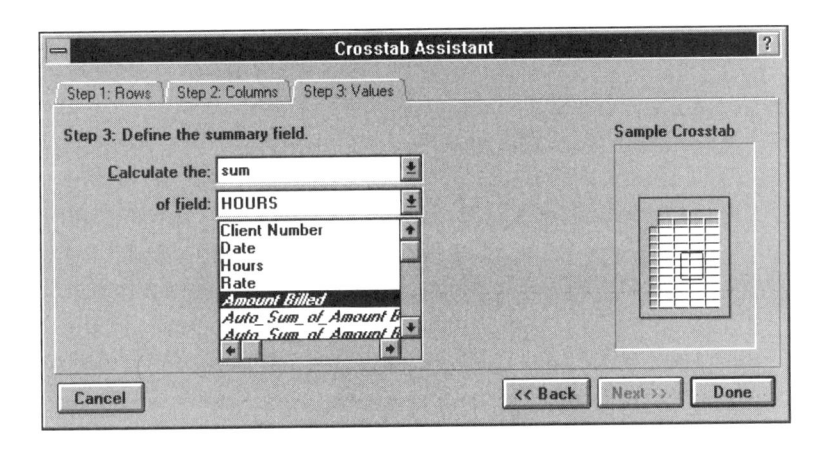

Figure 9.25 The Crosstab Assistant Step 3: Values.

Charts

The Chart Assistant gives you an easy of way of graphing your data. You can create two-dimensional and three-dimensional bar graphs, line graphs, area graphs, and pie graphs.

Creating a New Chart

Choose **Chart** from the Create menu to display the Chart Assistant (see Figure 9.26).

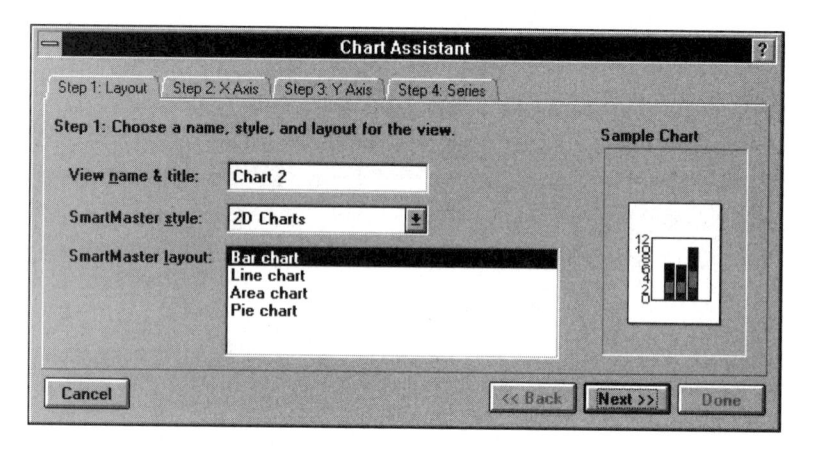

Figure 9.26 Step 1: Layout of the Chart Assistant.

As you can see in the figure, Step 1: Layout lets you enter a name and title for the chart, to choose **two-dimensional** or **three-dimensional** as the style, and to choose **Bar**, **Line Area**, or **Pie chart** as the layout. The same four layouts are available for both two and three-dimensional graphs. Approach displays a sample of the style and layout that you choose on the right side of this panel.

All of these types except the Pie chart graph data on an x and y axis. If you produced a bar graph of the amounts that you billed your clients for example, the x-axis (at the bottom of the chart) would list the names of all your clients, and the y-axis (at the left of the chart) would list dollar amounts; the bar above each client's name would indicate the amount that you billed that client.

Pie charts, on the other hand, simply show a circle divided in areas representing amounts. If you produced a Pie Chart of the amounts that you billed your clients, the entire circle would represent the total you billed all your clients. It would be divided into areas whose size showed how much you billed each client as a portion of the total.

Because they do not use an x and y axis, pie charts are created differently from other charts.

The Chart Assistant for Bar, Line, and Area Charts.

If you select **Bar Chart**, **Line Chart**, or **Area Chart** in the Step 1: Layout panel, then Step 2: X axis lets you choose a field used for the x-axis (see Figure 9.27). Step 3: Y axis lets you choose a field used for the y-axis and works identically to Step 2: X axis.

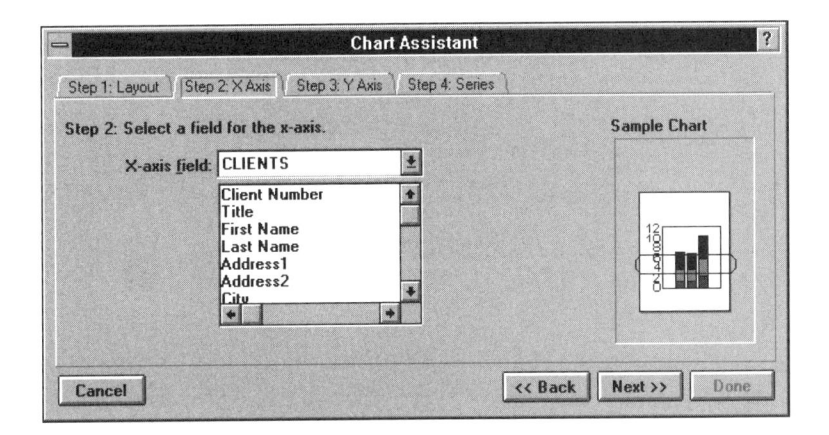

Figure 9.27 Choosing a field for the X axis.

Step 4: Series, which is optional, lets you choose a field that is used as the basis of a series. A series displays a number of values for each value in the x-axis. For example, if you are creating a bar graph of the amount you billed each client, you can use the calculated Billing Month field as the basis of a series; the chart displays a number of bars above each client's name, indicating the amount you billed the client each month.

The Chart Assistant for Pie Charts

If you select **Pie Chart** in Step 1: Layout the Assistant includes only one additional step (see Figure 9.28).

Use **Step 2: Pie Fields** to select the field that the chart is grouped on. If you were graphing the amounts you billed your clients, you would select **Client number**, so there would be one wedge for each client.

Use **Each wedge shows the:** to select the value that the chart represents, and use the drop-down to specify how it is summarized. For example, if you were graphing the amounts you billed your clients, you would select **Sum** from the drop-down and select the calculated **Amount Billed** field from the field list.

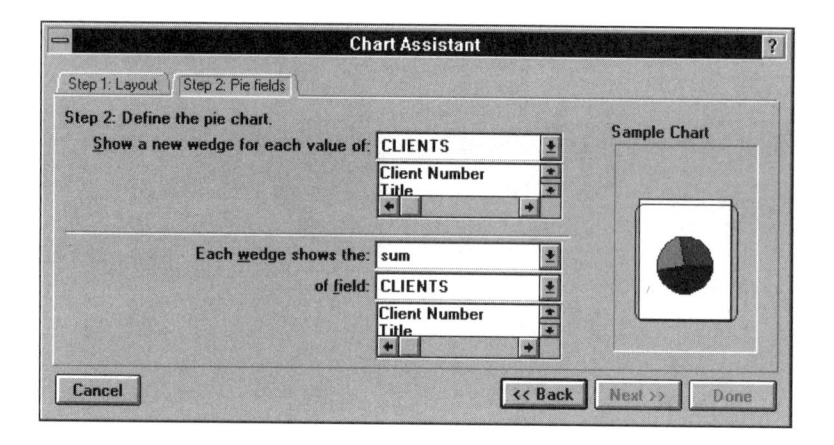

Figure 9.28 Creating a Pie Chart

Creating a Chart Based on a Crosstab

You may have noticed the similarity between the Chart and Crosstab assistant. You select a field for the x-axis and y-axis of a Bar, Line, or Area chart, just as you select values for the rows and columns of a crosstab.

SHORTCUT — You can create a chart based on a crosstab by choosing **Chart** from the Crosstab menu or clicking the **Chart** icon. The fields used for the crosstab's rows are used as the labels of the chart's x-axis. The fields in the columns are used as the basis of its y-axis.

Modifying a Chart

The Assistant creates a chart with the word *Title* as its title and (unless you created a Pie chart) the names of the fields you selected as the labels of its x-axis and y-axis.

These labels are simply text objects, and you can edit them in design mode just as you edit text objects in a Form or Report. Click the object to select it, and click it again to place an insertion point in it and edit it. You can also resize or move these text objects or add new objects to the chart.

Because it uses the Lotus Chart mini-application, which is included in a number of Lotus products, the Info Boxes of charts has a different look and feel than the Info Boxes used in other Approach views. For more information about the features of all the Info Boxes used by charts, see Approach's on-line help, which has comprehensive coverage of this subject.

Chapter 9: Analyzing Your Data: Worksheets, Crosstabs, and Charts

You can also modify the fields that the Chart is based on by choosing **Chart Data Source** from the Chart menu to display the Chart Data Source Assistant (see Figure 9.29). As you can see, this Assistant has panels like the ones in the Chart Assistant—for a pie chart, you can use it to change the pie fields, and for other types of charts, you can use it to select the fields that are the basis of the x-axis and y-axis and to create a series.

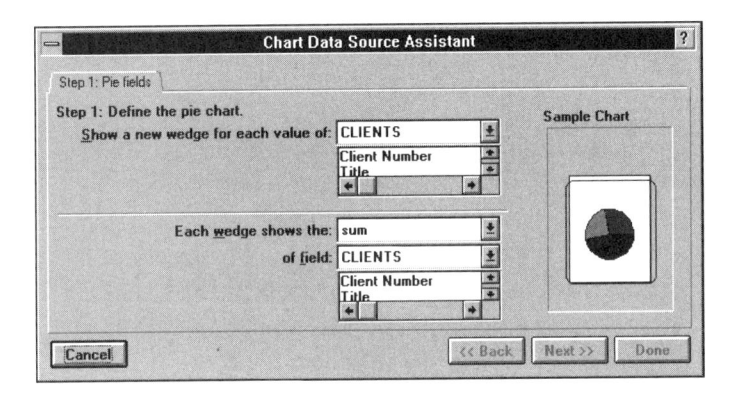

Figure 9.29 The Chart Data Source Assistant.

The Chart Menu

When you are using a Chart in Design mode, the Browse menu is replaced by the Chart menu (see Figure 9.30).

The Chart menu includes the following commands:

- *Style & Properties.* Displays the Info Box.
- *Chart Data Fields.* Displays the Chart Data Source Assistant, which lets you specify which fields should be used as the basis of the x-axis and y-axis or create a series (see Figure 9.29).
- *Arrange.* Is included on the menu only if an object is selected. Displays a submenu with the options **Bring to Front**, **Send to Back**, **Bring Forward**, **Send Backward**, which lets you change the stacking order of objects.
- *Align.* Is included on the menu only if an object is selected. Displays the Align dialog box, which lets you align objects vertically or horizontally.

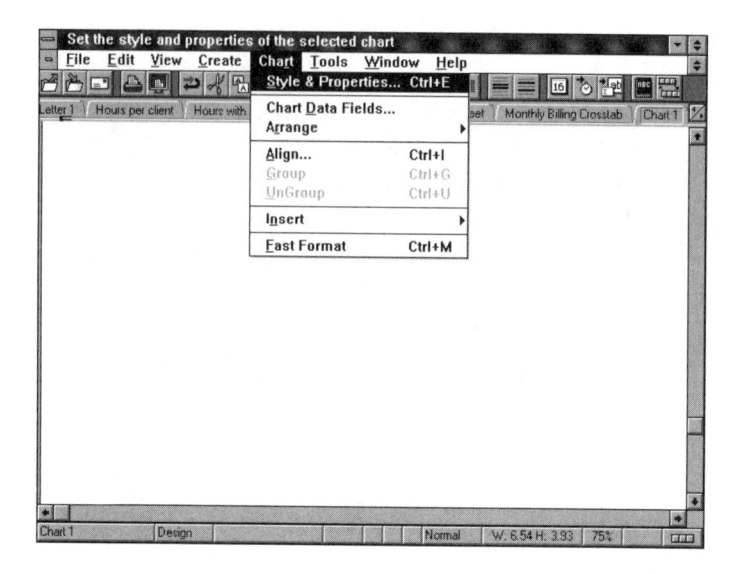

Figure 9.30 The Chart menu.

- *Group.* Is included on the menu only if an object is selected. Lets you group all the selected objects, so you can manipulate them as if they were a single object.
- *UnGroup.* Is included on the menu only if an object is selected. Lets you remove grouping that you created previously, so you can manipulate objects individually again.
- *Insert.* Displays a submenu that lets you insert the Date, Time or Page number in a text object.
- *Fast Format.* Lets you apply a fast format, as you can do when you are designing other views.

A Sample Chart

As a sample chart, you can do a Pie chart showing what portion of your hours you worked for each of your clients.

1. Choose **Chart** from the Create menu. As the SmartMaster layout, choose **Pie Chart**.

Chapter 9: Analyzing Your Data: Worksheets, Crosstabs, and Charts

2. Click the **Step 2** divider tab. In its top half, select **Client Number** as the field to show wedges for. In the bottom half, leave the sum as the summary function, select **Hours** as the database and Hours as the field (see Figure 9.31). Then select **Done**. Approach creates a chart (see Figure 9.32).

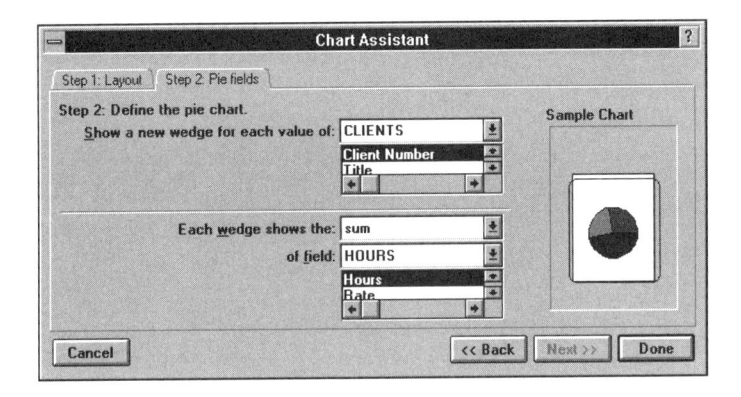

Figure 9.31   The Chart Assistant.

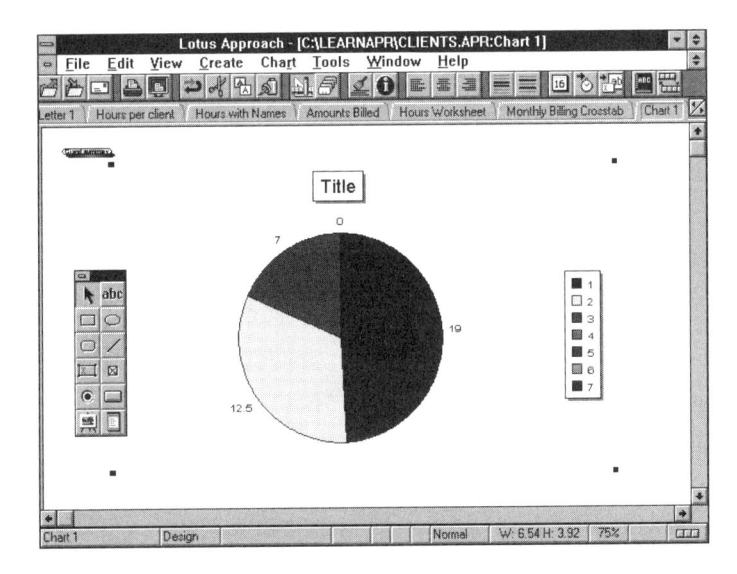

Figure 9.32   The finished Pie Chart.

The color-coded legend is not as clear in the illustration as it is on a color monitor. In color, this chart makes it very clear how your hours were divided among your clients—for example, that you worked about half of all hours for Client number 1.

If you want to experiment with the Approach charts, you can display the Info Box for this chart, edit its title, and change some of its other features.

Speeding Up Your Work with Macros

You can see that many operations you perform using Approach require a long series of commands. For example, to produce labels for your regular mailing, you might have to do a find based on the Mail To field, do a Sort based on the Zip field, switch the view so the mailing labels are displayed, and finally print the labels. In this chapter, you learn to automate this sort of repetitive task by using macros, which let you do all these things by making a single menu selection, pressing a single key, or simply by clicking a button or other object that you create. In this chapter, you learn:

- How to create, save and modify macros
- Which actions a macro can perform
- How to run macros using the menu or a function key
- How to attach macros to fields or views
- How to create chained macros

- How to add a push button to a form or other design and to create a macro that it runs
- How to attach an existing macro to a push button or other object in a design
- How to create a conditional macro
- How to use a formula in a macro to change the data in a field
- How to use a Variable field to control the execution of a macro

Creating and Using Macros

Macros in Approach are different from the macros that you may be familiar with from using other programs.

In older programs, macros hold a series of keystrokes, which all are executed automatically when you use the macro. You generally create a macro by making some menu selection to begin recording the macro, and then typing all the keystrokes that you want the macro to hold. Many Windows applications work in the same way, except that they turn off the mouse when you begin recording a macro, because it can only record keystrokes.

Approach macros are designed specifically for Windows users, who are more likely to use the mouse to execute commands than to use the keyboard. Rather than recording keystrokes, you use a dialog box to create a list of all the actions that the macro performs. You use the macro to perform all of the tasks that you specified, rather than performing each one individually.

Managing Macros

Choose **Macros** from the Tool menu to display the Macros dialog box (see Figure 10.1).

This dialog box is used to manage existing Macros as well as to create new ones. It contains a list of all the existing Macros in the current Approach file and the following push buttons:

- *Done.* Click this button to close the dialog box, saving all the changes you made.

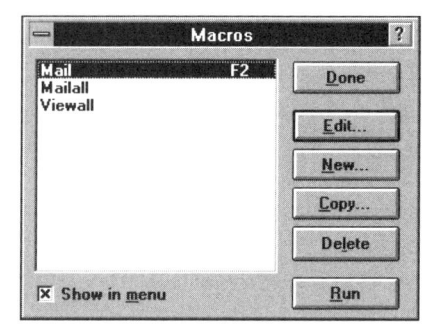

Chapter 10: Speeding Up Your Work with Macros   **365**

Figure 10.1   The Macros dialog box.

- *Edit.* Select a macro in the list and click the **Edit** button to display the Define Macro dialog box with macro's specifications, so you can modify it.
- *New.* Click this button to display the Define Macro dialog box to create a new macro.
- *Copy.* Select a macro in the list and click the **Copy** button to display the Define Macro dialog box with a copy of that macro's specifications. Initially, the macro has a name made up of the words **Copy of** followed by the name of the macro you copied. You can change the name and any of its specifications. This is the easiest way to create a macro similar to an existing one.
- *Delete.* Select a macro in the list and click the **Delete** button to delete the Macro.
- *Run.* Select a macro in the list and click this button to run the Macro.

As you will see later in this chapter you can run macros from the menu system, but it you select a macro in the Macros dialog box and deselect the **Show** checkbox, it is not displayed on the menu.

Notice that you cannot cancel changes by using the Macros dialog box. Many of its buttons display the Define Macro dialog box, however, and you can cancel the changes you make in the definition of a macro in that dialog box.

Defining a Macro

Create or modify a macro using the Define Macro dialog box (see Figure 10.2). As you can see, you use this dialog box to create a list of commands and to select options for each. When you run the Macro, Approach executes all the commands in the order they are listed.

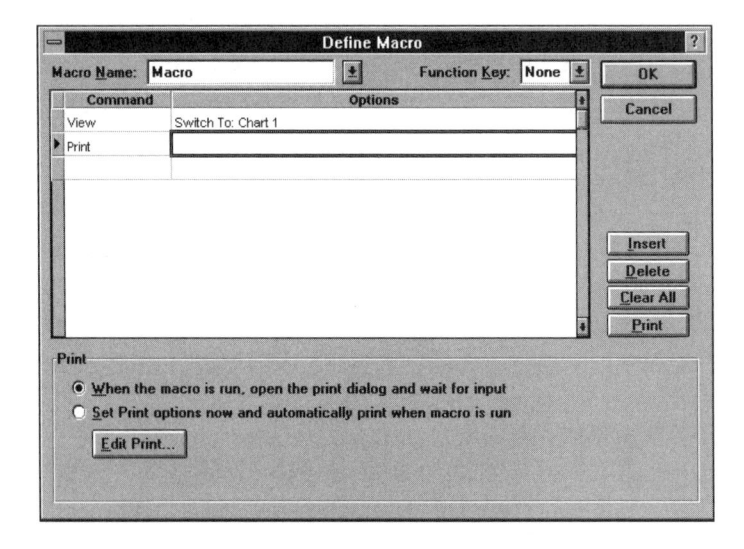

Figure 10.2 The Define Macro dialog box.

You can enter the name of a new macro in the Macro Name text box, or use the drop-down arrow to its right to select the name of an existing macro and display its actions in the list, so you can modify it.

> **NOTE** If you want to be able to run the Macro by pressing a function key, simply select that key from the Function Key drop-down.

Use the Command drop-down to select one of the commands macros can perform. There are many options available on this drop-down list (see Figure 10.3). Most of these Commands have options that are displayed in the panel in the bottom of the dialog box when you select the command from the drop-down. Options that you choose from this panel are displayed in the Options column of the Command list, to the right of each Command.

Chapter 10: Speeding Up Your Work with Macros

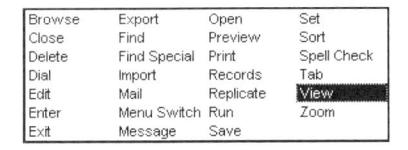

Browse	Export	Open	Set
Close	Find	Preview	Sort
Delete	Find Special	Print	Spell Check
Dial	Import	Records	Tab
Edit	Mail	Replicate	**View**
Enter	Menu Switch	Run	Zoom
Exit	Message	Save	

Figure 10.3 The Command drop-down list.

Add as many Commands as you want to the list in the same way, and specify options for each one. Approach always adds one blank row to the end of the list so you can add more commands.

You can change the order of commands already in the command list just as you do in the Field List of the Field definition dialog box:

- Click **Insert** to add a blank row above the current row.
- Select a row by clicking the indicator box to its left and click **Delete** to delete the row.
- Select a row by clicking the indicator box to its left and then click and drag the indicator box up or downward to move the row to another location in the list.
- Select **Clear All** to delete all the commands in the list.
- Select **Print** to display the Print dialog box and print the list. This can be useful for debugging, to let you look at the list while you are running the macro.

> **SHORTCUT**
> Approach automatically adds commands to this list if you perform them before using the Define Macro dialog box. If you switch the view and do a Find before defining a Macro, Approach automatically includes commands to switch to that view and perform that find at the beginning of the command list. The **Clear All** button is often useful to remove these commands.

Actions that Macros Can Perform

You can use the Command drop-down to include the following commands in Macros:

Browse

Select **Browse** from the drop-down to switch to the Browse mode. This is equivalent to choosing Browse from the View menu.

This command has no options.

Close

Choose **Close** from the drop-down to close the current Approach file. This is equivalent to choosing **Close** from the FIle menu.

This command has an option to automatically disconnect from the server if you are on a network.

Delete

Select **Delete** from the drop-down to delete records or a file (see Figure 10.4).

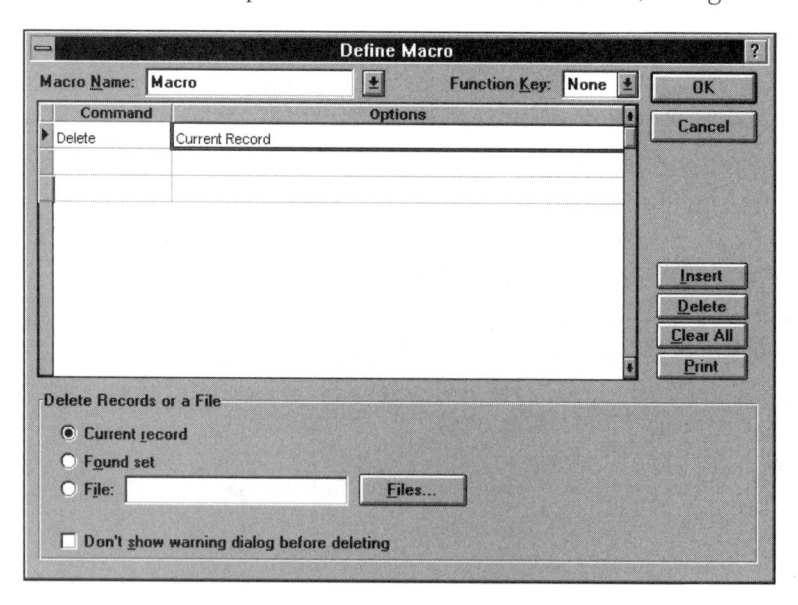

Figure 10.4 Options for the Delete Command.

This Command has the following options:

- Delete the current record.

- Delete all the records in the found set. Remember that you can include a Find in the macro before using the delete command.
- Delete a file. You can enter the name of the file in the text box or use the Files button to display a dialog box that lets you select it.

WARNING: By default, Approach displays a warning dialog box that lets you cancel the delete, but the checkbox in this panel lets you bypass the warning and delete the records or file immediately. Use this checkbox with caution.

Dial

Select **Dial** from the drop-down to dial a the telephone number in a field, assuming that you have a modem.

The options panel for this command displays a list of database fields, and you must select the field that holds the telephone number. Approach autodials the number in the current record.

Edit

Choose **Edit** from the drop-down to use any one of a number of editing commands (see Figure 10.5).

The edit Command has the options **Cut**, **Copy**, **Paste**, and **Select All**, which work in the same way as the equivalent commands of the Edit menu.

Of course, these are used in combination with each other. You can use Edit with the **Select All** option and then Edit with the **Copy** option to select and copy all the objects in a design, and later in the macro, use Edit with the **Paste** option to Paste those objects in a different Approach file.

This command also has an option to display the Paste Special dialog box for the user.

Enter

The **Enter** command of the drop-down is equivalent to pressing the **Enter** key.

This command has no options.

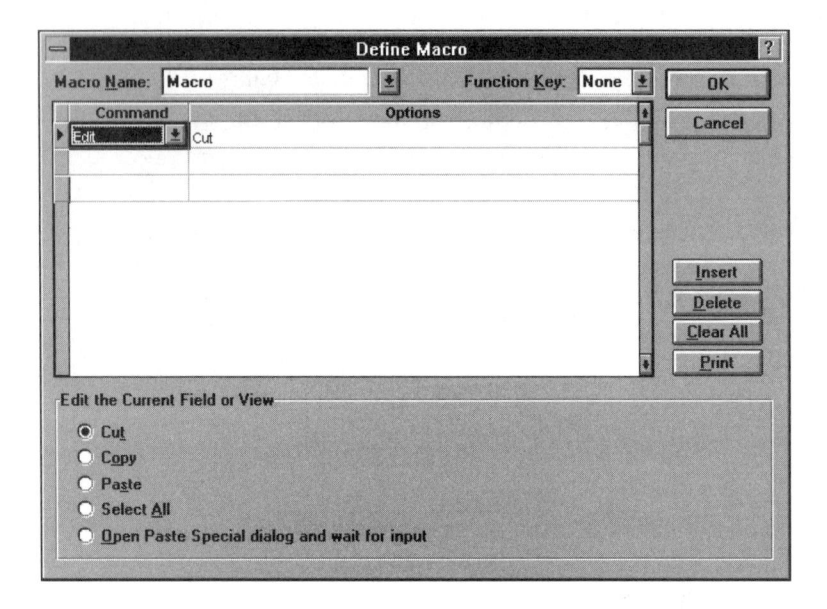

Figure 10.5 Options for the Edit Command.

Exit

Select **Exit** from the drop-down to quit Approach. This is equivalent to choosing **Exit** from the File menu.

This command has no options.

Export

Choose **Export** from the drop-down to export data so it can be used by another application. This command has two options:

- Display the Export Data dialog box as the Macro is running, so the user can specify how the data is exported.
- Sets the Export options while you are defining the macro.

This is equivalent to choosing **Export Data** from the File menu, which is covered in Chapter 12.

Find

Select **Find** to have the macro find a set of records (see Figure 10.6). This Command has the following options:

- *Perform stored find when macro is run:* You must click **New Find** or **Edit Find** while you are defining the macro, to display a find request and enter criteria for the find. The macro performs this find automatically,.
- *Go to Find and wait for input:* Displays a Find request while the macro is running and waits for the user to fill it out and press **Enter**. This is equivalent to choosing **Find** from the Browse menu.
- *Find Again and wait for input:* Displays a Find request with the criteria from the previous fiend. This is equivalent to choosing **Find Again** from the Browse menu.
- *Show all records:* Displays all the records. This is equivalent to choosing **Show All** from the Browse menu.
- *Refresh the found set:* Displays the current data in the found set, including changes that may have been made by other users of the network. This is equivalent to choosing **Refresh** from the Browse menu.

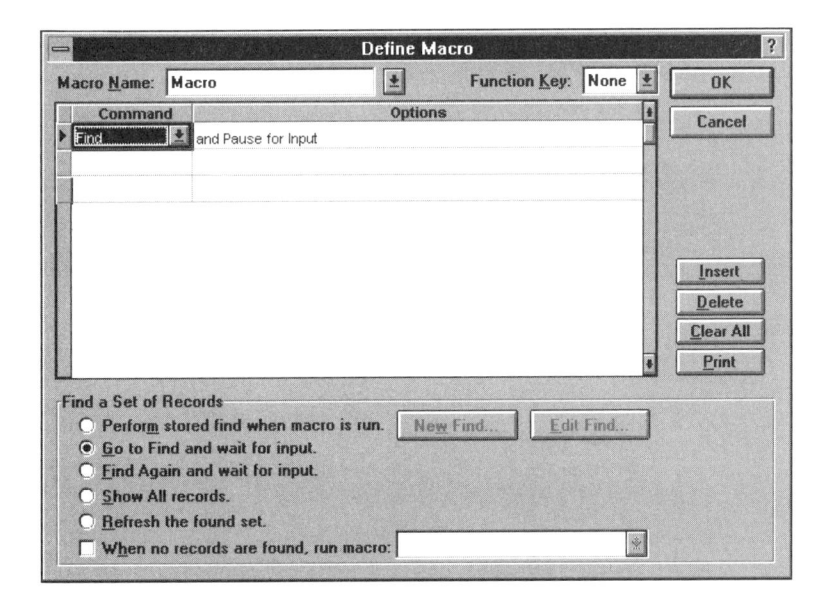

Figure 10.6 Options for the Find Command.

In addition to one of the above, you may specify a different macro to run if there are no records that match the criteria of the Find. Select the **When no records are found run macro:** checkbox and select a macro from the drop-down to its right.

Find Special

Select **Find Special** from the drop-down to find duplicate or unique records. This is equivalent to choosing **Find Special** from the Browse menu.

This Command has two options. You can use it to:

- Display the Find Special dialog box and wait for the user's input.
- Display the Find Special dialog box while you are defining the Macro. When the macro runs, it automatically performs the options you specify.

With either of these, you may specify a different macro to run if there are no records that match the criteria of the Special Find—choose **When no records are found run macro** and select a macro from the drop-down to its right.

Import

Select **Import** from the drop-down to import data from another application. This command has two options. You can use it to:

- Display the Import Data dialog box as the Macro is running, so the user can specify what data is imported.
- Set the Import options while you are defining the macro.

This is equivalent to choosing **Import Data** from the File menu, which is covered in Chapter 12.

Mail

Select **Mail** from the drop-down to send a Mail message

This command has two options. You can use it to:

- Display the Send Mail dialog box as the Macro is running, so the user can specify the message where the mail is sent and how the data is exported.

Chapter 10: Speeding Up Your Work with Macros 373

- Set the Send Mail options while you are defining the macro.

How this command is used depends on what mail application you have installed.

Menu Switch

Select **Menu Switch** from the drop-down to change the menu bar.

This Command has a drop-down that lets you display the Default menu, the Short menu, or a Custom menu, and a button that lets you display the Customize menus dialog box to create a custom menu. Short menus and custom menus are covered in Chapter 11.

Message

Choose **Message** from the drop-down to display a dialog box with a message for the user.

This Command has text boxes where you can enter a title for the dialog box and the text for the message that it displays (see Figure 10.7).

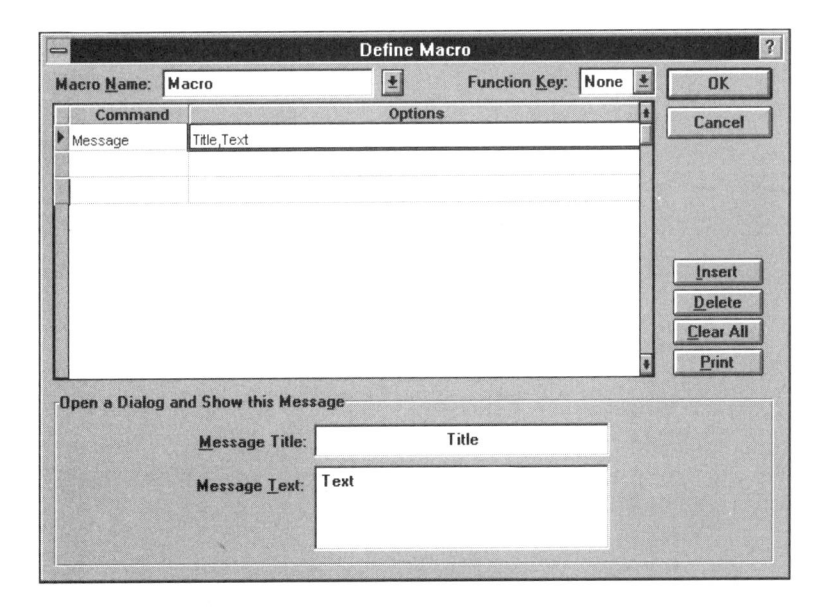

Figure 10.7 Options for the Message command.

Open

Select **Open** from the drop-down to Open a File.

This command is equivalent to choosing **Open** from the File menu and has two options. You can use it to:

- Display the File Open Export Data dialog box as the Macro is running, so the user can choose the file to be opened.
- Specify the file to open while you are defining the macro.

This is equivalent to choosing **Open** from the File menu.

Preview

Choose **Preview** from the drop-down to switch to Preview mode.

This command is equivalent to choosing **Preview** from the File menu and has no options.

Print

Select **Print** from the drop-down to print the current view.

This command has two options. You can use it to:

- Display the Print dialog box as the Macro is running, so the user can specify print options if necessary.
- Specify the Print options while you are defining the macro.

This is equivalent to choosing **Print** from the File menu.

Records

Select **Records** from the drop-down to move among, hide or duplicate records.

This Command has options that let you go to various records in the database, create a new (blank) record, hide the current record, or duplicate the current record (see Figure 10.8).

Replicate

Choose **Replicate** from the drop-down to replicate a notes Database. This command has two options. You can use it to:

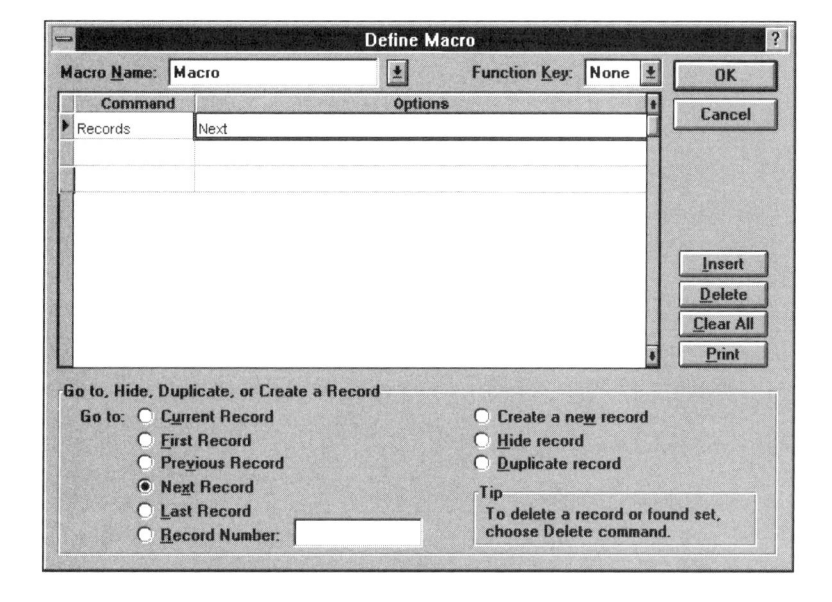

Chapter 10: Speeding Up Your Work with Macros 375

Figure 10.8 Options for the Records Command.

- Display the Replicate dialog box as the Macro is running, so the user can specify replication options.
- Set the Replication options while you are defining the macro.

Run

Select **Run** from the drop-down to run another macro from within the current macro. This is called *chaining macros*, and it is covered in more detail later in this chapter.

This Command has radio buttons that let you choose between two basic options (see Figure 10.9).

- *Run Macro.* Runs a macro that you select from the drop-down. Select the checkbox to its right to return to the next line of this macro after running the macro you selected.
- *If.* Runs macro only if a formula is true.

To create a conditional macro, select the **If** radio button and enter the formula in the text box or click the **Formula** button to use the Formula dialog box to generate it. This formula should return the value **True** or **False**.

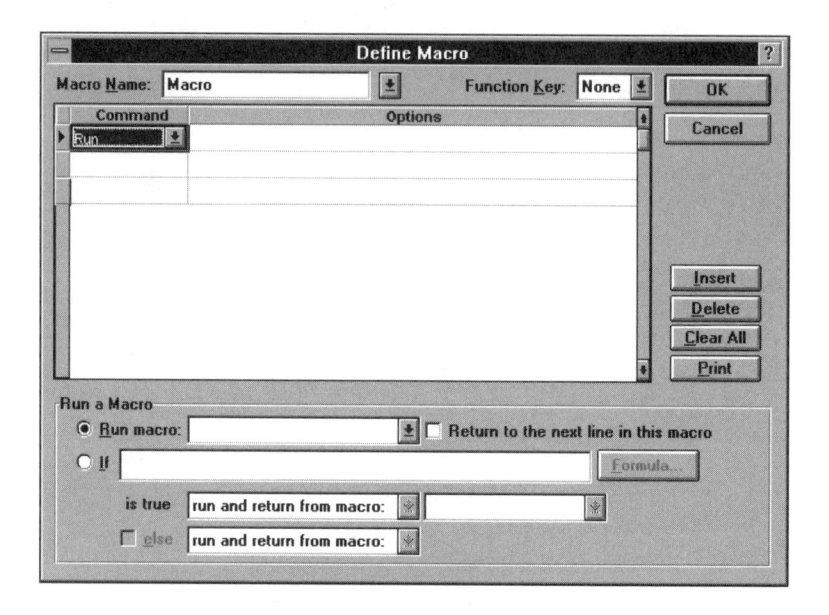

Figure 10.9 Options for the Run Command.

Use the is true drop-down to choose among several alternatives if the formula is true:

- *Run macro*: Use the drop-down to the right to select a macro to run if the formula is true.
- *Run and return macro*: Use the drop-down to the right to select a macro to run if the formula is true, and return to the next line in the current macro after it is done.
- *Continue this macro*: Run the remainder of the current macro.
- *End this macro:* Do not run the remainder of the macro.

You can use either of the first two to create a *conditional macro*. Use one of them as the first command, so that the macro does not run at all unless some condition is met.

Chapter 10: Speeding Up Your Work with Macros

You also have the option of selecting the **Else** check box and using the drop-down to its right to select some other alternative if the macro is false. This drop-down has the same options as the one above it, so you can run a different macro, run and return from a different macro, continue running this macro, or end this macro if the formula is false.

Save

Select **Save** from the drop-down to save the current Approach file.

This Command has two options. You can use it to:

- Save the current file under its own name. This is equivalent to choosing **Save Approach File** from the File menu.
- Display the Save As dialog box so the user can save a copy of the current Approach File with a different name and/or location. This is equivalent to choosing **Save As** from the File menu.

Set

Choose **Set** from the drop-down to enter a value in a field that is based on a Formula.

This Command has options that let you choose the field and specify a formula to give it a new value (see Figure 10.10).

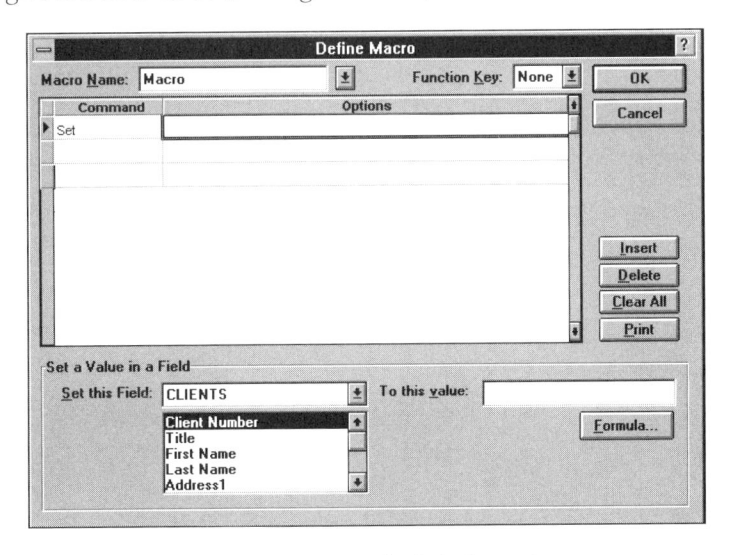

Figure 10.10 Options for the Set Command.

Sort

Select **Sort** from the drop-down to sort the records.

This command has two options. You can use it to:

- Display the Sort dialog box as the Macro is running, so the user can define a custom sort.
- Define the custom sort while you are defining the macro.

This is equivalent to choosing **Sort** from the Browse menu and **Define** from the submenu to create a custom sort.

Spell Check

Select **Spell Check** from the drop-down to open the Spell Check dialog box. This command has no options.

The Spell Checker is covered in Chapter 11.

Tab

Select **Tab** from the drop-down to tab to another field of Macro button.

This Command has options that let you tab forward or backward and specify the number of fields or macro buttons to move across (see Figure 10.11).

This is equivalent to pressing **Tab** or **Shift+Tab** one or many times.

View

Select **View** from the drop-down to switch the current view or to show or hide a view in Browse mode.

Zoom

Choose **Zoom** from the drop-down to change the size of the view displayed in the window. It has options to Zoom In, Zoom Out, or display the view in Actual Size, which are equivalent to choosing **Zoom In**, **Zoom Out**, or **Actual Size** from the View menu.

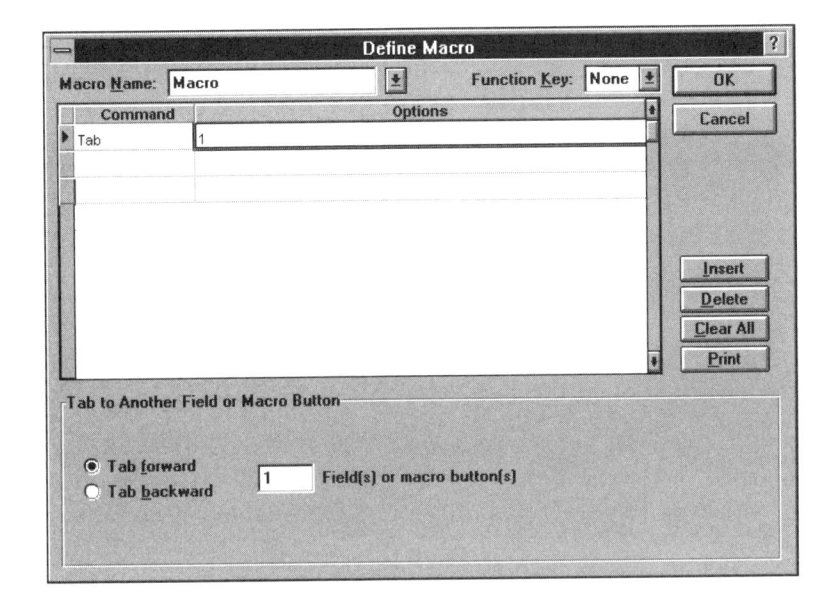

Figure 10.11 Options for the Tab Command.

Running a Macro

You can run a macro by using the Macros dialog box, the menu, a function key, or by clicking a push button or other object. You can also attach a macro to a field or a view, so it runs automatically when you switch in or out of the view or move the cursor into or out of the field.

Using the Macro Dialog Box

You can run a macro by selecting it in the Macro list of the macros dialog box and clicking the **Run** button.

Using the Menu

By default, any macro can be run using the menu. Choose **Run Macro** from the Tools menu to display a submenu listing the names of all defined macros (see Figure 10.12). Select the name of a macro from this submenu to run it.

Practical Approach, 3.0

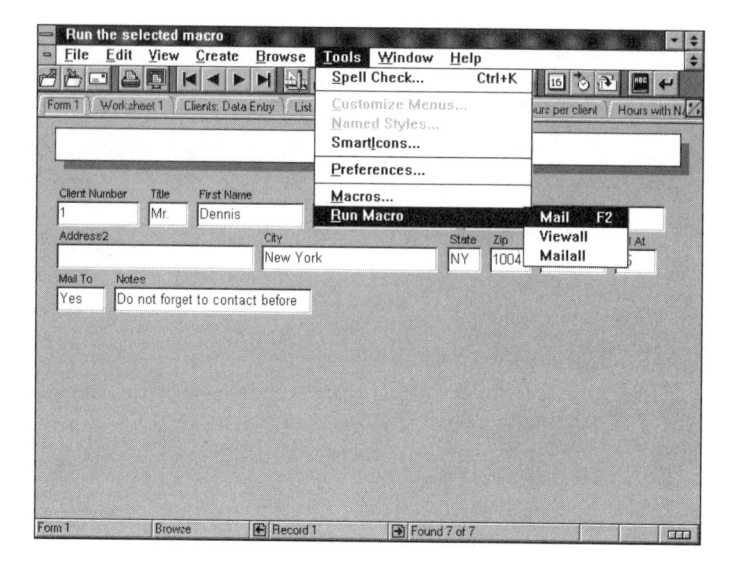

Figure 10.12 Run the selected macro.

If you do not want a macro to be displayed on the menu, select it in the Macros dialog box, and deselect **Show in**.

Using a Function Key

If you want to run the macro by pressing a function key, simply select the key from the Function Key drop-down list of the Define Macro dialog box, which lists all the function keys from F1 to F12. The key is displayed next to the macro's name on the menu.

Attaching a Macro to a Push button, other Object, or View

You can use drop-downs in the Macro panels of different Info box to:

- Attach a macro to a push button or other object in a design, so it runs when you click that object.
- Attach a macro to a field, so it runs automatically when you move the focus into or out of the field or change its data.
- Attach a macro to a view, so it runs automatically whenever you switch into or out of that view.

All of these are covered later in the Chapter.

Open and Close Macros

NOTE You can create a macro that runs automatically when you open or close an Approach File, simply by giving a macro the name Open or Close.

Sample Macros

Before going on to more advanced features of macros, you should create a sample macro that uses the basics that you have already learned.

As an exercise, try creating a macro to make it easier to do the regular mailing to your clients. Let's say that each time you do the mailing, you must do a Find to view just the records on the mailing list, then do a Sort to arrange these records in zip code order, then switch the view to display the mailing labels, and finally use the Print dialog box to print them. It is easy to create a macro that lets you do this with just one keystroke.

After you have used this macro for a while, you realize that you have to spend time afterwards switching back to the ordinary view that you use to work on your records; so you also want to create a macro to use this ordinary view, which is automatically run after the macro does the mailing.

As an exercise, create and try the macro that prints the mailing labels first. Then create the macro that restores the usual view and modify the mailing macro to run it. Begin by switching to the proper view and doing a find, so these steps are added to the macro automatically. Though you could add these steps while you are defining the macro, you may find it easier to do them first.

1. Begin by viewing the Clients database in Browse mode using the **Clients: Data Entry View**. Then choose **Find** from the Browse menu to display a Find Request. Click the **Mail To** checkbox so only records where it is selected are included in the found set (see Figure 10.13). Press **Enter** to do the Find, and note the status bar says *Found 4 of 7*. Then click the **Mailing Labels 1** divider tab to switch to that view.

2. Now, begin creating the macro. Choose **Macros** from the Tools menu to display the Macros dialog box, and click **New** to display the Define

Macro dialog box. Notice that the macro definition already has the View and the Find commands in its command list.

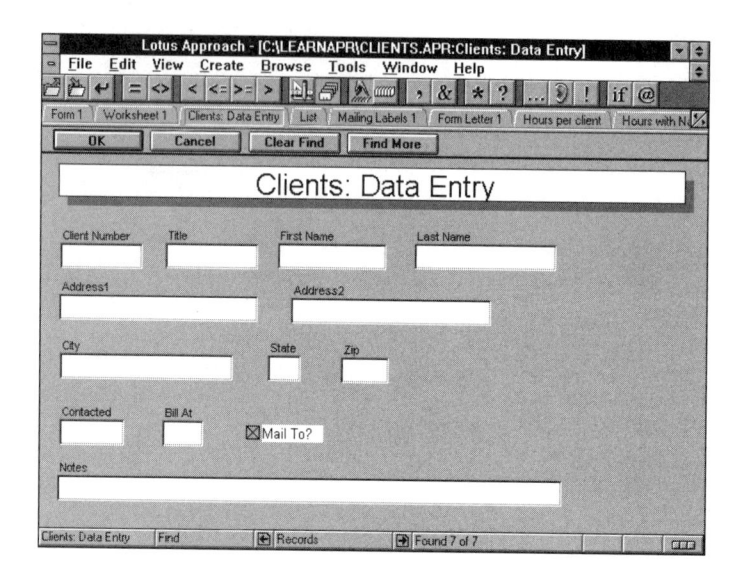

Figure 10.13 Do the Find before creating the macro.

3. In the Macro drop-down list, enter the name **Mail**. Use the Function Key drop-down list to select **F2**, so you can run the macro using a function key.

4. Now add more commands to the Command list. As the third command, use the drop-down to select **Sort**. Select the **Set sort now** radio button. Scroll through the field list and double-click the **Zip** field in the Fields list to add it to the Sort list (see Figure 10.14).

5. As the fourth command, use the drop-down to select **Print**. Leave the radio button selected so the user can set the print options and specifications of the macro (see Figure 10.15). Select **OK** to save it and return to the Macros dialog box, and then select **Done**.

Chapter 10: Speeding Up Your Work with Macros

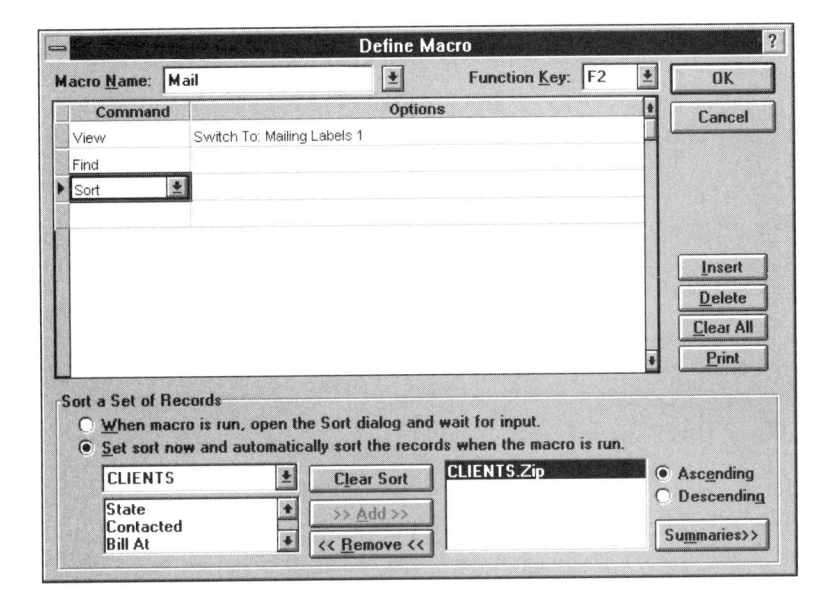

Figure 10.14 Defining the mail macro.

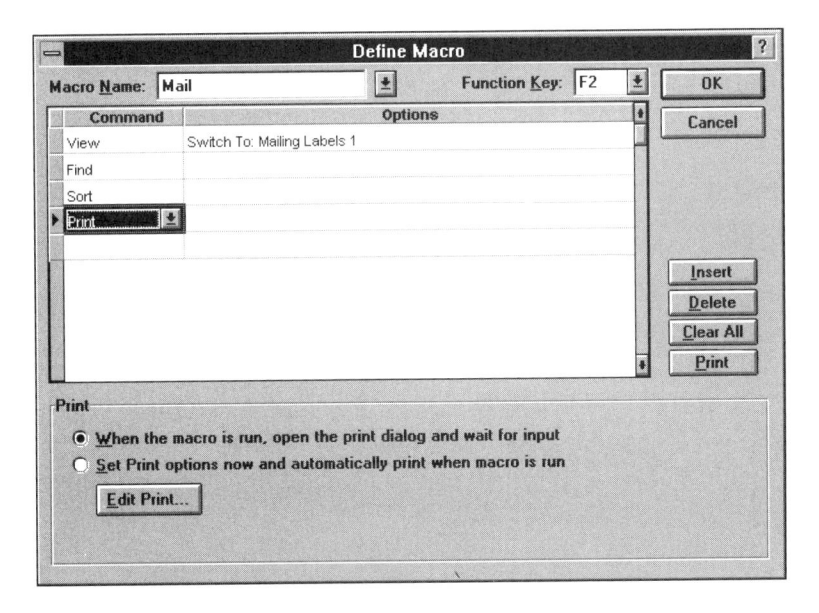

Figure 10.15 The final mail macro.

6. To try out the macro, first select the **Find All** icon to display all the records and select the **Form 1** divider tab. Then choose **Run Macro** from the Tools menu and **Mail** from the submenu. Approach displays the records in mailing label form, sorted by zip code; notice that the status bar says *Found 4 of 7* once again (see Figure 10.16). The Print dialog box is displayed; if you were actually doing the mailing, you would select **OK**, but since this is just a test, you can select **Cancel**.

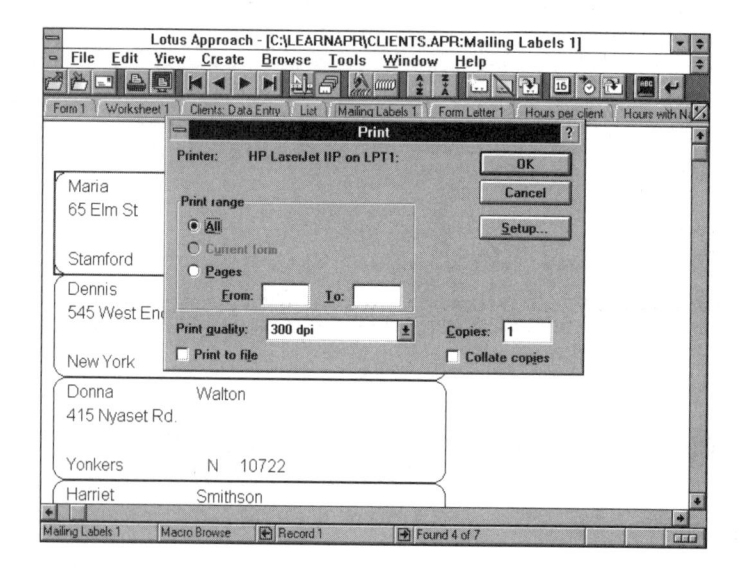

Figure 10.16 Running the macro.

7. Now, select **Show All**, click the **Clients: Data Entry** divider tab to display the database as you might want it after finishing printing mailing labels.

Lets say that, after you have done this mailing a few times, you realize it is foolish to switch views and show all records manually following each mailing. The macro also should do this for you automatically.

You could simply add a couple of extra steps to the existing macro to do this, but instead, you create a separate macro to do it and have the first macro run it.

Chapter 10: Speeding Up Your Work with Macros **385**

NOTE
The advantage of chaining macros in this way is that the second macro is available and can be run by any other macro you create, to switch back to your data entry form and show all the records, and this can be easier than adding the extra steps to each of the other macros. In this case, the macro is so short you would not save much work by having a number of macros use it, but you can save a significant amount of time by using chained macros with more steps.

1. Choose **Macros** from the tool menu to display the Macros dialog box, and click **New** to display the Define Macro dialog box. If necessary, click **Clear All** to remove commands from the list.

2. As the Macro Name, enter **Viewall**. As its first command, select **View** from the drop-down, and **Clients: Data Entry** as the View to switch to. As the second command select **Find** from the drop-down and **Show all** records as the option (see Figure 10.17).

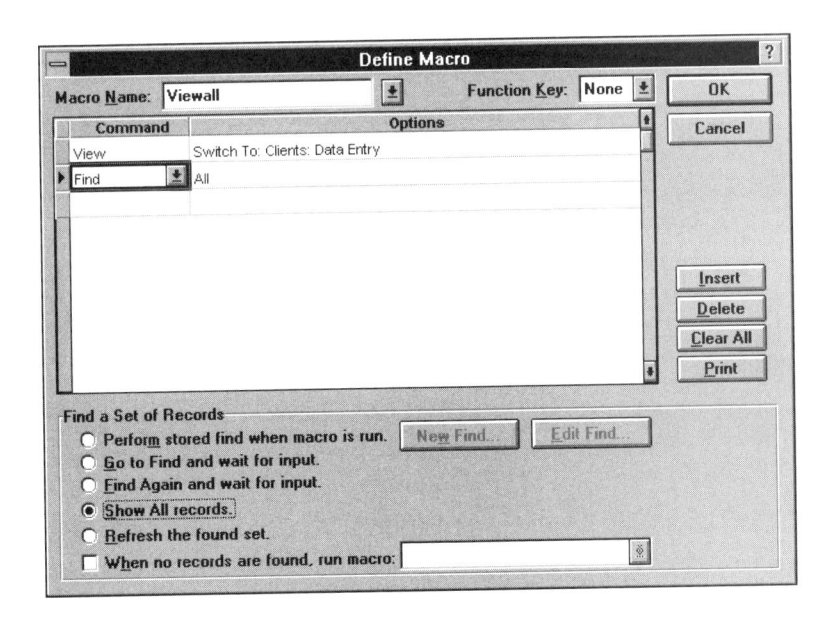

Figure 10.17 Defining the Viewall macro.

3. Now, you must change the earlier macro so it runs this macro when it is done. Select **Mail** from the Macro Name drop-down list, and select **Yes** to save the changes to Viewall. Use the drop-down to select **Run** as an

additional command added to the Mail macro at the end of its command list, and use the Run Macro drop-down to select **Viewall** (see Figure 10.18). Select **OK** to return to the Macros dialog box, and select **Done**.

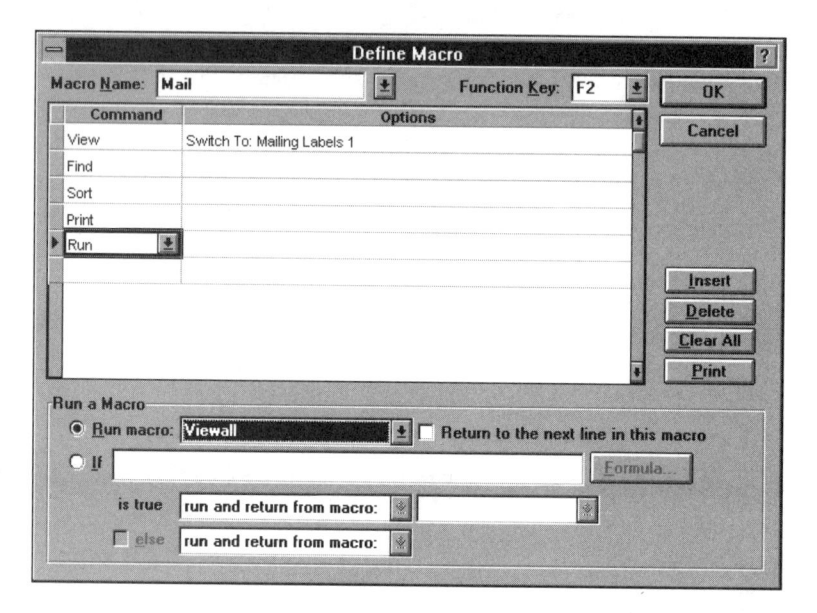

Figure 10.18 Using one macro to run another.

4. Now test the macro again. This time, press **F2** to run it. Approach displays the records in mailing label form, as previously. Select **Cancel** to bypass the Print dialog box. Approach automatically displays the records using the **Clients: Data Entry** form view, with all of the records included in the found set (see Figure 10.19).

Attaching Macros to Objects

Rather than using the menu or a function key to run a macro, you can attach macros to push buttons, other objects, or views.

Attaching Macros to Fields or Views

You can attach macros to fields or other objects in views or to views themselves by using the Macros panel of the Info Box.

Chapter 10: Speeding Up Your Work with Macros

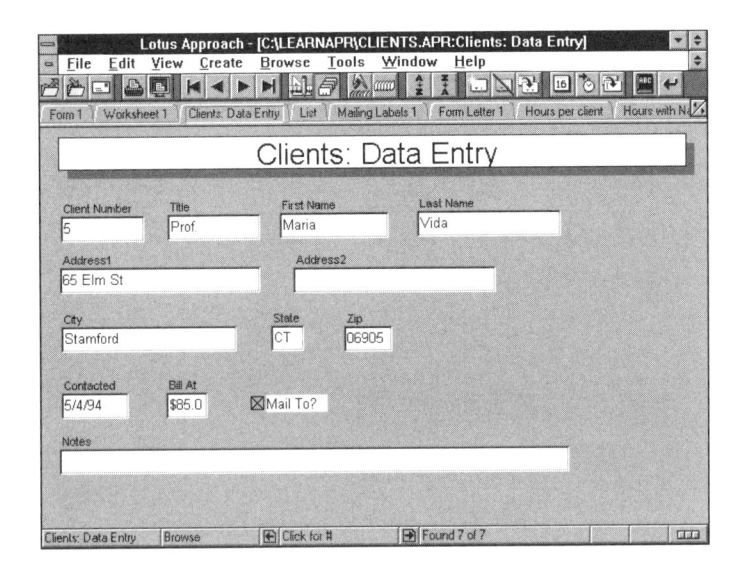

Figure 10.19 The Viewall macro automatically displays all records using Form 1.

In the Macros panel of a view Info box, select a macro from the **On switch to:** or **On switch out:** drop-down (see Figure 10.20). The macro runs automatically when you click the divider tab to display the view, or when you are finished using the view and click another divider tab to switch out of it.

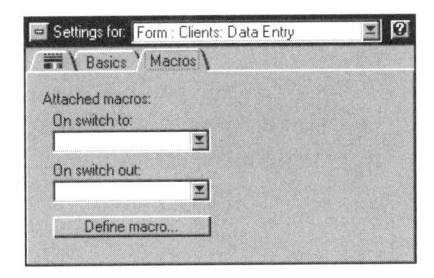

Figure 10.20 The Macros panel for a view.

For example, if you always want to view your mailing labels in zip code order, you could create a macro that sorts on the Zip field and select it from the On switch to drop-down of the Mailing Labels 1 View.

In the Macros panel of a field's Info box, select a macro from the **On tab into:** or **On tab out of:** drop-down to run that macro whenever the focus moves into or out of the field (see Figure 10.21). Select a macro from its **On data change:** drop-down to execute the macro when the focus moves out of the field only if the data has been changed. These are advanced features that most users do not need.

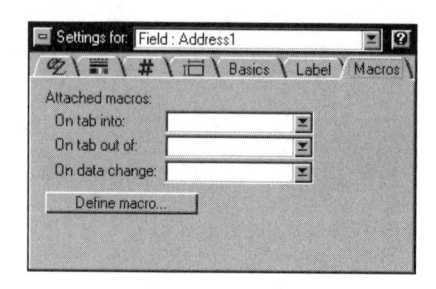

Figure 10.21 The Macros panel for a field.

Creating a Macro Button

The most common way for a user to add a macro to a design is by attaching it to a push button. In fact, push buttons that you create in Approach are usually called *Macro buttons*, because they are used only to run macros.

Add a macro button to a design in that same way that you add other objects. While you are in Design mode, click the **Macro Button** drawing icon. The pointer turns into crosshairs, and you can click and drag at any appropriate location in the design to place a push button there.

The Macro Button Info Box

When you release the mouse button after placing a push button in a design, Approach displays the macro button Info Box. You can display the Info Box for an existing macro at any time when you are in design mode, by selecting **Style & Properties** from the Form menu or clicking the **Info Box** icon.

Attaching a Macro to the Button

The Macros Panel of the Info Box is displayed initially when you create a macro (see Figure 10.22). Use the On clicked drop-down to select the macro that runs when the user clicks the push button.

Chapter 10: Speeding Up Your Work with Macros

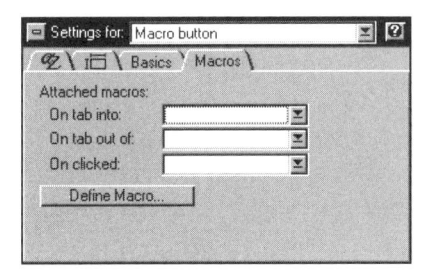

Figure 10.22 The Macro button Info Box.

WARNING

You can also attach a Macro to the push button, as you can to other objects, by using the On tab into or On tab out of drop-downs. The macro runs automatically when the user presses **Tab** or **Shift+Tab** to move the focus to the button. However, users do not expect push buttons to run in this way, and these drop-downs should only be used in special cases for example, to change a prompt line or display a message dialog box.

If the macro already exists, simply use the On clicked drop-down to select it. If you have not created the macro yet, select **Define Macro** to display the Macros dialog box.

Adding the Macro Button's Label

Use the Basics panel of a macro button's Info Box to specify the text that is displayed on its label (see Figure 10.23).

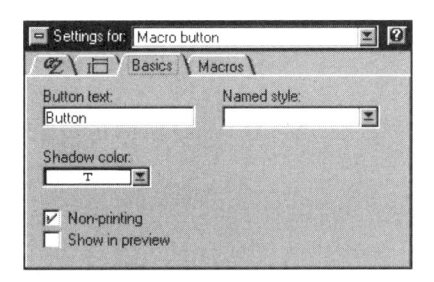

Figure 10.23 The Basics panel of the Macro button Info Box.

Simply type the label that you want to appear on the button in the Button text box.

As you can see, you can also use this panel to apply a Named style and shadow color to a button and to specify that it is non-printing. These are the same properties that are used for other objects, but buttons are Non-printing by default, since they are used to execute a command when you are looking at a view on screen, rather than to display data.

Other Styles and Properties of Macro Buttons

Use the first panel of the Info Box for Macro buttons to change the font of its label and other text effects.

The second panel indicates the size and location of the object, and lets you specify whether it should slide up or left when you print.

Manipulating Buttons

Buttons can be manipulated like any other objects in designs:

- Select a push button and click and drag its handles to resize it.
- Click and drag a push button to move it.
- Select a push button and then press **Del** or **Backspace** to delete it.

Choose **Undo** from the Edit menu immediately afterwards to undo any of these changes.

A Sample Push Button

Now, add a push button to Form 1 to run the macro you created to do your mailing.

1. Begin by viewing the database using the Clients: Data Entry form. If necessary, click the **Design** icon to switch to Design mode, and choose **Show Data** from the View menu to work with field names rather than data.
2. Click the **Macro button** drawing tool and click and drag to the right of the Zip field to place a push button there.
3. When you release the mouse button, the Macro button Info Box is displayed. Select **Mail** from the **On clicked** drop-down of its Macros

panel. Then click the **Basics** tab. As the Label for the button, type **Do Mail** in the button text box. Then close the Info Box. If necessary, click and drag to resize or move the push button (see Figure 10.24).

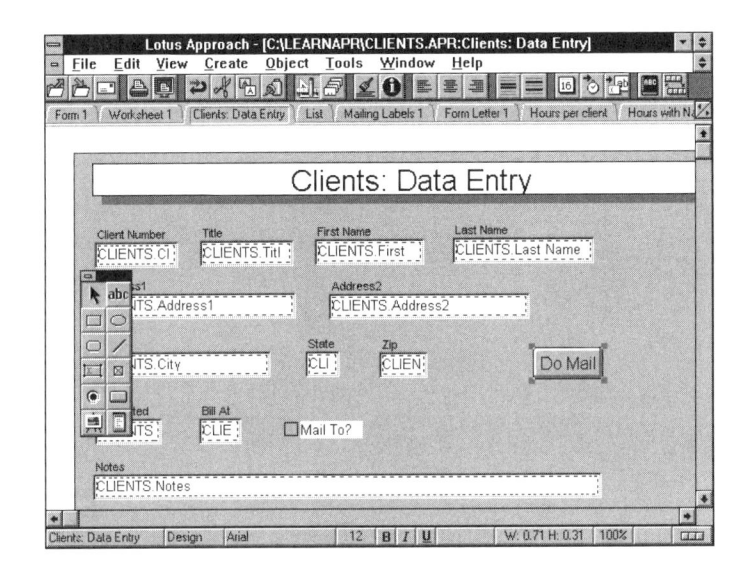

Figure 10.24 The push button placed in the design.

4. Now, click the **Browse** icon to return to Browse mode. Try clicking the **Arrow** icons to move among the records, so you can see that the button remains in place as the data changes. To test it, click the **New** push button. The macro runs, as before; click **Cancel** in the Print dialog box to return to Form 1.

Using Formulas in Macros

There are two important uses of formulas in macros. You can use a formula to specify whether a macro should run and whether an alternative macro should run under certain conditions. You can also use a formula to change the values of the data in a field, one of the most time saving uses of macros.

Conditional Macros

You can use the **Run** command to create macros or parts of macros that run only under certain conditions. When you select this command, Approach displays the If radio button, which lets you continue to run the macro only if a formula is true (see Figure 10.25). You can either enter the formula, or select **Formula** and generate the formula using the Formula dialog box.

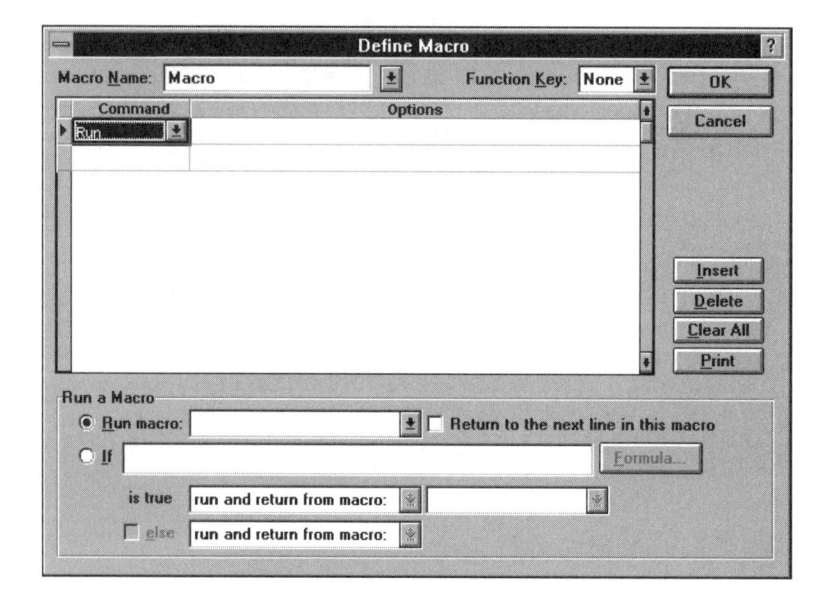

Figure 10.25 Options for the Run command.

> **NOTE** The formula must result in a Boolean value. If its value is **Yes**, the macro runs, and if its value is **No**, the macro does not run.

If you select this radio button, you can also select the **Else run macro** checkbox to specify another macro to run instead when the formula is not true. Use the drop-down list to its right to select the other macro.

Let's assume that you do mailings to everyone on your mailing list each month, using the Mail macro that you created earlier in this chapter. Each January, however, you want to do a mailing to all your clients, even the ones who are not on the mailing list. You already have the macro to do the monthly mailing set up, and you have a push button to run it while you have added to your data entry form. It is easy to change it so it automatically does the mailing to all your clients in January.

The formula you need to use to check whether to run the regular Mail macro is Month(Today( )) <> 1.

Remember that the Today( ) function returns the current date, and that the Month(date) function returns the month of the specified date in number form, with January returned as 1 and so on. Thus, Month(Today( )) returns 1 in January and some other number in any other month. If you change your Mail macro by adding a Run command before all of its other commands, selecting **Continue to run the macro** and entering the condition **Month(Today( )) <> 1** to its right, the Mail macro is not runs in January.

To do the mailing you need for January to run automatically, create a new macro named Mailall, which is the same as the Mail macro except it has **Show All** selected in the drop-down list to the right of the Find check box, so that it produces the mailing labels for all the records. You can create this macro almost effortlessly:

1. Select **Macros** from the Tools menu. In the Macros dialog box, select the name of the Mail macro and click **Copy** to display a copy of it in the Define Macro dialog box.
2. Edit the Macro Name so it is **Mailall**.
3. Click the **Find** command on its second line. Select **Show All** in the options panel (see Figure 10.26). Select **OK**.
4. Select the **Mail** macro from the Macro Name drop down. Approach displays a dialog box asking if you want to save changes to the current macro. Select **Yes** to save Mailall.

Now, you can add a **Run** command to the beginning of the Mail macro to make it a conditional macro that runs Mailall in January.

1. Place the focus in the first line of the command list of the Mail macro, and click **Insert** to add a new, blank first line. Then use the drop-down to select **Run** as the command for this new line.

Practical Approach, 3.0

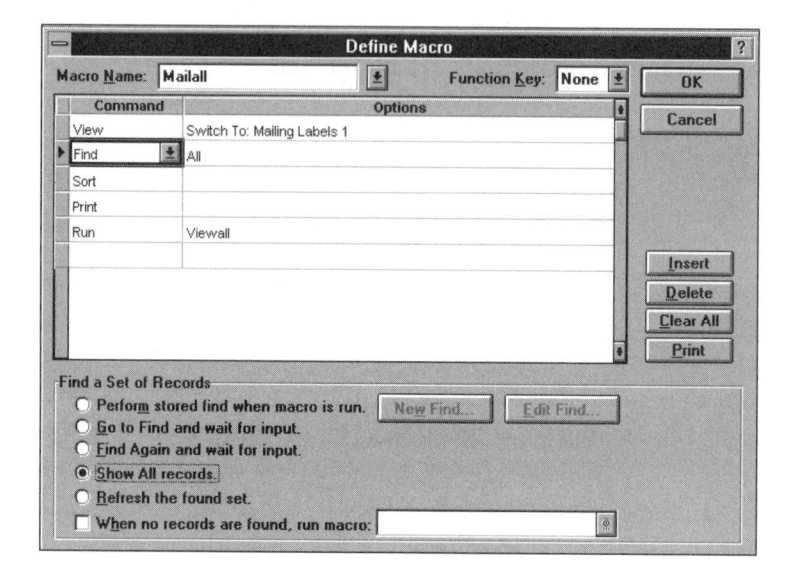

Figure 10.26 The Mailall macro.

2. Click the **If** radio button and, as the condition, enter **Month(Today( )) <> 1** in the text box to its right (or click **Formula** and use the formula dialog box to generate this condition).

3. From the **is true** drop-down, select **continue this macro**, so the rest of the macro runs if it is not January. Select the **Else** checkbox and select **Run macro** and select **Mailall** (see Figure 10.27).

Now, in January, when you click the **Mail** push button that you added to Form 1 to run the Mail macro, the Mailall macro runs automatically instead. Of course, you could also use the Mailall macro itself any time you want to do a mailing to all your clients.

Changing the Data in Records

One of the most convenient features of Macros is the **Set** command (see Figure 10.28). Select the field whose value you want to change from the field list and, if necessary, use the drop-down list of databases to use a field from another database). In the text box, enter a formula specifying the new value of the field or click **Formula** and use the Formula dialog box to generate the formula that is displayed in this text box.

Chapter 10: Speeding Up Your Work with Macros

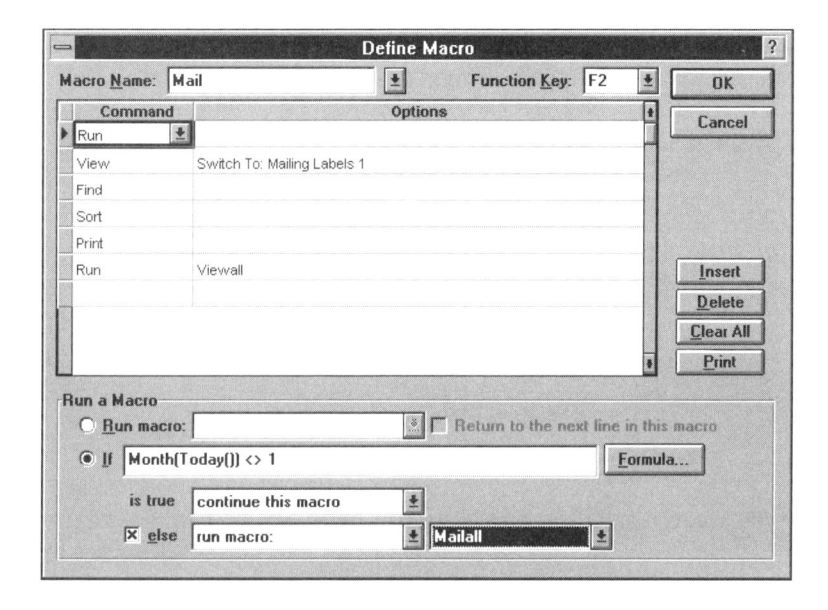

Figure 10.27 The final design of the macro.

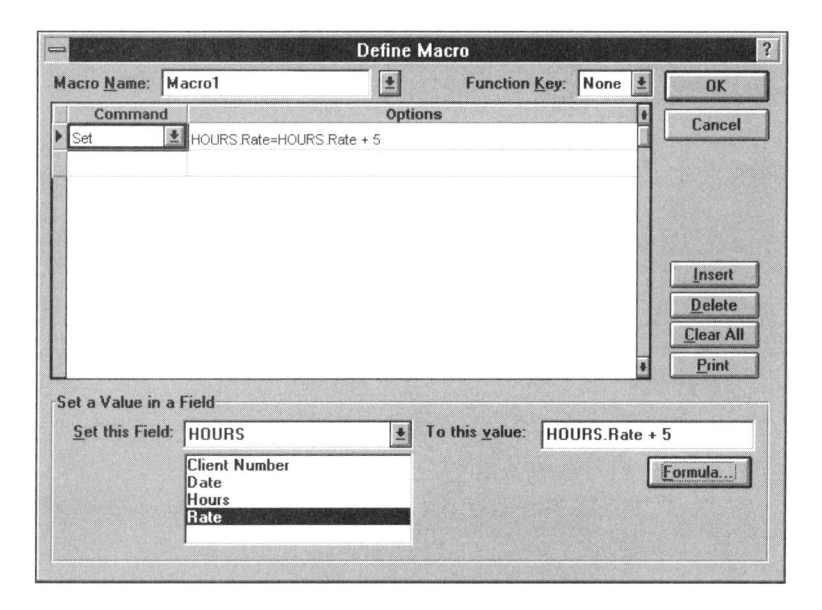

Figure 10.28 Options for the Set command.

If you want to put a simple value in all the fields of a database, you can use the **Fill Field** command of the Browse menu. The **Set** command, however, lets you make more sophisticated changes in data by using formulas.

For example, let us say that you are increasing the rate at which you bill all your clients by $5 per hour. You could use the macro, previously shown in Figure 10.28. It changes the value in the Rate field of the Hours table by using a formula that sets it to the current value in that field plus 5. Likewise, if you wanted to increase the rate by 10%, you could create a similar macro that uses the formula **1.1 * Hours.Rate**.

WARNING

In most cases, when using this type of macro, you need to use it only once. If so, you should delete it as soon as it is no longer needed. Otherwise, you may use it again in the future by mistake, and increase the value in this field again. Clients might not be pleased if you mistakenly ran this macro seven or eight times and raised the billing rate by over 100%.

This type of macro is created and used only once before it is deleted. However, it can save you a tremendous amount of time (compared with entering data in each record), if you are working with a large database.

Variables

The one field type you have not looked at yet is the **variable field**, which is generally used only in advanced applications, usually in macros.

To create a variable field, you define it in the usual way in the Field Definition dialog box. Enter its name, select **Variable** from the Field Type dropdown list, and select **Add** to add it to the Field list.

You may select **Options** to use the Variable Options panel for the new variable. There are also default options for a variable field (see Figure 10.29). You can see that its default type is Numeric, but you can use the Field Type dropdown list to make it Boolean, Date, Numeric, Text, or Time.

Optionally, you can use the Set default value text box to enter an initial value this variable field has when the Approach file is first opened; as you can see, it has no initial value by default.

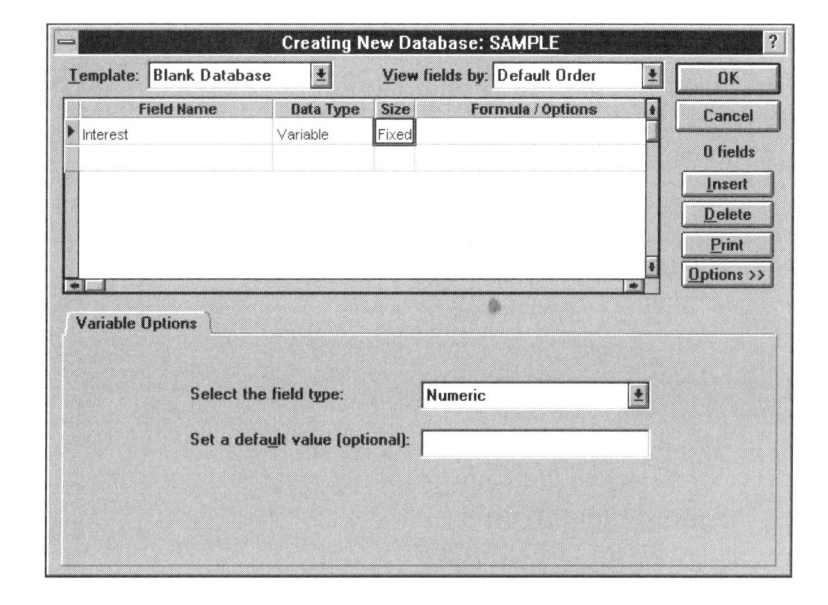

Figure 10.29   The Variable Options panel.

A variable field holds a value that is not saved in the database file and is not part of any record, but is accessible by all records. It is used to hold a temporary value that can be used in calculations or by macros. It is similar to a *Global Variable* in programming.

Using Variables in Calculations

If you had a database with a calculated field named Payment based on an amount of money held in a field called Debt multiplied times an interest rate, you could keep the interest rate in a variable field.

Name the variable field Interest. Use the **Variable Options** panel to give this field an initial value equal to the current interest rate; fill in the rate in the Value When Approach file text box. Then, use the formula **Debt * Interest** as the value of the Payment field. When the interest rate changes, display the **Variable Options** panel for the Interest field, and change the number in the Value When Approach file text box to the new interest rate. The value in all the Payment fields change accordingly, to reflect the new interest rate multiplied by the Debt in each record.

Using Variables in Macros

You can use variable fields in more sophisticated ways in macros, to do the sort of looping that is common in computer programming.

Let's say you had a macro that you must run twenty times. You can create a variable field named Counter and use the Variable Options panel to give it the initial value of 20. Then, at the end of the macro that you need to run repeatedly, add the **Run** command, and select the macro itself from the drop-down, so that when the macro is finished running, it runs itself again. If you just did this much, the macro would keep running forever. This is called an infinite loop.

> **NOTE** If you ever create this sort of infinite loop by mistake when you are defining a macro, you can click **Esc** in the dialog box displayed when it runs a macro or simply press **Esc** to cancel the macro. If it is moving through the records of a file, it automatically stops when it reaches the end of the file.

You can control how many times the macro runs, however, by including a Set command in the macro that changes the value of the variable. Select the variable field **Counter** from the field list to its right, and entering the formula **Counter - 1** as the value that it is changed to. In addition, make the macro conditional by selecting the **If** radio button of the Run command, and entering the condition **Counter > 0**. Now, each time the macro runs, the value of Counter is decreased by 1. After the first time it runs, Counter is 19, the second time it runs Counter is 18, and so on. After it runs 20 times, Counter is 0, the condition is no longer true, and so the macro is not run again.

If you need to change the number of times that this macro runs, just use the Variable Options dialog box to change the initial value of the variable.

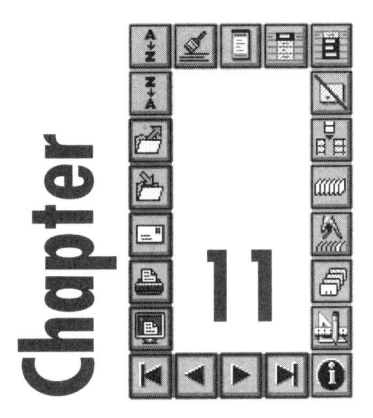

Using Approach Utilities

The Tools menu includes a number of utilities that are not necessary to run the program but that can give you added power or versatility. Many of these are used to customize Approach, either for your own use or to set up applications for beginning users. Chapter 10 covered macros, and this chapter covers the rest of the commands in the Tools menu, including:

- Using the Spell Checker
- Using Named Styles to design views that have a consistent appearance
- Creating custom menu systems
- Creating custom icon bars
- Using the Preferences dialog box to set up the Approach environment

The Spell Checker

Approach includes a built-in Spell Checker that can be used to check the spelling of the data in your data file or of text included in the design of your views:

- If you are in Browse mode, the Spell Checker checks spelling of data. This is particularly useful to check the spelling of long bodies of text entered in memo fields.
- If you are in Design mode, the Spell Checker checks the spelling of field labels and text objects.

How much text it checks depends on the selections you make in the Spell Check dialog box, which is displayed in different forms in Browse mode and Design mode.

Spell Check in Browse Mode

If you choose **Spell Check** from the Tools menu or click the **Spell Check** icon when you are in Browse mode the Spell Check dialog box is displayed as shown in Figure 11.1. You can use the radio buttons to limit the text that it checks as follows:

- *Selection.* Checks only the selected (highlighted) text in the current record. You must select the text before using the Spell Checker.
- *Current record.* Only text in the current record is checked.
- *Found set.* All the records of the found set are checked.
- *Selection across found.* Checks the selected (highlighted) text in every record in the found set.

NOTE
When you check spelling in Browse mode, the **Memo fields only** checkbox (which limits the spell check to text in memo fields) is selected by default. Because most field types contain names and other words that would not be in a dictionary, it is generally not useful to check their spelling. You can deselect this check box to check data in other fields.

Chapter 11: Using Approach Utilities   **401**

Figure 11.1   The Spell Check dialog box in Browse mode.

Spell Check in Design Mode

If you choose **Spell Check** from the Tools menu or click the icon when you are in Design mode, Spell Check dialog box is displayed as shown in Figure 11.2. The following radio buttons limit the text that is checked:

- *Selection.* Checks only the selected (highlighted) text in the design of the current view. You must select the text before using the Spell Checker.
- *Current view.* Checks all field labels and text objects in the current view.

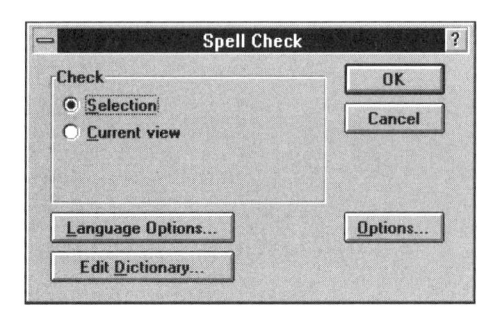

Figure 11.2   The Spell Check dialog box in Design mode.

Spell Check Options

Both of these dialog boxes include a Language Options button, which displays a dialog box with a drop-down that lets you select American or British spelling and other options if they are available.

Both the Browse and design modes contain an Edit Dictionary button, which lets you add words to the user dictionary: the Spell Checker compares spelling with a main dictionary, which you cannot edit, and a user dictionary, which you create yourself. The Edit Dictionary dialog box displays a list of all the words in the user dictionary (see Figure 11.3). You can add a word by entering it in the New word box and clicking **Add,** or delete a word by selecting it in the Current words list and clicking **Delete**.

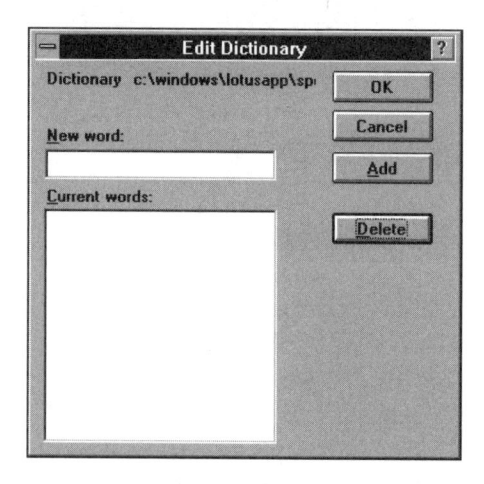

Figure 11.3 The Edit Dictionary dialog box.

Correcting Errors

Select **OK** to begin a Spell Check. When a word is found in the text that is not in one of its dictionaries, it displays the Spell Check dialog box (see Figure 11.4) The word that might be misspelled is displayed in the Unknown word box. If it is incorrect, you can edit it in the **Replace with:** text box, or select one of the alternatives the Spell Checker suggests to display that word in the replace with box. Then click **Replace** to correct this word or the **Replace All** button to replace all words that are misspelled in the same way.

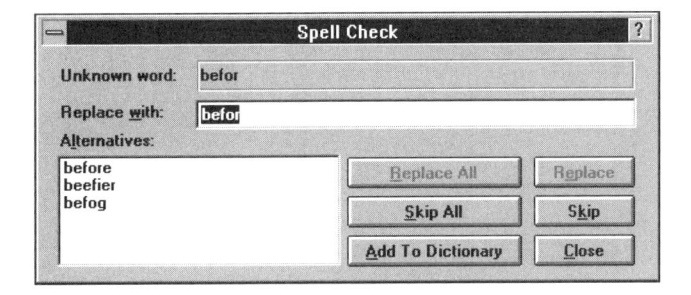

Figure 11.4 Correcting a spelling error.

If the Unknown word is not an error, you can click **Skip** to continue without correcting the word or **Skip All** to continue without correcting the word or flagging any future occurrences. You can also click **Add to Dictionary** to add the word to the user dictionary, so it is not flagged in future spell checks. It is added to the Current words list in the Edit Dictionary dialog box.

Click **Close** to end the Spell Check.

Named Styles

In Chapter 4, you learned about using the Info Box in Design mode to specify the properties and style of objects in views you are designing. You saw that objects have so many styles and properties that, if you wanted to change the appearance of all the fields or all the text objects in a view, it would take a long time to change the necessary styles and properties of each one individually.

Approach provides two shortcuts to save you time when you are applying the same format to a number of objects:

- *Fast Formatting*. Use the **Fast Format** command to copy all of the styles and properties of one object and apply them to another object. Select the object whose styles and properties you want to copy, and then choose **Fast Format** from the Object menu or click the **Fast Format** icon. The pointer is displayed as a paintbrush, and you can click other objects to apply the same style and properties to them. When you are done, choose **Fast Format** from the Object menu again to turn off the Fast Format feature.

- *Named Styles.* The Basic panel of Info Boxes has a Named style drop-down. Use the Named Styles utility to define a group of styles and properties and give them a name, and then, you can apply all of these styles and properties to an object simply by selecting that named style from this drop-down. You can also apply a named style to objects by using the Named Styles dialog box.

> **SHORTCUT** Fast Formatting was covered in Chapter 4, and it is adequate for most design work. If you are working with a single design, it is generally easier to apply a Fast Format to objects by clicking them than to go through the extra trouble of defining and managing fast styles and using the Info Box of each object to select its style.

Named Styles are useful primarily if you are developing a more complex application and you want consistency in objects in a number of views. For example, you might create one style named Field Style and another Title Style, and use the Named Style drop-down to select the first for all the field objects of all your views and the second for the text objects used as the titles of all your views.

As you can see, this feature is useful primarily for setting up an application, rather than for managing your own data.

Managing Named Styles

To create new Named styles or manage existing ones, switch to Design mode and choose **Named Styles** from the Tool menu to display the Named Styles dialog box (see Figure 11.5).

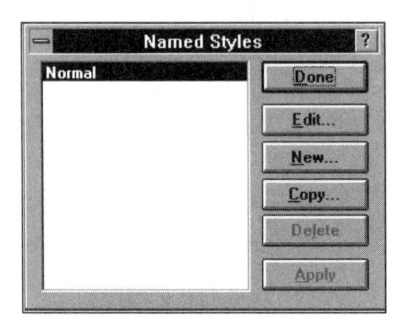

Figure 11.5 The Named Styles dialog box.

This dialog box is similar to the one used to create and manage macros. It contains a list of all the existing Named Styles in the current Approach file with the following buttons:

- *Edit.* Select a Named Style in the list and click **Edit** to display the Define Named Style dialog box with that Named Style's specifications, so you can modify it.
- *New.* Used to display the Define Named Style dialog box to create a new Named Style.
- *Copy.* Select a Named Style in the list and click **Copy** to display the Define Named Style dialog box with that a copy of that Named Style's specifications. Initially, the Named Style's name is **Copy of** followed by the name of the Named Style you copied. You can change the name and any of its specifications. This is the easiest way to create a Named Style similar to an existing one.
- *Delete.* Used to delete the selected Named Style.
- *Apply.* Use **Apply the selected Named Style** to the selected objects in a view. You must select the objects before choosing Named Styles from the Tool menu to display this dialog box.
- *Done.* Used to close the dialog box, saving all the changes you made.

SHORTCUT If you are applying a named style to a large number of objects in a design, it is easiest to select them all and then display the Named Styles dialog box and use its **Apply** button. The style is automatically selected in the Named Style drop-down of all the objects.

Defining a Named Style

When you select **Edit** or **New** in the Named Style dialog box the Define Style dialog box is displayed (see Figure 11.6).

Enter a name for a new style in the **Style Name:** text box or edit the name of an existing one. Or use this drop-down to select any existing style and display all of its specifications in the panels below.

Use the **Based on** drop-down to select an existing named style to be used as the basis of the style you are defining. All of its specifications are listed in the panels below.

Practical Approach, 3.0

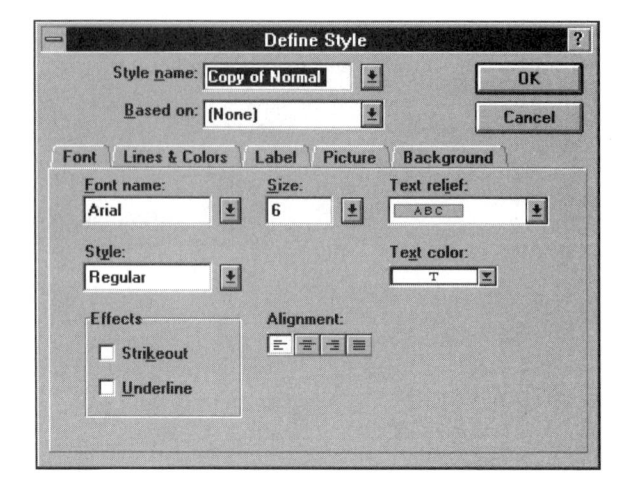

Figure 11.6 The Define Style dialog box.

> **NOTE** As you can see, the panels of this dialog box are similar to ones used in the Info Boxes of objects in designs. It includes panels equivalent to all the panels in the Info Boxes of all the objects in designs. Of course, when you apply a Named Style to an object, only the properties that can be used by that type of object are entered in its Info Box.

The Font Panel

The Font panel of the Define Style dialog box controls the following properties:

- *Font name:* Select a font from the Font name list. The options available in this list depends on which fonts you have installed under Windows.
- *Style:* Select styles such as **Bold** or **Italic** from the Style drop-down. Select **Regular** to remove these styles.
- *Effects*: Use the Effects checkboxes to **Underline** or **Strikethrough** text.
- *Size:* Select a size expressed in points from the Size list.
- *Alignment:* Use the Alignment buttons to specify if the text should be centered within its text frame, or aligned to the left or right edge of the text frame.

Chapter 11: Using Approach Utilities

- *Text relief:* Use this drop-down to select effects that make the text appear to be carved into or raised above its background.
- *Text color:* Use this drop-down to display a color palette, which lets you select the color of the letters used in the text object.

The Lines & Colors Panel

The Lines and Colors panel of the Define Style dialog box lets you specify settings for lines and colors (see Figure 11.7).

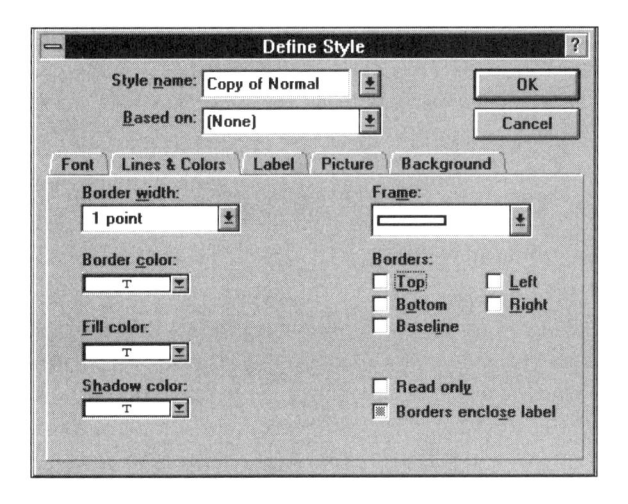

Figure 11.7 The Lines and Colors panel.

The settings for lines and colors are:

- *Border width:* Use this to select a border width between hairline and 12 points.
- *Border color, Fill color, and Shadow color:* All of these display color palettes you can use to select the color of the objects border, its fill color, and the color of its shadow. The palettes display a variety of colors, and you can click one to select it. The sample color on their upper left appears white but has the letter T in it to indicate that it is transparent. Choosing this color lets you see whatever is behind the object. For example, if you select **T** as the shadow color, the object's shadow is not visible.

- *Frame*: Displays graphics that let you use a solid line, double line, or several types of dotted lines for frames or to use shading that gives the frame a raised or lowered appearance.
- *Borders:* Use this to specify whether to display the Top, Bottom, Left and Right border of the object, and whether to display a baseline under the text in the object.
- *Read only:* Select this checkbox to prevent users from editing the object.
- *Borders enclose label:* This checkbox makes the borders enclose the label of a field. If it is not selected, the borders only enclose the data entry area for the field.

The Label Panel

The Label panel of the Define Style dialog box is used primarily to control the Font of the label of a field object (see Figure 11.8). It has the same features as the Font Panel, described above.

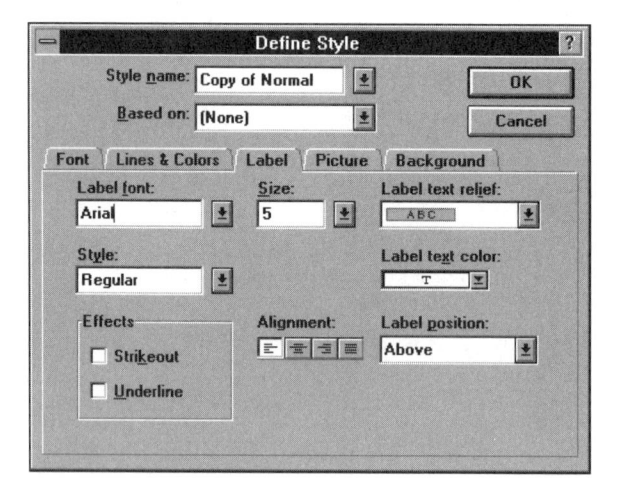

Figure 11.8 The Label panel.

This panel also lets you control the location of the label. Use the Label position drop-down to specify that the label should be Above, Below, Left or Right of the object, or the object should have no label. This drop-down also has a Don't change option, which lets you apply a style to an object but keep the original location of its label.

The Picture Panel

The Picture Panel of the Define Style dialog box is used to specify how pictures are handled that do not fit in the frame you created for the PicturePlus field (see Figure 11.9).

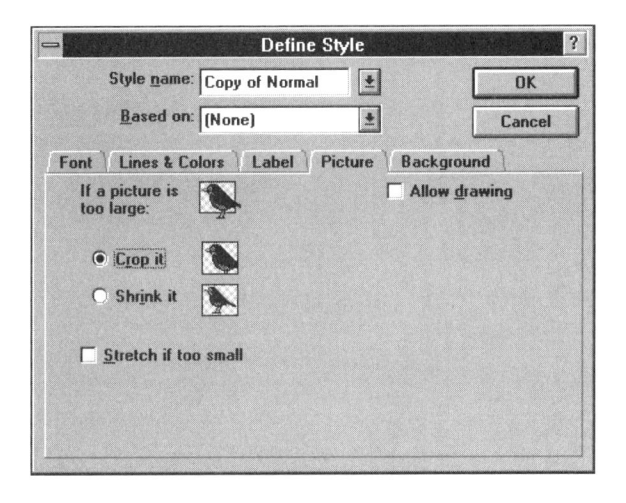

Figure 11.9 The Picture panel.

The radio buttons give you two options for handling pictures that are too large to fit in their frame:

1. You can crop the picture, so that it remains in its original size but not all of it is displayed.
2. You can shrink it, so all of it is displayed but in reduced size.

The checkbox gives you options for handling pictures that are too small. Select it to stretch the picture proportionally to fill the entire frame, or leave it unselected to leave the picture in its original size.

The **Allow Drawing** checkbox can be selected or deselected to control whether the user can draw a picture in the field with the mouse.

The Background Panel

The background panel of the Define Style dialog box controls features of the background of a view (see Figure 11.10). Its features are also included in the Lines & Colors panel, described above, but in this panel they are used to control the Borders, Fill color, and Shadow color of an entire page of the view, rather than of an object within the view.

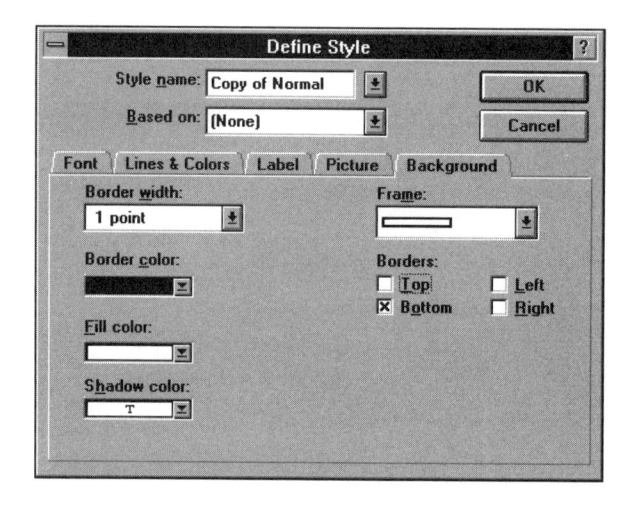

Figure 11.10   The Background panel.

Customizing Approach

There are a number of utilities on the Tools menu that let you customize the Approach environment. You can create custom menu systems, custom icon bars, and use the Preferences dialog box to customize many other features of Approach.

Most users are comfortable with the menus, icon bars, and preferences that Approach provides. It can be useful to customize one or two features of the interface to make it easier to work with the features you use frequently.

NOTE You may want to customize Approach for a novice. Approach provides a short menu system, designed to set up the system for novices and you may want to create custom menus and icon bars to let them perform special tasks.

Custom Menu Systems

You use two dialog boxes to create custom menu systems, one to manage menu systems, and the other to define custom menus.

Managing Menu Systems

To manage menu systems, choose **Customize Menus** from the Tools menu to display the Customize Menus dialog box (see Figure 11.11).

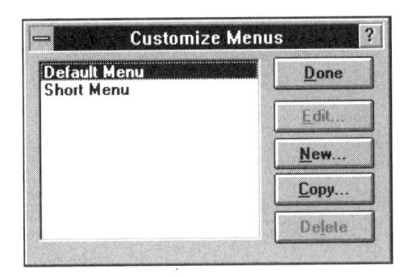

Figure 11.11 The Customize Menus dialog box.

As you can see, this dialog box is similar to the one used to create and manage macros and named styles. It contains a list of all the existing Menu systems in the current Approach file, which you manage using the following push buttons:

- **Done:** Closes the dialog box, saving all the changes you made.
- **Edit:** Select a Menu system in the list and click **Edit** to display the Define Custom Menu Bar dialog box with that Menu system's specifications, so you can modify it.
- **New:** Displays the Define Custom Menu Bar dialog box to create a new Menu system.
- **Copy:** Select a Menu system in the list and click **Copy** to display the Define Custom Menu Bar dialog box with a copy of that Menu system's specifications. You can change the name and any of its specifications. This is the easiest way to create a Menu system similar to an existing one.
- **Delete:** Select a Menu system in the list and click **Delete** to delete the Menu system.

The Default Menu and Short Menu system are listed in this dialog box initially, but they cannot be modified or deleted, like menu systems you define yourself.

Creating a Custom Menu

When you select **Edit**, **New** or **Copy** in the Customize Menus dialog box the Define Custom Menu Bar dialog box is displayed (see Figure 11.12).

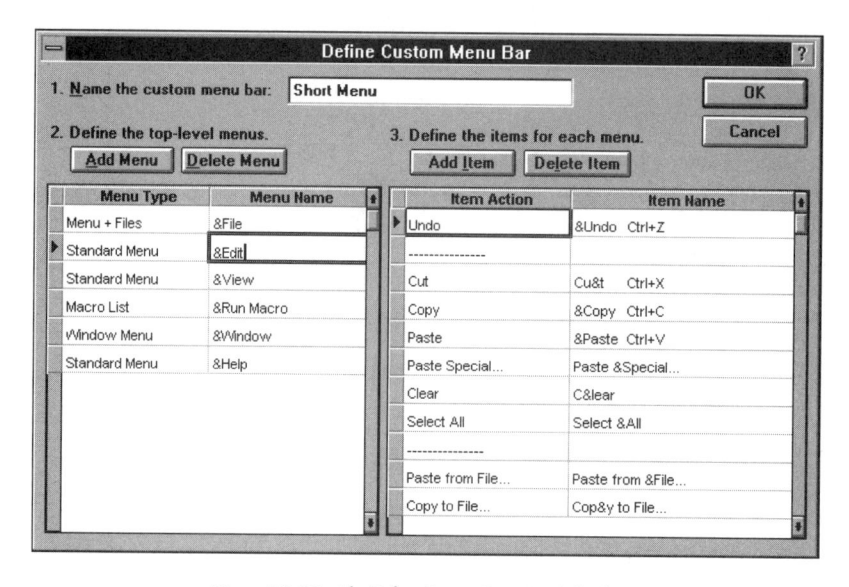

Figure 11.12 The Define Custom Menu Bar dialog box.

To create or modify a custom menu:

- Use **Name the custom menu bar** text box to name the custom menu.
- Use the **Menu Type** and **Menu Name** panel on the left to define the options available on the menu bar displayed at the top of the screen.
- Use the **Item Action** and **Item Name** panel to define the pop-up that is associated with each option on the menu bar.

When you place the focus in one of the rows in the Menu Type and Menu Name panel, all of the commands on its pop-up are listed in the Item Action and Item Name panel. In the illustration, the focus is on the Edit menu in the Menu Type/Menu Name panel, and **Undo**, **Cut**, **Copy Paste**, and the other common Edit menu commands are displayed on the right.

Defining the Menu Bar

To define the menu bar in the panel Menu Type/Menu Name use the drop-down in its left column to select among the following menu types:

- *Standard menu.* Lists the options defined in the panel to the right.
- *Menu + Files.* lists the options defined in the panel to the right plus the five Approach files opened most recently, like the Approach File menu.
- *Window menu.* Lists all open windows, to let the user switch among them.
- *Context menu.* Creates a menu that is displayed only in certain contexts, like the Approach Form, Report, or Object menu.
- *Macro List.* Lists all macros in the Approach file so the user can select one to execute it.
- *View List.* All Views in the current menu are listed so the user can select one to switch to it.

Enter a name for each in the column to its right, which are displayed on the menu bar.

You can modify the entries in this list as you do in other lists in Approach dialog boxes:

- Click **Add Menu** to add a new, blank row to this list.
- Click **Delete Menu** to delete the current row from this list.
- Click the selection box to the left of a row to select the row. The row is highlighted to show it is selected.
- Click and drag the selection box of a selected row upward or downward to change the order of records.

Defining the Menu Pop-Ups

When you click any of the items on the top-level menu in the Menu Name or Menu Type column on the left, the commands on its pop-up are displayed in the panel on the right, if it is one of the types that lets you define commands.

Modify this list in the usual way:

- Click **Add Item** to add a new, blank row to this list.

- Click **Delete Item to** delete the current row from this list.
- Click the selection box to the left of a row to select the row. Then click and drag the selection box of the selected row upward or downward to change the order of records.

Use the drop-down on the left, in the item Action column, to select the Action that the command performs. It includes all of the commands on the standard Approach menu, plus other commands. Enter the name of the command and a shortcut key to the right of each, which is included in the pop-up menu.

Defining Hot Keys and Shortcut Key Combinations

There are two ways of using the keyboard to make selections from Windows menus:

- *Hot Keys.* You can hold down **Alt** and press the underlined letter from the menu bar to display its pop-up. Once the pop-up is displayed, you can press the underlined letter on one of its commands to execute that command. For example, you can press **Alt+E** to display the Edit menu, and then press **P** to execute the Paste command.
- *Shortcut Key Combinations.* You can execute some commands instantly by using a key combination. For example, you can press **Ctrl+V** to execute the **Paste** command. It is displayed on the menu pop-up to the right of the option it is used for.

It is easy to specify both hot keys and shortcut key combinations on Approach custom menus.

To create hot keys, simply include **&** before a character when you enter its name in the Menu Name or Item Name list. That letter is underlined in the custom menu and works just as Hot Keys do in conventional Windows menus.

To create a shortcut key combination, simply type the combination to the right of the Command's name in the Item Name list, separated from the command with spaces, if you want. That combination is displayed to the right of the command in the pop-up and works just as shortcut key combinations do in conventional Windows menus.

Short Menus

Short menus are the one custom menu type that comes with Approach, in addition to the default menu. Short menus do not include any of the commands that

Chapter 11: Using Approach Utilities

let the user create or modify databases and views they also that omit difficult commands, such as **Import Data** and **Export Data** (see Figure 11.13).

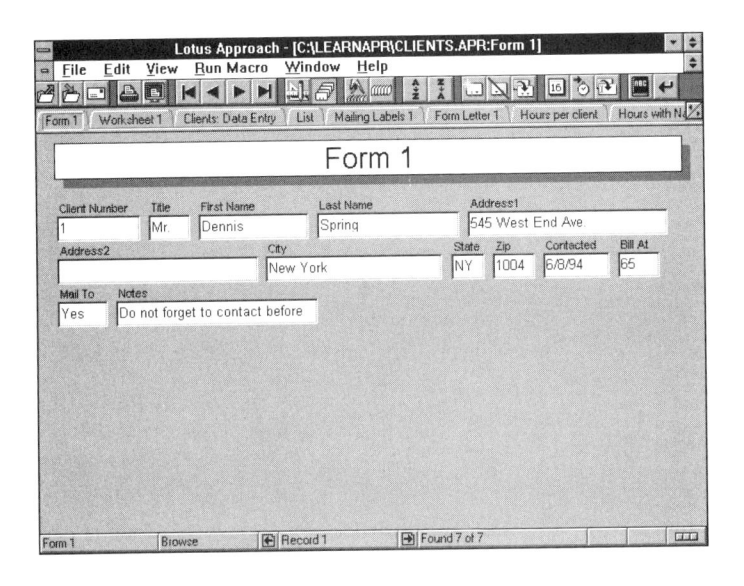

Figure 11.13 Using Approach with short menus.

Short menus are meant to be used with Approach applications that you set up for beginners. You create the databases and views, and the short menu system lets the user enter and edit data in them.

Its File, Edit, Window and Help menus have the options found on these menus in most Windows applications. Its View menu just lets the user zoom in and out. It also has a Run Macro menu, which includes a list of the macros in the Approach file. This makes it very easy to set up an application by creating macros for all the tasks that the user has to perform beyond the basics that are already on the menu.

Of course, you can also copy the Short menus and create a custom menu system based on them to set up a more specialized application for beginners.

> **NOTE** It is best to use password protection with this sort of application, to be sure that the user cannot display the full menu system. Password protection is covered in the section on *Preferences* in this chapter.

Using Custom Menus

After you have created custom menu systems, you can use them in several different ways.

You can use the Macro command Menu Switch to specify which menu bar is used. Simply select Default menu, the Short menu, or a custom menu from its Switch the menu bar drop-down. If you create a macro named Open that includes this command, you can control which menu is displayed when a user opens any Approach file.

You can also select a menu name from the Attached menu bar drop-down of any view to use it as the menu when that View is displayed. Thus, if you are setting up an application for novices, you can not only create the views that they need but precisely control which menu bar is displayed with each view.

Custom Icon Bars

To create custom Icon Bars, choose **SmartIcons** from the Tools menu to display the SmartIcons dialog box (see Figure 11.14).

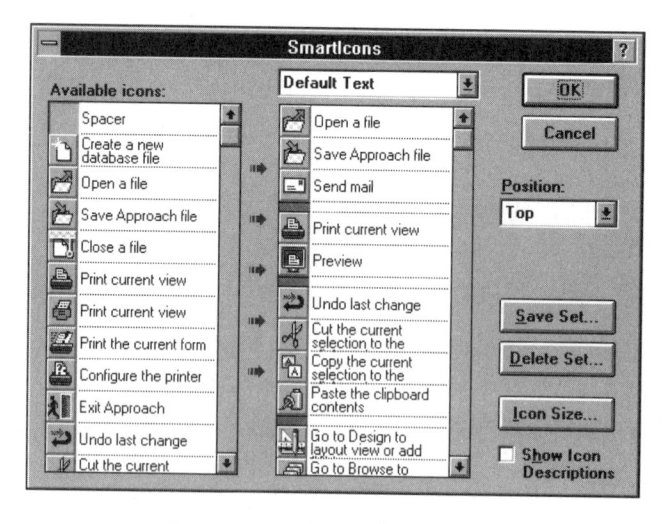

Figure 11.14 The SmartIcons dialog box.

If necessary, use the drop-down at the top of this dialog box to select the name of the Icon bar you want to customize. Its icons are displayed in the list below this drop-down.

All of the icons you can include in custom icon bars are displayed in the Available icons list, at the left of this dialog box. This includes many icons that are not available in any of the default icon bars. It begins with a Spacer icon, which you can use to add a space that is half the width of an icon between icons to group them.

You can modify an icon bar in the following ways:

- To add an icon, click and drag one of the icons from the Available icons list to the list of icons in the icon bar.
- To remove an icon, click and drag one of the icons from the list of icons in the icon bar to the Available icons list.
- To change the order of icons, click and drag icons up or down in the list of icons in the icon bar.
- To change the size of icons, click **Icon Size** to display the Icon Size dialog box, which you can use to select the size you want.

To name a new set of icons, click **Save Set**. Approach displays the Save Set of SmartIcons dialog box, where you can enter the name. The new set is added to the list names in the drop-down at the top of the SmartIcons dialog box.

> **NOTE** You can select **OK** to save changes you made in the current set of icons, or select **Save Set** to create a set with a new name in addition to the current icon set.

To delete a set of icons, select it in the drop-down and click **Delete Set**.

Use the **Position** drop-down to specify whether icons are at the left, right, top or bottom of the screen or to create a floating icon bar, which the user can click and drag to any location on the screen.

If you click **Show Icon Descriptions**, the help ballon for an icon is displayed whenever you move the pointer to it. By default, as you know, the balloons are displayed when you right-click an icon.

To use custom icons, click the **SmartIcons** box on the status bar to display a pop-up menu with the names of the icon bars you created and the standard icon bars (see Figure 11.15).

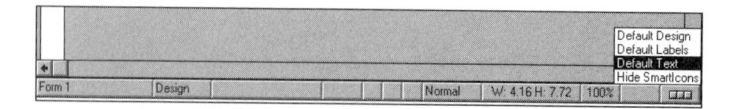

Figure 11.15 Selecting an Icon Bar in the SmartIcons dialog box.

Setting Preferences

You can customize many different aspects of the Approach environment by choosing **Preferences** from the Tools menu to display the Preferences dialog box.

The Display Panel

Use the Display panel to specify whether certain features of the Approach interface should be displayed (see Figure 11.16).

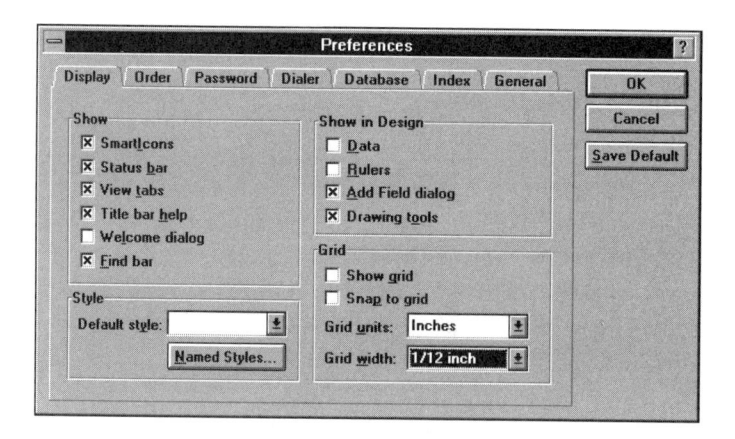

Figure 11.16 The Display Panel.

The Show area determines whether the SmartIcon bar, Status bar, View tabs, Title bar help, Welcome dialog box, and the Find icon bar are displayed.

The Style area lets you select a named style to be used as the default style when you create views.

The Show in Design area lets you specify whether Approach should show Data, Rulers, Add Field box, and Drawing tools by default in Design mode. You can see in the illustration that the Data and the Drawing tools are displayed by default, as you saw when you worked in Design mode.

The Grid area lets you specify whether Show grid and Snap to Grid are on by default, and also lets you specify the fineness of the grid. You can use the Grid units drop-down to determine whether the space between the grid lines should be measured in Inches or Centimeters. Then select the actual size of the space between gridlines from the Grid width drop-down.

The Order Panel

Use the Order panel to select a default Sort order for your records (see Figure 11.17). Use it like the Sort dialog box, which was described in Chapter 6. Add the Fields you want to use as the basis of the sort order in the Fields to sort on list, and select the **Ascending** or **Descending** radio button for each. Records are displayed in this order, if you do not sort them in some other way.

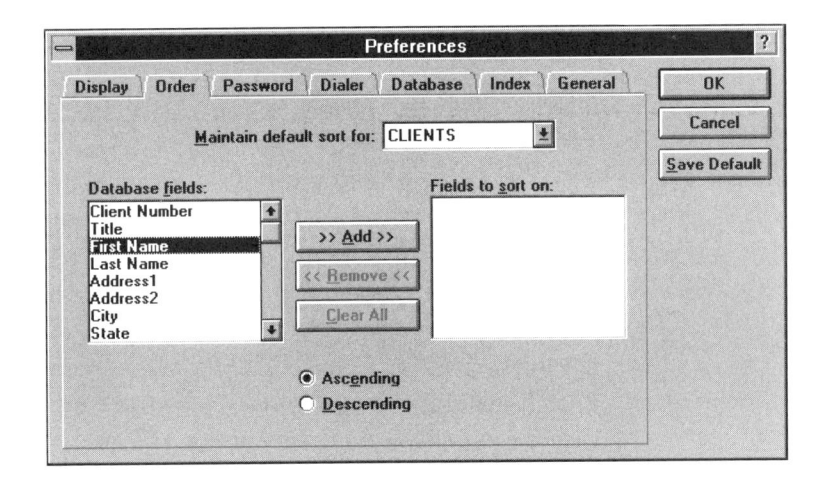

Figure 11.17 The Order panel.

The Password Panel

Use the Password panel to create or change the Password for the Approach file (see Figure 11.18).

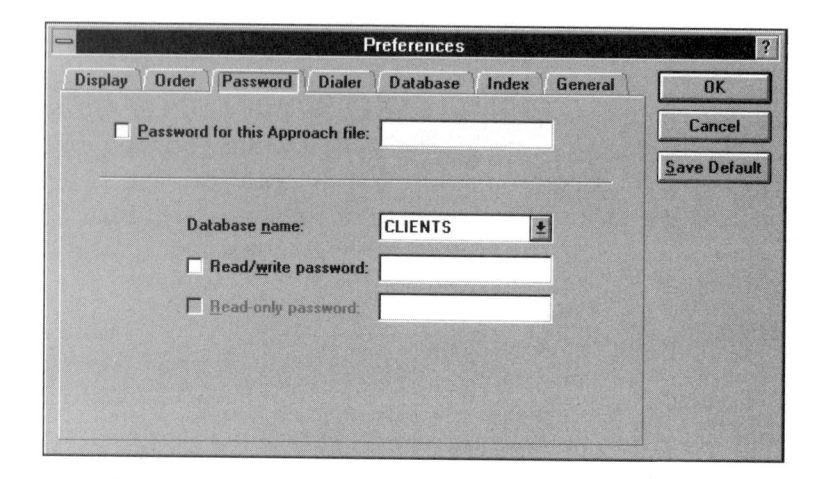

Figure 11.18 The Password panel.

The top half of this panel lets you create password protection for the Approach file, which is used to prevent other Approach users from changing the design views in this Approach file.

The bottom half of this dialog box lets you create two different levels of password protection for the data files underlying the Approach file. Both are used primarily to prevent unauthorized users from accessing the data on a network:

- Select **Set Read/Write Password** to make Approach ask for a password every time a database is opened. Enter the password in the text box to its right. The user must enter the password to have any access to the data at all.

- If you have created a Read/Write password, you can also create a second password, which gives users who do not know it the ability to view the data but not to modify it. To do so, select **Set Read Only Password** and enter a password in the text box to its right.

Approach displays either of these passwords as a series of asterisks, rather than displaying what you typed.

After you enter a password in any of these text boxes, when you click or tab to another control, Approach displays the Confirm Password dialog box, shown above in Figure 11.19, and you must reenter the password in the Retype Password text box and select **OK** to create the password.

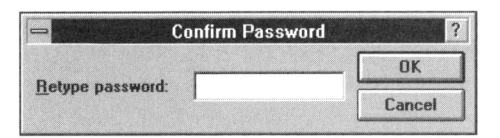

Figure 11.19 The Confirm Password dialog box.

Setting a Password Using Save As

You can also create a password for an Approach file by opening the file and then choosing **Save as** from the File menu, selecting the **Set Approach file password:** checkbox in the Save Approach File As Dialog box, and typing the password in the text box to its right (see Figure 11.20). Select the **Apr file only** radio button so Approach does not create a new data file.

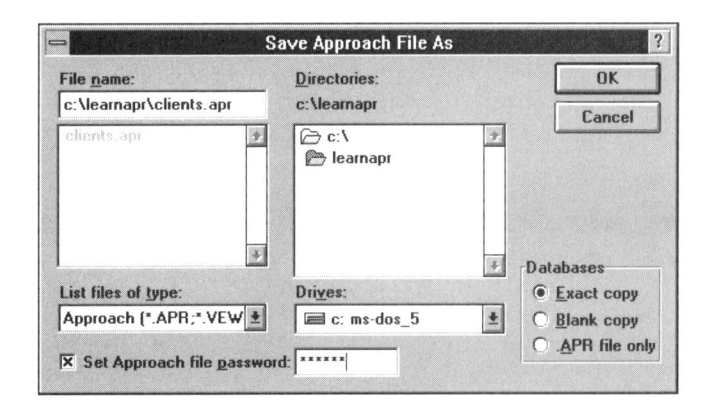

Figure 11.20 Using the Save Approach File As dialog box to create a password.

When you select **OK**, Approach displays the Confirm View Password dialog box, and you must retype the password to confirm it, as when you are using the Preferences dialog box.

This method can only be used to protect an Approach file, not a data file.

Removing Password Protection

Approach also displays this dialog box when you choose **Save As** from the File menu, so you cannot use this command to alter password protection unless you know the password.

Once you enter the password to use **Save As** you can remove password protection simply by deselecting **Set View Password**. Again, select **Same Data** so Approach does not create a new data file when you select **OK**.

> **WARNING**
>
> Approach does not password protect the Preferences dialog box, as it does the Save As dialog box. It is possible for an unauthorized user to remove password protection by choosing **Preferences** from the Tools menu, displaying its Password panel, and deselecting the Password for this Approach file check box. To prevent this from happening, you must use short menus or some custom menu that does not include the **Preferences** command.

The Dialer Panel

Use the Dialer panel to setup the autodialer to work with your modem (see Figure 11.21). Use the drop-downs to specify the port and baud rate of your modem, and the text boxes to specify dialing preferences. Use the Dial Type radio buttons to dial using tones for a touch-tone phone, or to dial using a pulse as old-fashioned dial phones do.

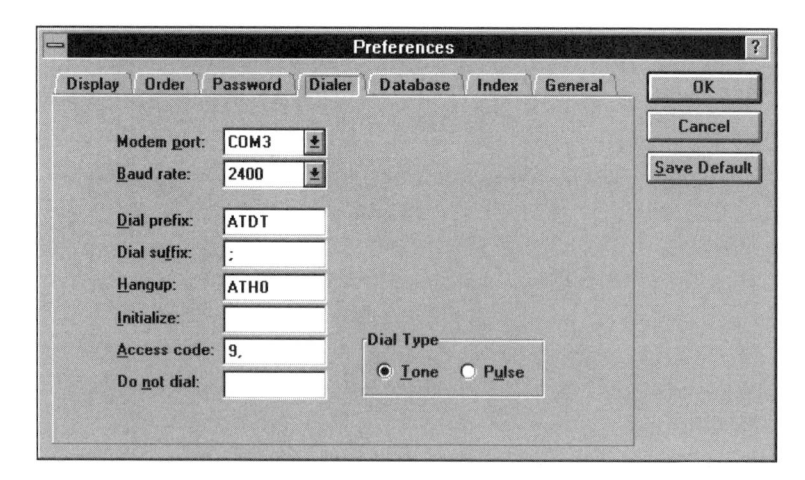

Figure 11.21 The Dialer panel.

The Database Panel

The database panel is displayed in several different forms, which let you set preferences for different types of data files.

Preferences for Xbase Files

If you are using a dBASE or FoxPro file, Approach displays the Database panel shown in Figure 11.22 to let you set database preferences.

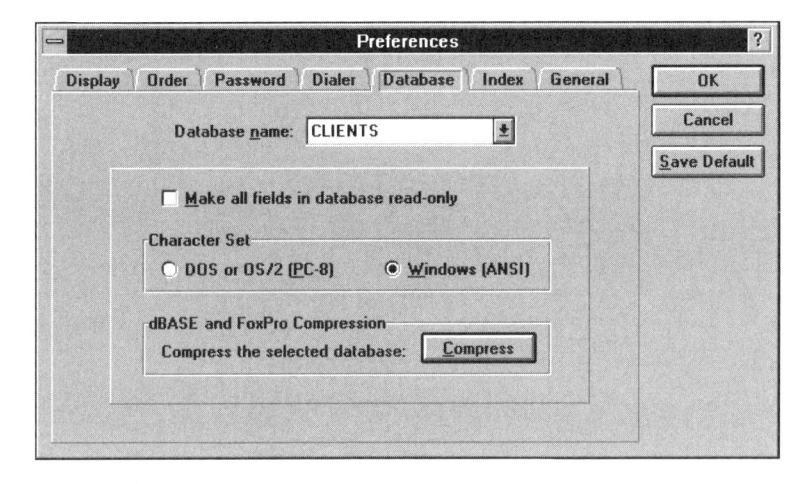

Figure 11.22 The Database panel for Xbase databases.

Select the database you want them applied to from the Database name drop-down. Use the checkbox to make a database read only, and the radio buttons to select its character set.

> **NOTE** Use the **Compress** button to permanently remove records from a dBASE or FoxPro database. When you delete records from this type of file, they are marked for deletion but are not removed from the file. Though they cannot be accessed in Approach, they can still be viewed if you use dBASE or FoxPro. This button makes a new copy of the file without the extra records, so they are permanently removed from the file. It is equivalent to using the PACK command in dBASE or FoxPro.

Preferences for Paradox Files

The Preferences panel for Paradox files has many of the same options as the Preferences Panel for Xbase files though it does not have a Compress button (see Figure 11.23). It also has radio buttons that let you specify whether Finds are case sensitive.

Practical Approach, 3.0

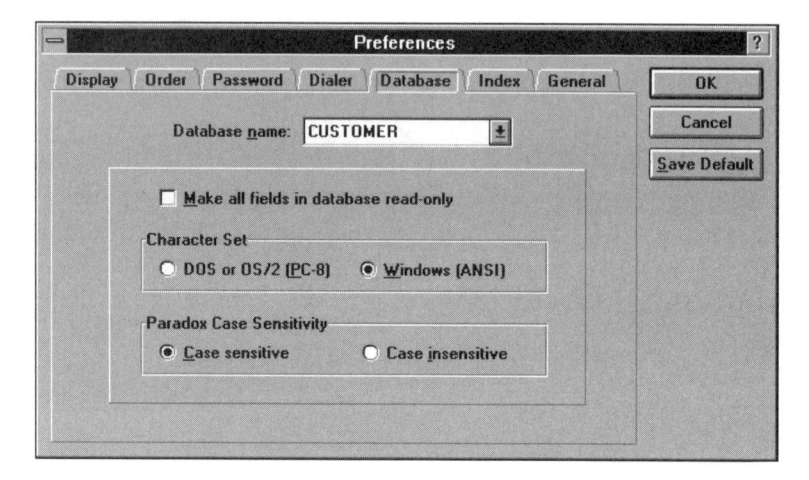

Figure 11.23 The Database panel for Paradox databases.

Preferences for SQL Tables

The Preferences panel for SQL tables has three checkboxes that you can use to set three options:

- *Read only.* Select this checkbox to make tables read only.
- *Include system tables.* Select this checkbox to include SQL systems tables in the lists of file names in Approach dialog boxes.
- *Cache table name.* Choose this checkbox to cache the table name the first time you open a SQL table.

> **NOTE** You may use the drop-down at the top of this dialog box to select any SQL table, but preferences that you select apply to all SQL tables that you create or use in Approach.

The Index Panel

The Index Panel differs for Xbase and Paradox Files.

Indexes for Xbase Files

If you are using dBASE or FoxPro databases the Index panel shown in Figure 11.24 is displayed, which lets you select dBASE and FoxPro indexes to be updated when you edit the database in Approach. Indexes must be updated if you are sharing files with dBASE or FoxPro users.

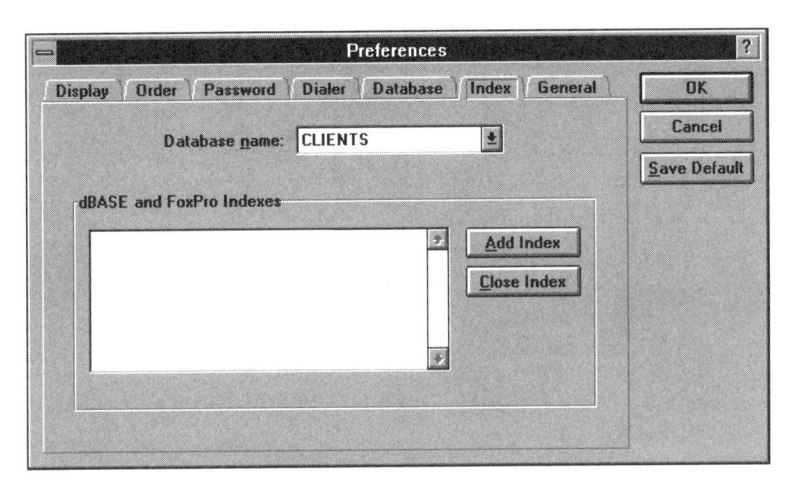

Figure 11.24 The Index Panel for Xbase databases.

Use the Database name drop-down to select the database. Click **Add Index** to display an Open dialog box, and use it to select indexes of that database. dBASE has indexes with the extensions NDX (single index files) and MDX (multiple index fields). Foxpro has indexes with the extensions IDX (single index files) and CDX (multiple index files).

If you no longer want an index updated, select it from the list and click **Close Index**.

Indexes for Paradox Files

If you are using a Paradox file the Index panel shown in Figure 11.25 is displayed, which lets you create secondary indexes.

A Paradox database has a primary index based on its key field; you must always specify a key field when you use a Paradox database in Approach.

Paradox also lets you use secondary indexes to speed queries and sorts. For example, Approach can sort a large database alphabetically by name in less time if you create a secondary index based on the Last Name and First Name field.

To create an index, click **Add Index** and enter its name in the Paradox secondary index list. Then select the fields that the index should be based on in the Database fields list and click **Add** to add them to the Fields to index list, or simply double-click them to add them to this list. As with other field pickers, you can remove a field from the Fields to index list by selecting it and clicking **Remove** or simply by double-clicking it.

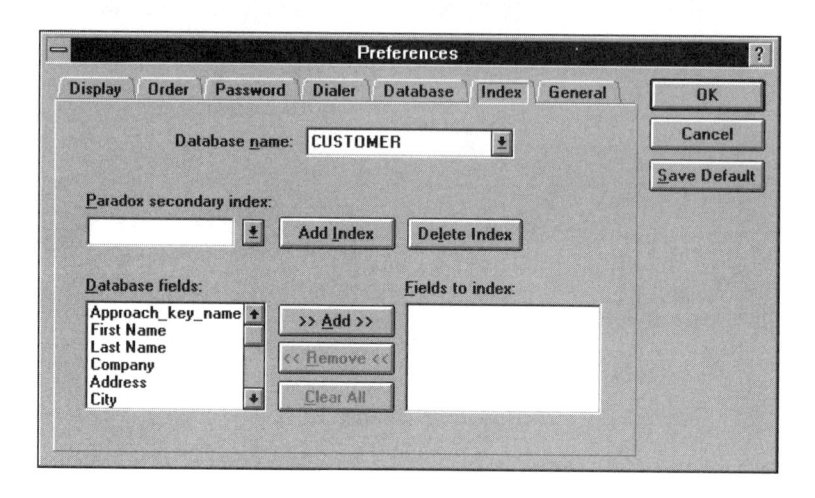

Figure 11.25 The Index Panel for Paradox databases.

To modify an existing index, use the drop-down to select it in the Paradox secondary index list, and use **Add and Remove** to change the fields in the Fields to index list.

To delete an index, use the drop-down to select it in the Paradox secondary index list, and click **Delete Index**.

NOTE: Approach automatically maintains all Paradox indexes. You do not decide which should be maintained, as you do with Xbase indexes.

The General Panel

Use the General panel to set miscellaneous preferences (see Figure 11.26).

The check boxes let you:

- Use **Enter** as well as the **Tab** key to move among fields in Browse mode.
- Show the **Add Fields** box after creating new fields, so you can add the fields to existing views. This is turned on by default.

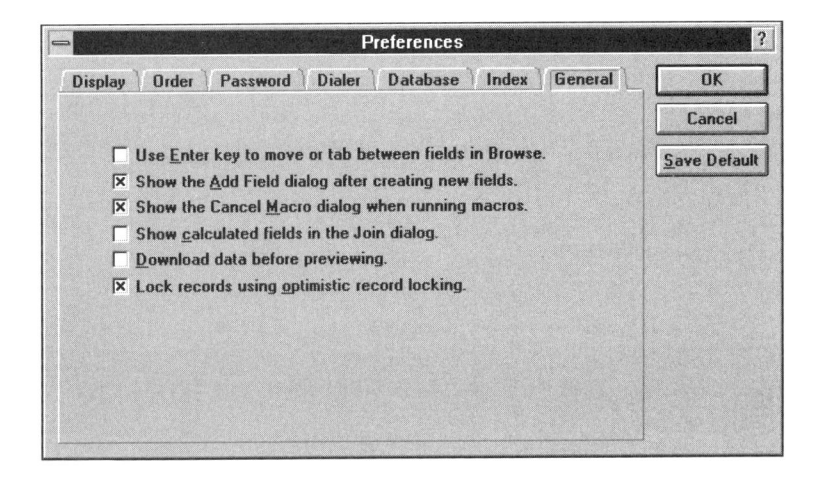

Figure 11.26 The Preferences General Panel dialog box.

- Display a dialog box that lets you cancel macros when they are running. This is turned on by default.
- Show calculated fields in the Join dialog box, so they can be used to relate databases.
- Download data before previewing.
- Use optimistic record locking.

The last two checkboxes are useful only on networks and so they are discussed in Chapter 12.

Chapter 12

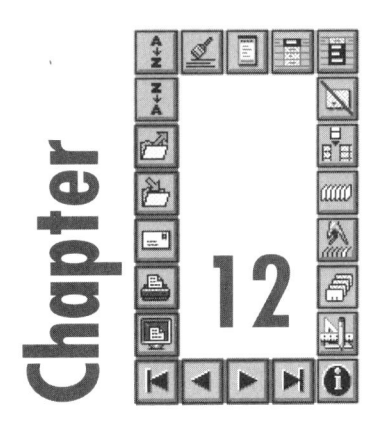

Working with Other Database Applications

As you learned at the beginning of this book, Approach creates and works directly with dBASE, FoxPro, Paradox and other types of data files. It uses the file types of these applications to hold data, and it overlays them with its own Approach files. In general, when you use Approach, you work with the Approach file rather than the actual database files, and so this book has focused on the field types and other features of the Approach files, rather than the underlying database files. This chapter covers some extra techniques that you should know if you want to use Approach data files in other database programs, or if you share them with users on a network who use other programs. This chapter covers:

- Special features of the three types of Xbase files used by Approach, dBASE III+, dBASE IV, and FoxPro files
- Special features of Paradox files
- Working with Lotus 1-2-3 and Lotus Notes data

- Working with ORACLE SQL, Microsoft SQL Server, DB2 files, and ODBC data sources
- How to use Approach to import and export data
- How to map fields of an Approach database
- How to copy a database to a network
- How to use the Refresh command to make sure you are viewing current data
- The difference between Optimistic and Pessimistic Record Locking, and how to use each
- How to speed printing and previewing of a design by using a network file

Files Types Used Directly by Approach

Approach creates and uses files from four different applications if you are working on a stand-alone microcomputer—dBASE III+, dBASE IV, FoxPro and Paradox. These applications fall into two categories.

* *Xbase.* Both FoxPro and dBASE IV are extensions of dBASE III+. They have some differences but most features are in common. These programs and other dBASE compatible programs are sometimes referred to collectively as Xbase.
* *Paradox.* On the other hand, Paradox is not compatible with Xbase, and its files have some features that are different from the other three.

If you are working on a network and have the appropriate software in addition to Approach, you can directly create and use ORACLE SQL, Microsoft SQL Server, and DB2 databases. Both SQL and DB2 are query languages, which programmers use to access data, but Approach acts as a front end to them. You can access the data by using Approach Views in all the ways you have learned earlier in this book, without knowing anything about the underlying language. You can create any of these files in the way that you learned in Chapter 2. Choose **New** from the File menu and select the type of file you want to create from the List Files of Type drop-down list. If you have the necessary software, ORACLE, SQL Server (short for Microsoft SQL Server), and DB2 are displayed as options in this drop-down list.

You can also work with any other databases that can be used as ODBC data sources. Open DataBase Connectivity (ODBC) is a convention adopted by most database applications to let them share data. However, ODBC is slower than the Powerkey technology that Approach uses to work with other file types directly.

The following sections discuss some technical features of these different file types. They are intended primarily for reference. Read only the ones that apply to the programs that you use.

Xbase Files

There are a couple of features you can use when working in Approach with any Xbase files, dBASE III+, dBASE IV, or FoxPro. All of these files have field naming conventions in Approach that are different than in the original application. With all of these file types, you must pack the file if you want to compress it by removing deleted records, and you have the option of adding indexes created in the Xbase application, so they are maintained when you modify the data in Approach.

Field Names

When you create a dBASE or FoxPro file in Approach, field names can be up to 32 characters long and can use any characters, including blank spaces and special characters such as commas and periods. However, dBASE and FoxPro themselves allow field names of up to 10 characters long, which can include letters, numbers, or the underscore character, but cannot include other special characters or blank spaces. If you create a dBASE field name in Approach that does not obey these rules, the field name is different if you use that file in another dBASE compatible application.

Database Preferences

To set preferences for Xbase files, choose **Preferences** from the Tool menu to display the Preference dialog box and then click the **Database** divider tab. If an Xbase file is selected its Database drop-down, the Database panel is displayed as shown in Figure 12.1.

Practical Approach, 3.0

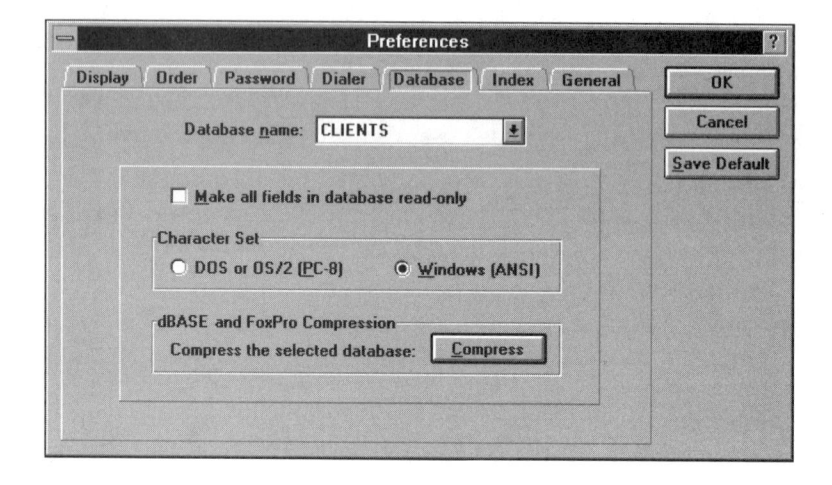

Figure 12.1 The Database panel.

You can use the checkbox to make a database read only, and the radio buttons to select its character set.

Packing Files

Use **Compress** to permanently remove records from a dBASE or FoxPro database.

All Xbase programs simply mark a record for deletion when you delete it. In order to improve performance, they do not actually remove it from the database file. Though deleted records are not accessible in Approach, they can still be used in Xbase compatible programs.

Failing to remove records from the file can leave you with bloated files. To remove the deleted records completely, use the **PACK** command of the Xbase language, which copies all the records that are not marked for deletion to a new file that is given the same name as the old one. Use **Compress** in the Database panel to pack any of the three Xbase file types in Approach.

Maintaining Indexes

You can update the indexes in dBASE or FoxPro in two ways:

- Update them in dBASE or FoxPro by entering the command **REINDEX** whenever you use them.

Chapter 12: Working with Other Database Applications

- Have Approach update them automatically whenever you modify the file in Approach, so they are always current and ready to use in dBASE or FoxPro.

WARNING In dBASE and FoxPro, you can explicitly create indexes to let you access records more quickly. If you use these files in Approach, it does not update their indexes by default. If you use the data in dBASE or FoxPro without updating the indexes, some records will be hidden when you view the data in dBASE or FoxPro in the order determined by these indexes.

There is always some overhead involved in maintaining an index, and if you have a large number of indexes that are maintained automatically, it slows down data entry and editing. In some cases, it would be better to re-index when you use the data again in another application, rather than updating the index as you enter data in Approach. In other cases, however, particularly if you are sharing the data on a network with other people who use different applications, it is best to keep the indexes up to date at all times.

To update indexes from Xbase applications in Approach, choose **Preferences** from the Tools menu to display the Preferences dialog box, and click the **Index** divider tab to display the panel shown in Figure 12.2.

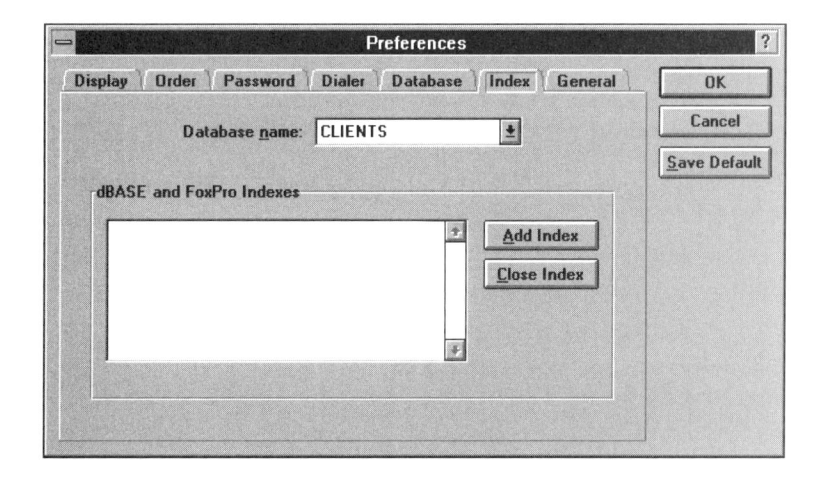

Figure 12.2 The Index panel for Xbase files.

To add and update an index to this Index Files list select **Add Index** to display the Add Index dialog box (see Figure 12.3). Use this in the familiar way to open an index file. Use the Directories list and the Drives drop-down to select the directory and drive where it has been saved. Use the List Files of Type drop-down list to select the type of file you are opening.

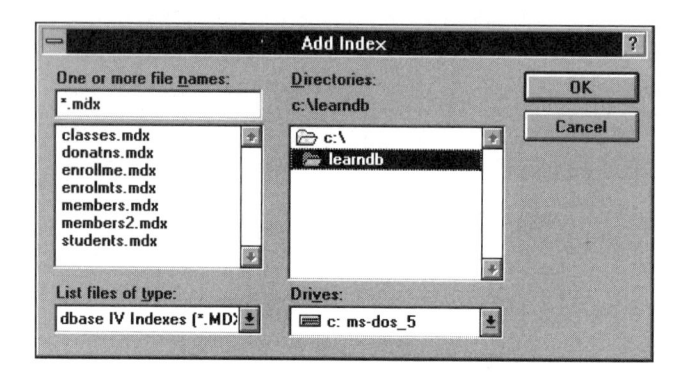

Figure 12.3 The Add Index dialog box.

You can update single index files and compound index files from both dBASE and FoxPro, which have the following extensions:

- *NDX files.* dBASE single index files. These were the only type of index available in dBASE III+.
- *MDX files.* dBASE multiple index files, which hold several index tags in a single file. These are the most common type of index used in dBASE IV.
- *IDX files.* FoxPro single index files. These are listed on the drop-down list as FoxPro 2.0 indexes, but they were available in FoxPro 1.0 and can still be created in FoxPro 2.0 and later versions.
- *CDX files.* FoxPro compound index files, which hold several index tags in a single file. These were added in Version 2.0 of FoxPro and now are the most commonly used type of FoxPro index.

When you select a file type, a field skeleton including its extension is displayed in the File Name text box, and all files in the current directory with that extension are listed below. Select the index you want maintained from this list, and select **OK** to add it to the index file list of the Database Options dialog box.

To remove an index from this list, select it and then select **Close Index**.

When all the indexes that you want to maintain are in the list, select **OK**. The indexes are updated to reflect changes you make in the data.

dBASE III+

dBASE III+ stores data in files with the extension DBF, and memos in files with the extension DBT. The memo field in the DBF file contains a pointer that indicates the location of the memo's text in the DBT file.

The maximum size of a record in a file is 128 fields and 4,000 characters. The maximum size of a file is 1 billion records and 2 billion characters. The maximum length of a memo is 5,000 characters.

Field Names

Names of fields can be up to 10 characters, including letters, numbers and the underscore character, but cannot include spaces or other special characters. If you create a file in Approach that does not following these field naming conventions, its field names will be altered when you use it in dBASE III+.

Incompatibilities of Approach and dBASE III+

Approach can use the data in any files created in dBASE III+. However, if you create files in Approach and then use them in dBASE III+, there are two incompatibilities:

- The editor of dBASE III+ does not let you view memo fields of more than 5,000 characters. If you attempt to edit them, it truncates the field and loses any data beyond this length.
- dBASE III+ cannot use Approach PicturePlus fields.

In addition, Time fields created in Approach are treated as character fields by dBASE III+.

dBASE III+ Networking Options

To specify networking options for any file, you select the **Connect** button of the New dialog box when you are creating the file, to display the dBASE or Paradox Network Connection dialog box. If you have specified a connection, you can change it by selecting the **Connect** button of the Open dialog box when you open the file. Approach displays the Network Connection dialog box, and you can change the specifications.

By default, Approach uses the dBASE IV network protocol for both dBASE III+ and dBASE IV files. However, you can make Approach use the dBASE III+ protocol for all dBASE files if you like. This is not done in a dialog box but rather, through the APPROACH.INI file. The APPROACH.INI file is a text file that contains commands and settings. When Approach is booted, it reads this file and uses these settings.

If you want to use the dBASE III+ protocol, go to the File Manager and find the Windows directory. Open the **APPROACH.INI** file. Add a line that reads:

```
SdBASEFile Sharing Method=dBASE3
```

Regardless of the protocol being used, Approach displays the dBASE Network Connection dialog box when you select the **Connect** button of the New dialog box and dBASE III+ or dBASE IV is selected in the List Files of Type drop-down list (see in Figure 12.4).

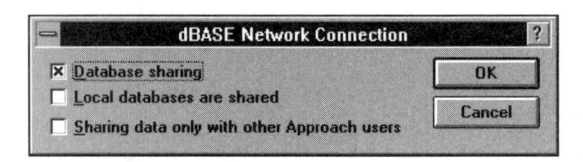

Figure 12.4 The dBASE Network Connection dialog box.

Its two options let you specify whether any database files are shared and whether local database files are shared, as follows:

- *Database sharing.* When the Database Sharing check box is selected (the default), other users are given access to your files at the same time you are using them. Deselect this check box to deny other users access to any files at the time you are using them.
- *Local Databases are shared.* When this checkbox is deselected (the default) other users are not able to access databases on your local drive while you are using them, even if the Database Sharing check box is selected, and even if your network lets you share files on your drive with

other users. Selecting this check box lets you use your local dBASE files with other applications at the same time you use them with Approach, and lets other users open your local dBASE files at the same time you are using them. However, you must use SHARE.EXE for this option to work.

- *Sharing Data only with other Approach users.* This option optimizes performance but can be used only if data is used exclusively by Approach.

> **WARNING**
> Selecting Local **Databases Shared** slows Approach's performance, and so it should only be used if necessary.

dBASE IV

dBASE IV stores data in files with the extension DBF and memos in files with the extension DBT. The memo field in the DBF file contains a pointer that indicates the location of the memo's text in the DBT file.

The maximum size of a record in a DBF file is 255 fields and 4,000 characters. The maximum size of a file is 1 billion records and 2 billion characters. The maximum length of a memo field is 64K (over 65,000 characters).

Field Names

Names of fields can be up to 10 characters, including letters, numbers and the underscore character, but cannot include spaces or other special characters. If you create a file in Approach that does not following these field naming conventions, its field names are altered when used in dBASE IV.

Incompatibilities of Approach and dBASE IV

Approach can use the data in any files created in dBASE IV, but it has one minor incompatibility with its data. dBASE IV can create two different types of fields to hold numbers:

- *Float.* This type holds floating point numbers, including digits, a decimal point and a leading minus sign. You must specify the total width of the field (including spaces for integer digits and, if necessary, a space for the decimal point and for decimal digits) and the number of decimal places. Maximum length is 20 digits, and calculations are accurate to 20 decimal places.

- *Numeric.* This type holds fixed point numbers, including digits, a decimal point and a leading minus sign. You must specify the total width of the field (including spaces for integer digits and, if necessary, a space for the decimal point and for decimal digits) and the number of decimal places. Maximum length is 20 digits, and calculations are accurate to 15 decimal places.

When Approach uses files created in dBASE IV, it uses both of these as numeric fields.

If you create files in Approach and then use them in dBASE IV, there are two incompatibilities:

- The editor of dBASE IV does not let you view memo fields of more than 64K characters.
- dBASE IV cannot use Approach PicturePlus fields.

In addition, Time fields created in Approach are treated as character fields by dBASE IV.

dBASE IV Networking Options

When you are creating a new file, to specify networking options, select **Connect** in the New dialog box after selecting dBASE IV from its List Files of Type drop-down list. The dBASE Network Connection dialog box is displayed (see Figure 12.4). If you have specified a connection, you can change it by selecting **Connect** in the Open dialog box when you open the file. Approach displays the Network Connection dialog box, and you can change the specifications.

The two options let you specify whether any database files are shared and whether local database files are shared, as follows:

- *Database sharing.* When this checkbox is selected (the default), other users are given access to your files at the same time you are using them. Deselect this check box to deny other users access to any files at the time that you are using them.
- *Local Databases are shared.* When this checkbox is deselected (the default) other users are not able to access databases on your local drive while you are using them. Even if the Database Sharing checkbox is selected and your network lets you share files on your drive, other

users cannot access the databases. Selecting this check box lets you use your local dBASE files with other applications at the same time you use them with Approach, and lets other users open your local dBASE files at the same time you are using them. However, you must use SHARE.EXE for this option to work.

> **WARNING** Selecting **Local Databases are Shared** slows Approach's performance, and so it should only be used if necessary.

FoxPro

Approach supports FoxPro through Version 2.1, and does not support the new General field type (used to hold OLE objects) that was added in Version 2.5.

FoxPro keeps data in files with the extension DBF. Memo fields are kept in files with the extension FPT. The Memo field in the DBF file contains a pointer to the location of the data in the FPT file.

Records can hold up to 255 fields and 4,000 characters. Files can hold up to 1 billion records and be up to 2 gigabytes in size for single-user files or multi-user files with a structural CDX index, or up to 1 gigabyte in size for other multi-user files.

FoxPro Memo fields have no length limit except for the limit on the disk space available. Unlike dBASE Memo fields, FoxPro memos can hold characters made of any combination of bits, including characters such as the null character (ASCII 0), and they can be used to hold binary data as well as text.

Field Names

Names of fields can be up to 10 characters long, including letters, numbers and the underscore character, but cannot include spaces or other special characters. If you create a file in Approach that does not following these field naming conventions, its field names are altered when you use it in FoxPro.

Incompatibilities of Approach and FoxPro

Approach can use the data in any files created in FoxPro through Version 2.0, but it cannot use the General field type added in FoxPro 2.5. In addition, FoxPro can create two different types of fields to hold numbers:

- *Float.* This type holds floating point numbers are held, including digits, a decimal point and a leading minus sign. You must specify the total width including the total width of the field (including spaces for integer digits and, if necessary, a space for the decimal point and for decimal digits) and the number of decimal places. Maximum length is 20 digits, and calculations are accurate to 20 decimal places.
- *Numeric.* This type holds fixed point numbers, including digits, a decimal point and a leading minus sign. You must specify the total width including the total width of the field (including spaces for integer digits and, if necessary, a space for the decimal point and for decimal digits) and the number of decimal places. Maximum length is 20 digits, and calculations are accurate to 15 decimal places.

When Approach uses files created in FoxPro, it uses both of these as Numeric fields.

If you create files in Approach and then use them in FoxPro, there are two incompatibilities:

- FoxPro cannot use Approach PicturePlus fields.
- FoxPro files cannot be shared at the same time by multiple users on a network.

In addition, Time fields created in Approach are treated as character fields by FoxPro.

> **NOTE** Note the tradeoff involved in using FoxPro rather than dBASE files. FoxPro does not have any limitation on the length of Memo fields it can read, unlike other versions of Xbase. However, Approach does not support networking with FoxPro files, as it does with other Xbase files. When you create a FoxPro file, **Connect** in the New dialog box is dimmed, so you cannot use the Network Connections dialog box.

Paradox Files

Approach supports Paradox 3.5, Paradox 4.0 and Paradox for Windows. Paradox 4.0 and Paradox for Windows include Memo fields and fields to hold OLE objects, but Paradox 3.5 does not.

Field Names

Names of fields can be up to 25 characters, including any character except the following: " [ ] { } ( ). In addition, the character # cannot be used by itself as a field name, though it can be used as part of a longer field name, and the characters -> cannot be used in combination, though either can be used separately. You can include spaces, but not as the first character of the field name.

If you are defining a Paradox file in Approach, the names of Boolean, Memo, Time and PicturePlus fields can be up to 7 characters long, including the same characters as other fields.

Database Preferences

To set preferences for Paradox files, choose **Preferences** from the Tool menu to display the Preference dialog box and click the **Database** divider tab. If a Paradox file is selected in its Database drop-down, the Database panel is displayed as shown in Figure 12.5.

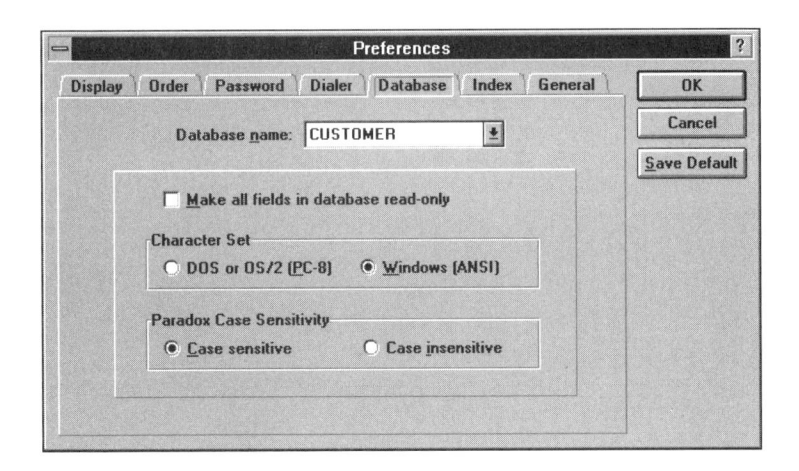

Figure 12.5 The Database panel for Paradox databases.

You can use the checkbox to make a database read only, and the radio buttons to select its character set. Use the radio buttons to specify whether Finds are case sensitive.

Creating Secondary Indexes

If you are using a Paradox file, you can choose **Preferences** from the Tools menu and click the **Index** divider tab to display the Index panel shown un Figure 12.6, which lets you create secondary indexes.

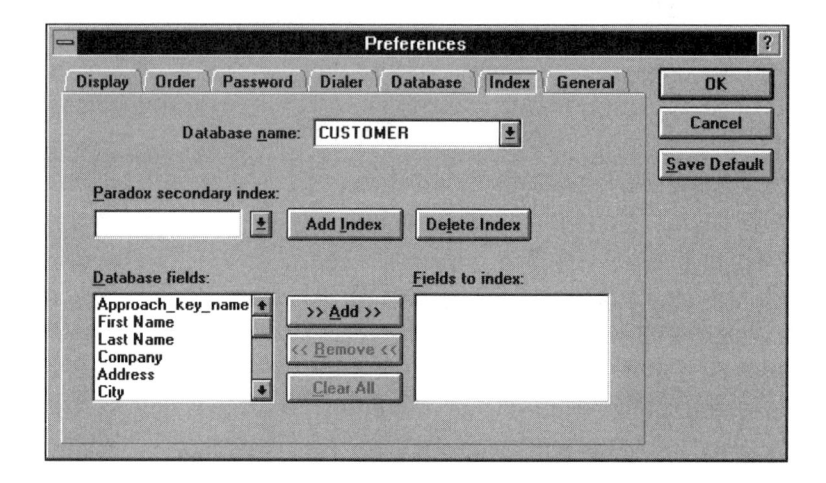

Figure 12.6 The Index Panel for Paradox databases.

A Paradox database has a primary index based on its key field. Paradox also lets you use secondary indexes to speed queries and sorts. For example, Approach can sort a large database alphabetically by name in less time if you create a secondary index based on the Last Name and First Name field.

To create an index, click **Add Index** and enter its name in the Paradox secondary index list. Then select the fields the index should be based on in the Database fields list and click **Add** to add them to the Fields to index list, or simply double-click them to add them to this list. As with other field pickers, you can remove a field from the Fields to index list by selecting it and clicking **Remove** or simply by double-clicking it.

To modify an existing index, use the drop-down to select it in the Paradox secondary index list, and use **Add** and **Remove** to change the fields in the Fields to index list.

To delete an index, use the drop-down to select it in the Paradox secondary index list, and click **Delete Index**. Approach automatically maintains all Paradox indexes.

Key Fields

All Paradox files that are created in Approach must have a key field. These are like the key fields in the one file of a relational database based on a one-to-many relationship; their value must be unique in each record. You can use either a single field or a combination of fields as this unique key.

When you are done defining a new Paradox database and select **OK** in the Define Fields dialog box, the Choose Key Field dialog box is displayed.

Select one of the fields in the fields list and select **OK** to specify that it is the key field. If no field or field combination in the database can be used as a key field, because none has a unique value in each record, you can select **Add Key Field** to add a field named Approach_key_name to the database. This is a Numeric field and, as its data, it is automatically given sequential numbers beginning with one.

When you add an Approach key field in this way, the label of the Add Key Field push button changes to Remove Key Field, and you can select it to remove the key field.

If you open an existing database file created in Paradox that does not already have a key field, Approach displays a warning, which says it cannot use this file because it does not have a key field and asks if you want to make a copy of it so you can add a key field. If you select **OK** to create a copy, it displays the New Database dialog box, which you can use to rename the Paradox file or save it under the same name, so it overwrites the original. It will create a copy of the file with the added Approach_key_name field.

The Approach_key_name field is not displayed on the default form of the Approach file created for this database, but it can be added to it like other fields.

Incompatibilities of Approach and Paradox

Approach can use the data in any files created in Paradox, but it has one minor incompatibility with its data. Paradox can create three different types of fields to hold numbers:

- *Numeric.* This type holds any number with or without decimals, up to 15 significant digits (including decimal places). Larger numbers are rounded and stored using scientific notation. Paradox automatically assigns the field length.

- *Currency.* This type holds any amount of money, up to 15 significant digits. It is like a Numeric field, except that amounts are automatically displayed with a dollar sign and two decimal places.
- *Short Number.* This type holds integers between -32K and 32K. This data type is used by programmers to conserve disk space.

  When Approach uses files created in Paradox, it uses all of these as Numeric fields. In addition, Approach calls Paradox picture fields an unknown field type and uses them for connected or imported data.

If you create files in Approach and then use them in Paradox, there are two incompatibilities:

- Approach Memo and PicturePlus fields cannot be viewed in Paradox 3.5, but they can be viewed in Paradox 4.0.
- Paradox files that do not include key fields cannot be used by Approach without a key field being added.

In addition, Time fields created in Approach are treated as alphanumeric fields by Paradox. Finally, Approach sorts and finds are case sensitive when a Paradox index exists.

Paradox Networking Options

When you are creating a new file, to specify networking options, select **Connect** in the New dialog box. After selecting **Paradox** from its List Files of Type drop-down list, to display the Paradox Network Connection dialog box (see Figure 12.7). If you have specified a connection, you can change it by selecting **Connect** in the Open dialog box when you open the file; Approach displays the Network Connection dialog box, and you can change the specifications.

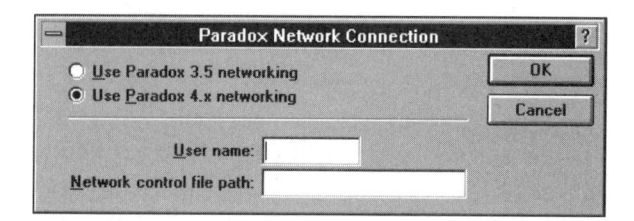

Figure 12.7 The Paradox Network Connection dialog box.

Use the radio buttons to specify whether you are using Paradox 3.5 or Paradox 4 Networking. If you are using Paradox for Windows, select Paradox 4.

Enter your user name in the User Name text box. You can also log on under another name if you want.

Enter the path name of your PARADOX.NET file in the Network control file text box. PARADOX.NET is a control file Paradox uses to keep track of all users on the network, and all users must specify its location. Enter the path name, but do not add the file name PARADOX.NET after it. All users must have access to the directory for this file.

Working with Other Lotus Applications

You can open and view data from Lotus 1-2-3 or Lotus notes in Approach.

You can open a Lotus 1-2-3 worksheet or a named range of a Worksheet just as you open a data file from any other application. Then you can create views in Approach to work with your Lotus 1-2-3 data.

You can open Lotus Notes views or forms in Approach. When you open a Notes view, it is read-only in Approach, but when you open a Notes form, you can edit its contents.

Working with SQL

You can use ORACLE or Microsoft SQL Server databases in either of two ways. You can log on to either server to open the databases in the usual way. The easier but less powerful way to use these databases is by opening a SQL Query file, which automatically logs on to the system for you but which can only let you read a copy of the database and cannot let you modify the data.

ORACLE SQL Server

To log on to ORACLE SQL Server, choose **Open** from the File menu and select **ORACLE** from the List Files of Type drop-down list to display the Connect to ORACLE dialog box (see Figure 12.8). You must use this dialog box before Approach displays a list of ORACLE database files.

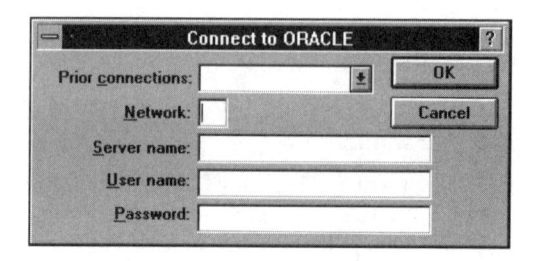

Figure 12.8 The Connect to ORACLE dialog box.

In the Network text box, enter the letter identifying the network protocol being used. Table 12.1 is a partial list of letters used to represent ORACLE protocols, but you should ask your network administrator if your system uses any others.

In the Server Name text box, enter the name of the server computer you want to log on to. In the User Name text box, enter your user name. In the Password text box, enter the password.

Table 12.1 Letters used to represent ORACLE Protocol.

Letter	Protocol
P	Named Pipes
X	SPX
B	NetBIOS
T	TCP/IP
D	DECNet
A	ORACLE Async

Select **OK** to return to the Open dialog box. The File list displays ORACLE databases, and you can open them as usual, except that different terms are used in ORACLE SQL than are used for Windows and DOS databases:

- A *connection* in ORACLE SQL is equivalent to a Drive in Windows terminology.

- An *owner* in ORACLE SQL is equivalent to a Directory in Windows terminology.
- A *Table Name* in ORACLE SQL is equivalent to a file name in Windows terminology.

ORACLE SQL Fields

ORACLE SQL Fields can have names of up to 30 characters, except that Boolean, Date, Picture and Time fields can only have up to 23 characters. These names can be made up of any characters except the double quotation mark, including spaces and special characters.

Text fields can be up to 255 spaces long. You do not specify the length of other field types, but Memo and Picture fields cannot be larger than 64K bytes in size, and you can have only one Memo or Picture field per database.

Incompatibilities of Approach and ORACLE SQL

There are three significant incompatibilities between Approach and ORACLE SQL:

- Approach PicturePlus fields cannot be viewed by other ORACLE SQL applications.
- Approach sorts place null and blank values before other characters. In ORACLE SQL null and blank values come after other field values in sorts.
- An ORACLE SQL Date field includes both a date and a time. Approach breaks this field type into two fields: a Date field with the same name as the ORACLE SQL field, and a Time field with that name followed by _TIME.

In addition, SQL finds and sorts are case sensitive. A field with only space characters in it is not considered to be blank by Oracle SQL or by Approach when it is using ORACLE SQL databases, though it is considered blank when Approach uses other file types.

Microsoft SQL Server

To log on to Microsoft SQL Server, choose **Open** from the File menu and select **SQL Server** from the List Files of Type drop-down list to display the Connect to SQL Server dialog box (see Figure 12.9). You must use this dialog box before Approach displays a list of SQL Server database files.

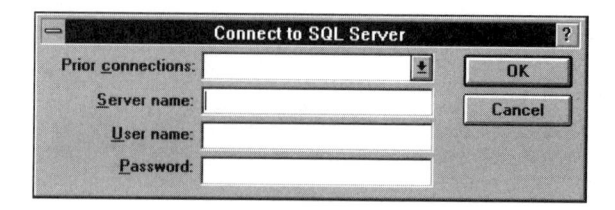

Figure 12.9 The Connect to SQL Server dialog box.

In the Server Name text box, enter the name of the server computer which you want to log on to. In the User Name text box, enter your user name. In the Password text box, enter the password, which is displayed as asterisks. You must get all this information from your network administrator before logging on.

Select **OK** to return to the Open dialog box. The File list displays Microsoft SQL Server databases, and you can open them as usual, except different terms are used in ORACLE SQL than are used for Windows and DOS databases:

- A connection in ORACLE SQL is equivalent to a drive in Windows terminology.
- An owner in ORACLE SQL is equivalent to a directory in Windows terminology.
- A Table Name in ORACLE SQL is equivalent to a file name in Windows terminology.

SQL Server Fields

SQL Server Fields can have names of up to 30 characters, except that Date, Picture and Time fields can have names of up to 24 characters. These names can be made up of letters, numbers, or the characters _ (underscore), $ (dollar sign), or # (number or pound sign), but their first character must be a letter, or the # or _ character.

If a table name begins with the # character, it is a temporary table; temporary table names are limited to 13 characters.

Text fields can be up to 255 spaces long. You do not specify the length of other field types. Memo and Picture fields can be up to 2 gigabytes in size, and you can have an indefinite number of them in a single database.

Incompatibilities of Approach and SQL Server

There are three significant incompatibilities between Approach and Microsoft SQL Server:

- Approach PicturePlus fields cannot be viewed by other SQL Server applications.
- An SQL Server Date field includes both a date and a time. Approach breaks this field type into two fields: a Date field with the same name as the ORACLE SQL field, and a Time field with that name followed by _TIME.
- SQL Server includes a field type for money, which Approach displays as a Numeric field.

SQL finds and sorts are case sensitive.

Preferences for SQL Tables

To set preferences for SQL tables, choose **Preferences** from the Tool menu to display the Preference dialog box and click the **Database** divider tab. If a SQL table is selected in its Database drop-down, the Database panel has three checkboxes you can use to set the following options:

- *Read only.* Select this checkbox to make tables read only.
- *Include system tables.* Select this checkbox to include SQL systems tables in the lists of file names in Approach dialog boxes.
- *Cache table name.* Select this checkbox to cache the table name the first time you open a SQL table.

NOTE: You may use the drop-down at the top of this dialog box to select any SQL table, but preferences that you select apply to all SQL tables you create or use in Approach.

SQL Query Files

A query file contains log on information that is used to connect you to the server, so Approach does not display a Connect dialog box to get this information from you. It also includes a SQL Select command, which specifies how you want to join files and which fields from the joined files you want to use.

Simply select **Query** from the List Files of Type drop-down list of the Open dialog box to display all files with a QRY extension in the File Name list, and open one in the usual way.

> **NOTE** Because you do not have to enter a password to log on when you use a query file, you do not have direct access to the data in the server. You can only view a copy of the data and cannot edit or modify it in any way.

The data requested by the Select statement is copied from the server to a temporary read-only file in your computer, which is automatically deleted when you close the file. When you open the query file again, another temporary file is created.

Saving the Data in a Query File

The only way to keep a permanent copy of the data in a query file is to save it as a different file type. Choose **Save As** from the File menu and use the List File of Type drop-down list to save the data in a different file format. Alternatively, select **Export Data** from the File menu, which is covered later in this chapter, to export it to a different file type.

> **WARNING** It is not a good idea to keep a local copy of the data on the server, however. There can be anomalies when you keep two copies of the same data. Your copy is likely to be out of date the next time you use it. Even worse, you may mistakenly make changes in your own copy of the data and think that you have updated the data on a network.

Making a local copy of network data in this way can be useful if you need to give a copy of the data to someone else. After sending it by modem, or saving it on a floppy disk to give away, delete it from your hard disk. Do not save a copy on your hard disk any longer than you need to.

Creating a Query File

To create a query file, use the SQL database it is based on, and choose **Save As** from the File menu. Choose **Query** from the List Files of Type drop-down list. You can also choose **Export** from the File menu. In the Export dialog box, select **Query** from the List Files of Type drop-down. The Export dialog box is covered later in this chapter.

Working with DB2-MDI

To log onto an IBM DB2-MDI server, choose **Open** from the File menu and select **DB2-MDI** from the List Files of Type drop-down list to display the Connect to DB2-MDI dialog box (see Figure 12.10). You must use this dialog box before Approach displays a list of DB2 database files.

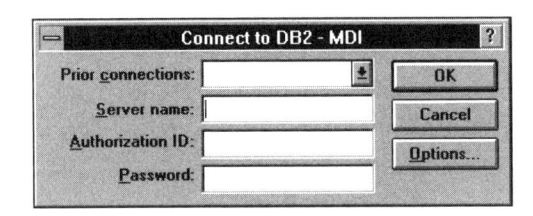

Figure 12.10   The Connect to DB2-MDI dialog box.

In the Server Name text box, enter the name of the server computer you want to log on to. In the Authorization ID text box, enter your ID. In the Password text box, enter the password.

Select **OK** to return to the Open dialog box. The File list displays DB2 databases, and you can open them as usual.

Working with ODBC Sources

The *Open Database Connectivity standard (ODBC)* has been adopted by most database vendors to allow data to be exchanged among their applications. To work with them, you must have another database application with an ODBC driver and Microsoft's ODBC Control Panel manager.

If you have a database application with an ODBC driver, it is included in the List files of type drop-down with the preface ODBC before the application name. You can select it from this drop-down in the New, Open, Save Database As, Import Data, or Export Data dialog box. The connect dialog box that is displayed depends on the ODBC driver.

ODBC Fields

All field names in ODBC must begin with a letter and be made up exclusively of letters and numbers. An ODBC key word may not be used as a field name.

The maximum length of field name depends on whether the ODBC driver supports its data type.

- If the driver supports the data type, the maximum length of the name is 30 characters or the limit imposed by the driver for all data types except PicturePlus, which can be up to 24 characters or 6 less than the limit imposed by the driver.
- If the driver does not support the data type Boolean fields may have names with up 23 characters or 7 less than the limit imposed by the driver, and Date and Time fields may have names with up to 24 characters or 6 less than the limit imposed by the driver.

You must specify a length for text fields. The maximum length depends on the limit imposed by the driver. All other fields are fixed length.

Incompatibilities of Approach and OBDC

There are a few significant incompatibilities between Approach and other applications that support ODBC:

- You can add a PicturePlus field to an ODBC data source in Approach only if it supports the Long Var Binary data type .
- You can add a Memo field to an ODBC data source in Approach only if it supports the Long Var Binary data type.
- Other applications cannot view Approach PicturePlus fields.
- All data types used to hold numbers in ODBC data sources are converted to Numeric fields in Approach.
- The Timestamp data type in ODBC includes both a date and a time. Approach converts a field of this type into two fields: one Date field with the same name as the original field, and one time field with the name followed by _TIME.

Importing and Exporting Data

You have looked at all the file types that you can create and use directly with Approach. You can interchange data with large number of other programs by importing and exporting data.

NOTE: When you use data from other programs directly, the data remains in the same file that it is in when the other program uses it, and the Approach file just overlays this data file. When you import or export data, you make a separate copy of data from another program in a format that Approach can use, or a copy of data from Approach in a format that the other program can use.

In addition to converting data to and from formats that Approach cannot use directly, importing data is useful to creating a copy of data in a file with different field names and field definitions than the original file, or to add data to an existing file from another file.

When you import data, you must *map* the fields of the original file against the fields of the file you are adding data to. That is, you must indicate which field in the original file corresponds to each field in the new file. Even if data is in a file that Approach can use directly, it is sometimes useful to change the file by mapping the fields in this way.

The Field Mapping dialog box is displayed only if the fields of the database being imported are different from the fields of the database that the data is being added to. If both databases have identical field definitions, the data is added without mapping.

Importing Data

Before importing data, you must have an Approach database with the appropriate fields to hold it. Then use this database in Browse mode, and choose **Import Data** from the File menu to display the Import Data dialog box to import data from another database file into it (see Figure 12.11). This option is available only if you are using a database file in Browse mode.

Use this dialog box to select the file from which the data is imported. Use the Directories list and the Drives drop-down list to select the directory and drive where it has been saved. Use the List Files of Type drop-down list to select the type of file you are opening. The file types that you can import data from and their extensions are:

- dBASE III+ (DBF)
- dBASE IV (DBF)
- FoxPro (DBF)

- Query (QRY)
- Paradox (DB)
- ORACLE
- SQL Server
- DB2
- ODBC Data Sources
- Delimited Text Files (TXT)
- Fixed Length Text Files (TXT)
- Excel (XLS)
- Lotus (WK1, WKS, WRK, WRI, WK3)

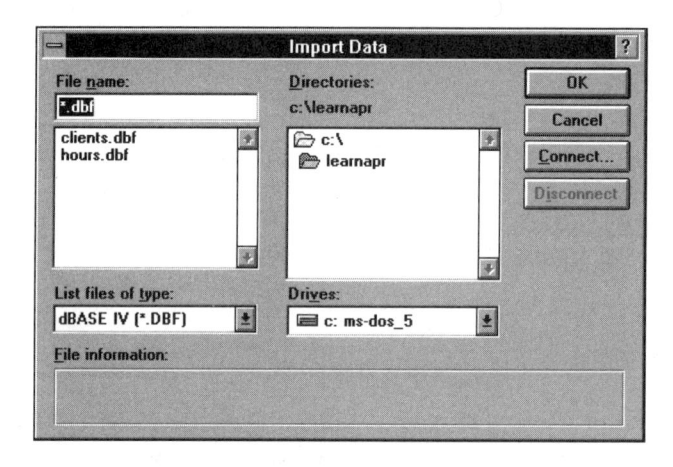

Figure 12.11 The Import Data dialog box.

If you select **Text-Delimited**, Approach displays the Text File Options dialog box when you open the file (see Figure 12.12). Use this dialog box to specify the delimiter used to separate fields in the file that you are importing data from. Use the radio buttons to specify comma-delimited, semicolon-delimited, space-delimited, or tab-delimited text files. Or, select **Other** and specify a character to its right to specify any other character as the delimiter that separates the fields. In addition, use **Character set** to specify whether the text file uses the Windows character set or the DOS and OS/2 character set. The final check box lets you specify whether the first row of the text file contains the names of its fields.

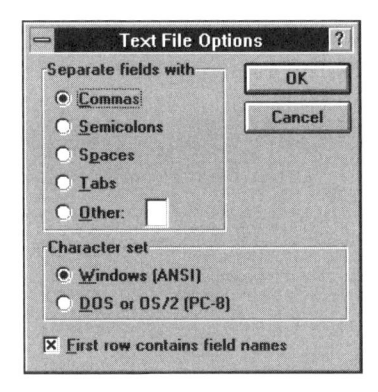

Figure 12.12 The Text Files Option dialog box.

When you select a file type, a field skeleton including its extension is displayed in the File Name text box, and all files in the current directory with that extension are listed in the box below it. Select the file that contains the data you want to import from this list (or just enter its name in the File Name text box).

Many other applications can convert their files into one of these types; for example, Q&A, SuperBase IV, AceFile, professional File, Reflex, DataEase, Rbase, Filemaker Pro, Microsoft Works, and Lotus Works can all convert their files into dBASE files. After converting the data to a dBASE file in the application, you can use the Import command of the File menu to import that dBASE file into Approach (if you want to map the data into fields in your database file rather than using it directly).

Import Setup

After you have selected **OK** on the Import Data dialog box, Approach displays the Import Setup dialog box (see Figure 12.13). You must use this dialog box to indicate which fields in another table are being imported, and which fields in the current table each one of them corresponds to.

To do this, simply click and drag the fields in the current table, which are listed in the right column of this dialog box, so they are lined up with the fields that they correspond to in the table that is being imported, which are listed in the left column of the dialog box. When they are lined up properly, you can click the center column of the selected row to add an arrow to it, indicating that the data from the field on the left will be imported into the field on the right

Practical Approach, 3.0

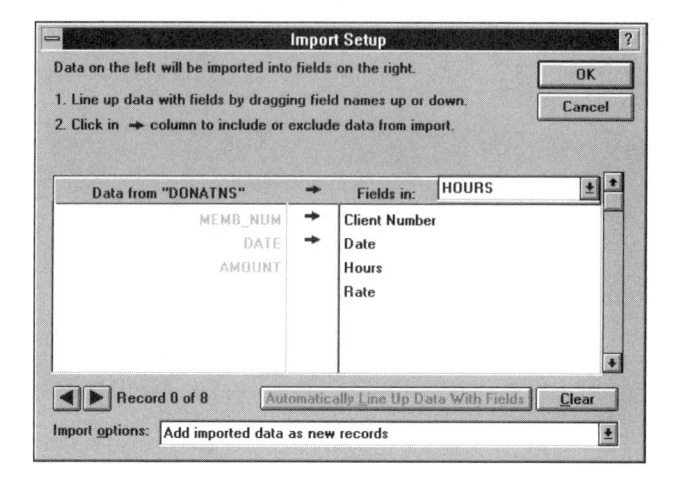

Figure 12.13 The Import Setup dialog box.

Exporting Data

Choose **Export File** from the File menu to display the Export Data dialog box, which lets you create a new file of a type used by other applications, and export data from the current database to it (see Figure 12.14). This option is available only if you are using a database file in Browse mode.

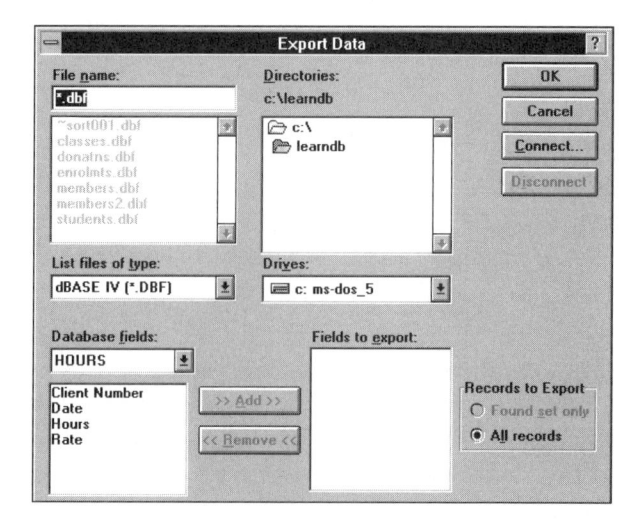

Figure 12.14 The Export Data dialog box.

Use this dialog box to specify the file to which the data is to be exported. Use the Directories list and the Drives drop-down list to select the directory and drive where it has been saved. Enter the name of the new file you want to create in the File Name text box; Approach adds the appropriate extension.

Use the **List Files of Type** drop-down list to select the type of file you are creating. The file types you can export data to and their extensions are:

- dBASE III+ (DBF)
- dBASE IV (DBF)
- FoxPro (DBF)
- Paradox (DB)
- Text Files (TXT)
- Excel (XLS)
- Lotus 1-2-3 (WK1)

If you select **Text**, Approach displays the Text File Options dialog box, which is the same dialog box used when you import a text file. Use this dialog box to specify the delimiter used to separate fields in the exported file. Use the radio buttons to specify comma-delimited, semicolon-delimited, space-delimited or tab-delimited text files; or select **Other** and specify a character to its right to use any other character as the delimiter that separates the fields. In addition, use **Character Set** to specify whether you want the text file to use the Window character set, or the DOS and OS/2 character set.

The bottom half of the Export Data dialog box lets you specify which fields to export. Select each field in the Database Fields list, and select **Add** to add it to the Fields to Export list. To remove a field from this list, select it and select **Remove**.

Approach creates a new file when you export data, which is designed so it can hold the data in all the fields you have added to this list, and is in the format used by the application that you are exporting to.

Use **Records to export** to specify whether you want to export the data in all the records of the current database or only in the records that are displayed as the result of a find. To export the data from only some of the records, you must perform a Find before choosing **Export** from the File menu, and then choose **Found Set Only**.

The Field Mapping Dialog Box

If the definition of the fields of a database is altered by another program, so that the fields are not the same as they were the last time they were used in Approach. When you open the database, Approach is displayed the same dialog box that it displays when you import data, with the title Field Mapping dialog box. Equivalent fields already mapped and included in the Mappings list. Use the dialog box in the same way that you would if you were importing an Approach file. Map the other fields that are in the database to the fields that were in it previously, so Approach know which data to display in those fields of forms, reports, and other designs.

Sharing Data on a Network

The sections earlier in this chapter that covered individual file types included instructions on how to log on to a network using each file type that Approach uses. This section covers a few other details about working with networks.

NOTE: Password protection is often useful on networks and was covered in the section on *Setting Preferences in* Chapter 11.

Copying a Database to a Network

To copy an existing Approach database to a network so that it is available to other users, use the Approach file and choose **Save As** from the File menu to display the Save Approach File As dialog box (see Figure 12.15). The Approach file is also retained with its original name, so that this option gives you two copies of the file.

If you want to rename the file, enter the new name for the file in the File Name text box. The List Files of the Type drop-down list includes only one option—Approach files. This dialog box also contains a Set Approach File Password checkbox and text box, which is was covered in Chapter 11. Use the Directories list and the Drives drop-down list to select the directory and drive where the database is to be saved.

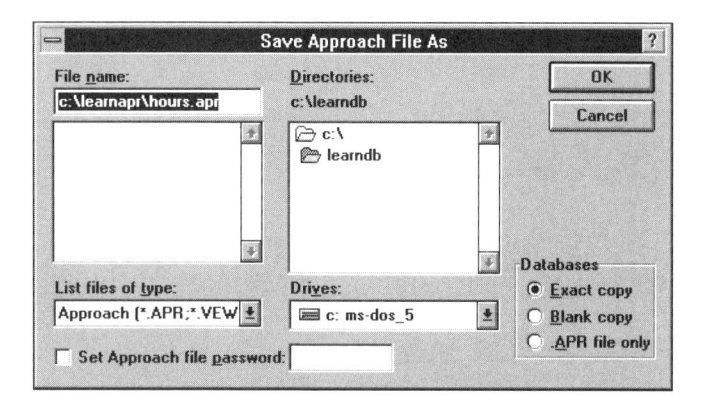

Chapter 12: Working with Other Database Applications

Figure 12.15 The Save Approach File As dialog box.

Select **Exact Copy** to create a duplicate of both the Approach file and the database file, including all of the data it holds. If multiple files are joined, all View and Database files are saved.

Select **OK** to display the Save Database As dialog box (see Figure 12.16). If you want to rename the file, enter the new name in the File Name text box. If necessary, select a different database type from the List Files of Type drop-down list. Finally, use the Directories list and the Drives drop-down list to select the network directory and drive where it is to be saved.

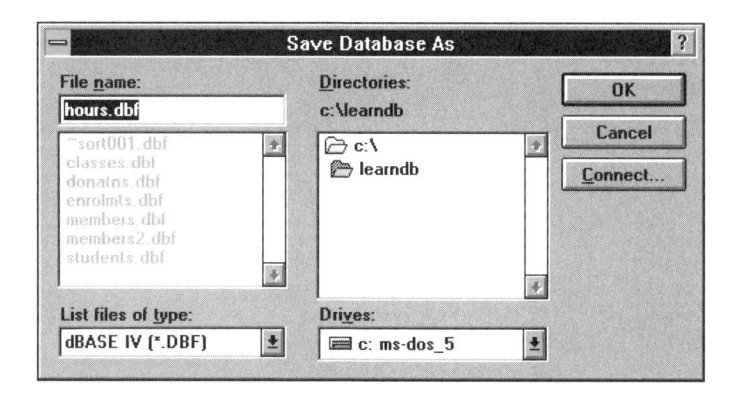

Figure 12.16 The Save Database As dialog box.

When you select **OK**, the database is copied to the network, with the name and file type you specified.

Refreshing Your Data

When you use files on a network, Approach places a copy of the data in your computer's memory. If you are editing data, changes are made to the actual database whenever you press **Enter** or move to a different record and are also reflected in the copy displayed on your screen. However, changes that other users make in the database are not always displayed on your screen.

Choose **Refresh** from the Browse menu to update the data that you are viewing, so it includes all changes to the data that other users have made. Refresh takes account of the sort order of your records and which records are included in the found set, if necessary.

Record Locking

Approach automatically locks records to avoid loss of data on a network, but it gives you the choice of two types of record locking.

To see how this data loss can occur, imagine that two users are editing the same record at the same time. The first user changes the last name and saves the record with the new name. The second user makes some other change and saves the record with this change but with the old last name, overwriting the change to the last name that the first user made. When you save a record, Approach saves the data that is displayed, so any changes made by other users since you last refreshed the screen would be lost if there were not record locking.

To avoid this problem, you can use either **Optimistic Record Locking** (the default in Approach), or **Pessimistic Record Locking**, which is also known as **Full Record Locking**. They have the following features:

- *Optimistic Record Locking* allows two users to modify the same record at the same time, but displays a dialog box warning the user that someone else has modified the record, and asking whether it should override the other person's changes. If the user selects **Yes**, all changes made in that record by other people on the network since the user last refreshed the screen are overwritten by the data that the user has in the record and are lost permanently. This includes changes in any field of the record you are working on, even fields that are not displayed in the form you are using. If the user selects **No**, the data is automatically refreshed to incorporate the changes made by other users. You can then save the record, with these changes included.

- *Pessimistic (or Full) Record Locking* does not let two users modify the same record at the same time. If one user is editing the record, Approach displays a dialog box telling any other users that the record is in use and is not available for them to edit.

Optimistic Record Locking gives you better performance than Pessimistic Record Locking, and is the default. You can switch to Pessimistic Record Locking by choosing **Preferences** from the Tools menu and clicking the **General** divider tab to display the General panel of the Preferences dialog box. The Lock record using Optimistic Record Locking is selected by default and you can deselect it to use Pessimistic Record Locking (see Figure 12.17).

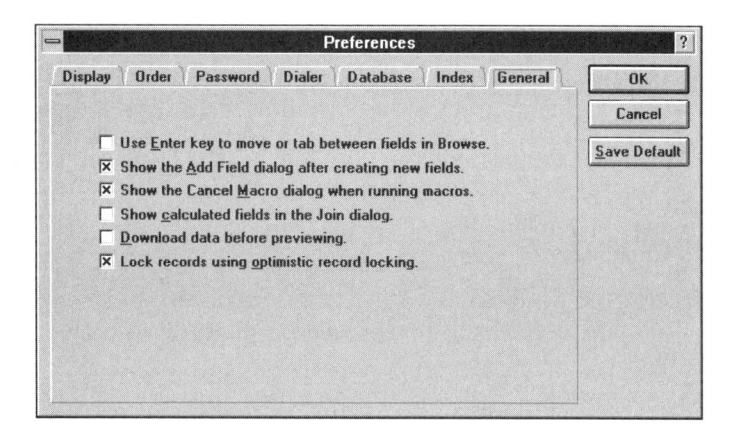

Figure 12.17 The Preferences dialog box using Optimistic record locking.

> **NOTE** All users on a network should use the same type of record locking.

Printing and Previewing Designs on a Network

There are two ways to speed print and preview to insure integrity of data when you are working with reports and other designs on a network. You can use the file as a single user, or download it to your disk. Though these methods are not usually necessary, you may find them useful on a heavily used network. They can also be useful to protect data integrity if you have a summary function in a Calculated field of a design, since locking of individual records does not protect the integrity of a summary function, which is based on a large number of records.

Exclusive Use of a Network File

You can use a network file as a single user by changing the Connect options when you open the file. Select the **Connect** button of the Open dialog box to display the Network Connection dialog box.

> **NOTE** If you use the database as a single user in this way, nobody else on the network is able to view the database for as long as you have it open. This can make printing and previewing noticeably faster. You must do this if you are changing the field definition of the file; to avoid confusion to other users, Approach does not let you change field definition when multiple users can access the file.

Downloading a Database to Your Disk

Rather than using the database as a single user, you can get similar benefits by downloading the database to your own computer's hard disk when you preview a report or other design. By default, Approach does not download to the disk in this way, because of the extra time it takes.

To download the database to your hard disk whenever you view the database in Print Preview mode, choose **Preferences** from the Tools menu and click the **General** divider tab to display the General panel of the Preferences dialog box. Select the **Download data before previewing** check box.

Part III

Appendices

Appendix A

Installing Approach

It is very easy to install Approach, because the installation program does almost all of the work for you. It creates a directory on your hard disk where the files are copied, and creates an Approach group in Windows with an icon that you click to run the program.

If you are installing on a stand-alone computer, you have the following options:

- *Full installation* installs the complete Approach product, sample, and template files.
- *Minimum installation* saves disk space by installing only the files needed to run Approach and leaving out utilities such as the spell checker.
- *Custom installation* lets you decide which files to install.

Unless you are short of hard disk space, it is best to use Full installation.

If you are installing on a network you have the following option:

- Install on a network node, where only a few files are needed.
- Install on a file server, where you can install the server version of Approach, which runs Approach on nodes.
- Install on the distribution version, which can be used to install the stand-alone version of Approach on other computers on the network.

System Requirements

Approach requires an IBM compatible computer with:

- An 80386 or higher processor
- A hard disk drive
- A floppy disk drive (for installation)
- A mouse
- Windows Version 3.1 or later
- At least 4 megabytes of RAM

To run Approach on a network, you must also have one of the following networking systems:

- Novell Advanced NetWare 2.0A or higher
- NetWare 386
- NetWare Lite
- LANtastic
- Microsoft LAN Manager
- IBM PC Local Area Network Program 1.12 or higher
- 3COM 3+Open
- Banyan VINES Network 2.1 or higher

Installing Approach

You can install Approach from the floppy disks supplied or from a distribution version of Approach that has already been installed on a network.

To install Approach:

1. Start your computer with Windows running.
2. If you are installing from floppy disks, place the Approach disk 1 in drive A (or in another drive).
3. From the Windows Program manager, choose **Run** from the File menu. Windows displays the Run dialog box, with the cursor in the Command Line text box. Enter the full path name of the INSTALL command. For example, to install from a floppy disk in the a: drive, type **A:INSTALL**, or to install from a network, type **PATHNAME\INSTALL** (where.PATHNAME represents the drive and directory where the the Approach INSTALL program is located). Then press **Enter** or click **OK** to run the command.
4. When the Approach installation screen is displayed, enter your name, and select **Next**.
5. The program guides you through the installation process and tells you when to insert new floppy disks if necessary. Follow the instructions until installation is complete.

When installation is done, the Windows program manager is displayed, with an Approach icon added to the group that you selected, and you can double-click this icon to start Approach.

Appendix B

Reference Guide

This appendix provides an overview of Approach, including a brief summary of the function of each menu command, dialog box, and Info Box, a listing of shortcut keys, and a listing of the operators, functions, and constants that can be used in Approach formulas. It is meant to be used as a reference—a quick way of looking up a menu option, icon, or function to refresh your memory of what you learned earlier in this book.

Menu and Dialog Box Reference

This section summarizes the full menu system of Approach. Dialog boxes are described with the menu commands you use to display them.

The File Menu

The File menu is used for the same type of file operations that it commonly performs in Windows applications, such as creating, opening, and closing files, and printing. It is also used to delete files, import and export data, and send mail.

New Command

Choose **New** from the File menu to use the New dialog box (see Figure B.1).

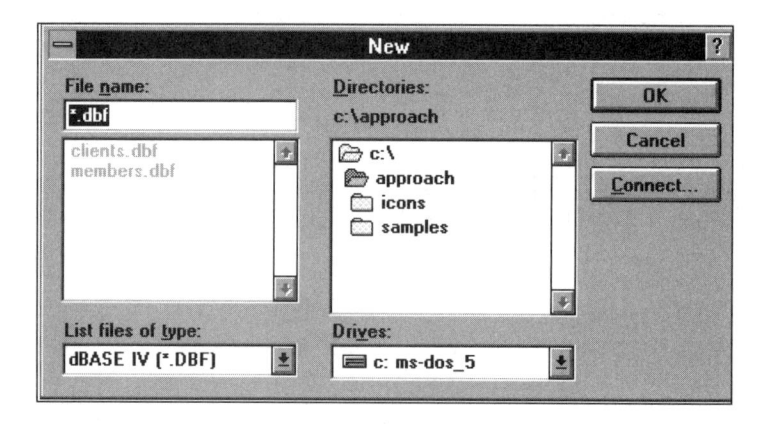

Figure B.1 The New dialog box.

This dialog box lets you create a new database file. Enter the name of the new file in the File Name text box. Use the Directories list and the Drives drop-down list to select the directory and drive where it is to be saved. Use the List Files of Type drop-down list to select the type of file that you are creating; the options are dBASE III+, dBASE IV, FoxPro, and Paradox. (If you have the appropriate additional software, ORACLE SQL, SQL Server, and DB2 will also be included on thids be included on this list.)

Network Connections

If you are creating a dBASE or Paradox file, click **Connect** to display the Network Connection dialog boxes to define a network connection (see Figures B.2 and B.3).

Appendix B: Reference Guide

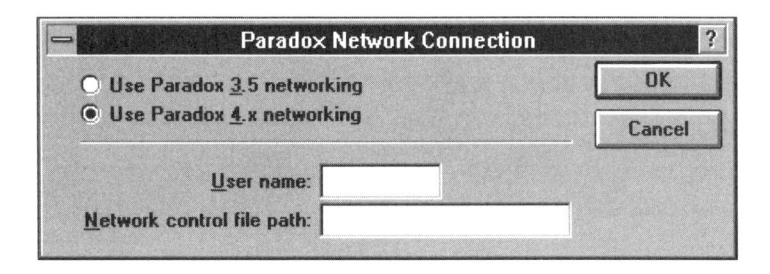

Figure B.2 The Paradox Network Connection dialog box.

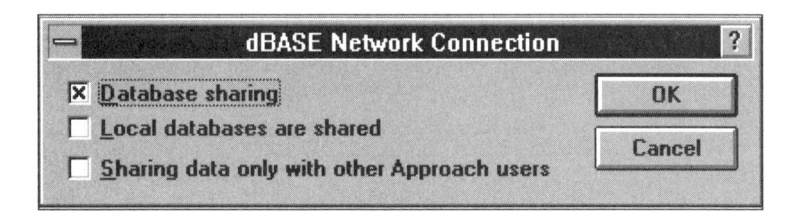

Figure B.3 The dBASE Network Connection dialog box.

The Field Definition Dialog Box

After you select **OK** from the New Dialog box the Field Definition dialog box is displayed (see Figure B.4). Its title bar includes the name of the file you are creating.

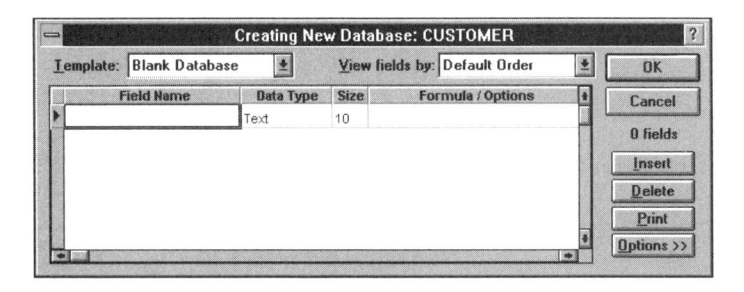

Figure B.4 The Field Definition dialog box.

Use the Field Name text box to enter the name of a field, the Data Type to select the field's data type, and the Size text box to specify the length of text and number fields.

To change the definition of a field you defined earlier, simply select and edit the specifications. To delete a field, select it and click **Delete**. To insert a new field in the structure of the table, click an existing field and click **Insert** to add a row above it to hold a new field.

You must use the database in expanded form to specify options for a field. You can click **Options** to expand the dialog box at any time, and it is expanded automatically if you create a Calculated field.

Options for Boolean, Date, Numeric, Text, and Time fields

Boolean, Date, Numeric, Text, and Time fields all have a Default Value panel and a Validation panel with the same options

The Default Value panel is used to specify a default value that is entered in a field automatically when you add a new record, though this value can be edited before the record is saved (see Figure B.5).

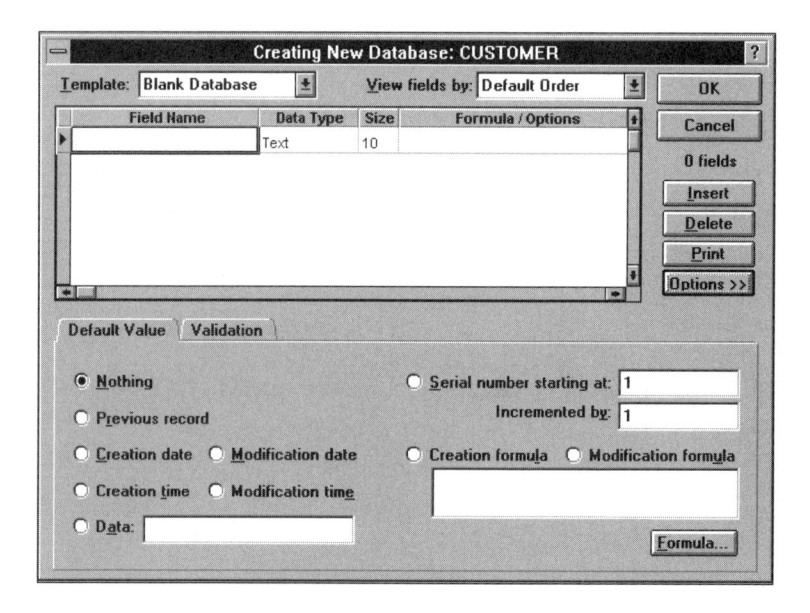

Figure B.5 Default Value panel.

It has the following options:

- The *Nothing* radio button is selected by default; nothing is added automatically.
- The *Previous* record radio button automatically enters data from the same field of the previous record in this field. It is useful if some fields of a table have repetitive data.
- The four radio buttons that follow let you automatically enter the date the record was created, the time it was created, the date it was modified last, and the time it was modified last.
- The *Data* radio button lets you enter some specific data in the field by default. Type the data in the text box to its right.
- The *Serial Number* radio button can only be used for number data and automatically enters a number larger than the number in the previous field. By default, the series of numbers that is entered automatically starts at 1 and is increased by 1 in each record. You can use the text boxes to the right of this radio button to specify a different starting number and a different amount that it is increased by.
- Use the *Formula* text box to enter a formula that will determine the default value of the field. You can also click **Formula** in order to use the Formula dialog box to generate this formula (described at the end of the menu section of this appendix). The radio buttons above the Formula text box let you specify whether this formula should be used as the default value when the record is first created or when it is modified.

Click the **Validation** divider tab to display the Validation panel, which lets you specify how Approach validates data that is entered in the field.

It has the following options:

- Select **Unique** to require a value in the field that is different from the value in that field in any other record of the database.
- Select the **From ... to** checkbox to specify a range of values that can be entered in the field. Enter the lowest acceptable value in the text box to its immediate right and the highest acceptable value in the text box further to the right.
- Select **Filled In** to require that some value be entered in the field; it cannot be left blank.

Practical Approach, 3.0

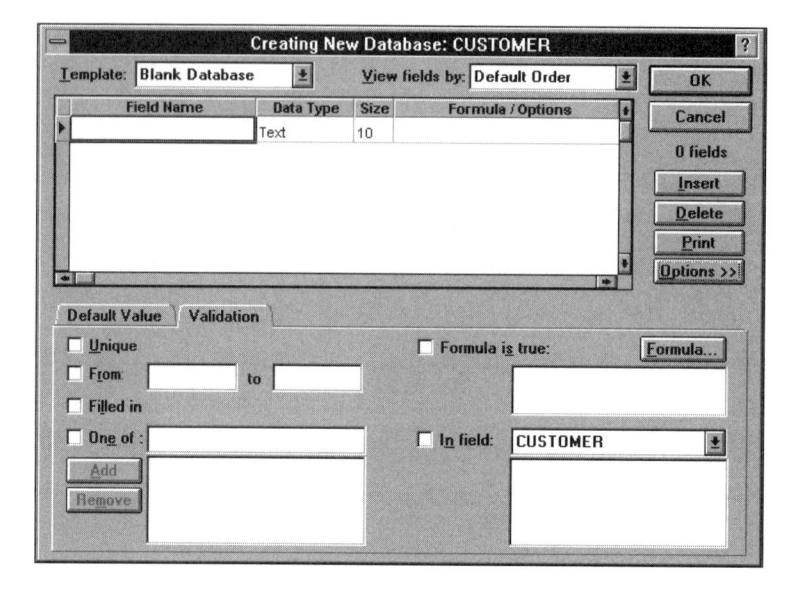

Figure B.6 Validation panel.

- Select **One Of** to specify a list of valid values for the field. Type each valid value in the text box to the right of this check box, and select **Add** to add it to the drop-down list of all valid values. To remove a value from this list, select it and select **Remove**.
- Select **Formula Is True** to require that the value satisfy a formula. You can enter this formula in the text box to its right or select the **Formula** push button to generate it using the Formula dialog box, which is discussed at the end of this menu and Dialog Box reference.
- Select **In Field** to specify that the value must be in some other field. This is most useful with relational databases, where the key field in the many file must be present in the one file. It is also lets you create look-up databases. You can create a database with a list of all states in one of its fields, and use it to validate entries in the State field of other databases.

Options for Calculated Fields

If you display the Field Definition dialog box in expanded form when the current field has the Calculated data type, Approach displays the Define Formula and Define Summary Panels.

The Define Formula panel specifies the formula that is used as the basis of the value in the field. It works like the Formula dialog box, which is discussed at the end of this menu and Dialog Box reference.

If you use a summary function in the formula, you can use the Define Summary panel to specify what data it summarizes (see Figure B.7).

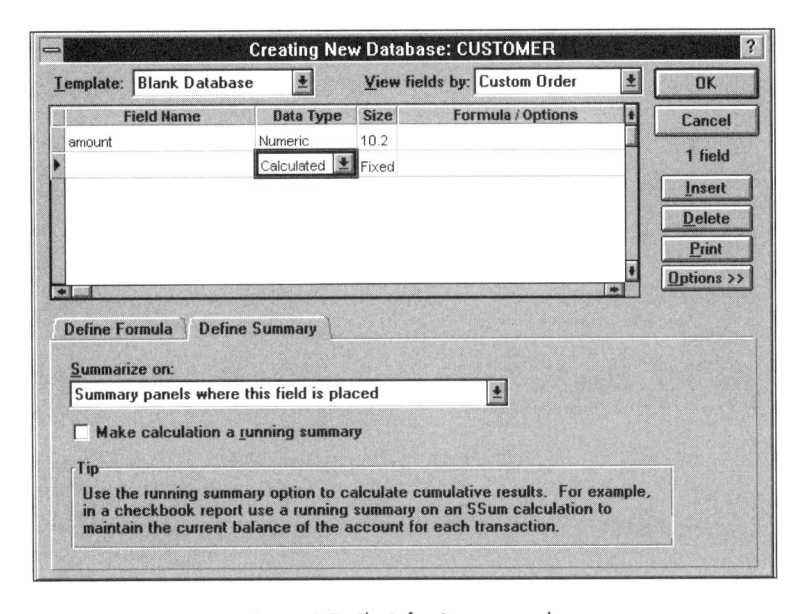

Figure B.7 The Define Summary panel.

By default, the summary depends on the panel where the field is placed. If it is in a group summary panel of a report it summarizes all the records in the group, and if it is in the grand total panel of a report, it will summarize all the records of the report. Use this drop-down to select some other set of records that the summary is based on.

The checkbox lets you make the calculation a running summary. You could use it if you want the total in a group summary panel to sum the values in all the records up to that point, rather than just the values in one group.

Memo Fields Options

Memo fields have no options. If you display the Field Definition dialog box in expanded form when the current field has the Memo data type, a blank options panel is displayed.

PicturePlus Fields Options

When you display the Field Definition dialog box in expanded form when the current field has the PicturePlus data type, Approach displays the PicturePlus Options panel (see Figure B.8).

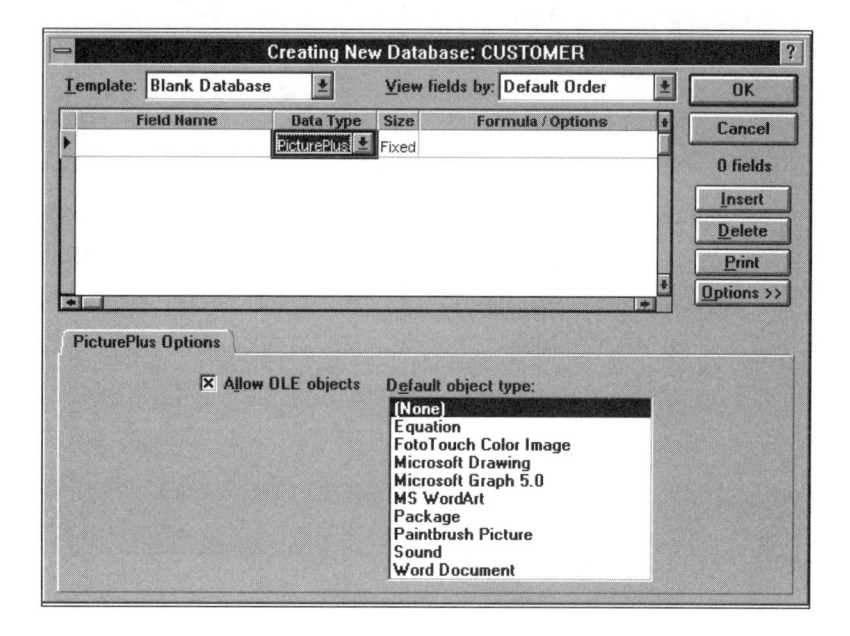

Figure B.8 The PicturePlus Options panel.

The panel features are:

- By default, OLE objects can be added to PicturePlus fields. You can deselect the **Allow OLE Objects** of the PicturePlus Options dialog box, to disallow OLE objects in PicturePlus fields.
- If OLE objects are allowed, you can also select a default object type from the list in this dialog box. Double-clicking a blank PicturePlus field automatically launches the application that lets you create the default object. The types of objects available as default objects depend on the other Windows applications you have.

Variable Fields Options

If you display the Field Definition dialog box in expanded form when the current field has the Variable data type, Approach displays the Variable Options panel (see Figure B.9).

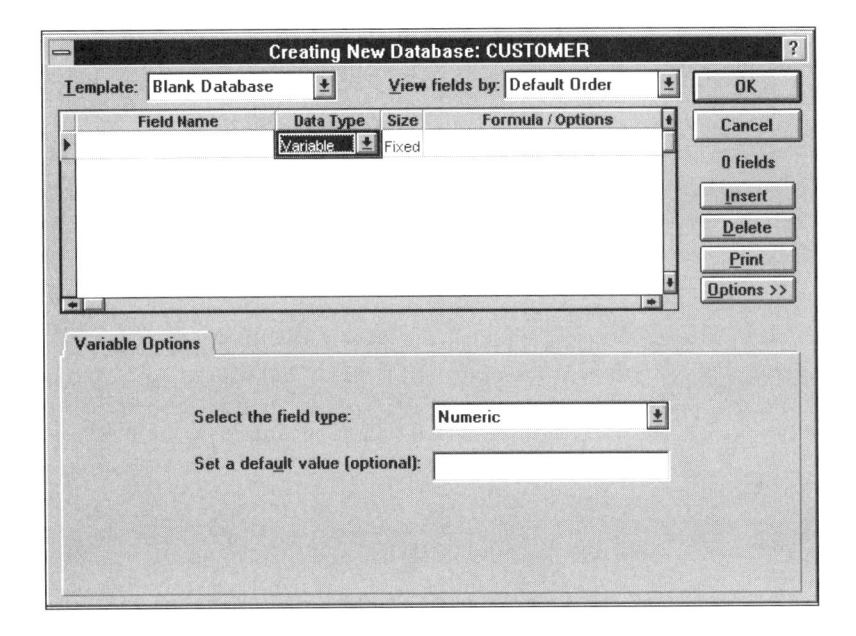

Figure B.9 The Variable Options panel.

The panel features are:

- The default data type of a Variable field is Numeric, but you can use the Type drop-down list to make it Boolean, Date, Numeric, Text, or Time.
- You can use the Set default value text box to enter an initial value that this variable field has when the Approach file is first opened. By default, it has no initial value.

Paradox Key fields

When you are done defining a new Paradox database and select **OK** of the Define Fields dialog box, The **Choose Key Field** dialog box is displayed. All

Paradox files that are created in Approach must have a key field or fields with a unique value in each record.

Select one or more of the fields in the fields list and select **OK** to specify the key field. If none of the fields in the database can be used as a key field, because no single field or group of fields has a unique value in each record, select **Add Key Field** to add a field named Approach Key Name to the database. This is a Numeric field and is automatically entered in sequential numbers beginning with one.

Open Command

Choose **Open** from the File menu to use the Open dialog box (see Figure B.10).

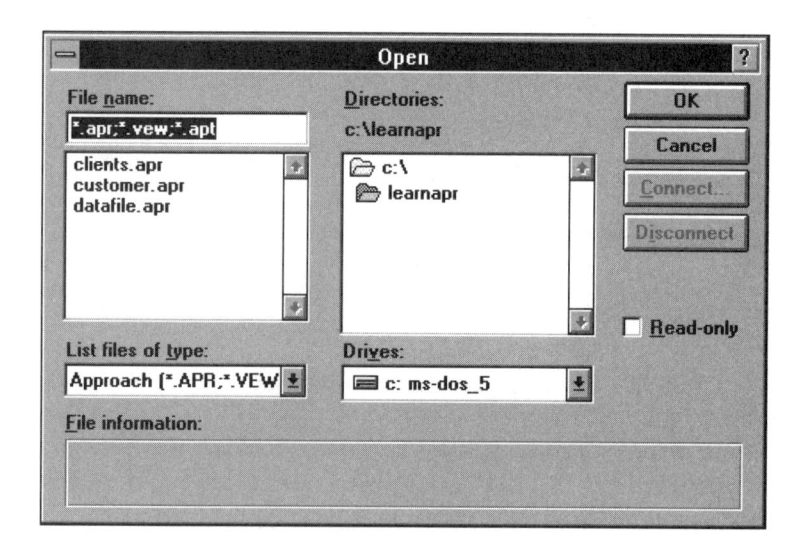

Figure B.10 The Open dialog box.

This dialog box lets you open an existing database file. Use the Directories list and Drives drop-down list to select the directory and drive where it has been saved. Use the List Files of Type drop-down list to select the type of file that you are opening. The options are Approach, III+, dBASE IV, FoxPro, Query, Paradox, ORACLE, ODBC: SQL Server, ODBC Data Sources, SQL Server, and DB2-MDI, Text-Delimited, Text-Fixed-Length, Excel, and Lotus 1-2-3. When you select a file type, a field skeleton including its extension is displayed in the File Name text box, and all files in the current directory with that extension are listed below. Select the file you want to open from this list (or just enter its name in the File Name text box). Select **Read-Only** to open it as a read-only file; you will be able to view but not to change its contents.

When you select **OK**, the file you have opened is displayed in a new window on the screen. You can open multiple files simultaneously; Approach creates a new window for each.

If you select **ORACLE**, **SQL Server**, or **DB2-MDI** from the List Files of Type drop-down list a dialog box is displayed to let you log on to the server.

Connecting to ORACLE

When you select **ORACLE** from List Files of Type, Approach displays the Connect to ORACLE dialog box (see Figure B.11).

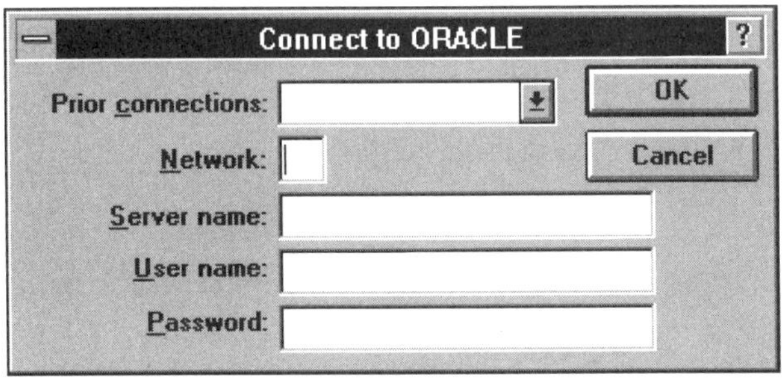

Figure B.11 The Connect to ORACLE dialog box.

In the Network text box, enter the letter identifying the network protocol being used. In Server Name enter the name of the server computer you want to log on to. In User Name enter your user name. In Password enter the password.

Select **OK** to return to the Open dialog box. The File list displays ORACLE databases, and you can open them as usual.

Connecting to SQL Server

When you select **SQL Server** from the List Files of Type the Connect to SQL Server dialog box is displayed (see Figure B.12.)

In the Server Name text box, enter the name of the server computer you want to log on to. In User Name enter your user name. In Password enter the password. Select **OK** to return to the Open dialog box.

The File list displays Microsoft SQL Server databases, and you can open them as usual.

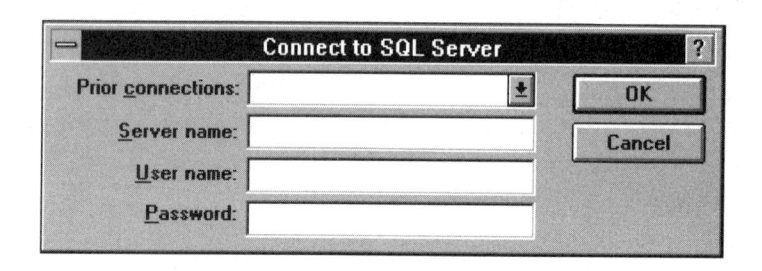

Figure B.12 The Connect to SQL Server dialog box.

Connecting to DB2-MDI

When you select **DB2-MDI** from the List Files of Type the Connect to DB2-MDI dialog box is displayed (see Figure B.13).

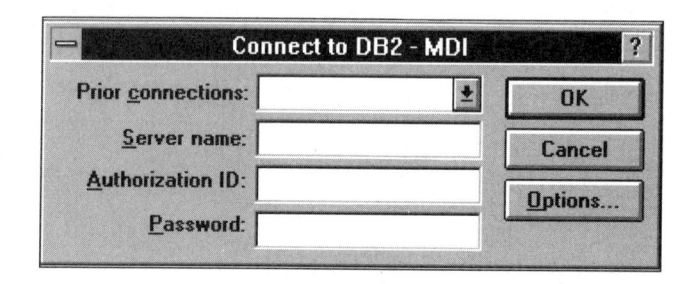

Figure B.13 The Connect to DB2-MDI dialog box.

In the Server Name text box enter the name of the Server Computer you want to log on to. In Authorization ID enter your ID. In Password enter the password. Select **OK** to return to the Open dialog box.

The File list displays DB2-MDI databases, and you can open them as usual.

Appendix B: Reference Guide

Close Command

Choose **Close** from the File menu to close the database file that is currently being used. The file's window is closed, revealing windows that are under it, if any.

Save Approach File Command

Choose **Save Approach File** from the File menu to save any changes you have made in the current Approach file. Data you enter is automatically saved in the appropriate database file as you enter each record. This menu option saves views that you have created in the Approach file.

If you save an Approach file that has not yet been named, the Save Approach File dialog box is displayed (see Figure B.14). Enter the name of the new file in the File Name text box. Use the Directories list and the Drives drop-down list to select the directory and drive where it is saved. The List Files of Type drop-down includes only one option–Approach files. The Set View Password checkbox lets you enter a password in the text box to its right to prevent unauthorized users from opening this Approach file.

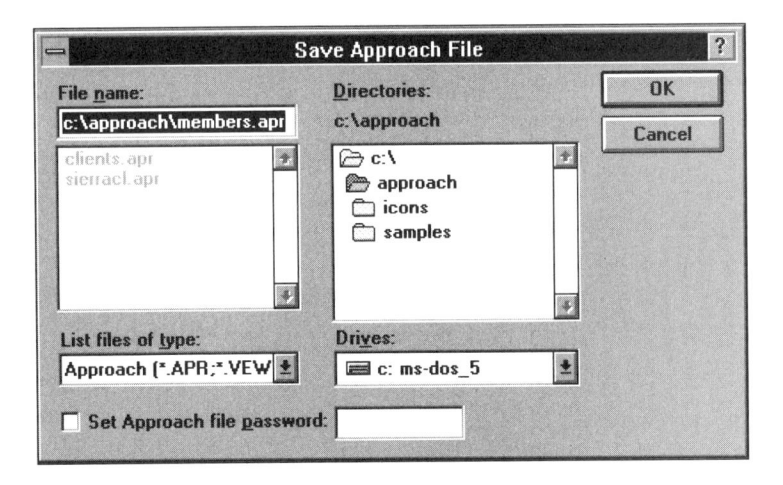

Figure B.14 The Save Approach File dialog box.

Save As Command

Choose **Save As** from the File menu to display the Save Approach File As dialog box that lets you save an Approach file under a different name or in a different location (see Figure B.15). The Approach file is also retained with its original name, so that this option gives you two copies of the file.

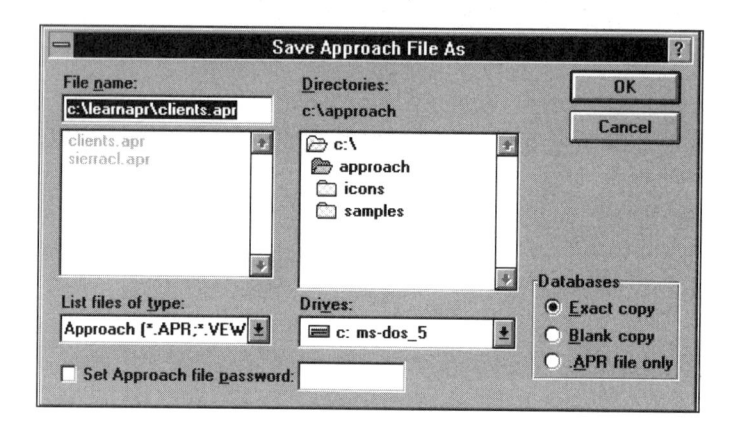

Figure B.15 The Save Approach File As dialog box.

The Save Approach FIle As dialog box has one additional feature that the Save Approach File dialog box does not have. The Databases radio buttons give you three options for saving your data files:

- *Exact Copy*. Creates a duplicate of both the Approach file and the Data file, including all of the data it is holding.
- *Blank Copy*. Creates a copy of the Approach file and Data file, but without any data.
- *APR file only*. Creates a copy of the Approach file but not of the Data file. The new Approach file still uses the old Data file.

In any case, the Save Approach File As dialog box lets you specify the location of the new Approach file.

Saving the Data File

If you select **Exact Copy** or **Blank Copy**, the two options that also create a new Data file, and select **OK**, the Save Database As dialog box is displayed (see Figure B.16).

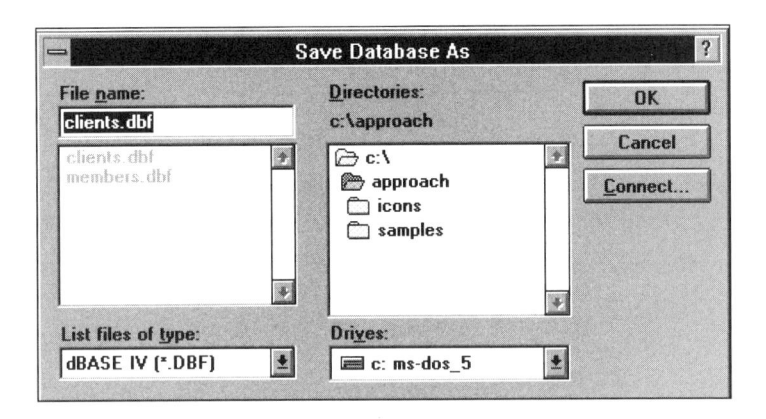

Figure B.16   The Save Database As dialog box.

Select **Connect** to use the Network Connection dialog box to define a network connection for the file type that is selected, as described in the section titled *Open Command*.

If you are displaying a view that is a relational database, the Save As dialog box is displayed for each of the files that the relational database uses.

Paradox Key Fields

If you select **Paradox** as the file type and the file does not have a key field, the Choose Key Field dialog box is displayed to let you specify a key field or fields that have a unique value in each record of the database.

Confirming a Password

If you select **Set View Password** and type the password in the text box to its right and select **OK**, the Confirm View Password dialog box is displayed (see Figure B.17). You must type the password again in the Retype View Password dialog box to confirm it. The Use Short Menus When View Opens dialog box is selected by default. Deselect it to display the full menu system for this database.

Practical Approach, 3.0

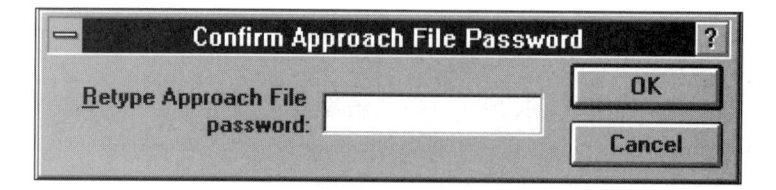

Figure B.17 The Confirm View Password dialog box.

Once you have added password protection, you cannot enter Design mode unless you know the password. If you click the **Design** icon, Approach displays the Enter View Password dialog box. If you enter an incorrect password, it does not let you enter Design mode.

Delete File Command

Choose **Delete File** from the File menu to display the Delete File dialog box that lets you delete an Approach or Data file (see Figure B.18).

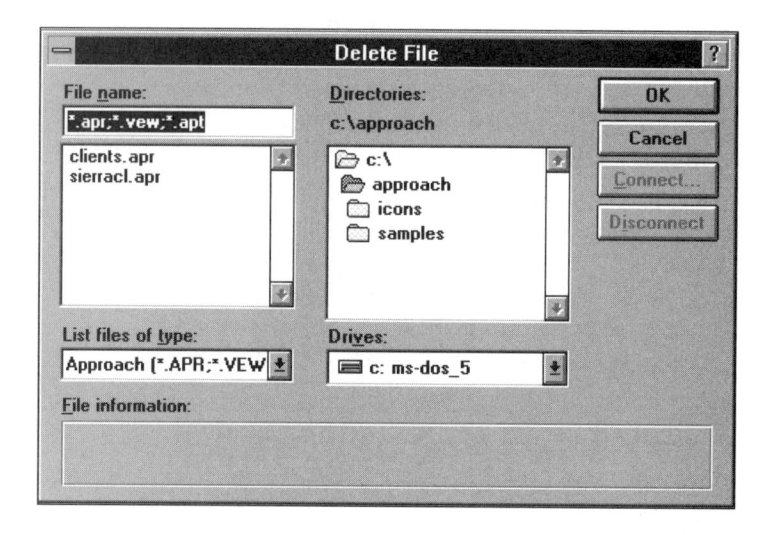

Figure B.18 The Delete File dialog box.

The options are Approach files, dBASE III+, dBASE IV, FoxPro, Query, and Paradox. When you select a file type, a field skeleton including the extension of the type you chose is displayed in File Name, and all files in the current direc-

Appendix B: Reference Guide

tory with that extension are listed below. Select the file you want to open from this list (or just enter its name in the File Name text box.) Files that are open cannot be deleted. Approach asks for confirmation before deleting the file.

Import Data Command

Choose **Import Data** from the File menu to display the Import Data dialog box, which lets you import data from another Database file into the current database (see Figure B.19). This option is available only if you are using a Database file in Browse mode.

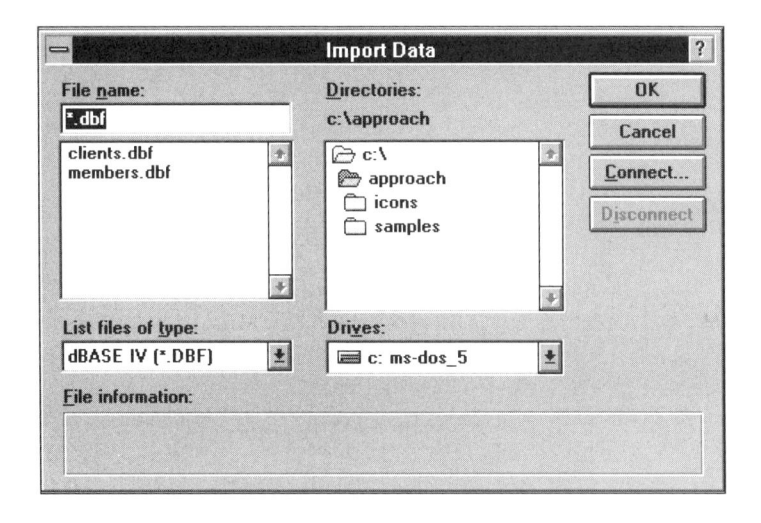

Figure B.19 The Import Data dialog box.

The file types that you can import data from and their extensions follow:

- dBASE III+ (DBF)
- dBASE IV (DBF)
- FoxPro (DBF)
- Query (QRY)
- Paradox (DB)
- ODBC-SQL Server
- ODBC Data Sources

- ORACLE
- SQL Server
- DB2-MDI
- Tex-Delimited (TXT)
- Text-Fixed Length
- Excel (XLS)
- Lotus (WK1, WKS, WRK, WRI, WK3)

If you select **Text-Delimited** the Text File Options dialog box is displayed (see Figure B.20). Use this dialog box to specify the delimiter used to separate fields in the file you are importing data from. Use the radio buttons to specify comma-delimited, semicolon-delimited, space-delimited, or tab-delimited text files. Or, select **Other** and specify a character to its right to specify any other character as the delimiter that separates the fields. In addition, use **Character Set** to specify whether the text file uses the Windows character set or the DOS and area OS/2 character set. The final check box lets you specify whether the first row of the text file contains the names of its fields.

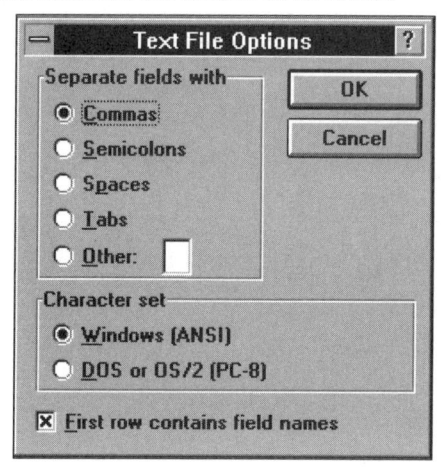

Figure B.20 The Text Files Option dialog box.

When you select a file type, a field skeleton including its extension is displayed in the File Name text box, and all files in the current directory with that extension are listed in the box below it. Select the file that contains the data you want to import from this list (or just enter its name in the File Name text box).

After you have selected **OK** from the Import Data dialog box the Import Setup dialog box is displayed (see Figure B.21). You must use this dialog box to indicate which fields in another table are being imported, and which field in the current table each one of them corresponds to. To do this, click and drag the fields in the current table (listed in the right column) so they are lined up with the fields that they correspond to in the table that is being imported, which are listed in the left column of the dialog box. When they are lined up properly, you can click the center column of the selected row to add an arrow to it, indicating that the data from the field on the left is imported into the field on the right.

Figure B.21 The Import Setup dialog box.

Import Approach File Command

When a database is displayed in Design (rather than Browse) mode, the File menu includes the option Import Approach file rather than Import Data. Choose **Import Approach file** from the File menu to display the Import Approach file dialog box (see Figure B.22). Use this dialog box in the usual way to select the file you want to import.

Practical Approach, 3.0

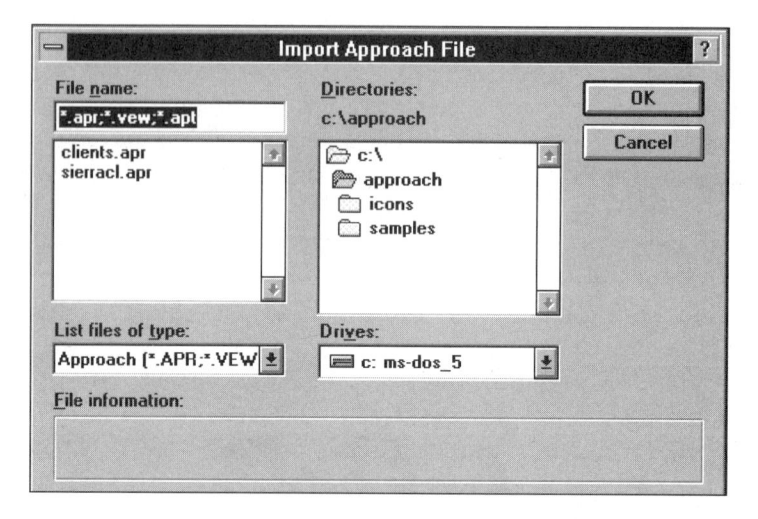

Figure B.22 The Import Approach file dialog box.

When you select **OK** the Import Approach File Setup dialog box is displayed (see Figure B.23). This dialog box works in the same way as the Import Setup dialog box illustrated in the section *Import Data Command*. The left column lists the fields of the database that you are importing, and the right column lists the fields in the current database. Click and drag the fields in the right column to line them up with the corresponding fields in the right column; when they are lined up, click the center column of a selected row to add an arrow to it.

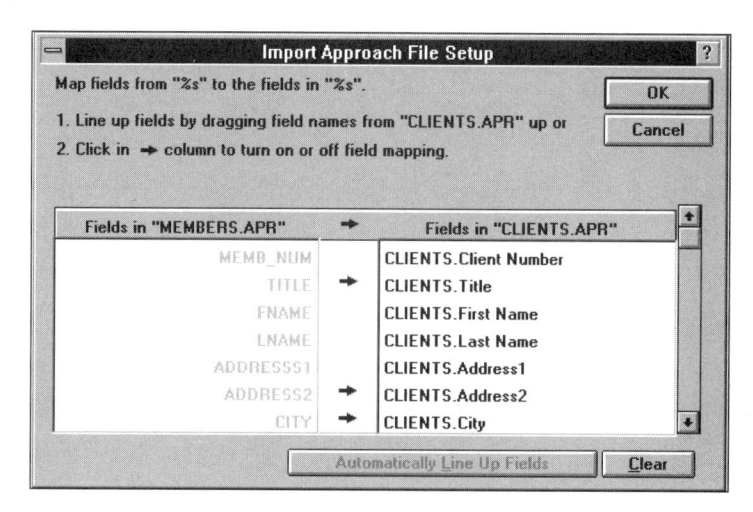

Figure B.23 The Import Approach File Setup dialog box.

Appendix B: Reference Guide

After importing the file, you are able to use its views in the current file.

Export Data Command

Choose **Export File** from the File menu to display the Export Data dialog box (see Figure B.24). This lets you create a new file of the type used by other applications, and to export data from the current database to it. This option is available only if you are using a Database file in Browse mode.

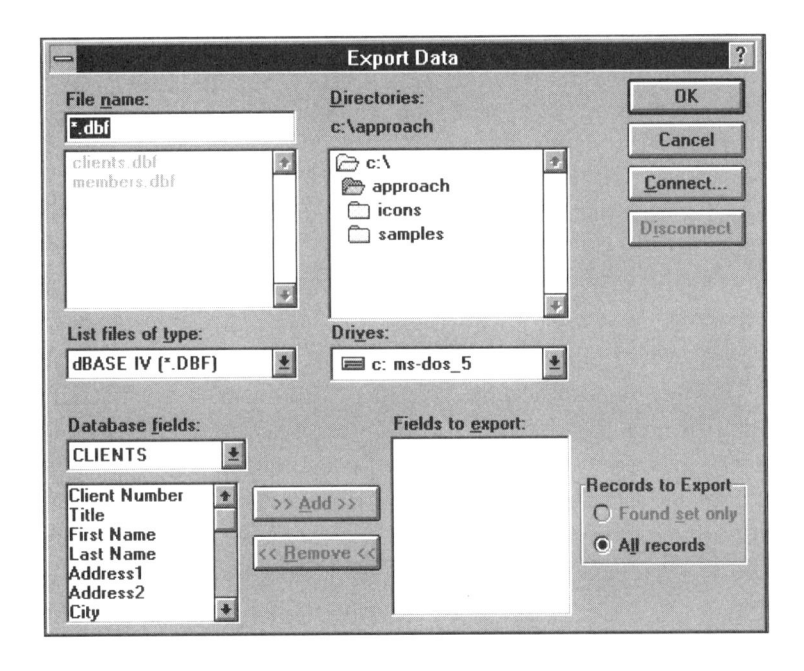

Figure B.24 The Export Data dialog box.

Enter the name of the new file you want to create, with the appropriate extension, in the File Name text box.

Use the List Files of Type drop-down list to select the type of file that you are creating. The file types that you can export data to and their extensions are:

- dBASE III+ (DBF)
- dBASE IV (DBF)

- FoxPro (DBF)
- Paradox (DB)
- Text-Delimited (TXT)
- Text-Fixed Length (TXT)
- Excel (XLS)
- Lotus 1-2-3 (WK1)

If you select **Text-Delimited**, the Text File Options dialog box shown in the *Import Data Command* section is displayed. Use this dialog box to specify the delimiter used to separate fields in the exported file. Use the radio buttons to specify comma-delimited, semicolon-delimited, space-delimited, or tab-delimited text files. Or, select **Other** and specify a character to its right to use any other character as the delimiter that separates the fields. In addition, use **Character Set** Area to specify whether you want the text file to use the Window character set or the DOS and OS/2 character set.

The bottom half of the Export Data dialog box lets you specify which fields to export. Select each field in the Database Fields list, and select **Add** to add it to the Fields to Export list. (To remove a field from this list, select it and select **Remove**.) The new file created when you export data is designed so it can hold the data in all the fields you have added to this list.

Use the radio buttons to the right of this list to specify whether you want to export the data in all the records of the current database or only in the records that are displayed as the result of a Find. To export the data from only some of the records, you must perform a find before choosing **Export** and you must select **Found Set Only** in this dialog box.

Approach File Info

Choose **Approach File Info** from the File menu to display the Approach File Info dialog box (see Figure B.25).

Appendix B: Reference Guide

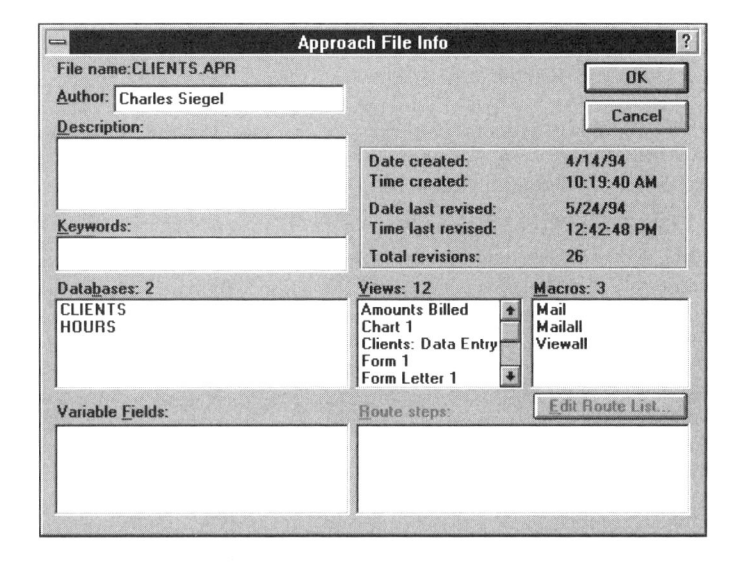

Figure B.25 The Approach File Info dialog box

This dialog box contains information on the date and time when the file was created and last revised, on the number of times it was revised, on the number of Databases, Views, Macro, and Variable fields it contains, and their names.

Add a description of the file to the Description text box, and it is displayed at the bottom of the Open dialog box, along with other File Info, when you open a file.

Send Mail

Choose **Send Mail** from the File menu to send e-mail. The dialog box that is displayed depends on the mail application that you have installed.

Preview Command

Choose **Preview** from the File menu to toggle to Print Preview mode.

Print Command

Choose **Print** from the File menu to display the Print dialog box (see Figure B.26). The name of the printer that is to be used is displayed at the top of this dialog box.

Practical Approach, 3.0

Use radio buttons in the Print Range area to select how much of the current database is printed. Select **All** to print the entire database, select **Current Form** to print the record currently being displayed, or select **Pages** and enter numbers in the From and To text boxes to specify which pages should be printed.

Use **Print Quality** to specify the resolution of the print out; you can use lower resolution to print a rough draft more quickly. Use the **Copies** text box to specify how many copies are printed. If you are printing multiple copies, you can select **Collate Copies** to have them collated.

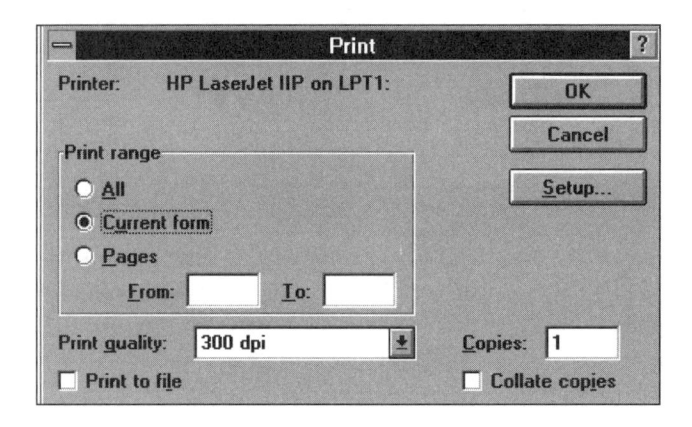

Figure B.26 The Print dialog box.

Select **Print to File** to save the formatted version of the document to a file rather than sending it to the printer. If you select this checkbox, then when you select **OK** to print the database the Print to File dialog box is displayed (see Figure B.27). Use this dialog box to specify the file where the document is to be saved. This file contains printer codes as well as data, so anyone can use this file to print the layout, even if they do not have Approach.

Select **Setup** to use the Print Setup dialog box.

Appendix B: Reference Guide **493**

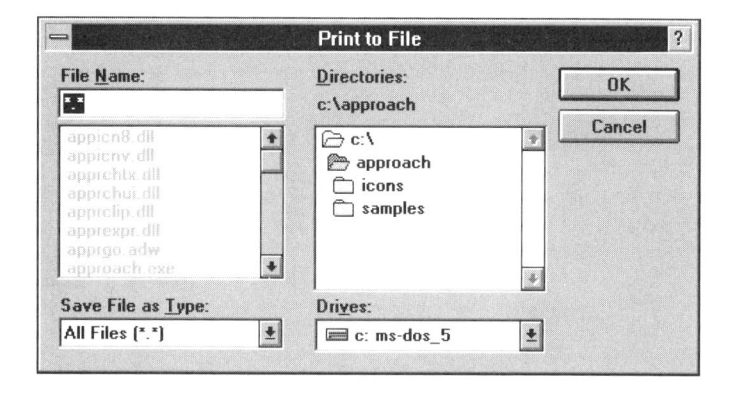

Figure B.27 The Print to File dialog box.

Print Setup Command

Choose **Print Setup** from the File menu to use the Print Setup dialog box (see Figure B.28). Use the radio buttons and drop-down list in the Printer area to select a printer, if you have more than one. Use the radio buttons in the Orientation area to select **Portrait** (upright) or **Landscape** (left-to-right) orientation. The drop-down lists in the Paper area lets you specify the size of paper that is being used (8.5" x 11" letter size, or 8.5" x 14" legal size), and the source of the paper the upper tray of the printer, the lower tray of the printer, or Manual Feed.

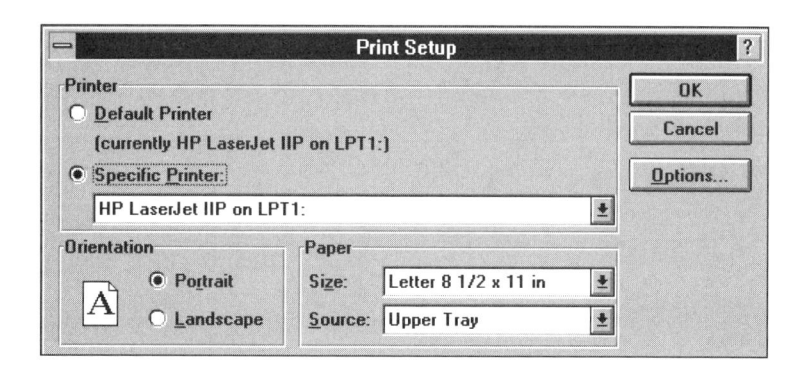

Figure B.28 The Print Setup dialog box.

When you choose **Options** it displays an Options dialog box, which varies depending on the printer being used. Select its **Help** button for information on the options it offers for your printer.

Exit Command

Choose **Exit** from the File menu to quit Approach. You can also quit by selecting **Close** from the Application Control menu.

File Names

The names of the five Approach files that have been used most recently are added to the end of the File menu. You can open a file by selecting its name.

The Edit Menu

The Edit menu is used for editor functions, such as Cut and Paste, that are common to Windows applications. It is also used to duplicate or delete a form.

Undo Command

Choose **Undo** from the Edit menu to undo the most recent editing operation performed. You can undo typing, undo a deletion, or undo a paste.

Cut Command

Choose **Cut** from the Edit menu to remove selected text or other selected objects from the document and place it in the clipboard instead.

Copy Command

Choose **Copy** from the Edit menu to leave selected text or other selected objects in the document, and place a copy of it in the clipboard.

Copy View Command

If no text or other objects are selected, the **Copy** from the Edit menu command is displayed as **Copy View**. If you are in Browse mode, you can choose it to display the Copy View to Clipboard dialog box (see Figure B.29).

Figure B.29 Copy View to Clipboard dialog box.

Use the radio buttons to specify if you want to copy only the current view or all views in the Approach file. If you select **Include data** then you can use the drop-down list to its right to specify whether you want the data from the current record, all the data from the found set, or all the data from the table.

You then can paste this into other applications, which treat it as an OLE object.

Paste Command

Choose **Paste** from the Edit menu to insert the contents of the clipboard at the current location of the cursor. You can paste the contents of the clipboard repeatedly.

Paste Special Command

Choose **Paste Special** from the Edit menu to use the Paste Special dialog box to paste an object on the clipboard into a PicturePlus field (see Figure B.30). This dialog box lets you choose the format of the object. For example, if it is an OLE object, you can embed it by selecting the **Paste** radio button, or link it by selecting **Paste Link**. Select the checkbox to display it as an icon rather than to display the actual object that you are pasting.

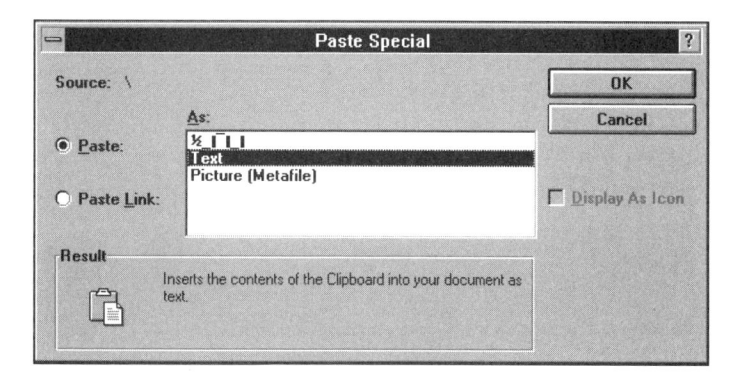

Figure B.30 The Paste Special dialog box.

Clear Command

Choose **Clear** from the Edit menu to delete selected text or to delete an object from a PicturePlus field.

Select All Command

Choose **Select All** from the Edit menu in Design mode to select all of the design of the current form or report.

Choose **Select All** from the Edit menu in Browse mode to select all of the records in the database or found set being displayed.

Paste from File Command

Choose **Paste** from the Edit menu to use the Paste from File dialog box to paste a picture or other object into the design of a View in Design modes or into the selected PicturePlus field of the current database if you are in Browse mode (see Figure B.31).

Use the List files of Type drop-down to select the type of file the picture or other object is in—Windows Bitmap files (BMP), Windows Metafiles (WMF), TIFF files (TIF), Paintbrush files (PCX) or Encapsulated PostScript files (EPS). When you make the selection, the files in the selected directory that have that extension are displayed in the File Name list, and you can select the one you want to paste into the field.

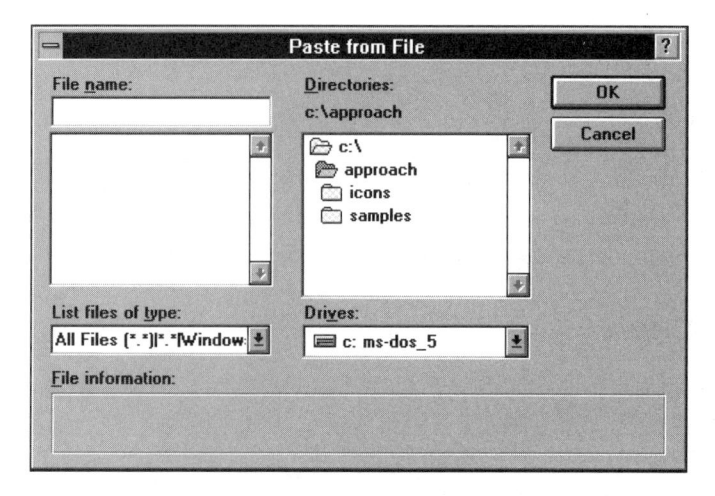

Figure B.31 The Paste from File dialog box.

Copy to File Command

Choose **Copy to File** from the Edit menu to use the Copy to File dialog box that lets you copy a PicturePlus field into a new file (see Figure B.32). Only Windows bitmap files are supported, and so there are no other options in the List Files of Type drop-down list.

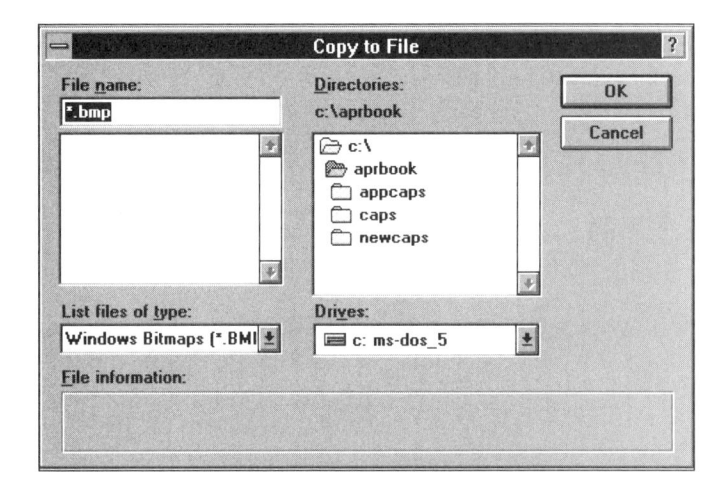

Figure B.32 The Copy to File dialog box.

Duplicate . . . Command

This option of the Edit menu is displayed as Duplicate Form, Duplicate Report, Duplicate Labels, Duplicate Worksheet, Duplicate Crosstab or Duplicate Chart, depending on the type of view currently being used. Select it to create a new view that is an exact duplicate of the current one, which you can then rename and modify. This option is available only in design mode.

Delete . . . Command

This option of the Edit menu is displayed as Delete Form, Delete Report, Delete Labels, Delete Worksheet, Delete Crosstab or Delete Chart, depending on the type of view that is currently being used. Select one of these options to delete the current design. This option is available only in design mode.

The View Menu

The View menu is used to toggle to Design or Browse mode, and to change the display in ways that may be convenient when you are creating a design.

Design Command

Choose **Design** from the View menu to toggle to Design mode. This option is equivalent to selecting the **Design** icon.

Browse Command

Choose **Browse** from the View menu to toggle to Browse mode. This option is equivalent to selecting the **Browse** icon.

Show Data

Choose **Show Data** from the View menu to specify whether or not data should be displayed when you are creating a design. This option is only accessible in design mode and is a toggle, with a check mark displayed to its left to indicate whether it has been selected.

Snap to Grid

Choose **Snap to Grid** from the View menu to specify whether objects should automatically be lined up with the grid of lines when you are creating a design. This option is only accessible in design mode and is a toggle.

Show Grid Command

Choose **Show Grid** from the View menu to specify whether you can see the grid of lines that objects are lined up with when you create a design. This option is only accessible in design mode and is a toggle.

Show Ruler Command

Choose **Show Ruler** from the View menu to display or eliminate rulers at the top and left of the window, which help you align objects in the design. This option is only accessible in design mode and is a toggle.

Show Drawing Tools Command

Choose **Show Drawing Tools** from the View menu to display or eliminate the toolbox of drawing tools that lets you add text, rectangles, lines, fields, checkboxes, and the like to a design. This option is only accessible in design mode and is a toggle.

Show Panel Labels Command

Choose **Show Panel Labels Tools** from the View menu to display labels identifying the panels of reports. This option is only accessible in design mode and is a toggle.

Show Data Entry Order Command

Choose **Data Entry order** from the View menu to display numbers that indicate the order in which the focus moves among fields of the design when you press **Tab** during data entry.

You can simply edit the numbers to change the data entry order. Alternatively, you can double-click the border of a one of the squares that holds these numbers to remove the numbers from all the squares; then simply click the squares in the order you want, and they are automatically numbered in that order.

This option is only accessible in design mode and is a toggle.

Show Smart Icons Command

Choose **Show SmartIcons** from the View menu to display or eliminate the icon bar of SmartIcons that you can use as shortcuts for many menu options. This option is a toggle.

Show Status Bar Command

Choose **Show Status Bar** from the View menu to display or eliminate the Status Bar from the bottom of the Approach Window. This option is a toggle.

Show View Tabs Command

Choose **Show View Tabs** from the View menu to display or eliminate the divider tabs that you use to Switch from one view to another. This option is a toggle.

Actual Size Command

Choose **Actual Size** from the View menu in Design View to display the design in its actual size. This option is only accessible if you previously enlarged or reduced the size of the design.

Zoom In Command

Choose **Zoom In** from the View menu in Design View to display the design in a larger size.

Zoom Out Command

Choose **Zoom Out** from the View menu in Design View to display the design in a smaller size.

The Create Menu

The Create menu is used to create new views and certain elements of views, as well as to join databases and change field definitions.

Form Command

Choose **Form** from the Create menu to display the Form Assistant, which is used to create a new form.

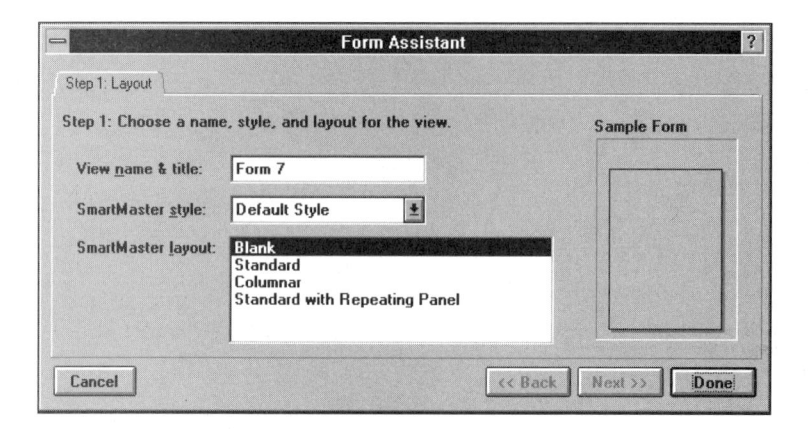

Figure B.33 Step 1 of the Form Assistant.

Step 1 is the Layout panel (see Figure B.33). Enter the name of the new form in the View name and title text box (or use the default name, such as Form 2, that Approach suggests).

Select a style from the SmartMaster style drop-down.

Select a layout from the SmartMaster layout list, which includes the following options:

- *Blank*: No fields or titles will be placed on the form initially. You must add them all manually.

- *Standard*: A standard form displays the fields one next another, with the name above each. As many fields as possible are placed on each line, so a record takes up as few lines as possible.

- *Columnar*: A columnar form displays the fields in one or more columns, with one field on each line, and its name to its left.

- *Standard with Repeating Panel*: Like a standard form, this option displays the fields one next to another, on as few lines as possible, with its name above each field. It also includes a repeating panel, with fields from a related table. If you select this option, a third step is added to the Assistant, which lets you add fields to the repeating panel. This option can only be used with a relational database—the one file must be used as the basis of the form, so one of its records is displayed at a time; all the related records from the many file are displayed below it in the repeating panel.

A sample of your selection is displayed in the Sample Form box to the right.

If you choose any option except Blank, you specify which fields it includes using Step 2, the Fields panel (see Figure B.34). Select each field to be included in the form from the Database Fields list, and select **Add** to add it to the Form Fields list. Alternatively, simply double-click a field in the Database Fields list to add it to the Form Fields list. If you are working with a relational database, use the Database drop-down list to display fields from other database files in the Database Fields list. You can add fields from all joined database files to the form.

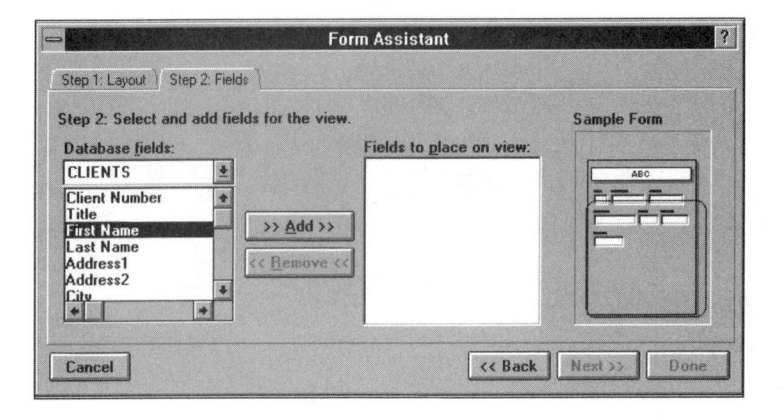

Figure B.34 Adding Fields to the Form.

If you selected **Standard with Repeating panel** as the SmartMaster layout in Step 1, Approach lets you specify which fields are used in the repeating panel by using Step 3: Panel (see Figure B.35). This step looks and works just like Step 2, and it is used for selecting the fields that are included in the repeating panel.

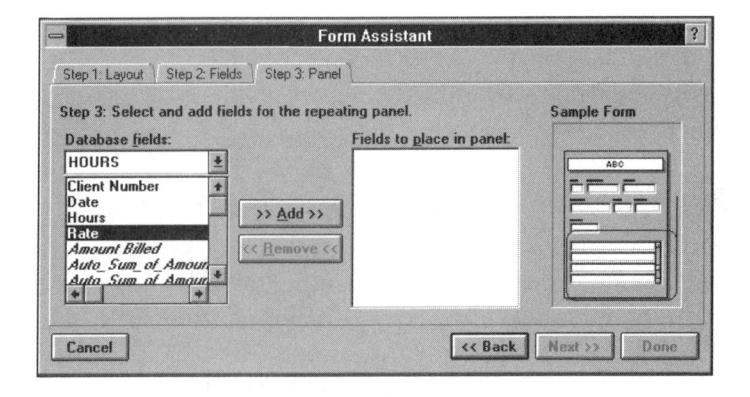

Figure B.35 Adding Fields to a repeating panel.

When you select **Done** a form with the name and fields you indicated is displayed, and you can make further changes in it.

Report Command

Choose **Report** from the Create menu to display the Report Assistant, which is used to create a new report (see Figure B.36).

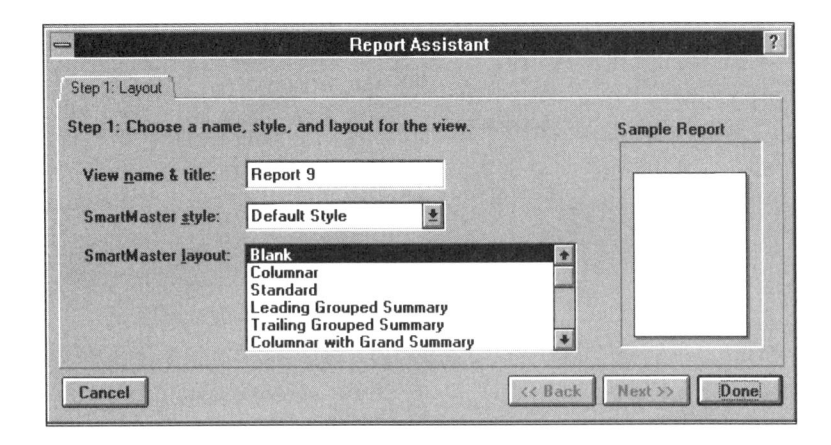

Figure B.36 The Report Assistant.

In Step 1 of this Assistant, enter the name of the new report in the View name and title text box (or use the default name, such as Report 2, that is suggested). Use the SmartMaster style drop-down to select a style.

Use the SmartMaster layout list to select which type of report you want to create, from the following options:

- *Blank Report*: No fields or titles are placed on the form initially. You must add them all manually.
- *Columnar*: A columnar report displays the fields in columns, so all the fields of each record are next to one another. The name of each field is displayed in the header at the top of each column. These titles continue to be displayed at the top of the screen as you scroll through the records, and they are printed at the top of each page if you print the report.
- *Standard*: A standard report displays the fields of each record next to each other, continuing on the next line when it reaches the right margin, so the entire record fits into the width of a page taking up as few lines as possible. Records are displayed one below another on the same page.

- *Leading Grouped Summary*: This layout produces a columnar report that is grouped by the contents of some field, with a summary for each. The summary is generally used to identify each group. For example, the records may be grouped by state, with the name of the state included at the beginning of each summary band .

- *Trailing Grouped Summary*: This layout produces a columnar report that is grouped by the contents of some field, with a summary for each group. The summary usually contains some calculation based on the records of the group. For example, the records may be grouped by state, with a total or average of the values in some numeric field for each state.

- *Columnar with Grand Summary*: This layout produces a columnar report with a grand total of the value in some field at the end of the report.

- *Summary Only*: A summary report includes only summary information for groups based on some field, and does not include the data in each record. For example, it might include the sum or average of the value in some field for each state, but not the value of this field in individual records.

If you select any of these options except Blank or Summary Only, the Fields step is added to the Assistant (see Figure B.37). Select each field to be included in the report from the Database Fields list, and select **Add** to add it to the Report Fields list. Alternatively, simply double-click a field in the Database Fields list to add it to the Report Fields list. If you are working with a relational database, use the Database drop-down list to display fields from other database files in the Database Fields list. You can add fields from all joined database files to the report.

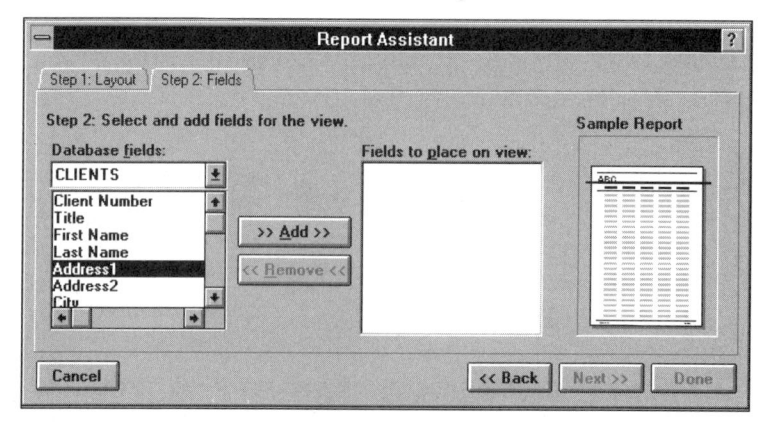

Figure B.37 The Fields Step of the Report Assistant.

If you select **Leading Grouped Summary**, Step 3: Leading Summary is added to the Assistant (see Figure B.38). To group the fields, select the check box in the top half of this panel and select the field that is used as the basis of the grouping. To add a summary field, select the check box in the lower half of the panel, use the drop-down to its right to select the type of summary (for example, average, sum, or number of items) and use the field list to select the field whose value is summarized.

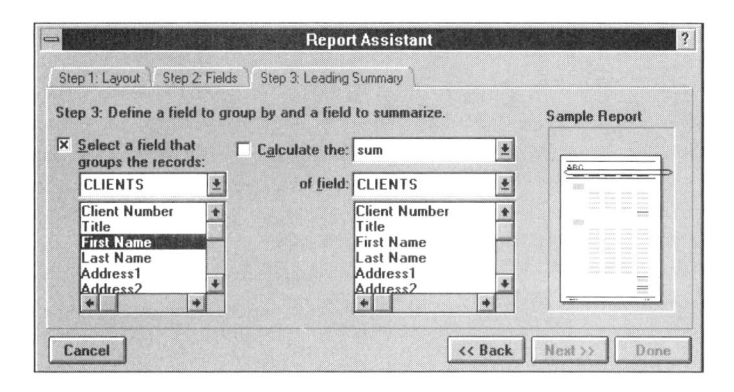

Figure B.38 The Leading Summary Step.

If you select **Trailing Grouped Summary**, Step 3: Trailing Summary is added to the Assistant (see Figure B.39). Use this in the same way as the Leading Summary step, described above, to specify how the records should be grouped and what type of summary should be used for each group.

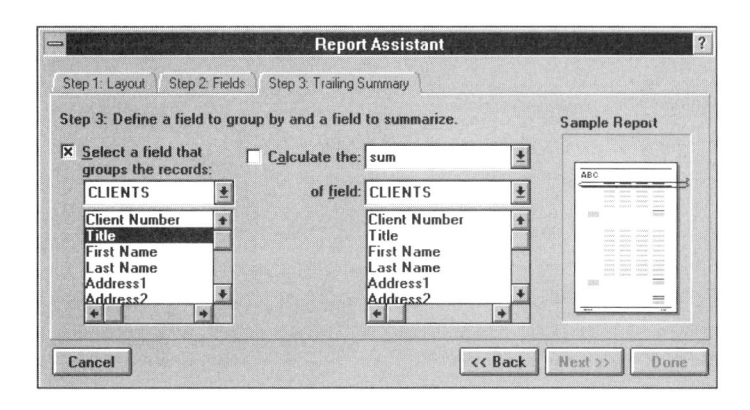

Figure B.39 The Trailing Summary Step.

If you select **Columnar with Grand Summary**, Step 3: Grand Summary, is added to the Assistant (see Figure B.40). Use it like the bottom half of the Leading Summary step, described earlier, to select the type of summary and the field whose values are summarized.

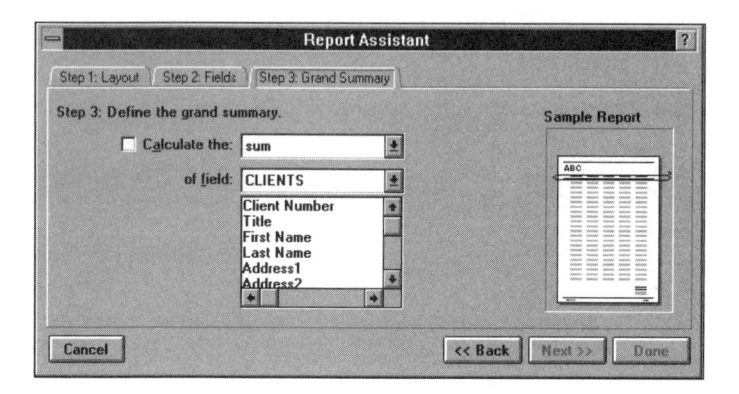

Figure B.40 The Grand Summary Step.

If you select **Summary only** in Step 1, Step 2: Trailing Summary, is added to the Assistant (see Figure B.41). Use it like the Leading Summary step, described above, to specify how the records should be grouped and what type of summary should be used for each group. The Fields step is not needed, because only the summary data is displayed.

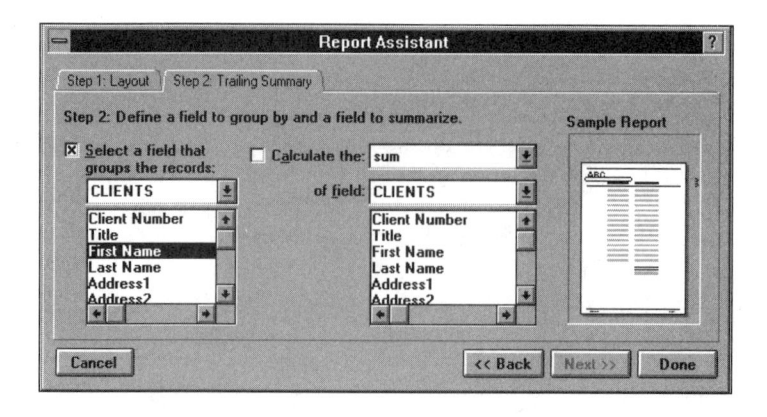

Figure B.41 The Trailing Summary Step for a summary only report.

Mailing Label Command

Choose **Mailing Label** from the Create menu to display the Mailing Label Assistant. The Basics panel of this Assistant is all you need to create most labels (see Figure B.42).

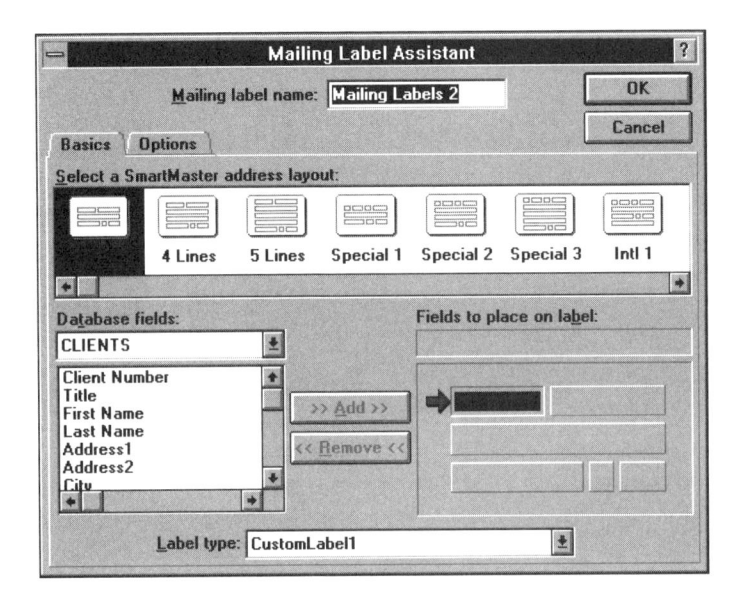

Figure B.42 The Mailing Label Assistant.

Enter the name of the new mailing labels in the Mailing label name text box or use the default name, such as Mailing Labels 2, that is suggested.

Select a SmartMaster layout, and that layout is displayed in the Fields to place on label box, at the lower right. Then select one of the spaces for fields in this layout to display an arrow to its left, select a field to be included in the labels from the Database Fields list, and select **Add** to add it where the arrow points. Alternatively, simply double-click a field in the Database Fields list to add it. When you add a field to the label, the arrow moves to the next space, so you can add another field.

To remove a name that has already been added, select it and select **Remove**, or simply double-click it.

If you are working with a relational database, use the Database drop-down list to display fields from other database files in the Database Fields list. You can add fields from all joined database files to the mailing labels.

Use the Label type drop-down list to select any standard Avery label layout, and your labels are automatically be sized to fit on that form.

Alternatively, if your labels are not a standard Avery layout, the Options panel lets you create custom layouts for labels (see Figure B.43).

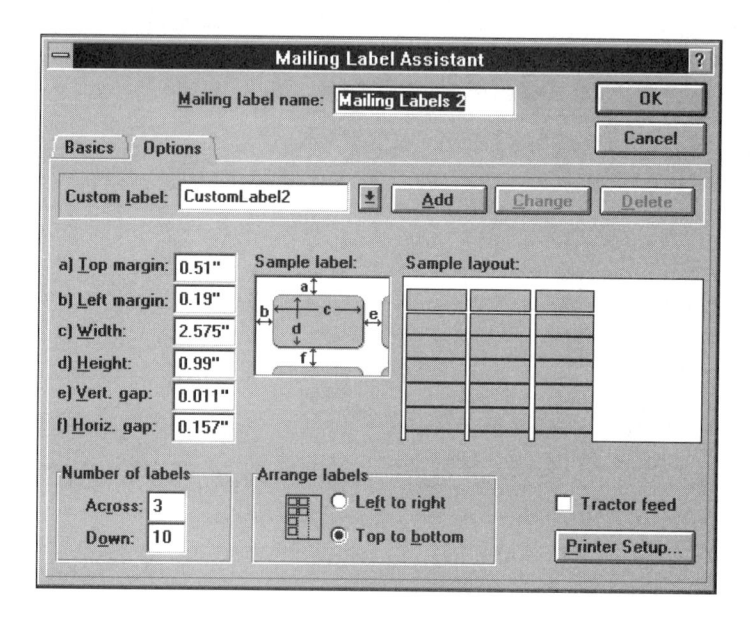

Figure B.43 The Options panel.

This panel is automatically filled out with the specifications of the Avery label selected in the Label Code drop-down list in the previous panel. If you are creating custom labels, you should begin by selecting the Avery labels that are the closest to what you need. Then use the text boxes to indicate the page margins, the width and height of each label, the size of the gaps between labels, and the number of labels across and down. The options you choose are displayed in the Sample layout area to the right.

Select **Printer Setup** to use the Print Setup dialog box described in the section on the *Print Setup Command* of the File menu.

Finally, you can use the radio buttons in the Arrange Labels area to specify the order in which records are printed or displayed in the label forms on the screen. Select **Left to Right** to have them printed across each row, beginning with the top row of each page. **Top to Bottom**, selected by default, prints them down each column, beginning with the left column of each page. Use the Number of Labels text boxes to change the number of labels across and down. Select **Tractor feed** if you use continuous form labels, rather than labels on separate, single-page forms.

When you select **OK** a mailing label with the layout and fields you indicated is displayed, and you can make further changes in it in Design mode.

Form Letter Command

Choose **Form Letter** from the Create menu to display the Form Letter Assistant.

Step 1 lets you enter a View name and title, select a SmartMaster style and a SmartMaster layout, like the first step of other Assistants (see Figure B.44). The style that you choose is displayed in the Sample Letter box to the right.

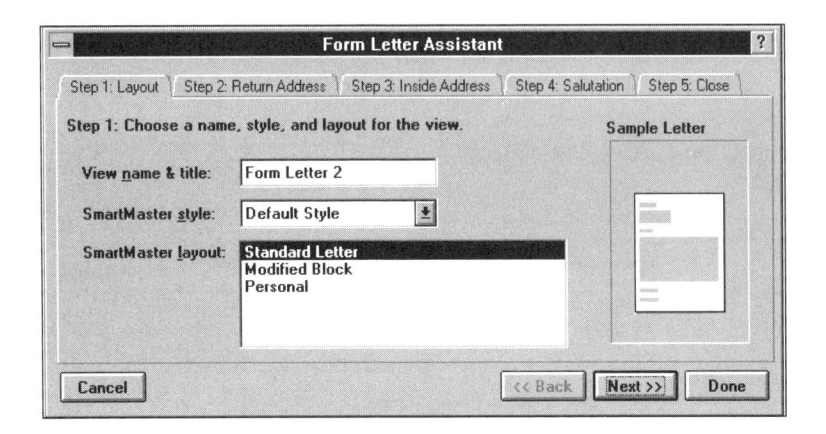

Figure B.44 Specifying the Layout of the Form Letter.

Step 2 lets you enter the return address—simply type it in the text box, or choose the None radio button to have no return address (see Figure B.45).

Practical Approach, 3.0

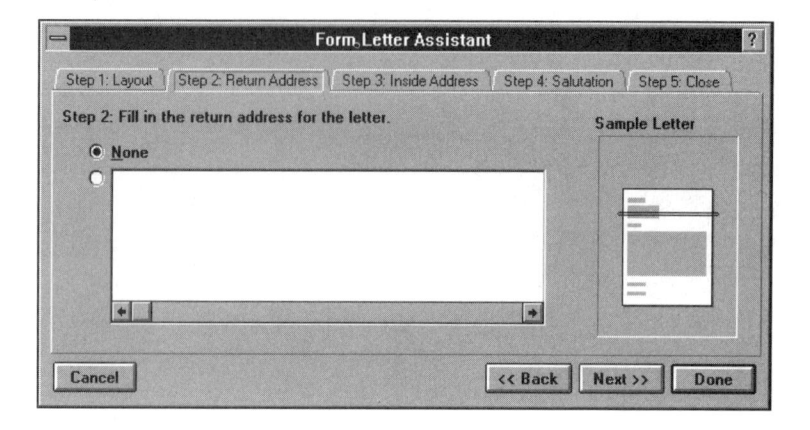

Figure B.45 The Return Address panel.

Step 3 lets you lay out the address you are writing to (see Figure B.46). This panel works like the Basics panel of the Mailing Label Assistant, described above. Use the drop-down to select a 3 line, 4 line, 5 line, or one of the special layouts. Then click a box of the layout to place an arrow to its left; select a field name and select **Add** (or double-click a field name) to place it in the box indicated by the arrow. When you add a name to a box, the arrow moves to the next box. To remove a name that has already been added, select it and select **Remove**, or simply double-click it.

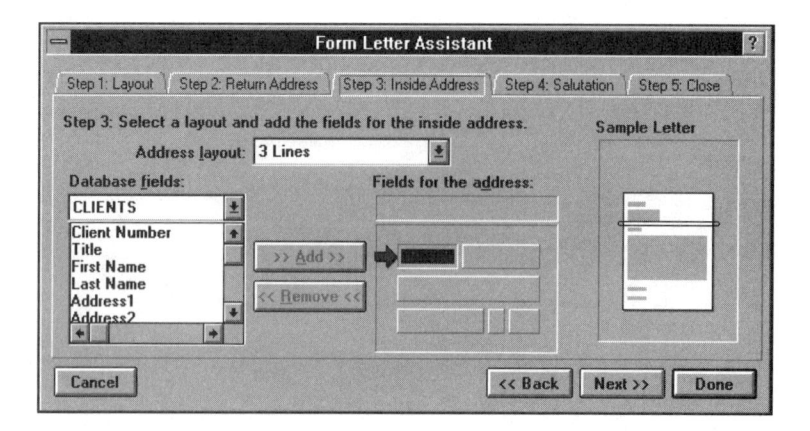

Figure B.46 The Inside Address panel.

Appendix B: Reference Guide

If you are working with a relational database, use the Database drop-down list to display fields from other database files in the Database Fields list. You can add fields from all joined database files to the mailing labels.

Step 4 lets you specify a salutation (see Figure B.47). You can include up to 2 fields and you can edit the word *Dear* and the colon in the text boxes before and after the fields. Select **None** if you do not want a salutation.

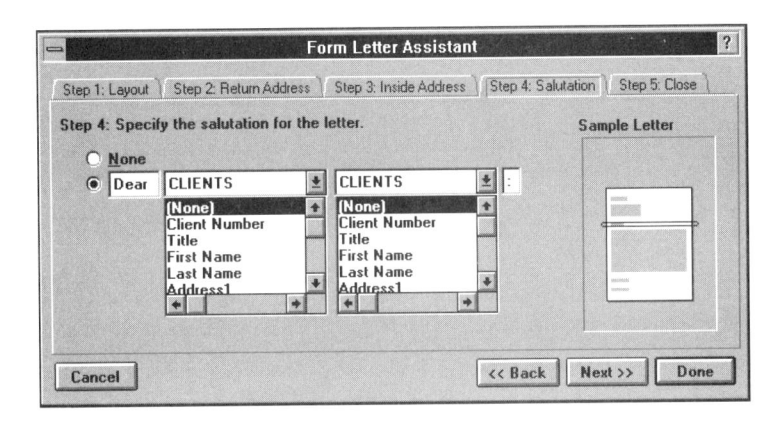

Figure B.47 The Salutation panel.

Step 5 lets you specify how the letter closes (see Figure B.48). Simply type the closing in the text box.

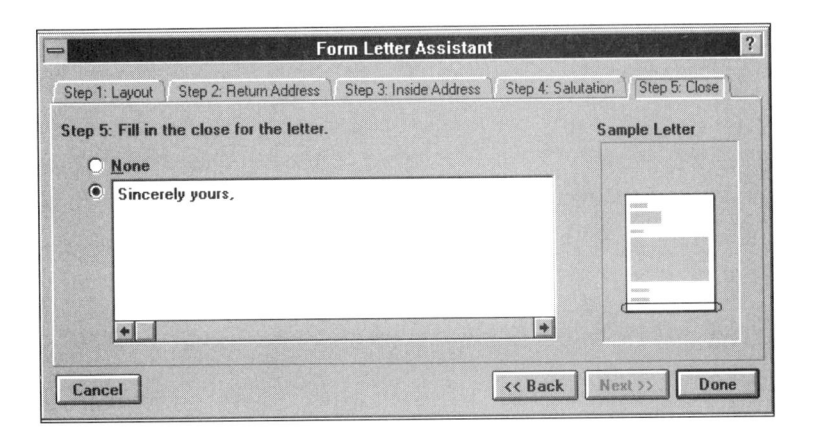

Figure B.48 The Close panel.

When you select **Done** a form letter with the specifications you indicated is displayed. You can type in text and make other changes to it in Design mode.

Worksheet Command

Choose Worksheet from from the Create menu to display the Worksheet Assistant, which has only one step, used to specify which fields are included in the Worksheet (see Figure B.49).

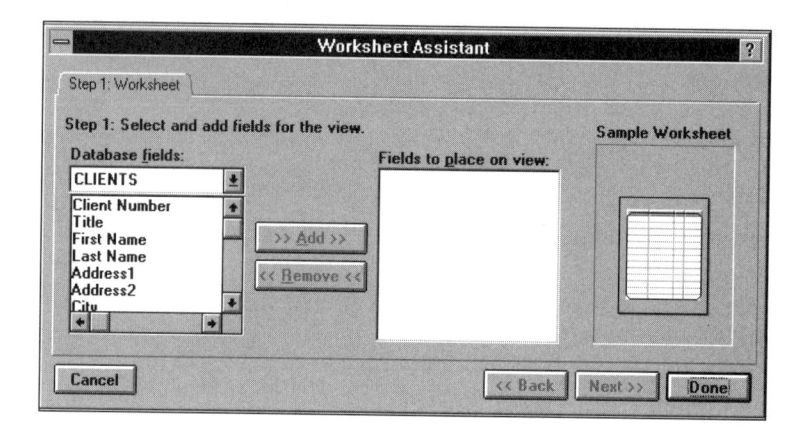

Figure B.49   The Worksheet Assistant.

To use this field picker, simply select a field in the Database fields list and click **Add** to add it to the Fields on view list; alternatively, you can just double-click a field to add it to the list. To remove a field that has already been added, select it and choose **Remove**, or simply double-click it.

If you are working with a relational database, use the Database drop-down list to display fields from other database files in the Database Fields list.

When you select **Done**, a Worksheet with the fields that you selected is displayed. You can make changes in either Browse or Design mode; in password protected Approach files, however, you can make changes in it only in Design mode.

Crosstab Command

Choose **Crosstab** from the Create menu to display the Crosstab Assistant.

Step 1 lets you specify which fields are used as the basis of rows in the Crosstab (see Figure B.50).

Appendix B: Reference Guide

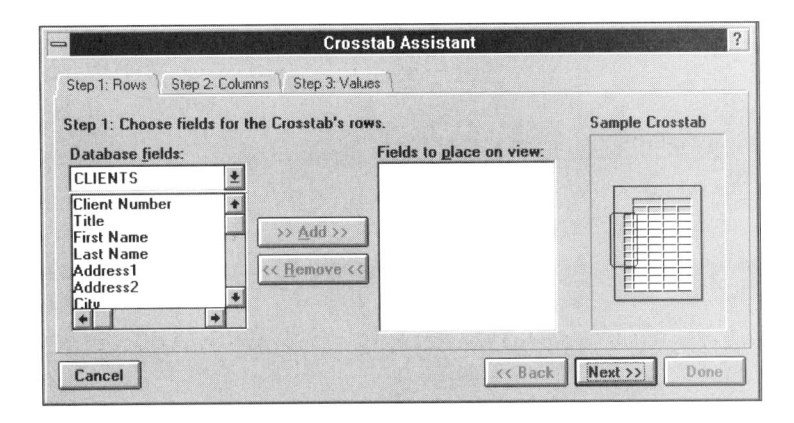

Figure B.50 The Rows panel of the Crosstab Assistant.

Use this like other field pickers. Select a field in the Database fields list and click **Add** to add it to the Fields to place on view list, or simply double-click a field to add it to the list. To remove a field that has already been added, select it and select **Remove**, or simply double-click it. If you are working with a relational database, use the Database drop-down list to display fields from other database files in the Database Fields list.

Use Step 2 to specify which fields are used as the basis of columns in the Crosstab (see Figure B.51). This step works just like Step 1.

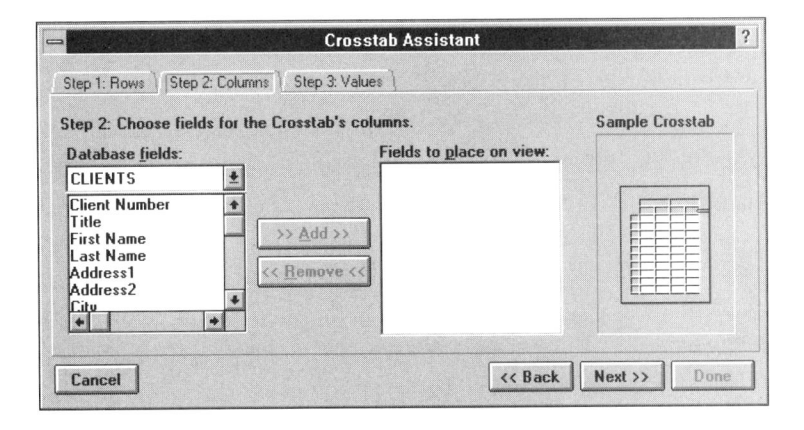

Figure B.51 The Columns panel of the Crosstab Assistant.

Step 3 lets you specify the values displayed in the cells of the Crosstab (see Figure B.52). Use the drop-down to select the type of calculation to be used, such as sum, average, or number or items, and use the drop-down and list below it to select the database table and field that the calculation is performed on.

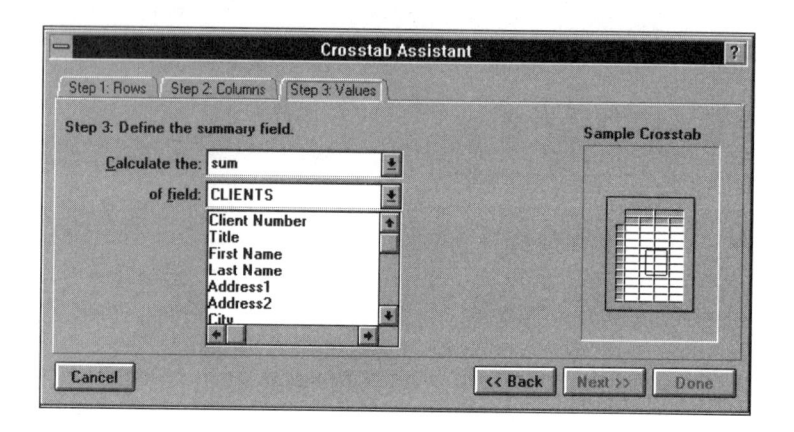

Figure B.52 *The Values Panel of the Crosstab Assistant.*

When you select **Done**, a Crosstab with the row headings, column headings and summary values specified is displayed, with an additional column summarizing the values in all the rows and an additional row summarizing the values in all the columns. You can make changes in either Browse or Design mode; in password protect Approach files, however, you can make changes in the Crosstab only in Design mode.

Chart Command

Chose **Chart** from the Create menu to display the Chart Assistant.

Step 1 lets you enter the View name and title, choose two-dimensional or three-dimensional as the SmartMaster style, and choose **Bar**, **Line**, **Area**, or **Pie chart** as the SmartMaster layout (see Figure B.53). The style and layout that you choose are shown in the Sample box to the right.

Appendix B: Reference Guide

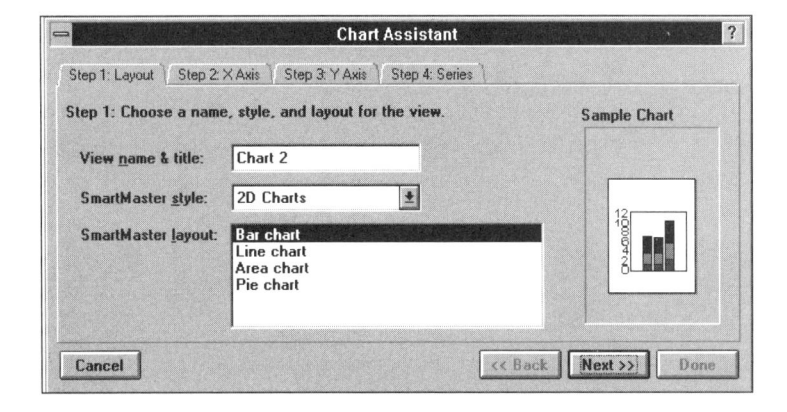

Figure B.53 Step 1 of the Chart Assistant.

If you select **Bar Chart**, **Line Chart**, or **Area Chart** as the layout in Step 1, then Step 2 of the Chart Assistant lets you choose a field used for the x-axis (see Figure B.54). Simply select the database from the drop-down, if necessary, and highlight the name of the field in the list.

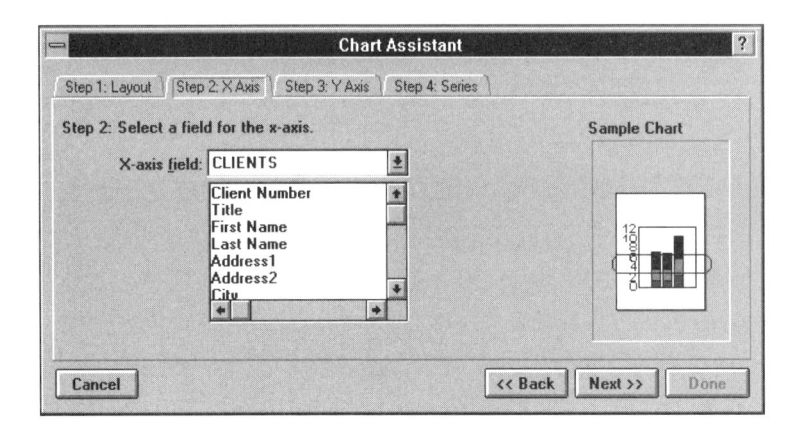

Figure B.54 The x-axis panel.

Step 3 lets you choose a field used for the y-axis and works identically to Step 2 (see Figure B.55).

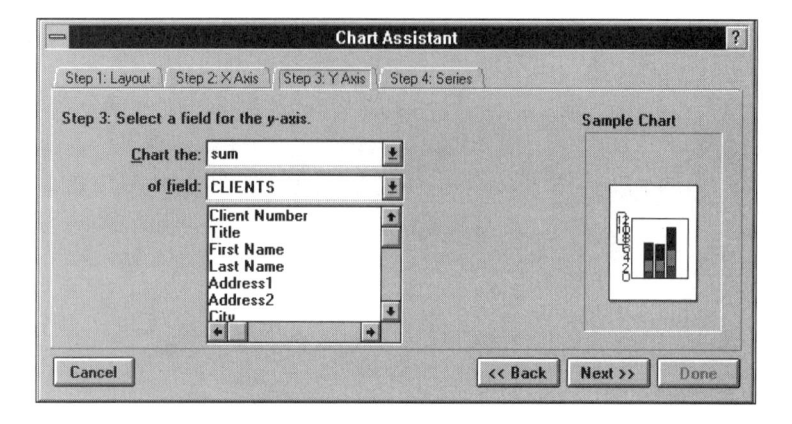

Figure B.55 The y-axis panel.

Step 4 is optional and lets you choose a field that is used as the basis of a series (see Figure B.56). A series displays a number of values for each value in the x-axis. For example, if you are creating a bar graph of the amount you billed each client, you can use the calculated Billing Month field as the basis of a series; the chart displays a number of bars above each client's name, indicating the amount you billed the client each month. To create a series, simply select the checkbox in this panel, select the database from the drop-down, if necessary, and highlight the name of the field the series is based on in the list.

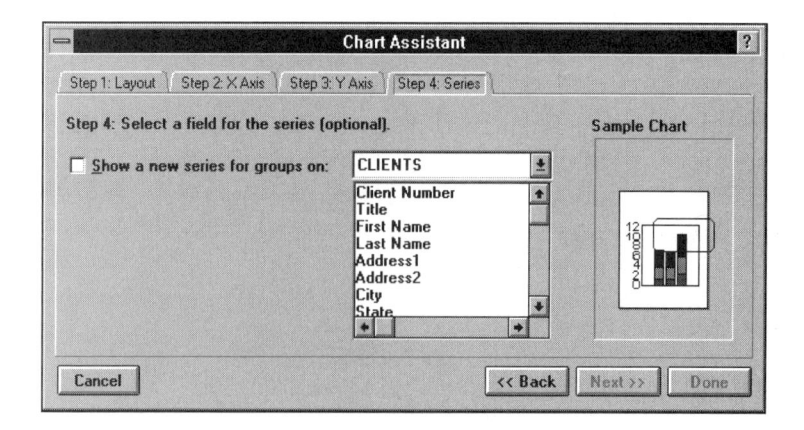

Figure B.56 The Series panel.

If you select **Pie Chart** as the layout in Step 1, then the Chart Assistant has only one other step, the Pie fields panel (see Figure B.57).

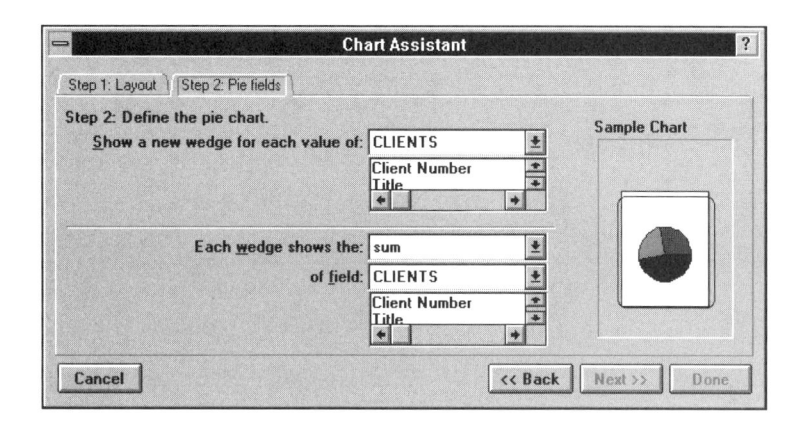

Figure B.57 The Pie fields panel.

Use the first field list to select the field that the chart is grouped on—if you are graphing the amounts you billed your clients, select **Client Number** here, so there would be one wedge for each client.

Use the second field list to select the value that the chart represents, and use the drop-down to specify how it is summarized. If you are graphing the amounts you billed your clients, select sum from the drop-down and select the calculated **Amount Billed** field from the field list.

When you select **Done** a Chart with the specifications you selected is displayed, and you can change its title and other labels in Design mode.

Repeating Panel Command

Repeating panels are useful for displaying relational databases with one-to-many relations. You can use the Form Assistant to create a form with a repeating panel, using the methods described above in the section on *The Form Command*. You can also use this command of the Create menu to add a repeating panel to an existing form.

Before adding a repeating panel, you must join the files and create the form for the one file, as always. Then display the form in Design mode and choose

Repeating Panel from the Create menu to display the Add Repeating Panel Dialog box (see Figure B.58).

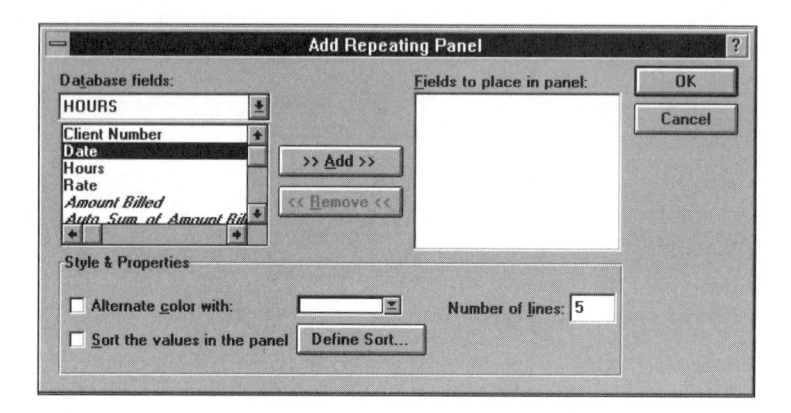

Figure B.58 The Add Repeating panel dialog box.

Use the top half of this dialog box in the same way you use other field pickers to select the fields to include in the repeating panel.

The Style & Properties panel of this dialog box lets you select properties of the repeating panel that you can also control using its Info Box:

- Select the *Alternate color with* checkbox to display alternating lines in the repeating panel with different background colors, if this makes it easier to view. Use the drop-down to its right to select a color or pattern that is used for every second line in the repeating panel. It alternates with white lines.

- Use the *Number of Lines* text box to specify how many lines should be included in the repeating panel. If there is more data than can be displayed in this number of lines, a scroll bar is added to the repeating panel, so you can scroll through all the data.

- Use the *Sort the values in the panel* checkbox if you want to control the order of the records in the panel. Click **Define sort** to display the Sort dialog box, and use it to define the sort order. The Sort dialog box is covered below in the section on *The Sort Command* of the Browse menu.

When you select **OK** from the Add Repeating Panel to Form dialog box, a repeating panel is added to the form, with all the fields that you selected in the dialog box included in it as individual field objects. You can work with the panel and the individual fields in Design mode, as you do with other objects in forms.

Summary Command

You can use the Report Assistant to create a report with a summary panel, using the methods described above in the section on *The Report Command*. You can also use this command to add a summary panel to an existing form.

Display the report in Design mode and choose **Summary** from the Create menu to display the Summary dialog box (see Figure B.59).

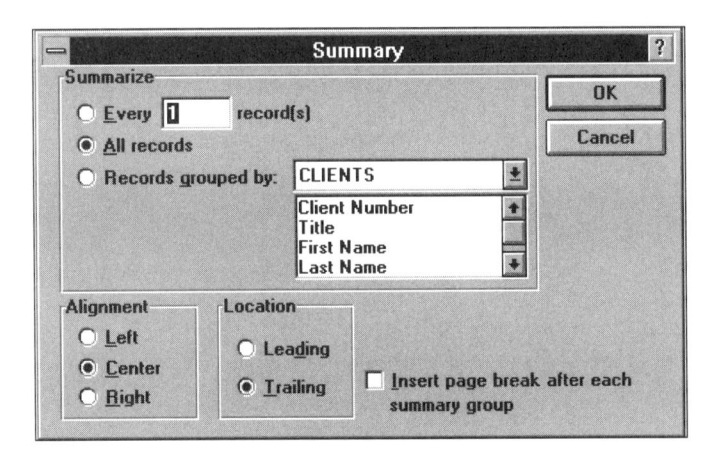

Figure B.59 The Summary dialog box.

Use this dialog box to specify how the report summarizes the data. The radio buttons in the Summarize area let you select what groups of records the summaries are based on:

- *Every __ record(s)*. Gives a summary for groups consisting of some group based on a number that you enter in the text box. If you enter **10** in the text box, the report includes summary information on every ten records in the database.

- *All Records.* Gives summary information on all the records in the database.
- *Records Grouped By.* Gives summary information based on some field that you specify. Select the field in the list of fields and if necessary, select the database from the drop-down list. The records are sorted on this field, and summary information is given for every value in the field.

The other two groups of radio buttons in this dialog box let you specify how the summary information is displayed. The Left, Center, and Right radio buttons display the information in the specified location. The Leading radio button displays the summary before each group of records, and the Trailing radio button displays the summary after each group of records.

Select **Insert page break** if you want each group to begin on a new page.

Drawing Command

Choose **Drawing** from the Create menu to display a submenu which has the following options

- *Line*: Used to add a line to the view. After selecting it, click and drag to place this graphic object.
- *Text:* Adds text to a design. After selecting it, simply click on the design and type text, or click and drag anywhere on the design to create a text box; then type the text in this box.
- *Ellipse:* Adds an ellipse to the design. After choosing it, click and drag to place this graphic object.
- *Rectangle:* Adds a rectangle to the design. After choosing it, click and drag to place this graphic object.
- *Rounded Rectangle:* Adds a rounded rectangle to the design. After choosing it, click and drag to place this graphic object.
- *Field:* Places a field in the design. After choosing it, click and drag anywhere in the design to place the field frame, and use the Info Box to specify which field it should hold. The same field can be placed in the design several times.
- *Radio Button:* Places radio buttons in the design. After choosing it, click and drag to locate the Radio buttons and use the dialog box that is displayed to define the Radio buttons. This dialog box is the same as the

one that is displayed when you use the Data Entry drop-down of the Field Info Box to add radio buttons to a design. It also has a drop-down and list to let you specify the field that the radio buttons represent.

- *Checkbox:* Places a checkbox in the design. After choosing it, click and drag to place the checkbox and use the dialog box displayed to define the field. This dialog box is the same as the one that is displayed when you use the Data Entry drop-down of the Field Info Box to add a checkbox to a design. It also has a drop-down and list to let you specify the field that the checkbox represents.
- *PicturePlus Field:* Adds a PicturePlus field to your design. After choosing it, click and drag to place the field frame, and use the Info Box to specify the field that it holds.
- *Macro Button:* Places a push button in the design. After choosing it, click and drag to place the button, and use the Info Box to attach a macro to the button.

These commands are equivalent to the drawing tools.

Object Command

Choose **Object** from the Create menu to use the Insert Object dialog box to add an embedded object to a PicturePlus field or a Design.

If the **Create New** radio button is selected the Insert Object dialog box is displayed in the form shown in Figure B.60.

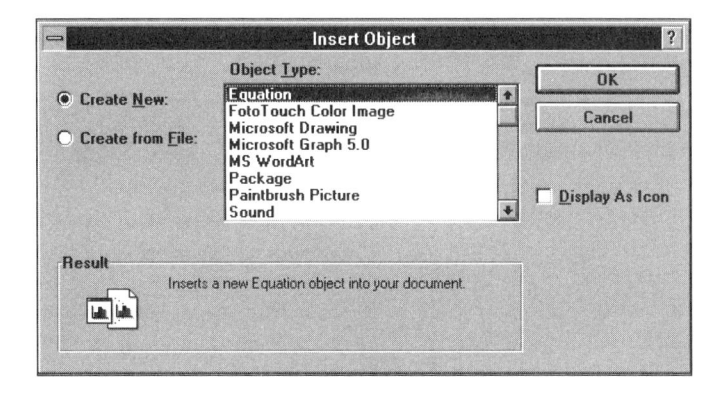

Figure B.60 Using The Insert Object dialog box to create a new object.

Select the type you want from the Object Type list (or simply double-click the object type in the list) to launch the application used to create that object. The Object Types that are available depend on what other Windows applications you have installed.

If you want the object to be displayed as an icon, double-click to display the actual picture or other data in the field, and select **Display as Icon**.

After you have finished using the other application to create and save the object, exit from that application. Most applications display a dialog box asking whether you want to update the object in Approach. Select **Yes** to embed the object in its current form.

If the **Create from File** radio button is selected, the Insert Object dialog box is displayed in the form shown in Figure B.61. Simply enter the name of the file that holds the object in the File text box, or click **Browse** to display the Browse dialog box. You can use it just like the Open dialog box to select a file.

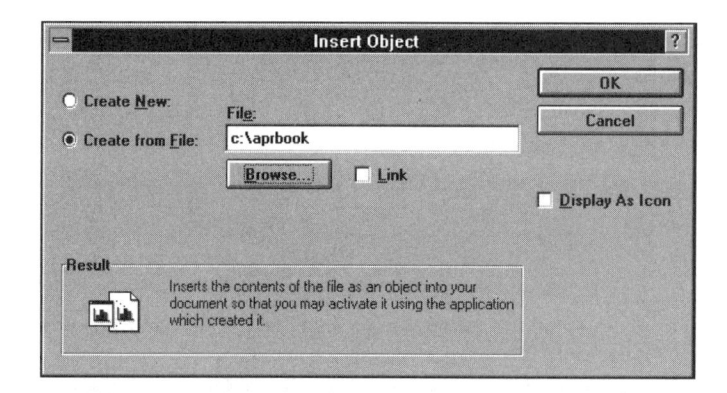

Figure B.61 Using the Insert Object dialog box to insert an existing object.

If you want the object to be displayed as an icon that the user must double-click to display the actual data in the field, select **Display as Icon**.

Select **OK** to insert the object in the PicturePlus field or Design. The object is embedded in Approach—you can double-click it at any time to call up the application where it was created so it can be modified.

Join Command

To join two Database files, first use one in Design mode. Then choose **Join** from the Create menu to display the Join dialog box (see Figure B.62).

Appendix B: Reference Guide

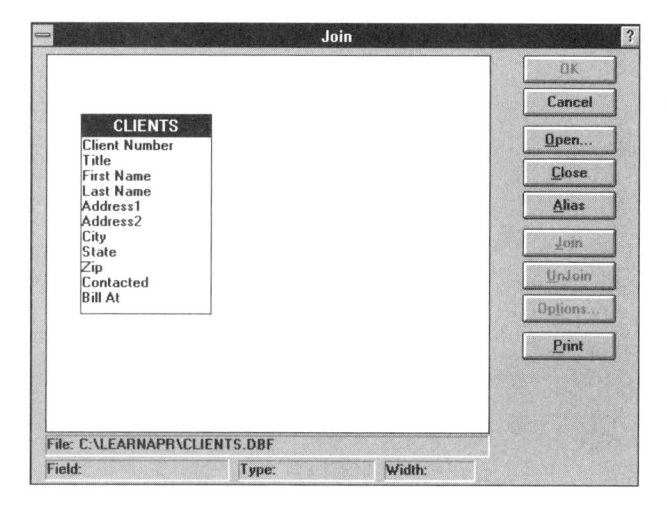

Figure B.62 The Join dialog box.

Select **Open** from this dialog box, to display the Open dialog box, shown in the section on the *Open Command* of the FIle menu. Select the file that you want to join to the first file from it in the usual way. When you select **OK**, the detail file is added to the Join dialog box. Select the key fields you want to use to join the files, and select **Join**. A line joins the two fields where the CLIENTS and HOURS Database files are joined using the CLIENT NUMBER field as the key field (see Figure B.63).

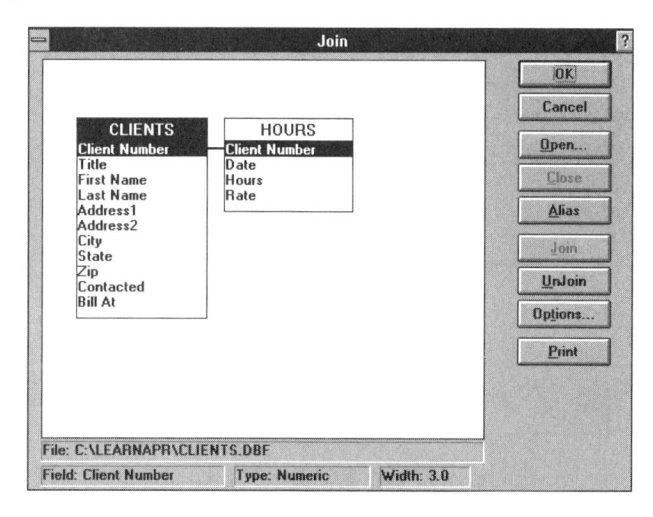

Figure B.63 Joining two files.

Practical Approach, 3.0

The Alias button of the Join dialog box lets you join a database to itself. If you click this button, it adds a second copy of the database to this dialog box. The numbers 1 and 2 are added to the name of the database in the title bar of the two lists in the Join dialog box. The name of the database does not change anywhere else in Approach. You can join these two copies of the same database just as you join any two databases. This is useful only in special cases.

To eliminate a Join you have created, first select it by clicking the line that represents the Join. A Join is automatically selected in this way when you first create it. When a Join is selected, the **UnJoin** button is enabled, and you can click it to eliminate the Join.

You can specify data entry options for a Join by selecting it and selecting **Options** to display the Relational Options dialog box (see Figure B.64). Use the checkboxes in this dialog box to automatically insert or delete records in both the detail and main file when records are inserted or deleted in the other file.

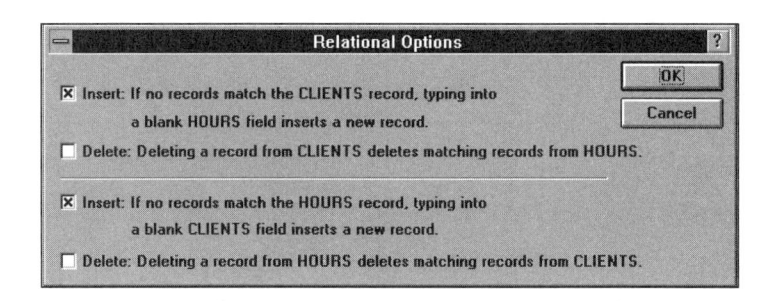

Figure B.64 The Relational Options dialog box.

Field Definition Command

Choose **Field Definition** from the Create menu to display the Field Definition dialog box. This dialog box is the same as the one you use to design a new file. For an illustration of it and information on using it, see the section on the *New Command* of the File menu.

The Browse Menu

The Browse menu is included in the menu system when you display a Form, Report, Mailing Label, or Form letter view in Browse mode. It is used to move through the records of the database, to add or delete records, and to perform Finds to isolate sets of records.

Find Command

Choose **Find** from the Browse menu to initiate a Find. Approach displays a Find Request—a copy of one record of the current view with no data in it. Enter an example of the data you want to find in one or more fields of this record and press **Enter**. Only the records that match the example you entered are displayed.

You can also enter multiple examples or use operators to perform more complex finds, described in Chapter 6.

Find Again Command

Choose **Find Again** from the Browse menu to reuse or modify the last Find you performed. A Find Request is displayed that is already filled out with the examples of data that you entered during the last Find. Leave the examples as they are, or modify them in any way you want, and press **Enter**. Approach displays only the records that match the example.

Find Special Command

Choose **Find Special** from the Browse menu to display the Find Special dialog box (see Figure B.65) which lets you find records that have or that do not have the same data in one or more fields.

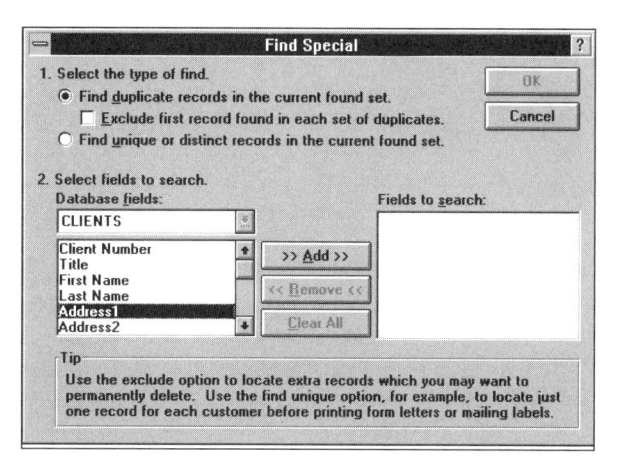

Figure B.65   The Find Duplicates dialog box.

Select **Find duplicate records** or **Find unique records** to specify whether you want the found set to include all the records with repetitive data or with unique data in the fields you are checking.

If you select **Find duplicate records** you can also select the check box under it to exclude the first record with a given value from the found set. Then, you can delete only duplications and keep one record with the each value in the fields.

You must specify the fields you want to checked for duplicates by adding them to the Fields to Search List. Select fields in the Database fields list and select **Add** or simply double-click fields in the Database fields list. If necessary, use the drop-down list above the Fields list to add fields from another file. To remove a field from the Fields to Search list, select it, and select **Remove** or double-click it. Select **Clear All** to remove all fields from this list and start over.

Show All Command

Choose **Show All** from the Browse menu to display all of the records in the database (rather than just the records selected by the last Find, or the records displayed after using the Hide Record command of the Browse menu).

Sort Command

For simple Sorts, move the cursor to the field that you want the sort to be based on. Then choose **Sort** from the Browse menu and **Ascending** or **Descending** from the submenu to sort on that field in Ascending or Descending order.

For more complex Sorts, choose **Sort** from the Browse menu and **Define** from the submenu to use the Sort dialog box to determine the order of the records (see Figure B.66). Select each field that the Sort is based on from the Fields list. If necessary, use the drop-down list above it to select the database the fields are in. Select **Add** to add the field to the Sort list. Use the **Ascending** and **Descending** for each field to determine if that field will be sorted from smallest to greatest, or from greatest to smallest value.

Appendix B: Reference Guide

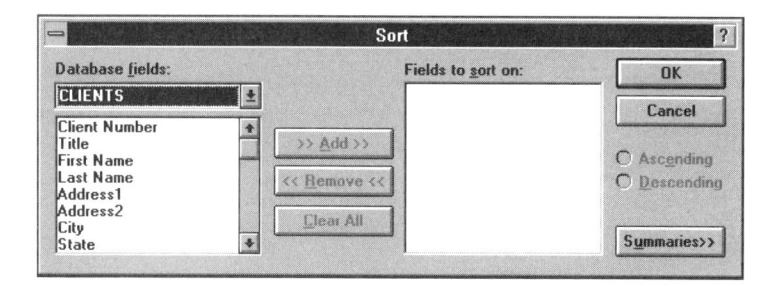

Figure B.66 The Sort dialog box.

To sort on a summary field, click **Summaries** to display the Sort dialog box in the expanded form that includes summary fields as well as ordinary database fields (see Figure B.67). Select a field in the Summary fields list and, if it is used in several panels, use the Summarized on drop-down to specify the one you want to use. Then add it to the Fields to sort on list just as you do ordinary fields.

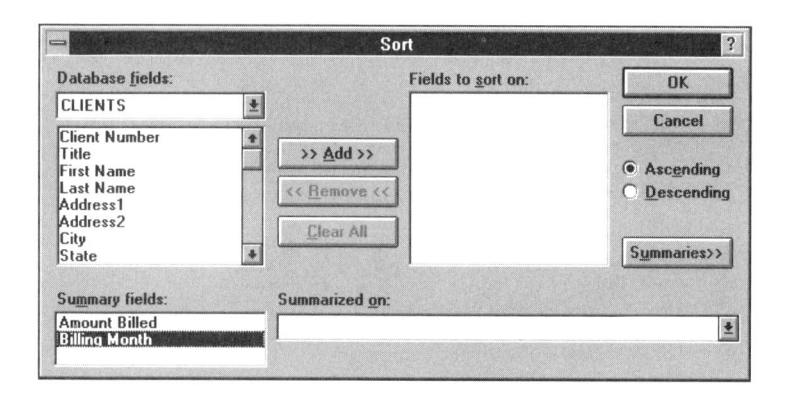

Figure B.67 The Sort dialog box with summary fields.

New Record Command

Choose **New Record** from the Browse menu to add a new blank record to the database.

Duplicate Record Command

Choose **Duplicate Record** from the Browse menu to add a new record to the database that is a duplicate of the current record.

Hide Record Command

Choose **Hide Record** from the Browse menu to hide the selected record, so it is not displayed and is not accessible in Reports, Finds, or Sorts. Ordinarily this hides just the current record, but you can also select multiple records by holding down **Shift** or **Ctrl** when you click them.

Delete Record Command

Choose **Delete Record** from the Browse menu to delete the selected record. Ordinarily this deletes just the current record, but you can also select multiple records by holding down **Shift** or **Ctrl** when you click them.

Delete Found Set Command

Choose **Delete Found Set** from the Browse menu to delete all the records that are displayed after doing a Find.

Fill Field Command

Choose **Fill Field** from the Browse menu to use the Fill Field dialog box to change the value of the selected field of all the records in the found set to the value you enter (see Figure B.68). Any previous data in these fields is lost.

Figure B.68 The Fill Field dialog box.

Insert Command

Choose **Insert**, from the Browse menu and **Todays Date**, **Current Time**, or **Previous Value** from the submenu, to enter the date, time or value from the previous record in the current field.

Refresh Command

Choose **Refresh** from the Browse menu to display the data with all changes included. This is useful if you are sharing data on a network and other users have made changes.

The Object Menu

When you display a Form, Report, Mailing Label or Form Letter view in Design mode and you select one or more individual objects in the view, the Browse menu is replaced by an Object menu, which helps you manipulate and work with objects.

Style & Properties

Choose **Style & Properties** from the Object menu to display the Info Box. Info Boxes are covered in detail in a later section of this Appendix.

Arrange Command

Choose **Arrange** from the Object menu to display a submenu that you can use to change the stacking order of objects, which objects seem to be in front of the others. The submenu has the following options:

- Choose **Bring to Front** to make the selected object appear to be in front of all other objects.
- Choose **Send to Back** to make the selected object appear to be behind all other objects.
- Choose **Bring Forward** to make the selected object appear one layer further forward compared with other objects.
- Choose **Send Backward** to make the selected object appear to be one layer further backward compared with other objects.

Align Command

Select a number of objects you want to align, and then choose **Align** from the Object menu to display the Align dialog box that lets you specify the alignment of the objects (see Figure B.69).

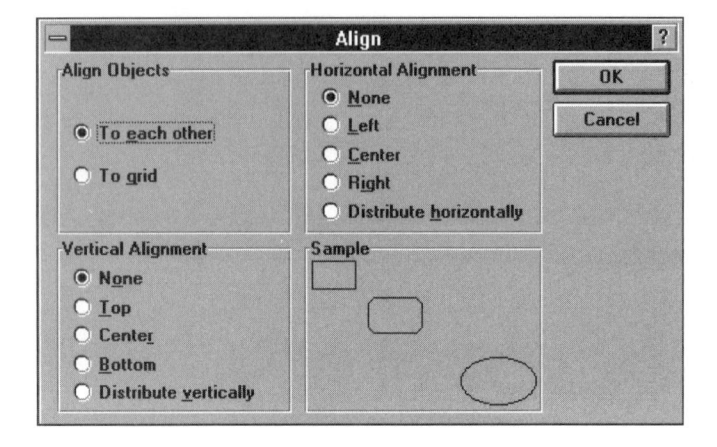

Figure B.69 The Align dialog box.

Use the radio buttons in the Align Objects area to determine if the objects will be aligned with each other or aligned with the lines of the grid. Use the radio buttons in the other areas to determine the vertical and horizontal alignment of the object with the grid, or with each other.

If you select **To Each Other** in the Align Objects area, and you select **Top** in the Vertical Alignment area, the top edges of the objects are lined up with each other. Likewise, if you select **Left** in the Horizontal Alignment area, the left edges of all the objects are lined up with each other.

On the other hand, if you select **To Grid** along with these other radio buttons, these edges of the objects are lined up with the grid lines.

The Distribute Horizontally and Distribute Vertically radio buttons arrange the objects with equal space between them.

The objects in the Sample area are arranged to illustrate the alignment chosen.

Group Command

Select a number of objects, and then choose **Group** from the Object menu to combine all of the selected objects into a group, which must be selected, moved and manipulated as a single object.

UnGroup Command

Select a group of objects you created using the **Group** command, and choose **Ungroup** from the Object menu to separate the objects, so each can be selected and manipulated individually.

Add Field Command

Choose **Add Field** from the Object menu to display the Add Field box. Then you can add Fields to the view by clicking and dragging them from this box.

This command is a toggle, and you can select it again to remove the Add Field box from the screen.

Insert Command

Choose **Insert** from the Object menu and **Todays Date**, **Current Time**, **Page #**, or **Field** from the submenu, to enter the date, time, page number, or value of a field in a text object.

Edit OLE Object Command

Choose **Edit OLE object** from the Object menu to display the source application of an OLE object included in the view, which you can use to edit it.

Fast Format Command

Select an object whose styles and properties you want to apply to other objects, and choose **Fast Format** from the Object menu to copy its style and properties. The pointer is displayed as a paintbrush, and you can simply click other objects to apply the same style and properties to them.

You can continue to select objects and fast format as many of them as you want to. When you are done, choose **Fast Format** from the Object menu again to turn off the Fast Format feature.

The Form Menu

When you display a form in design view and the entire form (rather than an individual object) is selected, the Browse menu is replaced by the Form menu.

Style & Properties Command

Choose **Style & Properties** from the Form menu to display the Info Box. Info Boxes are covered in detail in a later section of this Appendix.

Add Field Command

Choose **Add Field** from the Form menu to display the Add Field box. Then you can add Fields to the view by clicking and dragging them from this box. This command is a toggle, and you can select it again to remove the Add Field box from the screen.

Insert Command

Choose **Insert** from the Form menu and **Todays Date**, **Current Time**, **Page #**, or **Field** from the submenu, to add a text object to the Form which contains the date, time, page number, or value of a field.

Fast Format Command

Choose **Fast Format** from the Form menu to copy the style and properties of the select object. The pointer is displayed as a paintbrush, and you can simply click other views to apply the same style and properties to them. You can continue to select objects and fast format as many of them as you want. When you are done, choose **Fast Format** again to turn off the Fast Format feature.

The Panel Menu for Forms

When you select the repeating panel of a Form, the Browse menu is replaced by the Panel menu.

Style & Properties Command

Choose **Style & Properties** from the Panel menu to display the Info Box. Info Boxes are covered in detail in a later section of this Appendix.

Add Field Command

Choose **Add Field** from the Panel menu to display the Add Field box. Then you can add Fields to the view by clicking and dragging them from this box.

This command is a toggle, and you can select it again to remove the Add Field box from the screen.

Insert Command

Choose **Insert** from the Panel menu and **Todays Date**, **Current Time**, **Page #**, or **Field** from the submenu, to add a text object to the panel which contains the date, time, page number, or value of a field.

Fast Format Command

Select **Fast Format** from the Panel menu to copy the style and properties of the Panel. The pointer is displayed as a paintbrush, and you can simply click other objects to apply the same style and properties to them. You can continue to select objects and fast format as many of them as you want to. When you are done, choose **Fast Format** again to turn off the Fast Format feature.

The Report Menu

When you are working with a report in design mode, the Browse menu is replaced by a Report menu.

Style & Properties Command

Choose **Style & Properties** from the Report menu to display the Info Box. Info Boxes are covered in detail in a later section of this Appendix.

Add Field Command

Choose **Add Field** from the Report menu to display the Add Field box. Then you can add Fields to the view by clicking and dragging them from this box. This command is a toggle, and you can choose it again to remove the Add Field box from the screen.

Add Header Command

Choose **Add Header** from the Report menu to add a Header panel to the report. Objects that you add to the Header panel are printed at the top of each page of the report, and continues to be displayed at the top of the screen when you scroll through the report.

This command is a toggle, and you can choose it again to remove the Header panel from the report. If you do this, all objects in the header panel are also removed from the report and cannot be recovered.

Add Footer Command

Choose **Add Footer** from the Report menu to add a Footer panel to the report. Objects that you add to the Footer panel are printed at the bottom of each page of the report, and continue to be displayed at the bottom of the screen when you scroll through the report.

This command is a toggle, and you can choose it again to remove the Footer panel from the report. If you do this, all objects in the footer panel are also removed from the report and cannot be recovered.

Add Title Page Command

Choose **Add Title Page** from the Report menu to add a title page to the report. Any objects you add to it are printed on a separate page at the beginning of the report.

To view or work with the title page, use the **Show Title Page** command, following.

Insert Command

Choose **Insert** from the Report menu and **Todays Date**, **Current Time**, **Page #**, or **Field** from the submenu, to add a text object that contains the date, time, page number, or value of a field.

Sort Command

Choose **Sort** from the Report menu to display a submenu with the following options:

- Choose **Ascending** to sort in Ascending order on the current field.
- Choose **Descending** to sort in Descending order on the current field.
- Choose **Define** to display the Sort dialog box and use it to define the sort. The Sort dialog box is covered in the section on the *Sort Command* of the browse menu earlier in this Appendix.

You must select a field before you can use the Ascending or Descending option.

Show Title Page Command

Choose **Show Title Page** from the Report menu to view or work with a report's title page. To add the title page, use the **Add Title Page** command, discussed above.

This option is a toggle.

Turn On Columns Command

Choose **Turn On Columns** from the Report menu to work with columns. This command is only included on the menu of columnar reports.

When this option is on, you can select, move, and resize the columns of a report just as you do other objects. The **Show Data** option of the View menu must be on for you to work with columns.

This option is a toggle, and you can choose it again to make it impossible to work with columns.

Fast Format Command

Choose **Fast Format** from the Report menu to copy the style and properties of the Report. The pointer is displayed as a paintbrush, and you can simply click other views to apply the same style and properties to them. You can continue to select objects and fast format as many of them as you want to. When you are done, choose **Fast Format** again to turn off the Fast Format feature.

The Panel Menu for Reports

If you select a panel of a Report in Design mode, such as a Header, Footer, or Summary Panel, the Browse menu is replaced by a Panel menu. This Panel menu has the same options as the Report menu, all of which were discussed in the previous section.

The Mailing Label Menu

When you display a Mailing Label view in Design mode and the entire Mailing Label view (rather than an individual object) is selected, the Browse menu is replaced by the Mailing Label menu.

Style & Properties Command

Choose **Style & Properties** from the Mailing Label menu to display the Info Box. Info Boxes are covered in detail in a later section of this Appendix.

Add Field Command

Choose **Add Field** from the Mailing Label menu to display the Add Field box. You can add Fields to the view by clicking and dragging them from this box. This command is a toggle.

Insert Command

Choose **Insert** from the Mailing Label menu and **Todays Date**, **Current Time**, **Page #**, or **Field** from the submenu, to add a text object to the Mailing Label that contains the date, time, page number, or value of a field.

Sort Command

Choose **Sort** from the Mailing Label menu to display a submenu with the following options:

- Choose **Ascending** to sort in Ascending order on the current field.
- Choose **Descending** to sort in Descending order on the current field.
- Choose **Define** to display the Sort dialog box and use it to define the sort. The Sort dialog box is covered in the section on the *Sort Command* of the Browse menu earlier in this Appendix.

You must select a field before you can use the Ascending or Descending option.

Fast Format Command

Choose **Fast Format** from the Mailing Label menu to copy the style and properties of the selected object. The pointer is displayed as a paintbrush, and you can simply click other objects to apply the same style and properties to them. You can continue to click objects and fast format as many of them as you want to. When you are done, choose **Fast Format** from the Mailing Label menu again to turn off the Fast Format feature.

Appendix B: Reference Guide **537**

The Letter Menu

When you are working on a Form Letter in Design View the Browse menu is replaced with the Letter menu.

Style & Properties Command

Choose **Style & Properties** from the Letter menu to display the Info Box. Info Boxes are covered in detail in a later section of this Appendix.

Add Field Command

Choose **Add Field** from the Letter menu to display the Add Field box. Then you can add Fields to the view by clicking and dragging them from this box. This command is a toggle.

It is best to add fields to form letters as text objects, rather than using this method to add them.

Insert Command

Choose **Insert** from the Letter menu and **Todays Date**, **Current Time**, **Page #**, or **Field** from the submenu, to add the date, time, page number, or value of a field to the letter.

Fast Format Command

Choose **Fast Format** from the Letter menu to copy the style and properties of the selected object. The pointer is displayed as a paintbrush, and you can simply click other views to apply the same style and properties to them. You can continue to select objects and fast format as many of them as you want to. When you are done, choose **Fast Format** from the Letter menu again to turn off the **Fast Format** feature.

The Worksheet Menu

When you are using a worksheet, either in Browse or in Design mode, the Browse menu is replaced by the Worksheet menu.

Because it is displayed in either Browse or Design mode, this menu includes some commands that you are familiar with from the Browse menu, as well as some commands in common with the menus of other types of views and some special worksheet commands.

Style & Properties Command

Choose **Style & Properties** from the Worksheet menu to display the Info Box. Info Boxes are covered in detail in a later section of this Appendix.

Find Command

Choose **Find** from the Worksheet menu to display a submenu with the following options:

- Choose **Find** to display a Find Request—a copy of one row of the current worksheet with no data in it. Enter an example of the data you want to find in one or more fields of this record and press **Enter**. Approach displays only the records that match the example you entered. You can also enter multiple examples or use operators to perform more complex finds, which are described in Chapter 6. This option is equivalent to choosing **Find** from the Browse menu.

- Choose **Find Again** to reuse or modify the last Find you performed. A Find Request is displayed already filled out with the examples of data you entered during the last Find. Leave the examples as they are, or modify them in any way you want, and press **Enter**. Only the records that match the example are displayed. This option is equivalent to choosing **Find Again** from the Browse menu.

- Choose **Find Special** to display the Find Special dialog box, which lets you find records that have or do not have the same data in one or more fields. This option is equivalent to choosing **Find Special** from the Browse menu, and the dialog box.

- Choose **Show All** to display all of the records in the database. This option is equivalent to choosing **Show All** from the Browse menu.

Sort Command

For simple Sorts, move the cursor to the field that you want the sort to be based on. Then choose **Sort** from the Worksheet menu and **Ascending** or

Descending from the submenu to sort on that field in Ascending or Descending order.

For more complex Sorts, choose **Sort** from the Worksheet menu and **Define** from the submenu to use the Sort dialog box to define the sort. This dialog box was discussed earlier in this Appendix, in the section on *Sort Command*.

Records Command

Choose **Records** from the Worksheet menu to display a submenu with the following options:

- Choose **New Record** to add a new blank record to the database.
- Choose **Duplicate Record** to add a new record to the database that is a duplicate of the current record.
- Choose **Hide Record** to hide the selected record or records, so it is not displayed and is not accessible in Reports, Finds, or Sorts.

Delete Command

Choose **Delete Record** from the Worksheet menu to display a submenu with the following options:

- Choose **Selected Records** to delete the selected record or records.
- Choose **Found Set** to delete all the records in the current found set.

Add Field Command

Choose **Add Field** from the Worksheet menu to display the Add Field box. Then you can add a new column to the worksheet by clicking and dragging a them to a field from this box. This command is a toggle.

Add Column Command

Choose **Add Column** from the Worksheet menu to add a new, blank column to the Worksheet. You can use this column to hold a calculation.

Fill Field Command

Choose **Fill Field** from the Worksheet menu to use the Fill Field dialog box. This changes the value of the selected field of all the records in the found set to the value that you enter. This dialog box was discussed earlier in this Appendix, in the section on the *Fill Field Command* of the Browse menu.

Insert Command

Choose **Insert** from the Worksheet menu and **Todays Date**, **Current Time**, or **Previous value** from the submenu, to enter the date, time, or value from the previous record in a field.

Select Command

After you have selected a column of the worksheet, choose **Select** from the Worksheet menu and **Header only** from the submenu to select the column's header. Choose **Select** and **Cells only** from the submenu to select the column's cells.

Edit Column Label Command

After you have selected a column of the worksheet, choose **Edit Column Label** from the Worksheet menu to place an insertion bar in the header, so you can edit the label.

Refresh Command

Choose **Refresh** from the Worksheet menu to display the data with all changes included. This is useful if you are sharing data on a network and other users have made changes.

Fast Format Command

Choose **Fast Format** from the Worksheet menu to copy the style and properties of the selected object. The pointer is displayed as a paintbrush, and you can simply click other objects to apply the same style and properties to them. You can continue to fast format as many objects as you want. When you are done, choose **Fast Format** from the Worksheet menu again to turn off the Fast Format feature.

The Crosstab Menu

When you are using a Crosstab, either in Browse or in Design mode, the Browse menu is replaced by the Crosstab menu.

Because it is displayed in either Browse or Design mode, this menu includes some Commands in common with the Browse menu, the menus of other types of views and some special Crosstab commands.

Style & Properties Command

Choose **Style & Properties** from the Crosstab menu to display the Info Box. Info Boxes are covered in detail in a later section of this Appendix.

Find Command

Choose **Find** to display a submenu with the following options:

- Choose **Find** to display a Find Request. Enter an example of the data you want to find in one or more fields of this record and press **Enter**. Approach displays only the records that match the example you entered. You can also enter multiple examples or use operators to perform more complex finds, which are described in Chapter 6. This option is equivalent to choosing **Find** from the Browse menu.

- Choose **Find Again** to reuse or modify the last Find you performed. Approach displays a Find Request already filled out with the examples of data that you entered during the last Find. Leave the examples as they are, or modify them in any way you want, and press **Enter**. Approach displays only the records that match the example. This option is equivalent to choosing **Find Again** from the Browse menu.

- Choose **Find Special** to display the Find Special dialog box, which lets you find records that have or do not have the same data in one or more fields. This option is equivalent to choosing **Find Special** from the Browse menu.

- Choose **Show All** to display all of the records in the database. This option is equivalent to choosing **Show All** from the Browse menu.

Add Field Command

Choose **Add Field** from the Crosstab menu to display the Add Field box. Then you can add a new column to the Crosstab by clicking and dragging a field from this box. This command is a toggle.

Select Command

After you have selected a column or a row of the Crosstab, choose **Select** from the Crosstab menu and **Header only** from the submenu to select the column's or row's header, or choose **Select** from the Crosstab menu and **Cells only** from the submenu to select the column's or row's cells.

Edit Column Label Command

After you have selected a column of the crosstab, choose **Edit Column Label** from the Crosstab menu to place an insertion bar in the header, so you can edit its label.

Summarize Rows Command

Choose **Summarize Rows** from the Crosstab menu to add a new column to the right of the existing columns of the crosstab, which contains the sum of the values in each row.

Summarize Columns Command

Choose **Summarize Columns** from the Crosstab menu to add a new row under the existing rows of the crosstab, which contains the sum of the values in each column.

Chart Crosstab Command

Choose **Chart Crosstab** from the Crosstab menu to create a chart based on the crosstab. The fields used for the Crosstab's rows are used as the labels of the chart's x-axis. The fields in the columns are used as the basis of its y-axis.

Fast Format Command

Choose **Fast Format** from the Crosstab menu to copy the style and properties of the selected object. The pointer is displayed as a paintbrush, and you can

Appendix B: Reference Guide

simply click other objects to apply the same style and properties to them. You can continue to fast format as many objects as you want. When you are done, choose **Fast Format** again to turn off the Fast Format feature.

The Chart Menu

When you are using a Chart in Design mode, the Browse menu is replaced by the Chart menu. This can be used to work with objects in the Chart, and contains some commands from the Object menus of other views.

Style & Properties Command

Choose **Style & Properties** from the Chart menu to display the Info Box. Info Boxes for charts are part of a mini-application included in a number of Lotus products and are beyond the scope of this book. They are covered in detail in Approach's on-line help.

Chart Data Fields Command

Choose **Chart Data Fields** from the Chart menu to change the fields that the Chart is based on. Approach displays the Chart Data Source Assistant, which has panels like the ones in the Chart Assistant. For a pie chart, use it to change the pie fields. For other types of charts, you can use it to select the fields that are the basis of the x-axis and y-axis and to create a series. These panels were covered earlier in this Appendix, in the section on the *Chart command* of the Create menu.

Arrange Command

Choose **Arrange** from the Chart menu to display a submenu that you can use to change the *stacking order* of objects, which objects seem to be in front of the others. The submenu has the following options:

- Choose **Bring to Front** to make the selected object appear to be in front of all other objects.
- Choose **Send to Back** to make the selected object appear to be behind all other objects.

- Choose **Bring Forward** to make the selected object appear one layer further forward compared with other objects.
- Choose **Send Backward** to make the selected object appear to be one layer further backward compared with other objects.

The Align Command

Select a number of objects that you want Approach to align, and then choose **Align** from the Chart menu to display the Align dialog box, which lets you specify the alignment of the objects. This dialog box was discussed earlier in this section on the *Align Command* of the Object menu.

Group Command

Select a number of objects, and then choose **Group** from the Chart menu to combine all of the selected objects into a group, which must be selected, moved and manipulated as a single object.

UnGroup Command

Select a group of objects that you created using the **Group** command, and then choose **Ungroup** from the Chart menu to separate the objects, so each can be selected and manipulated individually.

Insert Command

Choose **Insert** from the Chart menu and **Todays Date**, **Current Time**, **Page #**, or **Field** from the submenu, to enter the date, time, page number, or value of a field in a text object.

Fast Format Command

Select an object whose styles and properties you want to apply to other objects, and then choose **Fast Format** from the Chart menu to copy its style and properties. The pointer is displayed as a paintbrush, and you can simply click other objects to apply the same style and properties to them.

You can continue to select objects and fast format as many of them as you want. When you are done, choose **Fast Format** from the Chart menu again to turn off the Fast Format feature.

The Tools Menu

The Tools menu includes utilities, used for checking spelling, creating custom menus and icon bars, creating named styles, customizing the Approach environment, and creating and running macros.

Spell Check Command

Choose **Spell Check** from the Tools menu to use Approach's Spell Checker. If you are in Browse mode, it checks the spelling of data. If you are in Design mode, it checks the spelling of field labels and text objects.

How much text it checks depends on the selections you make in the Spell Check dialog box, which is displayed in different forms in Browse mode and Design mode.

The Spell Check in Browse Mode

If you choose **Spell Check** from the Tools menu when you are in Browse mode, the Spell Check dialog box is displayed in the form shown in Figure B.70. You can use the radio buttons to limit the text that it checks:

- *Selection.* Checks only the selected (highlighted) text in the current record. You must select the text before using the spell checker.
- *Current record.* Checks only text in the current record.
- *Found set.* Checks text in all the records of the found set.
- *Selection across found set.* Checks the selected text in every record in the found set.

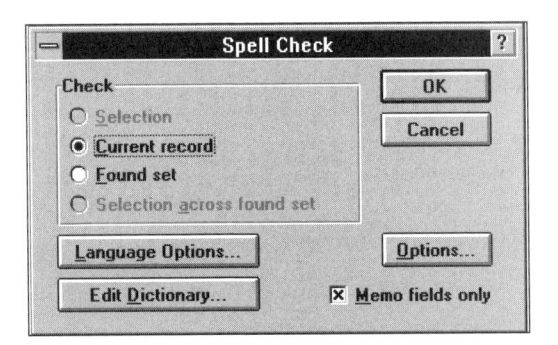

Figure B.70 The Spell Check dialog box in Browse mode.

When you check spelling in Browse mode, the Memo fields only checkbox, which limits the spell check to text in memo fields, is selected by default. You can deselect this check box to check data in other fields.

The Spell Check in Design Mode

If you choose **Spell Check** when you are in Design mode, the Spell Check dialog box is displayed shown in Figure B.71, and it includes the following radio buttons to limit the text that it checks:

- *Selection.* Checks only the selected (highlighted) text in the design of the current view. You must select the text before using the spell checker.
- *Current view.* Checks all field labels and text objects in the current view.

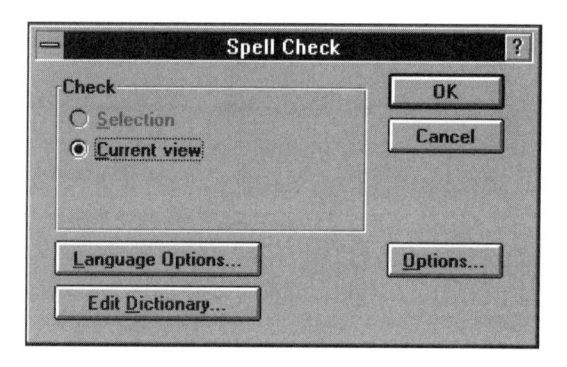

Figure B.71 The Spell Check dialog box in Design mode.

Other Features of the Spell Check Dialog Box

In either case the dialog box includes a Language Options button, which you can use to display a dialog box with a drop-down that lets you select American or British spelling and other options if they are available.

Both also contain an Edit Dictionary button which lets you add words to the user dictionary—the spell checker compares spelling with a main dictionary, which you cannot edit, and a user dictionary, which you create yourself.

Editing the Dictionary

The Edit Dictionary dialog box, displays a list of all the words in the user dictionary (see Figure B.72).

Appendix B: Reference Guide

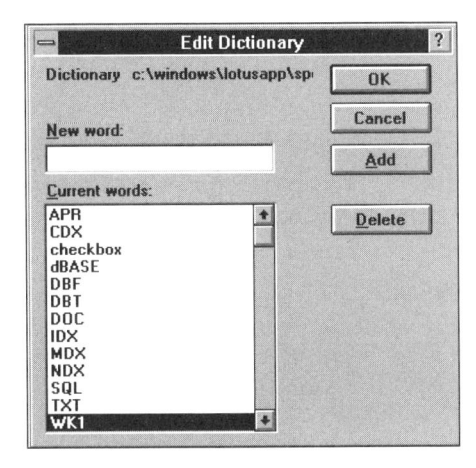

Figure B.72 The Edit Dictionary dialog box.

You can add a word by entering it in the New word box and clicking the **Add** button, or delete a word by selecting it in the Current words list and clicking the **Delete** button.

Correcting Errors

Select **OK** to begin the spell check. When a word in the text is found it is checking that is not in one of its dictionaries, it displays the Spell Check dialog box (see Figure B.73). The word that might be misspelled is displayed in the Unknown word box. If it is incorrect, you can edit it in the Replace with box, or select one of the alternatives that the spell checker suggests to display that word in the replace with box. Then click **Replace** to correct this word or **Replace All** to replace all words that are misspelled in the same way.

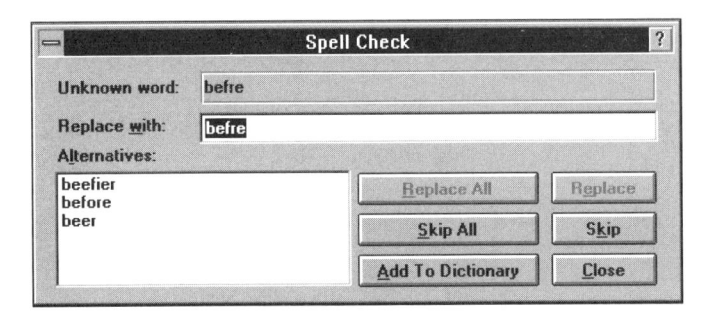

Figure B.73 Correcting a spelling error.

Practical Approach, 3.0

If the Unknown word is not an error, you can click **Skip** to continue without correcting the word or **Skip All** to continue without correcting the word or flagging any future occurrences of it. You can also click **Add to Dictionary** to add the word to the user dictionary, so it is not flagged in future spell checks. It is added to the Current words list in the Edit Dictionary dialog box.

Click **Close** to end the spell check.

Customize Menus Command

Choose **Customize Menus** from the Tools menu to display the Customize Menus dialog box that lets you manage custom menu systems (see Figure B.74).

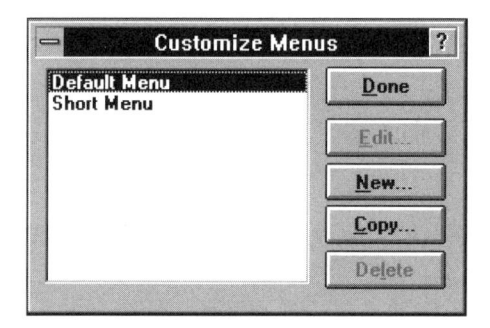

Figure B.74 The Customize Menus dialog box.

This dialog box contains a list of all the existing Menu systems in the current Approach file, which you manage using the following push buttons:

- Select a Menu system in the list and click **Edit** to display the Define Custom Menu Bar dialog box with that Menu system's specifications, so you can modify it.
- Click **New** to display the Define Custom Menu Bar dialog box to create a new Menu system.
- Select a Menu system in the list and click **Copy** to display the Define Custom Menu Bar dialog box with that a copy of that Menu system's specifications. You can change the name and any of its specifications. This is the easiest way to create a Menu system similar to an existing one.

- Select a Menu system in the list and click **Delete** to delete the Menu system.
- Click **Done** to close the dialog box, saving all the changes you made.

The Default Menu and Short Menu system are listed in this dialog box initially, but they cannot be modified or deleted like menu systems you define yourself.

Creating a Custom Menu

When you select **Edit**, **New**, or **Copy** in the Customize Menus dialog box, the Define Custom Menu Bar dialog box is displayed (see Figure B.75).

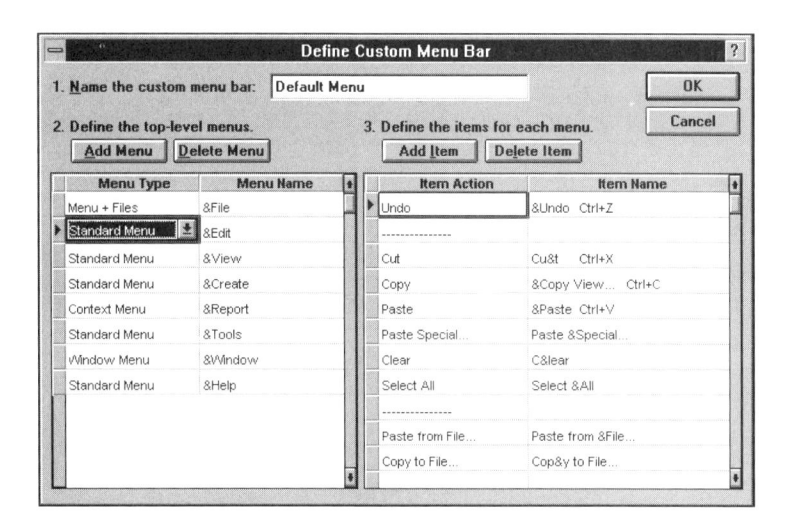

Figure B.75 The Define Custom Menu Bar dialog box.

To create or modify a custom menu:

- Use the Name text box to name the custom menu.
- Use the panel on the left to define the options available on the menu bar displayed at the top of the screen.
- Use the panel to the right to define the pop-up that is associated with each option on the menu bar.

When you place the focus in one of the rows in the left panel, all of the commands on its pop-up are listed in the right panel.

To define the menu bar in the panel on the left use the drop-down in its left column to select among the following the menu types:

- *Standard menu.* Lists the options defined in the panel to the right.
- *Menu + Files.* Lists the options defined in the panel to the right plus the five Approach files opened most recently, like the Approach File menu.
- *Window menu.* Lists all open windows, to let the user switch among them, like the Approach Window menu.
- *Context menu.* Displayed only in certain contexts, like the Approach Form, Report, or Object menu.
- *Macro List.* Lists all macros in the Approach file, so the user can select one to execute it.
- *View List.* Lists all Views in the current menu, so the user can select one to switch to it.

Enter a name for each in the column to its right, which is displayed on the menu bar.

You can modify the entries in this list as you do other lists in Approach dialog boxes:

- Click **Add Menu** to add a new, blank row to this list.
- Click **Delete Menu** to delete the current row from this list.
- Click the selection box to the left of a row to select the row. The row is highlighted to show it is selected.
- Click and drag the selection box of a selected row upward or downward to change the order of records.

When you click any of the items on the top-level menu in the panel on the left, the commands on its pop-up are displayed on the right, if it is one of the types that lets you define commands.

Modify this list in the usual way:

- Click **Add Item** to add a new, blank row to this list.
- Click **Delete Item** to delete the current row from this list.

- Click the selection box to the left of a row to select the row. Then click and drag the selection box of the selected row upward or downward to change the order of records.

Use the drop-down on the left to select the action that the command performs. It includes all of the commands on the standard Approach menu, plus other commands. Enter the name of the command to the right of each, which is included in the menu pop-up.

You can also create hot keys and shortcut keys for menu options:

- *Hot Keys.* To create hot keys, simply include **&** before a character when you enter its name in the Menu Name or Item Name list. If the hot key is used in a menu name, you are able to hold down **Alt** and press the underlined letter on an option on the menu bar to display its pop-up. If the hot key is used on in an item name, after the pop-up is displayed, you are able to press that letter to execute that command. This is the same way that hot keys work in all Windows applications, and hot keys are underlined in custom menus, as they are in other Windows applications.
- *Shortcut Key Combinations.* To create a shortcut key combination, simply type the combination to the right of the Command's name in the Item Name list, separated from the command with spaces if you want. You are able to execute the command instantly by using the key combination. That combination is displayed to the right of the command in the pop-up, as shortcut key combinations are in conventional Windows menus.

The Named Styles Command

To create new Named styles or manage existing ones, switch to Design mode and choose **Named Styles** from the Tool menu to display the Named Styles dialog box (see Figure B.76).

This dialog box contains a list of all the existing Named Styles in the current Approach file and the following push buttons:

- Select a Named Style in the list and click **Edit** to display the Define Named Style dialog box with that Named Style's specifications, so you can modify it.

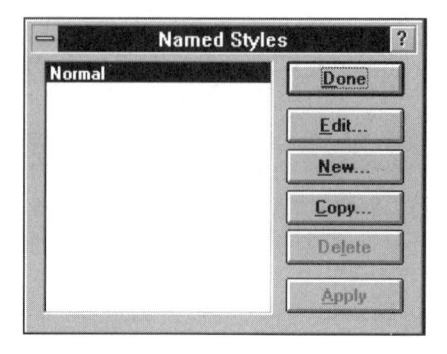

Figure B.76 The Named Styles dialog box.

- Click **New** to display the Define Named Style dialog box to create a new Named Style.
- Select a Named Style in the list and click **Copy** to display the Define Named Style dialog box with a copy of that Named Style's specifications.

  Initially, the Named Style has a name made up of the words **Copy of** followed by the name of the Named Style you copied. You can change the name and any of its specifications. This is the easiest way to create a Named Style similar to an existing one.

- Select a Named Style in the list and click **Delete** to delete the Named Style.
- Click **Apply** to Apply the selected Named Style to the selected objects in a view. You must select the objects before choosing Named Styles from the Tool menu to display this dialog box.
- Click **Done** to close the dialog box, saving all the changes you made. When you select **Edit** or **New** in the Named Style dialog box, the Define Style dialog box is displayed (see Figure B.77).

Use the text box of the Style name drop-down to enter a name for a new style or edit the name of an existing one. Or use this drop-down to select any existing style and display all of its specifications in the panels below.

Use the Based on drop-down to select an existing named style to be used as the basis of the style you are defining. All of its specifications are listed in the panels below.

Appendix B: Reference Guide   **553**

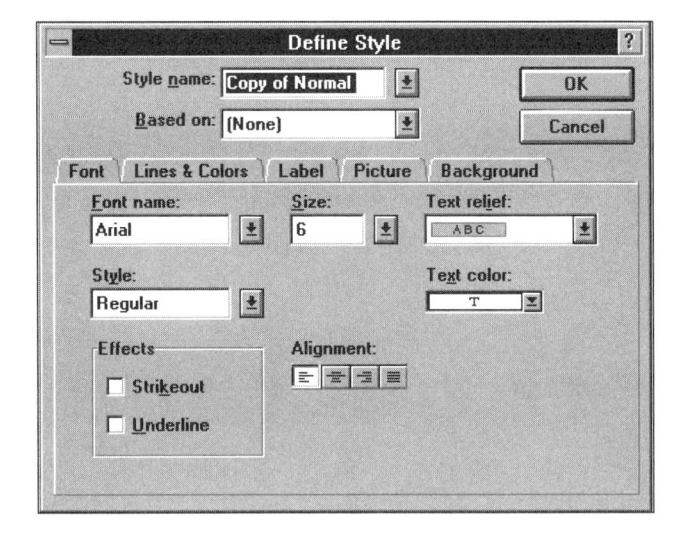

Figure B.77   The Define Style dialog box.

The Font Panel

The Font panel of the Define Style dialog box controls the following properties:

- *Font name.* Select a font, such as **Arial** or **Roman**, from the Font name list. The options available in this lists depend on which fonts you have installed under Windows.
- *Style.* Select styles such as **Bold** or **Italic** from the Style drop-down. Select **Regular** to remove these styles.
- *Effects.* Use the Effects checkboxes to Underline or Strikethrough text.
- *Size.* Select a size expressed in points from the Size list.
- *Alignment.* Use the Alignment buttons in the Alignment area to specify if the text should be centered within its text frame, or aligned to the left or right edge of the text frame.
- *Text color.* This drop-down displays a color palette, which lets you select the color of the letters used in the text object.
- *Text relief.* Use this drop-down to select effects that make the text appear to be carved into or raised above its background.

The Lines & Colors Panel

The Lines and Colors panel of the Define Style dialog box lets you specify the following settings for lines and colors (see Figure B.78).

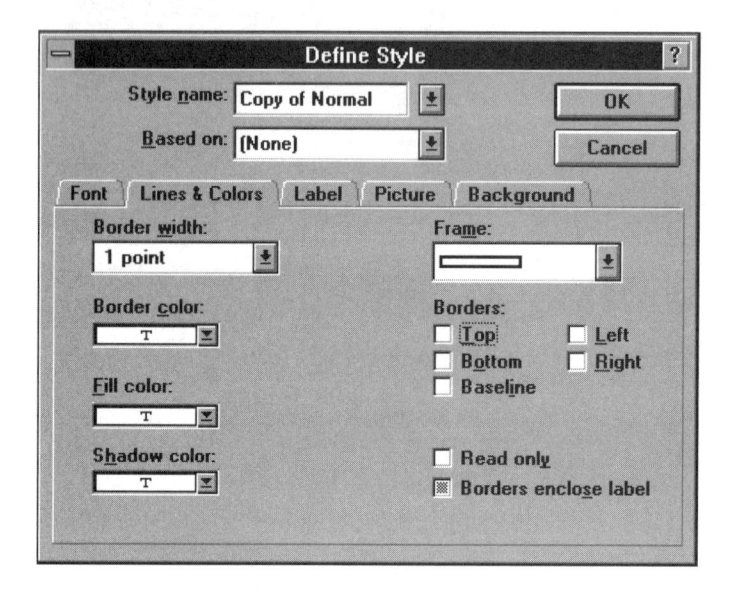

Figure B.78 The Lines and Colors panel.

- *Border width.* Use this drop-down to select a border width between hairline and 12 points,
- *Border color, Fill color, and Shadow color.* All of these drop-downs display color palettes that you can use to select the color of the object's border, its fill color, and the color of its shadow. All these palettes display a variety of colors, and you can click one to select it. The sample color on their upper left appears white but has the letter T in it to indicate that it is transparent. Choosing this color lets you see whatever is behind the object. If you select **T** as the shadow color, the object's shadow is invisible.
- *Frame.* The frame drop-down displays graphics that let you use a solid line, double line, or several types of dotted lines for frames or to use shading that gives the frame a raised or lowered appearance.

- *Borders.* Use the borders checkboxes to specify whether to display the Top, Bottom, Left and Right border of the object, and whether to display a baseline under the text in the object.
- *Read only.* Select the Read only checkbox to prevent users from editing the object.
- *Borders enclose label.* Select this checkbox to make the borders enclose the label of a field. If it is not selected, the borders only enclose the data entry area for the field.

The Label Panel

The Label panel of the Define Style dialog box is used primarily to control the Font of the label of a field object (see Figure B.79). It has the same features as the Font Panel, described above.

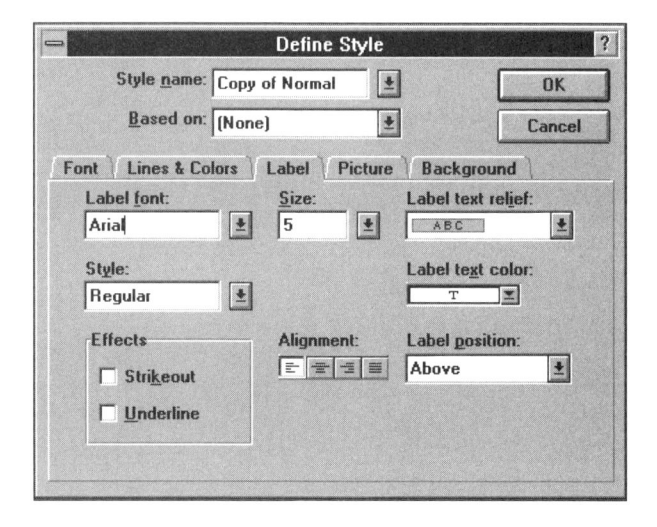

Figure B.79 The Label panel.

It also lets you control the location of the label. Use the Label position drop-down to specify that the label should be above, below, left or right of the object, or that the object should have no label. This drop-down also has a Don't change option which lets you apply a style to an object but keep the original location of its label.

The Picture Panel

The Picture Panel of the Define Style dialog box is used to specify how Approach handles pictures that do not fit in the frame you created for the PicturePlus field that holds them (see Figure B.80).

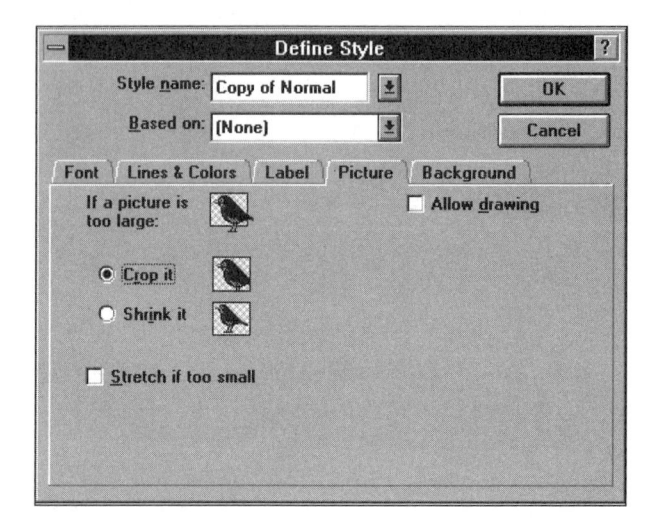

Figure B.80 The Picture panel.

The radio buttons give you two options for handling pictures that are too large to fit in their frame:

1. You can crop the picture, so that it remains its original size but not all of it is displayed.
2. You can shrink it, so all of it is displayed but in reduced size.

The checkbox gives you options for handling pictures that are too small. Select it to stretch the picture proportionally to fill the entire frame, or leave it unselected to leave the picture its original size.

In addition, you can use **Allow Drawing** to be selected or deselected to control whether the user can draw a picture in the field with the mouse, as described in Chapter 3.

The Background Panel

The background panel of the Define Style dialog box controls features of the background of a view (see Figure B.81). Its features are also included in the Lines & Colors panel, described above, but in this panel they are used to control the borders, fill color, and shadow color of an entire page of the view, rather than of an object within the view.

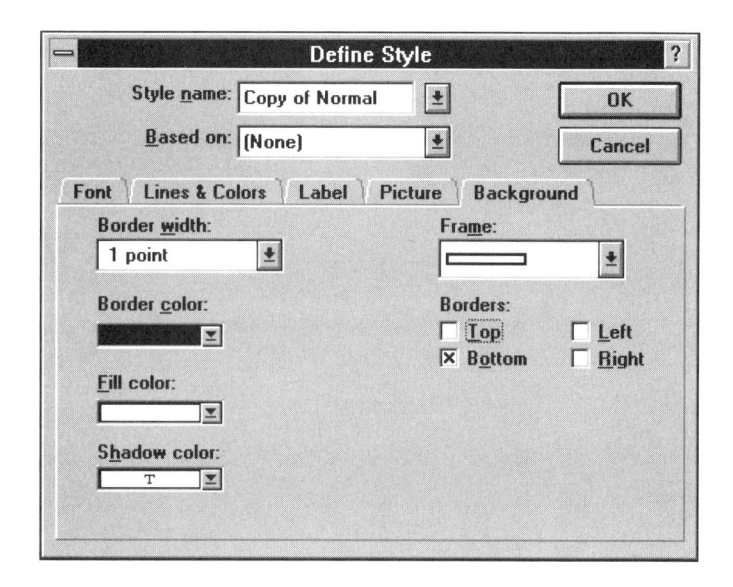

Figure B.81 The Background panel.

SmartIcons Command

Choose **SmartIcons** from the Tools menu to display the SmartIcons dialog box, which is used to create custom Icon Bars (see Figure B.82).

If necessary, use the drop-down at the top of this dialog box to select the name of the Icon bar you want to customize. The icons are displayed in the list below this drop-down.

All of the icons that you can include in custom icon bars are displayed in the Available icons list, at the left of this dialog box. This includes many icons that are not available in any of the default icon bars. It begins with a Spacer icon, used to add a space half the width of an icon between icons to group them.

Practical Approach, 3.0

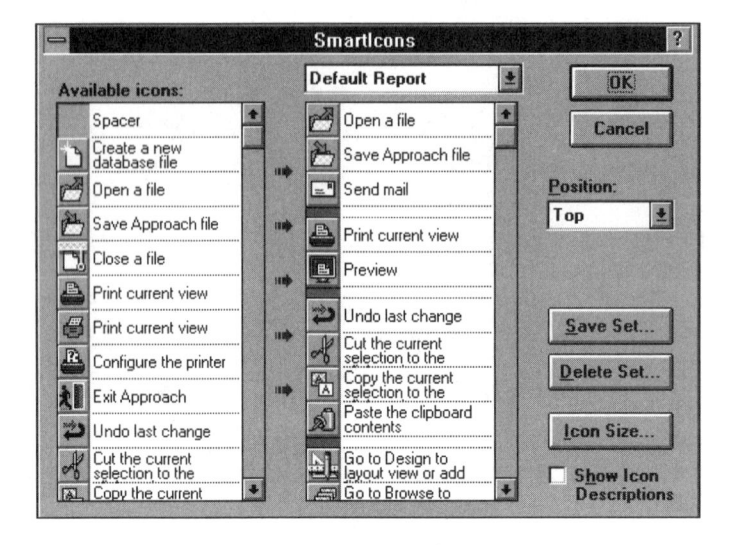

Figure B.82 The SmartIcons dialog box.

You can modify an icon bar in the following ways:

- To add an icon, click and drag one of the icons from the Available icons list to the list of icons in the icon bar.
- To remove an icon, click and drag one of the icons from the list of icons in the icon bar to the Available icons list.
- To change the order of icons, click and drag icons up or down in the list of icons in the icon bar.
- To change the size of icons, click **Icon Size** to display the Icon Size dialog box, which you can use to select the size you want.

To name a new set of icons, click the **Save Set** button. Approach displays the Save Set of SmartIcons dialog box, where you can enter the name. The new set is added to the list names in the drop-down at the top of the SmartIcons dialog box.

You can select **OK** to save changes you made in the current set of icons, or select **Save Set** to create a set with a new name in addition to the current icon set.

To delete a set of icons, select it in the drop-down and click **Delete Set**.

Use the **Position** drop-down to specify whether icons are at the left, right, top or bottom of the screen or to create a floating icon bar, which the user can click and drag to any location on the screen.

If you click **Show Icon Descriptions**, the help balloon for an icon is displayed whenever you move the pointer to it. By default, as you know, the balloons are displayed when you right-click an icon.

To use custom icons, click the SmartIcons box of the status bar to display a pop-up menu with the names of the icon bars that you created and of standard icon bars distributed with Approach.

Preferences Command

Choose **Preferences** from the Tools menu to display the Preferences dialog box, which you can use to customize many different aspects of the Approach environment.

The Display Panel

Use the Display panel to specify whether certain features of the Approach interface should be displayed (see Figure B.83).

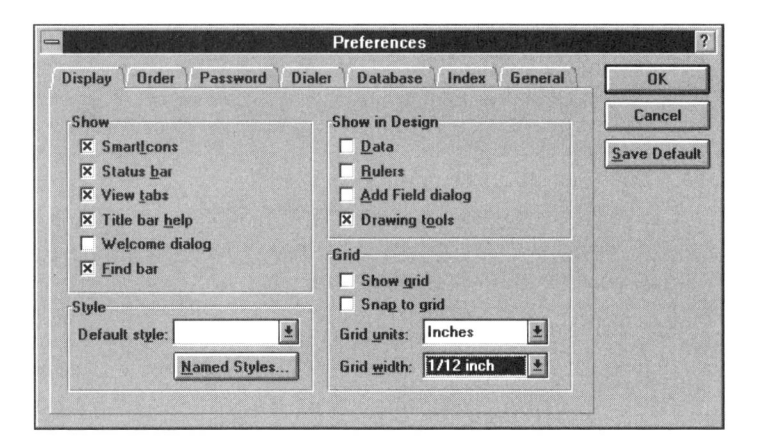

Figure B.83 The Display Panel.

The Show area determines whether the Icon bar, the Status bar, the View tabs, the Help messages displayed in the Title bar, the Welcome dialog box, and the special icon bar for Finds should be displayed.

The Style area lets you select a named style to be used as the default style when you create views. Named Styles were covered earlier in this chapter.

The Show in Design area lets you specify whether Approach should Show Data, Rulers, the Add Field box, and the Drawing tools by default in Design mode. You can see in the illustration that Data and the Drawing tools are displayed by default, as you saw when you worked in Design mode.

The Grid area lets you specify whether Show grid and Snap to Grid are on by default, and also lets you specify the fineness of the grid. You can use the Grid units drop-down to determine whether the space between the grid lines should be measured in Inches or Centimeters, and then select the actual size of the space between gridlines from the Grid width drop-down.

The Order Panel

Use the Order panel to select a default Sort order for your records (see Figure B.84). Use it like the Sort dialog box, which was described in the section on the *Sort Command* of the Browse menu. Add the Fields that you want to use as the basis of the sort order to the Fields to sort on list, and select the **Ascending** or **Descending** radio button for each. Records are displayed in this order, if you do not sort them in some other way.

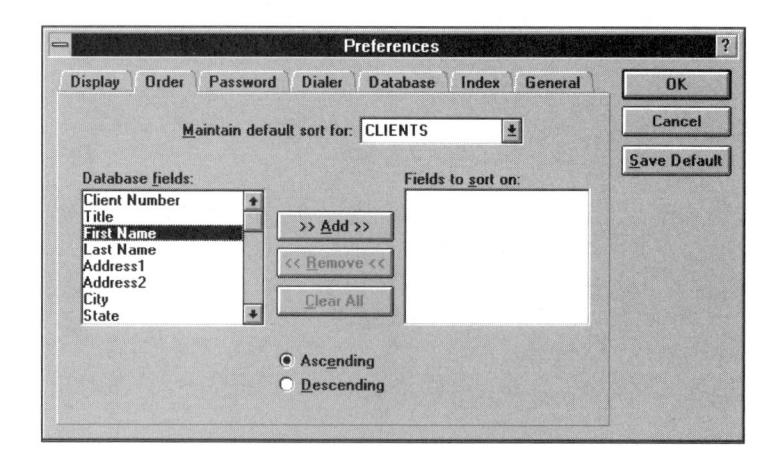

Figure B.84 The Order panel.

The Password Panel

Use the Password panel to create or change the Password for the Approach file (see Figure B.85).

Appendix B: Reference Guide

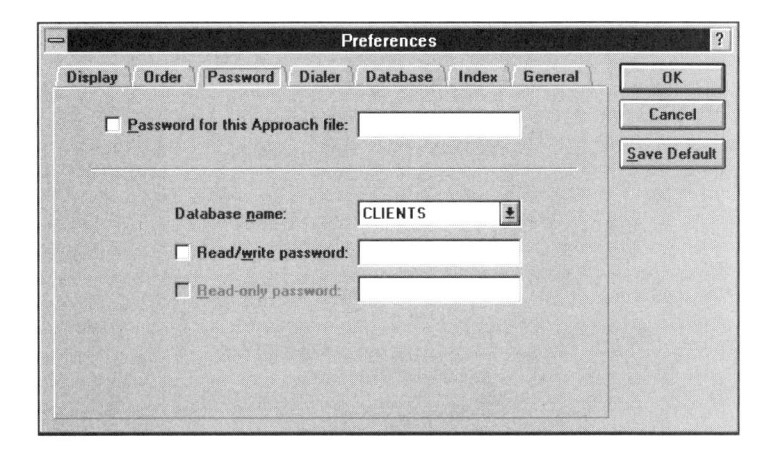

Figure B.85 The Password panel.

The top half of this panel lets you create password protection for the Approach file, which is used to prevent other Approach users from changing the design of views in this Approach file.

The bottom half of this dialog box lets you create two different levels of password protection for the data files underlying the Approach file. They are both used primarily to prevent unauthorized users from accessing the data on a network:

- Select **Set Read/Write Password** to make Approach ask for a password every time a database is opened. Enter the password in the text box to its right. The user must enter the password to have any access to the data at all.
- If you have created a Read/Write password, you can also create a second password, which gives users who know it the ability to view the data but not to modify it. To do so, select **Set Read Only Password** and enter a password in the text box to its right.

Approach displays either of these passwords as a series of asterisks, rather than displaying what you typed.

After you enter a password in any of these text boxes, when you click or tab to another control, Approach displays the Confirm Password dialog box. You must reenter the password in the Retype Password text box and select **OK** to create the password.

The Dialer Panel

Use the Dialer panel to setup Approach's autodialer to work with your modem (see Figure B.86). The Autodialer was discussed in Chapter 10. Use the drop-downs to specify the port and baud rate of your modem, and the text boxes to specify dialing preferences. Use the Dial Type radio buttons to dial using tones, as a touch-tone phone does, or to dial using a pulse, as old fashioned dial phones do.

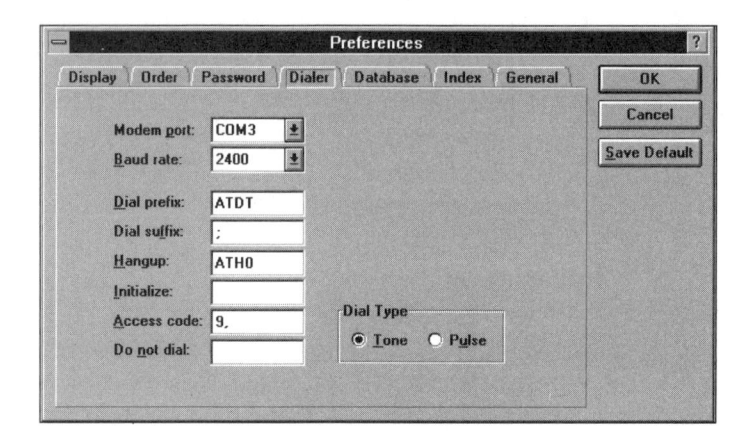

Figure B.86   The Dialer panel.

The Database Panel

The database panel is displayed in several different forms, which let you set preferences for different types of data files.

Preferences for Xbase Files

If you are using a dBASE or FoxPro file, Approach displays the Database panel in the form shown in Figure B.87 to let you set database preferences.

Select the database that you want them to apply to from the Database name drop-down. Use the checkbox to make a database read only, and the radio buttons to select its character set.

Use **Compress** to permanently remove records from a dBASE or FoxPro database. When you delete records from this type of file, they are marked for deletion but are not removed from the file. Though they cannot be accessed in

Approach, they can still be viewed if you use dBASE or FoxPro. This button makes a new copy of the file without the extra records, so they are permanently removed from the file. It is equivalent to using the PACK command in dBASE or FoxPro.

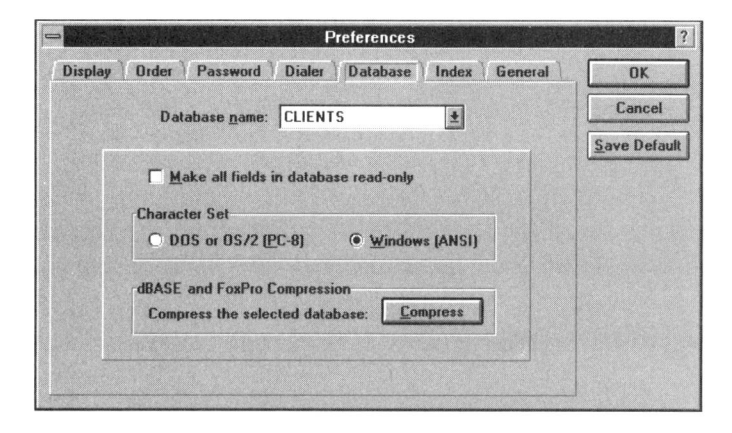

Figure B.87 The Database pane for Xbase databases.

Preferences for Paradox Files

The Preferences panel for Paradox files has many of the same options as the Preferences Panel for Xbase files, discussed in the previous section, though it does not have a Compress button (see Figure B.88). It also has radio buttons that let you specify whether Finds are case sensitive.

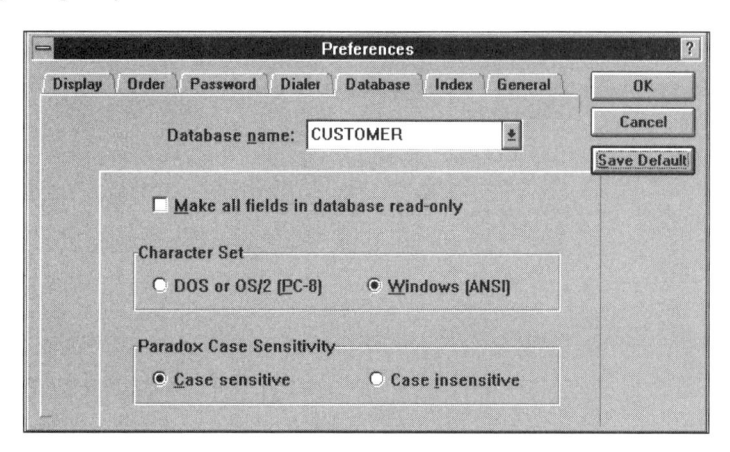

Figure B.88 The Database panel for Paradox databases.

Preferences for SQL Tables

The Preferences panel for SQL tables has three checkboxes that you can use to set three options:

1. *Read only.* Select this checkbox to make tables read only.
2. *Include system tables.* Select this checkbox to include SQL systems tables in the lists of file names in Approach dialog boxes.
3. *Cache table name.* Select this checkbox to cache the table name the first time you open a SQL table.

You may use the drop-down at the top of this dialog box to select any SQL table, but preferences that you select apples to all SQL tables that you create or use in Approach.

The Index Panel

The Index Panel differs for Xbase and Paradox Files.

Indexes for Xbase Files

If you are using dBASE or FoxPro databases, Approach displays an Index panel that lets you select dBASE and FoxPro indexes to be updated when you edit the database in Approach (see Figure B.89). Indexes must be updated if you are sharing files with dBASE or FoxPro users.

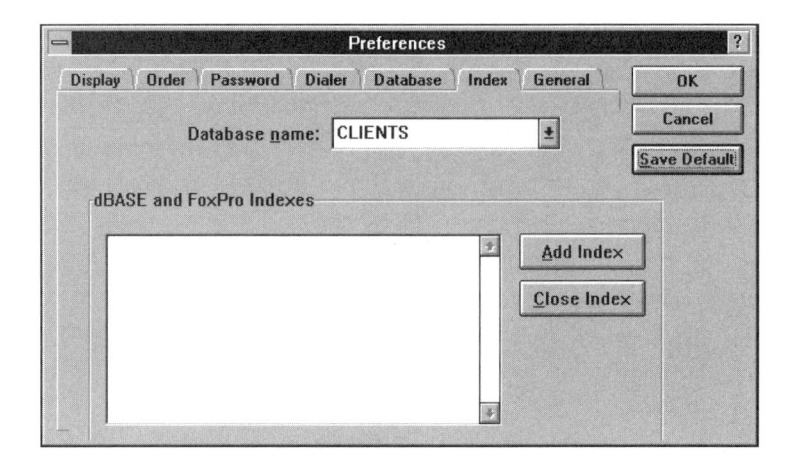

Figure B.89 The Index panel for Xbase databases.

Use the Database name drop-down to select the database. Click **Add Index** to display an Open dialog box, and use it to select indexes of that database. dBASE has indexes with the extensions NDX (single index files) and MDX (multiple index files). FoxPro has indexes with the extensions IDX (single index files) and CDX (multiple index files).

If you no longer want an index updated, select it from the list and click **Close Index**.

Indexes for Paradox Files

If you are using a Paradox file, the Index panel lets you create secondary indexes (see Figure B.90).

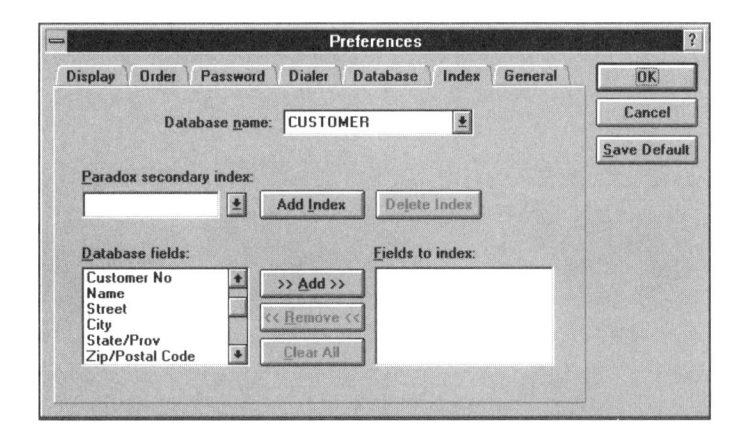

Figure B.90   The Index panel for Paradox databases.

A Paradox database has a primary index based on its key field; you must always specify a key field when you use a Paradox database in Approach.

Paradox also lets you use secondary indexes to speed queries and sorts. Approach can sort a large database alphabetically by name in less time, for example, if you create a secondary index based on the Last Name and First Name field.

To create an index, click **Add Index** and enter its name in the Paradox secondary index list. Then select the fields that the index should be based on in the Database fields list and click **Add** to add them to the Fields to index list, or simply double-click them to add them to this list. As with other field pickers, you can remove a field from the Fields to index list by selecting it and clicking **Remove** or simply by double-clicking it.

To modify an existing index, use the drop-down to select it in the Paradox secondary index list, and use **Add** and **Remove** to change the fields in the Fields to index list.

To delete an index, use the drop-down to select it in the Paradox secondary index list, and click **Delete Index**.

Approach automatically maintains all Paradox indexes. You do not decide which should be maintained, as you do with Xbase indexes.

The General Panel

Use the General panel to set miscellaneous preferences (see Figure B.91). The check boxes let you:

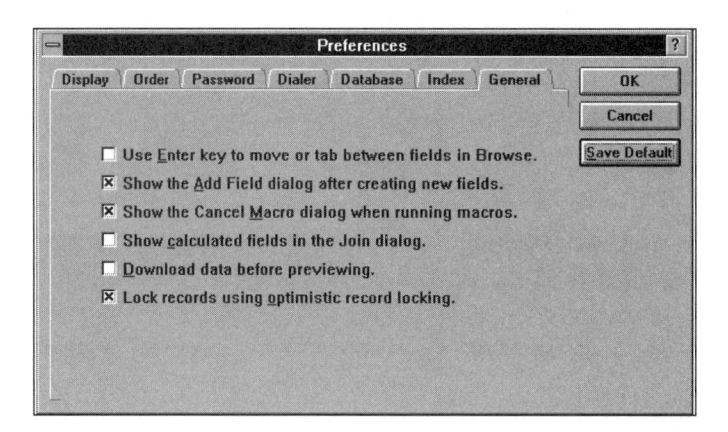

Figure B.91 The General Panel

- Use the enter key as well as the tab key to move among fields in Browse mode.
- Show the Add Fields box after creating new fields, so you can add the fields to existing views. (This is on by default).
- Display a dialog box that lets you cancel macros when they are running. (This is on by default.)

- Show calculated fields in the Join dialog box, so they can be used to relate databases.
- Download data before previewing.
- Use optimistic record locking.

The final two of these are useful only on networks.

Macros Command

Choose **Macros** from the Tools menu to display the Macros dialog box, which is used to manage existing Macros as well as to create new ones (see Figure B.92).

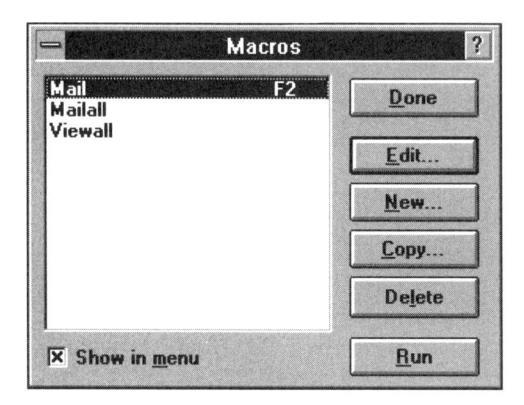

Figure B.92 The Macros dialog box.

It contains a list of all the existing Macros in the current Approach file and the following push buttons:

- Select a macro in the list and click **Edit** to display the Define Macro dialog box with that macro's specifications, so you can modify it.
- Click **New** to display the Define Macro dialog box to create a new macro.
- Select a macro in the list and click **Copy** to display the Define Macro dialog box with a copy of that macro's specifications. Initially, the macro has a name made up of the words **Copy of** followed by the name of the

macro you copied. You can change the name and any of its specifications. This is the easiest way to create a macro similar to an existing one.

- Select a macro in the list and click **Delete** to delete the Macro.
- Select a macro in the list and click **Run** to run the Macro.
- Click **Done** to close the dialog box, saving all the changes you made.

When you select **New**, **Edit**, or **Copy** in the Macros dialog box, you can create or modify a macro using the Define Macro dialog box (see Figure B.93). As you can see from the figure, you use this dialog box to create a list of commands and to select options for each. When you run the Macro, Approach executes all the commands in the order they are listed.

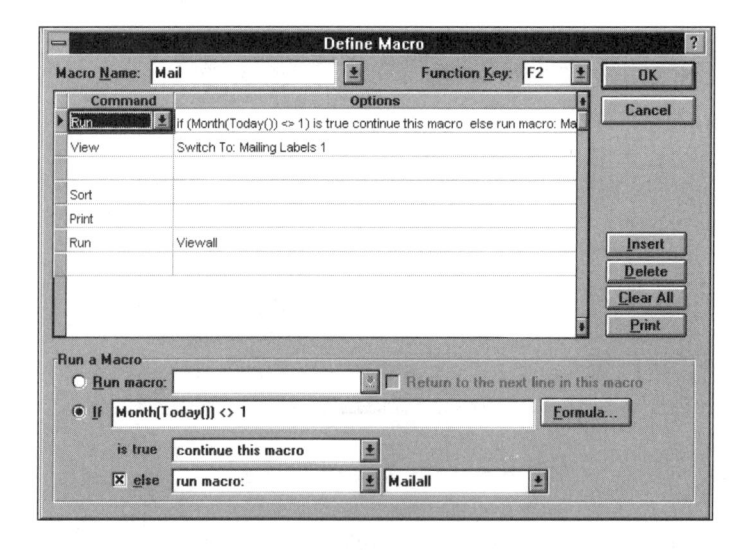

Figure B.93 The Define Macro dialog box.

You can enter the name of a new macro in the Macro Name text box, or use the drop-down arrow to its right to select the name of an existing macro and display its actions in the list, so that you can modify it.

If you want to be able to run the Macro by pressing a function key, simply select that key from the Function Key drop-down.

Use the Command drop-down to select one of the commands that macros can perform. Most of these Commands have options that are displayed in the panel in the bottom of the dialog box when you select the command from the drop-down. All these commands and options are described below.

Options that you choose from this panel are displayed in the Options column of the Command list, to the right of each Command.

Add as many Commands as you want to the list in the same way, and specify options for each one. Approach always adds one blank row to the end of the list so you can add more commands.

You can change the order of commands already in the command list as you do in the Field List of the Field definition dialog box:

- Click **Insert** to add a blank row above the current row.
- Select a row by clicking the indicator box to its left and click **Delete** to delete the row.
- Select a row by clicking the indicator box to its left and then click and drag the indicator box up or downward to move the row to another location in the list.
- Select **Clear All** to delete all the commands in the list.
- Select **Print** to display the Print dialog box and print the list. This can be useful for debugging, to let you look at the list while you are running the macro.

Approach automatically adds certain commands, such as Finds and switches of view, to this list if you perform them before using the Define Macro dialog box.

You can use the Command drop-down to include the following commands in Macros.

Browse

Select **Browse** from the drop-down to switch to Browse mode. This is equivalent to choosing Browse from the View menu.

This command has no options.

Close

Select **Close** from the drop-down to close the current Approach file.

This command has an option to automatically disconnect from the server if you are on a network.

Delete

Select **Delete** from the drop-down to delete records or a file (see Figure B.94).

This Command has the following options:

- Delete the current record.
- Delete all the records in the found set. Remember that you can include a Find in the macro before using the delete command.
- Delete a file. You can enter the name of the file in the text box or use the Files button to display a dialog box that lets you select it.

By default, Approach displays a warning dialog box that lets you cancel the delete, but the checkbox in this panel lets you bypass the warning and delete the records or file immediately.

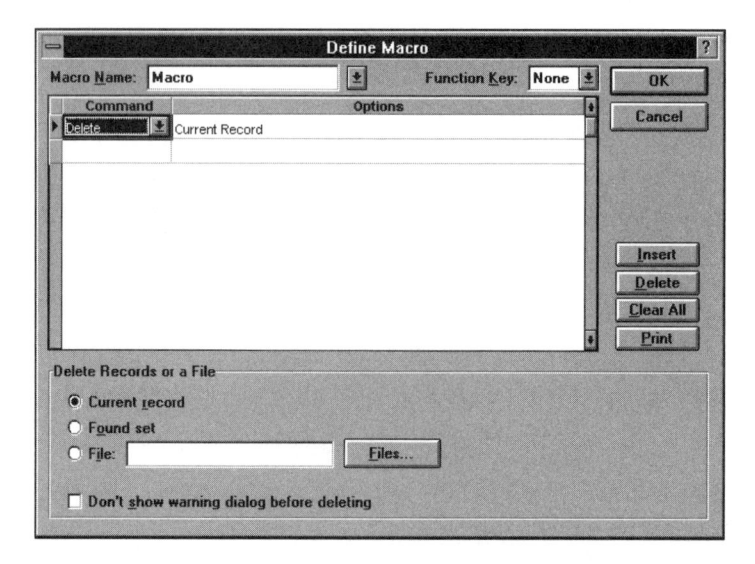

Figure B.94 Options for the Delete Command.

Dial

Select **Dial** from the drop-down to dial the telephone number in a field, assuming that you have a modem.

The options panel for this command displays a list of database fields, and you must select the field that holds the telephone number. Approach autodials the number in the current record.

Edit

Select **Edit** from the drop-down to use any one of a number of editing commands.

The **Edit** Command has the options **Cut**, **Copy**, **Paste**, and **Select All**, which work in the same way as the equivalent commands of the Edit menu (see Figure B.95).

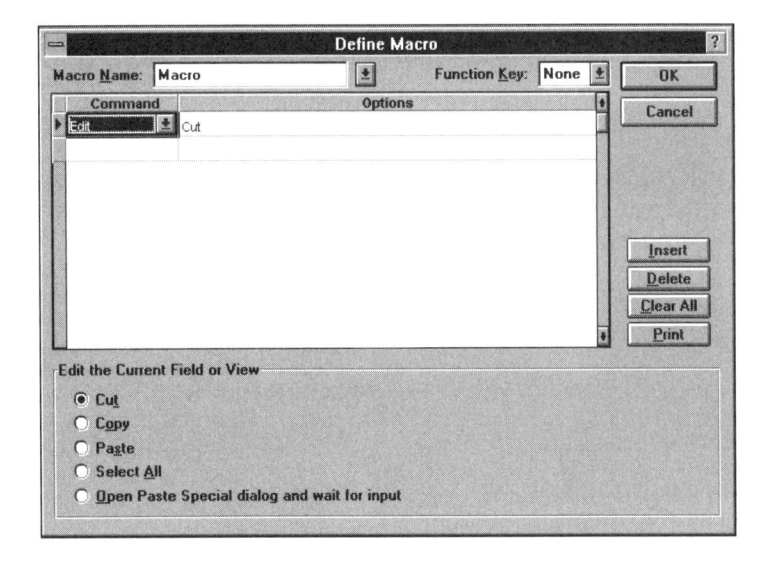

Figure B.95 Options for the Edit Command.

These are used in combination with each other. You can use Edit with the **Select All** option and then Edit with the **Copy** option to select and copy all the objects in a design. Later in the macro, use Edit with the **Paste** option to paste those objects in a different Approach file.

Enter

The **Enter** command of the drop-down is equivalent to pressing the **Enter** key.

This command has no options.

Exit

Select **Exit** from the drop-down to quit Approach. This is equivalent to choosing **Exit** from the File menu.

This command has no options.

Export

Select **Export** from the drop-down to export data so it can be used by another application. This command has two options:

* Display the Export Data dialog box as the Macro is running, so the user can specify how the data is exported.
* Set the Export options while you are defining the macro.

This is equivalent to choosing **Export Data** from the File menu.

Find

Select **Find** to have the macro find a set of records (see Figure B.96). This Command has the following options:

- *Perform stored find.* You must click **New Find** or **Edit Find** while you are defining the macro, to display a find request and enter criteria for the find. The macro performs this find automatically,.
- *Go to Find.* Displays a Find request while the macro is running and waits for the user to fill it out and press **Enter**. This is equivalent to choosing **Find** from the Browse menu.
- *Find Again.* A Find request is displayed with the criteria from the previous Find. This is equivalent to choosing **Find Again** from the Browse menu.
- *Show all.* Displays all the records. This is equivalent to choosing **Show All** from the Browse menu.

- *Refresh the found set.* The current data in the found set is displayed, including changes that may have been made by other users of the network. This is equivalent to choosing **Refresh** from the Browse menu.

In addition to one of the above, you may specify a different macro to run if there are no records that match the criteria of the Find—choose **When no records are found** and select a macro from the drop-down to its right.

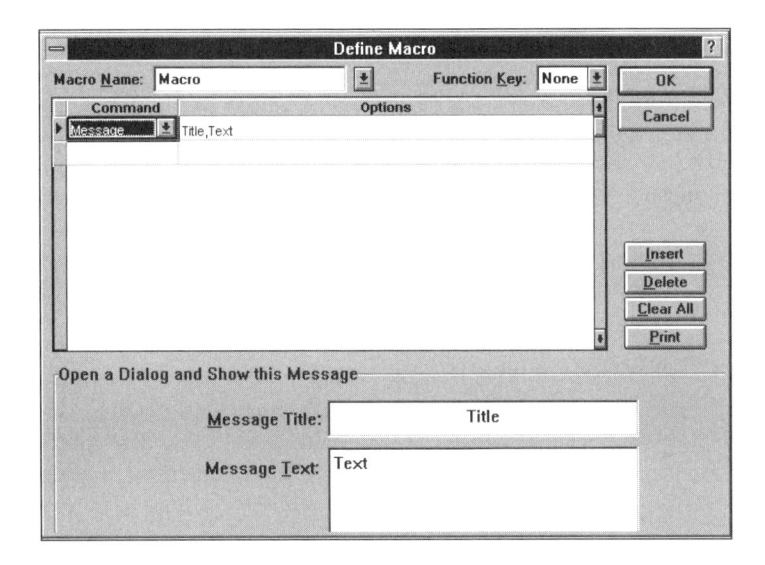

Figure B.96 Options for the Find Command.

Find Special

Select **Find Special** from the drop-down to find duplicate or unique records. This is equivalent to choosing **Find Special** from the Browse menu, covered in Chapter 6.

The Command options are:

- Displays the Find Special dialog box and wait for the user's input.
- Displays the Find Special dialog box while you are defining the Macro. When the macro runs, it automatically performs the options you specify.

With either of these, you may specify a different macro to run if there are no records that match the criteria of the Special Find—choose **When no records are found** and select a macro from the drop-down to its right.

Import

Select **Import** from the drop-down to import data so it can be used by another application. This command has two options:

* Displays the Import Data dialog box as the Macro is running, so the user can specify what data is imported.
* Sets the Import options while you are defining the macro.

This is equivalent to choosing **Import Data** from the File menu, which is covered in Chapter 12.

Mail

Select **Mail** from the drop-down to send a Mail message

This command has two options:

1. Displays the Send Mail dialog box as the Macro is running, so the user can specify the message and where the mail is sent, as well as how the data is exported.
2. Sets the Send Mail options while you are defining the macro.

How this command is used depends on what mail application you have installed.

Menu Switch

Select **Menu Switch** from the drop-down to change the menu bar.

This Command has a drop-down that lets you display the Default menu, the Short menu, or a custom menu, and a button that lets you display the Customize menus dialog box to create a custom menu.

Message

Select **Message** from the drop-down to display a dialog box with a message for the user.

Appendix B: Reference Guide   **575**

This Command this command has text boxes where you can enter a title for the dialog box and the text for the message that it displays (see Figure B.97).

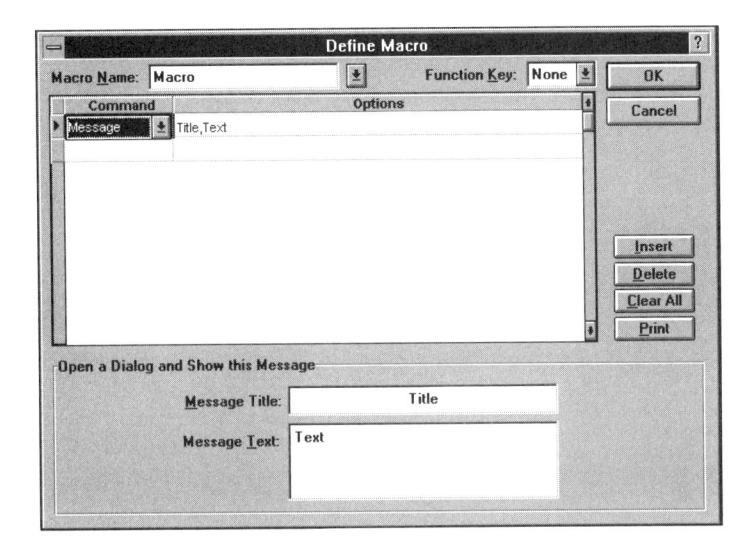

Figure B.97   Options for the Message Command.

Open

Select **Open** from the drop-down to Open a File.

This command is equivalent to choosing **Open** from the File menu and has two options:

* Displays the File Open Export Data dialog box as the Macro is running, so the user can choose the file to be opened.
* Specifies the file to open while you are defining the macro.

This is equivalent to choosing **Open** from the File menu.

Preview

Select **Preview** from the drop-down to switch to Preview mode.

This command is equivalent to choosing **Preview** from the File menu and has no options.

Print

Select **Print** from the drop-down to print the current view.

This command has two options:

- Displays the Print dialog box as the Macro is running, so the user can specify print options if necessary.
- Specifies the Print options while you are defining the macro.

This is equivalent to choosing **Print** from the File menu.

Records

Select **Records** from the drop-down to move among, hide or duplicate records.

This Command has options that let you go to various records in the database, create a new (blank) record, Hide the current record, or duplicate the current record (see Figure B.98).

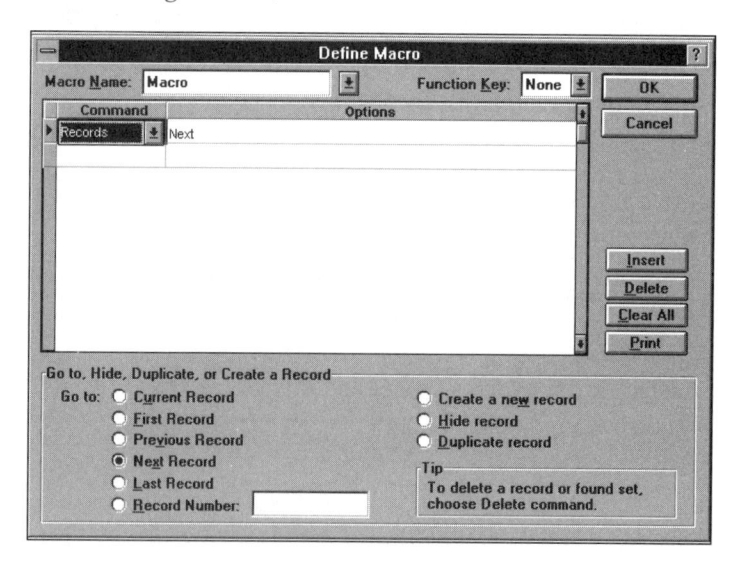

Figure B.98 Options for the Records Command.

Replicate

Select **Replicate** from the drop-down to Replicate a Notes Database. This command has two options:

Appendix B: Reference Guide

- Displays the Replicate dialog box as the Macro is running, so the user can specify replication options.
- Sets the Replication options while you are defining the macro.

Run

Select **Run** from the drop-down to run another macro from within the current macro (see Figure B.99).

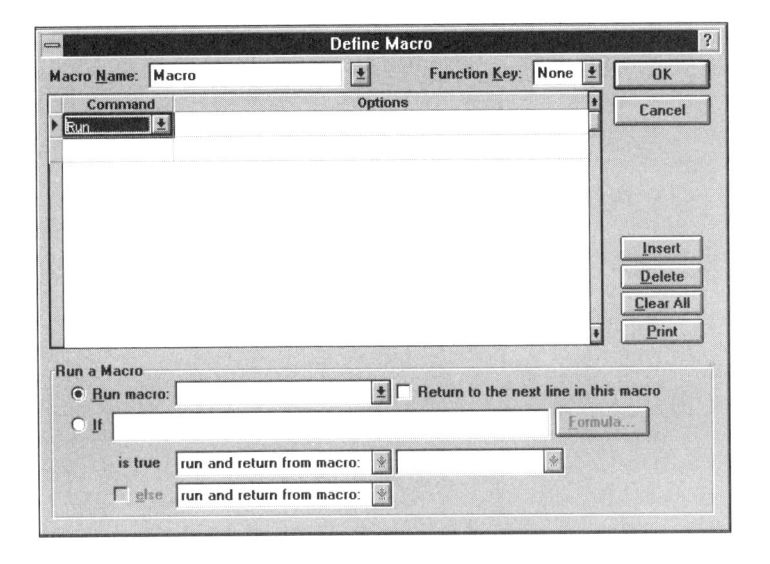

Figure B.99 Options for the Run Command.

This Command has radio buttons that let you choose between two basic options:

- *Run Macro.* Run a macro you select from the drop-down. Select the checkbox to its right to return to the next line of this macro after running the macro you selected.
- *If.* Run a macro only if a formula is true.

To create a conditional macro, enter the formula in the text box or click the Formula button to use the Formula dialog box to generate it. This formula should return the value True or False.

Use the drop down to choose among several alternatives if the formula is true:

- *Run macro.* Use the drop-down to the right to select a macro to run if the formula is true.
- *Run macro and return.* Use the drop-down to the right to select a macro to run if the formula is true, and return to the next line in the current macro after it is done.
- *Continue this macro.* Run the remainder of the current macro.
- *End this macro. Do* not run the remainder of the macro.

You also have the option of selecting **Else** and using the drop-down to its right to select some other alternative if the macro is false. This drop-down has the same options as the one above it, so you can run a different macro, run and return from a different macro, continue running this macro, or end this macro if the formula is false.

Save

Select **Save** from the drop-down to save the current Approach file.

This Command has two options:

- Save the current file under its own name. This is equivalent to choosing **Save Approach File** from the File menu.
- Display the Save As dialog box so the user can save a copy of the current Approach File with a different name and/or location. This is equivalent to choosing **Save As** from the File menu.

Set

Select **Set** from the drop-down to enter a value in a field that is based on a Formula.

This Command has options that let you choose the field and specify a formula to give it a new value (see Figure B.100).

Appendix B: Reference Guide

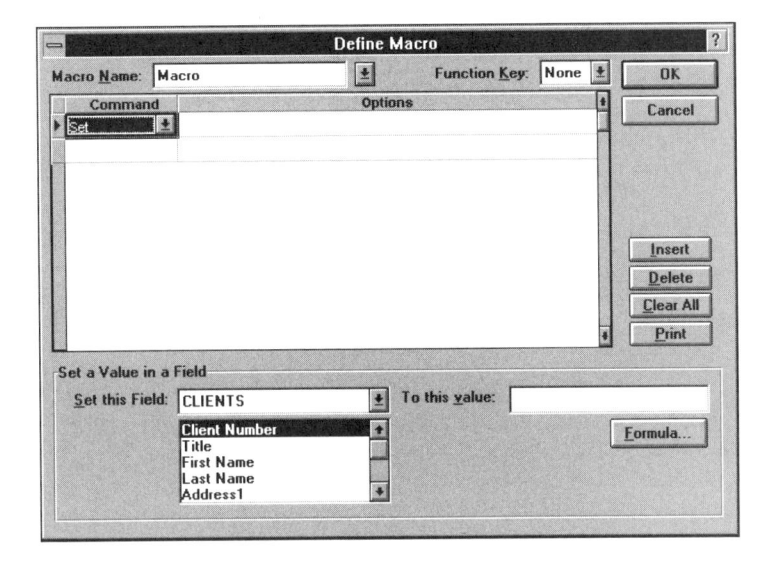

Figure B.100   Options for the Set Command.

Sort

Select **Sort** from the drop-down to sort the records.

This command has two options:

- Displays the Sort dialog box as the Macro is running, so the user can define a custom sort.
- Defines the custom sort while you are defining the macro.

This is equivalent to choosing **Sort** from the Browse menu and Define from the submenu to create a custom sort, covered in Chapter 6.

Spell Check

Select **Spell Check** from the drop-down to open the Spell Check dialog box. This command has no options.

The Spell Checker is covered in the section on the Spell Check command of the Tools menu.

Tab

Select **Tab** from the drop-down to tab to another field or Macro button.

This Command has options that let you tab forward or backward and specify the number of fields or macro buttons to move across (see Figure B.101).

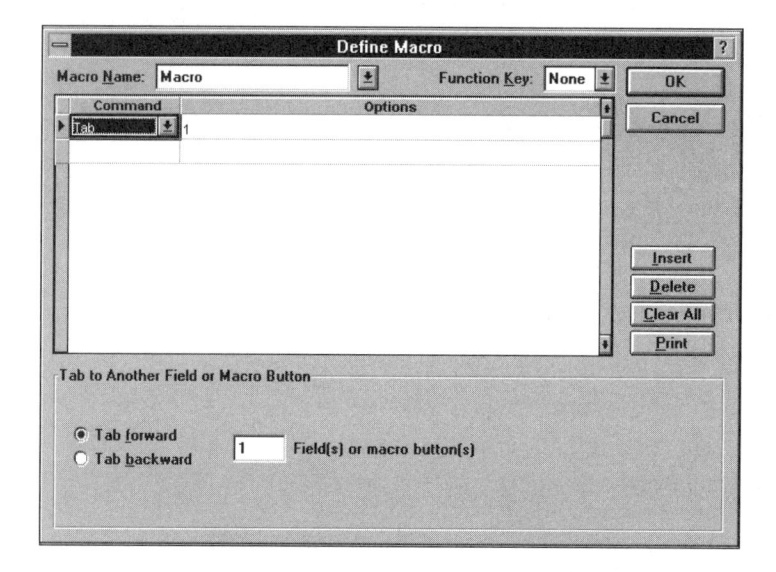

Figure B.101 Options for the Tab Command.

This is equivalent to pressing **Tab** or **Shift+Tab** one or many times.

View

Select **View** from the drop-down to switch the current view or to show or hide a view in Browse mode.

Zoom

Select **Zoom** from the drop-down to change the size of the view displayed in the window. It has options to Zoom In, Zoom Out, or display the view in Actual Size, which are equivalent to choosing Zoom In, Zoom Out, or Actual Size from the View menu.

Run Command

Choose **Run Macro** from the Tools menu to display a submenu listing the names of all defined macros. Select the name of a macro from this submenu to run it.

If you do not want a macro to be displayed on the menu, select it in the Macros dialog box, and deselect **Show**.

The Window Menu

Use the Window menu to arrange windows and move from one window to another.

Arrange Windows Command

Choose **Arrange Windows** from the Window menu to arrange all open windows within Approach so that they overlap, with the title bar of each visible.

Specific Windows

The name of any specific window that is open is added to the Windows menu, and you can select it to make that window the active window, which is displayed in front of all other open windows.

The Help Menu

Use the Help menu to get help about using Approach. Like other Windows applications, Approach uses the Windows Help system, with a special Help File provided by Approach.

Contents Command

Choose **Contents** from the Help menu to display the Help window (see Figure B.102). This is a separate application window, not a document window within Approach.

Practical Approach, 3.0

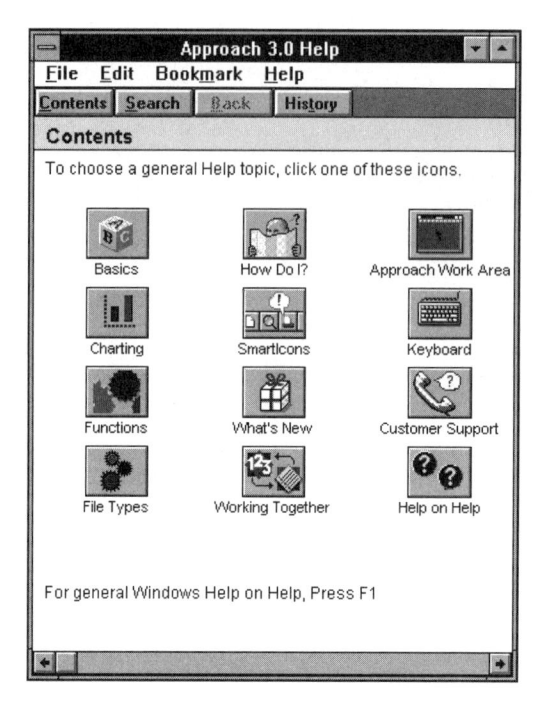

Figure B.102   Help Contents.

Move the pointer to the icon representing any of the general help topics listed and a help window with more specific topics appears (see Figure B.103).

Click one of these specific topics that is underlined with a solid line to jump to a window with help on that topic. Using the keyboard, you can press **Tab** to move from topic to topic, and press **Enter** to select the highlighted topic.

New Help windows displayed also have words underlined in the same way to show they are cross-referenced. You can click any underlined word to jump to the Help window describing it.

Other words are underlined with dotted lines. You can click these to display a definition of them in a small box. Click again to remove this box.

The push buttons at the top of this window help you navigate through the Help system after you have used cross-references to jump from one topic to another:

Appendix B: Reference Guide 583

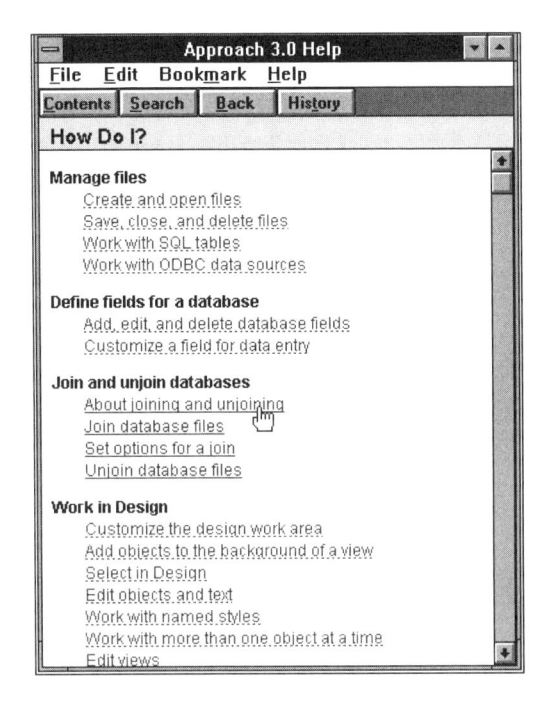

Figure B.103 More specific Help topics.

- Select **Contents** to display the table of contents of Help Topics that was displayed when you first opened the Help window.
- Select **Back** to display the last topic viewed.
- Select **History** to display a window with a list of the last forty Help Topics viewed. Select any topic from this list to view it again.
- Select << or >> to move to the previous or the next topic in a series of related topics that you are viewed.

Alphabetical Searches

The one remaining push button, **Search**, lets you do alphabetical searches. If you select this push button, Approach displays the Search dialog box (see Figure B.104).

Practical Approach, 3.0

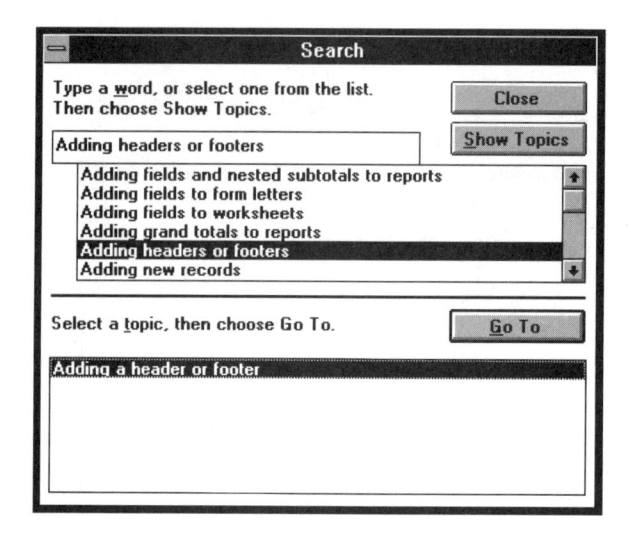

Figure B.104 The Search dialog box.

You can scroll through the list in the top half of this dialog box and select a word from it. Alternatively, type a word in the text box above this list. The list automatically scrolls to the nearest word as you type.

When you have found the word you want in the list, select **Show Topics**; the name of the topic that includes information on that word in the list in the bottom half of the dialog box is displayed. You can show more than one topic in this list if you want. At any time, you can select a topic from this list and select **Go To** to display Help on that topic.

The Help System has a Menu system of its own.

Help System File Menu

The File menu has features that are similar to the File menu of many Windows applications:

- *Open* lets you open another Help file if multiple Help files are available. Approach, however, provides only the file Approach.hlp, which is opened when you first use help.
- *Print Topic* prints the topic that is currently displayed. You must print the entire topic.

- *Print Setup* displays the dialog box that lets you control your printer. This dialog box is described in the entry under *File | Print Setup* earlier in this appendix.
- *Exit* closes the Help Window.

Help System Edit Menu

The Edit menu is also found on many windows applications, but in the Help system, it has only two options, because you cannot edit the text in the Help system itself:

- *Copy* displays the Copy dialog box, which includes all the text in the current topic. You can select text in this dialog box and then select **Copy** to copy it to the clipboard.
- *Annotate* displays a dialog box where you can you add your own notes (or annotations) to the current Help Topic. When you add a note, a paper clip icon is displayed to the left of the topic's title. You can view the annotation at any time by clicking this icon, or by tabbing to it and pressing **Enter**.

Help System Bookmark Menu

The Bookmark menu lets you add bookmarks to save your place in the Help system. It has the following options:

- *Define.* Displays a dialog box that lets you add a bookmark. It suggests a name for the bookmark based on the name of the current Topic, but you can edit it, and give it any name you want.
- *Bookmark names.* After you have defined bookmarks, their names are added to the Bookmark menu, and you can go to any one immediately by selecting it from this menu. If more than nine bookmarks have been defined, a More option is added, which you select to display all the bookmark names.

Help System Help Menu

The Help system itself includes a Help menu, which gives you help in using it. It has the following options:

- *How to Use Help.* Displays the contents for How to Use Help, which lets you use the Help system in Approach. This Help system works like the Approach Help system—you can search by topic or alphabetically, move back through the history of the windows displayed, and use the menu in the same way. It also includes a Glossary button, which displays a window with definitions of terms.
- *Always on Top.* Makes help windows always remain on top of any other windows that are displayed.
- *About Help.* Displays information on the current version of Windows Help you are using.

Help Search Command

Choose **Help Search** from the Approach Help menu to display the Search dialog box, which was shown above in Figure B.104. Use it as described in the section on *Alphabetical Searches*.

This option simply lets you do an Alphabetical search for a topic without displaying the Contents screen first. After you have displayed that topic, you can use it in all the ways described above.

Using Help Command

Choose **Using Help** from the Approach Help menu to display the contents for How to Use Help. You can also display this system by choosing **How to Use Help** from the Help menu within the Help system, and it was described in the section on the *Help System Help Menu*.

For Upgraders Command (Help Menu)

Choose **For Upgraders** to display special help for users who are upgrading from Approach 2.

Keyboard

Choose **Keyboard** from the Help menu to display a help system with instructions on using the key board, a list of the keyboard shortcuts, and a list of Direction keys and Selection keys.

Functions Command

Choose **Functions** from the Help menu to display a help system with descriptions of all the Approach Functions.

Appendix B: Reference Guide

Customer Support Command

Choose **Customer Support** from the Help menu to display a help system with information on the different forms of customer support that Lotus offers to Approach users.

About Approach Command

Choose **About Approach** from the Help menu to display the About Approach dialog box, which contains the version number and copyright date of the version of Approach that you are using.

The Formula Dialog Box

A number of dialog boxes displayed by using the menu selections described above include a Formula push button, which you can use to display the Formula dialog box (see Figure B.105).

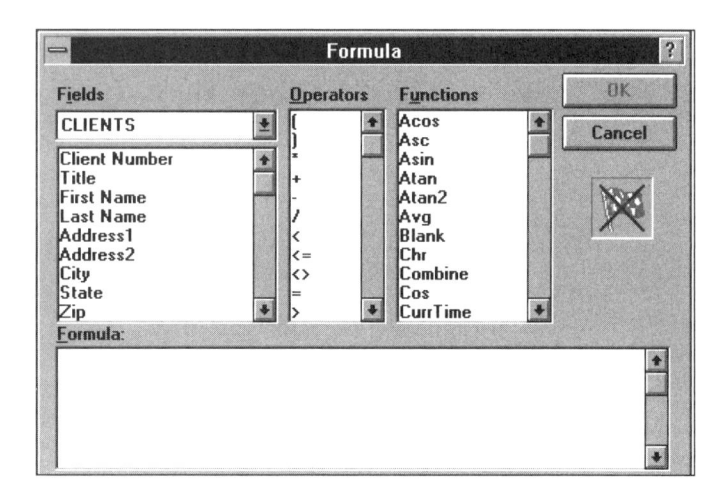

Figure B.105 The Formula dialog box.

A formula is calculation used by Approach. As you can see from this dialog box, Approach Functions consist of three elements that are added to the Formula text box when you select them from lists:

- Fields from a database, such as Last Name or Bill At.
- Operators, such as + (plus) or <> (not equal to).
- Functions, such as Abs (the absolute value of) or Avg (the average of).

In addition, you can use two other elements:

- *Constants* always have the same value, including numbers (such as 2), and words. These are not selected from lists but simply typed into the Formula text box.
- *Variables*, which you can add to formulas by including a variable field in your database.

You can simply select fields (including variable fields), operators, or functions from the lists in the Formula dialog box to add them to the formula. Constants must be typed into the formula.

Functions, operators, and constants are all discussed in detail in the next section of this appendix.

Operator, Constant, and Function Reference

Chapter 9 discussed Approach formulas, which can be made of fields, operators, constants and functions. This section lists Approach operators, summarizes the requirements for constants, and lists all Approach functions alphabetically for reference.

Operators

Approach includes three types of operators. The *arithmetic operators* are used to do addition, subtraction, and the like.

By default, multiplication and division are performed before addition and subtraction.

You can change the default by using parentheses, however, operations in parentheses are performed first. For example, by default, the formula 2 * 10 + 5 gives the result 25, but the formula 2 * (10 + 5) gives the result 30.

Appendix B: Reference Guide

The Comparison operators are used to check if a value is equal to, or smaller than another.

Table B.1 The arithmetic operators.

Operator	Meaning
+	addition
-	subtraction
*	multiplication
/	division
( )	precedence

Table B.2 The comparison operators.

Operator	Meaning
=	equal to
< >	not equal to
<	less than
>	greater than
< =	less than or equal to
> =	greater than or equal to

The Logical operators are used to combine Boolean values (Yes or No).

Table B.3 The logical operators

Operator	Meaning
AND	Yes if both values are Yes
OR	Yes if either value is Yes
NOT	Yes if the value is No; No if the value is Yes

Constants

Constants can be the same types as fields. Constants of different types are:

- *Text constants* must be enclosed in single quotation marks. For example, 'Smith'. Text constants are also called *strings*.
- *Date constants* must be enclosed in single quotation marks and entered as numbers separated by hyphens in the order month-day-year. For example, '2-14-93'. (This is the American order. The order may differ depending on your Windows International setting.)
- *Time constants* must be enclosed in single quotation marks and numbers, with hours, minutes, and seconds separated by colons, and hundredths separated by a decimal point. For example, '12:00:00.00.
- *Boolean constants* must be enclosed in single quotation marks and entered as either 'Yes' or 'No'.
- *Numeric constants* are simply entered as numbers. Scientific notation cannot be used.

Numeric constants were used in the examples above, because they are the simplest and do not require any explanation. Other constants may be used in the same way.

Functions

Most functions work on some value that you specify, which is called a *parameter* (or sometimes an *argument*) and placed in parentheses following the function. Different functions require parameters of different data types, and it is common to include the type of the parameter in parentheses after the function. Some functions have several parameters, which must be separated by commas.

You can also use formulas as the parameters of functions, if they return the correct data type. When one function is used as the parameter of another function in this way, they are called *nested functions*.

This section lists all functions alphabetically. Each begins with the function and the type of data it uses as parameters. In a few cases, there are parameters that are optional, and they are placed in square brackets. In some cases, there may be a list of parameters with an indefinite number of parameters. This is indicated by listing two parameters of that type followed by an ellipsis (...) to show that the list can continue indefinitely.

In the listings and examples, parameters are delimited by commas, but actually, Approach uses the delimiter specified in the List Separator setting in the International dialog box of the Windows' Control Panel. A comma is the standard delimiter in the United States, but many countries use a semi-colon (;) instead.

Abs(number)

The *Absolute Value* function returns the absolute value of a number, the positive equivalent of the number. For example, Abs(5) returns **5** and Abs(-5) returns **5**.

Acos (number)

The *Arccosine* function returns the trigonometric arccosine of a number in radians.

Asc(text)

The *ASCII* function returns the ASCII number of the first character of the text used as its parameter. Generally, a single character is used as the parameter. For example, Asc('A') returns **65** and Asc('Albert') returns **65**.

Asin(number)

The *Arcsine* function returns the trigonometric arcsine of a number in radians.

Atan(number)

The *Arctangent* function returns the trigonometric arctangent of a number in radians.

Atan2(Number1, Number2)

The *Arctangent2* function returns the arctangent of number1 / number2 in radians.

Avg(Number, Number, ...)

The *Average* function returns the average of all the parameters. There can be any number of parameters, all of which must be number values. For example, Avg(10,20,30) returns **20**.

Blank(FieldName, Value)

The *Blank* function returns the second value if the field is blank. Otherwise it returns the field's value. For example, Blank(Address2, 'xxx') returns **xxx** if the Address2 field is blank, or returns the content of the Address2 field if it is not blank.

Chr(number)

The *Character* function returns the ASCII character for a number. For example, Chr(65) returns **A**.

Combine(text, text ...)

The *Combine* function concatenates all the text strings used as parameters into a single text string. For example, Combine('Hello ', 'world') returns **Hello world**.

Cos(Number)

The *Cosine* function returns the cosine of an angle expressed in radians.

CurrTime( )

The *Current Time* function returns the time on the system clock.

Date(Number1, Number2, Number3)

The *Date function* converts numeric to date data. The three parameters represent month, day, and year, and they must make a valid date. Date(12, 15, 1993) returns **12-15-93**.

DateToText(Date, Format)

DateToText returns a date in text form. The format of the date is specified by a string, with repeated Ms representing the month, repeated Ds representing the day, repeated Ys representing the year, and spaces and commas or other delimiters included. For example, DateToText(Contacted,'MM. DD, YY') would return **Feb. 12, 94**, if 2/12/94 is in the Contacted field.

Day(Date)

The *Day* function returns the number of the day of the month from a date. For example, Day('12-15-93') returns **15**.

DayName(Number or Date)

The *DayName* function returns the name of the day of the week in text form. The parameter can be either a date or a number from 1 to 7, with 1 returned as **Sunday** and so on. For example, DayName('12-15-93') returns **Wednesday**, and DayName(2) returns **Monday**.

DayOfWeek(Date)

The *DayofWeek* function returns the day of the week in number form, with Sunday returned as 1 and so on. For example, DayOfWeek('12-15-93') returns **4**.

DayOfYear(Date)

The *DayOfYear* function returns the number of days from the beginning of the year to the specified date, with January 1 returned as 1 and so on. For example, DayOfYear('2-1-94') returns **32**.

Degree(Number)

The *Degree* function converts angles measured in radians to degrees. The parameter represents the number of radians. As the Acos( ), Asin( ), and Atan( ) functions all return angles measured in radians, they can be nested within the Degree( ) function to return the result in degrees.

Exact(Text1, Text2)

The Exact function does a case sensitive comparison of the two arguments, and returns **Yes** if they match and **No** if they do not.

If **SMITH** is entered in the Last Name field, then Exact(Last Name, 'SMITH') returns **Yes**, but Exact(Last Name, 'Smith') returns **No**.

Exp(Number)

The *Exponentiation* function calculates e to the power of the number value.

Factorial(Number)

The *Factorial* function returns the factorial of a number, that number multiplied by each smaller number. For example, Factorial(3) returns **6**, because 3 * 2 * 1 equals 6.

Fill(Text, Number)

The *Fill* function returns a text string containing the text that is specified repeated as many times as the number specifies. For example, Fill('x', 10) returns **xxxxxxxxxx**, and Fill('Hello ', 2) returns **Hello Hello**.

FV(Number1, Number2, Number3)

The *Future Value* function returns the future value of a series of periodic payments at a constant interest rate after the number of periods you specify. The first parameter is the periodic payment, the second parameter is the interest rate during each period, and the third parameter is the total number of periods. For example, if you invest $100 per month for a year at an annual interest rate of 12%, the periodic payment is 100, the interest rate per period is .01 (1% or 12% a year, divided by 12 months per year), and the total number of periods is 12. Thus, the value of the investment at the end of the year is: FV(100, .01, 12).

Hour(Time)

The *Hour* function returns a number representing the hour of a time value. For example, Hour('12:03:25.32') returns **12**.

Hundredth(Time)

The *Hundredth* function returns a number representing the hundredths of a second of a time value. For example, Hundredth('12:03:25.32') returns **32**.

If(Boolean Condition, Value1, Value2)

The *If* function returns the first value if the Boolean condition is Yes or the second value is No. The condition must be a Boolean value; the other two parameters can be any value. For example, If(Bill At > 90, 'Hello', 'Goodbye') returns **Hello** if the Bill At field contains an amount greater than 90 or returns **Goodbye** if it does not.

IsBlank(FieldName)

The *IsBlank* function returns **Yes** if the field is blank and **No** if there is data in it. For example, IsBlank(Address2) returns **Yes** if there is not a second address line in the record.

IsLastRecord( )

The *IsLastRecord( )* function returns **Yes** if the record is the last record in the found set in the current sort order and returns **No** if it is not.

Left(Text, Number)

The *Left* function returns a number of characters from the beginning of the specified text that is equal to the specified number. For example, Left('Hello world', 5) returns **Hello**.

Length(Text)

The *Length* function returns the number of characters in the specified text, including spaces, numbers, and special characters, as well as letters. For example, Length('John Smith') returns **10**.

Like(Text, Text)

The *Like* function compares the two text values and returns **Yes** if they are the same, or **No** if they are different.

The comparison is case insensitive. The second parameter can include the wildcard characters—a question mark (?) to represent any character, and an asterisk (*) to represent any number of characters (including zero characters). A few examples are:

- Like ("Last Name", 'SMITH') returns **Yes** if the name in the LAST NAME field is Smith.
- Like ("Last Name", 'SMITH*') returns **Yes** if the name in the Last Name field is Smith, Smithson, Smithers, or anything else beginning with Smith.
- Like("Last Name", 'SM?TH') returns **Yes** if the name in the LAST NAME field is Smith, Smyth, and so on.

All of these match regardless of capitalization of the name in the field.

Ln(Number)

The *Natural Logarithm* function returns the natural logarithm of a positive number—the logarithm to the base e. The value returned is the power to which e must be raised to produce the number.

Log(Number)

The *Logarithm* function calculates the common or decimal logarithm of a number—the logarithm to the base 10. The value returned is the power to which 10 must be raised to produce the number.

Lower(Text)

The *Lower* function converts all letters in text to lowercase but does not affect other characters. For example, Lower('Smith') returns **smith**.

Middle(Text, Number, Number)

The *Middle* function returns a string of characters taken from the specified text, beginning at the position specified by the first number, and containing the number of characters specified by the second number. For example, Middle('Smith',2,3) returns **mit**.

Minute(Time)

The *Minute* function returns a number representing the minutes of a time value. For example, Minute('12:03:25.32') returns **3**.

Mod(Number,Number)

The *Modulus* (*Remainder*) returns the remainder (modulus) left when the first number is divided by the second to give an integer result. For example, Mod(14,4) returns **2**, because 14 / 4 is 3 with a remainder of 2.

Month(Date)

The *Month* Function returns the month of the specified date in number form, with January returned as 1 and so on. For example, Month('12-15-93') returns **12**.

MonthName(Date or Number)

The MonthName function returns the month in text form. The parameter can be either a date or a number from 1 to 12, with 1 returned as **January** and so on. For example, MonthName('12-15-93') returns **December**, and MonthName(2) returns **February**.

NPeriods(Number1, Number2, Number3)

The *Number Of Periods* function returns the number of periods needed to pay the principal with a constant periodic payment at a constant interest rate. The first parameter is the interest rate, the second number is the principle that must be paid, and the third number is the periodic payment. For example, If you are paying a debt of $120,000 at 12% interest with a payment of $1000 per month, the monthly interest rate is .01 (1% or 12% divided by 12 months per year), the principal is $120,000, and the periodic payment is $1000, so the number of months you need to pay it is: NPeriods(.01, 120000, 1000).

NumToText(Number, Format)

The *NumToText* function returns a number in text form. The format of the text is determined by the Format parameter, which is made up of zeros specifying required digits and number signs representing optional digits.

For example, NumToText(2,#00.00) returns the text string **02.00**, and NumToText(2,###.00) returns the text string **2.00**

Pi( )

The *Pi* function returns 3.14159..., the ratio of the circumference to the diameter of a circle.

PMT(Number1, Number2, Number3)

The *PMT* function (payment) returns the amount of the periodic payment needed to pay off a specified principal at a constant periodic interest rate, with a specified number of periodic payments. The first parameter is the principal, the second parameter is the periodic interest rate, and the third parameter is the number of periods in which the principal must be paid. For example, if you are paying a debt of $120,000 at 12% interest by making monthly payments for 15 years, then the principal is $120,000, the monthly interest rate is .01 (1% or 12% divided by 12 months per year), and the number of periods is 180 (15 years times 12 months per year). The monthly payment is: PMT(120,000, .01, 180).

Position(Text, Text, Number)

The *Position* function searches the first text specified for the first occurrence of the second text specified, beginning at the location specified by the number.

Returns a number indicating its position. For example, Position('Smithson', 's', 2) returns **6**.

Pow(Number, Number)

The *Pow* function (power) returns the value of the first number raised to the power of the second number. For example, Pow(3, 2) returns **9**.

Prefix(Text, Text)

The *Prefix* function returns **Yes** if the characters at the beginning of the second text string match the first text string. For example, Prefix('Sm', 'Smith') returns **Yes**.

Proper(Text)

The *Proper* function converts the first letter of each word in text to uppercase and all other letters to lowercase. For example, Proper('JOHN Q. SMITH') returns **John Q. Smith**.

PV(Number1, Number2, Number3)

The *PV* function (Present Value) returns the present value of a series of periodic payments with a constant interest rate over a specified number of periods. The first number represents the periodic payment, the second number represents the periodic interest rate, and the third number represents the number of periods. For example, if an annuity pays $1000 per year for 10 years, and the discount rate is 10% per year, the periodic payment is $1000, the periodic interest rate is .1 (10%), and the number of periods is 10, so that the present value of the annuity is: PV(1000, .1, 10).

Radian(Number)

The *Radian* function converts angles measured in degrees to radians. The parameter represents the number of degrees. As the Cos( ), Sin( ), and Tan( ) functions all require parameters measured in radians, the Radian( ) function can be nested within them to use them on angles measured in degrees.

Random( )

The *Random* function returns a random number between 0 and 1. Often you multiply this by some power of ten and round the result to get the integer random number you really want to use.

Replace(Text, Number, Number, Replacement Text)

The *Replace* function replaces characters in the text with different characters. The first number specifies the starting position of the text that is being replaced, and the second number specifies the number of characters. The replacement text can be a different size than the number of characters it replaces. For example, Replace('of their party', 10, 4, 'countr') returns **of their country**, because it replaces part, four characters beginning with the tenth character of the string, with countr.

Right(Text, Number)

The *Right* function returns a number of characters from the end of the specified text that is equal to the specified number. For example, Right('Hello world', 5) returns **world**.

Round(Number, [Number])

The *Round* function returns the value of the first number rounded to the number of decimal places specified in the second number. If the second number is omitted (or if it is zero), Approach rounds the number to the nearest integer. For example:

- Round(2.643) returns **3**.
- Round(2.643,1) returns **2.6**.
- Round(2.643,2) returns **2.64**.

SAverage(Number Field)

The *SAverage* function (Summary Average) returns the average values of the specified field in the records in the range of the summary. The parameter must be a number field. For example, SAverage("Bill At") returns the average rate at which you bill clients.

SCount(Field Name)

The *SCount* function (Summary Count) returns the number of records that have a value in the specified field in the range of the summary. The parameter must be a field name. For example, SCount("Client Number") returns the total number of records in the range of the summary, as every record must have a client number.

Second(Time)

The *Second* function returns a number representing the seconds of a time value. For example, Second('12:03:25.32') returns **25**.

Sign(Number)

The *Sign* function returns -1 if the number specified is negative, 1 if the number specified is positive, and 0 if the number specified is zero. For example, Sign(15) returns **1** and Sign(-100) returns **-1**.

Sin(Number)

The *Sine* function returns the sine of an angle expressed in radians.

SLN(Number1, Number2, Number3)

The *Straight Line Depreciation* function calculates the straight line depreciation of an asset. The first number is the asset's cost, the second is its salvage value, and the third is its life. Straight line depreciation is calculated as (cost − salvage) / life. For example, if you by an asset for $1000 and scrap it after 3 years of use for a salvage value of $100, its yearly depreciation is SLN(1000, 100, 3).

SMax(Number Field)

The *SMax* function (Summary Maximum) returns the maximum value of the specified field in the records in the range of the summary. The parameter must be a number field. For example, SMax("Bill At") returns the highest rate at which you bill any client.

SMin(Number Field)

The *SMIN* function (Summary Minimum) returns the minimum value of the specified field in the records in the range of the summary. The parameter must be a number field. For example, SMin("Bill At") returns the lowest rate at which you bill any client.

SNPV(Number Field, Number)

The *SNPV* function (Summary Net Present Value) returns the net present value of a series of periodic future payments as a given discount rate. Future payments can be either negative (indicating money you must pay), or positive (indicating money paid to you), or both. The first parameter is the name of the field that holds the future payments. The second parameter is the discount rate. For example, If a field named Payments had one record for each year's projected net gain or loss on an investment in future years, and if the discount rate were 10% (.1), then you could calculate the present value of the investment as: SNPV(Payments, .1).

Soundslike (Text, Text)

The *Soundslike* function returns **Yes** if the first text string sounds like the second text string. For example, Soundslike ('Walton', 'Waldon') returns **Yes**.

Span(Text, Text)

The *Span* function returns the number of characters in the first text string before the first character that is not contained in the second text string. For example:

- Span('John Smith', 'Johnson') returns **4**.
- Span('54623456', '456') returns **3**.

Notice that the function ignores the order of the characters in the second test string.

SpanUntil(Text, Text)

The *SpanUntil* function returns the number of characters in the first text string before the first character that is also in the second text string. For example:

- SpanUntil('John Smith', 'Johnson') returns **0**.
- SpanUntil('54623456', '123') returns **3**.

Notice that the function ignores the order of the characters in the second test string.

Sqrt(number)

The *Sqrt* function (Square Root) calculates the square root of a number. For example, Sqrt(9) returns **3**.

SSTD(Number Field)

The *SSTD* function (Summary Standard Deviation) returns the standard deviation of the values in the field used as the parameter in all the records in the range of the summary. The parameter must be a Number field. Standard Deviation is a measure of how widely the values are dispersed from the average value.

SSum(Number Field)

The *SSum* function (Summary Sum) returns the sum of the values of the specified field in the records in the range of the summary. The parameter must be a Number field. For example, SSum(Hours) returns the total number of hours worked.

STD(Number, Number, ...)

The *STD* function (Standard Deviation) returns the standard deviation of all the parameters, a measure of how widely the values are dispersed from the average value. There may be any number of parameters, all of which must be Number values.

SVar(Number Field)

The *SVar* function (Summary Variance) returns the variance of the values in the field used as the parameter in the records in the range of the summary. The parameter must be a Number field.

Tan(Number)

The *Tangent* function returns the tangent of an angle radians.

TextToBool(Text)

The *TextToBool* function returns text as a Boolean value. It returns **No** if the first character in a string is F, f, N, n, or 0; otherwise, returns **Yes**.

TextToDate(Text)

The *TextToDate* function returns text as a Date value. The parameter must be a valid date in the format MM/DD/YY.

TextToTime(Text)

The *TextToTime* function returns text as a time value. The parameter must be a valid time in the format HH:MM:SS.00.

Time(Hours, Minutes, Seconds, Hundredths)

The *Time* function converts numeric to date data. The four parameters represent hour, minute, second, and hundredth of a second, and they must make a valid time.

Today( )

The *Today* function returns the current system date.

Translate(Text, Character, Character)

The *Translate* function in the specified text string replaces all occurrences of the first character with the second character. For example, Translate('6/23/93', '/', '-') returns **6-23-93**.

Trim(Text)

The *Trim* function returns the text without any leading or trailing blanks. For example, Trim(' John Smith ') returns **John Smith**.

Trunc(Number, [Number])

The *Trunc* function (Truncate) returns the first number truncated to the number of decimal places specified by the second number. If the second number is omitted (or if it is zero), Approach truncates the number to an integer. For example:

- Trunc(9.97463,1) returns **9.9**.
- Trunc(9.97463) returns **9**.

Upper(Text)

The Upper function converts all letters in text to lowercase but does not affect other characters. For example, Upper('Smith') returns **SMITH**.

Var(Number, Number, ...)

The *Var* function (Variance) returns the variance of all the parameters. There can be any number of parameters, all of which must be number values.

WeekOfYear(Date)

The *WeekOfYear* function returns the number of the week of the specified date, with January 1 being in week 1, and so on. For example, WeekOfYear('1-8-94') returns **2**.

Year(Date)

The *Year* function returns the year of the date in number form. For example, Year('12-15-93') returns **1993**.

Info Box Reference

You can change certain styles and properties of the objects in a View, parts of a view, such as columns or panels, or of a View as a whole by using the Info Box.

You can display an Info Box in several ways:

- Double-click an object, a panel, or a part of the view that does not have any objects.
- Choose **Style & Properties** from the Object menu.
- Click the **Info Box** icon.

Any of these display the Info Box for the selected object or panel or for the entire view.

Once the Info Box is displayed, it remains open until you select **Close** from its Control menu. As you select different objects, the Info Box changes and contains information on the style and properties of the object that is selected.

Appendix B: Reference Guide

Info Boxes have a *Divider tab interface* which lets you view and modify many different features of the object.

Styles and Properties of Graphic Objects

The styles and properties for graphic objects are among the simplest for any object. All have similar Info Boxes, except lines, which are even simpler than the others.

The Line Info Box

The first panel of the Info Box for a line, lets you specify settings for lines and colors (see Figure B.106). Use the drop-downs to:

- Select a line width between hairline and 12 points.
- Select a border color.
- Select a shadow color.
- Select a line style, such as solid line, double line, or several types of dotted lines.

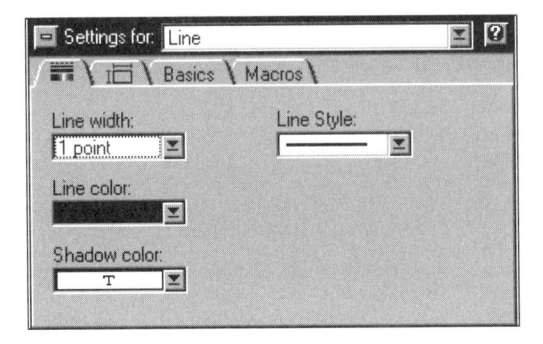

Figure B.106 The Lines and Colors panel of the Info Box for a line.

The drop-downs used to select colors simply display a palette with variety of colors, and you can click one to select it. The sample color on the upper left of each palette appears to be white but has the letter T in it to indicate that it is transparent. Choosing this color lets you see whatever is behind the object. When you place a graphic object, by default, its shadow is this color, so it is not visible; if you want the object to have a shadow, select any other Shadow color.

The second panel of the Info Box for a line displays indicates the size, location, and printing slide options of the object (see Figure B.107).

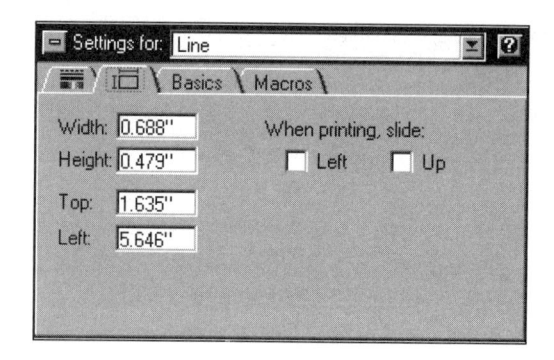

Figure B.107 The Size and Location panel of the Info Box for a line.

You can edit the numbers in the Width and Height text boxes to change the size of the object, or edit the numbers in the Top and Left text boxes to change its location. Generally, however, it is easier to change size and location by clicking and dragging the object itself—these numbers change accordingly.

The Left and Up check boxes in this panel can be used to close up spaces between objects when you print. If objects to the left or above the line change in size (for example, if the frame of a field shrinks because it has less data than the frame holds), you can select these check boxes to have the object slide left or up, so the space between objects remains the same.

The Basics panel for a line, includes a checkbox that lets you specify that it should not be printed (see Figure B.108). If you select **Non-printing**, the Show in preview checkbox is enabled, and you can select it if you want to display the object in print preview mode, even though it in not printed. This panel also includes a drop-down that lets you apply a named style to the object. Named styles are covered earlier in this appendix, in the section on the *Named Styles command* of the Tools menu.

The Macros panel for a line, lets you attach a macro to the line, so the macro is performed whenever the user clicks it (see Figure B.109). Use the Define Macro button to display the Macros dialog box to define or edit a macro—this dialog box was covered earlier in this Appendix, in the section on the *Macros Command* of the Tool menu.

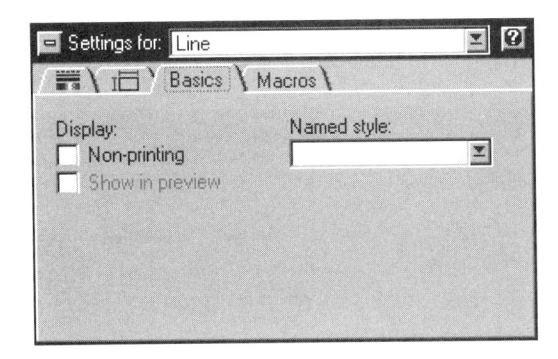

Figure B.108   The Basics panel of the Info Box for a line.

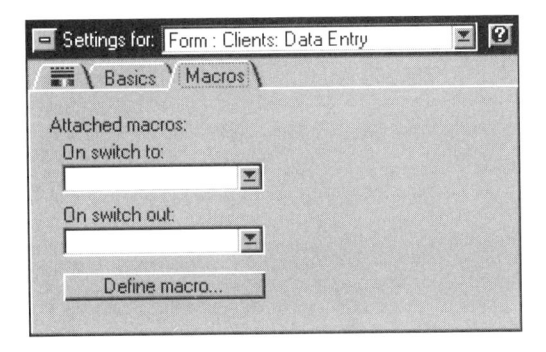

Figure B.109   The Macros panel of the Info Box for a line.

The Rectangle, Ellipse, or Rounded Rectangle Info Box

The Info Box for the other graphic objects, Rectangles, Ellipses, and Rounded Rectangles, are similar to the Info Box for Lines, but they have a few extra features, because these two-dimensional objects can have fill colors and effects lines cannot.

The first panel of the Info Box for a Rectangle, Ellipse, or Rounded Rectangle, lets you specify settings for lines and colors (see Figure B.101). Use the drop-downs to select:

- A line width between hairline and 12 points.
- A border color.

- A fill color.
- A shadow color.
- A frame style. The frame could be made of solid lines, double lines or several types of dotted lines, or could have special effects that make it appear to be raised or embossed.

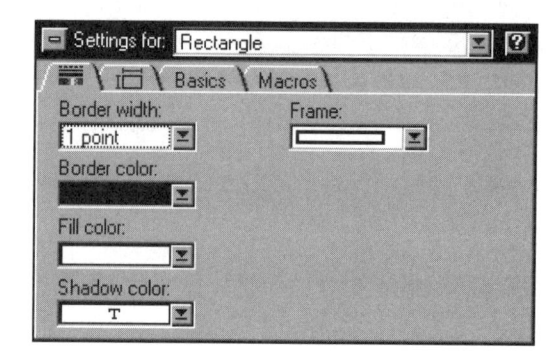

Figure B.110 The Lines and Colors panel of the Info Box for a Rectangle, Ellipse, or Rounded Rectangle.

The drop-downs used to select colors are simply palettes with a variety of colors, and you can click one to select it. The sample color on the upper left of each palette has the letter T in it to indicate that it is transparent. Choosing this color lets you see whatever is behind the object. When you place a graphic object, by default, its shadow is this color, so it is not visible.

The second panel of the Info Box for a Rectangle, Ellipse, or Rounded Rectangle, displays indicates the size, location, and printing slide options of the object (see Figure B.111).

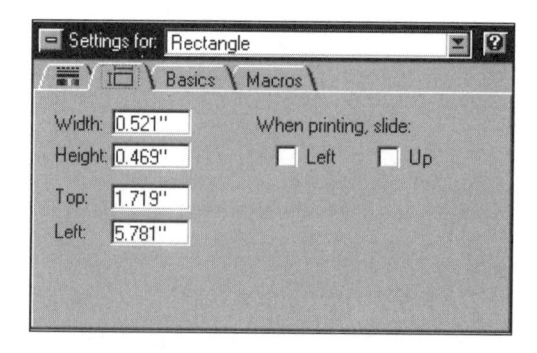

Figure B.111 The Size and Location panel of the Info Box for a Rectangle, Ellipse, or Rounded Rectangle.

You can edit the numbers in the Width and Height text boxes to change the size of the object, or edit the numbers in the Top and Left text boxes to change its location. Generally, it is easier to change size and location by clicking and dragging the object itself-these numbers change accordingly.

The Left and Up check boxes in this panel can be used to close up spaces between objects when you print. If objects to the left or above the Rectangle, Ellipse, or Rounded Rectangle change in size (for example, if the frame of a field shrinks, because it has less data than the frame holds), you can select these check boxes to have the object slide left or up, so the space between objects remains the same.

The Basics panel for a Rectangle, Ellipse, or Rounded Rectangle includes a checkbox that lets you specify that it should not be printed (see Figure B.112). If you select **Non-printing**, the Show in preview checkbox is enabled, and you can select it if you want to display the object in print preview mode, even though it in not printed. This panel also includes a drop-down that lets you apply a named style to the object. Named styles are covered earlier in this Appendix, in the section on the *Named Styles Command* of the Tools menu.

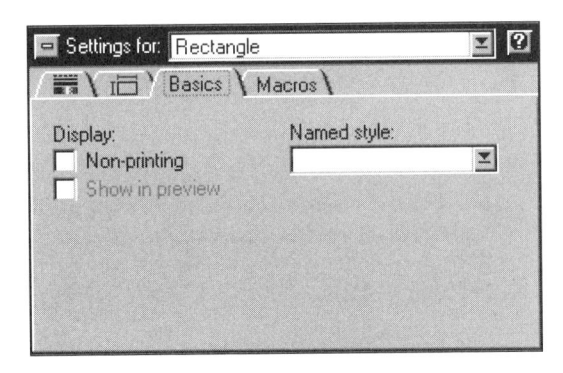

Figure B.112 The Basics panel of the Info Box for a Rectangle, Ellipse, or Rounded Rectangle.

The Macros panel for a Rectangle, Ellipse, or Rounded Rectangle, lets you attach a macro to the object, so the macro is performed whenever the user clicks it (see Figure B.113). Use **Define Macro** to display the Macros dialog box to define or edit a macro—this dialog box was covered earlier in this Appendix, in the section on the *Macros Command* of the Tools menu.

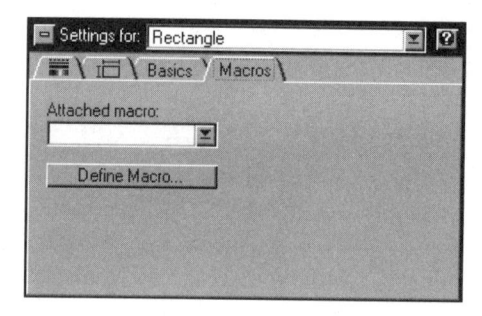

Figure B.113 The Macros panel of the Infor Box for a Rectangle, Ellipse, or Rounded Rectangle.

Style and Properties of Text Objects

Approach displays an Info Box that lets you control styles and properties of the text itself if there is an insertion point in the text object and you are editing it, and an Info Box that lets you control styles and properties of the text object as a whole when the object is selected but the text is not being edited in it.

The Text Editing Info Box

When you are editing a text object, Approach lets you use the Text Editing Info Box (see Figure B.114).

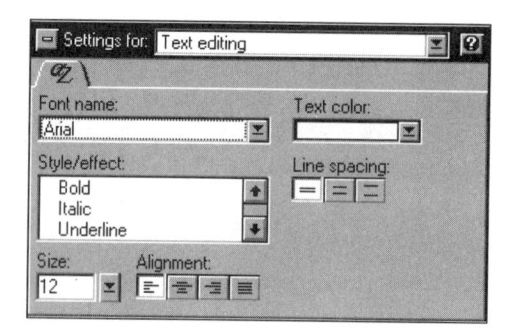

Figure B.114 The Text Editing Info Box.

Select a font, such as **Arial** or **Roman**, from the Font name list.

Select styles such as **Bold** or **Italic** or effects such as **Underline** or **Strikethrough** from the Style/effect list. You can select multiple styles and effects. When you select one, it is checked, and you can select it again to remove the effect.

Select a size expressed in points from the Size list. The options available in these lists depend on which fonts you have installed under Windows, and they may differ from the illustration.

Use the Alignment buttons to specify if the text should be centered within its text frame, or aligned to the left or right edge of the text frame. The Line spacing buttons let you select single space, one-and-a-half space, or double-space. The Text color drop-down displays a color palette that lets you select the color of the letters.

You can also use this dialog box to change the typeface of part of the text within a text object. First select (highlight) the text you want changed. Then choose **Text Style** from the Style menu to display the Info box. Changes you make in Font, Font Style, Size, and Effects apply only to the selected text, though changes in Alignment still apply to all the text in the object.

The Text Object Info Box

When you have selected a Text Object but are not editing the text, Approach displays the Text object Info Box (see Figure B.115). As you can see, the first panel of this Info Box is the same as the Text editing Info Box that you just looked at, which lets you control the font and other features of the text. See the section on *The Text Editing Info Box* immediately above for more information on this panel.

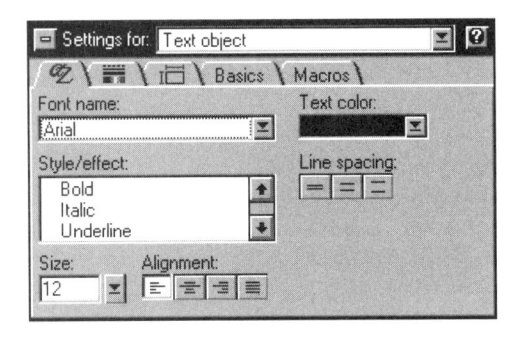

Figure B.115   The Font panel of the Info Box for a Text object.

The other four panels of this Info Box are similar to the ones used for a Rectangle, Ellipse, or Rounded Rectangle.

The second panel of the Info Box for a Text Object lets you specify settings for lines and colors (see Figure B.116).

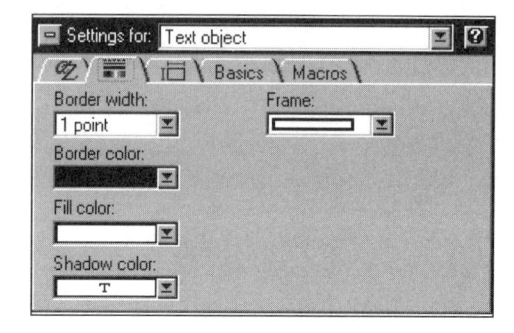

Figure B.116   The Lines and Colors panel of the Info Box for a Text object.

Use the drop-downs to select:

- A line width between hairline and 12 points.
- A border color.
- A fill color.
- A shadow color.
- A frame style. The frame could be made of solid lines, double lines or several types of dotted lines, or could have special effects that make it appear to be raised or embossed.

The drop-downs used to select colors are simply palettes with a variety of colors, and you can click one to select it. The sample color on the upper left of each palette has the letter T in it to indicate that it is transparent. Choosing this color lets you see whatever is behind the object. When you place a graphic object, by default, its shadow is this color, so it is not visible.

The third panel of the Info Box for a Text Object, displays indicates the size, location, and printing slide options of the object (see Figure B.117).

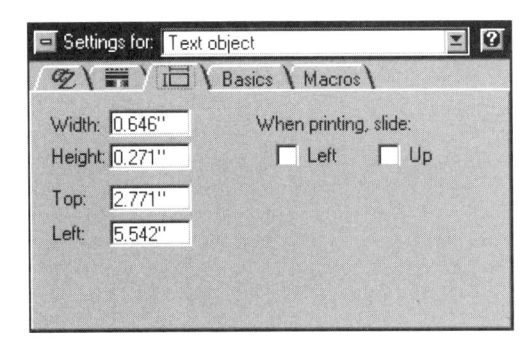

Figure B.117 The third panel of the Info Box for a Text object.

You can edit the numbers in the Width and Height text boxes to change the size of the object, or edit the numbers in the Top and Left text boxes to change its location. Generally, it is easier to change size and location by clicking and dragging the object itself—these numbers change accordingly.

The Left and Up check boxes in this panel can be used to close up spaces between objects when you print. If objects to the left or above the Text Object change in size (for example, if the frame of a field shrinks, because it has less data than the frame holds), you can select these check boxes to have the object slide left or up, so the space between objects remains the same.

The Basics panel of the Info Box for the Text Object includes a checkbox that lets you specify that it should not be printed (see Figure B.118). If you select **Non-printing**, **Show in preview** is enabled, and you can select it if you want to display the object in print preview mode, even though it in not printed. This panel also includes a drop-down that lets you apply a named style to the object. Named styles are covered earlier in this appendix, in the section on the *Named Styles command* of the Tools menu.

The Macros panel for a Text Object, lets you attach a macro to the object, so the macro is performed whenever the user clicks it (see Figure B.119). Use **Define Macro** to display the Macros dialog box to define or edit a macro—this dialog box was covered in this Appendix, in the section on the *Macros command* of the Tools menu.

Practical Approach, 3.0

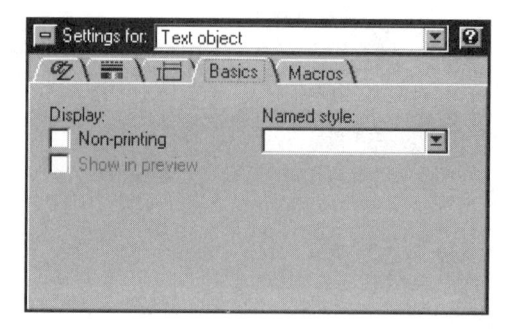

Figure B.118   The Basics panel of the Info Box for a Text object.

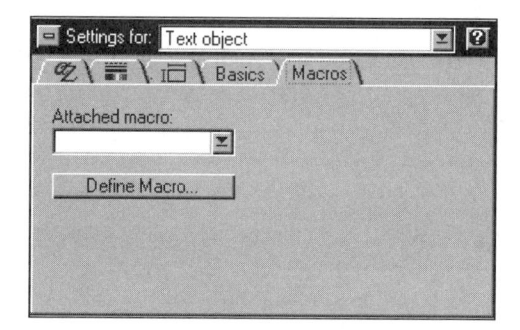

Figure B.119   The Macros panel of the Info Box for a Text object.

Styles and Properties of Fields

Approach has different Info Boxes for PicturePlus fields than for other fields. PicturePlus fields are covered after other fields.

The Field Info Box

The Info Box for fields is more complex than for other objects. It has the same panels as text objects, but it also has panels that let you control the Format of the data in the field and the way its label is displayed.

The Font Panel of the Field Info Box

The Font panel lets you control the font used to display the data (see Figure B.120). There are a separate set of controls used to control the font of the fields label in the Label panel.

Appendix B: Reference Guide   **615**

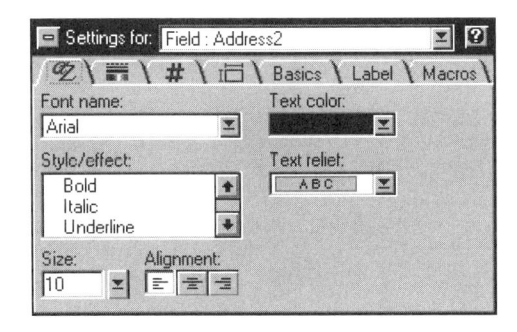

Figure B.120   The Font panel of the Info Box for a Field.

Select a font, such as **Arial** or **Roman**, from the Font name list.

Select styles such as **Bold** or **Italic** or effects such as Underline or Strikethrough from the Style/effect list. You can select multiple styles and effects—when you select one, it is checked, and you can select it again to remove the effect.

Select a size expressed in points from the Size list. The options available in these lists depend on which fonts you have installed under Windows.

Use the Alignment buttons in the Alignment area to specify if the data should be centered within the field's borders, or aligned to the left or right edge of the field.

The Text color drop-down displays a color palette that lets you select the color of the letters.

The Text relief drop-down lets you make the text in the field appear to be flat, raised above the background, or carved into the background.

The Lines and Colors Panel of the Field Info Box

The second panel of the Info Box for a Field lets you specify settings for lines and colors (see Figure B.121).

Use the drop-downs to select:

- A line width between hairline and 12 points.
- A border color.
- A fill color.
- A shadow color.

- A frame style. The frame could be made of solid lines, double lines or several types of dotted lines, or could have special effects that make it appear to be raised or embossed.

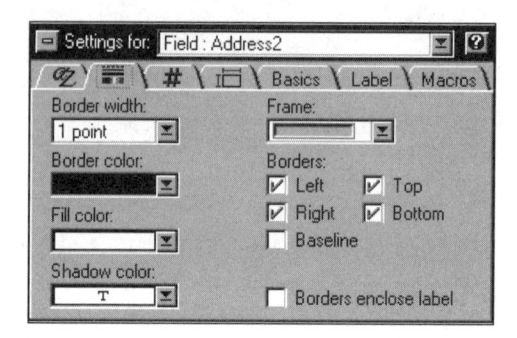

Figure B.121 The Lines and Colors panel of the Info Box for a Field.

The drop-downs used to select colors are simply palettes with a variety of colors, and you can click one to select it. The sample color on the upper left of each palette has the letter T in it to indicate that it is transparent. Choosing this color lets you see whatever is behind the object. When you place a graphic object, by default, its shadow is this color, so it is not visible.

Use the Left, Right, Top and Bottom checkboxes to specify whether the border should be displayed on each edge of the field. Select **Baseline** to underline the data itself.

Select **Borders enclose label** if you want the field's label to be inside of its borders, with the data.

The Format Panel of the Field Info Box

The third panel of the Info Box for a Field lets you control how its data is formatted. Its options differ, depending on the Data Type of the field and on the Format type you choose for it. You must use the Format type drop-down to choose among the Format types that are available for each Data Type.

Fields that are the Text data type can use any Format because a Text field can hold any characters. You can use it for numeric, date, or time data, as well as text data. Most other Data Types only give you the option of one format type besides the default format. Memo fields cannot be formatted.

After you choose a Format type from this drop-down, controls are displayed in the panel that let you specify all the options for formatting that type of data.

When you do any formatting, the Info Box displays a sample of the format you are creating, in its lower left corner.

Fields of every data type have a Display as entered option on this drop-down, you can choose display data without formatting. You can use this option to remove formatting that you specified previously.

The panel has no other controls when this option is selected from the drop-down (see Figure B.122).

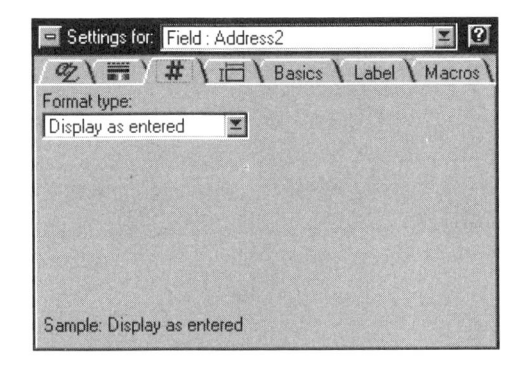

Figure B.122   Using the Format type drop-down to remove formatting.

Date Formats

If you are formatting a field that is the Date or Text Data Type, you can select **Date Format** from the Format type drop-down to display the options shown in Figure B.123.

The Current Format drop-down controls what is displayed in the rest the Info Box. The first three options, Day-Month-Year, Month-Day-Year, and Year-Month-Day, control the order of the drop-downs in the right half of the Info Box. As you can see in the Figure, by default, Day-Month-Year is selected, and the drop-downs to the right, under the Day of week drop-down, are in this order, as is the sample date at the bottom of the panel. In America, it is most common to begin a date with the month—if you select Month-Day-Year, the drop-downs under Day of the week and the sample date changes to this order. Likewise, if you choose Year-Month-Day, which some computer applications use for sorting chronologically, the order of the drop-downs and the sample date changes accordingly.

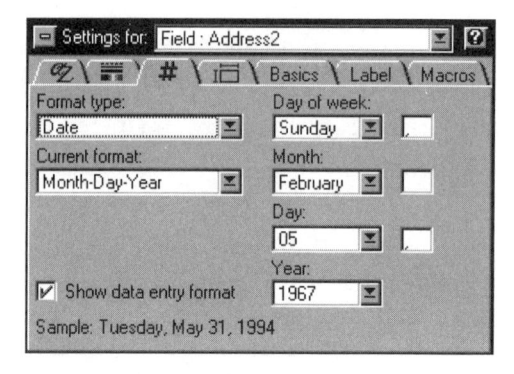

Figure B.123 Formatting dates.

The fourth option on the Current format drop-down, Other, gives you a different set of controls to create different types of date format. For example, you can display the quarter of the year a date is in.

Day, Month, and Year Formatting

In most cases, you want to display the month, day and year of a date. Use the Current format drop-down to select Day-Month-Year, Month-Day-Year, or Year-Month-Day, to control the order of the date elements. Then choose the formats for each element from the drop-downs to its right, and enter the separators you want to use between date elements in the text boxes next to them. You have the following options:

- *Day of the week*. Select a three-letter abbreviation of the day (such as Sun), the full name of the day (such as Sunday) or select the blank option if you do not want to display the day.
- *Date*. Select a display with or without leading zeros or no display.
- *Month*. Select a three-letter abbreviation (such as Feb.), the full name of the month (such as February) the number of the month with leading zeroes (such as 02), the number of the month without leading zeroes (such as 2) or no display of the month.
- *Year*. Select the full year including the century, the last two numbers of the year without the century, or no display of the year.

Enter any (or no) characters in the text boxes between these data elements to be used as separators.

Other Date Formatting

If you select **Other** in the Current format drop-down, Approach displays the controls you use to specify a format that represents different periods of the year: quarters, trimesters. or halves of the year (see Figure B.124). You can format a date so Approach displays it as Third Quarter 1993 or as 2nd Trimester 1993.

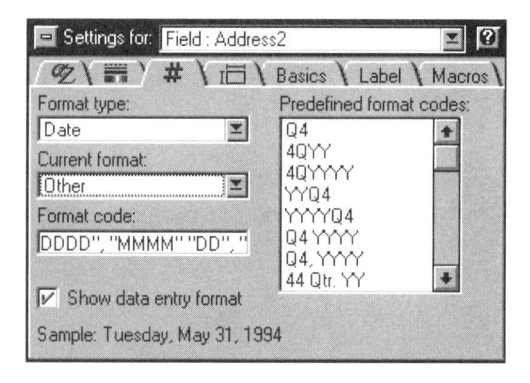

Figure B.124 Specifying other date formats.

The Format code text box contains a code that specifies how a date is formatted, which consists of three parts: a number, text, and a year format.

The number specifies how many periods the year is broken up into, and how the number of the period is displayed:

- Which number is used determines how many periods there are. Use the numbers 4 to display quarters, 3 to display trimesters, 2 to display halves, or 1 to display the year.
- How many numbers are used determines how the number of the period is displayed. Use one number to display it as a number such as 1, two numbers to display it as an ordinal number such as 1st, and three numbers to display it in a written out form, such as first.

The second part of the code is text, and it is used literally in the display. You could use the Quarter or Trimester display that is part of the result.

The third part of the code is a year format, either YY to display the last two digits, or YYYY to display all four digits of the year.

Thus, the code 4 Qtr YY would display a result such as **1 Qtr 93** or **3 Qtr 92**, and the code 333 Trimester YYYY would display a result such as **First Trimester 1993** or **Second Trimester 1992**.

You can either select the format you want from the list of Predefined format codes list or type a custom format in the Format Code text box.

Time Formats

If you are using the Info Box for a Time or a Text field, you can choose **Time** as the Format type to display the controls shown in Figure B.125.

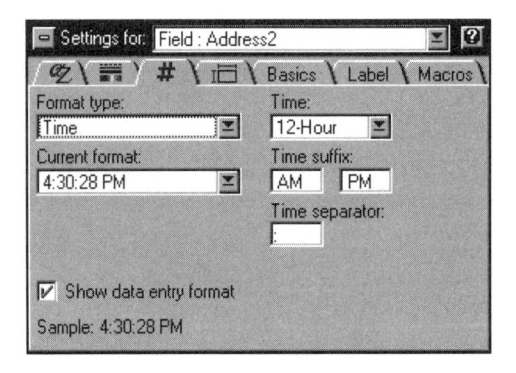

Figure B.125 Formatting times.

Use the Current format drop-down to select which elements of the time are displayed. You can display time accurate to the hundredth second, to the second, to the minute, or just display the hour.

Use the Time drop-down to specify whether to use 12-hour or 24-hour time.

If 12-hour time is used, you can edit the Time suffix text boxes below it to change the usual AM and PM that is displayed by default following times in the morning and afternoon. Enter up to three letters to be used, instead of each. If 24-hour time is used, only one Time suffix text box is displayed, and you can enter a suffix in it that is displayed following all times. You can leave these boxes blank if you do not want any suffix displayed, and this is the default for the 24-hour clock.

Use the Time separator text box to specify separators used between these elements. By default, a colon is used, but you can enter any character or series of characters to be used as a separator. The separator is only be used between hours, minutes, and seconds; hundredths of a second are preceded by a decimal point if they are included.

Numeric Formats

If you are using the Info Box for a Numeric or a Text field, you can choose **Numeric** as the Format type to display the controls shown in Figure B.126.

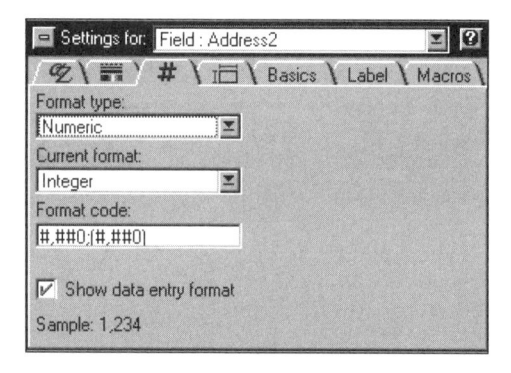

Figure B.126   Formatting numbers

Use the Current format drop-down to select one of Approach's built-in formats. Options include:

- *Integer.* Uses a comma separator and does not display decimal places.
- *General.* Uses a comma separator and displays two decimal places.
- *Currency.* Is like Integer but with a leading dollar sign.

You can also choose Currency decimal, which is like General but with a leading dollar sign, percentage with and without decimal, and scientific (exponential) notation.

The Current format drop-down also includes formats for Telephone numbers, Social Security numbers, and extended Zip codes. To use these, however, the data must have been entered only as numbers, and the hyphens or parentheses must be added by the formatting.

When you select any of these Format types, in addition a code for it is displayed in the Format code text box. In these codes, 0 (zero) specifies a digit that is always displayed—it is displayed as a zero if there is no number in that location—and # (the number sign) specifies an optional digit that is displayed only if there is a number in that location. You can edit these codes to fine tune the format types that Approach provides—for example, to display more or fewer digits, to change the separator, and the like.

Text Formats

If you are using the Info Box for a Text field, in addition to all the other Format types, you can choose Text as the Format type to display the controls shown in Figure B.127.

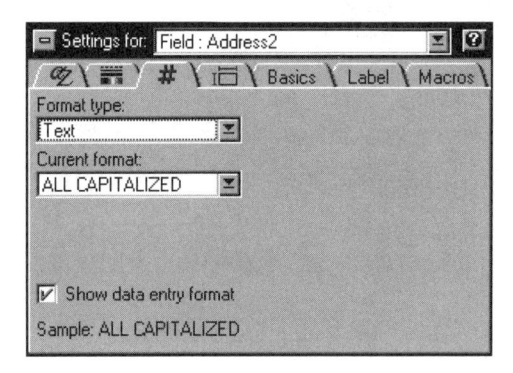

Figure B.127 Formatting text.

The Current format drop-down is simply used to specify whether text is displayed in all capital letters, all lowercase letters, or lowercase letters with a capital letter at the beginning of each word. Its options are self-explanatory: ALL CAPITAL LETTERS, all lowercase letters, and First Letters Capitalized.

The Size and Location Panel of the Field Info Box

The fourth panel of the Info Box for a Field, displays indicates the size, location, and printing slide options of the object (see Figure B.128).

You can edit the numbers in the Width and Height text boxes to change the size of the object, or edit the numbers in the Top and Left text boxes to change its location. Generally, it is easier to change size and location by clicking and dragging the object itself—these numbers change accordingly.

Appendix B: Reference Guide

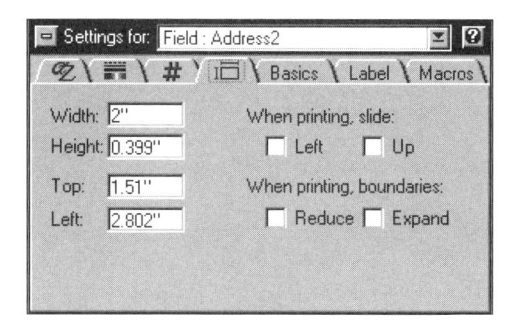

Figure B.128   The Size and Location panel of the Info Box for a Field.

The Left and Up checkboxes in this panel can be used to close up spaces between objects when you print. If objects to the left or above the Field change in size (for example, if the frame of a field shrinks, because it has less data than the frame holds), you can select these check boxes to have the object slide left or up, so the space between objects remains the same.

The Basics Panel of the Field Info Box

The Basics Panel of the Info Box has a Field drop-down and list that you can use to change the field that is displayed in this field frame (see Figure B.129). You can think of the field that is displayed in it as one property of the field frame, which you can change as you do any other property.

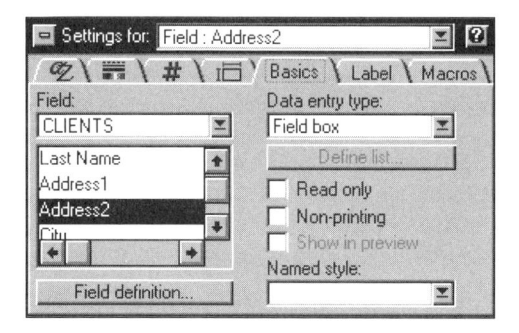

Figure B.129   The Basics panel of the Info Box for a field.

The Basics panel also includes the following features:

- A checkbox to make the Field read-only, which you can select to prevent users from editing the field.
- A checkbox that lets you specify that it should not be printed. If you select **Non-printing**, the **Show in preview** is enabled, and you can select it if you want to display the object in print preview mode, even though it in not printed.
- A drop-down that lets you that apply a named style to the object. Named styles are covered in this Appendix, in the section on the *Named Styles command* of the Tools menu.

In addition, the Data entry type drop-down lets you create drop-down lists, checkboxes, and other special controls to make it easier to enter data in the field. All of its uses are covered below.

Drop-Down Lists

You can use the Data entry type drop-down of a field's Info Box to create a drop-down list that lets the user select the values to add to the field. There are two types of drop-down list available:

- Select **Drop-down list** if you want to restrict the user to only the values that can be selected from the drop-down list.
- Select **Field box & list** if you want the user to have the option of either typing in the text, or selecting one of the options of a drop-down list.

Either of these can speed data entry. The first gives you complete control over the values that the user can enter, ensuring that valid data is entered.

When you select one of these options, Approach displays the Drop-Down List dialog box, or the Field Box and List dialog box, which is identical to it (see Figure B.130). Either of these lets you specify the values in the drop-down list: the only difference is whether the final control also includes a Field Box.

You can specify the values that can be chosen from the drop-down list by creating custom values or by using values that are in a database field. Creating custom values is a very simple process. Using database field values can sometimes be more complex but often can speed your work. First, look at how to add values in these two different ways. Once they are added, the values in the list can be manipulated in a similar way.

Appendix B: Reference Guide

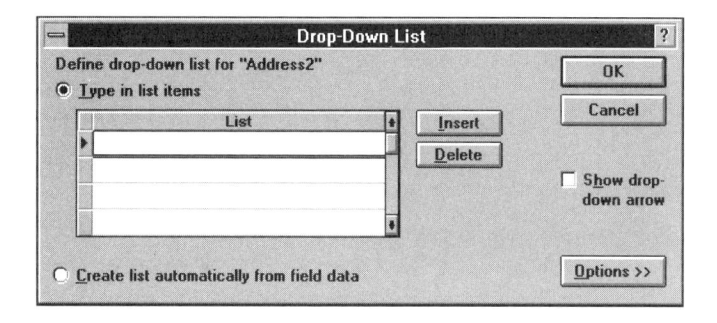

Figure B.130 The Drop-down List dialog box.

To create custom values, simple enter them in the list. You can modify this list in the same way that you do a field definition list. Click the Insert button to its right to insert a new, blank row above the current one. Use the field selection box at the left of each row to select (highlight) a row. Once a row is selected, click **Delete** to remove it, or click and drag its selection box to change field order. Apart from that, use the usual Windows editing keys to enter or change data.

When you are done, select **OK** to create a drop-down list that lets the user select from the values that you typed. That is all that you need to do to create most drop-down lists.

If you have a longer list of values, you can often save time by selecting the **Create list automatically from field data** radio button. Approach automatically adds all of the values currently in this field to the List. Then you can edit the list in the usual ways, to add more values or remove existing ones.

In most cases, this is all you need to do to create a value list instantly. There are a few cases, however, where you must use the expanded form of the dialog box (see Figure B.131).

If there are no values in the field, Approach automatically displays the expanded form of this dialog box when you select the **Create list automatically** radio button. You can also display the dialog box in this form by selecting the Options push button. This enlarged form of the dialog box lets you add values from fields other than the current one to the value list simply by selecting that field in the Field list. The values in the field you select replace any values already in the value list.

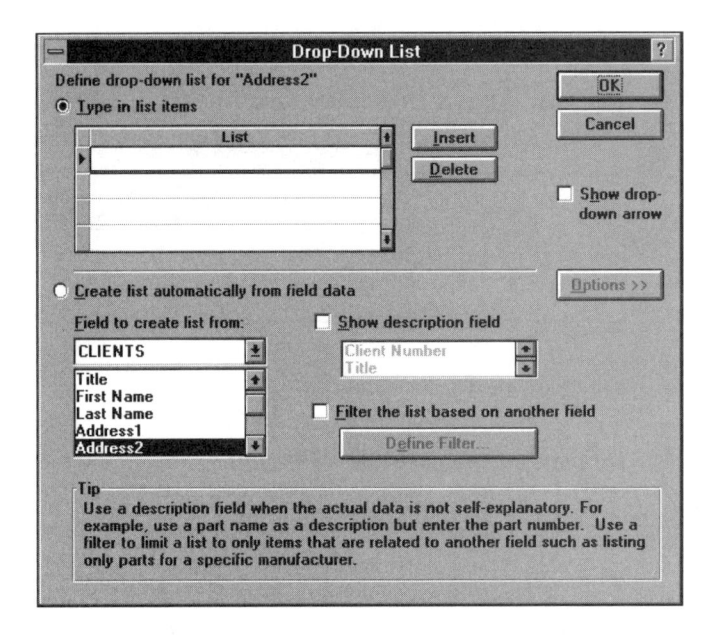

Figure B.131 The Expanded drop-down List dialog box.

If you select **Show description field**, the Field list under it is activated and can be used to add descriptions from a field to the List, which are used to represent the actual values stored in this field. For example, you can select the Client Number field from the list on the left (as the actual value to be entered), and select the Last Name field from the list on the right (as the value to be used as a description). Then the List displays the last names of clients, but when you select one the client number is entered in the field.

Descriptions from fields obviously cannot be used to enter new data. This feature is meant to be used when the data is already in another database file. Note that to use it, you must be sure that there is a unique value in each description field. You could not actually use it to enter Client numbers as described in the example above, because some Clients have the same last names. You could use it to enter a Part Description field and enter values in a Part Number field, as the tip in the dialog box says, only if each part has a unique description.

You can use **Define Filter** to limit the list. When you select it, Approach displays the Define Filter dialog box, which simply lets you choose a field to filter by. This feature is also useful only in relational databases. If you have one database that lists teachers and the courses they teach, you can use a filter to create a drop-down with only the courses taught by one teacher. Relational databases are discussed in Chapter 7.

After you have finished defining a drop-down list, you can no longer display its dialog box by using the Data entry type drop-down. If you want to modify its definition, select **Define list** under this drop-down to display its dialog box, and change it using the methods described above.

Check Boxes

Choose **Checkboxes** from the Data entry type drop-down of a Field's Info Box to display the Define Checkbox dialog box (see Figure B.132).

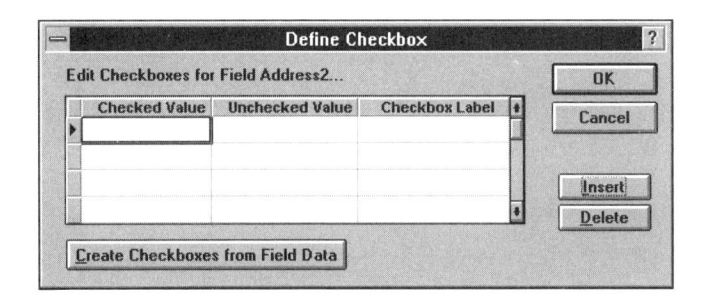

Figure B.132 The Define Checkbox dialog box.

To define a checkbox, you generally enter a Checked Value, Unchecked Value, and Checkbox label in one row of the list in this dialog box. Checkboxes are generally used to enter values in Boolean field—enter **Yes** as the Checked Value, **No** as the Unchecked Value, and some Label that explains to the user what the checkbox does.

It is also possible to create a group of checkboxes associated with a single field by entering multiple rows in this list. You can edit the values in the list as you do in the Drop-down dialog box, and you can automatically fill the list with all the values already in some field by clicking **Create Checkboxes** from Field Data button. If you do this, you should give each row of the list a Checked Value, no Unchecked Value, and a Label that indicates what the checked value is, so that users can select one of the checkboxes in the group to enter its value in the field.

However, users are not accustomed to using checkboxes in this way. To let the user choose among multiple values in this way, it is best to create a group of radio buttons to avoid confusion.

Radio Buttons

Choose **Radio buttons** from the Data entry type drop-down of a Field's Info Box to display the Define Radio Buttons dialog box (see Figure B.133).

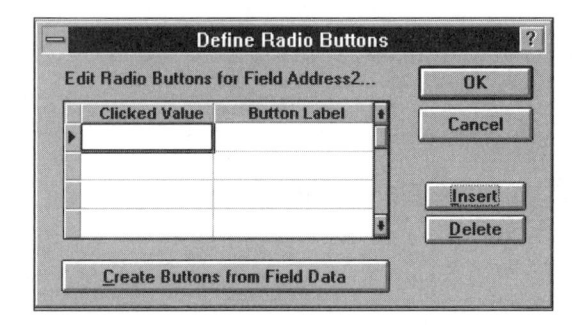

Figure B.133 The Define Radio Buttons dialog box.

To define a group of Radio Buttons, you should simply enter a list of Clicked Values and a Label associated with each. You can edit the values in the list as you do in the Drop-down dialog box, and it is sometimes useful to fill the list with all the values already in some field by clicking **Create Buttons** from Field Data push button.

Approach creates a group of radio buttons, and the user can select one to enter its value in the field. As with all radio buttons, one and only one must be selected. Selecting one automatically deselects others.

The Label panel of the Field Info Box

The Label panel lets you specify how the field's label is displayed (see Figure B.134):

- Control the font, color, and other typographical effects of the label, as you do with any text. For more details on these controls, see the Fonts panel of this Info Box in the section on *The Info Box for Fields*.

Appendix B: Reference Guide

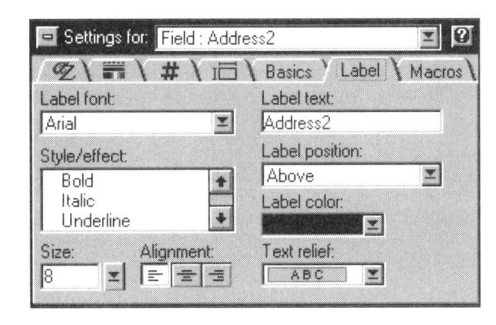

Figure B.134 The Label panel for a field.

- Change the label of the field by editing it in the Label text box. By default, the field's name is used as the label and displayed in this box.
- Use the Label position drop-down to locate the label above, below, left, or right of the field; or choose No label from this drop-down to eliminate the label.

The Macros panel of the Field Info Box

The Macros panel of the Field Info Box includes three drop-downs that let you attach a macro to the field (see Figure B.135). It runs when the focus enters the field (before the user edits its value), when the focus leaves the field (after the user has had the chance to edit its value), or when data changes. This makes it possible to control the data entered in a field very closely.

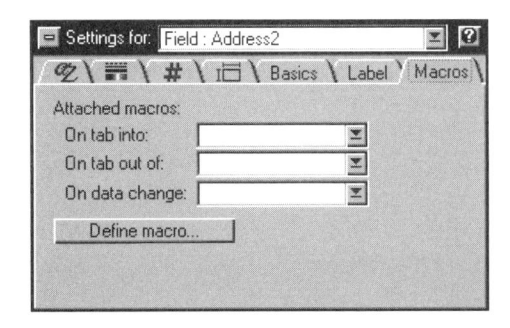

Figure B.135 The macros panel of the Info Box for a field.

Simply select existing macros from these drop-downs or, to create or edit a macro, click **Define macro** to display the Macros dialog box, covered earlier in the section on the *Macro Command* of the Tools menu.

The Checkbox group and Radio Button Group Info Boxes

You can control the style and properties of a checkbox or radio button group that you have created to speed data entry by using the Checkbox group or Radio button group Info Boxes, which are identical.

The first panel of the Info Box for a Checkbox or Radio Button Group lets you specify settings for lines and colors (see Figure B.136).

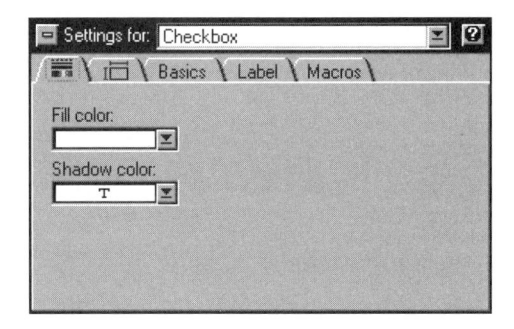

Figure B.136 The Lines and Colors panel of the Info Box for a Checkbox or Radio Button Group.

Use the drop-downs to select:

- A fill color.
- A shadow color.

The drop-downs used to select colors are simply a palette with a variety of colors, and you can click one to select it. The sample color on the upper left of each palette has the letter T in it to indicate that it is transparent. Choosing this color lets you see whatever is behind the object. When you place a graphic object, by default, its shadow is this color, so it is not visible.

The second panel of the Info Box for a Checkbox or Radio Button Group, displays indicates the size, location, and printing slide options of the object (see Figure B.137).

Appendix B: Reference Guide **631**

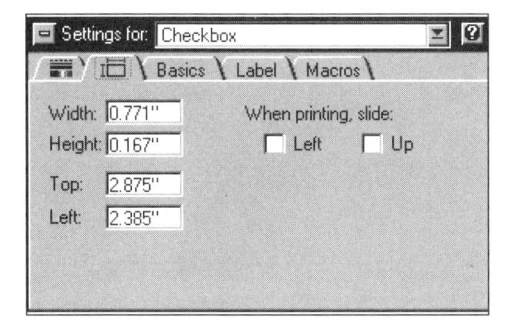

Figure B.137 The Size and Location panel of the Info Box for a Checkbox or Radio Button Group.

You can edit the numbers in the Width and Height text boxes to change the size of the object, or edit the numbers in the Top and Left text boxes to change its location. Generally, it is easier to change size and location by clicking and dragging the object itself—these numbers change accordingly.

The Left and Up check boxes in this panel can be used to close up spaces between objects when you print. If objects to the left or above the Checkbox or Radio Button Group change in size (for example, if the frame of a field shrinks, because it has less data than the frame holds), you can select these checkboxes to have the object slide left or up, so the space between objects remains the same.

The Basics panel of the Info Box for a Checkbox or Radio Button Group, is identical to the Basics panel for a field (see Figure B.138). For all the features of this complex panel, see the section on *The Basics Panel of the Field Info Box*.

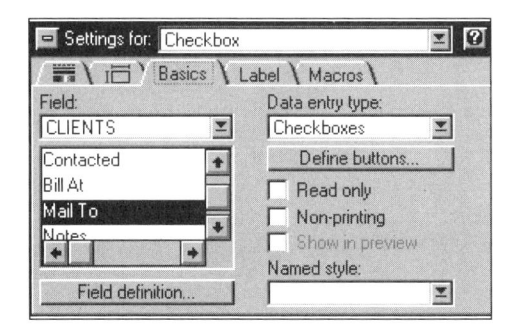

Figure B.138 The Basics panel of the Info Box for a Checkbox or Radio Button Group.

The Macros panel of the Checkbox group or Radio button group Info Box, includes three drop-downs that let you attach a macro to the field (see Figure B.139), so it runs when the focus enters the field (before the user edits its value), when the focus leaves the field (after the user has had the chance to edit its value), or when data changes. This makes it possible to control the data entered in a field very closely.

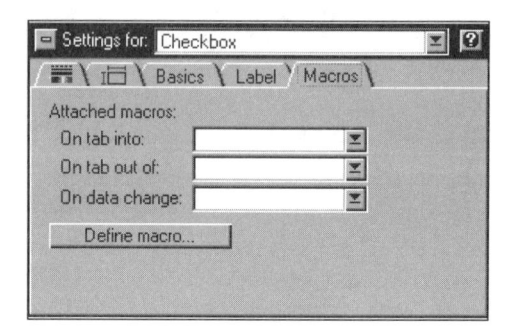

Figure B.139 The Macros panel of the Info Box for Checkbox or Radio Button group.

Simply select existing macros from these drop-downs or, to create or edit a macro, click **Define macro** to display the Macros dialog box, which was covered earlier in this Appendix, in the section on *Macro Command*.

The PicturePlus Info Box

The first panel of the Info Box for a PicturePlus field lets you specify settings for lines and colors (see Figure B.140).

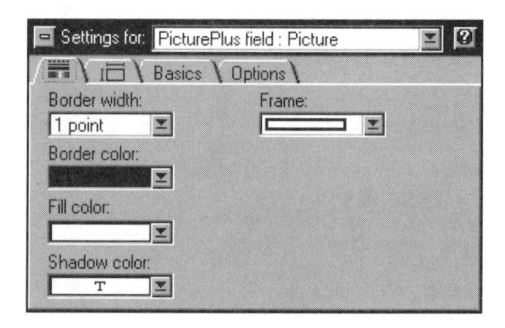

Figure B.140 The Lines and Colors panel of the Info Box for a PicturePlus field

Use the drop-downs to select:

- A line width between hairline and 12 points.
- A border color.
- A fill color.
- A shadow color.
- A frame style. The frame could be made of solid lines, double lines or several types of dotted lines, or could have special effects that make it appear to be raised or embossed.

The drop-downs used to select colors are simply palettes with a variety of colors, and you can click one to select it. The sample color on the upper left of each palette has the letter T in it to indicate that it is transparent. Choosing this color lets you see whatever is behind the object. When you place a graphic object, by default, its shadow is this color, so it is not visible.

The second panel of the Info Box for a PicturePlus field, displays indicates the size, location, and printing slide options of the object (see Figure B.141).

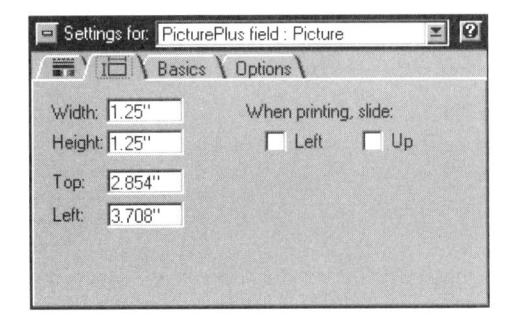

Figure B.141 The Size and Location panel of the Info Box for a PicturePlus field.

You can edit the numbers in the Width and Height text boxes to change the size of the object, or edit the numbers in the Top and Left text boxes to change its location. Generally, it is easier to change size and location by clicking and dragging the object itself—these numbers change accordingly.

The Left and Up checkboxes in this panel can be used to close up spaces between objects when you print. If objects to the left or above the PicturePlus field change in size (for example, if the frame of a field shrinks, because it has less data than the frame holds), you can select these check boxes to have the object slide left or up, so the space between objects remains the same.

The Basics panel includes a Field list that you use to select the PicturePlus field that holds the picture or other object that are displayed in this PicturePlus frame (see Figure B.142). If necessary, use the drop-down list to select a different database file.

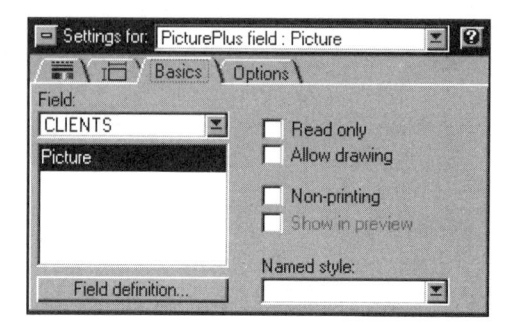

Figure B.142 The Basics Panel of the Info Box for a PicturePlus Fields.

If necessary, use **Field Definition** to display the Field Definition dialog box, which can change the definition of the fields in the database. This dialog box was covered in the section on the *New Command* of the TFile menu.

The Basics panel of the Info Box for a PicturePlus field controls the following styles and properties:

- *Read-Only* can be selected to prevent the user from launching the applications the OLE object was created in and editing it.
- *Allow Drawing* can be selected or deselected to control whether the user can draw a picture in the field using the mouse.
- *Non-printing* can be selected if you do not want the PicturePlus field to be printed. If you select this checkbox, the Show in preview checkbox is enabled, and you can select it if you want to display the object in print preview mode, even though it in not printed.

Use the Options panel of this Info Box to specify how Approach handles pictures that do not fit in the frame you created for them (see Figure B.143).

Appendix B: Reference Guide   **635**

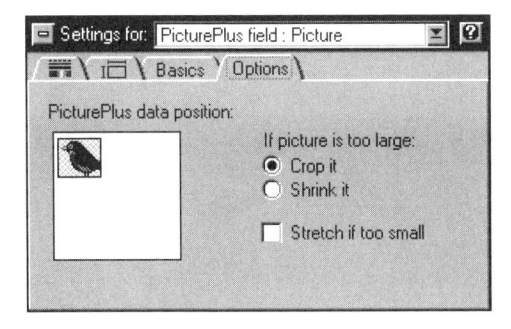

Figure B.143   The Options panel of the Info Box for a PicturePlus field.

You can specify what is done both for pictures that are too large and for those that are too small:

- *Too Large.* The radio buttons give you two options for handling pictures that are too large to fit in their frame. You can crop the picture so that it remains its original size but not all of it is displayed, or you can shrink it, so all of it is displayed but in reduced size.
- *Too Small.* The checkbox gives you options for handling pictures that are too small. Select it to stretch the picture proportionally to fill the entire frame, or leave it unselected to leave the picture its original size.

The Macro Button Info Box

The Font panel of the Macro Button Info box lets you control the font used for the text that is displayed on the button (see Figure B.144).

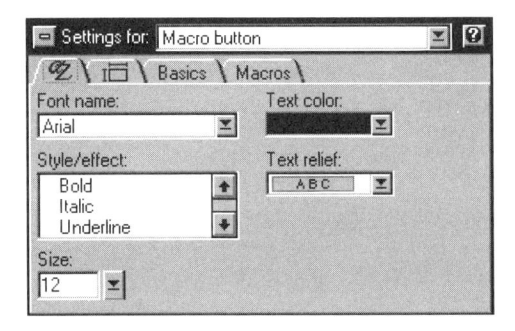

Figure B.144   The Font panel of the Info Box for a Macro Button.

Select a font, such as Arial or Roman, from the Font name list.

Select styles such as **Bold** or **Italic** or effects such as Underline or Strikethrough from the Style/effect list. You can select multiple styles and effects: when you select one, it is checked, and you can select it again to remove the effect.

Select a size expressed in points from the Size list. The options available in these lists depend on which fonts you have installed under Windows.

Use the Alignment buttons in the Alignment area to specify if the data should be centered within the field's borders, or aligned to the left or right edge of the field.

The Text color drop-down displays a color palette that lets you select the color of the letters.

The Text relief drop-down lets you make the text in the field appear to be flat, raised above the background, or carved into the background.

The second panel of the Info Box for a Macro Button, displays indicates the size, location, and printing slide options of the object (see Figure B.145).

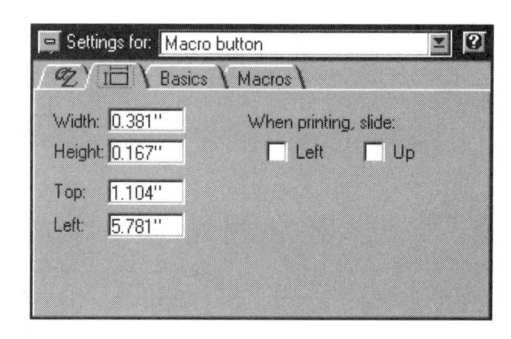

Figure B.145 The Size and Location panel of the Info Box for a Macro Button.

You can edit the numbers in the Width and Height text boxes to change the size of the object, or edit the numbers in the Top and Left text boxes to change its location. Generally, it is easier to change size and location by clicking and dragging the object itself—these numbers change accordingly.

The Left and Up check boxes in this panel can be used to close up spaces between objects when you print. If objects to the left or above the Macro button change in size, you can select these check boxes to have the Macro button slide left or up, so the space between objects remains the same.

Appendix B: Reference Guide

The Basics panel of a Macro Button's Info Box lets you specify several features of how the buttons is displayed (see Figure B.146).

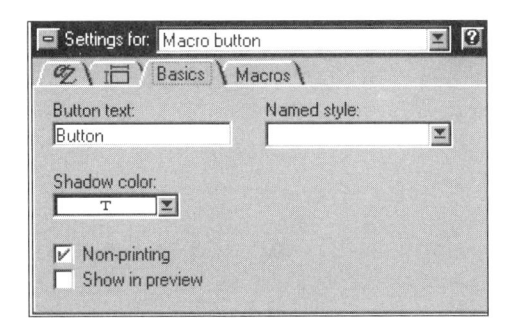

Figure B.146 The Basics panel of the Info Box for Macro Button.

Most important, it lets you specify the text displayed on the button. Simply type the label you want to appear on the button in the Button text box.

You can also use this panel to apply a Named style and shadow color to a button and to specify that it is non-printing. Unlike other objects, Macro buttons are Non-printing by default, since they are used to execute a command when you are looking at a view on screen, rather than to display data.

The Macros Panel of the Info Box lets you attach a macro to the button (see Figure B.147).

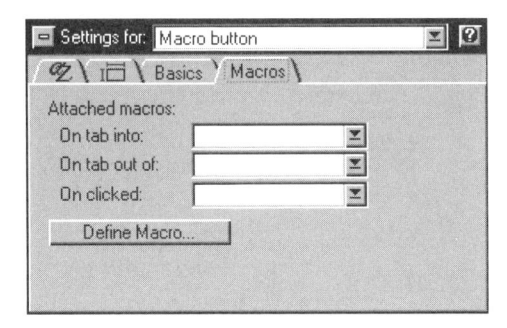

Figure B.147 The Macros panel of the Info Box for a Macro Button.

Use **On clicked** to select the macro that runs when the user clicks the push button. You can also attach a Macro to the push button, as you can to other objects, by using the On tab into or On tab out of drop-downs—the macro runs automatically when the user presses **Tab** or **Shift+Tab** to move the focus to the button. However, users do not expect push buttons to run in this way, and these drop-downs should only be used in special cases.

If the macro already exists, use **On clicked** to select it. To create or modify the macro, select **Define Macro** to display the Macros dialog box covered earlier in the section on the *Macros Command* of the Tools menu.

Styles and Properties of Views and their Components

The earlier sections of this appendix covered styles and properties of individual objects that can be used in many different types of views. The remainder of the appendix covers the styles and properties of the views themselves and of components of a view, such as the repeating panels that can be added to Forms, the Summary Panels of Reports, and the Rows and Columns of Crosstabs.

The Form Info Box

If an entire form (rather than an individual object) is selected, the Form Info Box is displayed.

The first panel of this Info Box, lets you specify settings for lines and colors (see Figure B.148).

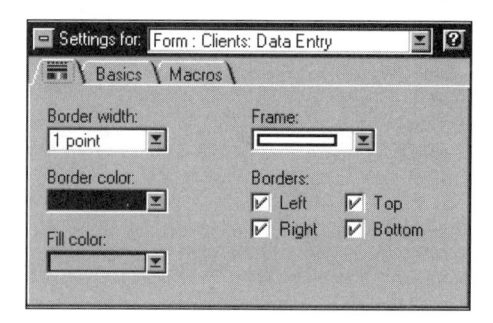

Figure B.148 The Lines and Colors panel of the Info Box for a Form.

Use the drop-downs to select:

Appendix B: Reference Guide **639**

- A line width between hairline and 12 points.
- A border color.
- A fill color.
- A shadow color.
- A frame style. The frame could be made of solid lines, double lines or several types of dotted lines, or could have special effects that make it appear to be raised or embossed.

The drop-downs used to select colors are simply palettes with a variety of colors, and you can click one to select it. The sample color on the upper left of each palette has the letter T in it to indicate that it is transparent. Choosing this color lets you see whatever is behind the object. When you place a graphic object, by default, its shadow is this color, so it is not visible.

Use the Left, Right, Top and Bottom checkboxes to specify whether the frame should be displayed on each edge of the field.

The Basics panel of this Info Box lets you control basic features of the Form (see Figure B.149).

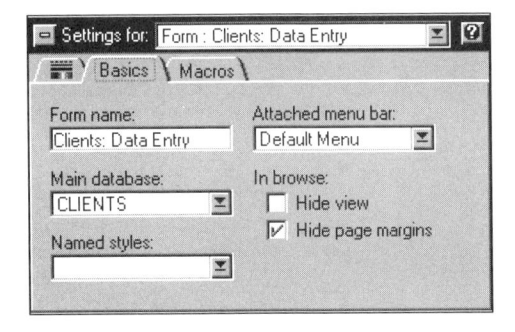

Figure B.149 The Basics panel of the Info Box for a Form.

The features are:

- *Form name.* Use the Form name text box to modify the name of the form. Simply edit the existing name, or replace it with a new name. The new name is displayed on the Form's divider tab.
- *Main database.* This drop-down lets you control the main database of a form. This is used only if you are working with a relational database.

- *Named styles.* This drop-down lets you apply a named style to the form, like the equivalent drop-down for individual objects. Named styles were covered in the section on the *Named Styles command* of the Tools menu.
- *Attached menu bar.* Use this drop-down to display the short menus or a custom menu rather than the default menu whenever the user switches to this view.
- *Hide view.* Select this checkbox if you do not want this view to be displayed in Browse mode. This feature is useful only if you are setting up an application for a novice.
- *Hide page margins.* This checkbox is selected by default. If you deselect it, the margins will be displayed in Browse mode: the fields on the form will be shifted right, for example, because the left margin in included in the screen.

The Macros panel of this Info Box, includes two drop-downs that let you run a macro automatically whenever the user switch into or out of this view (see Figure B.150). Simply select an existing macro, or, to create or edit a macro, click **Define macro** to display the Macros dialog box.

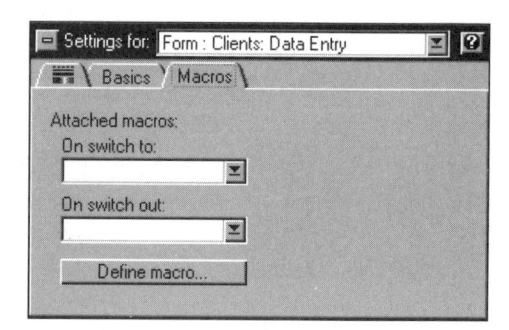

Figure B.150   The Macros panel of the Info Box for a Form.

The Repeating Panel Info Box

If the **Repeating panel of a Form** is selected, the Repeating Panel Info Box is displayed.

The first panel of the Info Box for a Repeating panel of a report, lets you specify settings for lines and colors (see Figure B.151).

Appendix B: Reference Guide **641**

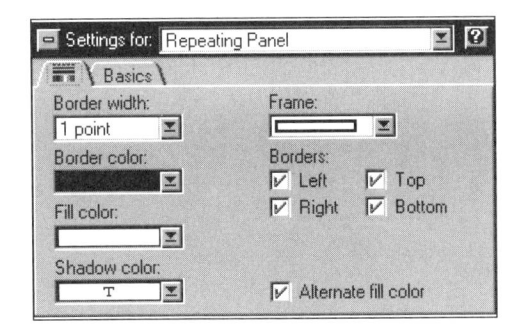

Figure B.151 The Lines and Colors panel of the Info Box for the Repeating panel of a Form.

Use the drop-downs to select:

- A line width between hairline and 12 points.
- A border color.
- A fill color.
- A shadow color.
- A frame style. The frame could be made of solid lines, double lines or several types of dotted lines, or could have special effects that make it appear to be raised or embossed.

The drop-downs used to select colors are simply palettes with a variety of colors, and you can click one to select it. The sample color on the upper left of each palette has the letter T in it to indicate that it is transparent. Choosing this color lets you see whatever is behind the object. When you place a graphic object, by default, its shadow is this color, so it is not visible.

Use the Left, Right, Top and Bottom checkboxes to specify whether the border should be displayed on each edge of the Repeating panel. By default, it is not displayed, and selecting these checkboxes adds a visible frame around the Repeating panel.

Select **Alternate Panel Background With** to display alternating lines in the repeating panel with different background colors, if this makes it easier to view. If you select this option, the color selected in the Fill color drop-down is used for every second line in the repeating panel. It alternates with white lines.

Use the Basics panel of the Info Box to specify the properties shown in Figure B.152.

Practical Approach, 3.0

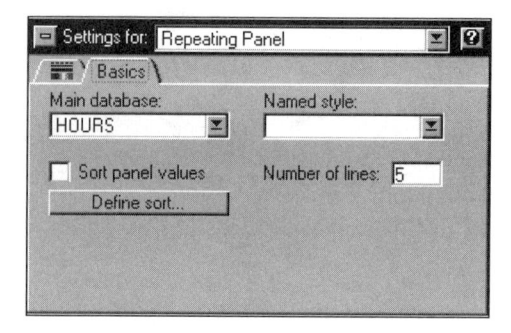

Figure B.152 The Basic panel of the Info Box for the Repeating Panel of a form.

- Use **Main database** to select the main database of the panel. **Do not confuse this with the main database of the entire form**, which is the one database of the one-to-many relationship. The main database of the panel is the many database of the one-to-many relationship that the form is based on. You might want to change the main database of the panel if you are using a more complex relationship, that has other databases joined to the fields displayed in the panel, such as the many-to-many relationship described above.

- Use **Number of Lines** to specify how many lines should be included in the repeating panel. If there is more data than can be displayed in this number of lines, a scroll bar is added to the repeating panel, so you can scroll through all the data.

- Use **Named style** to apply a named style to the panel. Named styles are covered in the section on the *Named Styles Command* of the Tools menu.

- Use **Sort panel values** if you want to control the order of the records in the panel. Click **Define sort** to display the Sort dialog box, and use it to define the sort order. The Sort dialog box is covered in the section on the *Sort Command* of the Browse menu.

The Report Info Box

If an entire report (rather than an individual object) is selected, the Report Info Box is displayed.

The Basics panel of this Info Box (see Figure B.153) lets you control the following features of the report:

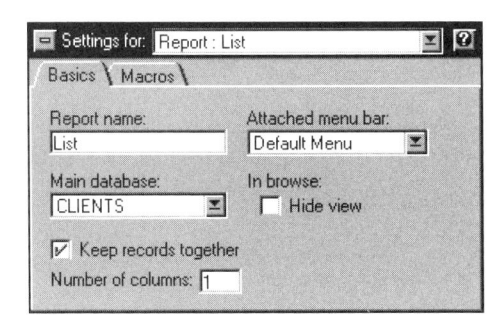

Figure B.153 The Basics panel of the Info Box for a Report.

- Use **Report name** to modify the name of the report. Simply edit the existing name, or replace it with a new name. The new name is displayed on the Report's divider tab.
- The **Main database** lets you control the main database of a report. This is used only if you are working with a relational database.
- If **Keep Records together** is selected, the report will not be printed with one record broken up on two pages. If there is not enough room at the bottom of the page for the entire record, Approach will begin printing it on the next page.
- **Number of columns** lets you specify the number of columns in the report. Rather than creating a columnar report with a separate column for each field, you can create a report with the data in just a few columns. Specify the number of columns you want to use, begin with the standard report layout, and then move some fields to the other columns, or copy the data to repeat it across the page.
- Use **Attached menu bar** to display the short menus or a custom menu rather than the default menu whenever the user switches to this view. Attached Menus are covered in the section on the *Customize Menus Command* of the Tool menu.

The Macros panel of this Info Box includes two drop-downs that let you run a macro automatically whenever the user switch into or out of this view (see Figure B.154). Simply select an existing macro, or, to create or edit a macro, click **Define macro** to display the Macros dialog box.

Practical Approach, 3.0

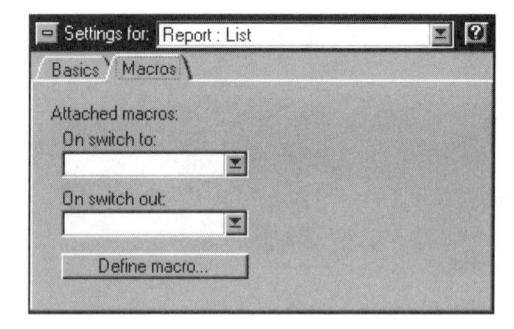

Figure B.154 The Macros panel of the Info Box for a Report.

The Body Info Box

If the Body Panel of a report is selected, the Body Info Box is displayed.

The first panel of the Info Box for a Body Panel of a report lets you specify settings for lines and colors (see Figure B.155).

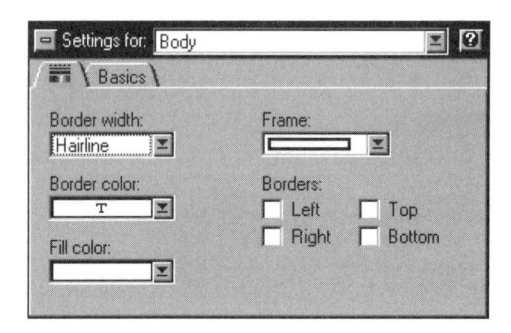

Figure B.155 The Lines and Colors panel of the Info Box for The Body Panel of a Report.

Use the drop-downs to select:

- A line width between hairline and 12 points.
- A border color.
- A fill color.
- A shadow color.

- A frame style that could be made of solid lines, double lines or several types of dotted lines, or could have special effects that make it appear to be raised or embossed.

The drop-downs used to select colors are simply palettes with a variety of colors, and you can click one to select it. The sample color on the upper left of each palette has the letter T in it to indicate that it is transparent. Choosing this color lets you see whatever is behind the object. When you place a graphic object, by default, its shadow is this color, so it is not visible.

Use the Left, Right, Top and Bottom checkboxes to specify whether the border should be displayed on each edge of the body panel. By default, it is not displayed, and selecting these checkboxes adds a visible frame around each record of the report.

Use the Basics Panel of the Info Box for the Body Panel of a Report, to apply a Named style to the Body panel (see Figure B.156).

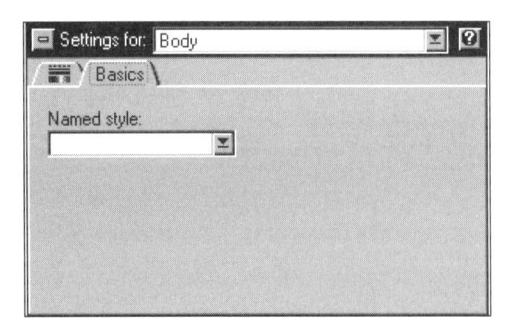

Figure B.156 The Basics panel of the Info Box for the Body Panel of a Report.

The Summary Panel Info Box

If the Summary panel of a report is selected, the Summary Panel Info Box is displayed.

The first panel of the Info Box for a Summary panel of a report lets you specify settings for lines and colors (see Figure B.157).

Use the drop-downs to select:

- A line width between hairline and 12 points.
- A border color.

- A fill color.
- A shadow color.
- A frame style that could be made of solid lines, double lines or several types of dotted lines, or could have special effects that make it appear to be raised or embossed.

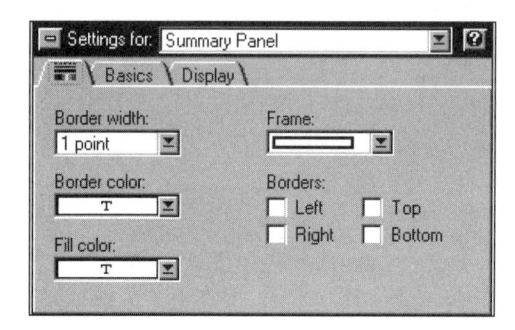

Figure B.157   The Lines and Colors panel of the Info Box for Summary panel of a Report.

The drop-downs used to select colors are simply palettes with a variety of colors, and you can click one to select it. The sample color on the upper left of each palette has the letter T in it to indicate that it is transparent. Choosing this color lets you see whatever is behind the object. When you place a graphic object, by default, its shadow is this color, so it is not visible.

Use the Left, Right, Top and Bottom checkboxes to specify whether the border should be displayed on each edge of the Summary panel. By default, it is not displayed, and selecting these checkboxes adds a visible frame around the summary panel.

Use the Basics panel of the Info Box for a Summary Panel of a report to control how this panel summarizes the data (see Figure B.158).

The radio buttons in the Summarize area let you select what groups of records the summaries are based on:

- *Every __ record(s)*. Gives a summary for groups consisting of some group based on a number you enter in the text box. For example, if you enter 10 in the text box, the report includes summary information on every ten records in the database.
- *All Records*. Gives summary information on all the records in the database.

Appendix B: Reference Guide   **647**

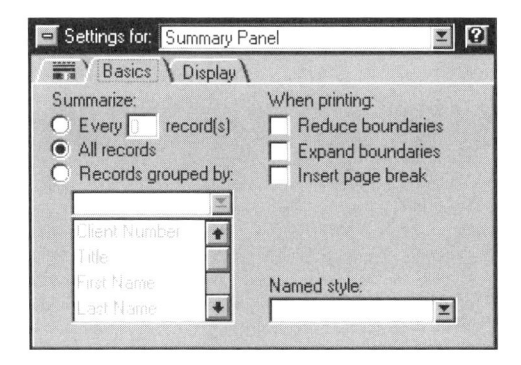

Figure B.158   The Basics panel of the Info Box for a Summary Panel of a Report.

- *Records Grouped By*. Gives summary information based on some field that you specify. Select the field in the list of fields and if necessary, select the database from the drop-down list. The records are sorted on this field, and summary information is given for every value in the field.

Select **Reduce boundaries** if you want the panel to be reduced in size if there is not enough information to fill it. Select **Expand Boundaries** to expand the size if there is too much information to fit in it when you print the report. Select **Insert page break** if you want each summary panel to be printed on a new page.

Use the Named style drop-down to apply a Named style to the Summary panel. Named styles are covered earlier in the section on the *Named Style Command* of the Tools menu.

Use the Display panel of the Info Box for a Summary Panel of a report, to control how where the summary is displayed (see Figure B.159).

It includes the following controls:

- Use **Alignment** to Left justify, right justify, or center the summary panel on the page.
- Use the **Leading** radio button to display the summary before the group of records it applies to. The **Trailing** radio button displays the summary after the group of records that it applies to.

Practical Approach, 3.0

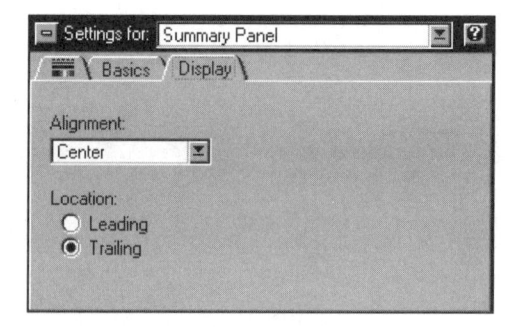

Figure B.159 The Basics panel of the Info Box for a Summary Panel of a Report.

The Mailing Labels Info Box

If an entire Mailing Label view (rather than an individual object) is selected, the Mailing Labels Info Box is displayed.

The first panel of this Info Box lets you specify settings for lines and colors (see Figure B.160).

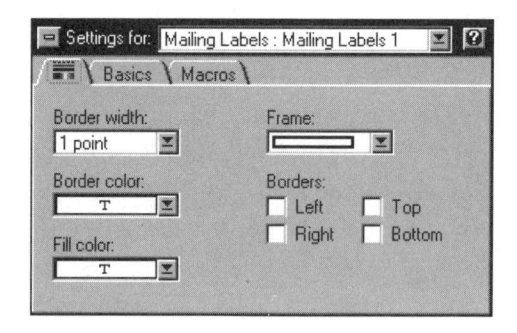

Figure B.160 The Lines and Colors panel of the Info Box for Mailing Labels.

Use the drop-downs to select:

- A line width between hairline and 12 points.
- A border color.
- A fill color.

- A shadow color.
- A frame style could be made of solid lines, double lines or several types of dotted lines, or could have special effects that make it appear to be raised or embossed.

The drop-downs used to select colors are simply palettes with a variety of colors, and you can click one to select it. The sample color on the upper left of each palette has the letter T in it to indicate that it is transparent. Choosing this color lets you see whatever is behind the object. When you place a graphic object, its shadow is this color, by default, so it is not visible.

Use the Left, Right, Top and Bottom checkboxes to specify whether the frame should be displayed on each edge of the mailing label view. (This frames the entire view, not individual labels.)

The Basics panel of this Info Box (see Figure B.161) lets you control the following features of the Mailing Label:

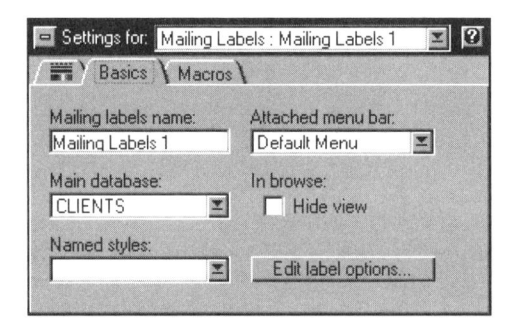

Figure B.161 *The Basics panel of the Info Box for Mailing Labels.*

- Use **Mailing Labels name** to modify the name of the Mailing Label. Simply edit the existing name, or replace it with a new name. The new name is displayed on the Mailing Label's divider tab.
- The **Main database** drop-down lets you control the main database of a Mailing Label. This is used only if you are working with a relational database.
- The **Named styles** drop-down lets you apply a named style to the Mailing Label, like the equivalent drop-down for individual objects.

- Use the **Attached menu bar** drop-down to display the short menus or a custom menu rather than the default menu whenever the user switches to this view.
- Select **Hide view** if you do not want this view to be displayed in Browse mode. This feature is useful only if you are setting up an application for a novice.
- Select **Edit label options** to display the Mailing Label Options dialog box, shown in Figure B.163. This dialog box is identical to the Options panel of the Mailing Label Assistant. It can be used to change options of existing labels, just as the Assistant is used to create options for new labels. This dialog box is useful if you have laid out mailing labels, printed a test copy of them, and found there are minor differences from your mailing labels. You can change the layout without starting again from scratch. Its features covered in the section on the *Mailing Label Command*.

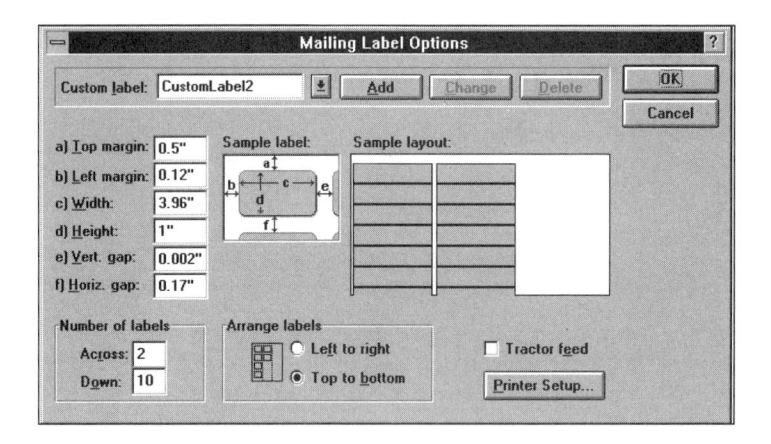

Figure B.162 The Mailing Label Options dialog box.

The Macros panel of this Info Box includes two drop-downs that let you run a macro automatically whenever the user switches into or out of this view (see Figure B.163). Simply select an existing macro, or, to create or edit a macro, click **Define macro** to display the Macros dialog box, which is covered in the section on the *Macros Command* of the Tools menu.

Appendix B: Reference Guide **651**

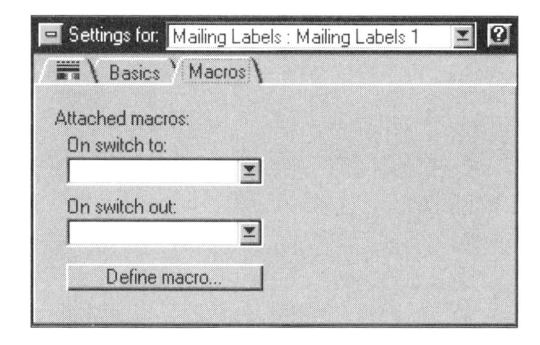

Figure B.163 The Macros panel of the Info Box for Mailing Labels.

The Borders of Mailing Labels

The borders of each mailing label is a rounded rectangle. If you select it, the Rounded rectangle Info Box is displayed.

The Form Letter Info Box

If an entire Form Letter (rather than an individual object) is selected, the Form Letter Info Box is displayed.

The first panel of this Info Box lets you specify settings for lines and colors (see Figure B.164).

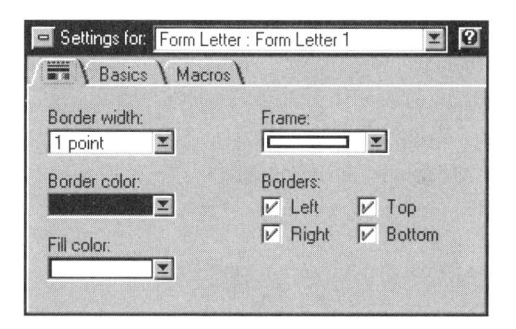

Figure B.164 The Lines and Colors panel of the Info Box for a Form Letter.

Use the drop-downs to select:

- A line width between hairline and 12 points.
- A border color.
- A fill color.
- A shadow color.
- A frame style that could be made of solid lines, double lines or several types of dotted lines, or could have special effects that make it appear to be raised or embossed.

The drop-downs used to select colors are simply palettes with a variety of colors, and you can click one to select it. The sample color on the upper left of each palette has the letter T in it to indicate that it is transparent. Choosing this color lets you see whatever is behind the object. When you place a graphic object, by default, its shadow is this color, so it is not visible.

Use the Left, Right, Top and Bottom checkboxes to specify whether the frame should be displayed on each margin of the form letter.

The Basics panel of this Info Box (see Figure B.165) lets you control the following features of the Form Letter:

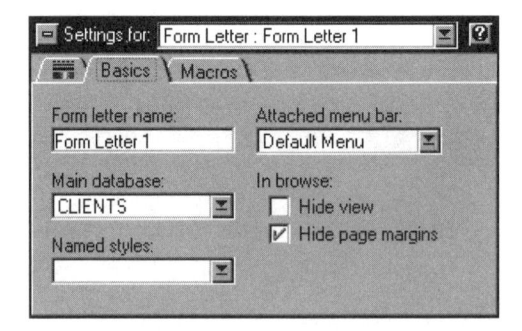

Figure B.165 The Basics panel of the Info Box for a Form Letter.

- Use **Form Letter name** to modify the name of the Form Letter. Simply edit the existing name, or replace it with a new name. The new name is displayed on the Form Letter's divider tab.

- The **Main database** drop-down lets you control the main database of a Form Letter. This is used only if you are working with a relational database.
- The **Named styles** drop-down lets you apply a named style to the Form Letter, like the equivalent drop-down for individual objects.
- Use the **Attached menu bar** drop-down to display the short menus or a custom menu rather than the default menu whenever the user switches to this view.
- Select **Hide view** if you do not want this view to be displayed in Browse mode. This feature is useful only if you are setting up an application for a novice.

The Macros panel of this Info Box includes two drop-downs that let you run a macro automatically whenever the user switch into or out of this view (see Figure B.166). Simply select an existing macro, or, to create or edit a macro, click **Define macro** to display the Macros dialog box.

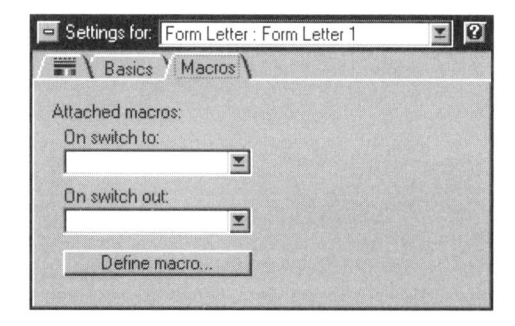

Figure B.166 The Macros panel of the Info Box for a Form Letter.

The Worksheet Info Box

The Basics panel of the Worksheet Info Box (see Figure B.167) lets you control the following features of the Worksheet:

- Use the **Name** text box to modify the name of the Worksheet. Simply edit the existing name, or replace it with a new name. The new name is displayed on the Worksheet's divider tab.

Practical Approach, 3.0

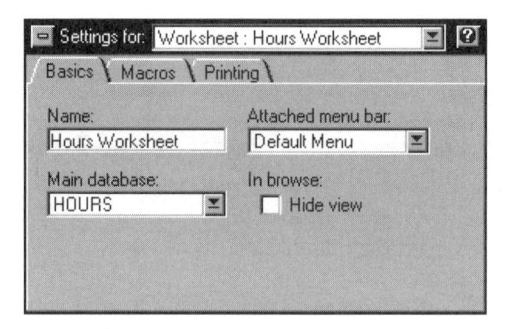

Figure B.167 The Basics panel of the Info Box for a Worksheet.

- The **Main database** drop-down lets you control the main database of a Worksheet. This is used only if you are working with a relational database.
- Use the **Attached menu bar** drop-down to display the short menus or a custom menu rather than the default menu whenever the user switches to this view.
- Select **Hide view** if you do not want this view to be displayed in Browse mode. This feature is useful only if you are setting up an application for a novice.

The Macros panel of this Info Box includes two drop-downs that let you run a macro automatically whenever the user switch into or out of this view (see Figure B.168). Simply select an existing macro, to create or edit a macro, click **Define macro** to display the Macros dialog box.

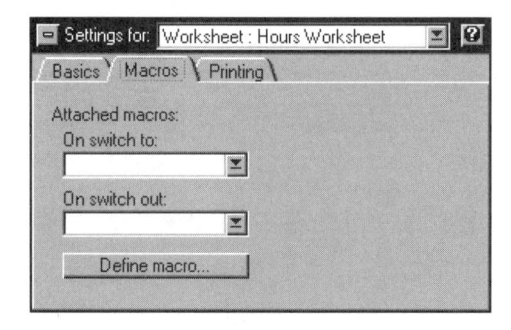

Figure B.168 The Macros panel of the Info Box for a Worksheet.

The Printing panel of this Info Box lets you set the following specifications, that are useful when you print the Worksheet (see Figure B.169).

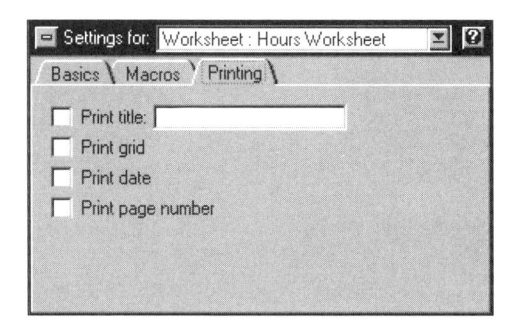

Figure B.169 The Printing Panel of the Info Box for a Worksheet.

- Select **Print title** and enter a title in the text box to its right if you want a title above the printout of the worksheet.
- Select **Print grid** if you want the printout to include the grid of lines between the cells of the Worksheet.
- Select **Print date** and **Print Page number** if you want the printout to include the current date and page numbers.

The Column Info Box

If one or more columns of a Worksheet are selected, or if only the header or the cells of the column are selected, the Column Info Box is displayed.

The Fonts panel lets you select the typeface, size, style, alignment and other effects of its font used to display the data (see Figure B.170).

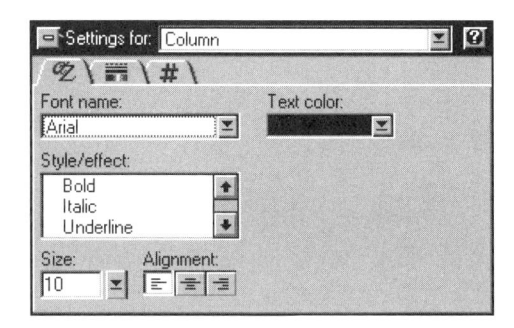

Figure B.170 The Fonts panel for a column of a Worksheet.

The Lines and Colors panel lets you select the fill color and border color of the column (see Figure B.171). This border color applies to the entire column, not to individual cells.

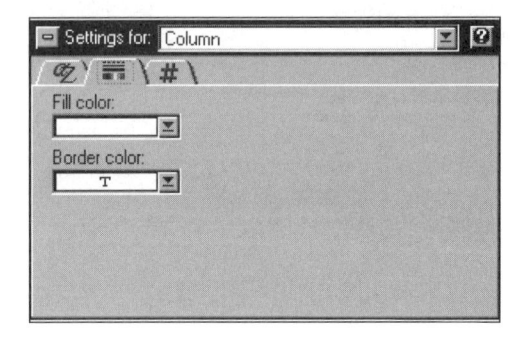

Figure B.171 The Lines and Colors panel for a column of a Worksheet.

The Format panel lets you format data. Its options depend on the data type of the field in the column. It works like the Format panel of the Info Box for Fields.

The Header Info Box

If you are editing the header of the column of a Worksheet, you can use the Header Info Box to change its style and properties.

The Fonts Panel of the Header Info Box lets you select the typeface, size, style, alignment and other effects of its font used to display the data (see Figure B.172).

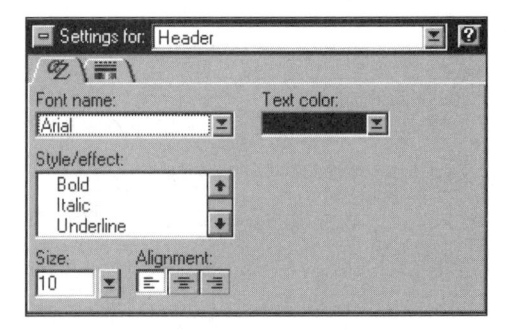

Figure B.172 The Fonts panel of the Info Box for a Header.

Appendix B: Reference Guide

The Lines and colors panel of the Header Info Box lets you control the Fill color and border color of the header (see Figure B.173).

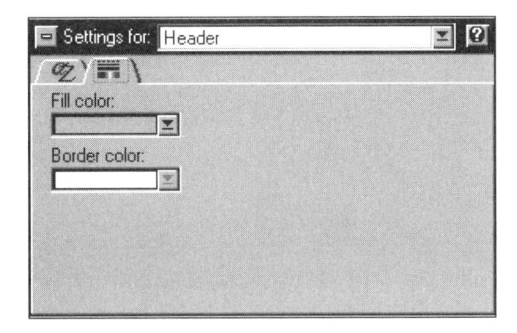

Figure B.173 The Lines and Colors panel of the Info Box for a Header.

Info Boxes for Crosstabs

Crosstabs have the same Info Boxes as Worksheets:

- If the entire **Crosstab** or a single cell is selected, the Crosstab Info Box is displayed, which is identical to the Worksheet Info Box (see Figure B.174).

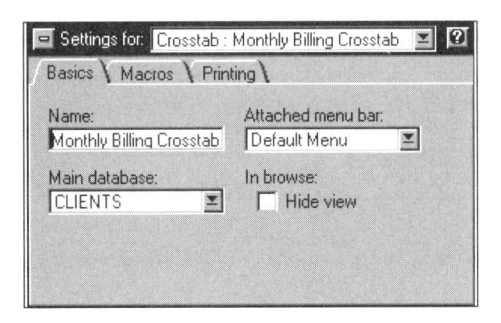

Figure B.174 The Crosstab Info Box.

- If a row or column is selected, the Row Info Box or the Column Info Box is displayed (see Figure B.175). Both of these are identical to the Column Info Box for a Worksheet.

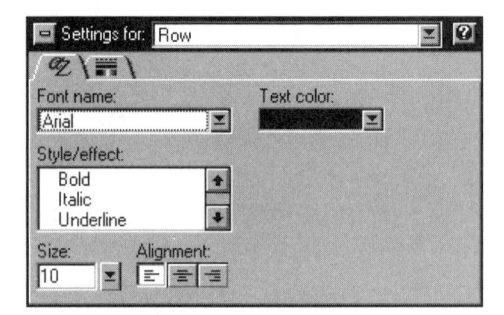

Figure B.175   The Row Info Box.

- If the header of a row or column is selected, the Header Info Box is displayed, which is identical to the Header Info Box for a Worksheet (see Figure B.176).

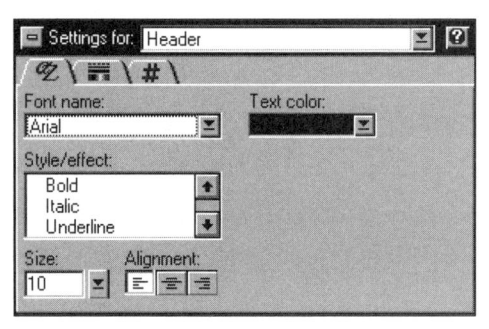

Figure B.176   The Header Info Box.

For more information on any of these, see the sections on *Worksheet Info Box*, *Column Info Box*, and *Header Info Box*.

Shortcut Keys

You can use shortcut keys as a substitute for many menu selections in Approach. To use menu shortcut keys, hold down **Ctrl** while you press some other key or key combination. All of these are listed on the menus, to the right of the menu selection. Generally, you can learn the keys of the menu selections that you use frequently without any effort. Table B.4 summarizes these Ctrl key shortcuts for reference.

Appendix B: Reference Guide

Table B.4   Ctrl Key Shortcuts.

Menu Selection	Shortcut Key
Actual Size (100%)	Ctrl+1
Alignment	Ctrl+I
Browse	Ctrl+B
Copy	Ctrl+C
Cut	Ctrl+X
Delete Record	Ctrl+Del
Design	Ctrl+D
Fast Format	Ctr+-M
Find	Ctrl+F
Go To Record	Ctrl+W
Group	Ctrl+G
Hide Record	Ctrl+H
Insert Time	Ctrl+Shift+T
Insert Previous Value	Ctrl+Shift+V
Insert Time	Ctrl+Shift+D
New Record	Ctrl+N
Open	Ctrl+O
Paste	Ctrl+V
Preview	Ctrl+Shift+B
Print	Ctrl+P
Refresh	Ctrl+R
Save Approach File	Ctrl+S
Show All	Ctrl+A
Show Drawing Tools	Ctrl+W
Show Ruler	Ctrl+J
Snap to Grid	Ctrl+Y
Sort	Ctrl+T
Style & Properties	Ctrl+E
Undo	Ctrl+Z
Ungroup	Ctrl+U

Shortcut Keys for Moving through the Database

There are a few options on the Browse menu that let you move through the database file, which have shortcut keys based on the cursor movement keys. These are summarized in Table B.5.

Table B.5 Shortcut Keys for Movement through the Database File.

Menu selection	Shortcut keys
First Record	Ctr+-Home
Last Record	Ctrl+End
Previous Record	PgUp
Next Record	PgDn

Alternative Editor Shortcut Keys

Finally, there are alternative shortcut keys for several editor functions, that can be used instead of the ones displayed on the menus, which were listed in Table B.6. These are included for compatibility with earlier Windows programs, where they were the most common shortcut keys for these functions. They are listed in Table B.3.

Table B.6 Alternative Editor Shortcut Keys.

Menu selection	Shortcut keys
Copy	Ctrl-Ins (same as Ctrl-C)
Cut	Shift-Del (same as Ctrl-X)
Paste	Shift-Ins (same as Ctrl-V)
Undo	Alt-Backspace (same as Ctrl-Z)

Finally, **Alt+** the first letter of any menu option can be used as a shortcut key combination to pull down that menu. Once the menu is pulled down, the underlined letter of any menu option may be used as a shortcut key to select that option.

Appendix C

Windows Basics

This Appendix is meant for readers who are not already comfortable with the features found in most Windows applications. It describes how to make selections from the pop-up menus found in Windows applications, change the size of a Window, use the different controls found in the dialog boxes of Windows applications, and other basics.

Windows applications are generally easy to learn because these features are common to all of them. Readers who are familiar with other Windows applications do not need to relearn the basics covered in this appendix.

Mouse Actions

You constantly use the mouse when you are working with Windows applications, and there are four basic actions that you must perform with it:

- *Click.* Move the pointer to the appropriate location, and then press and release the left mouse button quickly.
- *Double-click.* Move the pointer to the appropriate location, and then click the left mouse button twice in very rapid succession.
- *Click and Drag.* Move the pointer to the location where the action begins, and then press and hold down the left mouse button. Move the pointer to the location where the action ends, then release the mouse button.
- *Right-click.* Move the pointer to the appropriate location and click the right mouse button.

You usually use the left mouse button. The right button is used only in special cases.

Pop-Up Menus

Windows applications all use what are called pop-up or pull-down menus. A menu bar with all of the Main menu options is always displayed at the top of the application. When you select one of the items on the menu bar, a submenu pops up, and you can make selections from it.

Some items on the pop-up submenus have an arrowhead to their right. If you select them, an additional submenu pops up to present you with more options. After the user has selected **Create** from the Main menu and then selected **Drawing** from the Create pop-up menu, for example, another submenu pops up to let you choose among a number of different types of drawing that you can create (see Figure C.1).

Appendix C: Windows Basics

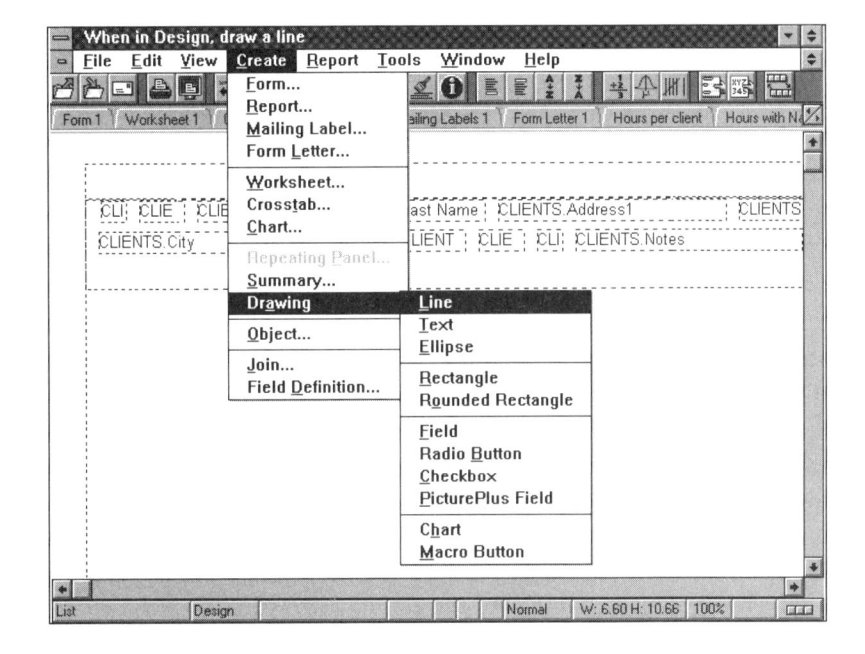

Figure C.1 Using pop-up menus.

Making Selections Using the Mouse

To choose an option from the menu using the mouse, simply click the item on the Main menu bar to display the pop-up submenu. Then click the option that you want to choose on the pop-up submenu. Click anywhere else to make the submenu disappear without making any choice.

Alternatively, click the item on the Main menu to pop up a submenu, keep holding the mouse button down, and drag downward to highlight the submenu option you want. Release the mouse button to choose the highlighted option.

Making Selections Using the Keyboard

An easy way to make a selection using the keyboard is to hold down the **Alt** key and press the underlined letter of the Main menu option you want to display on its submenu. For example, press **Alt+F** to display the File menu pop-up menu. Then press the underlined letter of the submenu option you want. After popping up the File menu, for example, simply press **O** to choose Open.

You can also press **Alt** to move the highlight to the Main menu bar without displaying a submenu. Press the **Right Arrow** and **Left Arrow** to move among the options on the menu bar; a help line describing each one is displayed in the status bar. Press **Enter** to choose one and to display its submenu.

After displaying a pop-up submenu, you can use the **Up Arrow** and **Down Arrow** to move among its options (rather than pressing the underlined key of one of the options). Again, as you move the highlight among the menu options, a help line is displayed in the status bar describing what each one does. Press **Enter** to choose the highlighted option.

Press **Esc** to back out of the menu without selecting an option. If you press **Esc** once, the pop-up disappears, but an option of the menu bar is still highlighted. Press **Esc** again to back out of the menu system entirely.

Shortcut Keys

Many menu options also have Control-key shortcuts, which are the quickest and easiest way to select. The shortcut key is displayed to the right of the option on the menu pop-up.

For example, pressing **Ctrl+O** is equivalent to choosing **Open** from the File menu.

As you use the menus, notice the shortcut keys for the options you use most frequently. You will learn them with little or no effort.

Common Features of Windows Menus

The Main menu bars of virtually all Windows applications have the following options in common:

- The *File menu*, on the far left, is used for opening, closing, and saving files.
- The *Edit menu*, second from the left, is used for cutting, copying, pasting, and for other editing functions.

- The *Window menu*, second from the right, is used to move among windows of the application, (after you have opened several windows in the same application).
- The *Help menu*, on the far right, is used to access the help system.

When you go on to other Windows applications, you will find that they have these menus, and that you are already familiar with some of their options.

Dialog Box Controls

Many menu options have an ellipsis (...) to their right to indicate that, if you select them, the option displays a dialog box that presents you with more choices. These dialog boxes have a variety of controls (see Figure C.2).

Using the keyboard, you can press **Tab** and **Shift+Tab** to move among these controls. The current control is highlighted, and you can generally select it by pressing the **Spacebar**. Most controls also have shortcut keys, which are underlined—you can select them immediately by pressing **Alt** plus the shortcut key.

Of course, it is easier and more usual to select controls by simply clicking them with the mouse.

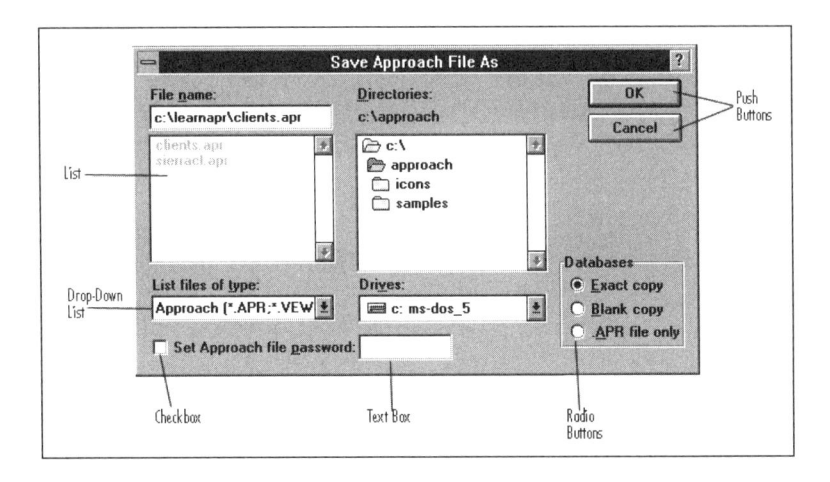

Figure C.2 Dialog box controls.

Most of these controls are used for indicating your choices. After you have selected the choices you want, you select **OK** to initiate some action.

Text Box

You enter text in a text box. Either click it, or tab to it, and then simply type text in it.

In some cases, you can generate an entry in a text box by making a selection from a list that is under (or near) it.

In more complex cases, you sometimes can generate entries in a text box by using a push button that is next to it to display another dialog box. Make the appropriate selections in that dialog box, and select **OK** to return to the original dialog box, with the text added to the text box.

In either case, you can type the text in instead of generating it, or you can edit the text that you generated.

Lists

A list lets you choose among a large number of options.

If a list is too long to fit in the space allotted to it, the scroll bar to its right is activated. You can use it to scroll through the list in the same way that you scroll through a window; (scroll bars are described in the section entitled *Working with Windows*). You can also use the **PgUp** and **PgDn** keys or the Arrow keys to scroll through the list.

Drop-Down Lists

To save space, many lists are not displayed in full. Instead, *drop-down lists*, which work a bit like pop-up menus, are used.

Only the option that is selected is displayed. Click the arrow at the right of a drop-down list to display all the options. After you select the option you want, only it is displayed.

Checkboxes

Checkboxes are used for options where there are only two choices. If the box has an X or checkmark in it, the option is turned on; if it has no checkmark the option is turned off.

Click the text box to add a checkmark—or to remove it if it is already there. Using the keyboard, tab to the checkbox and press **Spacebar** to add or remove the checkmark.

Radio Buttons

Radio buttons are used when you must choose one and only one of a number of options. A set of radio buttons is a series of circles with a dot in the center of one.

Click any one of them to move the dot to it and remove it from the one that was selected previously.

Using the keyboard, tab to the group of radio buttons. Then use the Arrow keys to select the one you want.

Push Buttons

Push buttons are used to take some action. For example, to move an item from one list to another, you generally would select it in the first list, and then select a **Move** push button to move it.

Often, you use a push button to display another dialog box.

To select a push button, simply click it. Using the keyboard, tab to it and press the **Spacebar**, or use its shortcut key.

There are two push buttons that are included in virtually all dialog boxes:

- The **OK** button closes the current dialog box and takes the action that you indicated by the options that you selected in it.
- The **Cancel** button closes the dialog box without taking any action.

You can click them or, using the keyboard, simply press **Enter** to select **OK**, or press **Esc** to select **Cancel**.

Working with Windows

There are two different types of windows that you work with when you are using Windows applications.

- The *Application Window* holds the program itself.
- *Document Windows* hold features used within the program. For example, databases in Approach, letters you are typing in a word processing program, or worksheets in a spreadsheet program.

The Application window has the name of the program, Approach, in its title bar, and the Document window has the name of the database it holds in its title bar (see Figure C.3).

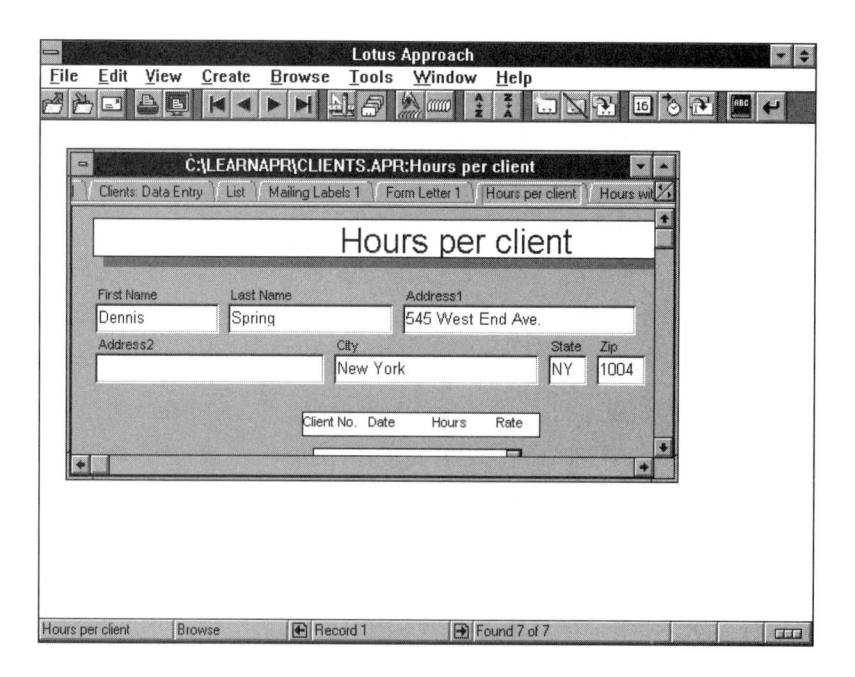

Figure C.3 Features of Windows.

Resizing and Moving Windows

It is easy to rearrange windows to make them more convenient to work with. You can change their size and move them, so you can see all of the applications and all of the documents you need to use. Once the windows are arranged in this way, you can use whichever window you want simply by clicking it.

Moving Windows

You can move a window simply by clicking and dragging its title bar. Move the mouse pointer to the title bar, hold down the mouse button while you drag the mouse, and release it when the window is situated where you want it.

Resizing Windows

To resize windows, just click and drag their bottom or right border to make them larger or smaller. You can also click and drag the lower right corner to control both the height and width of the window. When you move the mouse pointer to one of these borders, it becomes a double-headed arrow—press the mouse button, hold it down while you drag the mouse, and release it when the window is the size you want.

The Maximize, Minimize, and Restore buttons in the upper right corner of the window let you change the size of the window instantly. Click **Maximize** to make the application window fill the entire screen, or to make a Document window fill its entire Application window. Click **Restore** to return the window to the size it was before you maximized it. Click **Minimize** to reduce the window to an icon.

If the window is maximized (like the Application window in Figure C.3), only the Minimize and Restore buttons are displayed. If a window is not maximized (like the Document window in Figure C.3), the Minimize and Maximize buttons are displayed. If a Document window is maximized, its title bar is combined with the title bar of the Application window.

Control Menus

Both the Application window and Document windows have Control menus, which you can use by clicking the box in the upper-left corner of the window.

You can also use the Control menu of the Application window by pressing **Alt+Spacebar**, and you can use the Control menu of the current document window by pressing **Alt+hyphen**.

Both the Application and the Document Control menus give you another way of moving and resizing windows (see Figure C.4 and Figure C.5). If you select **Size**, you can use the Arrow keys to move the borders of the window to resize it, instead of clicking and dragging with the mouse. You can select **Restore**, **Minimize**, or **Maximize** instead of using the equivalent buttons. You can move the window by selecting **Move** and using the **Arrow** keys, instead of clicking and dragging the title bar.

Selecting **Next** from a Document Control menu lets you cycle among all the Document windows that are open within the application—keep choosing **Next** from the Control menu until you are using the window you want.

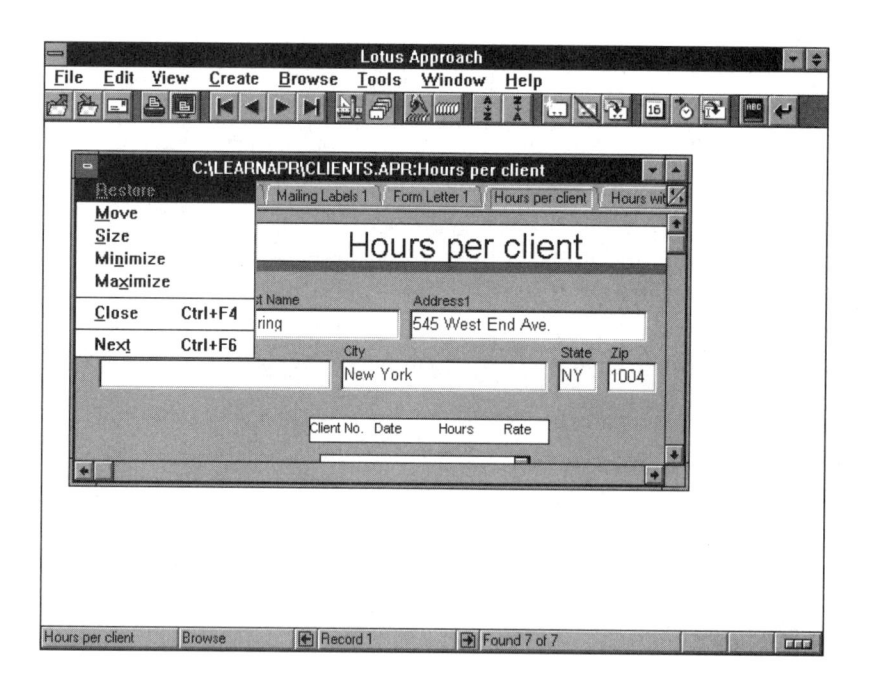

Figure C.4 The Application Control Menu.

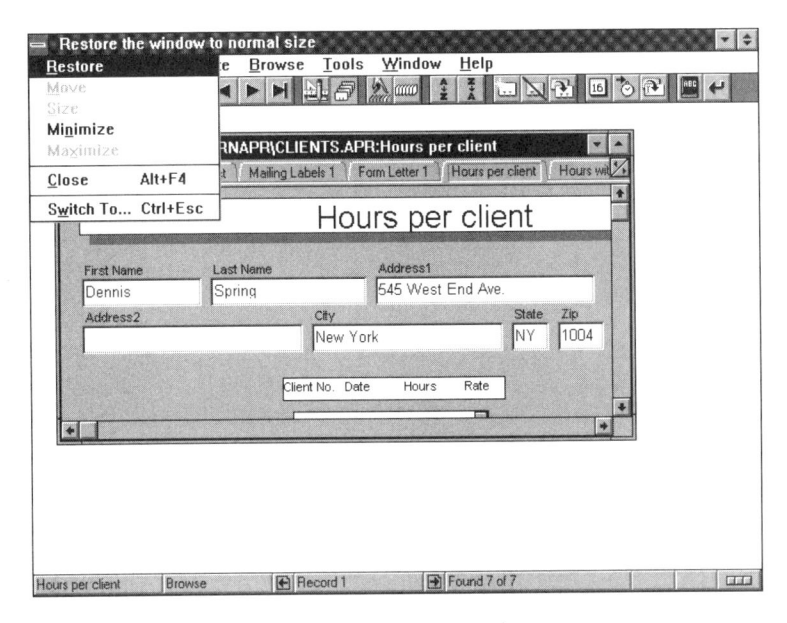

Figure C.5 The Document Control Menu.

The Application Control menu also has a Switch To option which you can use instead of the Next option. Select **Switch To** from the Control menu to display the Task list, (a list you can use to select and switch to any other application that is currently open). You can also display the Task list by pressing **Ctrl+Esc**.

Choose **Close** from the Control menu to close a window. If you select this from the Application Control menu, it is the same as exiting from the application.

If you have minimized a window, you can display its control menu by clicking the icon that represents it, then choosing **Restore** or **Maximize** from the Control menu to display the window again. Alternatively, you can restore the window by double-clicking the icon.

The Scroll Bars

If a document in a window is too large to be displayed fully, you can use the scroll bar at the right of the window to move up and down through the document; use the scroll bar at the bottom of the window to move right and left in the document. These scroll bars work similarly, though only the vertical scroll bar is described below, you can use the horizontal scroll bar in the same way.

Click the **Arrow** at the top or bottom of the scroll bar at the right of the window, to scroll one line up or one line down in the document. Click anywhere between the scroll box and the **Up Arrow** or **Down Arrow** to scroll one window up or one window down in the document.

The location of the scroll box indicates which part of the document is currently displayed. For example, the beginning of the document is being displayed, it is at the top of the scroll bar. You can click and drag the scroll box to move instantly to any location in the document. Drag the scroll box to the bottom of the scroll bar in order to move to the end of the document.

The Editor

Several features used for editing text are common to Windows applications.

You can click anywhere within text to place an *insertion point* (also called a *cursor*) there. Anything you type is added at the insertion point. Working with the keyboard, use the following cursor movement keys:

- The *Arrow* keys move the cursor one character to the right or one character to the left, or one line up or one line down.
- The *Home* or *End* keys move the cursor to the beginning or to the end of the line.
- The *PgUp* or *PgDn* keys move the cursor one window up or one window down (and scroll the contents of the window at the same time).
- The *Del* key deletes the character to the right of the cursor.
- The *Backspace* key deletes the character to the left of the cursor.
- The *Ctrl* key is often used in combination with one of the cursor movement keys to magnify the movement. For example, the **Right Arrow** key moves the cursor one character to the right, and **Ctrl+Right Arrow** moves the cursor one word to the right.

Selecting Text

You can select (or mark text) by clicking and dragging over it. You can also select text by using cursor movement keys in combination with the Shift key.

For example, pressing **Shift+End** moves the cursor to the end of the line and marks all the text between its original position and the end of the line.

In either case, the text is highlighted to show it is selected.

Once text is selected, any character that you type replaces all selected text. To replace a name for example, you can select it and type the new name. As soon as you begin, the original name is replaced with what you type. Likewise, pressing **Del** or **Backspace** deletes all selected text.

Using any cursor movement key, such as an Arrow key, deselects all selected text (unless you hold down the **Shift** key at the same time). Clicking with the mouse outside of the selected text also deselects all selected text as it places the cursor.

Cut and Paste

The most powerful use of selected text is cutting or copying and pasting.

Once text is selected, you can copy it to the clipboard by choosing **Cut** or **Copy** from the Edit menu. Cutting removes the original text, and Copying leaves the original text; but both place a copy in the clipboard.

Then, choose **Paste** from the Edit menu at any time to place the text you put in the clipboard at the current location of the cursor. You can move to another document, or even to a different Windows application. You can also paste the same text repeatedly, an indefinite number of times. As long as you do not cut or copy something new to the clipboard, the text remains there and can be pasted anywhere.

Undoing Errors

Because you delete all selected text when you type any new characters, you are bound to make occasional errors when you are using the Windows editor. For this reason, Windows applications have Undo as the first option of their Edit menu. Choosing **Undo** from the Edit menu undoes the last change that you made.

New Windows users tend to keep typing after making an error. You must choose **Undo** from the Edit menu immediately after you make an error in order to recover the text that you accidentally deleted.

The Help System

The help system of Approach is similar to the help systems of other Windows applications. It uses the Windows Help System, with a special Help File provided by Approach.

If you choose **Contents** from the Help menu, the Help window is displayed (see Figure C.6). This is a separate Application window, not a Document window within Approach.

There are two basic ways of searching for help: by topic and alphabetically.

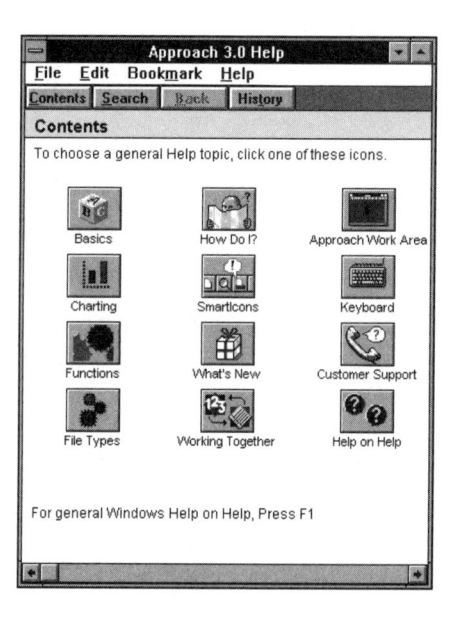

Figure C.6 Help Contents.

Searching by Topic

The main Table of contents of the Help system contains icons that represent general topics (see Figure C.6). Click any of these icons to display a help window with more specific topics on that topic (see Figure C.7).

Appendix C: Windows Basics   **677**

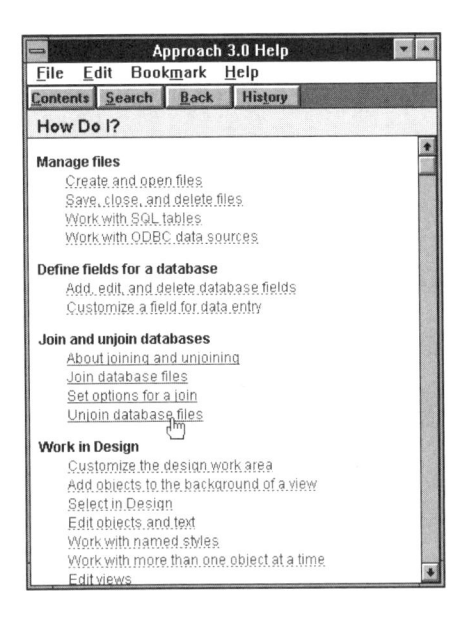

Figure C.7   More specific Help topics.

When you move the pointer to any of the underlined topics, it is displayed as a hand with the index finger extended (see Figure C.7). Simply click to jump to a window of text on the topic. Using the keyboard, you can press **Tab** to move from topic to topic, and press **Enter** to select the highlighted topic.

This new Help window also has words *underlined* in the same way to show they are cross-referenced. You can click any underlined word to jump to the Help window describing it.

Other words are underlined with *dotted lines*. You can click these to display a definition of them in a small box. Click again to remove this box.

The push buttons at the top of this window help you navigate through the help system after you have used cross-references to jump from one topic to another:

- *Contents* displays the table of contents of Help Topics that was displayed when you first opened the Help window.
- *Back* displays the last topic viewed.
- *History* displays a window with a list of the last forty Help Topics viewed. Select any topic from this list to view it again.

- *<< and >>* moves to the previous or the next topic in a series of related topics that you have viewed.

You can select any of these either by clicking or by pressing its underlined shortcut key.

Alphabetical Searches

The one remaining push button, the Search push button, lets you do alphabetical searches. If you select this push button, Approach displays the Search dialog box (see Figure C.8).

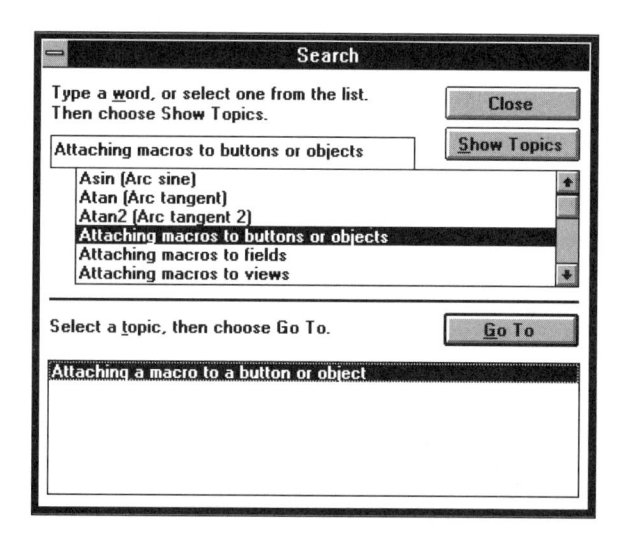

Figure C.8 The Search dialog box.

You can scroll through the list in the top half of this dialog box and select a key word from it. Alternatively, you can type a word in the text box above this list; the list automatically scrolls to the nearest key word as you type.

When you have found the word you want in the list, select the **Show Topics** button. Approach displays the name of all the topics that include information on that word in the list in the bottom half of the dialog box. At any time, you can select a topic from this list and select **Go To** to display Help on that topic.

The Help System Menus

You have learned how to search for Help. The Help System's menus give you extra power or convenience in using the Help System.

The File Menu

The Help System's File menu has features that are similar to the File menu of many Windows applications:

- *Open* lets you open another Help file if multiple Help files are available. Approach, however, provides only the file Approach.hlp, which is opened when you first use help.
- *Print Topic* prints the topic that is currently displayed. You must print the entire topic.
- *Print Setup* displays the dialog box that lets you control your printer. This dialog box is described in Chapter 5 of this book.
- *Exit* closes the Help window.

The Edit Menu

The Edit menu is also found on many Windows applications, but in the Help System's Edit menu it has only two options, because you cannot edit the text in the Help System itself.

- *Copy* displays the Copy dialog box, which includes all of the text in the current topic. You can select text in this dialog box and then select **Copy** to copy it to the clipboard.
- *Annotate* displays a dialog box where you can add your own notes (also called *annotations*) to the current help topic. When you add a note, a paper-clip icon is displayed to the left of the topic's title. You can view the annotation at any time by clicking this icon, or by tabbing to it and pressing **Enter**.

The Bookmark Menu

The Bookmark menu lets you add bookmarks to save your place in the Help System:

- *Define.* Displays a dialog box that lets you add a bookmark. It suggests a name for the bookmark based on the name of the current topic, but you can edit it and give it any name you want.
- *Bookmark names.* After you have defined bookmarks, their names are added to the Bookmark menu, and you can go to any one immediately by selecting it from this menu. If more than nine bookmarks have been defined, a More option is added, which you select to display all the bookmark names.

The Help Menu

Finally, the Help System itself includes a Help menu, which gives you help in using it:

- *How to Use Help* displays the Contents for How to Use Help, which lets you use the Help System for the Approach Help System. This Help System works like the Approach Help System. You can search by topic or alphabetically, move back through the history of the windows displayed, and use the menu in the same way. It also includes a Glossary button, which displays a window with definitions of terms.
- *Always on Top* makes Help windows always remain on top of any other windows that are displayed.
- *About Help* displays information on the current version of Windows Help you are using.

Index

& operator 234
... operator 229
<<#>> 125
<<Back 14, 161
<<Date>> 125
<<Time>> 125
<> operator 230, 232
= operator 229, 231, 238
@ Functions 242

A

Abs(number) 591
Absolute Value function 312
Acos() 315
Acos(number) 591
Action Column 414
Actual Size 149, 378, 580
Add 92, 164
    and Remove 426
    button 191, 242
    Column 344
    Field 25, 166, 186, 195, 203, 344, 353
        Box 24, 62, 103, 108, 111, 125, 127, 146
        Dialog tool 127
        Footer 187-188
        Header 187
        icon 333
        Index 442, 565
    Item 550
    Key Field 43, 443, 478

Menu 413
    objects 99
    Title Page 187, 535
    to Dictionary 548
add 16
    data 2, 64, 66
    new objects 24
    pictures 112
    records 65
    summary data 172
    text 24
adding fields 126
addition 294-295, 588
additional fields 47
Address layout 199
Agv(Number,Number,...) 591
algebra 295
Alias
    button 269, 524
    dialog box 154
    Objects 154
        area 530
Alignment 406
    area 123
    buttons 123, 611, 615, 636
    Drawing 147, 409, 556
    radio button 182, 209
Allow OLE objects 476
alphabetical order 215-216
Alt+F 56
An Existing File 54
analyzing data 16
AND 296
Application Control menu 494, 673

Apply Format icon 148
Approach
    Assistants 157
    File 40, 53-54, 57, 171, 350, 420, 569
        As dialog box 60
        Close 108
        Info dialog box 490
    files 9-10
    Formula 182
    Functions 586
    Help menu 586
    icon bar 70
        bar SmartIcons 70
    interface 559
        Current View 12
        Divider tab scroll buttons 12
        Edit 12
        File 12
        Icon Bar 12
        Menu Bar 12
        Status Bar 12
        View indicator 12
        Views 12
    Memo 444
    View file 11
    views 341, 430
APR extension 10, 53
Arccosine function 314
Arcsine function 314
Arctangent function 314
Arctangent2 function 315
area graphs 18
argument 299, 590

arithmetic
    operators 293-294, 588
    formulas 294
    signs 39
Arrange 153
    command 153
    Labels 193, 509
    Window 56, 581
Asc(text) 591
Ascending 187, 218
    icon 248
    order 534, 539
        Descending order 526
    radio button 560
    sorts 215
ASCII
    character 303
    function 303
    number 303
    order 218
Asin() 315
Asin(number) 591
Assistant 13-14, 159-162, 164, 166, 174, 181, 200, 270, 319, 329, 504, 509
    Form 13
asterisk 304
Atan() 315
Atan(number) 591
Atan2(Number1,Number 2) 591
Attached menu 165, 185
    bar 194
Authorization ID text box 451
autodialer 422, 562

autodials 369
automate 95
    data entry 38
automating 94
    data entry 97
automation 97
Average 176
    function 311
Avery
    forms 190
    label 191, 193
    layout 191
    number 191

B

Back 70
    Arrow 21, 70
background 615
    panel 557
Bad Field Reference 319
Bar
    Chart bar 356
    graphs 18
Based on 405
baseline 616
basic features 7
Basics 2, 168
    panel 87, 120, 128-129, 139, 146, 149, 159, 164, 184, 190, 202, 265, 279, 284, 350, 507, 606
    tab 391

Blank
　Copy 483
　Database 34, 50-51
　Form 162
　function 307
　Option 205
blank
　column 333, 335
　fields 48
　form 163
　record 22
　row 141, 345
　spaces 37, 39
　values 62
Blank(FieldName,Value) 592
Body
　Info Box 644
　panel 180
Bold 123-124
boldface 124
Bookmark
　menu 585, 679
　names 585
　　Define 585
Boolean 40, 51, 396, 447, 472
　condition 307
　constants 298
　field 167, 215, 221, 323
　fields 39, 67, 452
　value 293, 296-297, 302, 392, 589
border
　color 119, 341, 407, 607, 615
　width 407
borders 25, 119, 129, 165, 202, 410, 557
　panel 275

boundaries 130
break down 46
Bring Forward 153, 359, 529, 544
　icon 153
Bring to Front 153, 359, 529, 543
Browse 20-21, 28, 86
　dialog box 86
　icon 170, 196, 207, 281, 391
　　Send Mail 20
　　Show All 22
　　Sort Ascending 22
　　Sort Descending 22
　　Start Arrow 20
　　View 580
　menu 63, 65, 67, 76-78, 166, 244, 524-529, 531-532, 535, 537, 573
　　Delete Found Set 78, 244
　　Delete Record 528
　　Duplicate Record 77
　　Fill Field 528
　　Find 525
　　Find Again 525
　　Find Special 525
　　Hide Record 528
　　Insert 79, 528
　　New Record 527
　　Refresh 77, 529
　　Set command 396
　　Show All 220, 526
　　Sort 526
　　submenu 79
　　submenu Current Time 79
　　submenu Previous Value 79
　　submenu Today's Date 79

mode 6-7, 19, 22, 27, 64-65, 70, 80, 87, 102, 105, 112, 158, 170, 343, 400, 426, 453, 524, 537, 566, 569
mode icon 20-22
  Back Arrow 21
  Browse 21
  Delete Record 22
  Design 21
  End Arrow 21
  Find 21
  Forward Arrow 21
  New Record 22
  Open file 20
  Preview 20
  Print 20
  Save Approach File 20
  screen 221
business applications 3, 312
Button text box 390, 637

C

Cache table name 449
Calculated 40, 59
  data type 474
  field 315-316, 318, 462
calculation 40-41
Cancel 58, 60, 93-94
  button 43, 221
capitalization 218, 221
case sensitive 216, 563

cell 341
  range of 332
  single 332
cells 342, 514
Cells Only 333, 540
Character
  function 303
  set 432, 454, 486
Chart 13, 28, 355
  Area 356, 515
  Assistant 355, 514, 517, 543
  Bar 515
  Crosstab 353
  Data Source 359
  icon 358
  Line 151, 356
  menu 359, 543-544
    Align 359
    Arrange 359, 543
    Chart data Fields 359, 543
    Fast Format 360, 544
    Group 360, 544
    Insert 360, 544
    Style & properties 359, 543
    UnGroup 360, 544
  Pie 357, 517
chart 2, 7, 18, 157, 516
charts
  area graphs 18
  bar graphs 18
  line graphs 18
  pie graphs 18
checkbox 25
  Allow Drawing 86
  Create as Icon 85

drawing tool 143
Filled in 92
label 144, 168
Set Approach File Password 54
Set View Password 59
checkboxes 97, 100, 669
Checked Value 144
Choose Key Field 477
    dialog box 443
Chr(number) 592
circumference 313
Clear 87
    All 526, 569
    Find 221
clipboard 112, 116
Close 56-58, 110, 368
    button 268
    Index 435
code 136
Collate Copies 210, 492
color
    border 605
    palette 407, 611
    panel 275, 341
    shadow 605
colors 119, 165, 202
column 8, 16, 332
    header 333-334
    restore 337
Column Info Box 655
Columnar
    form 162, 166
    report 157, 173, 176, 178, 180, 184
    summary report 173
    with Grand Summary 174, 596
columns 351
    multiple 332
Combine(text, Text...) 592
command
    Arrange 153
    Fast Format 148
    Insert 79
    list 366, 569
    New 65
    Paste Special 83
    Show Grid 151
    Undo 103, 108
Commands 366-367
Comparison
    formulas 296
    operators 226, 293, 295
Compress 562
    button 423
Confirm Password dialog box 420, 561
Connect 440, 447
    button 37, 435-436, 462
    dialog box 449
constants 292, 298, 317, 469, 588
    Boolean 298, 590
    Date 298, 590
    Numeric 298, 590
    Text 298, 590
    Time 298, 590
Context menu 550
Control menu 56, 81, 103, 671
    Close 103
    panel 591
controls 667

Index

Conversion functions 302
copies 210
  multiple 285
Copy 29, 81, 83-84, 103, 105, 108,
      112, 365, 567
  data 60
  icon 115
  of 567
    to File 497
  View 494
Cos(Number) 592
Cosine function 315
Counter 398
Create 28
  a new file 35
  Buttons 628
    from Field Data button 145
  Chart 28
  Crosstab 28
  Directory 30
    dialog box 30
  Form 28
    Letter 28
  Formula 325
  from File 522
    button 85
  Mailing Label 28
    dialog box 193
  menu 13, 61, 85, 88, 95, 159-160,
      167, 172, 182, 190, 196,
      266, 270-271, 285, 288, 316,
      321, 500, 514, 517, 520-522,
      524
    Chart 355, 360, 514
    Crosstab 348, 512
    Drawing 520

Field Definition 88, 326, 524
Form 159 , 500
Form Letter 159, 509
Join 277
Mailing Label 159, 507
Object 521
Report 159, 503
Summary 519
Worksheet 512
New 521
  button 85
  radio button 521
Report 28
Worksheet 28
create 46
  controls 126
  forms 2
  mailing labels 197
  menu 110, 227
  new database 2
  reports 48
  worksheets 2
Creating New Database 37
Creation
  Date 90
  Formula button 91
criteria 234, 237, 573
Crop it 147
cross tabulated form 18
crosshairs 388
Crosstab 13, 28, 157, 330, 354, 513-
    514, 541
  Assistant 348-349, 353, 358, 512
  Info Box 657
  menu 541-542, 355
    Add Field 542

    Cells Only 542
    Chart Crosstab 542
    Fast Format 542
    Find 541
    Select 542
    Styles & Properties 541
    Summarize Columns 542
crosstab 2, 7, 18, 347-348
Ctrl 72
Ctrl+End 71
Ctrl+Home 71
Ctrl+N 65, 73, 171
Currency 138, 444, 621
    decimal 168, 621
    with decimals 138
Current
    Field 78
    Format 137, 206, 347, 617-618
        list 135
        menu 8, 134, 139
        menu Currency 138
        menu Currency with decimals 138
        menu General 138
        menu Integer 138
        menu Percent with decimals 138
    Time 79, 528
        function 309
    View 12
    words 547
current database 61, 162, 456
    date 298, 339
    directory 30, 36
    field 65-66, 71, 79, 214, 489
    format 168
    month 67
    record 22, 77
    system date 323
    table 455
    time 298
    view 19, 27, 401, 576
    year 67
Currtime() 592
cursor 66
Custom
    icon bars 410
    labels 193
    layouts 157
    mailing labels 15
    menu 185, 373
        define 411
        system 410, 411, 416
    Order 45
    sort order 214
    values 141
        create 635
Customize Menus 411, 549
    dialog box 574
Cut 28, 81, 83, 103, 105, 112, 115, 675
    icon 115

D

Data 90, 96
    entry 168
        menu 139
        type 129

Index

Entry Options
    Changing 94
    Options dialog box 94
    view 227
  file 59
  Type 38, 40-41, 45, 51, 616
    Boolean 40
    Calculated 40
    Date 40
    list 51
    Memo 40
    menu 40
    Numeric 41
    PicturePlus 41
    Text 41
    Time 41
    Variable 41
data 46, 75
  add 2, 66
  edit 2, 19
  entry
    automate 38, 95, 97
    forms 10
    speed 2
    validate 95
  file 9, 13, 33
  lose 62
  type 33, 49, 472
  validating 97
Database
  divider tab 431, 441, 449
  Fields list 163, 192
  menu 61
  Options dialog box 434
  panel 423, 432

  Sharing 436
database
  applications 2
  design 47
  designing 49
  field 141, 191
    values 141
  file 46, 50, 57
    creating 45
  management
    programs 9
    systems 158
  normalization 257
  panel 562
  programs 53
  sharing 438
  theory 48, 257
Databases Shared 437
Date 40, 125, 195, 472
  constants 298
  data 303
  entry 140
  field 67, 69, 92
  Format 134, 617
  function 302, 307
  specified 308
Date(Number1,Number2,Number3)
    592
dates 294
DateToText 302
DateToText(Date, Format) 592
Day(Date) 592
Day-Month-Year 134-135
DayName function 308
DayOfWeek function 308

DayOfWeek(Date) 593
DayOfYear function 308
DayOfYear(Date) 593
DB2-MDI 451, 480
   databases 480
   dialog box 451
dBASE 10, 42-43, 55, 429, 434, 455,
     562-564
   compatible application 431
   databases 40, 424
   file 49-50
dBASE III + 9, 36, 39
dBASE IV 9, 36, 39, 58, 425
   file 49,53
DBF 50
   extension 53
   file 58, 435
decimal 41
   digits 438
   places 42-43, 62, 166, 168, 314,
     438, 440, 444,
   point 42-43, 437-438
Default menu 373, 416, 426, 549,
     574
   Order 45
   Value panel 63, 89, 97, 324, 472
     tab 96
default
   form 75
   formats 134
   name 159, 172, 196
   printer 210
   value 89, 325
Define 187
   Checkbox dialog box 143
   Custom Menu Bar dialog box 412

Filter 626
   button 143
   dialog box 143
   Formula panel 354, 475
   List 627
   Macro 389, 609, 613
     button 606
     dialog box 366, 567, 569
   Named Style 552
   Radio Button dialog box 145
   Style dialog box 408, 553
   Summary panel 317, 474-475
Degree function 315
Degree(Number)593
Del 66
Delete 44, 56-57, 94, 141, 344, 365
   button 44
   File 58, 484
     dialog box 56
   Form 159
   Found Set 78, 244
   Index 426, 442, 566
   Item 414, 550
   Labels 159
   menu 413
   objects 99
   Record 22, 72, 159
     icon 72
   Set 417, 558
delimiter 301, 454
dependent calculated field 319
Descending 187
   order 534, 539
   radio button 560
   sorts 215, 218
Design 19, 20-21, 100, 126, 149, 487

Index

button 100
Form Letters 100
icon 109, 167, 188, 204, 279
Mailing Labels 100
mode 7, 19, 22, 24, 64, 87, 99,
      102, 104-105, 108-109, 112,
      159, 167, 194, 331, 343,
      418, 519, 535, 537
    Delete Form 159
    Delete Labels 159
    Delete Report 159
    Spell Check 546
    reports 2, 100
    window 121, 150
  View 25, 28, 107, 178, 271, 537
    Forms 164
    Window 117, 149, 151
designing a database 49
detail database 265
  file 265
Dial 369
  Type radio buttons 422
Dialer panel 422, 562
dialing preferences 562
dialog box 53, 94, 266, 270, 667
  Align 154
  Approach File As 60
  Browse 86
  Create
    Directory 30
    Mailing Labels 193
  Data Entry Options 94
  Define
    Checkbox 143
    Custom Menu bar 549

Filter 143
  radio Button 145
Delete File 56
Drop-Down List 140, 144
Edit Dictionary 402
Export 370
Field Definition 33-34, 37, 43, 50,
    61, 82, 88-89, 95-97, 111
Find Special 573
Formula 91, 293. 326
Go To Record 72
Icon Size 417
Import data 574
Insert Object 85
Join 269, 277, 567
Key Field 43
List 140, 168
Macros 364, 379
Mailing Label Options 194
Network Connection 436, 440
New 33, 37, 50, 56
Open 54, 57
Paradox Network Connection 444
Print 209
  to File 210
Save Approach File 54
Save Database As 60
Save View 56, 58, 60
Send Mail 372
Sort 187, 215
Spell Check 400
Summary 183
Variable Options 399
warning 369, 460, 570
Welcome 34, 50, 56, 58

diameter 313
Directories list 35-36, 50, 57, 59-60, 80, 453, 457
directory 29
  current 30, 35
  new 31
  root 29, 36, 50
  tree 31
Directory Create 30
disk space 48
Display 133
  as Icon 522
    checkbox 85
  panel 559
  rulers 151
divider tab 12, 64, 75, 104
  interface 14, 25, 104, 161, 605
  new 158
  scroll buttons 12
  Validation 95
division 295, 588
Do Mail 391
Document
  Control menus 672
  Window 56
Done 164
  button 161
DOS 50, 454
  prompt 210
double line 119
Download data 567
Drawing tool 24-25, 28, 103, 108, 110, 117, 127, 140, 418-419, 560
  Add Field 25
  Checkbox 25

Field 24
Graphics 24
Macro Button 25
Picture 25
Radio Button 25
Text 24
Drives menu 35, 60, 80
Drop-down List 100, 104, 140, 144, 668
  dialog box 140
  menus 97
Duplicate
  Form 159
  labels 159
  Record 77, 159
    icon 77
  values 244

E

Edit 12, 28-29, 365, 567
  Column Label 344, 353
  command 571
    Copy 571
    Cut 571
    Paste 571
    Select All 571
  Cut 28
  Dictionary
    button 546
    dialog box 402, 546
  Find 572
  label 194

Index

menu 53 , 80-81, 83, 87, 103, 105, 108, 110, 112, 115-116, 159-160, 415, 494, 496-497, 585, 666, 679
    Clear 496
    command 494
    Copy 83, 105, 494
    Copy of File 497
    Cut 83, 105, 115, 494
    Delete Chart 497
    Delete Crosstab 497
    Delete Form 497
    Delete Labels 497
    Delete Report 497
    Delete Worksheet 497
    Duplicate Chart 497
    Duplicate Crosstab 497
    Duplicate Form 497
    Duplicate Labels 497
    Duplicate Report 497
    Duplicate Worksheet 497
    Paste 105, 112, 116, 494-496
    paste from File 112
    Paste Special 83, 495
    Select All 496
    Undo 87, 103, 337-338, 494
  OLE object 87
  Paste 28
  submenu 29
edit 16, 66, 126
  data 2, 19
  fields 158
  menu Clear 87
editing
  commands editing 369
  text 123
    editing 674

Effects 123, 406
Else 377, 578
  run macro 392
embedded OLE objects 82
Embedding 82
Encapsulated PostScript Files 80
End 71
  Arrow 21, 81
enlarge 107
Enter 65-66
  command 572
  icon 65, 22
  key 369
  View Password 484
EPS 80
Esc 53, 66, 70
Exact Copy 459, 483
Exact(Text1, Text2) 593
Excel 82
  spreadsheets 82
Exit 31, 171, 572
Exp(Number) 593
Expand 1313
  Boundaries 184, 647
Export 573
  Data 415, 450, 573
    dialog box 370, 451, 456, 490
  File 456
  options 370, 572

F

Factorial function 312
Factorial(Number) 593

Fast Format 166, 186, 196, 203, 344,
    353, 403, 537, 543
  command 148
Field 8, 24, 125
  Box 139-140
  Definition 61, 88, 95, 288, 316,
      326, 634
    button 111, 128
    dialog box 37, 43, 50, 61, 82,
        88-89, 95-97, 111, 277,
        288, 322
  frame 129
  Info Box 129, 132
  list 95
  Mapping dialog box 453, 458
  Name 38, 45
    column 51
    text box 51
  objects 202
  read-only 128
  style 276
  tool 127
field 44, 48, 66
  formatting 351
  frame 623
  length 62
  name 40
  numeric 41
  object 276
  single 47
  type 40, 62, 69, 439
fields 47, 103, 120, 292
  adding 126
  additional 47
  to Search list 242

File 12, 28
  Manager 31, 84
  icon 30
  menu 30-31, 50, 53, 56-59, 73,
      108, 171, 177, 209, 225,
      415, 470, 478, 482, 485,
      489, 523, 575, 584, 666
  Approach File Info 490
  Close 57-58, 368, 481
  Delete 56
  Exit 31, 370, 496, 572
  Export File 489
  Import Data 485
  New 470
  Open 57, 59, 478, 575
  Preview 491, 575
  Print 225, 491, 576
  Print Setup 493
  Save Approach File 59, 481, 578
  Save As 450, 482
  Send Mail 491
file
  Approach 10
  data 9, 33
  Approach View 11
  new 34
  server 466
  type 36, 49, 80
File Name 478
  List 36, 55, 450, 496
  text box 37, 55, 80, 86, 434, 489
Fill
  Field 78
    command 396
    function 303

Index

In checkbox 95
fill color 119, 275, 280, 341, 557, 607, 611, 615
Fill() function 300
Fill(Text,Number) 594
Filled In checkbox 92
Fills Menu systems 410
Financial function 309
Find 19, 21, 27, 78, 223, 233, 235, 344, 353, 367, 371, 572
   Again 221, 371, 572
   All icon 27, 220, 225
   command 382, 393
   Duplicate
     radio button 244
     records 526
   icon 222, 237
     bar 418
   mode 7, 27, 219
   More
     button 237
     option 237
   operation 219
   Request 27, 220-222, 224, 227-228, 232-233, 240, 242, 525, 538, 541
     Form 219, 221
   simple 219
   Special 242, 538, 541, 573
   unique records 526
Finds 76-77, 213, 221, 226-227, 291, 323, 441, 563, 569
Find\Find Again 541
fixed point numbers 440
Float 436

floating point number 437, 440
folders 29
Font 123, 611, 614
   list 207
   Names 406
   Panel 408, 553, 555, 614
   Style 123
Fonts 341, 351
   panel 206
footer 173, 187
Footer panel 534
For Upgrades 586
Form 13, 28, 159-160, 164, 167, 270, 529
   Assistant 13, 160, 163, 167, 172, 177, 500
   Info Box 638
Form 1 52, 58, 64, 102, 108-109, 158, 160
   Divider 75
Form Letter 7, 13, 28, 99-100, 159, 198, 201, 524, 529, 537
   Assistant 198-200, 517
     Step 1 199
     Step 2 199
     Step 3 199
     Step 4 200
     Step 5 200
   design 16
   divider tab 652
   Info Box 651
   menu 28, 105, 110, 127, 164, 166, 186, 531
     Add Field 110, 127, 166, 186, 532

Close 110
Fast Format 166, 186, 532
Insert 166, 186, 532
Style & Properties 166, 186, 532
  name 165, 639
  Report 524
  standard 8, 13
  view 14
form 117, 162
  columnar 162
  letter 2, 9-11, 16, 47-46
    Edit 202
  standard 15, 64, 73, 99, 161
format 10, 73, 126, 302, 619
  labels 190
Format code 168
  text box 136, 619, 622
  type 132, 137-139, 168, 206, 355, 616-617, 620, 622
Formats 130
Formatting 138
  Fields 130
  panel 201
forms 7, 14, 99-100, 157
  create 2
  data entry 10
  new 99
Formula 91, 473, 587
  button 93, 577
  dialog box 91, 292-293, 326, 392
  Is True 93, 325, 474
  text box 292
formula 2, 228, 242, 291-292, 299, 315, 391, 578

Constants 292
variables 292
Formula/Options column 38, 96, 316
formulas combine 297
formulas complex 324
Forward 71
  Arrow 21, 71
Found
  message 220
  Set 227, 369, 539
    Only 457
four-line form 196
FoxPro 9-10, 36, 39, 42-43, 425, 429, 434, 440, 562-564
  databases 40, 424
  Memo 439
Frame 408
  style 612
From...to 92
Full Record Locking 460
function 40, 226 291-292, 298, 300, 469, 588
  Absolute Value 591
  Arccosine 591
  Arcsine 591
  Arctangent2 591
  ASCII 591
  Average 591
  Blank 592
  Character 592
  Combine 592
  Cosine 592
  Current Time 592
  Date 592
  Day 592

Index

DayName 593
DayOfWeek 593
Degree 593
Exact 593
Exponentiation 593
Factorial 593
Fill 594
Future value 594
Hour 594
Hundredth 594
If 594
IsBlank 594
IsLastRecord() 595
key 363, 380, 382, 568
Left 595
Length 595
Like 595
logarithm 596
Lower 596
Middle 596
Minute 596
Month 596
MonthName 596
Natural Logarithm 595
nested 590
Number Of Periods 597
NumToText 597
Pi 597
PMT 597
Position 597
Pow 598
Prefix 598
Proper 598
PV 598

Radian 598
Random 598
Second 600
Sine 600
SMax 600
SMin 600
SNPV 601
Soundslike 601
Span 601
SpanUntil 601
Sqrt 602
SSTD 602
SSum 602
STD 602
SVar 602
Tangent 602
TextToBool 602
TextToDate 603
TextToTime 603
Time 603
Today 603
Translate 603
Trim 603
Trunc 603
Upper 604
Var 604
WeekOfYear 604
Year 604
Fund Again 538
Future
    Value 310
    payments 311
FV(Number1,Number2,Number3) 594

G

General 138, 621
   divider tab 462
   panel 426, 461, 566
Global variable 397
Go To Record dialog box 72
Grand Summary
   created 181
   Summary panel 176
graphic objects 24, 99, 103, 119, 607
Graphics 24
grid 100, 151
   area 419, 560
   option 151
   Show 419
   Snap to 419
gridlines 106, 151
Group 152
   change 631
   command 531
   icon 152
   Summary 182
      panel 318

H

handles 118, 169
header 173, 184, 187, 332, 345
   Info Box 656, 658
   panel 180, 533
   report 534
Help 12, 28
   <<or>> 583
   Annotate 585
   back 583
   button 12, 211, 494
   Contents 583
   Copy 585
   file 581, 584
   Go to 584
   History 583
   menu 415, 581, 586
      Contents 581
      Custom Support 587
   messages 559
   next topic 583
   Search 586
   System 584-585, 676, 680
      File Menu 679
   topic 583, 585
   window 581, 583
      Exit 585
hide 106, 222
   page margins 165
   record 78, 225
   rulers 151
   View 165, 185, 194
Horizontal
   Alignment 154, 530
   lines 151
Hot Keys 414, 551
Hour function 309
Hour(Time) 594
Hundredth function 309
Hundredth(Time) 594

I

Icon Bar 12, 124, 246
  create 557
  Size 417, 558
    dialog box 417
icon 19, 29-30, 125, 151, 226, 469
  Add 247
    Field 333
  Arrow 281
  Ascending 248
  Asterisk 247
  At 247
  Available 558
  Back Arrow 21
  bar 22, 27, 65, 79, 100, 107, 149, 183, 220, 283, 558
    floating 558
  Bring Forward 153
  Browse 21, 170, 189, 196, 207, 247, 281
  Chart 358
  Copy 115
  Cut 115
  Delete Record 22, 72
  Design 21, 109, 167, 247, 279
  Duplicate Record 77
  Ellipsis 247
  End Arrow 21
  Enter 222, 246
  Equals 246
  Exclamation Point 247
  Fast Format 148
  File Manager 30
  Find 21, 222, 237, 247
    All 27, 220, 225, 247
  Forward Arrow 21
  Greater Than 246
    Or Equal To 246
  Group 152
  If 247
  Info Box 103, 164, 201, 205, 274
  insert Column 335
  Less Than 246
    Or Equal To 246
  Line 207
  magnifying glass 149
  New Record 22, 170
  Not Equal 246
  Open file 20, 246
  Or 247
  Paste 112, 116
  Preview 20, 248
  Print 20
  Printer 209
  Question Mark 247
  Save
    Approach File 20, 59
    File 246
  select Header 338
  Send
    Backward 153
    Mail 20
  Show
    All 22
    Next SmartIcon 151-153
  Show/Hide Grid lines 151
  SmartIcon 125

Sort
- Ascending 22, 188, 287
- Descending 22, 188

Sounds Like 247
Spell Check 400
Start Arrow 20
Trailing Summary Panel 182
Undo 110, 116
Ungroup 152
Zoom
- In 149
- Out 149

If 375
- function 307
- radio button 376, 394
- Searches 324

IF() function 307, 324
If(Boolean Condition, Value1, Value2) 594
Import 574
- Approach File 487
- Data 415
  - Command 488, 490
  - dialog box 372, 451, 453, 455
- options 574
- Setup 487
  - dialog box 455

importing data 453
In field 93
indefinite number 240
independent object 125
Index
- create secondary 442
- delete 442
- divider tab 433, 442
- list 425
- panel 425, 564
- primary 442, 565
- secondary 565

indicator box 367
Info Box 25-26, 28, 68-69, 86, 100, 103-105, 117-119, 124, 128, 133-134, 137, 139, 144, 149, 159, 164-166, 177, 181, 194-195, 202, 206, 276, 532, 604-608, 610, 612, 614, 622
- Attached menu 165
- Form name 165
- Hide
  - page margins 165
  - view 165
- icon 103, 164, 201, 205, 274, 279, 604
- Line 605
- Main database 165
- Named styles 165
- tool 123

Insert 79, 125, 166, 186, 195, 203, 344, 367, 569
- button 44
- Column icon 335
- command 79
- Date icon 205
- Object dialog box 85
- page break 520
- new field 44

insertion bar 226, 338, 540
- point 66, 122, 189

install 465
- Custom 465

Full 465-466
  Minimum 465
    disk space 465
    spell checker 465
    utilities 465
  program 465
  screen 467
installing 2
Integer 42, 138, 313, 444, 621
  digit 168, 437
interest rate constant 310
interface 12, 106
  divider tab 14, 25, 104
invalid
  data 93, 289
  entry 70
IsBlank function 307
IsBlank(FieldName) 594
IsLastRecord function 307
IsLastRecord() 595
isolate data 2
Italic 123-124
Item
  Action 412
  name 412

J

Join 266, 277, 523
  button 267
  dialog box 267, 269, 277, 524, 567
  files 263

K

Keep records together 185
Key Field 43, 48, 92, 255, 267, 287
  dialog box 43
  fields 93
  combinations 658
  feature 160
keyboard 586, 665

L

Label 99, 145, 197
  Code 193
  custom mailing 15
  mailing 15
  Options dialog box 194
  panel 131, 145, 408, 555, 614
  printing 15
  text box 131
landscape 211, 493
Language Options button 401, 546
last record 78
Leading
  blanks 306
  summaries 182
  zero 68
Left and Up boxes 120
Left function 304
Left(Text,Number) 299, 595
Length function 304

Length(Text) 595
Letter menu 201, 203, 537
   Add Field 203, 537
   Fast Format 203
   Insert 203, 537
   Styles & Properties 203, 537
Like function 304
Like(Text,Text) 595
Line
   graphs 18
   icon 207
   tools 24
Lines 103, 117-119
   and Colors panel 554
      Border color 544
      Border width 554
      Borders 555
      Borders enclose label 555
      Fill color 554
      Frame 554
      Read only 555
      Shadow color 554
   diagonal 118
   horizontal 118
   vertical 118
Linked OLE objects 83
Linking 82
List 168, 668
   dialog box 140, 168
   divider tab 217, 223, 225, 248
   File Name 36
   Files of Type 453, 496
      menu 55, 58, 80
   separator 301
   view 227
Ln(Number) 595

Lock Record 461
Log(Number) 596
Logarithm 298
   function 313
Logical
   AND 232-234
   function 307
   operators 293, 296
   OR 232-233, 235, 237
lose data 62
Lotus 587
   Notes 429, 445
Lotus 1-2-3 429, 445
   worksheet 445
Lower function 304
Lower(Text) 596
lowercase 216, 304
   letters 238

M

Macro 28, 132, 166, 195, 389, 573, 576, 579
   attach 380
   Button 25, 388, 390, 580
      Info Box 635
   dialog box 364, 567, 654
      Copy 568
      Edit 568
      New 568
   List 550
   Run 375, 379, 577

macro 59, 121, 293, 323, 364, 372
  chaining 375
  chaining 385
  conditional 376
  current 577
  execute 388
  panel 350, 121, 166, 338, 386-387, 609, 613
  Run 394, 578
magnifying glass icon 140
Mail 382, 390, 394,
  message 372
  To 167
  merge 207
  Label 28, 524, 529
    Assistant 190, 192, 199, 507, 510
    divider tab 649
    menu 105, 535
    menu Add Files 536
    menu Fast Format 536
    menu Insert 536
    menu Sort 536
    menu Styles & Properties 536
    name 194
    Options 650
    view 535
  Mailing Labels 1 196
  Mailing Labels 2 191
  Mailing Labels 7, 100, 159, 190-191
    dialog box 195
    Info Box 194, 648
      Attached menu bar 194
      Edit label 194
      Hide View 194
      Mailing label name 194

      Main 194
      Named Styles 194
    menu 195
      Add Field 195
      Insert 195
      Sort 196
      Style & Properties 195
mailing label 1-2, 9-11, 13, 15, 117, 157, 215
  printed 195
mailing list 46, 393
main 30, 194
  database 165, 286, 321
  menu 664-665
    bar 666
    options 664
  file 261
manage menu systems 411
manipulate 122
  objects 22, 105, 117
many file 264
many-to-many relationship 259, 260
many-to-one relationship 47, 255, 261, 266, 276, 284, 285-286
map 453
Mappings list 458
margin 116, 194, 202
maximize 56
maximum 88
Memo 40, 51, 447-448
  data type 475
  fields 39-40, 68, 452, 475, 616
  only 400
menu
  bar 166, 550, 574
  Browse 28, 63, 76-78, 166

Chart 359
Control 56, 81, 103
Create 13, 28, 61, 85, 88, 95, 110,
    167, 172, 183, 190, 196,
    266, 271, 288, 320
Crosstab 355
Current Format 134, 138-139
Customize 574
Data
    entry 139
    Type 40
Database 61
default 416, 574
Drives 35, 60, 80
Edit 28, 53, 80-81, 87, 103, 105,
    108, 110, 112, 115-116, 159
File 28, 30-31, 50, 53, 56-59, 73,
    108, 171, 277
    menu Close 56
Form 28, 105, 110, 127, 164, 166,
    186
    Letter 105
Help 28, 415, 585
Letter 201, 203
List Files of Type 55, 58, 80
Mailing Label 105, 195
Name 412
Object 28, 87, 105, 125, 127,
    148-150, 152-153, 186
Open 54, 56, 58
option 152, 469
Report 28, 105, 184, 184, 187-188
short 185, 574
Style 190
Switch 373, 574
systems 7, 28, 399, 548

Copy 411
Delete 411
Done 411
Edit 411
New 411
Template 44, 51
Text 123-125, 201
Tool 364
Type 412
View 19, 22, 28, 100, 102, 106-
    107, 109, 133, 149-152, 155,
    158, 167
    Design View 500
    fields 45
Window 28, 30,s 56
Worksheet 335
Message 373, 574
methods 122, 143
Middle function 304
Middle(Text,Number,Number) 596
Minimize 56
minimum 88
Minute(Time)596
Mod() 326
Mod(Number,Number) 596
mode
    Browse 7, 19, 22, 27, 64-65, 80,
        96, 105, 150, 170
    Design 7, 19, 22, 24, 64, 87, 99,
        105, 108-109, 159
    Find 7, 27
    Indicator 19
    Preview 7, 20, 26
modem 571
Modification
    Date 90

Formula 325
   button 91
modify reports 177
Modulus (Remainder) function 312
Month 135
   function 308
Month(Date) 596
Month-Day-Year 134-135, 617
MonthName 308
Month\Name(Date or Number) 596
Move 56, 99
move columns 184
multi-select objects 152
multiple
   Approach files 56
   criteria 227
   fields 163
   files 48
   records 162, 177-178
     display 172, 174
     prints 172, 174, 178
     viewing 172
multiplication 294-295, 588

N

Named Styles 120, 149, 165, 194, 275, 404, 551-552, 559
   Styles dialog box 405
     Apply 405
     Copy 405
     Define 405

     Delete 405
     Done 405
     Edit 405
     New 405
   utility 149
Natural Logarithm function 313
negative 314
nested
   functions 300
   parentheses 297
network 2, 10, 36, 430, 458, 461, 567, 570
   administrator 446
   node 466
   protocol 446
   text box 446
Network Connection dialog box 436, 440, 444, 470
New 50, 65, 365
   command 65
   Data 60, 66
   database 44, 52
     create 2
   dialog box 33, 35, 37, 50, 56, 435, 471
     connect 438
     new 34
   Find 371, 572
   Help window 582
   Record 22, 54, 96
     icon 170
   Word box 547
new
   directory 31
   divider tab 158

field type 62
file 34, 50
Forms 99, 157
length 62
record 65, 89, 171
worksheet create 331
Next SmartIcon
  Bar tool 183
  icon 125
next record 71
Next>> 14, 161
non-numeric
  character 67, 69
  entry 70
non-printing 124, 147
  checkbox 120
  field 129
NOT operators 297
Notes field 73
Nothing radio button 90
nudge 115
number
  fields 90
  random 313
  specifics 136
  specified 304
  text 619
  truncated 314
  value 312
Number of
  columns 185
  Lines 274
  Periods function 310
Numeric 41-42, 51, 137, 168, 347, 438, 440, 472
  field 41, 62, 69-70, 444

formula 309
NumToText function 302
NumToText(Number,Format) 597

O

Object 28, 85
  Linking and Embedding see OLE
  menu 87, 105, 125, 127, 148-150, 153, 186, 529-531, 544
    Add Field 127, 531
    Align 154, 529
    Arrange 153, 529
    Edit OLE object 531
    Fast Format 403, 531
    Group 152, 530
    Insert 531
    Styles & Properties 529, 604
    Ungroup 152
  Type List 85, 522
object
  Add 162
  deselect 113
  independent 125
  manipulate 150
  select 113
ODBC 451
  Control Panel manager 451
  data source 452
  driver 451, 453
  key word 451
OLE 63
  object 81-82, 85, 146, 476

On Switch 387
One of 92
one file 261
one-to-many relationship 257, 259-261, 266, 278, 284, 255
one-to-one relationship 47, 49, 253, 262-263
Open 57, 59
   Database Connectivity Standard see ODBC
   dialog box 54, 56-57, 266, 277, 523, 565
      Connect 444
   file 20
   menu 54, 56, 58
operators 40, 226, 246, 291-292, 469, 588
   arithmetic 293-294
   comparison 226, 293, 295, 297, 589
   Logical 293, 296, 589
   relational 226
   special 227
   unusual 226
Optimistic Record Locking 460-461
Options 88, 141, 268, 288, 325, 396, 494
   button 38, 82, 191
   column 569
   dialog box 211
   divider tab 192
   panel 147, 193, 508, 571
OR 296
ORACLE 445, 479
   databases 479
Oracle 9

Order panel 419, 560
Orientation area 211
original size 147
OS/2 character set 454
ovals 117

P

page number 125, 186, 195, 339
Page# 125
Pages radio button 209
paintbrush 148, 532-533
   Files 80
palettes 119, 407, 605, 608, 612
Panel menu 532-533, 535
   Add Field 532
   divider 342
   Fast Format 533
   Insert 533
   Style & Properties 532
Paradox 9-10, 36, 39-41, 429, 441, 443, 445, 483
   databases 477
   file 43, 425, 564-565
      Preferences panel 563
   indexes 426
   Network Connection dialog box 444
parameter 299, 302
Part Description field 626
password 332, 420, 450, 479, 561
   checkbox 458
   panel 419, 422, 560

protection 331-332, 415, 561
   text box 451
Paste 28, 81, 84, 103, 105, 108, 675
   from File 112
   icon 112, 116
   Link 495
      button 84
   radio button 84
   Special 83
      command 83
Payment function 310
PCX 80
Percent with decimals 138
periodic interest rate 309
Pessimistic Record Locking 461
PgDn 71, 207
PgUp 71
Pi function 313
Pi() 597
Picture 25
   fields 448
   panel 409, 556
PicturePlus field 25, 39, 41, 63, 67, 72, 76, 79, 80-82, 84-85, 87, 110, 126, 409, 449, 495, 497, 521, 556, 614, 633
   Drawing tool 110, 112
   field 111
      Info box 86
   file 496
   Info Box 632
   menu 87
   object 146, 476
   Options panel 82, 476
   tool 146
pictures 99

Pie Chart 356-357
   graph 18, 356
PMT(Number1,Number2,Number3) 597
pointer 44, 273, 388, 537, 582
pop-up menus 28
port Assistant 172
Portrait 211, 493
Position function 305
Position(Text,Text,Number) 597
Pow(Number,Number) 598
Power
   function 313
   key technology 9
Predefined format 136
   format codes list 620
Preferences 415, 564
   dialog box 399, 410, 421, 441, 449
   panel 424
Prefix function 305
Prefix(Text,text) 398
Present Value function 310
Preview 20, 462
   icon 248
   mode 7, 20, 26, 374, 575
Previous
   column 43
   record 71, 90
   Value 79, 528
principal 310
Print 20, 209, 225, 374, 381, 569, 576, 613
   button 270
   data 15
   dialog box 209, 270, 386, 569

Index

Grid 339
options 576
Preview 197, 207, 209
   mode 197
Quality 209, 492
Setup 208, 210, 492, 585
   Command 508
title 339
to File 492
   dialog box 210
topic 584
Printer
   codes 492
   icon 209
   Setup 193, 508
printing
   labels 15
   panel 350
   slide options 512
prints 172
Proper function 305
Proper(Text) 598
protocol
   network 446
   ORACLE 446
push button 25, 103, 669
PV(Number1,Number2,Number3) 598

Q

QRY extension 450
Query 450

R

Radian function 315
Radian(Number) 598
radio button 25, 97, 100, 103, 126, 144, 669
   drawing tool 145
Random function 313
Random() 598
range of values 92
Read Only 146, 408
   field 284
Read/Write password 420
rearrange 19
record 8, 48, 65, 344, 374, 576
   add 65
   addresses 49
   current 77, 570
   delete 269
   Duplicate 539
   Hide 539
   individual 177
   insert 269
   last 78
   Lock 461
   locking 437
   maintaining 254
   multiple 162
   New 96, 282, 539
   next 71
   previous 71
   sample 75
   Selected 539
   to export 457

rectangle 24, 117, 119
Reduce 107, 130-131
   Boundaries 184, 647
reference guide 2
Refresh 344, 353, 460, 573
relational
   database 2, 28, 48-49, 92-93, 128, 141, 143, 162, 243, 253, 255-256, 261, 263, 265, 276, 501, 508, 511, 643
   management system 1
   operators 226
Relational Options dialog box 268, 524
Remove 92, 163-164, 192, 566
   button 243
Repeating Panel 261, 268, 271, 275, 280, 282-283, 518
   Info Box 640
Replace function 305
Replace(Text,Number,Number,Replacement Text) 599
Replicate 374
   dialog box 576
   options 375
Replicated 576
Report 7, 9-11, 13, 15, 28, 78, 99-100, 117, 159, 172, 529
   Assistant 175-176, 180, 182, 285, 503, 519
   design 2
   Fields list 504
   Info Box 185, 642
      Attached menu 185
      Hide View 185
      Keep records together 185
      Main Database 185
      Number of columns 185
      Report Name 185
   menu 28, 105, 184, 187-188, 533, 535
      Add Field 533
      Add Footer 534
      Add Header 533
      Add Title Page 534
      Fast Format 535
      Insert 534
      Show Title Page 535
      Sort 187, 534
      Turn On Columns 535
   modify 177
   Name 185
   print 179
   standard 178, 180
   summary 319
   Trailing Grouped Summary 319
Resize 56, 19, 184, 273, 276, 280
   window 671
resolution 209, 492
Retype
   Password text box 420, 561
   View Password 483
Right
   Alignment 347
   function 305
Right(Text,Number) 599
Root directory 29, 36, 50
Round function 313
Round(number,[Number]) 599
rounded rectangles 24, 117

Index

row 16, 332, 351
   blank 141, 345, 413, 550
   current 550
   marker 332
rulers 106
rules 100
Run 365
   button 379
   command 392
   Macro menu 415

S

Salutation 204, 511
Same
   Data 60
   page 172
sample
   chart 360
   color 119, 607
   database 48
   file 49, 53
   folders 29
   Form
      box 501
      letter 203
   records 75
Save 577
   Approach File 20, 53, 59, 108, 171, 377
      As 482
      As dialog box 458

button 59
   dialog box 54
   icon 59
As 59, 377, 421, 458, 578
   dialog box 60
Set button 558
View dialog box 56, 58, 60
SAverage(Number Field) 599
Scientific
   notation 443
   applications 311
SCount(Field Name) 599
screen 9, 13, 160, 172-173
scroll bar 50, 673
Search 231, 583
   Request 324
Second function 309
Second(Time) 600
Select 344, 353
   All of the Borders 280
   header icon 338
   group 114
Selection
   Point 110
   box 141
Send Backward 153, 359, 529, 544
Send Mail 20, 574
   dialog box 372
   options 373, 574
Send to Back 153, 359, 529, 543
send e-mail 491
separate fields 46-47
separator 137, 618, 621
Serial Number 95
   radio button 90

automatically 95
Server
  computer 480
  Name 448
    text box 446, 451, 480
Set 578
  Approach File Password 54, 421
Set
  Default 477
  Read/Write Password 561
  View Password 422, 483
    checkbox 59
shadow color 119, 407, 410, 612
Shift 72, 114
Shift+Tab 43, 66, 283, 580
Short
  menu 165, 373, 414-415, 574
    System 410, 412
  Numbers 444
Shortcut Key Combination 414, 551
shortcut keys 658, 660
Show 581
  All 22, 27, 77, 371, 384, 393, 538, 541, 572
  data 22, 102, 109, 125, 167, 188, 535
    Entry Order 155
    off 1988
    option 133, 272
  description field 142
  Fields 204
  grid 560
  Grid command 151
  Icon Description 417, 559
  in Preview 120, 147, 613, 624
  Next SmartIcon icon 151-153

Panel Labels 177
Ruler 151
SmartIcons 152
Status Bar 152
Title Page 187, 534
Topics 584
View Tabs 152, 158
Show/Hide Grid lines icon 151
Showing
  Data 100
  Drawing Tools 152
  Next SmartIcon 150
Shrink it 147
Sign function 314
Sign(Number) 600
simple
  database 8
  Find 219
Sin(Number) 600
Sine function 315
single field 47
single-file database 48-49
Size 123-124, 406
  column 41
  list 207
  text box 472
Slide Left 190
SLN(Number1,Number2,NUmber3) 600
SmartIcons 70, 106, 416, 499
  Back Arrow 70
  bar 428
  box 559
  dialog box 558
  End Arrow 71
  Forward Arrow 71

Index

Start Arrow 70
SmartMaster 161, 173
   layout 161, 173, 176, 191, 270,
      360, 501-503, 507, 509, 514
   style 501, 509, 514
SMax(Number Field) 600
SMin(Number Field) 600
Snap to Grid 151, 560
Snpv(Number Field,Number) 601
solid line 119
Sort 2, 22, 25, 46-47, 76-78, 129,
     180, 187, 196, 213-215, 254,
     287, 344, 363, 378, 381-382,
     526, 538, 579
   Ascending 22, 188, 214, 217, 248,
     287, 536
   custom 378
   Descending 22, 188, 214, 536
     icon 188
   dialog box 187, 215-217, 419,
     527, 534, 539, 579
   list 214-215, 218, 288
   option 187
   order 460, 560
   panel 275
   simple 538
Soundslike function 306
Soundslike(Text,Text) 601
Spacer icon 557
Span function 306
Span(Text,Text) 601
SpanUntil function 306
SpanUntil(Text,Text) 601
Special Find 574
   dialog box 372

special
   cases 270
   characters 69, 246
   design tools 100
   features 76
   layout tools 108
   operators 227
   worksheet commands 538
Specific Painter 210
speed data entry 2
Spell Check 378, 401, 546, 579
   Current record 545
   dialog box 400
     Add to Dictionary 403
     Replace 420
     Replace All 402
     Replace with 402
     Skip 403
     Skip All 403
   Found set 545
   icon 400
   Replace 547
   Replace All 547
   Selection 545, 546
   Skip 548
   Skip All 548
Spell Checker 399-400
spreadsheet 16, 330
SQL
   data 216
   files 41
   Query file 445
   Select command 449
   Server 9-10, 447, 449, 479
     Fields 448

tables 424, 564
Sqrt(number) 602
Square Root function 314
SSTD(Number Field) 602
Ssum() function 317
SSum(Number Field) 602
stacking order 149, 153, 543
   change 153
standard 52
   data entry from 52
   Deviation function 311
   Form 8, 13, 15, 64, 73, 99, 161, 174, 178
   formats 15
   report 174
   summary report 173
   Worksheet 6, 8, 13
Start 70
   Arrow 20, 70
Statistical function 311
Status Bar 12, 19, 26, 55, 72, 106, 124, 150, 220, 418
Std(Number,Number,...) 602
Straight Line Depreciation function 311
Strikethrough 123
string 240, 298, 305
Style & Properties 87, 122, 164, 166, 185-186, 195, 203, 343, 353
Styles 124, 406
   area 559
   Bold 124
   menu 190
   Underline 124
subdirectories 29, 36

submenu 110, 187, 201, 205, 520, 539
   options 153
subtraction 294-295, 588
sum 321
summaries 177, 181, 317, 527
   Columns 353
   Rows 353
summarize 318
Summary 174, 183, 348
   Average function 301
   Count 301
   dialog box 183
   function 349
   Info Box 645
   Maximum function 301
   Minimum function 301
   Net Present Value function 311
   Only 174, 176, 504, 506
   Panel 183, 646
   Standard Deviation function 312
   Sum function 302
   variance function 312
summary
   calculation 182
   data 18
   field 175, 216
   function 182, 317, 475
   information 519
   panel 181-182
   report 157, 175, 180, 291, 504
SVar(number Field) 602
Switch 81, 499, 654
symbol @ 323

Index

T

Tab 65-66, 73, 158
   order 155
      order changing 155
      numbers 155
table 8
tabular form 13, 16, 75
Tan(Number) 602
Tangent function 315
Task List 81
technical details 2
Template 44, 51
   drop-down menu 44
   menu 51
   selecting 45
text 24, 41, 51, 473
   box 93, 668
      Field Name 51
      File 86
      File Name 37, 55, 80
      Format code 136
      Formula 292
      Label 131
      Time separator 137
      Top and Left 119
      Width and Height 119
   color 407
   constants 298, 323
   editing 123
   Editing Info Box 123, 610
   field 40-43, 62, 68-69, 137
      Options dialog box 454, 457
   frame 121, 130
   create 121
   functions 303, 305
   menu 103, 123-125, 201
   Object 124, 129, 611
      Info Box 124
   relief 407
   searching 221
   specified 304
   string 303, 305-306
      specified 306
   Style 123
   tool 122
Text-Delimited 454, 486, 490
TextToBool function 302
TextToBool(Text) 602
TextToDate function 303
TextToDate(Text) 603
TextToTime(Text) 603
Three-dimensional 356
TIF 80
TIFF Files 80
Time 41, 125, 137, 186, 195, 294
   constants 298
   fields 39
   function 303, 309
   separator text box 137
   suffix 137
   value 303, 309
Time(Hour,Minutes,Seconds,Hundreths) 603
Timestamp data type 452
Title
   bar 559
   Field 46, 51
To Grid 154, 530

Today function 308
Today's Date 79
Today() 299, 393, 603
Today() function 323
Todays Date 528
Tool
  Info Box 123
  menu 364
    named Styles 404
    Preferences 431, 441, 449
  Text 122
toolbox 103
Tools
  drawing 24
  Line 24
  menu 379, 384, 399, 401, 410, 545, 548, 551, 606, 609
    Customize Menus 411, 548
    Macros 567
    Preferences 418, 433, 442, 461-462, 559
    Run Macro 581
    SmartIcons 557
    Spell Check 401, 545, 579
Top to Bottom 193
Tractor Feed 509, 193
Trailed Grouped Summary 175, 321, 505
Trailing 182
  blanks 306
  Group 174
  Summary 175
    Panel icon 182
Translate function 306
Translate(Text,Character,Character) 603

trigonometric
  arccosine 314
  arctangent 314
  functions 300
Trim function 306
Trim(Text) 603
Trunc(Number,[Number]) 603
Truncate function 314
truncated 62
tutorial 2
two-dimensional 356
Type Style 126
typeface 124, 206

U

Unchecked Value 144
Underline 123-124
underlined topics 677
underlining 124
Undo 53, 87, 110
  command 103, 108
  Edit menu 675
  icon 110, 116
Ungroup 152, 531
  icon 152
Unique 92
  checkbox 95
  identifier field 43
  values 243
Unjoin button 268
unusual operators 226
Upper function 299, 306

Index

Upper(Text) 299, 604
uppercase 216, 299
User Name text box 446
Using Help 586
utilities 2, 28

V

validate
   data entry 95
   date 93
validating data 97
   entry 94
Validation 97
   divider tab 91, 95, 288, 326, 473
   panel 92, 94, 288, 325, 472
   Rules 92, 94
      panel 97
   tab 96
value list 141
Var(Number,Number,...) 604
Variable 41, 396
   data type 477
   fields 59
   Options 397
      dialog box 398
      panel 398, 477
Variables 292-293, 588
Variance function 312
Vertical
   Alignment 530
   lines 151

VEW 10
View 22, 28, 75, 131, 150, 167, 171
   current 27
   data 16
   Design 25, 28
   divider tab 222
   Drawing tools 28
   fields menu 45
      Custom Order 45
      Data Type 45
      Default Order 45
      Field Name 45
   Form 14
   indicator 12
   Info Box 28
   List 550
   menu 19, 22, 100, 102, 106-107,
      109, 133, 149-152, 155, 158,
      167, 498-500, 580
      Actual Size 500
      Data Entry Order 499
      Design 498
      Grid 151
      Show Data 498
      Show Drawing Tools 499
      Show grid 498
      Show Panel Labels Tools 499
      Show Ruler 151, 498
      Show SmartIcon 499
      Show Status Bar 499
      Show View Tabs 499
      Snap to Grid 151, 498
   Worksheet 14
      Zoom In 500
   Tabs 106

view 19
Viewall 385-386
Views 7, 12, 19, 59, 193, 198, 202

W

warning dialog box 369
WeekOfYear function 308
WeekOfYear(Date) 604
Welcome dialog box 34, 50, 56, 58, 418, 559
Width and Height text boxes 119
wildcard 240
   character 36, 240
Window 28
   editors 341
   menu 30, 56, 415, 550
      Main 30
Windows
   applications 7, 53, 59, 67, 663-664, 666, 670
   basics 2
   Bitmaps 80
   Clipboard 81, 83
   editor keys 66
   File Manager 7, 29, 50
   Metafiles 80
   Paintbrush 80
   Program Manager 30, 467
Without data 100
WMF 80
word protection 484
word-wrapped 125

Worksheet 7, 13, 16, 28, 64, 157, 329, 333-334
   add 16
   Assistant 330, 345
   Box Printing panel 350
   edit 16
   Info Box 350, 653
      Basics panel 350
      Macros Panel 350
   menu 335, 339, 537-539
      Add Column 539
      Add Field 539
      Delete record 539
      Edit Column Label 540
      Fast Format 540
      Fill Field 540
      Find 538
      Insert 540
      Record 539
      refresh 540
      Styles & Properties 538
   pane divider 343
   separate panes 342
   special commands 343
   standard 8, 13, 64, 75
   view 14
      data 16
Worksheet 1 52, 58, 75

X

x-axis 358

Y

y-axis 358
Year 135
   function 308
   format 136
Year(Date) 604
Year-Month-Day 134-135, 617
Yes button 53

Z

Zoom 378
   In 149, 378, 580
     icon 149
   Out 117, 149, 378, 580
     icon 149
     sizes 26